HISTORY

OF

NEW ENGLAND.

A New Plan of ye Great Town of BOSTON in New England in AMERICA
With the many Additionall Buildings, & New Streets, to the Year 1743.
To His Excellency Jonathan Belcher Esqr Capt General and Governour in Chief of His Majesties Provinces of the Massachusets Bay & New Hampshire in New England and Vice Admiral of the same this Plan of the great Town of BOSTON is humbly dedicated by Yr Excellencies Most obedient & humble Servt William Price
Printed for & Sold by Wm Price at ye Kings Head & Looking Glass in Cornhill, Near the Town House in Boston, Where is Sold a Large New South East Prospect of Boston Neatly done & A Prospect of the Colledg's in Cambridge New England. And Great Variety of Mapps & Prints of all Sorts in Frames & Glass or without
Bartons Point
Charles River
Ferry to Charles-Town
is about half a Mile over
Mill Pond
N. Water Mill
Gee's Ship Yd
Fox Hill
Powder House
Watch House
COMMON
Pleasant Street
School
Cornhill
Middle Street
Ship Street
Long Wharfe
Old Wharfe
Fort Hill
S. Battery
Hills Wharf
Wind Mill Point
HARBOUR
Scale of ½ a Mile
The Names of the Wards
Charter Street Ward
North St. Ditto
Fleet St. Ditto
Pond Ward
Anne St. Wd.
Hanover Ditto
Cambridge D.
Kings St. D.
Cornhill D.
Malbrough D.
Summer St. D.
Orange St. D.
BOSTON N.E. Planted An. Dom. 1630
EXPLANATION.
A. The Old Meeting ... 1630
B. Old North M. ... 1650
C. Old South M. ... 1669
D. Annabaptist M. ... 1680
E. Kings Chappel Foun.d 1688
F. Brattle St. M. ... 1699
G. Quakers M. ... 1710
H. New North M. ... 1714
I. New South M. ... 1716
K. French M. ... 1716
L. New N.o Brick M. ... 1721
a. Town House.
b. Governours House.
c. South Graman School.
d. North Graman School.
e. Writing School.
f. Writing School.
g. Alms House.
h. Bridewell.
I. Town Granery.
The Wards Military Companies Distinguished by the Prickt Line thus ...... From N.o 1 to 12.
Great Fires.
First ... 1653
Second ... 1676
Third ... 1679
Fourth ... 1683
Fifth ... 1690
Sixth ... 1691
Seventh ... 1702
Eigth ... 1711
Genll Small Pox.
First ... 1640
Second ... 1666
Fifth ... 1702
Sixth ... 1721
Seventh 1730
M. Christ Church Founded 1723.
N. Irish Meeting House 1731
O Hollis Street Meeting 1731.
P Trinity Church Founded 1734.
Q Lynds Street Meeting built 1736.
R Work House built 1738.
S. Bennet Street Meeting built 1742.
T. Faneuil Hall & Market house, a handsom large brick building Worthy of the Generous Founder Peter Faneuil Esq. who in the Year 1742 Gave it to the Town for the use of a Market.

HISTORY

OF

NEW ENGLAND.

BY

JOHN GORHAM PALFREY.

VOLUME IV.

BOSTON:
LITTLE, BROWN, AND COMPANY.
1875.

Cambridge:
Press of John Wilson and Son.

HISTORY

OF

NEW ENGLAND

FROM THE

REVOLUTION OF THE SEVENTEENTH CENTURY.

BY

JOHN GORHAM PALFREY.

Moribus antiquus res stat Romana virisque.
— Ennius, *apud Cic. de Rep. V.* 1.

BOSTON:
LITTLE, BROWN, AND COMPANY.
1875.

Cambridge.
Press of John Wilson and Son.

TO

CHARLES FRANCIS ADAMS,

EMINENT AMONG THOSE SONS OF NEW ENGLAND

BY WHOM SHE IS

"A NAME AND A PRAISE AMONG ALL PEOPLE OF THE EARTH,"

THIS TREATISE IS INSCRIBED.

PREFACE

TO THE FOURTH VOLUME.

I HAD just made arrangements for putting into type a continuation of my History of New England, intending, as the work proceeded, to make additions to the text as it had been composed, and to adjust and amplify the body of notes of which I had a rough draught, when, in November, 1873, I was arrested by illness. When I regained some strength, the question occurred, whether I should attempt a prosecution of my plan under the disadvantages which would attend it. Should I do so, I must expect to fall short of the ideal which I had proposed to myself, and be content to produce what would not bear a rigorous criticism. But I decided that these considerations should not deter me, because materials which I had been long collecting, and which remained in a state unfit for any use but my own, would then be lost. As long as I should be able to apply myself to the task, I might hope to be putting into shape what would serve the convenience of future students, however it might be found to fail in completeness and even in accuracy.

The history of New England is considered to be dry and unpicturesque. But by peculiar titles it deserves, beyond the records of dynastic intrigues and wars, to be known to the philosophical student of man and society, of divine Providence, and of the progress of the race. In more stirring narratives one may read of the conflicts of furious human passions, of the baseness of men in high degree, of revolutions due to nothing worthy and issuing in nothing profitable. In the colonial history of New England we follow the strenuous action of intelligent and honest men in building up a free, strong, enlightened, and happy State. With sagacity, promptitude, patience, and constancy they hold their ground from age to age. Each generation trains the next in the lessons of liberty, and advances it to further attainments; and, when the time comes for the result of the modest process to be disclosed, behold the establishment of the political independence of America, and the boundless spread of principles which are working for good in the politics of the world.

The administration of the controlling colonies of New England illustrates the power, wisdom, and virtue that may reside in a society of undistinguished men. Sometimes, though not often, those to whom this people gave their confidence proved untrustworthy, and sought and used office for selfish ends; but the popular manhood generally defeated them. It was not to the agency of leaders that the progress of New England was mainly due, nor did that community furnish many such persons for commemoration in biographies. It was the popular good principles and good sense transmitted from parent to son which brought the excellent results to pass.

Of the friends who have helped me in the progress of this work, some are now no more. Among those to whom I have been recently indebted, I have especially to acknowledge obligations to Mr. HOADLY of New Haven, and Mr. GOODELL of Salem, who allowed me the use of the proof-sheets of their respective publications of colonial documents; to Mr. DEANE of Cambridge, whose stores of knowledge have been freely imparted to me; and to Mr. TRUMBULL of Hartford, who has materially assisted my study of that history of Connecticut, which he is so richly qualified to write.

I have devoted much time to the Archives of Massachusetts. But such is the ingenious disorder in which, some thirty-five years ago, the precious documents in that collection were dispersed, that the search among them is laborious and unsatisfactory to a vexatious degree. Nor till the liberality of some future Legislature shall cause them to be replaced in a chronological series, will it be possible for a student to assume that he has found every thing contained in them that is material to his inquiries.

Since the following pages constitute a sequel to my three volumes of History of New England during the Stuart Dynasty, I believe that I have consulted the reader's convenience in references in the notes, by enumerating the volumes from I. to IV. as all belonging to one work. In these notes, the references in the present volume, as in the preceding, to "British Colonial Papers," indicate papers now in the custody of the Master of the Rolls, and mostly included in the two voluminous collections entitled respectively "Board of Trade," and "America and West Indies." These papers are not arranged in the precise order of the dates; but consultation of them will be easy after the completion of Mr. SAINSBURY'S Calendar, which as yet is brought down no further than to the year 1660. In my references to them, as well as in other notes, I shall be thought to have gone excessively into details; and I cannot dispute the justness of the criticism; such, at present, is the uncontrollable tendency of my mind.

The map which makes the frontispiece to this volume, reduced from the sheet published by William Price in 1743, represents the chief town of New England as it was at the close of the administration of Governor Belcher, and essentially as it remained for sixty years longer. I have some recollection of Boston before 1805, and it was not then very materially different from the delineation of it in Bonner's map of 1722. On the whole, the population of the town, gaining and losing from time to time, grew but little during the latter half of the past century. At the time of the capture of Louisburgh in 1745, it was reckoned at 20,000. The Federal census of 1800 reported it to be 24,937.

The plan of my work would be accomplished by the completion of one more volume, bringing down the narrative to the opening of the War of Independence.

J. G. P.

CAMBRIDGE, MASSACHUSETTS;
1875, *May* 2.

CONTENTS

OF THE FOURTH VOLUME.

BOOK IV.

PROGRESS IN THE REIGNS OF KING WILLIAM THE THIRD AND QUEEN ANNE.

CHAPTER I.

CHAPTER II.

CHAPTER III.

Provincial Charter of Massachusetts.

CHAPTER IV.

CHAPTER V.

CHAPTER VI.

CHAPTER VII.

CHAPTER VIII.

CHAPTER IX.

CHAPTER X.

CHAPTER XI.

BOOK V.

PROGRESS UNDER THE HANOVERIAN KINGS.

CHAPTER I.

CHAPTER II.

CHAPTER III.

CHAPTER IV.

CHAPTER V.

CHAPTER VI.

CHAPTER VII.

APPENDIX.

BOOK IV.

PROGRESS IN THE REIGNS OF KING WILLIAM THE THIRD AND QUEEN ANNE.

HISTORY OF NEW ENGLAND.

BOOK IV.

PROGRESS IN THE REIGNS OF KING WILLIAM THE THIRD AND QUEEN ANNE.

CHAPTER I.

THE early dreams in New England of an independence of the parent country had faded away. A discouraging experience in the past, and new views of existing advantages and dangers, had combined to allay that enthusiasm for absolute liberty which prompted the emigrations. Religion was no longer, in the same degree as formerly, the central principle of public conduct. Economical interests had come to rival the interests and to modify and complicate the plans of politics. The local unanimity had been dissolved. Permanent parties had been formed with opposing judgments both upon local questions and upon questions of the relations of the Colonies to the empire; the men qualified to lead opinion were not, as formerly, agreed in opinion among themselves.

Politics and parties in New England

The question may occur, why, in the dark times of the last two Stuart kings, the Puritan emigration had not been renewed, restoring the unanimity while it reinforced the numbers and the energy of New England. That such an enterprise should have such a revival is not in any hitherto experienced, or probable, course of things. The spirit which has stimulated it, dying a natural death, has no resurrection. The brief course of splendid triumph of Puritanism in England had been brought to an end by its own mismanagement. Even if champions like Eliot and Hampden should again appear, what mind among them so sanguine as to believe that a second combination for the recovery of English freedom would issue more prosperously than the now frustrated struggle which they had inaugurated? When the worthless sensualist Charles the Second ascended the throne, English Puritans were no longer in a condition for joint counsels and common action. They were dispirited by a dismal defeat, incurred, as it seemed, by their own faults and discords. The early part of that reign was for them a time of merely helpless stupor and amazement. The Corporation Act, the Act of Uniformity, the Conventicle Act, and the Five-Mile Act constituted a succession of outrages that impoverished, scattered, and disarmed them.[1] Then the King's leaning to measures of Comprehension and Indulgence,[2] which would favor papist as well as sectary, crippled their power by dividing their sentiments, as it did in the succeeding reign. The Test Act[3] had scarcely renewed the severity and the consternation, when the fiction of the Popish plot[4] came to the aid of the patriot party, and all but secured the exclusion of the Romanist Duke of York from the succession to the throne. When that tide turned, only a little time passed before the seizure of the charter of Massachusetts into the King's hands; and the consequent establishment of a despotism in that Colony forbade English patriots to look thither for a refuge. Possibly, had the enterprise of the Prince of Orange failed, there might have been a second emigration of patriotic and religious Englishmen to the western world. But it would not have been projected in circumstances so inspirit-

Improbability of further immigration.

1661, 1662, 1663, 1665.

1667, 1672.

1673.

1678.

1684.

[1] See above, Vol. II. 435-437.
[2] See above, Vol. III. 7, 18.
[3] See above, Vol. III. 19.
[4] See above, Vol. III. 241.

ing as what were thought to attend the first, nor could the materials for it have been of a character so substantial. Richard Baxter might have made the voyage, and have brought some companions of a like earnest spirit. But a large number of men like Winthrop and Cotton, or like those who guided the Long Parliament and the Westminster Assembly, were not at that day to be found in England. Statesmanship there, as well in the patriot circle as in that of the court, was, in the time of King James and his son-in-law, of a type widely different from what it had been in the first half of the same century.[1] And though the circle of Bates, Calamy, and Howe was composed of worthy Christian men, their virtue was not distinctly of the sort which welcomes danger, conflict, and sacrifice.

As bodies politic, the Colonies of New England were now disabled. The most powerful and restiff of them, after triumphing in a sharp contest with the Ministry of King Charles the Second, had afterwards been stricken to his feet. The charter of Massachusetts, the only unquestionable title of her citizens to any rights, proprietary, social, or political, had been vacated by regular process in the English courts. The condition of the four towns which were collectively called New Hampshire was undefined; they were awaiting a new organization. Plymouth, never endowed with a charter, was at the royal mercy, as indeed she always had been except so far as she had been protected by the influence or the imputed power of Massachusetts. The charters which Connecticut and Rhode Island had owed to Lord Clarendon's jealousy of the confederacy and hatred of Massachusetts were understood to have been surrendered — the latter with little reluctance — to the usurpations of Randolph and Andros. They had been resumed, but it

Improbability of further resistance.

[1] "No part of English history is read, upon the whole, with less satisfaction than those thirteen years during which William the Third sat upon his elective throne." (Hallam, Constitutional History, Chap. XV.)

was uncertain whether that anomalous proceeding would be allowed in England.

On the other hand, the reasons which had quickened the desire for independence did not now exist in the same strength as in earlier times. Except in the twenty years that intervened between the assembling of the Long Parliament and the restoration of King Charles the Second, New England, through her whole history, had been agitated by fears for her religious freedom. She had been disquieted from the first to the last of that history by apprehension of encroachments from the English hierarchy, and during no small part of it by alarm lest the government that claimed her allegiance should itself fall into vassalage to the Roman see. On the British throne she at length saw a prince not only unquestionably Protestant, but understood to be strictly orthodox after the standard of her own doctrines and forms, — an unflinching Dutch Calvinist according to the pattern of the Synod of Dort.

Character and position of King William.

King William the Third was indeed no enthusiast for the creed in which he agreed with the colonists. No ardor possessed him but for the humiliation of France. During the seventeen years since he had been summoned, at the age of twenty-two, to direct the defence of his country against a devas-

1672.

tating invasion of the French king, a succession of intrigues and wars against that monarch had been his perpetual occupation. Louis the Fourteenth, in his declining life, was after his incongruous manner a furious devotee to the Romish religion which he had always professed; and the safety of the reformed faith in England, Holland, and the North of Europe depended on successful resistance to his power. But the Protestantism of William of Orange was not so fastidious as to withhold him from alliances with the King of Spain, with the Emperor of Germany and other Catholic princes of the empire, and even with the Pope; nor was it so hearty as to make him willing to protect suffering Protestants at the cost of his political convenience, as was mournfully manifested by his desertion of the French confessors in the treaty of Ryswick. It might be true that, though the doctrine of predestination was dear to him as it made an uncalculating courage easy, his religious belief, on the whole, had no strong hold of his mind; for he was no brooder upon theories, but a busy man of affairs. But if in that case his Calvinistic subjects might not hope encouragement from him as a sympathizer, they might expect from him toleration as an indifferentist. Toleration had on the whole been the policy of his race, though his rough predecessor, Maurice, had broken the continuity of the tradition. William's position as Protestant head of coalitions composed of Catholics on the one hand, and on the other of Protestants of different names, imposed upon him as a necessity the disavowal of intolerant sentiments. And he had given reason to believe that he would favor such legislation for the Church of England as should offer easy terms of comprehension to dissenters. The disaffection with which the new settlement of the kingdom was regarded by many of the clergy inclined him to favor the sectaries, who were warmly its friends.[1]

Still, if King William was head of the Church of England, that body was constituted of warring members; nor would the degree of respect with which the rights of nonconformity were to be treated in his colonies be determined by his friendship or his discretion. In the danger which had lately distressed the Church, the dissenters, to whom the Church had all along been so cruel, had helped in its extrication. Had the Church learned moderation and lenity, and was it capable of grat-

Prospects as to the new ecclesiastical administration.

[1] "Their [the clergy's] disaffection made the King more inclinable to favor the dissenters, whom he generally looked upon as better affected to his person and title." (Kennett, History of England, III. 518.)

itude? and, if it should be indisposed to relent, how far would it prove able to overrule or to persuade a tolerant sovereign? The "Claim of Right," which constituted the settlement for Scotland, contained an express declaration against episcopacy in that kingdom;[1] if one form of dissent from the established religion of England might be established in Scotland, might the precedent be followed and another form be permitted in Massachusetts?

1689. April 11.

The leaning of the King's mind in respect to the religious administration was thought to be indicated when presently after his accession he gave the bishopric of Salisbury, the only see then vacant, to Gilbert Burnet, a frank and active enemy to all intolerance, and even reputed to be a doubtful churchman. And the appointment of a successor to Archbishop Sancroft, when that impracticable prelate refused to take the oath of allegiance, afforded a further acceptable assurance of the bias of the royal mind. It was impossible that the enlightened and generous Tillotson should ever lend himself to a vexatious treatment of dissent.

Accordingly the course of religious administration in this reign was such as, if it did not give complete satisfaction to the dissenters of New England, yet afforded them sufficient practical security. An early proceeding of the convention which, after recognizing the Prince and Princess of Orange as King and Queen of England, resolved on the same day to declare itself a parliament, was to pass an Act commonly known as the Toleration Act, "for exempting their Majesties' Protestant subjects from the penalties of certain laws." It left the Corporation Act and the Test Act still in force. But all Trinitarian Protestants who should take the oaths of allegiance and supremacy, and make the prescribed declaration against popery, were now permitted to absent themselves from church and to attend

1689. Feb. 13.

Toleration Act. May 24.

[1] Fifth Article, ibid., 588.

conventicles, provided that their places of meeting should be open during religious services, and that their preachers should subscribe the doctrinal articles of the Church of England.[1] It has been supposed that the terms of the Toleration Act were negotiated by John Locke. His writings show that he must have considered them inadequate to the ends of justice.[2]

Defeat of measures of Comprehension.

A repeal of the Test Act, and a measure of *Comprehension*, as it was called, including such alterations of the Liturgy and Articles as might satisfy the consciences of orthodox non-conformists and bring them into the Church, were both proposed. Patrick, Tillotson, Burnet, and Tenison were among the eminent churchmen who favored the concession.[3] But difficulties which proved to be insurmountable intervened. Even Whigs could not be persuaded to a unanimous agreement upon measures of so radical a character. Lord Nottingham, whose vast influence in the ecclesiastical circle might have brought about a generous indulgence, was well disposed to a comprehension, but the Test Act he was more inclined to strengthen than to rescind. The embarrassing subject was gotten rid of by a shift which only saved both parties from the mortification of confessing a defeat. The Houses petitioned the King to summon a Convocation of the clergy to give their advice. The Convocation met, and its temper was shown when Dr.

April.

Nov. 20.

[1] Hansard, Parliamentary History, V. 263; compare Hallam, Constitutional History, 584–586.

[2] Herbert Skeats, History of the Free Churches of England, 133, 196. — It was in the year of the landing of the Prince of Orange in England that Locke wrote, in Latin, his first Letter on Toleration. (Lord King, Life of Locke, I. 327.)

[3] "They proposed a new selection of lessons; . . . . . they left it to the minister's option to substitute the Apostles' for the Athanasian creed; new collects were drawn up; . . . . . a fresh version of the Psalms was made, more conformable to the original; words and phrases that had been objected to were collected out of the Liturgy, and others, clearer and plainer, and less exceptionable, proposed in their room. Suggestions were offered for meeting other scruples of the dissenters, especially in regard to baptism and ordination." (John James Tayler, Retrospect of the Religious Life of England, 75.)

Jane, the chief Oxford champion of the doctrine of passive obedience in the late reign, was chosen Prolocutor of the lower House by a majority of two to one over the liberal Tillotson.[1] The bishops, as a body, were not averse to some indulgence to non-conformists. But the inferior clergy, disinclined to any accommodation of the sort, interposed all sorts of obstacles to the transaction of business. They wearied out the other party, and nothing was done. The favorable time for action by the civil government had been lost, for in the next Parliament the Tory party was so strongly reinforced that there was no encouragement so much as to propose any plan of ecclesiastical reform, and the exclusive system of the Church of England remains in vigor to this day.

For the present, according to appearance, the danger to religious liberty in New England which had formerly been so appalling had passed away. Henceforward it was civil freedom that required securities. As well at home as in the Colonies, charters had been arbitrarily dissolved; would justice prevail for their restoration, now that liberty was won? or would the new government profit by the misconduct of the old, and refuse to redress wrongs which it never would have ventured to inflict? or would right be accorded to the strong and withholden from the weak, and London be reinstated while Massachusetts was denied? In the recent controversies, the colonists had claimed an interest,

Prospects as to civil administration.

[1] "All the storm which was raised in Convocation the last year by those who will be the Church of England was on my account." (Archbishop Tillotson in Letters of Rachel Lady Russell, II. 46. In three or four letters of 1689 and 1690, preserved in this interesting collection, Tillotson gives a circumstantial account of the King's urgency to overcome his reluctance to accept the primacy; a fact especially noteworthy, on account of its connection with the other fact, that Tillotson's desire for a comprehension was the cause of the bitter hostility to him on the part of the parochial clergy.) Heads of Argument assented to (in 1692) by the United Clergy (Presbyterian and Independent); comp. Dalrymple, Memoirs, &c., Part II. 23; Calamy, Historical Account of my own Life, &c., I. 211.

which the Crown lawyers had disallowed, in the Great Charter; would the claim be still rejected, or would the birthrights of Englishmen to life, liberty, and property be henceforward understood in Westminster Hall as rights of Englishmen living in a colony? The colonists were well able to manage their internal affairs; would their discretion and public spirit be respected, or would they be embarrassed and teased by a meddlesome policy at court? Would the Privy Council continue to superintend them with an intermitting and lax control, or would they be placed, as repeatedly in former times, under a special jurisdiction likely to be more vigilant and more vexatious? Would this new close alliance with Holland, or would any consequences of the great change in England, affect the strictness of that administration of the Navigation Laws which had lately threatened so much trouble?

If ever the people of New England imagined that in their King, born the citizen of a republic, they were to find a friend by reason of his being a friend to popular institutions, no calculation could have been more illusory. Hard experiences had strengthened that love of power which belonged to his stern, self-relying, and ungenial nature. His life had been a long lesson of the inconvenience of restraints, and of divided authority, to one fated to act a great part. His enemy, the King of France, was master of his own resources; he could keep his secrets in his own breast; he could choose his agents; he could conceive and shape his own plans, mature them with his own silent observations, and put them in execution whenever he saw the time to be ripe. William's moment of greatest apparent power was when he was at the head of the most numerous coalition which for the time being he had been able to form. But, the more parties he had won to his alliance, the more unmanageable had he made it. In projecting a negotiation or a campaign, he must consult

The King's leaning to arbitrary power.

and persuade a cabinet of equals, with rival interests to be conciliated; with stupidity and ignorance in sovereigns and ministers to be cautiously approached; with whimsical apprehensions and jealousies to be allayed; with conceit to be humored; with sensitive obstinacy to be overcome or soothed or eluded. He who has thus felt the embarrassments of restricted authority naturally comes to covet absolute authority with a disinterested ambition. If he is prompted by generous aims, the restraints which disable him are felt with the more impatience and resentment. He is doomed to become tenacious and greedy of power.

Nor was it to be expected that in the prosecution of any political projects the new King would be restrained by sentimental scruples. Generosity, delicacy, sympathy, tenderness, are not looked for as royal attributes; and the Prince of Orange was a person uncommonly unembarrassed by any weakness of the sort. Harsh, as well as unfaithful, to a wife who resigned herself to him with so romantic a devotion that it cost her no pang to sacrifice her filial duty to his ambition; alienating, by his arrogance and caprices, those friends of his youth who, notwithstanding, never ceased to labor for his greatness with assiduous fidelity, — no vein of human sensibility seemed to throb in him. In him the kingly qualities seemed to be petrified.[1] And as to any feeling of kindness for the

[1] Few readers but must feel that the facts as to the tragedy of Glencoe (Feb. 13, 1692) are too stubborn for even Lord Macaulay's masterly management. And why labor a hopeless interpretation, as if a complicity in that brutal transaction was not altogether accordant with the King's sullen, strong, impatient, domineering nature? The man who, at twenty-five, might have prevented, but did not prevent, the assassination of the illustrious De Witt, would hardly think much, at forty, of the treacherous massacre of a few scores of savage McDonalds. The man who for twenty years had been studying refinements in the art of politics could not be expected to be much shocked by a little stratagem. Nor does Namur or Steenkirke tell the story of one who, through softness of heart, was chary of human life. Nor, when the affair of Glencoe raised a loud outcry, did William seem to be so much as concerned

Colonies which so lately as in his boyhood had dispossessed his native country — the only country which he loved — of the best of its foreign possessions, what was there, when he never so much as took pains to disguise his aversion to England,[1] to make him an indulgent father to her children on the other side of the water?

As it could not be supposed that the imported King was well acquainted with the conditions of English administration, his choice of advisers was a matter of immediate interest to his colonial subjects. And its interest increased as his own qualities and tastes became better known. Though a brave and skilful, he had not been an eminently successful soldier. But he was the ablest political manager in Europe. He knew all the schemes, intrigues, and factions of all the courts, and had gauged the abilities and characters of all the controlling courtiers. It followed that the special function which he assumed for himself, when seated on the throne of England, was the charge of the foreign relations of his realm. This department of affairs, including the military arrangements incident to it, he not only superintended,

New official organization.

for any ill reputation which it might attach to him. — Jan. 23, 1689, Evelyn records (Memoirs, III. 269), as among the obstacles to a settlement of the kingdom, "the morose temper of the Prince of Orange, who showed little countenance to the noblemen and others, who expected a more gracious and cheerful reception when they made their court." It is remarkable how coldly he is characterized by the genial Burnet, than whom he had no more devoted English friend. (History of his own Time, IV. 561.) Lord Dartmouth, in a note to this passage (ibid.), adds a trait or two. "He had a very ungraceful manner of laughing, which he seldom did unless he thought he had outwitted somebody, which pleased him without measure. Therefore, when there was a direct way to what he aimed at, and another that was less so, he constantly chose the latter. . . . . . I was told in Holland of some instances . . . . . that showed a cruelty in his nature hardly to be paralleled." "King William distrusted human virtue, contemned human nature, and knew not human sympathy." (Wallace, History of England, in Lardner, Cyclopædia, IX. 146.)

[1] When Queen Anne, at her accession, told the House of Lords, "I know my own heart to be entirely English," and, "You will always find me a strict and religious observer of my word," no one misunderstood her flings at the brother-in-law whom she detested. (Sir John Dalrymple, Memoirs, &c., Part IV. 244.)

but personally conducted, with not much consultation and not much aid. For other business of the government he proved to have little taste or preparation, and to allow himself but little time, leaving it mainly to his great Ministers of state. When matters relating to it were necessarily brought to his notice, he was apt to make a summary disposition of them; the governing principle of his decisions being to take care that what the Revolution had left of the royal prerogatives[1] should not be further abridged, and that such opportunities for extending the sovereign's power as the existing jealous state of the public mind admitted should not fail of being put to use.

Of the official advisers of the King, the Treasurer and the Secretaries of State were those whose action would most affect the interests of the Colonies. Danby, formerly Lord High Treasurer, was not enough trusted to be restored to that post, though he had materially aided in the recent Revolution. The Treasury was put in commission, the eccentric Lord Mordaunt, afterwards Earl of Peterborough, being nominally at its head; while its efficient chief was Sidney Godolphin, under whose administrations, while formerly holding the same place at two different times, Randolph and Andros had perpetrated their odious usurpations. The Earl of Sunderland, from whom the Colonies could have expected no kindness, was not at first reinstated in the office which he imagined to have been earned by his treachery to his late master. The new Secretaries of State were the Earl of Nottingham and the Earl of Shrewsbury. The latter was too young to be yet

[1] "In England his principal aim was the upholding of the prerogative." (Ranke, Englische Geschichte, VI. 576 *et seq.*) Ranke sketches King William's character and policy at large with vigor and discrimination. Says Michelet, "Libéral en religion par son indifférence, il eut été despote en politique, s'il avait pu. Au fond, il sympathizait fort peu avec nos Calvinistes, dont Rohan avait dit, 'Ils sont républicains.' Il sut se servir d'eux, mais il trouvait en eux une déplaisante ressemblance avec les Puritains anglais." (Histoire de France, XIII. 444; comp. 169, 189, 408, 418.)

known except for his brilliant personal qualities, and for the brave part which he had taken in the subversion of King James's despotism. Lord Nottingham was a grave and moderate Tory; an undisguised lover of prerogative, though his loyalty had not been proof against recent exigencies; and a fanatical devotee of the Church of England.

The legal proceedings which terminated in the vacating of the charter of Massachusetts had been conducted in the Court of King's Bench and the Court of Chancery, and had been pressed on by Sir Robert Sawyer, as Attorney-General. The new constitution of those tribunals was an occasion of concern to the Colonies. The Great Seal was intrusted to a commission; the chief commissioner being Sir John Maynard, a statesman nearly ninety years old, universally respected in that corrupt age for courageous probity, and recognized as the greatest lawyer of his time. He had been a prominent member of the Long Parliament on the popular side, and one of the prosecutors of the Earl of Strafford. The new Chief Justice of the King's Bench was John Holt, a young man just risen into professional eminence and general esteem. He was known to entertain liberal sentiments in politics, and for his contumacy in respect to the dispensing power had been removed by King James from the office of Recorder of London.[1] The first Attorney-General under the new order of things was Sir George Treby, who, as spokesman for the corporation of London, had greeted the Prince on his arrival there as the representative of a line "consecrated from generation to generation to the high office of defending truth and freedom against tyrants."[2]

A signally important measure, affecting the position of the Colonies, appeared to meet with favor on all sides, and if it had been matured in Parliament would probably in

[1] Campbell, Lives of the Chief Justices, II. 129.

[2] Macaulay, History, II. 455.

the circumstances have encountered no opposition from the King, though on this subject he had practised a somewhat suspicious reserve, saying nothing in his "Declaration of Right" of either the restoration of charters or the colonial mal-administration of King James.[1] In a bill which was introduced for the restoration of their charters to corporations which had been wrongfully deprived in the late reign, the Colonies of New England were expressly provided for. The bill was lost by the indiscretion of its advocates, who insisted on attaching to it some provisions of an unreasonably vindictive character. The King did not like this far-reaching severity against Tories, and, being at the same time displeased at some expressions in the House of Commons of disapprobation of an intention which he had announced of going over to command his troops in Ireland, he suddenly prorogued the Parliament. It was presently dissolved, and writs were issued for another election. The opportunity had gone by. The Whig party, which had taken the lead in the recent Revolution, was offended and weakened by the want of a more liberal confidence on the King's part; and this demoralization, and the displeasure produced by the harsh tenor of measures proposed by it in the late Parliament against political offenders, gave the control of the new Parliament to the Tories, whose sensibility to the abuses of the late reign was already blunted.

Proposed restoration of charters.

1690. Jan. 10.

February.

March 20.

The question about the charters was to be soon resolved, but from this time another element of discord in the relation of the Colonies to the parent country was to assume a prominence permanently hostile to a good understanding between them.

Colonial system.

With the Revolution which seated the Prince of Orange

[1] First of William and Mary, Second Session, Chap. II.; Commons' Journal, X. 17; comp. McPherson, Annals of Commerce, II. 640; Chalmers, Revolt, &c., I. 231, note.

on the English throne, the commercial interest in England obtained new importance, and the colonial system attracted increased attention. The colonial empire of England, now so vast, at that time comprehended not very much more than the settlements on the eastern seaboard of North America between Florida and Newfoundland, and a few islands of the West Indies, though already there were factories and forts on the Spanish Main, on the Gold Coast of Africa, and on both sides of the peninsula of Hindostan.[1]

At so late a time as almost in the last days of the colonial subjection of New England, Edmund Burke — the work in which the words occur is now ascertained to be his — set forth the accepted theory of the relation of colonies to their metropolis in terms expressing no sense of the vicious character of that system: "The ends to be answered are to make the new establishment as useful as possible to the trade of the mother country; to secure its dependence; to provide for the ease, safety, and happiness of the settlers; to protect them from their enemies; and to make an easy and effectual provision to preserve them from the tyranny and avarice of their governors, or the ill consequences of their own licentiousness; that they should not, by growing into an unbounded liberty, forget that they were subjects, or, lying under a base servitude, have no reason to think themselves British subjects. This is all that colonies, according to the present and best ideas of them, can or ought to be."[2] Adam Smith recognized the fact of the

[1] The Bermudas were acquired in 1609; Barbadoes, in 1625; St. Christopher, Antigua, Nevis, and Montserrat, in 1632; Jamaica, in 1655; and the Bahamas, in 1672. (Roberts, History of the Colonial Empire of Great Britain, 7.) There was also an inconsiderable colony at Honduras, on the Spanish Main, and factories and forts (since 1620) on the Gold Coast of Africa, and (since 1656 and 1661) on the river Hoogly, in Bengal, and on the island of Bombay.

[2] Account of the British Settlements in America, II. 301. — Nor on this point, notwithstanding his general leaning to liberal notions, was

application of this theory in the dealings of England with her colonies in North America. "The first regulations," he says, "which she made with regard to them had always in view to secure to herself the monopoly of their commerce; to confine their market, and to enlarge her own at their expense; and consequently rather to damp and discourage than to quicken and forward the course of their prosperity." And he made no secret of his opinion of the character of this policy. He called it one of the "mean and malignant expedients of the mercantile system." "To prohibit a great people," he said, "from making all that they can of every part of their own produce, or from employing their stock and industry in the way that they judge most advantageous for themselves, is a manifest violation of the most sacred rights of mankind."[1]

Navigation Laws. The legislation for controlling colonial trade for the profit of the native Englishman began as far back as the time of the Commonwealth, when, by the
1651. Oct. 9. "Act for Increase of Shipping and Encouragement of Navigation," commonly called the First Navigation Law, the colonist, prohibited from shipping his goods except in vessels built in Britain or a British

Governor Pownall wiser than his great contemporary. Setting forth "the duty of the mother country to nourish and cultivate, to protect and govern the colonies," he explains that the "nurture and government should precisely direct its care to two essential points: 1. that all the profits of the produce and manufactures of these colonies centre finally in the mother country; and, 2. that the colonies continue to be the sole and proper customers of the mother country." (Administration of the Colonies, 27.) "The principles on which the Act of Navigation is founded are just, and of sound policy." (Ibid., 181; comp. Herman Merivale, Lectures on Colonization and Colonies, &c., Lect. III.; Arthur Mills, Colonial Constitutions, Chap. XLI.) — It might be added that, as colonies grew in importance, they were found to have the further uses of yielding supplies of men and munitions for war, and of profitable places for official patronage. (Comp. "Notes and Queries," No. 301, p. 273.)

[1] Wealth of Nations, II. 387, 434. For an intelligent exposition of the character of this system, see Sydney Smith Bell's "Colonial Administration of Great Britain," especially the third chapter, entitled "Causes in the Administration of the British North American Colonies which produced their Rebellion, and Ultimate Independence."

colony, was restrained from making his bargain for freight wherever it could be had on the most favorable terms.[1] From regulating commerce as to the mode of transportation, the legislation of King Charles the 1660.
Second passed to regulating the destination of the cargoes. By an Act of the first year after his restoration, colonial produce could be carried nowhere else till it had first been landed in England; in other words, the colonial producer was obliged to sell his property on such terms as he could get from the native Englishman, or else to charge himself with a double freight, and with port dues and other expenses for entry and clearance in England.[2] From thus compelling the colonists to sell in England, the next step was to compel them to buy from that country, which was done by another law for- 1663.
bidding importations into the colonies of "any commodity of the growth, production, or manufacture of Europe," except from "England, Wales, or Berwick-upon-Tweed," and in vessels built in England.[3] To a 1673.
strict execution of these laws the colonial governors were bound by their official oath, and local revenue officers appointed in England for the colonies were invested with all the same powers as in the parent country.[4] Acts of King William's third Parliament confirmed 1696.
the existing regulations of trade, and increased their oppressiveness by some minor provisions.[5] The cupidity of the landholder was stimulated by that of the merchant. An apprehension arose that the industry of

[1] See above, Vol. II. 282; Vol. III. 276–281; Chalmers's History of the Revolt, &c., I. 99.

[2] See above, Vol. II. 444. The Act is of the twelfth year of Charles the Second, Chap. IV.; comp. XVIII.

[3] See above, Vol. II. 445. The Act is of the fifteenth year of Charles the Second, Chap. VII. §§ 2, 3; comp. S. S. Bell, Colonial Administration, &c., 47.

[4] See above, Vol. III. 33, 34. The Act is of the twenty-fifth year of Charles the Second, Chap. VII.; comp. Chalmers, Annals, I. 317, 318.

[5] Acts of the seventh and eighth years of King William, Chaps. VII. and XXII.; eighth and ninth years of King William, Chap. XX. § 69.

the colonial grazier and weaver would "sink the value of English land;" and a law of one of the last years of this reign forbade the loading "in any ship or vessel," or "upon any horse, cart, or other carriage," of "any wool, or manufacture made or mixed with wool, being the produce or manufacture of any of the English plantations in America," to be conveyed "to any other of the said plantations, or to any other place whatsoever."[1]

1699.

1675. March 12. Committee of the Privy Council for the Colonies.

For fourteen years before King William came to the throne the colonial administration had been conducted by a committee of the Privy Council. The new committee appointed from that body on his accession pronounced the management to have been unsatisfactory. They represented that "the present circumstances and relation the Colonies stood in to the government of England was a matter worthy of the consideration of Parliament, for the bringing of those proprieties and dominions under a nearer dependence on the crown, as his Majesty's revenue in the plantations was very much concerned therein."[2] He had too many affairs on his hands to be able to spare attention for questions that might be deferred; and a reference to Parliament, which might involve a concession of prerogative, was not to be made without consideration. Complaints from the merchants of Bristol and Liverpool,

1689. May 9.

1 Act of tenth and eleventh of King William, Chaps. X., XIX.; comp. Act of eleventh and twelfth, Chap. XIII. § 9. — The growth and manufacture of wool still continued to be the great business of England. It had immensely increased of late, and the encouragement of it was a primary object of legislation. In 1697, when the population of England was about five millions, the value of the wool yearly shorn in that kingdom was computed at two millions of pounds sterling, and that of manufactured woollen goods at eight millions. (Davenant, Discourse on the East India Trade, in Works, II. 146.)

2 Privy Council Register, *sub die.*— The Committee of the Privy Council constituted by the new King, Feb. 14, 1689, consisted of the Earls of Danby, Halifax, Devonshire, Shrewsbury, and Nottingham, the Bishop of London, Lord Mordaunt, afterwards Earl of Peterborough, and five other persons. (O'Callaghan, Docs. Rel., &c., III., xiv.; Lucas, Memoranda towards a History of the Earlier Colonial Administration of Great Britain, 9–12.)

that the Navigation Laws were evaded to their private loss and to the damage of the commercial interests of the realm,[1] awoke a new jealousy on the subject of colonial lawlessness; and steps were taken in Parliament towards the establishment of a *Council of Commerce*,[2] which it was thought would have been followed up but for a diversion of public attention to a plot for the assassination of the King. Taking the question into his own hands, he proceeded to revive the ancient *Board of Trade and Plantations*,[3] with authority to ascertain the condition of the colonies in respect both to internal administration and to commerce; to examine the instructions which had been given to colonial governors, and propose amendments; to recommend suitable persons for colonial appointments; and to scrutinize the acts of colonial legislatures. The Board, now constituted of sixteen commissioners, continued to exist till the close of the war of American Independence.[4] John Locke, who had been Secretary to the Council for Trade in the time of King Charles the Second,[5] was one of the commissioners now appointed; but he soon withdrew,[6] finding the studious habits which he cherished inconsistent with the active duties of the place, and with the necessity which it imposed of converse with numbers of men.[7]

Reinstitution of the Board of Trade. 1695. Dec. 16.

1696. May 15.

1672.

1697. Jan.

The name of the authority now created for the superintendence of the colonies expressed what was intended to be the spirit of colonial administration. The colonies were to be made auxiliary to English trade. The Englishman in America was to be employed in making the

[1] Privy Council Register for January 12, 1690; comp. Chalmers, Revolt, &c., I. 269 *et seq.*

[2] Chalmers, Ibid., I. 270.

[3] See above, Vol. III. 33.

[4] O'Callaghan, Docs. Rel., &c., III., xv.

[5] See above, Vol. III. 33, note 2.

[6] King, Life of John Locke, II. 7.

[7] Letter to Lord Somers, Ibid. Dr. Watts addressed to him some lines on that occasion. (Horæ Lyricæ, Book II.)

fortune of the Englishman at home. It was not by its own fault that the Board of Trade proved to be an inefficient agency. It had no authority to act directly on the colonies, but only to make recommendations to the King in Council. It generally had good information, and was always watchful and intelligent. But it was thought by the higher power to be disposed to magnify its office imprudently, and its counsels were often set aside by denial, and oftener by neglect.[1] The strict enforcement of the Navigation Laws was the theoretical policy of the Board. In a certain sense, also, this was a point of honor with the Parliament and the nation; and occasionally, in commercial exigencies, it was passionately urged by English owners of plantations in the sugar islands, and English merchants who dealt with the planters and had a common interest with them. But in practice the object was never pursued with persistency. During all the long periods while the New England Colonies were fighting the French, it would have been imprudent for the parent government to cripple and to offend them by a vigorous interference with the business which furnished so large a part of their livelihood; the uncertainty which existed as to the amount of resistance that might be offered to too harsh measures was always so great as to render them of questionable prudence; the profit of the extra-legal commerce of New England with

Imperfect enforcement of the Navigation Laws.

[1] Chalmers's Revolt, &c., *passim.* "The Board of Trade and Plantations, in theory, possessed as extensive functions as those which pertain by a subsequent arrangement to its modern substitute, the Colonial Office. At the same time, it will appear that its actual intent was limited to the enforcement of the Navigation Acts, and of those commercial regulations which were then thought essential to the maintenance of the commercial prosperity of Great Britain." (Lucas, Memoranda, &c., 3.) "The confusion of the rights of the empire and of the colonies increased the difficulties of the Board where it could act, and materially diminished its opportunities of acting." (Ibid., 4.) According to Governor Pownall, Lord Somers's intention, in constituting the Board of Trade, was to create a tribunal of great dignity and efficiency. (Administration of the Colonies, 20, 21.)

foreign countries supplied abundant means for the purchase of English manufactures, which in the absence of that trade could not have been paid for; and, after all, a stern enforcement of the Navigation Laws upon an unwilling people was troublesome and expensive, even when the attempt at enforcement was not defeated by the artifices of parties concerned or by the contumacy of jurors. So that, through much of the time, the officious stubbornness of Randolph and his coadjutors, agents of the Board of Trade, led to nothing but disappointment to themselves and their masters, and irritation and suspicion in the Colonies.

CHAPTER II.

THE emancipation from the tyranny of Governor Andros and of his infatuated master was an immense relief to New England; but it would have been without a parallel among political revolutions, if it had been followed at once by a satisfactory condition of affairs. In Massachusetts, the government which was set up was on all hands understood to be provisional merely. This admission was unfortunate for the public repose, both as indicating timidity on the part of the persons at the head of affairs, and as keeping alive a question which left the obligations of citizens undetermined. The case of Massachusetts differed from that of Rhode Island and Connecticut in the very important particular that her charter had been formally vacated by legal process. But this had been done with circumstances of such injustice, and so resembling those which in England had excited extreme resentment when the municipal corporations were the sufferers, that the new King and his servants would not probably have taken offence, had Massachusetts, like her two sister communities, reconstituted her ancient government as still of right existing; while the local administration would have derived respect and authority from the confidence displayed in that pretension.[1]

Provisional government of Massachusetts.

[1] May 24, 1689 (see above, Vol. III. 589), the Magistrates resolved to assume the function urged upon them by the Delegates, "until by direction from England there be an orderly settlement of government;" and for greater explicitness they indorsed upon their vote, "It was declared by the gentlemen subscribing that they do not intend an assumption of charter government, nor would be so understood." This did not satisfy the Delegates; and, encouraged by the arrival, before the week's end, of Sir William Phips and of orders to proclaim the new King, they organized

The first General Court constituted according to the ancient charter adjourned after a five weeks' session, having first declared the laws to be provisionally revived which were in force at the time of the inauguration of the Council under Dudley's presidency, instructed the judicial courts to resume their functions as exercised at that time, and confirmed subordinate officers, military and civil, in their places. This was all which for the present could be done; and things remained in a state of great uncertainty till, near the end of the year, Bradstreet was able to communicate to the Court a letter from the King giving authority to the persons now in office to "continue the administration of the government" till his further pleasure should be made known. His further pleasure was not announced till after nearly three years more; but meanwhile this order fortified the temporary government, and produced a more satisfactory condition of affairs.

1689. July 13.

June 22.

July 5.

Dec. 3.

Aug. 12.

Instead of retaining their places by virtue of this missive, as it seems they would have been justified in doing, the Magistrates chose to interpret it as authority for maintaining the old charter government; and annual elections

themselves as a House of Deputies, and on the next day, after choosing a Speaker, sent a memorial (June 6) to the Governor, Lieutenant-Governor, and Assistants, praying them "to accept government according to our charter rules by the names of 'Governor and Council for the Massachusetts Colony,' . . . . . until further orders from England." The Magistrates dismissed their scruples, and took the oaths of office the same day. (Mass. Col. Rec., *sub die.*) — "For about seven weeks after the Revolution, here was not so much as a face of any government. . . . . . But at length the Assembly prevailed with those that had been of the government to promise that they would reassume, and accordingly a proclamation was drawn; but, before publishing it, it was underwritten, that they would not have it understood that they did reassume charter government. So that between government and no government this country remained." (Calef, More Wonders of the Invisible World, 95.) — Oct. 26, 1689, Bradstreet explained to the Earl of Shrewsbury the reasons which had dictated the provisional resumption of the government "according to the rule of the charter, being that," he said, "under which these colonies have happily grown and flourished." (British Colonial Papers.)

were accordingly ordered and held for the present as in former times, resulting in three successive designations of Bradstreet and Danforth to the two highest offices. The
1690 General Court must have considered itself as in-
Feb. 12. creasing its chances for a renewal of the vacated charter when it modified the law for admission to the franchise, reducing the amount of the pecuniary qualification, and repealing the provision which required a testimonial to the candidate's religious character from his minister, a certificate from selectmen to the effect that he was "not vicious in life" being now recognized as an equivalent.[1] Bradstreet was probably infirm in
1689. Dec. 4 health during the first winter of his new adminis-
-1690. May 28. tration, as he appears to have been absent from all the meetings of the Magistrates for six months. By the same conveyance which brought authority from
1689. England for a provisional reinstitution of the gov-
Nov. 24. ernment had come an order to the Governor to send Andros and his fellow-prisoners to England.[2] Danforth and four others were directed by the House
Dec. 7. to draw up complaints against them, in order to an arraignment before the Privy Council.[3] Elisha Cooke and Thomas Oakes were appointed to proceed to England, to be associated with Mather in his agency.[4]

[1] Mass. Col. Rec., *sub die.*

[2] Randolph wrote to the Commissioners of Customs, Dec. 12, 1689, that, though the order for the conveyance of the prisoners by the first ship to England had been received nearly three weeks before, no notice of it had been given them, "nor had they liberty to go out of gaol to provide necessaries." — Jan. 29, 1690, Bradstreet wrote to Lord Shrewsbury that he had given orders for sending the prisoners to England by the Rose frigate. As to domestic affairs, he expressed his fears of trouble from the Indians in the spring. (British Colonial Papers.)

[3] Jan. 2, 1690, Stoughton, Gedney, Brown, and others, were added by the Council to this Committee. (Mass. Col. Rec., *sub die.*) Depositions against Andros are in the Archives of Massachusetts, CXXVII. 143, &c.

[4] Mass. Col. Rec. for Dec. 3, 1689, Jan. 18 and 24, 1690. — Elisha Cooke was now fifty-two years old. He was graduated at Harvard College in 1657, and became a physician, but took to politics early. In 1681 and 1682 he was a Representative from Boston in the General Court, and espoused the popular cause so warmly as to occasion a special report against him from Randolph to his masters in England.

The degree of good order which prevailed during this long suspension of a legitimate government gave evidence, on the whole, of the peaceable disposition of the people, and of their attachment to the leaders whom they had empowered for the existing crisis.[1] But it was impossible that quiet and content should be complete, while questions of such moment were unsettled. Would the old charter be restored, with or without alteration of its grants? If not, what frame of government would succeed it? What degree of self-government would be allowed? What force would be conceded, not only to acts of the existing provisional authority, but to the colonial legislation of two generations, during which the powers conveyed by the charter had been differently understood in the Colony and in England? Nor was there wanting a party spirit to take advantage of the solicitude excited by such uncertainties. Besides persons who were prompted by considerations of direct personal advantage, there was a class not inconsiderable for numbers or capacity, among the recent immigrants especially,[2]

Unsettled condition of Massachusetts.

(See above, Vol. III. 354, note 2.) In 1683 he was Speaker of the House; and in the three following years he was an Assistant, taking the place of Dudley, whose sycophancy to the court had caused him to be left out. Cooke in his turn was passed over, when Dudley became President. Cooke was rich and well connected. He married a daughter of Governor Leverett. He was forward in the measures for the deposition of Andros, and became one of the Council for the Safety of the People and Conservation of the Peace. He was now again an Assistant in the provisional government, to which dignity Oakes also was raised, while abroad, in the spring of 1690. Oakes had before been Speaker of the House. He was younger than Cooke, being five years after him in college, but as early as 1682 had distinguished himself sufficiently on the patriot side to be included with him in Randolph's maledictions. (Ibid.) Oakes, like Cooke, was a physician. Lawyers do not appear in the House till after more than another generation.

[1] "For divers weeks from the arrest of Andros the Colony continued without any pretence to civil government. Yet, through the mercy of God, all things were under such good inclinations among us that every man gave himself the laws of good neighborhood, and little or nothing extravagant was all that while done." (A. B., "Account of the Late Revolution," &c., 11.)

[2] Oct. 26, 1689, Bradstreet writes to Lord Shrewsbury of the efforts of "many strangers that have come in amongst us" to embarrass the gov-

who, either from genuine sympathy with the absolutist party in England, or making what appeared to them the better choice among evils, disapproved the recent rising, and who, when not venturing on active measures to obstruct the patriot authorities, viewed them with a malign or suspicious eye, and at best afforded them no cheerful support.

The embarrassments thus occasioned could not but perplex a government which had not, in a high degree, the strength of personal ability and character. Well-meaning and painstaking as he was, the now aged Governor had never been eminently fit for difficult occasions. Danforth, besides being in only a secondary place, was occupied with his special business in the administration of Maine;[1] and, except him, no other Counsellor possessed capacity equal to that of some of the partially disaffected persons, who, like Stoughton, retained more or less traditional hold upon the public confidence. So loose, in fact, proved the bonds of authority, that a press of men for military service was sometimes resisted.[2] So was, in repeated instances, the collection of taxes.[3] A court constituted for Middlesex County, under commissions from Governor Andros, persisted in exercising its jurisdiction, and was only stopped by its members being sent to gaol.[4]

Sept. 24.

ernment and create disorder. (British Colonial Papers.)

[1] See above, Vol. III. 595, note 1.

[2] "Few or none will own the authority of a press." (Letter from Boston, of July 13–30, 1689, in British Colonial Papers; comp. Mass. Archives, CVII. 184.)

[3] "The people . . . . . openly disown the power of government, and refuse to pay rates and taxes, which it is presumed to collect in their Majesty's name." (Randolph to the Lords of Trade, Oct. 15, 1689, in British Colonial Papers.) This fact, though Randolph overstates it, actually existed to some extent.

[4] Thomas Greaves, of Charlestown, "Judge of the Inferior Court of Pleas" for Middlesex, in a letter to James Russell, of Charlestown (Sept. 2, 1689), protested against Russell's intention "to keep a pretended court of jurisdiction, not having any lawful authority from our sovereign Lord and Lady King William and Queen Mary." Greaves was summoned before the Council, Sept. 24, for "contriving, framing, and publishing under his hand a seditious writing highly contemning the government of this their Majesty's Colony." (British Colonial Papers. The warrant for his commitment is in Mass. Archives,

One consequence of this uncomfortable state of affairs was the inefficient prosecution of the war in which Andros had had such imperfect success. To the hostile movements made by the natives in the last summer of his administration he had at first attached little importance, though they appeared in a different light to his associates in the government. The indulgence which he preferred to practise towards the savages had so little of the expected effect that he presently felt obliged to abandon that policy, and undertake a winter campaign in the eastern country. The recall, by the provisional government, of the troops which he had posted there, however justified by other considerations, had an unfavorable influence on the prospects of the war.[1]

War with the Eastern Indians.

1688, 1689.

The number of Indians remaining within the closely settled portions of New England was not now considerable enough to require any special precautions against disaffection which might arise among them. Four years before the Revolution, Governor Hinckley estimated their number, including all ages, in Plymouth, where they were much more numerous than in other parts of the country occupied by Englishmen, at less than six thousand.[2] Thirteen years later it was believed that in Massachusetts proper there were not many more than two hundred.[3] They were all reckoned among *praying*

1685.

1698.

XXXV. 35, 48.) Greaves, Richard Sprague, and ten other malecontents, sent a petition to the King for redress. (British Colonial Papers.) Feb. 4, 1691, the General Court issued a summons to Lawrence Hammond to appear and show cause why he withheld the records of the Middlesex County Court. He neglected to appear, and a warrant was issued for his arrest. (Mass. Col. Rec.)

[1] See above, Vol. III. 564, 567, 587.

[2] New England Memorial (Davis's edition), 412.

[3] This was the estimate of the ministers Grindal Rawson and Samuel Danforth in their Report to the Society for Propagating the Gospel in New England. They reckoned an Indian population of about 1300 in what had been Plymouth Colony, and of 1500 or 1600 in Martha's Vineyard and the neighboring islands. But this was an enumeration of Christian converts and their families. (Mass. Hist. Col., X. 129, &c.) I do not find satisfactory materials for an account of the remnant of unconverted savages after Philip's

Indians, though experience had shown that in respect to security for their harmlessness their small numbers were to be more regarded than their religious profession. But the force of the tribes which roamed over the wide tracts now occupied by Maine, New Hampshire, and Vermont, was still almost unbroken, and had probably even been largely increased by the resort of savages who had been expelled from their seats in the war which had been waged almost continuously since the outbreak of King Philip.[1]

Leaving out of view the seven outlying towns on Connecticut River, which, in some sort, though imperfectly, were covered by New York and the friendly Iroquois Indians, the frontier of Massachusetts at this time may be traced by a line beginning at Falmouth on Casco Bay, and running along the towns of Scarborough, Saco, Wells, York, Amesbury, Haverhill, Andover, Dunstable, Chelmsford, Groton, Lancaster, and Worcester. The withdrawal of the troops from the eastern country was a signal to the tribes in that quarter to renew their turbulence. Of the four towns of New Hampshire, Portsmouth and Hampton lay a little out of the track of the marauders as they passed

war. No doubt a considerable portion of those who had been in hostility were frightened away to their friends at the eastward and in Canada, and many became domestic servants in English families, and many sought amnesty by taking up the profession of praying Indians. (See above, Vol. III. 221, 222.)

[1] John Eliot, the Indian "Apostle," lived long enough to witness the sad frustration of the high hopes which had animated the labors of his middle life. (See above, Vol. II. 190 *et seq.*; 334 *et seq.*) He died at Roxbury, May 20, 1690, having lived to be eighty-six years old. Eliot and Richard Baxter were close friends for twenty years or more. Portions of their correspondence are preserved in Dr. Williams's Library, Red Cross Street, London. Baxter wrote to Eliot two years before his death (Feb. 5, 1688), "I thank you for your condescending communications to your unworthy brother, than whom few more value and honor your labors above all other men's, and who daily prayeth to God for your further success, and should much rejoice to hear more of it before my pained, languishing body lie down in the dust, and my soul shall quit this sinful world. And sometimes remember in your supplications to our Father your weak and worthless fellow-servant." The letter is dated "From my poor obscure recess, where I have been since I came out of prison for preaching and not taking their Oxford oath."

westward from their chief places of strength on the Penobscot and the Kennebec; and Portsmouth had numbers and defences which afforded it some security. It is matter of wonder that the brave inhabitants of the other two towns should have persevered to maintain their position through that miserable war which raged during the greater part of King William's reign of thirteen years.[1]

The reader remembers that the relations between these people and the French dated from an early period of the appearance of Frenchmen in the western hemisphere. A son of De Monts' lieutenant, Poutrincourt, visited the region about the Kennebec eight years before the English settlements at Plymouth. He was accompanied by a Jesuit priest, who, "with the help of one of them, who understood some French, announced Jesus Christ" to the savages thereabouts. He found them "a teachable people, who listened to him with respect, and seemed to be not far from the kingdom of God."[2] It is not recorded that this transient visit had any immediate effect; but the Abenaquis were attracted by their vicinity to the French settlements on the St. Lawrence, and the passage from the head waters of the Kennebec to those of the Chaudière was not difficult at favorable seasons of the year. In time they made application for a priest. It was arranged that the Jesuit Father Druillettes should reside among them;[3] and the mission which he originated "promised the same fruits of benediction as were gathered in the most flourishing establishments of the faith."[4] The fruit was ripe when intelligence of the havoc made by Philip's people in Plymouth and Massachusetts reached the eastern country; and the Abenaquis, with whom the Etetchemins were now so

1612.

The French and the Abenaquis.

1646.

[1] "Decennium Luctuosum," the *Woful Decade*, is Cotton Mather's not ill-chosen title for his history of that long distress, in Magnalia Christi, &c., VII. 60 *et seq.*

[2] Charlevoix, Histoire, &c., I. 130.

[3] Ibid., 280; comp. above, Vol. II. 304.

[4] Charlevoix, Histoire, &c., I. 281, 310.

closely allied that the two families were no longer distinguished, devastated the settlements in that quarter, till they were with difficulty reduced to a surly submission after three years' resistance.[1] The struggle, renewed in the time of Governor Andros,[2] was still going on when his government was overthrown and the different communities which it embraced were remitted to their original condition of independence of one another. Considerable numbers of Abenaqui converts had meanwhile been collected by the priests into settlements of their own in Canada, as at Besancour, near Three Rivers, and St. François, near Quebec.[3]

1675–1678.

The settlement of Dover, lying at the lowest convenient fording-place of the Piscataqua, and with an ungarrisoned territory to the north of it, had been kept in perpetual alarm through a great part of its early history. In the first days of the anarchy, as it may be strictly called, which in New Hampshire followed upon the deposition of Andros,[4] the Indians undertook an enterprise, dictated, it seems, by resentments which had been nursed through thirteen years. At Dover, by the lower falls of the tributary river Cochecho, were five of those *garrison-houses*, as they were called, which were common at outposts; that is, houses slightly fortified for the purpose of receiving a number of neighbors in case of any alarm. One of these belonged to Major Waldron, who by a stratagem had made prisoners of four hundred Indians towards the close of Philip's war.[5] To

Sack of Dover by the Indians.

[1] See above, Vol. III. 206–214. — It is remarkable how the French historian passes over these important transactions.

[2] See above, Vol. III. 539, 564, 567.

[3] Charlevoix, Histoire, &c., II. 109; comp. Maine Hist. Col., VI. 207 *et seq.*; Gallatin, Synopsis, &c., in Archæologia Americana, II. 31 *et seq.*

[4] It was not till March 19, 1690, that New Hampshire was incorporated into Massachusetts, by a vote of the General Court of the latter Colony, founded upon a petition from inhabitants of the former. (Mass. Col. Rec., *sub die.*)

[5] See above, Vol. III. 209.

each of these houses on a summer evening came two Indian women, and begged for a lodging, which was refused them at only one. When the other inmates were asleep, the women unbarred the doors, and whistled a signal to their confederates, who had been approaching in the darkness. A hand-to-hand fight with the whites was what the Indians always shunned, but they had now an advantage while the just awakened sleepers were groping for their arms. One house was alarmed by the barking of a dog, in time for the inmates to rally and defend it. Among them was the minister of the hamlet, who threw himself on his back with his feet against the door, and so held it till the muskets of his friends began to take effect. The house which had not admitted the spies seemed safe, but its owner was son of his next neighbor, whom the savages brought within his hearing, and threatened to kill if a surrender continued to be refused. Filial affection prevailed, and the occupants of both houses were put together in a separate building, to be carried away to the eastern country. But they were negligently guarded, and managed to escape.

1689. June 27.

Both of the two other garrison-houses were burned. Waldron's was, of course, the object of special attention. He was eighty years old. At the first disturbance he leaped from his bed, and, seizing his sword, drove before him some Indians who had already entered his chamber. While he returned for fire-arms, one of the savages followed him closely and struck him on the back of the head with a hatchet. The blow of the coward was feeble, and Waldron was only stunned; but while for the moment he was helpless the Indians dragged him into his hall, and tied him in a chair placed upon a table. Then they gashed his body with their knives, one saying after another, "I cross out my account." They cut off his nose and ears, and crammed them into his mouth, and at length put an end to his sufferings with his own sword.[1] Twenty-three white people were killed at this time, and twenty-nine made prisoners. Several of the latter were sold to the French in Canada, being, as has been believed, the first English captives who were thus disposed of.[2]

August. The easy success which had attended this enterprise invited a repetition of it, and within two months another part of Dover called *Oyster River* (now Durham) was attacked. Eighteen men were killed while at work in the fields. Two boys, who with some women and young children were in a house where there were fire-arms, defended it till it was set on fire, when they surrendered on a promise that their lives should be spared. The conquerors impaled one of the children, killed two or three others, and carried away the rest of their prisoners. A gang of Indian strollers murdered four Englishmen at Saco, but, firing upon a party which went out to bury the bodies, were driven off with loss.[3] The important post at Pemaquid was assailed by a party from the mouth of the Penobscot, where Father Thury, "a good worker, and a man of capacity," had a considerable mission. The officer in command surrendered himself and his fifteen men on the condition of being dismissed in safety; but several of

July.

Aug. 2.

Indian war in Maine.

[1] The way in which these particulars of Waldron's fate became known may be inferred from a statement respecting the captivity of Mary Gerrish in Belknap's New Hampshire (Farmer's edition), 129, note ‡; comp. Niles, History of the French and Indian Wars, in Mass. Hist. Col., XXVI. 206 *et seq.*

[2] Mather, Magnalia Christi Americana, VII. 64–66; New Hampshire Provincial Papers, II. 49 *et seq.* — Four or five days before this disastrous affair, Major Henchman of Chelmsford wrote to the Governor in Boston that he had information from some Indians that there was trouble brewing on the Piscataqua, and notice was sent to Waldron, but the messenger was detained at Newbury ferry, and did not reach Dover till the morning after the massacre. (N. H. Provincial Papers, II. 48–53.) The affair is described in letters written the day after. (Mass. Hist. Col., XXI. 85–91.)

[3] Mather, Magnalia, &c., VII. 65.

the garrison were put to death or led away captives.[1] The scattered settlers east of what is now Portland (if *settlements* their places of precarious habitation can be called) withdrew into a few poorly fortified houses.

In the course of these operations there was treacherous communication, not suspected at the time, between French priests in Canada and Indians about Boston. It was this which, according to a statement of the French Governor-General, accomplished during the summer the massacre of no fewer than two hundred Englishmen, and the capture of sixteen fortified places, with twenty cannon.[2]

The General Court of Massachusetts, suddenly convened by the Governor, resolved to raise six hundred men for service in the eastern country, and appointed Jeremiah Swayne, a Counsellor, to the command. The enlistment for this service did not proceed with energy, owing partly to causes that have just been explained, and partly perhaps to want of confidence in the commander, who had his military reputation still to make. But a considerable body of Massachusetts troops took the field, under Major Church, the soldier of Philip's war, who brought from Plymouth and Rhode Island a reinforcement of two hundred and fifty men, English and Indians. Church's former good fortune did not follow him. He went by sea to Casco, and thence marched as far as the Kennebec, fighting on the way an indecisive action, in which he sustained considerable loss. He proceeded some distance up that river without finding the enemy, and before winter, having settled some garrisons,

Aug. 21.

September.

[1] So secure was the garrison that the answer to the summons was that the commander was tired, and was going to sleep. (Charlevoix, Histoire, &c., I. 557, 558.)

[2] Charlevoix, Histoire, &c., III. 418. — "M. de Nonville reported that, in consequence of the good understanding, which he had had through two Jesuits, with those Indians who occupy the woods in the neighborhood of Boston, who are disposed to become Christians, he had been afforded the means to seize, exclusive of Penkuit [Pemaquid], sixteen forts during the summer, in which were twenty cannon." (O'Callaghan, Documents, &c., 438, 440.)

sent back the rest of his troops in the transports, and himself returned by land to Boston;[1] and the autumn passed without further alarm.

These were but operations of a *little war*, though of a grievously distressing one. In the next year there appeared openly a new party to it, occasioning it thenceforward to be conducted on a vastly larger scale. The New England people now began to be acquainted with the price they were to pay for the happiness of seeing the Calvinistic Prince of Orange on the British throne. He had not reigned three months when England declared war against France; and a series of wars between New England and New France began, which with only one long interval lasted for seventy years, both parties availing themselves of aid from the savages, — the French especially, who by their missionaries succeeded best in establishing an interest with the tribes.

King William's war with France.

May 7.

A line of French stations, admitting of communication, though in some instances far apart, already extended through the interior of the continent from the mouth of the St. Lawrence to the mouth of the Mississippi, enclosing the whole line of English colonies on the Atlantic shore.[2] From the rivers Mississippi and Ohio, France pressed upon Carolina and Virginia with her Indian allies; from the Great Lakes, on New York; from the Penobscot and the upper waters of the Connecticut, on Massachusetts. In her relations to the North American tribes, proselyting was her object everywhere, her agents being Jesuit and Récollet missionaries. In her relations to the tribes of the North she had two further objects, the command of the cod-fishery and of the fur-trade.

The population of Canada at this time did not amount to more than twelve thousand persons,[3] or about one eighth part of the population of New Eng-

Condition of Canada.

[1] Church, Entertaining Passages, II. 55–66; Williamson, History, I. 614.

[2] See above, Vol. III. 563, note 2.

[3] From time to time a census was

land.[1] For nearly thirty years the government, relinquished
by a partnership of adventurers which was insti- 1663.
tuted by Cardinal Richelieu under the style of the 1627.
Hundred Associates, had been supervised for the King by Colbert and Louvois, who found most efficient auxiliaries in the ecclesiastics congregated at Quebec and Montreal and scattered thence over the hunting-grounds of the native tribes. M. de Callières, royal Governor of Montreal, and commander-in-chief of the forces in Canada, was in France when the news of the English Revolution reached that country. He immediately submitted to the Minister of
Marine a plan for a general attack on the north- 1689.
ern English Colonies.[2] He had already in his January.
government thirteen or fourteen hundred regular soldiers. With them and six hundred militia he proposed to capture, first, Albany, approaching it by the way of Lake Champlain, and then New York. The scheme was approved, and to execute it an officer who had formerly for
several years had experience as Governor of New June 7.
France was restored to that position.[3] Louis de Buade, Comte de Frontenac, now nearly seventy years old, was a man of energy and talent equal to the great occasion created by these circumstances.[4] His instructions required

taken of the population of Canada. In 1679 it was rated at 9400 souls; in 1719 at 22,530. (O'Callaghan, Documents, IX. 136, 896.) Bouchette (British Dominions in North America, I. 347) places it in 1688 at 11,249. Comp. Charlevoix, III. 387; Murdock, History of Nova Scotia, 276.

1 Holmes, American Annals, I. 448, 465; Chalmers, Revolt, &c., I. 207. — "An Abstract of the Militia or Train-bands in New England," reported, May 13, 1690, by Sir Edmund Andros to the Board of Trade, represented the number to be 13,220, of whom 7975 belonged to Massachusetts, 3061 to Connecticut, 1392 to Plymouth, and 792 to Rhode Island. (British Colonial Papers.)

2 See the Memoir in the "Documentary History of New York," I. 177; or in O'Callaghan, Documents, &c., IX. 404. Charlevoix describes it. (Histoire, &c., III. 392.)

3 Royal Instructions to the Count de Frontenac in "Documentary History of New York," I. 183.

4 He succeeded the Sieur de Nonville, who was now recalled to an employment about the persons of the King's sons. (Charlevoix, I. 543; comp. Colden, History of the Five Indian Nations, I. 102. De Non-

him to execute the conquest, if possible, in season to return to Canada before winter with as many of his troops as should not be required to secure the new possessions. He was at the same time "to profit by circumstances to conclude a solid and advantageous peace with the Iroquois."[1]

Confederacy of the Five Nations.

Iroquois was the collective name given by the French to those tribes of Indians which, called by the English the *Five Nations*, acted from this time forward so important a part in the conflicts between New England and New France. When they first became known to Europeans, these tribes, bearing severally the names of Mohawks, Oneidas, Onondagas, Cayugas, and Senecas, possessed most of the territory which now constitutes the State of New York, extending themselves in the order in which they have been named from Hudson River to Lake Ontario and Lake Erie, while by conquests in their perpetual wars they had spread their power on the one side over a considerable region north of those lakes, and, in the opposite direction, to the western borders of Virginia and Maryland. From an early time the New England colonists had had some knowledge of the Mohawks, who claimed a sort of jurisdiction over the Mohegans of Connecticut,[2] but it was not till a half-century after the colonization that New Englander and Iroquois were brought face to face.

The Indians of the Five Nations were a superior race to the aboriginal people of New England. Though not less ferocious and cruel, they had more sense of truth, more intelligence, and more courage. That permanent alliance of the tribes with each other, which constituted them so great a power, could only have existed on the basis of some capacity for political organization. Each

ville had been Governor since 1684.) The reason of the qualified terms in which the Jesuit describes Frontenac is that that able ruler chafed at and occasionally repelled the assumptions of the priests.

[1] O'Callaghan, IX. 426.

[2] See above, Vol. I. 24, 469.

nation was in the last resort independent of the rest; and, moved by interests or passions of its own, a single nation would sometimes contract engagements and pursue measures at variance with the objects of the confederacy. But interferences on the part of one or more tribes with the policy of the rest as to peace or war were a departure from their normal course of action.

Owing to various causes, such as their physical constitution, their perpetual and destructive wars, their occupation as hunters, which required large spaces of land, and their wretched domestic habits, giving to their progeny a poor chance for life, the population of the Five Nations was small in comparison with the extent of their domain. Their whole number was never rated at above ten thousand persons, of whom their males of military age were believed to be three thousand, or less than one third part. But, in the rivalry of European interests in America, their friendship or enmity was of the utmost consequence to the contending parties. For they occupied in force the high interior of the hitherto discovered portion of the continent, and, according to the direction of the rivers which had their springs in the Iroquois hunting-grounds, there was communication with the Great Lakes, with the Gulf of Mexico, and with the Atlantic coast.

Their friendship for the English.

The Iroquois were generally friends to the English, though not without those fluctuations which belong to the caprice and impressibility of savages. They found the best customers for their furs in the foreigners who commanded the mouth of the Hudson; and, on the other hand, their jealousy was constantly reawakened by the persistency of the French in attempts to establish themselves on their soil by means of posts on the way from the Great Lakes to the outlet of the Mississippi.

Under a sudden impulse of confidence in one rival, or of uneasiness respecting the purposes of the other, chiefs of

the Mohawks and Oneidas came to Albany, and made a treaty by which their lands and castles were
1684. placed under the protection of the King of England. In the same year, De Barre, Governor-General of Canada, bent on chastising an attack of the Senecas upon some French whom they accused of supplying their savage enemies with fire-arms, led a force of fifteen hundred men into the country of that tribe. By the time that he had reached the south-east corner of Lake Ontario,
Hostilities between them and the French. he found his soldiers so much disabled by the fatigue of the march and the heat of the summer as to make pacific measures prudent; and he undertook a negotiation, the result of which was that the Indians contemptuously allowed him to withdraw without further damage.[1]

The Marquis de Nonville, succeeding to the government of Canada, came resolved to remove the discredit
1685. which had fallen on his master's power. With an army of fifteen hundred French and five hundred friendly
1687. Indians, he penetrated as far as the country of the
June. Senecas, the tribe which was the special object of his resentment. There, falling into an ambuscade, he met with heavy loss, and was compelled to a precipitate retreat. The Indians did not pursue their advantage with the vigor which they might have exerted had they had proper support from the Governor of New York, to whom the King had given orders dictated by his subserviency to the crown of France. As it was, after some fruitless attempts of the
1689. French to obtain a pacification by treaty, twelve
July 26. hundred Iroquois warriors came to the island of Montreal, and spread a terrible devastation around that

[1] Colden, History of the Five Indian Nations, &c., I. 64. Colden's work must be used with much caution. Writing long after the period of some of the most important events which he relates, he falls into inaccuracy as to dates, and accordingly as to the mutual influences of events. The best means of correcting it are afforded by Charlevoix, for the time prior to that of newspapers.

city, burning the houses, and killing, it was said, more than a thousand of the people.[1] A further consequence of these transactions was, that for the time the French lost most of the Indian allies, whose fidelity to them had hitherto been steady.

This took place just after the overthrow of the government of King James the Second in the parent country, and of Governor Andros in New England. New France appeared to be in an almost desperate condition. Her pecuniary distress was not what in similar circumstances was brought about in New England, for the King took care of her military outlays. But her loss of men in the war had been severe; her husbandry had unavoidably been neglected; her interior trade was cut off; and an exasperated savage enemy was at her doors, scarcely less powerful, in numbers, than her own people; well united together, for the present, by a common hate and fear; with plenty of recent experience in the kind of warfare in which it was most formidable; animated to new action by its recent success.[2]

If New France in such circumstances seemed scarcely equal to cope with the vigorous Five Nations alone, its doom might appear to be certain when, war having been declared by King William against France, the hostile savage power was backed by the equally interested hos-

[1] Charlevoix, Histoire, &c., I. 549. Charlevoix's relation of this affair has a few touches that help our conception of the character of Indian war, unless, indeed, we should consider them as due to the lively French imagination of the writer. "Ils commencèrent par massacrer tous les hommes; ensuite ils mirent le feu aux maisons. Par-là tous ceux qui y étaient restés tombèrent entre les mains de ces sauvages, et essayèrent tout ce que la fureur peut inspirer à des barbares. Ils la poussèrent même à des excès dont on ne les avait pas encore crus capables. Ils ouvrirent le sein des femmes enceintes, pour en arracher le fruit qu'elles portoient. Ils mirent des enfans tout vivans à la broche, et contraignèrent les mères de les tourner pour les faire rôtir. Ils inventèrent quantité d'autres supplices inouïs, et deux-cent personnes de tout âge et de tout sexe périrent ainsi en moins d'une heure dans les plus affreux tourmens." (Comp. Smith, History of New York, 100.)

[2] Colden, History, &c., I. 92, 93.

tility and superior military efficiency of New York and New England. But precious time passed and nothing was done. After the deposition of Governor Andros, the governments of New England remained in an undefined and ineffective state.[1] In New York, incapacity in the successive rulers, party spirit and turbulence among the English people, and the chronic dissensions and jealousies between them and their more numerous Dutch fellow-citizens, were at the all-important crisis fatal obstacles to strenuous action. The behavior of the Dutch colonists in these times was such as to provoke from the contemporary historian the comment that "many of them had none of the virtues of the country of their origin, except their industry in getting money," and that "they sacrificed every thing other people think honorable or most sacred to their gain."[2]

The threatening attitude of the Five Nations, and the recent demonstrations of their strength and boldness, necessarily embarrassed and postponed the enterprise with which the new Governor of New France was
1689. charged.[3] Immediately on arriving at Quebec
Oct. 2. he proceeded to Montreal, whence he sent emissaries to endeavor to engage the tribes in a negotiation for

[1] Of course, one result of this was financial disorder. One of the first representations brought to the Board by Cooke and Oakes, on their arrival in England, was that "the charge of the war hath hitherto been maintained by the disbursements of particular persons, there being no public treasure to be found upon the Revolution, and that the public stores of ammunition were very inconsiderable; that nothing since had been raised there but what had been advanced by way of loan, to carry on the public charges of the war." (Journal of the Board of Trade for Feb. 25, 1690.)

[2] Colden, History, &c., I. 100.

[3] La Hontan, Voyages, &c., I. 198, &c. Charlevoix (Histoire, &c., II. 117) speaks bitterly of the Protestant La Hontan. — According to a Memoir in the French "Bureau de la Marine," the slowness of Frontenac's movements was owing to an instruction from the King respecting an attempt to make peace. "The ill-founded hope of peace with the Iroquois caused the inactivity in which the last campaign had been passed." (O'Callaghan, IX. 431, 433.) King James (treacherously to England) had set his heart on bringing about this pacification between the French and the Iroquois. (Charlevoix, Histoire, &c., II. 330, 376, 401, 403.)

a peace,[1] with the less chance, however, of success, as at a great council at Albany the chiefs had just been renewing their engagements with the English.[2] At Onondaga they held another council to consider his proposals, and its result was a renewed declaration of their purpose to "adhere to the old chain" with Corléar (the planters of New York), and to prosecute the war against Onondio (the French). But the military arrangements of one division of their allies did not satisfy them. They thought they saw a more promising course of action. "Brother Kinshon," they said to the messengers present from New England (which country they symbolized by the Oneida word for *fish*), "we hear you design to send soldiers to the eastward against the Indians there, but we advise you, now so many are united against the French, to fall immediately on them. Strike at the root; when the trunk shall be cut down, the branches fall of course. Corléar and Kinshon, courage! courage! In the spring, to Quebec! Take that place, and you will have your feet on the necks of the French, and all their friends in America."[3]

September.

1690. Jan. 22.

But, while they announced and counselled so correct a policy in relation to the French, they were not prepared for such action as would have made them immediately useful to New England. At the conference which had lately been held with them by commissioners from Massachusetts, Plymouth, and Connecticut, while the chiefs were profuse of protestations of friendship, they

1689. September.

[1] Charlevoix, Histoire, &c., II. 76; Colden, History, &c., I. 106 *et seq.*

[2] Colonel John Pynchon, Major Thomas Savage, and Captain Andrew Belcher, appointed Aug. 21, 1689 (Mass. Col. Rec., *sub die*), to treat with the Mohawks at Albany, had proceeded immediately on their mission.

[3] Colden, History, &c., I. 113 *et seq.* — At this juncture, Feb. 13, 1690, Wait Winthrop was restored to the command of the militia of Massachusetts. (Mass. Col. Rec., *sub die.*) This may be guessed to have been a measure of conciliation at a time too much in need of union to admit of the cherishing of any needless jealousies. (See above, Vol. III. 581.)

French intrigues with the Eastern Indians.

could not be brought to undertake hostilities against the Eastern Indians, with whom they said they had no quarrel.[1] Frontenac's good information concerning these Eastern tribes gave him encouragement as to the use which they might be made to serve. "The Abenakis or Cannibas . . . . . ordinarily reside on the river Quinebaqui [Kennebec], and disperse themselves for the purpose of hunting as far as Quebec, whither they have been attracted by the missionaries. Of all the Indians these are the bravest and most formidable to the English. The experience of what they effected last year by the capture of Fort Pemkuit [Pemaquid] and sixteen palisaded settlements ought to be an assurance of what may be expected from them, were they to receive some assistance for the expeditions on which they can be led against the Iroquois in the direction of Quebec, and against the English towards Acadia. . . . . . The preservation of Acadia is due to these Cannibas. They alone have prevented the English invading and settling it; and its security depends for a solid foundation on the continuance of the war they will wage against the English." Such was part of a report submitted to the King by the Governor, who, with no loss of time, concerted his measures accordingly. The King concurred in his opinion. "As the settlement of the Cannibas," he wrote, "is particularly towards Acadia and in the vicinity of the New England settlements, where they seized Fort Pemkuit and several fortified posts, they ought to be encouraged to continue the war there."[2]

As the new French Governor viewed the circumstances in which he stood, he found it material to give the English colonists employment at home, so as to restore the spirit of his own people by action, and to re-establish with the savages the credit of the French arms. To quell the pre-

[1] Colden, Five Nations, I. 109.

[2] Louis the Fourteenth to the Comte de Frontenac. (O'Callaghan, IX. 453.)

sumption of the Iroquois, it was necessary to convince them that their reliance on the protection of the Governor of New York was insecure,[1] and that, notwithstanding present appearances, the pledges by which they expected to avert unfriendliness in that quarter would expose them to at least equal trouble from the resentment of the French. Proceeding on these considerations, Frontenac organized three parties for attacks on as many points, distant from each other, of the English border.[2]

Sack of Schenectady by French and Indians.

Schenectady, called by the French *Corléar*,[3] — by which name, believed to have been the name of a Dutch inhabitant of the place, the Indians also designated the Colony of New York, — lies twenty miles north-west from Albany. At the time now treated of, it contained perhaps five hundred inhabitants. A party of a hundred and ten Frenchmen and about as many natives reached the place by a difficult march of three or four weeks from Montreal. The French were "bush-lopers or Indian traders;" the natives were mostly renegade Iroquois, settled by their priests at a place near Montreal, called Cocknawaga.[4] The invaders were so exhausted when they reached their destination as to be all ready to surrender, had they encountered any resistance. But to their great joy they found the place unguarded.[5]

[1] Charlevoix, Histoire, &c., II. 43.

[2] Frontenac's characteristic energy and promptness are observable on this occasion. The assault on Schenectady was made in less than three weeks after the treaty of the English with the Indians at Onondaga.—The transactions of the French for a year, beginning in November, 1689, are detailed at length, in a perspicuous manner and with good information, in a Memoir by M. Monseignat, Comptroller-General of the Marine in Canada, believed to have been prepared for Madame de Maintenon. (O'Callaghan, IX. 462–491.)

[3] Colden, History, &c., I. 32.

[4] Smith, History of New York, 61; Colden, Five Nations, I. 120 *et seq.*; Charlevoix, II. 45 *et seq.* Monseignat says in his account of the affair (Documentary History of New York, I. 186) that this party "may have been composed of about two hundred and ten men: viz., eighty savages from the Sault and from La Montagne; sixteen Algonquins; and the remainder Frenchmen."

[5] La Hontan, Voyages, &c., I. 204; Colden, History, &c., I. 121.

Urgent as the necessity was for strict discipline and vigilance, there was too much irritation between the partisans of Leisler and his opponents to admit of their cordial joint action;[1] and it was said, moreover, that the inhabitants had not believed such an invasion to be possible, and on account of the inclement weather had allowed their sentries to be withdrawn.

The surprise was complete. At two o'clock of a severely
1690. cold morning the assailants entered through a gate
Feb. 8. which they found open. "The massacre," according to the French officer's report, "lasted two hours." "There were upwards of eighty well-built and well-furnished houses in the town," of which all were burned but two. "The lives of between fifty and sixty persons, old men, women, and children, were spared," they having escaped the first fury of the attack. Thirty prisoners were led away. A list is preserved of the names, mostly Dutch, of sixty persons who were killed, of both sexes and all ages. Of the two gates of the town, the invaders had not been able in the darkness to find that which opened towards Albany, and by it some of the miserable people escaped through "snow above knee-deep," several of them being so frozen on the way as to be maimed for life. Of fifty horses which they captured, the victors had to kill almost all for food on their return march. The details of the massacre are of the most revolting description.[2]

Of the three parties despatched at the same time by
Jan. 18– Count Frontenac for depredations in different
March 18. quarters, another, mustered at Besancour or

[1] Captain Bull had been sent with a company from Connecticut for the protection of Albany. Writing to the government of Massachusetts of the disaster at Schenectady, he does not spare the misbehavior of the factious New-Yorkers. (Mass. Archives, XXXV. 236, 237; comp. Documentary History of New York, II. 103; O'Callaghan, III. 692, 695, 708.)

[2] They are to be found (in full, it is to be hoped) in the "Documentary History of New York" (I. 186 *et seq.*), in the letter from M. de Monseignat. Comp. Mass. Archives, XXXVI. 111.

Three Rivers, was led by an experienced officer, named Hertel de Rouville, and consisted of fifty men, of whom one half were Indians. By a winter march of two months they reached the village of Salmon Falls (Semenfels), in Dover, a neighborhood with which they had become but too well acquainted in the preceding summer. Making their attack just before daylight, as was their practice, they found their victims unprepared. They killed thirty men, burned the twenty-five or thirty houses of the village, and led away more than fifty prisoners, most of whom were women and children.[1]

Renewed invasions of New Hampshire and Maine.

The Indians and their civilized neighbors, both French and English, had become acquainted with the line of transit by the Chaudière and the Kennebec, as well as with that by Lake Champlain and the Hudson. The third party of invaders, four or five hundred strong, mostly consisting of Frenchmen, left Quebec on the day of the departure of the last mentioned from Three Rivers, and, taking such a direction towards the coast as to traverse a formerly inhabited region of Maine, reached Casco Bay (Kaskebé) after a tramp of four months, prolonged by a want of provisions which forced them to supply themselves by the chase.[2] At Falmouth, where they came to the sea, seventy Englishmen were collected in an intrenchment, which was mounted with eight pieces of cannon. Observing the French to be preparing to push a siege with regular approaches, the garrison surrendered on the fourth day of the investment. "Women and children, and especially the wounded, were cruelly murdered" by the victors.[3] The surviving prisoners were marched to Quebec.[4] The fort was demolished, and all the buildings around it reduced to ashes. The flag had scarcely been

May 17.

[1] Charlevoix, Histoire, &c., II. 50 *et seq.*

[2] Ibid., 52.

[3] Letter of Captain Sylvanus Davis in Mass. Hist. Col., XXIV. 101–112.

[4] La Hontan, Voyages, I. 204; Charlevoix, Histoire, &c., II. 50.

struck, when four vessels sent from Boston to relieve the place appeared in the offing.[1] There was nothing for them but to put to sea again. A portion of the victorious party took the ill-fated Dover on their way back. There, at a hamlet called Fox Point, they captured six persons, killing twice as many, and burning some houses. Later in the summer a party of Indians fell upon Exeter, where on one day they killed eight persons whom they found mowing in a field, and in the next put to death as many more belonging to a garrison-house, from which, however, the savages were repulsed. Two companies of English, following an Indian track, found at Wheelwrights' Pond, in Dover, a superior force, which they attacked without success, being obliged to draw off after the loss of several men, of whom twelve were killed. Forty more Englishmen were murdered within the week, along the Massachusetts line.[2]

July 4.

July 6.

The alarm was great throughout New York and New England,[3] the greater because the Mohawks, disgusted with what they considered the pusillanimity of the Dutch and English, many of whom, terrified by the disaster at Schenectady, had moved down the river to be out of harm's way, seemed to be wavering in fidelity to their alliance.[4]

[1] Charlevoix, Histoire, &c., II. 54.

[2] Magnalia, VII. 72-75. — 1690, May 28, David Jeffries writes from Boston, to John Usher in London, of the "miserable condition" of the Eastern people, and their "cries for relief." Counsellor Bullivant writes of the distressed condition, and says that Danforth answered to applicants for relief that "the Lord Jesus was King of the earth as well as the heaven, and if he did not help them, he could not." (British Colonial Papers.)

[3] A change of Counsellors which was made at the election of May, 1690, is perhaps to be interpreted as an indication of popular uneasiness. Wait Winthrop, Sir William Phips, and Dr. Oakes were substituted for Shrimpton, Richards, and Pynchon. (Mass. Col. Rec., *ad loc.*)

[4] Colden, History, &c., I. 123, 125, 130. But there was more than hesitation among the Mohawks, since no fewer than eighty of that furious tribe had been with the French in the assault on Schenectady. Charlevoix gave the Iroquois credit for an astute policy. "Ils ne veulent pas qu'aucune des deux nations Européennes, entre lesquelles leur pays est situé, prenne une trop grande supériorité sur l'autre, persuadés qu'ils en seroient bientôt les victimes." (II. 89; comp. 138.)

Connecticut, not herself immediately exposed, sent troops to secure Albany and the upper towns on Connecticut River. The General Court of Massachusetts invited a consultation of commissioners from the several Colonies as far south as Virginia, appointing William Stoughton and Samuel Sewell on her own part.[1] Delegates from Massachusetts, Plymouth, Connecticut, and New York, met at New York, and part of the result of their deliberations is to be seen in the expedition against Quebec which is presently to be described. Meanwhile a spirited enterprise was proceeding, which Massachusetts had set on foot. That Colony despatched seven or eight hundred men in eight small vessels for an attack on Port Royal (afterwards Annapolis), in Acadia, from which place privateers had been fitted out to prey upon her commerce. The expedition was under the command of Sir William Phips, who was now for the first time made a freeman, having "voluntarily offered himself" for the service.[2] It had complete success. Port Royal, surprised and unprepared for resistance, surrendered at the first summons; and Phips followed up his good fortune by capturing and destroying the French fort at the mouth of the river St. John.[3]

May 1.

April 28.

Capture of Port Royal.

May 23.

¹ Mass. Archives, XXXVI. 4, 5.

² Mass. Col. Rec.

³ O'Callaghan, IX. 455; Murdock, History of Nova Scotia, 183, 185; Charlevoix, Histoire, &c., II. 65–72. According to Charlevoix, the garrison of Port Royal consisted of but eighty-six men, and they had but eighteen guns, and those not mounted. He understood the four English vessels which appeared before Falmouth just after its capture to have been part of Phips's squadron. (Ibid., 65.) — "The expedition cost £3000 more than the plunder amounts to." (Letter of Jan. 8, 1691, from James Lloyd of Boston, in British Colonial Papers.) — In 1690, "A Journal of the Proceedings in the Late Expedition to Port Royal," &c., was "printed for Benjamin Harris at the London Coffee House." I have not seen the piece. — The reader will remember that, since the Treaty of Breda, in 1667, Nova Scotia had been a possession of the crown of France. (See above, Vol. II. p. 630.)

Among the late Mr. Sparks's papers in the library of Harvard College is a copy by George Chalmers of a Journal of Phips's expedition to Port Royal, sent some seventy

Unfortunately, this gratifying exploit gave new encouragement to the more ambitious scheme, the consideration of which had hitherto been only approached with a reasonable and warning conviction of its difficulty and hazards. The conquest of Canada was indeed no new idea. The project had formerly found favor in England;[1] and, encouraged by the remembrance of this approval, the General Court sent a vessel to solicit from the King a supply of arms and ammunition, and the aid of a naval force,[2] — the first time that ever Massachusetts asked military help from England, and now with the purpose of a foreign conquest for the crown. The fruitlessness of the application did not defeat the enterprise. The present time, if any, seemed in some respects highly suitable for its prosecution. It was believed that Quebec was not in a good condition for defence. The existing animosity of the Five Nations against the French promised a formidable auxiliary force, and their urgency for the movement was even such as it might not be prudent to oppose.[3] The conquest would be an immense benefit to Massachusetts, in respect to her security for the future against disturbances from the Eastern Indians, as well as to hostile relations always likely to exist with the French, whose aggressions had hitherto been so brutal. A special reason for energetic action at the present moment was presented by the position of Massachusetts at the British Court. Soliciting as she was from the King a restoration of her charter, in no way could she better recommend herself to his good-will than by laying at his feet the dominion of Canada, the conquest of her arms. A solemn proclamation was sent out, exhort-

Expedition against Canada.

March 12.

years later by Governor Bernard to the Board of Trade. After Phips's conquest a President and Council were appointed to reside on the spot, and report to the Governor of Massachusetts.

[1] See above, Vol. II. 630; III. 114.

[2] Mass. Col. Rec., *sub die.*

[3] Colden, History, &c., I. 117.

ing the people to seek by repentance for sin the Divine intervention, never needed more. We "are now arriving," it declared, "to such an extremity that an axe is laid to the root of the trees, and we are in imminent danger of perishing."[1]

March 12.

The expedition was projected on a scale proportioned to the magnitude of the object. Its costliness presented a formidable difficulty. The government issued a proposal to persons who should advance the money that they should be remunerated with half the net proceeds of the spoils, besides being repaid the amount of their outlay.[2] This plan did not find favor, and the sums immediately necessary were borrowed on the simple credit of the Colony. An embargo was laid to prevent intelligence and to detain supplies.[3] Sir William Phips's recent achievement caused him to be appointed General, and John Walley of Barnstable was made Lieutenant-General, of the forces to be sent by sea.

June 6.

June 12.

March 22.

The fleet, consisting of thirty-two vessels, the largest mounting forty-four guns, sailed from Nantasket, near Boston, having been detained till too near the autumn, waiting for the supplies which it was hoped would come from England; but it was the summer of the battle of the Boyne, and there was too much going on just then to allow the home government to concern itself about America. Phips's fleet conveyed two thousand men, with provisions for four months. The stock of ammunition was scanty.[4] The plan of the campaign contemplated a diversion to be made by an assault on Montreal by a force composed of English from Connecticut and New York, and of Iroquois Indians, at the same time with the attack

Aug. 9.

1 Mass. Col. Rec., *sub die.*

2 Mass. Archives, XXXVI. 111.

3 Mass. Col. Rec., *sub die.* Letter of John Usher (July 4) in British Colonial Papers.

4 "Ammunition little enough." (Letter of Major Savage, Feb. 2, 1691, in Mass. Hist. Col., XIII. 256.)

on Quebec by the fleet. And a second expedition into Maine under Captain Church was to threaten the Eastern tribes, whose incursions had during the last summer been so disastrous. At the same time that their maraudings along the northern border were to be checked and punished, they were to be kept occupied, so as to be disabled from carrying assistance to Quebec.

As is so apt to happen when a plan involves the simultaneous action of distant parties, the condition of success failed. The movement of Church, who had with him but three hundred men, proved ineffective as to any contribution to the descent upon Canada. In the peril in which he found himself, Frontenac could not afford to

September.

send his Abenaqui allies any succor; nor was it, on the other hand, to be imagined that the English commander with so small a force should penetrate across the country in time to make himself useful on the St. Lawrence. Landing in an inlet of Casco Bay, in what is now the town of Brunswick, Church went forty miles up the Androscoggin, taking two or three Indian forts, killing a few scores of the savages, and liberating a number of their captives. Leaving a hundred men at Wells, he returned by sea to Boston, to meet there a cold reception, which he thought cruelly unjust.[1] Certainly he had achieved nothing brilliant. But it may have been in consequence of his inroad, against which the savages found that they got no aid from Quebec, that they sent some of their saga-

Nov. 29.

mores to the Kennebec, who agreed with commissioners of Massachusetts on a truce for five months, and a restoration of their prisoners. Only three towns, Wells, York, and Kittery, all close to the south-western corner of Maine, now remained to the English in that province.

It was not till after a voyage of more than six weeks

[1] Church, Entertaining Passages, 107–117; Williamson, History, &c., I. 624–627; Letter of Benjamin Church to Thomas Hinckley, in Mass. Hist. Col., XXXV. 271 *et seq.*

that the fleet from Boston cast anchor within the mouth of the river St. Lawrence, and meanwhile the overland expedition against Montreal had miscarried. Sept. 23. The commanders respectively of the Connecticut and the New York troops had disagreed, and could not act effectively together. The troops were bewildered by false reports, which Frontenac contrived to have spread among them, of obstructions in their way. The Indian auxiliaries were, or pretended to be, frightened by rumors of the appearance of small-pox. The supply, both of boats and of provisions, was found to be insufficient. The disastrous result was that a retreat was ordered, without so much as an embarkation of the troops on Lake Champlain.[1]

Frontenac was at Montreal, whither he had gone to superintend the defence, when the intelligence, Sept. 30. so unexpected, reached him from Quebec; and presently after came the tidings of Phips's fleet being in the St. Lawrence.[2] Nothing could have been Oct. 1. more opportune than this coincidence, which gave the Governor liberty to hasten down to direct his little force of two hundred soldiers at the capital.[3] The French historian says that, if he had been three days later, or if the English fleet had not been delayed by contrary winds, or had had better pilots in the river, where in fact it was nearly a fortnight more in making its slow way,[4] Frontenac would have come down from the upper country only to find the English commander in his citadel.[5] As it was, there ensued a crushing mortification and sorrow to Massachusetts. New France was made much more formidable than ever. More than sixty years were to pass before Quebec should receive an English garrison.

[1] Charlevoix, Histoire, &c., II. 88, 89.

[2] I use the dates of the New England writers. They differ from those of the French by ten days, the French nation having adopted the Gregorian calendar more than a century before this time.

[3] La Hontan, Voyages, I. 324; Colden, Five Nations, &c., I. 134 *et seq.*

[4] Mather, Magnalia, II. 48.

[5] Charlevoix, Histoire, &c., II. 76.

When by a hasty and perilous passage down the river Frontenac reached his capital, he learned that the English fleet was already close upon him. Major Provot, a capable officer in command there, had used actively the little time since the first alarm in constructing defences, and making dispositions of the neighboring militia, who were directed not to retreat into the fort till they should have done their best to repulse any landing which might be attempted below. Frontenac had left orders with the commander at Montreal to follow him with all speed with the soldiers who could be spared from that place, and with as many militia as he could collect by the way. The day after the Governor's arrival, the English ships were only four leagues from the town; and at dawn of the day following they doubled Point Levi, and came to anchor beneath that magnificent cliff which now bears the name of Cape Diamond. According to the French Governor's official account, they "numbered thirty-four sail, four of which were large ships, some others of inferior size, and the remainder small vessels." He supposed them to have brought "no less than three thousand men."

Oct. 4.

The English fleet before Quebec.

Oct. 5.

Oct. 6.

Early in the forenoon a boat showing a white flag put off from the admiral's ship with a messenger, who, when brought blindfolded to head-quarters, through streets which were made to seem to him thronged with people and noisy with notes of preparation, delivered a summons expressed in peremptory terms. Phips wrote that, without regard to the war between the two crowns, "the destruction made by the French and Indians upon the persons and estates of their Majesties' subjects of New England . . . . . might, upon the present opportunity, prompt unto a severe revenge," but that he, acting for "their most excellent Majesties William and Mary, King and Queen of England, Scotland, France, and Ireland, Defenders of the Faith, and by order of their aforesaid Majesties' government of the Massachusetts Colony in New England," desired to avoid unnecessary carnage in obtaining the unconditional surrender of the garrison with its stores and "the persons and estates" of the colonists. This surrender made, he added, "You may expect mercy from me as a Christian, according to what shall be found for their Majesties' service and their subjects' security. Which if you refuse forthwith to do, I am come provided, and am resolved, by the help of God in whom I trust, by force of arms to revenge all wrongs and injuries offered, and bring you under subjection to the crown of England, and, when too late, make you wish you had accepted of the favors tendered." And "upon the peril that would ensue" a positive answer was demanded within an hour. The messenger showed his watch, which indicated ten o'clock, and said he could not wait after eleven.[1]

Frontenac replied that he would not trouble him to stay so long. "Tell your general," said he, "that I do not acknowledge your King William, and that the Prince of Orange is a usurper who has violated the most sacred rights of blood in wishing to dethrone his father-in-law. . . . . . Though your general had offered me better terms, and I was disposed to accept them, how could he suppose that so many brave men as there are here [the Governor stood surrounded by his officers] would advise me to place confidence in the word of a man who has violated the capitulation he had entered into with the Governor of Port Royal;[2] a rebel who has failed in the fidelity he owed to his lawful king, forgetful of all the favors conferred upon him?" The messenger asked for a written answer. "No," said the spirited Governor, "I have no answer to

[1] O'Callaghan, IX. 455, 462, 484; La Hontan, Voyages, &c., I. 338, 339.

[2] The particulars of Phips's alleged violation of the capitulation of Port Royal are given by Charlevoix (II. 68).

give your general, but from the mouths of my cannon and musketry, that he may know that a man of my rank is not to be summoned after this fashion."

The messenger was no sooner on the deck of his vessel than the prompt veteran opened his fire, and the first shot happened to carry away the English general's ensign. During the rest of this day the invaders were inactive. On the evening of the next day, the officer left in command at Montreal came into Quebec with the welcome
Oct. 7. reinforcement of eight hundred men. The English had prepared to go on shore, but a high wind obstructed the movement, and one of their vessels, carrying sixty men, ran aground, and was with difficulty floated off. The day following, Phips landed a large number of men
Oct. 8. (supposed by the Governor to be no fewer than two thousand, but said by the English to be "twelve or thirteen hundred") on the left bank of the river, two miles below the town, and did some little skirmishing; and the fleet cannonaded the fort, but to little purpose on account of its great height above the water. A second cannonading was so well returned from the work as greatly
Oct. 9. to encourage the assailed party, two of the four largest ships appearing to have suffered severely, while the other two changed their moorings to a place a league above the town. Then an attempt was made at
Oct. 10. an assault by the troops on shore, but it was intercepted and discomfited by a party which had been placed in an ambuscade; and a second trial had the same
Oct. 11. ill success. The night after this second failure the English went on board their vessels, abandoning in their retreat five pieces of cannon and a quantity of ammunition; and the fleet dropped two leagues down the river.[1]

[1] Major Walley's Journal, in Mather, Magnalia, II. 48 *et seq.*; Hutch. Hist., I. 554 *et seq.*; Charlevoix, Histoire, &c., II. 76 *et seq.*; O'Callaghan, IX. 455 *et seq.*

The small-pox had appeared among the crews. The cold had set in with a severity unusual for the early autumn, and "several of the men were so frozen in their hands and feet as to be disabled from service." It was believed that the expedition to Montreal, on which so much reliance had been placed, had miscarried and been abandoned; and a deserter reported that Frontenac had reinforced the garrison "with no fewer than thirty hundred men," — nearly twice as great a force as that of the assailants. The weather was getting constantly worse; the ships, with unskilful pilots, were in a perilous situation, among storms of snow that fell day by day. A council of war determined that, in such circumstances, to persist in the enterprise would be a tempting of Providence. An arrangement was made to give up some prisoners taken during the week, in exchange for English captives, who had been brought into Quebec by the Indians.[1] Tempestuous weather damaged the fleet on the voyage home. One vessel was wrecked in the river; two or three foundered at sea; some others were blown off to the West Indies. The number of men lost in the expedition, by disease and casualties, was estimated at two hundred, though only thirty fell by the hands of the enemy before Quebec.[2] The money sacrificed by Massachusetts was reckoned at fifty thousand pounds.[3]

Its repulse and dispersion.

Phips came back to Massachusetts mortified and distressed. There had been trouble enough

Nov. 19.

[1] Frontenac's report to his superiors of his great success (Nov. 12, 1690) is in O'Callaghan, IX. 459.

[2] Such was the English statement. (Sir William Phips, as reported by Hutchinson, Hist., I. 401.) But Charlevoix supposed that six hundred English had fallen in the three actions. (Histoire, II. 89; comp. O'Callaghan, IX., 455, 459, 492.)

[3] According to Jeremiah Dummer (Defence of the Charters, 37), the expedition "cost £150,000 in money, and, what was infinitely more valuable, the lives of 1000 men." A thousand men would have been more than one in three of the force that went from Boston. Elsewhere (Letter to a Noble Lord, 13) he says that the cost was £50,000. It is surprising to find a man like Dummer falling into such an inaccuracy.

there before his departure. This dismal discomfiture brought it almost beyond the point of possible endurance. The money for the outfit of the expedition had been mostly borrowed, in the imprudent expectation of a reimbursement from the enemy's spoils. The colonial treasurer had no funds. The returning soldiers needed their pay, and were almost in a state of mutiny. A heavy tax was assessed, but time would be necessary to collect it, and a delay of payments was out of the question. The government had recourse to an expedient which proved fruitful of mischief to the Colony through two generations.

Dec. 10.

They issued a paper currency, called *bills of credit*, in denominations from two shillings to ten pounds. These bills were receivable in payment of sums due to the treasury. They fell at once, so that the soldier who received them for their nominal value had to part with them at a discount of one third.[1] At the time when the outcry was loudest, Phips showed his generosity, and at the same time did something to avert the odium which naturally fell upon him, by exchanging a considerable amount of hard money for those securities.

Issue of a paper currency.

It may be guessed that he was not a little relieved when it was presently decided that he should go to England on business for the Colony. The ostensible object was to obtain aid towards the renewal of the enterprise against Quebec. But it was also believed that he might be useful at court in soliciting the restoration of the ancient charter. It was fully time that something was done towards

[1] "Many people being afraid that the government would in half a year be so overturned as to convert their bills of credit altogether into waste paper, the credit of them was thereby very much impaired, and they who first received them could make them yield little more than fourteen or sixteen shillings in the pound, from whence there arose those idle suspicions in the heads of many rude, ignorant, and unthinking folks concerning the use thereof, which to the incredible detriment of the province are not wholly laid aside unto this day." (Mather, Magnalia, II. 52, 55.) Mather was not deep in the theory of finance.

restoring a legitimate and acknowledged government. The people were in that state of distress and alarm in which a questionable authority does not suffice.[1] An exulting and ferocious enemy was mustered all along their border. Mourning was already in many of their houses. They had spent more than all their available money, and they had paid it for a miserable defeat. The war between France and England interfered with their supplies from the latter country, and the Navigation Laws forbade them to seek supplies elsewhere. While the vessels which they had been at so much cost to arm for the disastrous foreign expedition were prevented by the stormy weather from returning for their protection, their property, afloat along all the coast, was the prey of a swarm of French privateers, which had been so bold as even to land marauders on both shores of Long Island Sound.[2] Heavy taxes were to be paid, and the paper substitute for money which was to pay them was driving out of the country what little remained of the coin which intelligibly expressed the worth of property and furnished a safe basis for the transactions of business.

Depressed condition of Massachusetts.

[1] "Report," wrote a malecontent from Boston, "cannot make their circumstances bad enough. . . . . . One great author of our mischief is about to embark to solicit our further ruin. . . . . . It pleased God to retaliate their perfidies by the most fatal and shameful overthrow that ever was heard of." (Letter of Dec. 31, 1690, in the collection of British Colonial Papers.)

[2] Divers letters sent this autumn from Newport and Boston, among the British Colonial Papers.

CHAPTER III.

On his return to England, where, almost two years before, he had left Increase Mather making interest at court for the restoration of the old charter,[1] Phips found small encouragement to hope that that object would prove attainable.

1691. February.

This was not the fault of Mather, who had been unwearied in his exertions. At first the new King seemed to make fair professions, but they were in general terms;[2] and the ministers, in their hurry of business, had little thought to spare for New England. The convention, which presently declared itself a parliament, was advised by Sir Robert Sawyer, the Attorney-General, that "cities, universities, and the plantations" ought to "be secured against *quo warrantos* and surrenders, and their ancient rights restored."[3] But the principle did not obtain a place in the Claim of Right, presented to the candidate for the throne.[4] In an order issued by the new Privy Council for proclaiming the King and Queen in the plantations, "New England was passed over, the further consideration thereof being respited until the business of taking away the charter there shall be heard by the committee, and the true state thereof reported to his Majesty."[5] The Committee for Trade and Plantations,

Plans for a new government in Massachusetts.

1689. Feb. 2.

Feb. 19.

Feb. 14.

[1] See above, Vol. III. 564–566; Mather, Magnalia, II. 56.

[2] Increase Mather, Brief Account concerning several of the Agents, &c., 5.

[3] Commons' Journals, X. 17.

[4] Commons' Journals of Feb. 4–12, and Lords' Journals of Feb. 9–12.

[5] Privy Council Register, *sub die.*

then just appointed from the Privy Council,[1] consulted the Attorney-General, who reported to them that there was no law to prevent the placing of a Governor over Massachusetts forthwith; and they matured a measure to that effect.[2] This, however, as well as the earlier scheme for reinstating Andros, Mather succeeded by the royal favor in defeating. The King in Council, having considered a petition presented by Mather and Phips, ordered that the committee should prepare a new charter, and that, instead of a successor to Andros as Governor, two commissioners should be empowered "to take upon them the administration of the government there, with directions immediately to proclaim the King and Queen."[3]

Feb. 22.

Feb. 26.

The directions were sent, but not the commissioners. The scheme of a General Governor, with the extensive jurisdiction which had been given to Andros, was still entertained. Lord Shrewsbury, Secretary of State, was instructed by the Council, "upon inquiry from those who have the most considerable interest in New England, New York, and the Jerseys, to present to the King the names of such as may be thought fit at this time to be Governor and Lieutenant-Governor of those parts,"[4] — an arrangement which the Council judged conducive to the efficiency of the Colonies in the war now on foot with France. But they entertained a doubt, which they reserved for future examination, of "his Majesty's right to appoint a General Governor for those parts."[5]

April 18.

May 2.

May 9.

[1] Register of the Privy Council; O'Callaghan, &c., III. 578, 722.

[2] See above, Vol. III. 591, note 1; 592, note 2.

[3] Privy Council Register, *sub die;* comp. Cotton Mather, Parentator, 121; Petition of Mather and Phips against Andros, in Mass. Archives, CXXIX. 317, 345. — Mather and Ashurst petitioned (Feb. 13, 1689) for the restoration of the charter, the removal of Andros, and the securing and punishment of John Usher, now in England, for illegal acts as the Colony's Treasurer. (Mass. Hist. Col., XXXVIII. 117.)

[4] Privy Council Register, *sub die.*

[5] Ibid.

Reception in England of the news of the Revolution.

The arrival of the important news of the Revolution in New England awakened at court a new interest in the affairs of that country. John Riggs, Andros's servant,[1] appeared before the Privy Council with his and his master's account of what had taken place, and a copy of the "Declaration" of the insurgents;[2] and Randolph's wife and others presented petitions for the deliverance of their friends who were in durance at Boston.[3] Randolph had written at length to the Board of Trade and to the Privy Council in his elaborate and venomous manner.[4] Captain George, of the Rose frigate, made his complaint to Pepys, Secretary of the Admiralty. The Commissioners of the Customs asked for an order prohibiting the exportation of powder to Boston, "not knowing in what condition the government of New England at present stands."[5] But the prompt measures which had been taken by the provisional government in Massachusetts prevented any hasty acts of resentment in England. The addresses to the King and Queen from the "President and Council for safety of the people and conservation of the peace," and from the "Governor and Council, and Convention of Representatives," had come over as early as the complaints of the other

July 22.

May 29.

June 12.

July 15.

May 20.

[1] Though generally mentioned as a servant, Riggs was probably a subaltern officer, and attached to Andros in some such capacity as that of secretary. Among allowances made March 14, 1701, to persons who served the King in Andros's time, was one to "John Riggs, an ensign in his Majesty's service." (British Colonial Papers.) But this may have been a rank acquired subsequently to 1689.

[2] Riggs went from New York in the middle of May (O'Callaghan, I. 244), and returned December 10 (Ibid., 246).

[3] O'Callaghan, III. 578; Memorials of Sarah Randolph, John Trefoy, and others, in British Colonial Papers. Sarah Randolph says that her husband has served the crown these thirty years; . . . . . that he has "no other means whereby to maintain himself but by his said employment [of Secretary of Massachusetts]; and that, if he loses that, she and her five children must perish."

[4] O'Callaghan, III. 578; Proceedings of the Mass. Hist. Col. for 1871, 113.

[5] British Colonial Papers.

party; and they had had such good effect, that, as has already been told, the King in Council author- June 6. ized Bradstreet and his associates to continue to Aug. 10. administer the government till further orders. Riggs was sent back with an instruction to "such as for the July 25. time being take care for the preserving the peace and administering the laws in Massachusetts," to "set at liberty or send in safe custody into England" the late Governor and his fellow-prisoners, taking care in the latter case that they should be civilly used in their passage.[1] Before this order arrived, Andros had made a second, and this time a successful, attempt to Aug. 2. escape from his imprisonment. He got as far as Rhode Island, where he may have imagined that he would be safe; but he was arrested there, and was brought back under the guard of a troop of horse despatched after him from Boston.[2]

The war was now hot both in Scotland and in Ireland; matters of the first consequence relating to the settlement of the internal administration were pending in England, and the government had again no leisure to attend to Massachusetts. In better heart, as the prospect that his position would be recognized seemed to brighten, Oct. 26, Bradstreet wrote to Lord Shrewsbury setting forth the useful operation of the charter government Oct. 30. while it was in force, the difficulties which it had encountered from the discontent and misconduct of new- July 13. comers, and the present danger to the province Aug. 3. from French hostility; and his representations of Oct. 24. the exposed state of the country were seconded by various memorials of private parties.[3]

Weary of the delays which had occurred, Mather was

[1] Privy Council Register, *sub die.*

[2] He escaped August 2, 11 P.M. (Mass. Archives, I. 89), and got to Newport, August 3 (Randolph's letter of September 5, to the Board of Trade, in British Colonial Papers.)

[3] British Colonial Papers.

led to consider whether he might not have a better chance with the legislature than with the King and his ministers; and by the advice of English friends of the Colony he determined to pursue his object by first soliciting a reversal by Parliament of the decree in Chancery against the old charter. That obtained, he proposed to proceed by applying to the King for the grant of some new privileges, to cure the defects of that instrument in respect to its applicability to the existing state of things. At one moment the former point seemed gained. As has been before related, the House of Commons passed, first, a resolve declaring the abrogation of charters in the late reign, both within the realm and in New England, to be "illegal and a grievance," and then a bill for restoring them.[1] The bill went up to the House of Lords, where there was equally good reason to expect that it would be carried. But, before there was time for that House to act upon it, Parliament was prorogued; and, presently after, it was dissolved.

Prospects for a renewal of the charter.

1690. Jan. 10.

Jan. 27.

An opportunity was lost which could not present itself a second time. Mather's endeavors had all along been obstructed by an opposition which, so far from having yet spent its force, was constantly growing more formidable. In letters from their prison in Boston, Randolph and his allies had been plying their English friends with earnest dissuasives from according any favor to the colonists; and other letters to the like effect came from persons less liable to the suspicion of being goaded by personal resentment. Randolph wrote: "This people having dared to proceed to this height upon hope only of receiving their charter privileges (as they term them), what can we expect upon the arrival of their agents laden with such favors,

Obstacles to a renewal.

1689. July 23.

[1] A letter of Mather to Bradstreet, Sept. 3, 1689 (in N. H. Hist. Col., I. 252), briefly related the transactions thus far.

but that they proceed to try us upon their laws; or, if it be his Majesty's pleasure to direct other methods for governing this country, the guilt of their crimes already done, and the fear of deserved punishment, is such that they will massacre us, and at the same time cast off their allegiance to the crown, accounting themselves his Majesty's nominal and not real subjects, as one of their chief ministers lately declared in public." He hoped that the King had already "sent hither a sufficient force to quiet the present disorders, and reduce this country to a firm dependence upon the crown. Here," he reported, "is no government, no law; customs, excise, and the Acts of Trade and Navigation are cried down. All things are carried on by a furious rabble, animated and encouraged by the crafty ministers." He contrasted the inefficiency of the late operations against the Indians Sept. 5. with those which had been conducted by Andros, to show "the desolation brought upon the country by the tumultuous designs of an anti-monarchial faction;" and he "humbly proposed it absolutely necessary for the honor and interest of the crown, and for the lasting well-being of New England, that fifteen hundred, or at least a thousand, good soldiers be speedily sent hither to reduce this people to a firm dependence upon the crown, and to regain what is already lost."

Randolph played on a variety of stops. To the Lords of Trade he wrote that the Massachusetts people Oct. 15. paid "no regard to the Acts of Trade," and "held fast the anti-monarchial principles spread among them by Sir Henry Vane, Hugh Peters, &c.; and Venner, who made the insurrection in London soon after the Restoration, had his education here also." He irritated the ecclesiastical sensibility of the Bishop of London, who Oct. 25. was a member of that board, by informing him that "Mather's book against the Common Prayer" had

"persuaded the people that we were idolaters, and therefore not fit to be intrusted longer with the government;"
Oct. 26. and that the ministers had encouraged the widow of an officer in her refusal "to let him be buried in the burying-place of the Church of England, though wished in his will, and the grave ready." He bespoke the
Dec. 12. vengeance of the Commissioners of Customs by acquainting them with the arrival in Boston of cargoes excluded by the Acts of Trade. As the time
1690. drew near for his embarking for England agree-
Jan. 10. ably to the royal instruction, he urged that no decision on the old charter should be made before his arrival, and that in the mean time its inconsistency with past practices under it should be considered. Mr. Ratcliffe, too, had come over, the angry minister of the Episcopal chapel in Boston. The King's "most loyal and
February. dutiful subjects of the Church of England in Boston" represented their grievances and apprehensions in acrimonious language.[1] John Usher, Andros's
1689. treasurer, a plausible opponent, was himself in
September. England, in no good temper, within six months after his dismissal from that office.[2]

While the political complexion of the new Parliament was so different from that which it succeeded as
1690. March 20-May 23. to discourage the bringing of the business of New England to its notice in the same form as it had been presented in before, the royal command respecting Andros, Randolph, and their friends, had taken effect, and

[1] Letters in British Colonial Papers; comp. Greenwood, History of King's Chapel, 44. — The Address of Episcopalians, signed by Miles, the clergyman, and Foxcroft and Ravenscroft, church-wardens, is in Mass. Hist. Col., XXVII. 193.

[2] In a petition to the Privy Council, Sept. 26, 1689, Usher described the Revolution of April 19, recited proceedings of the provisional government against him, and prayed that he might not be molested or troubled in his person or estate, "upon the account of his being Treasurer and Receiver-General of his Majesty's revenue in New England." (Privy Council Register.)

they had arrived in England, prepared to exert themselves to the disadvantage of the Colony.[1] About the same time came Oakes and Cooke, deputed by the March. General Court to be associates of Mather in his agency. The agents on the one part, with Sir Henry Ashurst, who had before been acting with Mather under an appointment from Massachusetts, and on the other part Andros, Dudley, Randolph, West, Graham, Palmer, Sherlock, and others, being summoned before the Lords of the Committee, the agents asked for time to prepare April 10. their charges against King James's officers.[2] A week being allowed them for that purpose, the singular result followed that the agents declined to sign April 17. a statement of the grievances of their constituents, which had been prepared by Humphreys, their legal counsel. The Lords accordingly "agreed to offer their opinion to his Majesty that Sir Edmund Andros and the persons lately imprisoned in New England, and now attending his Majesty, be forthwith discharged and set at liberty; and that the paper or charge which had not been signed or owned might be dismissed."[3] The Privy Council passed an order to that effect, and Andros and his fellow-culprits were accordingly set free. Their April 24. liberty was not all that they recovered. Before the end of the year, Dudley sailed for Boston with a commission as Counsellor of New York; and Andros, 1692. Feb. 11. though not until after longer waiting, was made Governor of Virginia. The restoration of Ran- December. dolph to his power of annoyance in America was for a time deferred.

[1] Feb. 9, 1690, a receipt was given for the party by the captain of the Rose frigate, which had now been refitted by orders from the Admiralty. (Mass. Archives, XXXV. 230; comp. Letter of Bradstreet to Lord Shrewsbury, Jan. 29, 1690, in British Colonial Papers.) The indictment of the General Court against Andros and his friends is preserved in Mass. Archives, XXXV. 255, &c.

[2] British Colonial Papers.

[3] Privy Council Register, *sub die*; comp. Parentator, 132; Increase Mather, Brief Account, &c., 7; Whitmore, Andros Tracts, II. 173.

As to the abandonment of the complaints, the truth was that Somers, with whom the agents advised, thought it unsafe for them to pursue the investigation in the existing state of the home government. Of the same nature with the charges against Andros were charges which could be brought against Lord Danby, and others now by the restoration of Tory ascendency at the height of power, but of a power felt by themselves to be insecure. It was of the first importance to avoid the opposition of these great men; but their good-will would be forfeited by persistence in a prosecution which would turn the public attention, now peculiarly sensitive, upon themselves.

The occupation of all minds during the summer with the momentous campaign in Ireland allowed the agents no good opportunity for a hearing, even if the influences of the new Parliament had been less unpropitious. It is likely, also, that they were willing to await the issue of the expedition against Canada, which they hoped would be such as to recommend them to the royal favor. Their suit would be greatly facilitated if they should prove able to back it with intelligence of the conquest of Quebec by their constituents. Nor in that case might it prove necessary for them to stop with urging that Massachusetts desired the restitution of her old charter. They might perhaps further represent with confidence that it would be for the King's interest to add the conquered New France to her domain.

Meanwhile their opponents were not idle. The dis-
1690. charged prisoners now presented an "Address of
Jan. 25. divers gentlemen, merchants, and other inhabitants of Boston and the adjacent parts," signed by seventeen "very considerable persons," who prayed the King for a union of "those little provinces, and the appointment of a Governor and Council to prevent further ruin and losses."[1] "An ingenious merchant of Boston" wrote

[1] British Colonial Papers. — The list of these subscribers, with a statement of their fortunes, gives us a notion of what was accounted

that "a great many good ingenuous men there, with some of the rising generation, were clearly for a General Governor and to live under the laws of England;" and that "if they should have their charter, all the superstitious party, as they reckon the Church-of-England men, must move to New York" and elsewhere.[1] Andros told his own story, largely and artfully, in an elaborate memorial presented to the Lords of Trade.[2] Randolph renewed his complaints against the irregularities of trade in New England.[3] Carefully prepared memoirs on both sides were presented, the authorship of many of which is now unknown.[4] One pamphlet exhibited an "Abstract of the printed laws of New England, which are either contrary or not agreeable to the laws of England, which laws will immediately come in force in case the bill in Parliament for the restoring the charters of the plantations doth pass." Another, entitled "Considerations humbly offered to the Parliament, showing that those charters relating to the plantations were taken away upon quite different occasions from those in England," undertook to prove that the charters were "seized for the abuse of their power in destroying, not only the woollen and other manufactures, but also the very laws and navigation of England, and making themselves, as it were, independent of this crown."[5]

May 16.

May 27.

June 12, June 19.

wealth in those days. The estates of two (Shippen and Page) are estimated at £12,000 each; of two (Bowden and Brinley), at £10,000; of three, at £6000; of two, at £5000; and of two, at £4000.

[1] Ibid.

[2] R. I. Rec., III. 281; O'Callaghan, III. 722, &c. The answer of the agents to this paper (May 30, 1690) is in Mass. Archives, XXXVI. 96.

[3] Privy Council Register.

[4] Several of these remain in manuscript; and several, both published and unpublished before, are in the very valuable collection of "Andros Tracts," made by Mr. W. H. Whitmore, for publication by the Prince Society. The MS. copy, in the collection of British Colonial Papers, of "New England's Faction Discovered," is in the handwriting of Randolph, who also indorsed upon it: "The printing of this paper will more justify us than if I should trouble their Lordships with many letters. E. R."

[5] It is instructive to learn from the warm language of this passage, what indeed there are plenty of other indications of, that a morbid apprehen-

The business of the agents made no progress in the direction last pursued. They turned their attention next to devising some method for bringing it, by a writ of error, before the Court of King's Bench, where Holt was presiding, with a view to a revision of the Chancery decree; but this was found impracticable. "There was now but one way left," Mather concluded, "for the settlement of New England, scil., — to implore the King's royal favor. It was not in the King's power to reverse the judgment against the old charter; nevertheless, his Majesty had power to reincorporate his subjects, thereby granting them a charter which should contain all the old, with new and more ample privileges."[1] When the King came back from the battle of the Boyne and his decisive campaign in Ireland, the Parliament was about to begin its second session. As soon as its approaching prorogation released something of his attention, the agents proceeded with the method now determined on.

Sept. 6.

Oct. 2.

On the general principles of government the King had his well-matured notions, and they were far from being liberal. Probably the special subject of colonial administration was new to him. His Dutch compatriots had pursued the method of managing their colonies by incorporated companies, which had scarcely any subordination to the States-General beyond a liability to inspection. And, as to desert, it is not likely that his partial or indifferent eye

sion of a commercial rivalry on the part of New England was felt by the British merchants at this early time. It was this fear of competition, as much as any thing else, that created the great sensibility in England in respect to the Navigation Laws. And to this unreasonable panic on the part of the merchants, annoying the government with its complaints and clamors, it is natural to ascribe whatever energy the reluctant government manifested in the execution of those laws.

1 Brief Account, &c., 6.—Nov. 29, 1690, Bradstreet informed the agents of the dissatisfaction that was felt, because in nine months of absence they had reported nothing "that might have been a direction in the conduct of public affairs." He interpreted the failure of the Quebec expedition as a stern frown of Providence. "Shall our Father spit in our face, and we not be ashamed?" (Mass. Archives, XXXVI. 228.)

would distinguish unfavorably between the rough dealers in gin and peltry at the mouth of the Hudson, and the representative of cultivated English thought and manners on the coast of Massachusetts Bay. The agents, in their ignorance of the temper and habits of their monarch, hoped not a little from the influence of his religious Queen.[1]

Their petition for a new charter with additional provisions was referred to the law officers of the crown, who, through the Chief Justice, reported favorably upon it, though in general terms; and in this new form the subject was again placed by the Privy Council in the hands of the Lords of Trade.[2] It was just after this time that Phips arrived from Massachusetts. The King had immediately gone off to Holland to confer with commissioners of his allies on the management of the war with France. With the interval of only a couple of weeks, he remained on the continent till the autumn; and the agents could not reach him with personal solicitations. Mather, however, lost no opportunity for advancing his business. Lord Monmouth, and especially Lord Wharton, rendered him constant good offices. Archbishop Tillotson and Bishop Burnet were among his assiduous friends. Just before the King came to England for a short visit in the spring, Mather obtained an audience of the Queen, in which he entreated her Majesty's good offices for her subjects in Massachusetts, and she replied, "I shall be willing to do all I can for them."[3] The King admitted him to two audiences, saying at the latter of them

Suit for a new charter.

1691. February.

Oct. 19.

April 9.

April 28.

[1] Increase Mather's letter of Sept. 2, 1690, is in Mass. Archives, XXXVI. 83. — Abraham Kick, an Amsterdam correspondent of Mather, was in favor there with the Princess of Orange, and took an interest in securing her favor for his friend. His letter to her for that purpose is in Whitmore's Andros Tracts, II. 165.

[2] Mather, Brief Account, &c., 6; Parentator, 124.

[3] Brief Account, &c., 7; Parentator, 127–130.

that he would see what might be done when he should receive a report he was expecting from the Lords of Trade.[1]

Meanwhile the malecontents in Massachusetts had excited themselves into new activity. Sixty-one "merchants and other inhabitants of Boston, Charlestown, and places adjacent," sent an Address to the King representing "the deplorable state and condition of the territory," occasioned by "the tumultuous removal of the late government under Sir Edmund Andros, and the distractions and divisions arising therefrom."[2] On consideration of this paper, the Board of Trade called upon the Massachusetts agents for an account in writing of the existing state of that Colony, and the Council had had before them Sir William Phips and other persons "concerned in New England" to give "a relation of the late proceedings and expedition of the people of New England against Canada under his command."[3] The Lords reported to the Privy Council that before proceeding further it was necessary for them to know whether it was the King's "pleasure to have a Governor or single representative, of his own appointment from time to time, to give his consent to all laws and acts of government." The King being understood to declare that such was his pleasure, it was "ordered that the Lords of Trade forthwith prepare the draft of a new charter upon that foundation."[4] On their advice, the duty of framing the charter was committed to the Attorney-General, Sir George Treby.[5]

April 9, 21.

April 30.

May 14.

[1] Brief Account, 7, 8; Parentator, 131, 132.

[2] In an Address of the General Court to the King (Oct. 14, 1691), this paper is spoken of as proceeding from "about sixty disaffected persons, ... some out of other colonies, and not a few of the rest mere strangers and sojourners among us, ... scarcely any of the issue of the first planters." (Mass. Col. Rec., *sub die.*)

[3] Privy Council Register; Journal of the Board of Trade, *sub dieb.*

[4] Privy Council Register, *sub die.*

[5] Ibid.

Mather insisted that the King had been misunderstood as to a determination to have a Governor in Massachusetts of his own appointment. He obtained the concurrence of some members of the Privy Council in this view, and wrote to Lord Sidney, who, having succeeded Lord Shrewsbury as Secretary of State, was in attendance on the King in Flanders, to urge it upon the royal attention.[1] But he obtained no answer. King William was no more disposed than King James to relax the dependence of Massachusetts on the crown. The Attorney-General's draft of a charter was silent as to a power of the Governor to arrest a law by his negative, and it empowered the freemen "to choose the Deputy-Governor and the other general officers."[2] This did not please the Lords of Trade. and the Attorney-General was instructed to make another draft with provisions more favorable to the prerogative in these particulars. Mather and Ashurst waited upon him to protest, and the former went so far as to declare "that he would sooner part with his life than consent to the minutes, or any thing else that did infringe any liberty or privilege of right belonging to his country." On reflection he thought he had "expressed his dissatisfaction, perhaps, with a greater pathos than he should have done." His language gave offence, and he was told on the part of the ministers that his "consent was not expected nor desired; for they did not think the agents from New England were plenipotentiaries from another sovereign state, but that, if they declared they would not submit to the King's pleasure, his Majesty was resolved to settle the country, and they must take what would follow."[3]

May 27.

Scheme for a new charter.

June 8.

There was no doubt that they were dealing with a per-

[1] Dec. 26, 1690, Henry, Viscount Sidney, succeeded Lord Shrewsbury after the latter's service of less than two years.

[2] Parentator, 133; Brief Account, &c., 9.

[3] Parentator, 134; Brief Account, &c., 9, 10.

son apt to be as good as his word, when his word was a threat. The Attorney-General presented his amended draft. The Lords applied themselves diligently to the consideration of it, and in a fortnight's time came to a final decision respecting the main features, as they are presently to be described, of the instrument to be recommended to the King.[1] On a conference with the Attorney-General, the agents reduced their objections to two. They urged that judicial as well as other officers should be appointed by the General Assembly, and not by the Governor in Council, and that the choice of Counsellors ought to be made as formerly by the two branches of the Court, without being subject to a revisal by the Governor. The agents drew up a statement of their views, which they submitted in one copy to the Privy Council, while another was sent to the King in the Netherlands, with a request, which was also urged upon the Queen, that proceedings might be stayed till his return to England.[2] The Queen was understood to engage her influence with him in favor of their application. But the answer from the other side of the channel was "not only that the King did approve of the minutes agreed unto by the Lords of the Committee, but that he did by no means approve of the objections which the agents of New England had made against them."[3]

July 2—July 17. July 30. July 29. Aug. 20.

Nothing seemed further to be practicable in respect to the great point of saving for Massachusetts something like its former degree of independence of the parent state. "Resolved," however, "to get as much good and prevent as much hurt to the country as possibly might be," the agents presented a petition to the effect, "that no property belonging to that Colony, or to any therein,

Aug. 27.

[1] Journal of the Board of Trade, *sub dieb.*

[2] Brief Account, &c., 10, 11; Parentator, 135.

[3] British Colonial Papers.

might by the new charter be taken from them, nor any privileges which they had a right unto; that the province of Maine might be confirmed; Nova Scotia added to the Massachusetts;" and that New Hampshire, which, at the request of its own people, had been annexed to Massachusetts in the first year after the Revolution,[1] might be placed by the royal authority under that government.[2] Mather was also authorized by Plymouth to represent that, failing to obtain a separate charter, that Colony desired to "be united to Boston rather than to New York." He prevailed in obtaining two amendments to the instrument which had been prepared. "That phrase of corporal oath was altered, that so no snare may be laid before such as scruple swearing on the book;" and a clause was added, confirming past grants made by the General Court, "notwithstanding any defect that might attend the form of conveyance, that so men's titles to their lands might not be invalidated, only for that the laws which gave them their right had not passed under the public seal in the time of the former government."[3] These arrangements finished the transaction. The Privy Council directed Lord Nottingham, as Secretary, to "prepare a warrant for his Majesty's royal signature, for passing said charter under the great seal of England in the usual manner."[4] Sept. 17.

The charter of King Charles the First, which, after being fifty-five years in force, was dissolved by a legal judgment, had created a corporation of Englishmen under the name of the "Governor and Company of Massachusetts Bay." By the charter of King William the Third a community of Englishmen was invested, in law, as a body politic, with certain privileges, and restrained within certain limits of action, under the name of the "Province of Massachusetts Bay." The Province so constituted embraced

[1] Mass. Archives, XXXV. 328.

[2] Parentator, 136; Brief Account, &c., 12.

[3] Journals of the Board of Trade, from July 24 to September 16.

[4] Privy Council Register, *sub die.*

the old Colonies of Massachusetts and Plymouth, and the territories of Maine and Nova Scotia, with all lands lying between the two last-named jurisdictions. Except for the little interruption at the mouth of the Piscataqua, the coast line of Massachusetts, as now constituted, extended from Martha's Vineyard and Nantucket at the south, to the mouth of the St. Lawrence at the north; while, with the exception of a narrow strip along the Hudson, recognized as belonging to New York, her territory reached westward to the Pacific Ocean.

The new Constitution.

The charter provided that there should be a Governor, Lieutenant-Governor, and Secretary, to be appointed from time to time by the King. There was to be a Legislature, or General Court, in two branches; namely, a House of Representatives chosen as heretofore annually by the towns, and a Council, consisting of twenty-eight members, to be selected in the first instance by the King, and afterwards, from year to year, on the last Wednesday in May, by the General Court, subject to the Governor's rejection. Eighteen, at least, of the Counsellors were to be inhabitants or landholders in Massachusetts proper, four in what had been Plymouth Colony, three in Maine, and one in the country between the Kennebec and Nova Scotia; and seven were to be a quorum for the transaction of business. It was required of the Representatives to be freeholders, and each town for the present was to have two Representatives and no more; but this limitation was made subject to be changed by law.

Bills passed by the Council and Representatives were subject to be rejected by the Governor. Laws approved by him went at once into effect, but were to be forthwith reported to the King, who might annul them at any time within three years from their enactment. The Governor was to be commander-in-chief of the militia, and to appoint military officers. He was also, with the consent of the Council, to appoint judges and all other officers connected with the courts.[1] The General Court was to constitute judicial courts (except courts of Admiralty, which were reserved for the jurisdiction of the crown, and except Probate courts,

[1] It is remarkable that the great question respecting the tenure of judicial office — whether judges held their places *quamdiu sese bene gesserint* or *durante beneplacito* — remained in dispute to the very end of the provincial period. Douglas — no good authority, however — says (Summary, I. 472), "They [the Governors] nominate *durante beneplacito* all judges," &c. The charter does not touch the point, nor do the terms of the commissions issued to successive judges. Only two years before the war of the Revolution broke out, there was a controversy (Life and Works of John Adams, I. 118) between John Adams and Brattle, a Cambridge lawyer of reputation, as to a fact which, whatever it was, might be supposed to be familiar and notorious; the latter maintaining that judicial place had always been held under the charter *during good behavior*, the former that it had been held in dependence on the King and his Governor. In the silence of the charter, the laws, and the judicial record, Brattle argued that "what right, what estate vests in them [the judges], the common law of England, the birthright of every man here as well as at home, determines, and that is an estate for life, provided they behave well." (Ibid., III. 518.) Adams maintained that "the common law of England is so far from determining that the judges have an estate for life in their office, that it has determined the direct contrary." (Ibid., 521.) An Act of the year 1700 (twelfth and thirteenth of William the Third, Chap. II.) provided that "judges' commissions be made *quamdiu se bene gesserint.*" But there is no reason to believe that this Act was ever regarded as applicable to the Colonies. Certainly, the judges of Massachusetts were practically at the mercy of the General Court at least, for the General Court voted their salaries from year to year. Till the reign of King George the Third (Acts of first of George the Third, Chap. XXIII.), all civil offices, conferred by royal writ, including those of the judges, were vacated at the demise of the King. Consequently, as often as a King died before this time, new judicial appointments might be made in Massachusetts. (Comp. Hutch. History, III. 96.) Governor Belcher, in 1730, pretending an analogy between the accession of a new sovereign and of a new Governor, claimed and exercised the right of making new nominations; but the measure was opposed in Council (Hutch. Hist., II. 376), and never was repeated, though Shirley, Belcher's successor, renewed the claim. As was pointed out at the time, and was urged afterwards by Mr. Adams, the judges, by the terms of their commissions, were not the Governor's officers, but the King's, and therefore not liable to be affected in their position by a change of Governors. (Adams, III. 569, &c.; comp. Hutch. History, II. 375, 376; III. 96, 390; Chalmers, Opinions of Eminent Lawyers, &c., 249, 258.) John Dickinson, on the eve of the American Revolution, understood the judges in all the Colonies to hold their places during the King's pleasure. (Letters from a Farmer, &c., 87.) The Provincial Act for a re-constitution of the courts in Lord Bellomont's time required new appointments, which were accordingly made July 17, 1699. (Prov. Council Rec., *sub die.*) Dudley, whose assumption of the government was contem-

which were to be constituted by the Governor in Council); to appoint, with the Governor's concurrence, all officers, besides such as were military or judicial; and to levy taxes on all proprietors and inhabitants. A General Court was to come together on the last Wednesday in May of every year, and at other times when summoned by the Governor, who might also adjourn, prorogue, or dissolve it. A great step was, that the religious element was eliminated from the government; the qualification of a voter was no longer to be membership of a church, but the possession of a free-hold worth two pounds sterling a year, or of personal property to the amount of forty pounds sterling.[1] This measure put an end to what yet survived of the old clerical ascendency in politics.[2] Liberty of conscience and of worship was secured to all Protestants; and it was provided that, in litigated civil cases not affecting real estate, appeals might be made from the courts to the King in Council when the amount in controversy exceeded three hundred pounds. Natives and inhabitants of the Province were to enjoy "all liberties and immunities of free and natural subjects . . . . . as if they were born within the realm of England." Trees of two feet in diameter at a foot's distance from the ground, growing on common land, were to belong to the King, for the use of the royal navy.[3]

poraneous with the accession of a new monarch, immediately (June 29, 30, 1702) revised the list of judges. (Ibid.) The position and the action of Governor Bernard in 1761 were similar. — Governor Bernard, in the temporary disability of a judge, appointed a substitute (February, 1762) for the trial of a single cause. (Quincy's Massachusetts Reports, 551.) Other persons had from time to time been appointed for special service and limited terms. (Washburn, Judicial History of Massachusetts, 155, 156.)

[1] It has been forcibly argued by Mr. Ellis Ames, the learned associate editor of the Provincial Laws, that this word "forty" in the engrossed charter was a clerical error for fifty. (Proceedings of the Mass. Hist. Col. for 1768, 370; Province Laws, I. 363.)

[2] Hutchinson says (Hist., I. 337) that, when they persuaded the people to refuse to give up the old charter (see above, Vol. III. 381, &c.), "the clergy turned the scale for the last time. The balance which they had held from the beginning they were allowed to retain no longer."

[3] This provision is likely to have been suggested by Phips, who, as a

The Governor, Lieutenant-Governor, and Secretary were not to be the only crown officers in Massachusetts. Admiralty judges, and the prosecutors and other officers in their courts, — King's Advocates, Registrars, and Marshals, — were designated by the Lords of the Admiralty. The colonial wealth in naval stores had called for the employment of a Surveyor of the Woods, and Edward Randolph had held the office among his other annoying functions.[1] The last provision of the new charter brought it into fresh prominence, and it was kept up at the cost of many embarrassments, as will hereafter be seen. Managers of the Post-Office, among whom also Randolph secured a place,[2] were appointed by, and accountable to, the General Post-Office in England.

More important than any of these officials were those who represented the English custom-house. An ordinance of the Long Parliament[3] had exempted the plant- 1643.
ers of New England from paying duties on mer- March 10.
chandise brought by them from the parent country, or exported thither; and they were equally excepted from the operation of the later Navigation Law. At 1645.
an early period Massachusetts imposed a duty on May 14.
imported wines for the benefit of her own treasury;[4] and in later times this form of revenue was made to 1668.
embrace various articles, and to yield a consider- Nov. 7.
able amount.[5] When, after the accession of King 1669.
Charles the Second, the dispensation in favor of May 19.
New England was withdrawn, and measures were taken for

shipbuilder, understood its importance particularly well.

[1] He was commissioned for the service in 1685, with an annual stipend for it of £50. (British Colonial Papers.)

[2] See above, Vol. III. 484.

[3] It is entered in the Record of the Massachusetts General Court for May 10, 1643. (See printed Records, II. 34.)

[4] Ibid., 106; III. 51; comp. above, Vol. II. 11; Vol. III. 50; Chalmers, Letter to Lord Mansfield, in Sparks's Manuscript Collection, 21, 120, 122.

[5] Mass. Rec., IV. (Part 2), 410, 418.

an extensive and rigorous execution of the Navigation Laws,[1]
1661. Aug. 7. the General Court of Massachusetts had anticipated complaints by successive Acts directing the
1663. May 27. Oct. 21. enforcement of those Laws within their jurisdiction.[2] The Act of Parliament usual on the accession of a monarch, by which the avails of custom dues called *tonnage and poundage* were settled on King Charles the Second, provided that these duties should be collected in every part of the King's dominions by officers appointed in England. A later Act regulated the appoint-
1674. May 8. ment of these officers,[3] and it was in the capacity of Collector of the Customs that Edward Randolph
1678. made his second visit to New England.[4] Meanwhile the regulations of the Colony for local revenue remained in force. Imposts due to the English exchequer were to be paid to the King's collectors, while imposts levied by the colonial law continued to be received by the colonial naval officers.[5] These two businesses were different; but they were sufficiently alike and sufficiently connected to admit and to tempt frequent interferences and collisions.

Its unsatisfactory character.

The conditions of the franchise established by the new charter, and the power given to the King to repeal the laws, — for this was the sense of his right to revise them, — to entertain appeals from the courts of justice, and to appoint a Governor with prerogatives liable to pernicious abuse, — these provisions were enough to make the instrument intensely unpalatable to Mather and to many of the best men of that constituency for which

[1] See above, Vol. II. 444; Vol. IV. 19.

[2] See above, Vol. II. 513, 530; Vol. III. 276, 311; Mass. Rec., IV. (Part 2) 31; comp. 73, 87; V. 155, 236, 262, 337, 383.

[3] See above, Vol. III. 310, 323; Vol. IV. 19; comp. Chalmers's Political Annals, I. 318, 320, 400, &c.

[4] See above, Vol. III. 317, 333, 350. His commission as "Collector, Surveyor, and Searcher" for the New England Colonies (July 9, 1678) is in Mass. Hist. Col., XXVII. 129.

[5] See above, Vol. III. 352.

he was acting. The powers were dangerous in the best of circumstances. In any hands they were susceptible of being used in ways to humble and distress the Province. Neither the character of the reigning sovereign, — though as yet that was little known, — nor the influences which surrounded him, afforded assurance that even by him they would be leniently used. But what might they become — though this was a consideration which the agents could not urge — if the insecure throne of the Dutch adventurer should be overturned, and his father-in-law should again be able to wreak his anger on the Puritan colony which had so affronted him? He who could so act without law as King James had done in the usurped government of Andros, how would he act when on his side he should have law which the most upright judges of England must respect and enforce?

Its recommendations.

On the other hand, there were features of the constitution of the Legislature of a favorable aspect to popular rights. The first branch was to be nominated by electors, of which the second branch, consisting of Representatives of the towns, constituted the major part, though the nomination did not constitute a choice without the Governor's approval. Further, by the provincial charter the power of the purse was formally given to the General Court. The Court, and not the Governor, might impose and levy taxes; and moneys could not be drawn by the Governor from the treasury, except by a warrant issued with the advice and consent of the Council. By the charter the Governor could have no money from Massachusetts except what the people of Massachusetts might see fit to grant him. Here, in the last resort, was the security for what remained of the measure of independence which had been once possessed. Herein consisted the guaranty for some degree of self-government. Future circumstances might be such as to require in Massachusetts a repetition of the experiment, made in England a half-century before, to determine whether executive usurpation could be checked by the money-granting power.

Of the new arrangement touching the extent of her territory, Massachusetts had no reason to complain. If she had failed of retaining New Hampshire, she had received the government of the more congenial people of Plymouth; her title to Maine, fruitlessly opposed again by the heir of Gorges while the charter was in dispute, was quieted by it; and the whole extensive territory of Nova Scotia, and of what is now New Brunswick, was a new acquisition, however questionable its value might be when estimated in relation to the cost of its defence, and to the fact that, by virtue of the treaty of Breda, it was still a property of the King of France.[1]

1691. July 9.

The agents well knew what disapprobation awaited them at home for whatever share they had had in bringing their constituents into this new condition of formal and definite subjection to England. Cooke and Oakes could not bring themselves to express any assent to the transaction. With sincere, and not, as many thought, simulated reluctance, Mather made up his mind to accept the arrangement as the best that it was possible to obtain. It was not by any means without its advantages

Reluctant acceptance of it.

[1] Massachusetts, however, did not at any time take possession of Nova Scotia, further than to occupy Port Royal (Annapolis) and St. John. Nova Scotia had declined in population and in consequence since it was the scene of the contest between La Tour and D'Aulnay. (See above, Vol. II. 144, 285 *et seq.*) According to a census taken in 1689, the year before the capture of its capital by Phips, the whole number of the white inhabitants of the province was but eight hundred and three. (Murdock, History of Nova Scotia, 177; comp. Douglas, Summary, I. 306.) Its occupation, whether by French or English, was hitherto of no consequence to either party, except for its vicinity to the cod-fishery and its possession of convenient naval stations. — Richard, Lord Gorges, now renewed his claim to Maine and other territory of New England. But, on a hearing of him and of the agents by counsel, he was "left to take his remedy at law concerning the same;" which it does not appear that he ever undertook. (Privy Council Journal for July 30, 1691; British Colonial Papers.)

as compared with a mere recovery of the old charter unaltered. It expressly made some things lawful which had hitherto been assumed by more or less violent construction, as the right to tax non-freemen, to conduct the public business by representatives, to inflict capital punishment, to create courts of justice, and to prove wills.[1] But independently of substantial reasons for apprehending that under some future sovereign of England, if not in the present reign, the new charter might be made an instrument of practical misrule, it was a heavy blow to the pride of patriots who had scarcely ceased to cherish the vision of ultimate independence.[2]

But what could be done? Mather was assured with united voice by the lawyers with whom he advised, that the annulling of the charter which had taken place was unquestionably valid in law, hasty and unjust as the proceedings had been; that to obtain a legal reversal of it was at present impossible; and that an attempt to do so, if encouraged by any future circumstances, would not be prejudiced by his accepting the present settlement, inasmuch as neither could his assent bind the Colony, nor could the present submission of the Colony bar a future demand for its rights.[3] It was plain that any attempt to

[1] Mauduit, in Mass. Hist. Col., IX. 272. — "It was likewise considered," says Mather (Brief Account, &c., 15), "that some persons in England were endeavoring to get a patent for all mines, minerals, gums, &c., in New England, which design was of late likely to have taken effect, only the new charter has most happily prevented that which would have been of pernicious consequence to all that territory." This refers to a project long pressed upon the government by Sir Matthew Dudley and partners of his in both countries (see below, 395, note 2). — On this course of transactions, Cotton Mather circulated in manuscript a little *jeu d'esprit*, not without merit, under the title of "Political Fables." In it he figures under the name of Orpheus, and his father under that of Mercurius. It is in print in Mass. Hist. Col., XXI. 126, &c., and Whitmore's "Andros Tracts," II. 325; comp. Jasper Mauduit's Observations, in Mass. Hist. Col., *ubi supra*.

[2] See Dummer, Defence of the Charters, 8; Brief Account, &c., 12–20.—According to Calef (More Wonders, &c., 149, 150), Cotton Mather had obstructed the resumption of the old charter in 1689. But I have seen no proof of it.

[3] Brief Account, &c., 13.

persuade the King to further concession would be hopeless. It was with no good grace that he had come into the arrangement now proposed. To solicit any amendment of it would be but to offend him, and risk its withdrawal.

Direct resistance to the royal pleasure was out of the question. There was not even an approach to unanimity in the Colony. Even among native citizens there was not a preponderance of agreement as to any one right policy for the time. Besides native citizens, there were now in Massachusetts numbers of people of English birth — and they important and active, Church and King men — who cared nothing for her interest or her pride. Many of her rich inhabitants were probably merchants recently come over, who sympathized with prerogative. She was helpless through her poverty. Her public treasury was empty. She stood alone, without an ally in New England. Rhode Island, besides having little power, and having never had a generous policy, had strong motives for compliance with the English court. She was contented with her charter; she was not immediately threatened with the loss of it; and, in order to keep it, it seemed her interest to stand well with the King's servants. The position of Connecticut in respect to her charter was the same. The feeble Colony of Plymouth, which had never had a charter, was soliciting one from the King's indulgence. Massachusetts could hope for no help from friends in England. The experiment had shown it. Danby and the Tories ruled in Parliament; and, as to the liberal religious party, it had, even with the King for its well-wisher, been miserably defeated in the Convocation, and had as much as it could do to secure its own immunity.

Nor must it be forgotten how great was the anxiety which was relieved by a settlement of any tolerable kind. The annulling of the old charter placed the Colony at the sovereign's mercy, and in that condition it remained down to the time when the provincial charter was bestowed. How mischievous might be the exercise of this despotism the Colony had well learned from Sir Edmund Andros; and while the existing state of things should last, there was no security against the repetition of a rule like his, except in the uncertain favor of King William, or of the sovereign who might succeed him. Nor was usurpation on the King's part the only probable source of trouble while the government remained unsettled. During three years of dissolution of the bonds of regular authority, a self-respecting people had kept the peace with exemplary self-control; but who so sanguine as to predict that an orderly anarchy could long subsist?

Earlier than the final action of the Privy Council, Mather must have made up his mind as to the course necessary to be taken; for, a fortnight before the order came for the charter to pass the seals, Sir Henry Ashurst had applied to him for a nomination of the persons to be appointed to office by the King, — a singular trust, which appears to have been committed by the Ministry to Mather alone.[1] His nominations were adopted, the new government being in that respect constituted in exact conformity with his wish.[2] He was probably understood by the courtiers to be the most considerable man in Massachusetts, and the most important to be gratified. Phips was made Governor, and sworn into office by the Privy Council;[3] a man whom, alike by reason of the close intimacy between them, and of his moderate abilities and superficial character, Mather might well promise himself

Sept. 3.

Royal appointments under it.

Sept. 28.

Dec. 31.

[1] Letter of Ashurst to Mather, in Hutch. Hist., I. 413. — Phips was nominated September 28. (Journal of the Board of Trade, *sub die.*)

[2] Journals of the Board of Trade, *sub die.* — October 12, the pecuniary claims of Governor Andros and of Treasurer Usher on Massachusetts were referred to the Governor and Council, who were "directed to satisfy them out of the public stock what might appear to be justly due unto them." (Privy Council Register, *sub die.*)

[3] Ibid.

that he should have little difficulty in managing. Stoughton was selected to be Lieutenant-Governor. After all his misdeeds, he remained a favorite with the clergy, to whose order he had formerly, in a certain sense, belonged; and he had regained some credit with the people by taking part with them, though in his own reserved and churlish way, in the rising against Andros. Isaac Addington, who in the last two elections under the old charter had first been made Speaker of the House and then an Assistant, was appointed Secretary, in which capacity he had served the provisional government since the Revolution. Bradstreet's name stood first in the new list of Assistants. Such as in the old board had been strenuous friends of the old charter — Danforth, though lately Deputy-Governor, and Elisha Cooke and Thomas Oakes, though lately associated with Mather in the agency — were not included.

Nov. 4. When the King came back to England, Mather obtained an audience, at which "on the behalf of New England he most humbly thanked his Majesty" for having "been pleased by a charter to restore English liberties unto them; to confirm them in their properties; and to grant them some singular privileges."[1]

In Plymouth, after the resumption of its ancient government,[2] Thomas Hinckley was chosen to be Governor each year till the end of the separate existence of that Colony. An address of congratulation was promptly sent to the King and Queen on their accession.[3] Plymouth responded with spirit to an application from Massachusetts to take a part in the operations against the Indians in the summer after the Revolution, appointing Captain Church to the command of its volunteers and impressed men,[4] for whose outfit and pay Plymouth, with better judgment than was

1689. June 6.

Transactions in Plymouth.

Aug. 14.

[1] Parentator, 144; Hutch. Hist., II. 5-12.

[2] See above, Vol. III. 596.

[3] Mass. Hist. Col., XXXV. 199; Plymouth Colony Records, VI. 209.

[4] Ibid, 212-216.

shown by Massachusetts on the same occasion, provided by a tax amounting, according to the valuation of the time, to one thirteenth part of the whole property of her citizens.[1] Concurring with the plan of the Congress at Albany, Plymouth raised sixty men "to be sent by water to Albany or elsewhere, to join with the forces of New York, Massachusetts, or Connecticut, &c., for the defence of said places or other service of their Majesties against the common enemy."[2] On further information from Massachusetts respecting the proposed expedition against Canada, another levy was made of a hundred and fifty English soldiers and fifty Indians.

Oct. 2.

1690. May 20.

June 5.

Being informed from England that the design of annexing their Colony to New York had been defeated by Mather, and that the plan for attaching it to Massachusetts had been for the present postponed in consequence of the remonstrances of their agent, Mr. Wiswall,[3] the General Court voted to call meetings of the towns for deliberation on the subject, "that it be known whether it be their minds we should sit still and fall into the hands of those that can catch us, without using means to procure that which may be for our good, or prevent that which may be our inconvenience; or

Dec. 1.

June 24.

1 A tax of £750 (£560 sterling) was levied (Plymouth Rec., VI. 220). The whole valuation of the Colony was then £35,900. Scituate was the most populous and the richest town, being rated for £88. Plymouth and Barnstable came next, each paying £60. — December 25 (Ibid., 229), the Court "ordered that Major Church shall have ten pounds allowed him (besides what he hath received from the Bay) more than his wages by the week, and that his weekly wages as Major in the late expedition shall be forty shillings." (Plymouth Colony Records, VI. 249, 254, 255.)

2 Plymouth Colony Records, VI. 231.

3 Mr. Wiswall sailed from Boston to England, as agent for Plymouth, in February, 1690. (Letter of Governor Hinckley to Increase Mather, in Mass. Hist. Col., XXXV. 229; Letter of Cotton Mather to Governor Hinckley, Ibid., 248.) Oct. 17, 1690, writing to Hinckley under great discouragement as to the prospect of a separate charter, Wiswall advised the Colony to "remember 10 Ecclesiastes, 19." (Ibid., 277; comp. Plymouth Col. Rec., VI. 259.)

if they will act, then to know what instruments they would improve, and what money they can raise; and must also know that if a patent can be procured, it will not take up less than five hundred pounds sterling, which will take nearly seven hundred pounds of our money."

"Though the Colony labored under many inconveniences, being small in number, low in estate, and great public charges," it preferred still greater straits to a loss of its independence.[1] A hundred pounds sterling were "sent unto Sir Henry Ashurst, towards the charge of procuring a charter," besides gratuities to himself of fifty pounds, and of twenty-five pounds each to Mather and Wiswall. But it was too late for any effective endeavor in that direction. Wiswall naturally thought that, in comparison with himself and his meritorious Colony, Massachusetts and her agents were treated with undue consideration. "You know," he wrote home, "who it is that is made to trot after the *Bay* horse."[2]

1691. March 3.

Phips, while in England, had not been forgetful of the business with which he was charged, relating to a renewal of the expedition against Canada. In the King's absence he presented a memorial to the Queen, setting forth that, in order to secure his conquest of Nova Scotia, it was indispensable to "send over a frigate, and a quantity of warlike ammunition," and that "the inhabitants of New England had their hearts filled with thankfulness and zeal for his Majesty's service by reason of the preparation and passing of a charter, and would set out the frigate at their own expense with a number of war

Renewal of the plan against Quebec.

June 30.

Dec. 11.

[1] In disgust against the probability of annexation to New York, people in Plymouth refused to pay rates. (Ibid., 208.) Many times distraint was resorted to and resisted. (Comp. Hinckley's letters to Mather and Wiswall, in Mass. Hist. Col., XXXV. 287, 292.)

[2] Wiswall's Letter to Hinckley, in Mass. Hist. Col., XXXVI. 299. The pun, however, is as old as Cudworth's time. (Backus, History, &c., 319; comp. Plymouth Rec., VI. 259, 260.) Wiswall, with Oakes and Cooke, arrived in Boston, October 23. (Sewall's Diary.)

and other ships, not only to preserve Nova Scotia, but also to reduce Quebec and the other parts of Canada." He prayed to be placed in command of an expedition for these purposes, and he presented the "names of harbors and races in the eastern part of New England and in Nova Scotia fit for settlement in townships, every town consisting of at least thirty thousand acres of land."[1] But he does not appear to have obtained much attention to this scheme, and not improbably his own interest in it may have abated when other interests were awakened in his mind by his recent high promotion.

Nov. 10.

He still lingered with Mather in England. Perhaps they did not incline to disturb the existing government of the Colony before the time when in due course it would be dissolved by the expiration of the political year. Besides, Mather liked to lengthen out his stay in a society from which he received much flattering attention, and he may well be supposed to have shrunk from the cold reception which he too well knew awaited him at his home.

At length, the Governor, with his colleague in the agency, arrived in Boston. The easy transfer of the chief magistracy to him had been provided for. Bradstreet, at his last inauguration, only a few days before, had taken "the oath of his place or office for this year, or until there be a settlement of government from the crown of England."[2] At the town-house, whither the new Governor was conducted with imposing civil and military parade, the new charter was first read in the presence of the General Court, and then the Governor's commission. The oaths of office were administered first to him, and then by him to the Counsellors, and writs were issued for an election of Deputies to come together in the following month. Before separating, the Court appointed "a day of solemn thanksgiving to Almighty God

1692. May 14.

May 4.

Inauguration of the Provincial Charter.

May 24.

[1] British Colonial Papers.

[2] General Court Records, *sub die*.

for granting a safe arrival to his Excellency our Governor, and the Reverend Mr. Increase Mather, who have industriously endeavored the service of this people, and have brought over with them a settlement of government in which their Majesties have graciously given us distinguishing marks of their royal favor and goodness."[1] With such courteous words were the chagrins of the time glozed over. One thing was certain, — that, in a sense different from that of earlier times, Massachusetts was now a dependency of the British crown.

[1] The Earl of Nottingham was assured by Phips (Letter of May 29, in British Colonial Papers) of "the good disposition of the people;" and Mather wrote to him (June 23, Ibid.) that "the generality of their Majesty's subjects received with thankfulness the favors granted to them by the new charter." (Comp. Mass. Hist. Col., XXXII. 307.) In the following May, Mather preached the annual election sermon before the government. He prefaced the printed edition of it with a defence of his conduct in the agency, entitled Address to the Inhabitants of the Province of the Massachusetts Bay. (Whitmore, Andros Tracts, II. 303, &c.)

CHAPTER IV.

The aged and feeble Bradstreet must have been quite as well pleased to retire from the government of the Province as his enterprising successor was to assume it. The management of the war had been too much for his failing strength. The administration of the last three years had been honest and careful, and in the circumstances the degree of good order which was maintained was highly creditable to the people. But it was impossible that a government which from the beginning had been declared by itself to be only temporary should be capable of a vigorous rule; and respect for it, though partially reinforced by the royal order in the summer of the Revolution, had been again weakened during the unexpectedly long agitation of the question of a permanent settlement.

French and Indian war.

The war had languished for a time after the defeat of the invasion of Canada. The strenuous Governor of that country would have followed up his advantage by a movement against New York, and he applied to his court for reinforcements for that purpose; but he was told that the King had now employment nearer home for all his forces, and for the present it was necessary that his views for New France should be confined to measures of defence.[1] While the exhausted condition of Massachusetts forbade a renewal of offensive operations on her part, the French Governor's chief immediate solicitude was for the

[1] "His Majesty not being in a condition at present," &c. (Letter of the King to the Count de Frontenac, of April 7, 1691, in O'Callaghan. IX. 494; comp. Charlevoix, I. 528, 561.)

conduct of the Iroquois Indians; and the year after the repulsed invasion was mostly passed by him in a succession of unsatisfactory negotiations and indecisive hostilities with that crafty, capricious, and formidable confederacy,[1] though New England was at the same time annoyed with a desultory maritime war.

Though the result of Colonel Church's expedition into Maine had disappointed expectation, it appeared to have been not without a salutary effect in alarming the Indians in that quarter; for it was scarcely over, when some of their chiefs appeared at the town of Wells, with proposals for a pacification. A treaty was accordingly made between three commissioners from Boston and six representatives of the Abenaqui tribes. The Indians restored ten English captives; and agreed to deliver up their remaining prisoners at Wells and contract for a permanent peace at the end of five months, and meanwhile to abstain from hostilities and to give notice of any which they might know to be meditated by the French. On the day appointed, President Danforth, with some members of his Council and a guard, came to meet the chiefs at Wells; but, the favorable season for their inroads having returned, the savages had changed their minds, and, after waiting for them a sufficient time, Danforth withdrew to York. A reinforcement of thirty-five men sent by him to Wells reached that place in season to repel an attack which, within an hour after their unexpected arrival, was made upon it by a band of two hundred Indians. The defeated party fell upon an outlying settlement of York, which they satisfied their vengeance by burning, along with a vessel anchored there, of which they massacred the greater portion of the crew. Their further movements were for the present arrested by a detachment of four companies who, landing in their rear at the

1690. October.

Nov. 29.

Operations in Maine.

1691. May 1.

June 9.

July.

[1] Charlevoix, II. 92 *et seq.*

head of Casco Bay, went in pursuit of them as far as Pejepscot (Brunswick). Some Indians came in canoes to a detached settlement, now the town of Rye, and carried away twenty-one of the inhabitants. On or about the same day they murdered four men and two women at Dunstable. York and Wells, with Kittery, which was protected by its contiguity to Portsmouth, were still the only towns remaining to the English in Maine.[1]

Sept. 29.

At York, which was a place of some consequence, having three or four hundred inhabitants, there were several fortified houses. Early in a winter morning the town was surprised by a numerous party of French and Indians, who had made their march on snow-shoes. A brave but unorganized defence was overcome. Seventy or eighty of the English were killed. A larger number were miserably dragged away to Canada, freezing, hard driven, and half famished. Four of the houses were resolutely defended, till the enemy were tired out, and, setting on fire the buildings they had taken, withdrew into the woods. The fate of the minister, Mr. Dummer, was much deplored. He was found on the doorstep of his house, dead by a gunshot wound. His wife, one of the prisoners, died of fatigue and misery.[2]

Indians at York. 1692. Jan. 25.

At Wells, with fifteen soldiers, sent to aid the inhabitants in its defence, was the brave Captain Converse, who

[1] Port Royal, Phips's recent conquest, neglected by the English ministry, now fell back again into the hands of the French. Villebon, Governor of Acadia, returning from a visit to France, whither he had been to represent the importance of recovering his lost post, came with a frigate to Port Royal, which he found ungarrisoned, and resumed possession of it (November 26) without firing a gun. (Charlevoix, II. 110; O'Callaghan, IX. 526; Journals of the Board of Trade for Jan. 11, 1692; Privy Council Register for January 14.)

[2] Mather, Magnalia, VII. 76, 78. — Mather's epitaph on Dummer is as follows: —

"Dummer, the Shepherd Sacrific'd
By Wolves, because the Sheep he priz'd.
The Orphans Father, Churches Light,
The Love of Heav'n, of Hell the Spight.
The Countries Gapman, and the Face
That Shone, but knew it not, with Grace.
Hunted by Devils, but Reliev'd
By Angels, and on high Receiv'd.
The Martyr'd Pelican, who Bled
Rather than leave his Charge Unfed.
A proper Bird of Paradise,
Shot, and Flown thither in a Trice."

had repulsed the Indians from it just a year before. The Sachem Moxus, then defeated, was brother of Madockawando, who was reported by a redeemed captive to have strongly resented that mishap, and to have threatened a bloody vengeance. At Wells, as at York, there were several fortified houses, built of timber, with angles adjusted with some skill. Five hundred French and Indians now came against the place, guided by the two brother chiefs. The day before, three small English vessels had arrived, bringing the relief of their freight of provisions and ammunition, besides the seasonable reinforcement of the fourteen men who navigated them. Two days the enemy pushed the assault. They fired from behind breastworks of timber filled in with hay. They attempted the vessels unsuccessfully with blazing rafts. They rolled up to within a few yards of the fortification a large cart, faced with thick planks, which gave protection from musketry. But the English had two or three twelve-pound cannon, which were gallantly served, the men loading and pointing them, and the women, who brought ammunition, lighting the fuse. On the evening of the second day the assailants were discouraged and withdrew. They had sustained considerable loss, while they had killed only one Englishman, a seaman, who accidentally fell into their hands as he went on shore from one of the vessels. Out of temper by reason of their disappointment, they treated him ferociously, hacking him in pieces with their knives, and inserting lighted splinters into the wounds. In the mean time Lieutenant Wilson, with eighteen men, had destroyed a party which had imprudently made another attack on Dover.[1]

Indians at Wells.

June 9.

June 10, 11.

[1] Mather, Magnalia, VII. 78–81. — Charlevoix is silent upon this affair, as well as upon the calamity of York in January. Comp. Niles, History of the French and Indian Wars, in Mass. Hist. Col., XXVI. 225–230.

Such was the state of the war at the time of the accession of the new Governor. In other respects there had been little change in the outward appearance of affairs since his departure eighteen months before. But there was as yet no beginning of a recovery from the great depression and embarrassments which had been experienced; and, though a certainty had now succeeded to the grievous anxieties respecting the fate of the charter, it was by no means attended with a universal sense of relief. The bankruptcy of the treasury, in consequence of the expenses of the ill-fated expedition to Quebec, was a fact but too well ascertained. The public creditors, including all persons employed by the public alike without as with their own consent, had to put up with paper money in payment of their dues. As time proceeded, bearing with it the necessity of further outlays, there was a multiplication of public promises to pay in the form of treasury bills, and a continually deteriorating currency came into the place of whatever coin had been in circulation. In the general poverty the payment of heavy taxes was extremely burdensome, and, as has been before told, the collecting of them sometimes required compulsion, which was sometimes resisted. Military service against the French and Indians was in the circumstances indispensable, but the prevailing discouragement rendered it unattractive, and sometimes it was refused, and could only be obtained by the use of force. The authority of the tribunals of justice was disputed, and a sort of mutiny, got up by a court which had been commissioned before the Revolution, was for a while obstinately maintained. In this disturbed and enfeebled condition of the Colony, there were well-founded apprehensions of an attack in force from the French, much more serious than the annoyance of the cruisers which through the last two years had been marauding in Massachusetts Bay and Long Island Sound. Industry, in every form except the mere tilling of the

Depression and disorders.

ground, was brought almost to a stand. The fear of real want impending was not simply imaginary.

Witchcraft in New England.

A yet worse trouble confronted the new Governor. He found a part of the people whom he was to rule in a state of distress and consternation by reason of certain terrible manifestations during the last few weeks before his coming, attributed by them to the agency of the Devil, and of wicked men, women, and children, whom the Spirit of Darkness had confederated with himself, and was using as his instruments.

The people of Massachusetts in the seventeenth century, like all other Christian people at that time, — at least, with extremely rare individual exceptions, — believed in the reality of a hideous crime called *witchcraft*. They thought they had Scripture for that belief, and they knew they had law for it, explicit and abundant; and with them law and Scripture were absolute authorities for the regulation of opinion and of conduct.

In a few instances witches were believed to have appeared in the earlier years of New England. But
1651. the cases had been sporadic. They appear to have first presented themselves among the planters at Springfield.[1] In Plymouth Colony they fared well. There
1660, 1676. were two prosecutions, which resulted in acquit-

[1] Johnson, Wonder-working Providence of Sion's Saviour, 199; comp. Upham, Salem Witchcraft, I. 417–420.

I am indebted to my learned friend, Mr. J. H. Trumbull, for the following extract from a letter published in the "Mercurius Publicus" (London newspaper), of Sept. 25, 1651. It is dated "From Natick in New England, 4 July, 1651." It is neither signed nor addressed, but there can be no doubt that the writer was John Eliot; and it was probably sent to Edward Winslow, then in London. It seems to settle the question of the execution of Martha Parsons at Springfield in 1651. Hutchinson did not credit the fact (II. 16), which he erroneously supposed Johnson to report as belonging to the year 1645. Eliot writes: —

"The state of things here amongst us seems more troublesome, and we have had sad frowns of the Lord upon us, chiefly in regard of fascinations, and witchcraft; for now God calls his people into near communion with himself in visible and explicit Covenant with him, only he doth not love it should be visible. Four in Springfield were detected, whereof

tals.[1] Jane Walford, of Portsmouth, New Hampshire, was charged with being a witch; but she prosecuted one of her accusers for slander, and obtained a verdict.[2] The first instance of an execution for witchcraft is said to have occurred in Connecticut, soon after the settlement; but the circumstances are not known, and the fact has been doubted.[3] A year later, one Margaret Jones, of Charlestown, in Massachusetts, and, it has been said, two other women in Dorchester and Cambridge, were convicted and executed for the goblin crime.[4] These cases appear to have excited no more attention than would have been given to the perpetration of any other felony, and no judicial record of them survives. A case much more observed was that of Mrs. Ann Hibbins, the widow of an immigrant of special distinction. He had been agent for the Colony in England, and one of the

1656.

1647. May 30.

one was executed for murder of her own child and was doubtless a witch, another is condemned, a third under trial, a fourth under suspition."

A further extract from the same letter of Eliot I should have used in another connection, had I been acquainted with it in time.

"Here are also other sorts of Fascination by strange errors, not a few; and of late there are at *Salon* [Salem] a sort of people (some Church Members) whom they call *Shakers*, who seem to be taken with strange gripings and fits, and afterwards they speak foolish and strange words; but some speak wiser, and are conceited of revelations. The Church hath given some of them admonition."

Two weeks after this letter was written, John Clark, John Crandall, and Obadiah Holmes, coming to the region where these "fascinations" and "strange gripings" were going on, were arrested on a warrant from Salem; and it was a part of their offence that "they did administer the Sacrament of the Supper to one excommunicate person, to *another under admonition*," &c. (See above, II. 352.) Is not here a gleam of cross-light on the history of Clarke's "Ill News from New England"? The brethren from Rhode Island came to help on the "fascination," at a season when magistrates and elders were trembling under "frowns of the Lord," and specially disinclined to open doors to emissaries of the evil one.

1 Sears, Pictures of the Olden Time, &c., 334.

2 N. H. Hist. Col., I. 255.

3 Winthrop, History of New England, II. 307; comp. Kingsley, Historical Discourse, &c., 53, 100; Conn. Rec., I. 171. Other executions for witchcraft appear to have taken place in Connecticut in 1651 (Ibid., 220), in 1654 (New Haven Col. Rec., II. 78), and in 1662 (I. Mather, Illustrious Providences, 137).

4 Hutchinson, I. 150; II. 16; Winthrop, II. 326.

Assistants.[1] He had lost his property, and the melancholy and ill-temper to which his disappointed wife gave way appear to have exposed her to misconstructions and hatred,
1656. June. in the sequel of which she was convicted as a witch, and after some opposition on the part of the Magistrates was hanged.[2]

With three or four exceptions, — for the evidence respecting the asserted sufferers at Dorchester and Cambridge is imperfect, — no person appears to have been punished for witchcraft in Massachusetts, nor convicted of it, for more than sixty years after the settlement, though there had been three or four trials of other persons suspected of the crime.[3] At the time when the question respecting the
1681. May. colonial charter was rapidly approaching an issue, and the public mind was in feverish agitation, the ministers sent out a paper of proposals for collecting facts concerning witchcrafts and other "strange apparitions."[4] This brought out a work from President Mather entitled
1684. Jan. 1. "Illustrious Providences," in which that influential person related numerous stories of the performances of persons leagued with the Devil.[5]

The imagination of his restless young son was stimulated,[6] and circumstances fed the flame. In the last year
Witchcraft in Boston. 1688. of the government of Andros, a daughter, thirteen years old, of John Goodwin, — a mason living at the South End of Boston, — had a quarrel

[1] Winthrop, II. 321; see above, I. 613.

[2] According to a story which has come to us through Hutchinson (Hist., &c., I. 187), John Norton, of the First Church, said she was hanged "only for having more wit than her neighbours;" by which he explained himself to mean that she "unhappily guessed that two of her persecutors, whom she saw talking in the street, were talking of her."

[3] The case, however, of Mary Oliver, mentioned by Hutchinson (Ibid., II. 16), may have been another case of conviction, somehow proving harmless. (Comp. Cotton Mather, Magnalia, VI. 66, &c.)

[4] Increase Mather, Illustrious Providences, Preface.

[5] Ibid., Chaps. V. and VI.

[6] Cotton Mather had been but three years out of college, and was not twenty years old when the "Proposals" were published.

with an Irish washerwoman about some missing clothes. The woman's mother took it up, and scolded provokingly. Thereupon, the wicked child, profiting, as it seems, by what she had been hearing and reading on the mysterious subject, "cried out upon her," as the phrase was, as a witch, and proceeded to act the part understood to befit a bewitched person, in which behavior she was presently joined by three others of the circle, one of them only four or five years old. Now they would lose their hearing, now their sight, now their speech; and sometimes all three faculties at once. They mewed like kittens; they barked like dogs. "One while their tongues would be drawn down their throats; another they would be pulled out upon their chins to a prodigious length." The joints of their faces and limbs would be dislocated, "and anon they would clap together with a force like that of a spring-lock." "Sometimes they were kept from eating their meals by having their teeth set when they carried any thing into their mouths." They could read fluently in Popish and Quaker books, in the "Oxford Jests," and in the "Book of Common Prayer," but not in the "Westminster Catechism," nor in books of President Mather, nor in John Cotton's "Milk for Babes." "Dr. Thomas Oakes found himself so affronted by the distempers of the children, that he concluded nothing but an hellish witchcraft could be the original of these maladies." Through all this, "about nine or ten at night they always had a release from their miseries, and ate and slept all night for the most part indifferently well." Cotton Mather prayed with one of them; but she lost her hearing, he says, when he began, and recovered it as soon as he finished. Four Boston ministers and one of Charlestown held a meeting, and passed a day in fasting and prayer, by which exorcism the youngest imp was "delivered." The poor washerwoman, crazed with all this pother, — if in her right mind before, — and defending herself unskilfully in

Nov. 27.

her foreign gibberish and with the volubility of her race, was interpreted as making some confession. A gossiping witness testified that, six years before, she had heard another woman say that she had seen the accused come down a chimney. She was required to repeat the Lord's Prayer in English, — an approved test of innocence; but, being a Catholic, she had never learned it in that language. She could recite it, after a fashion, in Latin; but she was no scholar and made some mistakes. The helpless wretch was convicted and sent to the gallows.

Cotton Mather took the oldest "afflicted" girl to his house, where she dexterously played upon his self-conceit to stimulate his credulity. She satisfied him that Satan regarded him as his most terrible enemy, and avoided him with especial awe. When he prayed or read in the Bible, she was seized with convulsion fits. When he called to family devotion, she would whistle, and sing, and scream, and pretend to try to strike and kick him; but her blows would be stopped before reaching his body, indicating that he was unassailable by the Evil One.[1] Mather's account of these transactions, with a collection of other appropriate matter, was circulated not only in Massachusetts, but widely also in England, where it obtained the warm commendation of Richard Baxter; and it may be supposed to have had an important effect in producing the more disastrous delusion which followed three years after. His conclusion was: "I am resolved after this never to use but just one grain of patience with any man that shall go to impose upon me a denial of devils or of witches. I shall count that man ignorant who shall suspect, but I shall count him downright impudent if he assert the non-existence

[1] "There then stood open the study of one belonging to the family, into which entering, she stood immediately upon her feet, and cried out, 'They are gone; they are gone! They say that they cannot, God won't let 'em come here.' She also added a reason for it, which the owner of the study thought more kind than true." (Cotton Mather, Late Memorable Providences, 27.)

of things which we have had such palpable conviction of. I am sure he cannot be a civil (and some will question whether he can be an honest) man that shall go to deride the being of things which a whole country has now beheld a house of pious people suffering not a few vexations by. But if the Sadducee, or the Atheist, have no right impressions by the Memorable Providences made upon his mind, yet I hope those that know what it is to be sober will not repent any pains that they may have taken in perusing what records of these witchcrafts and possessions I thus leave unto Posterity."[1] The Goodwin children soon got well; in other words, they were tired of their atrocious foolery; and the death of their victim gave them a pretence for a return to decent behaviour.[2]

Mr. Samuel Parris was minister of a church in a part of Salem which was then called *Salem Village*, and which now as a separate town bears the name of Danvers. He was a man of talents, and of repute for professional endowments, but avaricious, wrong-headed, and ill-tempered. Among his parishioners, at the time of his installation and afterwards, there had been angry disputes about the election of a minister, which had never been composed. Neighbors and relations were embittered

Witchcraft in Salem.

[1] Late Memorable Providences, &c., 41.

[2] The younger Mather's treatise, entitled "Late Memorable Providences relating to Witchcrafts and Possessions," &c., was "finished June 7, 1689" (p. 44). The first edition, of which I have not seen a copy, was published in London in that year. The second (London, 1691) has a dedication to Wait Winthrop; an Epistle "to the reader" by Morton, minister of Charlestown, and Allen, Moody, and Willard, of Boston, in which they maintain "that there is both a God, and a Devil, and witchcraft" (Epistle, 3), and assert the trustworthiness of Mather's work; and, lastly, a "Preface," in which that oracle of Puritans, Richard Baxter, affirms that "he must be a very obdurate Sadducee that will not believe" the narratives of the book (Preface, 3). — I follow Mather's account of the case of the Goodwin children. The account given by their father (Ibid., 46) is less circumstantial and less picturesque. Another version of the story, with additional narratives of a similar description, was published by Mather in London in 1702, making Chap. VII. of the Sixth Book of the Magnalia.

against each other. Elizabeth Parris, the minister's daughter, was now nine years old. A niece of his, eleven years old, lived in his family. His neighbor, Thomas Putnam, the parish clerk, had a daughter named Ann, twelve years of age. These children, with a few other young women, of whom two were as old as twenty years or thereabouts, had become possessed with a wild curiosity about the sorceries of which they had been hearing and reading, and
1691, used to hold meetings for study, if it may be so
1692. called, and practice. They learned to go through motions similar to those which had lately made the Goodwin children so famous. They forced their limbs into grotesque postures, uttered unnatural outcries, were seized with cramps and spasms, became incapable of speech and of motion. By and by, they interrupted public worship.
March 20. Abigail Williams, Parris's niece, called aloud in church to the minister to "stand up and name his text." Ann Putnam cried out, "There is a yellow bird sitting on the minister's hat, as it hangs on the pin in the pulpit."[1] The families were distressed. The neighbors were alarmed. The physicians were perplexed and baffled, and at length declared that nothing short of witchery was the trouble.[2]

[1] Increase Mather, Further Account of the Trials of the New England Witches, &c., 2. The materials for this tract were "collected" by Deodat Lawson, a minister who had a large agency in promoting the excitement. An Appendix consisted of Increase Mather's "Cases of Conscience concerning Witchcraft," published in London in 1693.

[2] In the summer before these transactions, Richard Baxter published in London (the preface is dated June 20, 1691) a volume, now exceedingly rare, of two hundred and fifty pages, on "The Certainty of the World of Spirits, fully evinced by Unquestionable Histories of Apparitions and Witchcrafts," &c. Baxter says: "They that will read Mr. Increase Mather's book, and especially his son's, Mr. Cotton Mather's, book, of the witchcrafts in New England, may see enough to silence any incredulity that pretendeth to be rational."

Among the principal contemporary authorities for the transactions in Essex County in relation to witchcraft are the judicial records in the clerk's office at Salem; a volume of original papers in the Massachusetts Archives; Increase Mather's Further Account, &c.; Cotton Mather's Wonders of the Invisible World; Calef's More Wonders of the Invisible World. In later times, Hutchinson, in his

The kinsfolk of the "afflicted children" assembled for fasting and prayer. Then the neighboring ministers were sent for, and held at Mr. Parris's house a prayer-meeting which lasted through the day. The children performed in their presence, and the result was a confirmation by the ministers of the opinion of the doctors. Of course, the next inquiry was by whom the manifest witchcraft was exercised. It was presumed that the unhappy girls could give the answer. For a time they refused to do so. But at length, yielding to an importunity which it had become difficult to escape unless by an avowal of their fraud, they pronounced the names of Good, Osborn, and Tituba.

Tituba — half Indian, half negro — was a servant of Mr. Parris, brought by him from Barbadoes,[1] where he had formerly been a merchant. Sarah Good was an old woman, miserably poor. Sarah Osborn had been prosperous in early life. She had been married twice, and her second husband was still living, but separated from her. Her reputation was not good, and for some time she had been bedridden, and in a disturbed nervous state. In the meeting-house of Salem Village, with great solemnity, and in the presence of a vast crowd, the three accused persons were arraigned before John Hathorne and Jonathan Corwin, of Salem, members of the Colonial Council. The "afflicted children" were confronted with them; prayer was offered; and the examination proceeded with a questioning of Sarah Good, the other prisoners being for the time withdrawn.

March 1.

When Good declared that she was falsely accused, Hathorne "desired the children all of them to look at

History, told the story at length (II. 25 *et seq.*), and Mr. Charles W. Upham much more fully and circumstantially in his very interesting volumes entitled "Salem Witchcraft." Some original papers of the time have been transmitted through private hands. A specimen of such is in the Proceedings of the Mass. Hist. Col., 1860, 31. A copy of minutes of the Danvers Church in the years 1692 and 1693 is printed in Mass. Hist. Col., XXIII. 169 *et seq.*

[1] Fowler, Life of Samuel Parris, 1.

her; . . . . . and so they all did; . . . . . and presently they were all tormented." The prisoner was made to touch them, and then their torment ceased, the received doctrine being that by this contact the Satanic influence which had been emitted from the witch was drawn back into her person. Similar proceedings were had with the other two prisoners. Tituba, whether in collusion with her young mistress, or, as was afterwards said, in consequence of having been scourged by Mr. Parris,[1] confessed herself to be a witch, and charged Good and Osborn with being her accomplices. The evidence was then thought sufficient, and the three were committed to gaol for trial.

Martha Corey and Rebecca Nourse were next cried out against. Both were church-members of excellent charac-
March 21. ter; the latter, seventy years of age. They were examined by the same Magistrates, and sent to
March 24. prison, and with them a child of Sarah Good, only four or five years old, also charged with diabolical prac-
April 3. tices. Mr. Parris preached upon the text, "Have not I chosen you twelve, and one of you is a devil?" Sarah Cloyse, understanding the allusion to be to Nourse, who was her sister, went out of church in displeasure, and was accordingly cried out upon, examined, and committed. Elizabeth Procter was another person
April 11. charged. The Deputy-Governor and five Magistrates came to Salem for the examination of the two prisoners last named. Procter appealed to one of the children who was accusing her. "Dear child," she said, "it is not so; there is another judgment, dear child;" and presently they denounced as a witch her husband, who
April 18. stood by her side. A week afterwards, warrants were issued for the apprehension of four other suspected persons; and a few days later for that of three others, one of whom, Philip English, was the principal merchant of Salem. On the same day, on the infor-

[1] Calef, More Wonders of the Invisible World, 91.

mation of one of the possessed girls, an order was sent to Maine for the arrest of George Burroughs, a graduate of Harvard College, formerly Parris's rival as candidate for the ministry at Salem Village, and now minister of Wells. The witness said that Burroughs, besides being a wizard, had killed his first two wives and other persons whose ghosts had appeared to her and denounced him.

Charges now came in rapidly. George Jacobs, an old man, and his grand-daughter, were sent to prison. "You tax me for a wizard," said he to the Magistrates; "you may as well tax me for a buzzard; I have done no harm." They tried him with repeating the Lord's Prayer, which it was thought impossible for a witch to do. According to Parris's report, "he missed in several parts of it." His accusers persisted. "Well, burn me or hang me," said he, "I will stand in the truth of Christ; I know nothing of the matter, any more than the child that was born to-night." Among others, John Willard was now apprehended. As a constable he had served in the arrest and custody of some of the reputed witches. But he came to see the absurdity of the thing, and was said to have uttered something to the effect that it was the Magistrates that were bewitched, and those who cheered them on. He was forthwith cried out against as a wizard, and committed for trial.

May 10.

May 18.

Affairs were in this condition when the King's Governor arrived. About a hundred alleged witches were now in gaol, awaiting trial. Their case was one of the first matters to which his attention was called. Without authority for so doing, — for, by the charter which he represented, the establishment of judicial courts was a function of the General Court, — he proceeded to institute a special commission of Oyer and Terminer, consisting of seven Magistrates, first of whom was the hard, obstinate, narrow-minded Stoughton.[1]

May 14.

Executions of witches.

[1] For the commissions constituting this court, see the Journal of the Provincial Council.

The commissioners applied themselves to their office without delay. Their first act was to try Bridget Bishop,[1] against whom an accusation twenty years old, and retracted by its author on his death-bed, had been revived. The court sentenced her to die by hanging, and she was accordingly hanged at the end of eight days. Cotton Mather, in his account of the proceedings, relates that, as she passed along the street under guard, Bishop "had given a look towards the great and spacious meeting-house of Salem, and immediately a dæmon, invisibly entering the house, tore down a part of it."[2] It may be guessed that a plank or a partition had given way under the pressure of the crowd of lookers-on collected for so extraordinary a spectacle.

June 2.

At the end of another four weeks the court for the witchcraft investigation sat again, and sen-

June 30.

[1] Perhaps the reason of the selection of Bridget Bishop for the first trial was that, twelve years before, she had been arraigned on a similar charge, and there remained a prejudice against her.

[2] Mather, Wonders of the Invisible World, 52. — In Mass. Hist. Col., XXXVIII. 391 *et seq.*, is a letter which, two days before this first trial, Cotton Mather wrote to his parishioner, John Richards, one of the judges. Mather was in a state of nervous agitation, different from his habitual sanguine mood. "I am languishing under such an overthrow of my health, ... the least excess of travel or diet, or any thing that may discompose me, would at this time threaten perhaps my life." He could not, therefore, as he tells his friend, go to Salem. "Excuse me from waiting upon you, with the utmost of my little skill and care to assist the noble service whereto you are called of God this week, the service of encountering the wicked spirits in the high places of our air, and of detecting and confounding their confederates."

In the four weeks' recess of the court after the conviction of Bridget Bishop, the Governor and Council submitted the case to several ministers of Boston and its neighborhood, who replied (June 15), recommending "the speedy and vigorous prosecutions of such as have rendered themselves obnoxious, according to the directions given in the laws of God and the wholesome statutes of the English nation for the detection of witchcrafts," and at the same time the exercise "of a very critical and exquisite caution," and an observance of "the directions given by such judicious writers as Perkins and Barnard." (Hutch. Hist., II. 50, 51.) The views expressed in this paper were presented in an enlarged and more elaborate form in October of this year, in a tract, composed by Increase Mather, and signed by fourteen ministers, published under the title, "Cases of Conscience concerning Evil Spirits personating Man."

tenced five women, two of Salem, and one each of Amesbury, Ipswich, and Topsfield, all of whom were executed, protesting their innocence. "At the trial of Sarah Good one of the afflicted fell in a fit, and after coming out of it she cried out of the prisoner for stabbing her in the breast with a knife, and that she had broken the knife in stabbing of her. Accordingly a piece of the blade of a knife was found about her. Immediately, information being given to the court, a young man was called who produced a haft and part of the blade, which the court having viewed and compared saw it to be the same. And upon inquiry the young man affirmed that yesterday he happened to break that knife, and that he cast away the upper part, this afflicted person being then present. The young man was dismissed, and she was bidden by the court not to tell lies; and was improved after (as she had been before) to give evidence against the prisoners."[1] For another of these convicts, Rebecca Nourse, a matron eminent for piety and goodness, a verdict of acquittal was first rendered. But Stoughton sent the jury out again, reminding them that, in her examination, in reference to certain witnesses against her who had confessed their own guilt, she had used the expression, "they came among us." Nourse was deaf, and did not catch what had been going on. When it was afterwards repeated to her, she said that by the *coming among us* she meant that they had been in prison together. But the jury adopted the court's interpretation of the words as signifying an acknowledgment that they had met at a witch orgy. The Governor was disposed to grant her a pardon. But Parris, who had an ancient grudge against her, interfered and prevailed. On the last communion-day before her execution, she was taken into church, and formally excommunicated by Mr. Noyes, her minister.[2]

July 19.

[1] Calef, More Wonders, &c., 101.

[2] Mather's "Wonders of the Invisible World" belongs to this second recess of the court. It was, as a

Of six persons tried at the next session of the court, the Reverend George Burroughs was one. At a certain point of the proceedings the young people pretending to have suffered from him stood mute. Stoughton asked who hindered them from telling their story. "The Devil, I suppose," said Burroughs. "Why should the Devil be so careful to suppress evidence against you?" retorted the judge, and with the jury this encounter of wits told hardly against the prisoner. His behaviour at his execution strongly impressed the spectators in his favor. "When he was upon the ladder, he made a speech for the clearing of his innocency, with such solemn and serious expressions as were to the admiration of all present. His prayer (which he concluded by repeating the Lord's Prayer) was so well worded, and uttered with such composedness, and such (at least, seeming) fervency of spirit as was very affecting, and drew tears from many, so that it seemed to many the spectators would hinder the execution. The accusers said the Black Man stood and dictated to him."[1]

Aug. 5.

Aug. 19.

sermon, "uttered (in part) on August 4, 1692."

[1] George Jacobs, an old man, was one of those who suffered with Burroughs. A witness against both was a young woman, grand-daughter of the former, who had previously confessed herself to be a witch. The day before their execution she obtained permission to visit them, when she acknowledged to them the falsehood of her charge, and received their forgiveness, Burroughs praying with and for her. The day after she wrote the following letter to her father: —

"From the Dungeon in Salem-prison, April 20, '92.

"Honored Father, — After my humble duty remembered to you, hoping in the Lord of your good health, as blessed be God I enjoy, though in abundance of affliction, being close confined here in a loathsome dungeon, the Lord look down in mercy upon me, not knowing how soon I shall be put to death, by means of the afflicted persons, my grandfather having suffered already, and all his estate seized for the King. The reason of my confinement is this, I having, through the Magistrates' threatenings, and my own will and wretched heart, confessed several things contrary to my conscience and knowledge, though to the wounding of my own soul, the Lord pardon me for it; but oh! the terrors of a wounded conscience who can bear. But blessed be the Lord, He would not let me go on in my sins, but in mercy, I hope, to my soul would not suffer me to keep it in any longer, but I was forced to confess the truth

In the course of the next month, in which the Governor left Boston for a tour of inspection in the Eastern country, fifteen persons — six women in one day, and on another eight women and one man — were tried, convicted, and sentenced. Eight of them were hanged. The brave Giles Corey, eighty years of age, being arraigned, refused to plead. He said that the whole thing was an imposture, and that it was of no use to put himself on his trial, for every trial had ended in a conviction, — which was the fact. It is shocking to relate that, suffering the penalty of the English common law for a contumacious refusal to answer, — the *peine forte et dure*, — he was pressed to death with heavy weights laid on his body. By not pleading he intended to protect the inheritance of his children, which, as he had been informed, would, by a conviction of felony, have been forfeit to the crown.

Sept. 9. Sept. 17. Sept. 22. Sept. 19.

In the following month the malady broke out in another neighborhood. One Ballard, of the town of Andover, whose wife was ill in a way that perplexed their medical friend, sent to Salem to see what light could be obtained from the witch-detectors there. A party of them came to his help, and went to work with vigor. More than fifty persons at Andover fell under accusation, some of the weaker-minded of whom were brought to confess themselves guilty not only of

Witchcraft in Andover. October.

of all before the Magistrates, who would not believe me, but 'tis their pleasure to put me in here, and God knows how soon I shall be put to death. Dear father, let me beg your prayers to the Lord on my behalf, and send us a joyful and happy meeting in Heaven. My mother, poor woman, is very crazy, and remembers her kind love to you, and to uncle. So leaving you to the protection of the Lord, I rest your dutiful daughter,

"MARGARET JACOBS."

(Upham, History, &c., II. 318.) — Vol. CXXXV. of the Archives is full of papers of this description, which cannot now be read without tears. See, for instance, the petitions of Mary Esty (Archives, CXXXV. 121) and Rebecca Fox (Ibid., 76).

afflicting their neighbors, but of practising such exercises as riding on animals and on sticks through the air.[1]

There were no executions, however, after those which have been mentioned as occurring on one day of each of four successive months. There had been twenty human victims, Corey included, besides two dogs, their accomplices in the mysterious crime. Fifty persons had obtained a pardon by confessing; a hundred and fifty were in prison awaiting trial; and charges had been made against two hundred more.[2] The accusers were now flying at high quarries. Hezekiah Usher, known to the reader as an ancient Magistrate of consideration, was complained of, and Mrs. Thacher, mother-in-law of Corwin, the justice who had taken the earliest examinations.[3] Zeal in pushing forward the prosecutions began to seem dangerous; for what was to prevent an accused person from securing himself by confession, and then revenging himself on the accuser by arraigning him as a former ally?

Multiplication of charges.

Mrs. Hale, wife of the minister of Beverly who had been active in the prosecutions, and Dudley Bradstreet, of Andover, the old Governor's son, who had granted warrants for the commitment of some thirty or forty alleged witches,[4] were now accused. The famous name of John Allyn, Secretary of Connecticut, was uttered in whispers.[5] There had even begun to be a muttering about Lady Phips, the Governor's wife, and Mr. Willard, then minister of the Old South Church in Boston, and afterwards head of the College, who, after yielding to the infatuation in its earliest stage, had made himself obnoxious and suspected by partially retracing his steps.[6] People began now to be almost

[1] Mass. Hist. Col., V. 71 *et seq.*

[2] Calef, More Wonders, &c., 110.

[3] Mass. Hist. Col., V. 69.

[4] Ibid., XXI. 124.

[5] Hutch. Hist., II. 60.

[6] Willard was one of the signers of the "Epistle to the Reader" prefixed to Mather's "Memorable Providences." Comp. Upham, History, &c., II. 458.

as wild with the fear of being charged with witchcraft, or having the charge made against their friends, as they had been with the fear of suffering from its spells. The visitation, shocking as it had been, had been local. It had been almost confined to some towns of Essex County. In other parts of the Province the public mind was calmer, or was turned in the different direction of disgust at the insane tragedies, and dread of their repetition. A person in Boston, whose name had begun to be used dangerously by the informers at Andover, instituted an action for defamation, laying his damages at a thousand pounds; a measure which, while it would probably have been ruinous to him, had he made a mistake in choosing his time, was now found, at the turning of the tide, to have a wholesome effect.

After the convictions which were last mentioned, the court which had conducted the trials adjourned for two months. Thanks to the good sense of the people, it never met again. Before the time designated for its next session, the General Court of the Province assembled, and the cry of the oppressed and miserable came to their ear. The General Court superseded the court of Special Commission, the agent of all the cruelty, by constituting a regular tribunal of supreme jurisdiction. When that court met at the appointed time, reason had begun to resume her sway, and the grand jury at once threw out more than half of the presentments. They found true bills against twenty-six persons. The evidence against these was as good as any that had proved fatal in former trials; but only three of the arraigned were found guilty, and all these were pardoned.[1] One of them may have owed her

Action of the General Court. Oct. 12.

Nov. 25.

1693. Jan. 3.

[1] Calef, More Wonders, &c., 142. According to Cotton Mather (Parentator, 166), the cause of this executive lenity and of the popular "turn of the tide" was his father's "very learned 'Cases of Conscience concerning Witchcraft,' in which treatise he did, with incomparable reason and

conviction to a sort of rude justice; she had before confessed herself a witch, and charged her husband, who was hanged on her information.[1] Stoughton, who now, under the regular organization of the courts, had been made Chief Justice, showed his disapprobation of the pardons by withdrawing from the bench with passionate anger. Feb. 21. Phips wrote to the Lords of Trade a disingenuous letter in which he attempted to divert from himself, chiefly at Stoughton's expense, whatever blame might in some quarters be attached to the recent transactions; it even appeared to imply, what was Nov. 21. contrary to the fact, that the executions did not begin till after his departure from Boston to the Eastern country.[2] 1692. September.

reading, demonstrate that a devil may appear in the shape of an innocent and a virtuous person, to afflict those who suffer by diabolical manifestations, and that the ordeal of the sight and the touch is not a conviction of a covenant with the devil."

[1] Calef, More Wonders, &c., 141.

[2] "On my arrival here I found the prisons full of people committed upon suspicion of witchcraft, and complaints were continually made to me that many persons were grievously tormented by witches, and that they cried out upon several persons by name as the cause of their torments. The number of these complaints increasing every day, by advice of the Lieutenant-Governor and the Council, I gave a Commission of Oyer and Terminer to try some of the suspected witches, ... and I depended upon the court for a right method of proceeding in cases of witchcraft. At that time I went to command the army at the eastern part of the Province. . . . . . When I returned, I found people much dissatisfied at the proceedings of the court; for about twenty persons were condemned and executed, of which number some were thought by many persons to be innocent. The court still proceeded in the same method of trying them, which was by the evidence of the afflicted persons, who, when they were brought into the court, as soon as the suspected witches looked on them, instantly fell to the ground in strange agonies and grievous torment; but when touched by them upon the arm or some other part of their flesh, they immediately revived and came to themselves, upon which they made oath that the prisoner at the bar did afflict them, and that they saw their shape or spectre come from their bodies, which put them to such pains and torments. When I inquired into the matter, I was informed by the judges that they began with this, but had human testimony against such as were condemned, and undoubted proof of their being witches; but at length I found that the Devil did take upon him the shape of innocent persons, and some were accused of whose innocency I was well assured, and many considerable persons of unblamable life and conversations were cried out upon as witches and wizards. The Deputy-Governor, not-

The drunken fever-fit was now over, and with returning sobriety came profound contrition and disgust; emotions not due to any new-born distrust of the reality of the crime which had been aimed at, but to

Subsidence of the excitement.

withstanding, persisted vigorously in the same method, to the great dissatisfaction and disturbance of the people, until I put an end to the court, and stopped the proceedings. . . . . . When I put an end to the court, there was at least fifty persons in prison, in great misery by reason of the extreme cold and their poverty. Most of them having only spectre evidence against them, and their *mittimus* being defective, I caused some of them to be let out upon bail, and put the judges upon consideration of a way to relieve others, and prevent their perishing in prison, upon which some of them were convinced and acknowledged that their former proceedings were too violent, and not grounded upon a right foundation, but that, if they might sit again, they would proceed after another method; and whereas Mr. Increase Mather and several other divines did give it as their judgment that the Devil might afflict in the shape of an innocent person, and that the look and the touch of the suspected persons was not sufficient proof against them, these things had not the same stress laid upon them as before; and upon this consideration I permitted a special superior court to be held at Salem, in the county of Essex, on the third day of January, the Lieutenant-Governor being chief judge. Their method of proceeding being altered, all that were brought to trial, to the number of fifty-two, were cleared, saving three; and I was informed by the King's Attorney-General that some of the cleared and condemned were under the same circumstances, or that there was the same reason to clear the three condemned as the rest, according to his judgment. The Deputy-Governor signed a warrant for their speedy execution, and also of five others who were condemned at the former Court of Oyer and Terminer; but, considering how the matter had been managed, I sent a reprieve, whereby the execution was stopped until their Majesties' pleasure be signified and declared. The Lieutenant-Governor upon this occasion was enraged and filled with passionate anger, and refused to sit upon the bench at a superior court, at that time held at Charles Town; and, indeed, hath from the beginning hurried on these matters with great precipitancy, and by his warrant hath caused the estates, goods, and chattels of the executed to be seized and disposed of without my knowledge or consent. The stop put to the method of the first proceeding hath dissipated the black cloud that threatened this Province with destruction. For whereas this delusion of the Devil's did spread, and its dismal effects touched the lives and estates of many of their Majesties' subjects, and the reputation of some of the principal persons here, and indeed unhappily clogged and interrupted their Majesties' affairs, which hath been a great vexation to me.

"I have no new complaints, but people's minds, before divided and distracted by different opinions concerning this matter, are now well composed." (Letter of Phips to the Earl of Nottingham, of Feb. 21, 1693, in British Colonial Papers.)

It would be interesting to know what part or interest Joseph Dudley took in these transactions, of which

compassion for the bitter misery which had been inflicted, and to a sense of the hard and reckless unfairness with which the designated victims had been judged and doomed. A few still held out against the return of reason. There are some men who never own that they have been in the wrong, and here and there is a man forever incapable of seeing it. Stoughton, with his bull-dog stubbornness, that might in other times have made him a Saint Dominic, continued to insist that the business had been all right, and that the only mistake was in putting a stop to it.[1] Cotton Mather was always infallible in his own eyes. In the year after the executions, he had the satisfaction of studying another remarkable case of possession in Boston;[2] but

he could not have been ignorant. He was still, in the summer of 1692, Chief Justice of New York, where it must be presumed that he was in communication with his friend Stoughton. But he also appears to have had, more or less, his home in Massachusetts at that time.

[1] A reprieve coming to Salem for seven witchcraft convicts in January, 1693, "so moved the judge that he said to this effect: 'We were in a way to have cleared the land of them: who it is that obstructs the cause of justice I know not. The Lord be merciful to the country!' And so went off the bench, and came no more into that court." (Upham, II. 359.)

[2] This was the case of Margaret Rule, who began to be "afflicted" Sept. 10, 1693. Among other marvellous experiences, she lived many days without food, and Mather and others affirmed that they had seen her "lifted up from her bed, wholly by an invisible force, a great way towards the top of the room where she lay." (Calef, More Wonders, &c., 23.) Mather, who was "himself a daily witness of a large part of these occurrences," wrote an account of them, "not with the design of throwing it presently into the press, but only to preserve the memory of such memorable things." Circulated in manuscript, it fell into the hands of "Robert Calef, merchant, of Boston," who entered into an investigation of the matter, which brought him into an angry controversy with Mather, and involved him in a prosecution for slander. (Ibid., 16, 18.) The dispute led to the publication by Calef of his work, dated in August, 1697, in which he treated at large the witchcraft cases in Salem.

Mather's narrative of Margaret Rule's possession is entitled "Another Brand Plucked out of the Burning." This title refers to an earlier treatise entitled "A Brand Plucked out of the Burning," in which he had set forth another case which occurred earlier in Boston, just after the tragedies in Essex County. It is in manuscript in the library of the Antiquarian Society. Mercy Short, the heroine, had formerly been a captive of the Indians. Her behaviour seems that of a distracted, ignorant woman repeating, in a fragmentary way, with the cunning of insanity, what rumor had brought to her of the proceed-

when it and the treatise which he wrote upon it failed to excite much attention, and it was plain that the tide had set the other way, he soon got his consent to let it run at its own pleasure, and turned his sprightly activity to other objects.[1] The Corporation of Harvard College, to which body both the Mathers belonged, had not had enough of wonders, nor could their dignity well bear that their recent position should be wholly compromised. They issued certain "Proposals to the Reverend Ministers of the Gospel in the several churches of New England" for a collection of "apparitions, possessions, and enchantments."[2] But the movement was abortive; there was not now stomach for such a work. Saltonstall, horrified by the rigor of his colleagues, had resigned his place in the commission at an early period of the operations. After a stubborn resistance on his part, Parris, the Salem minister, was driven from his place by the calm and decent, but irreconcilable indignation of his parishioners.[3] Noyes, his

1694. March 5.

ings at Salem. Sarah Good, while lying in gaol in Boston, had asked her for "a little tobacco," and Mercy "affronted her by throwing an handful of shavings at her, and saying, 'That's tobacco good enough for you;'" whereupon "poor Mercy was taken with just such or perhaps much worse fits as those which held the bewitched people then tormented by invisible furies in the county of Essex." With an interval or two, they continued for five months, under Mather's frequent inspection. Short's familiar spirits, visible to her, but not to bystanders, were, like those of the Goodwin jade, accustomed to express "a very particular provocation and malignity against a certain person in the town,"—Mather's euphemism for himself. Perhaps the most salient feature of the piece is his frequently holding up, *in terrorem*, to readers, his knowledge, communicated by Short, of the guilt of hitherto unsuspected persons, — knowledge, however, which as yet he professed himself disinclined to divulge. Short's power of living without food was marvellous, as were her voluble reasonings from Scripture with her tormentors.

[1] The account of the Salem witchcraft, published in 1702, in Mather's Magnalia (VI. 79), is not from his pen. His taste for the business had probably been impaired by this time. "Having in my hands a most unexceptionable account thereof, written by Mr. John Hales, I will here content myself with the transcribing of that." He tries his hand again at the subject, but daintily, as late as 1724. (Parentator, 161.)

[2] Magnalia, VI. 1. "I must complain that unto this hour (eight years after) there have not half ten considerable histories been transmitted to us in answer to these proposals."

[3] Calef, More Wonders, &c., 97–104.

well-intentioned but infatuated neighbor in the First Parish, devoting the remainder of his life to peaceful and Christian service, caused his church to cancel, by a formal
1712. and public act, their excommunication of the blameless Mrs. Nourse, who had died his peculiar victim.

Hideous as the retrospect of such horrors was, it was again and again repeated, under the goad of a remorse which demanded at least expression, though reparation could not be. Members of some of the juries, in a written public declaration, acknowledged the fault of their wrongful verdicts, entreated forgiveness, and protested that, "according to their present minds, they would none of them do such things again, on such grounds, for the whole world, praying that this act of theirs might be accepted in way of satisfaction for their offence."[1]

Retrospection and reaction.

On a day of General Fasting, proclaimed by authority to be observed throughout the jurisdiction, the people were invited to pray that "whatever mistakes on either hand had been fallen into, either by the body of this people, or by any orders of men, referring to the late tragedy raised among us by Satan and his instruments, through the awful judgment of God, he would humble them therefor, and pardon all the errors of his servants and people."[2] On
1696. that day, Judge Sewall rose in his pew in the Old
Jan. 14. South Church in Boston, handed to the desk a paper acknowledging and bewailing his great offence and asking the prayers of the congregation "that God would not visit the sin of him or of any other upon himself or any of his, nor upon the land," and remained standing while it was read by the minister. To the end of his long life, the penitent and much-respected man kept every year a private day of humiliation and prayer on the same account. Twenty-eight years after, he prays in an entry in his diary in reference to the transaction: "The good and gracious God be pleased to save New England, and me and my family!"

[1] Calef, More Wonders, &c., 144.

[2] Mass. Prov. Rec., *sub die*.

Ann Putnam, one of the three beginners of the mischief, after thirteen years, came out of the long conflict between her conscience and her shame, with a most affecting declaration of her remorse and grief, now on record in the books of the Danvers Church.[1] Twenty years after, the General Court annulled the convictions and attainders, and made grants to the heirs of the sufferers, in acknowledgment of their pecuniary losses.[2] "Some of them [the witch accusers] proved profligate persons," says Governor Hutchinson, "abandoned to all vice; others passed their days in obscurity and contempt."[3]

1710. Oct. 17.

Occasion of the outbreak.

It is not to be supposed that at this day the testimony can be elucidated or the juggles exposed, which beguiled so many people, otherwise discerning and right-minded, almost two centuries ago. Nor does it properly belong to the province of an historian of New England to account for phenomena which have been exhibited on a much larger scale in other times and places than those of which he writes. Governor Hutchinson recounted these transactions seventy years after their occurrence, when the traditions relating to them were fresh. He had heard the story of them told by not a few contemporaries, and he had a mass of writings in relation to them which now have perished. He was a man eminent for force and acuteness of mind. As head of the judiciary of Massachusetts, he had had large practice in

[1] Upham, Salem Witchcraft, II. 509, 510.

[2] Mass. Prov. Rec., *sub die.* But even this did not finish the business in the legislature. The case of George Burroughs was called up and reviewed, under a petition for an allowance to his family, as late as nearly sixty years after his murder. (Mass. Prov. Rec. for May 31, 1749.)

[3] Hutch. Hist., II. 62. See also Calef (Epistle Dedicatory, last paragraph but two). He says some of the witnesses were "as vile varlets as not only were known before, but have been further apparent since by their manifest lives, whoredoms, incest, &c." — Thirty years after the performances at Salem, three young girls at Littleton went through a similar series of feats of imposture. The oldest of them after a while avowed at large to Mr. Turell, of Medford, their methods of proceeding, which seemed simple when explained. (Turell, Case of Witchcraft in Littleton; comp. Mass. Hist. Col., XX. 6.)

the weighing of evidence; and his judgment on the whole matter was, "that a little attention must force conviction that the whole was a scene of fraud and imposture, begun by young girls, who at first perhaps thought of nothing more than being pitied and indulged, and continued by adult persons, who were afraid of being accused themselves. The one and the other, rather than confess their fraud, suffered the lives of so many innocents to be taken away, through the credulity of judges and juries. There are," he says, "a great number of persons who are willing to suppose the accusers to have been under bodily disorders which affected their imaginations. This is kind and charitable, but seems to be winking the truth out of sight."[1] Recent investigations have further established a strong probability that in the principal scene of the tragedy, after the cruel facility of the tribunals had been manifested in the course of the first trials, more or fewer of the charges were instigated by personal vindictiveness and malice growing out of quarrels which had existed in the preceding years.[2] In short, impudent craft, on the one part, under one or another wicked excitement, had practised upon a preparation, on the other part, for being grossly and disastrously deluded.

Worthlessness of the confessions.

The confessions made by the accused in numerous instances — fifty or more — were in the early trials received as weighty evidence; nor, taking fairly into view the state of opinion at the time, ought this estimation of them to create surprise. It was not long, however, before circumstances disclosed their worthlessness. It soon became manifest that, an accusation once made, confession was both the sure and the only way to save life. Without exception, in the first trials, every person arraigned was convicted; and every person who confessed was spared; and all who did not confess were executed. In some instances confessions were retracted,

[1] Hutch. Hist., II. 62. [2] Upham, Salem Witchcraft, I. 242 *et seq.*

though, as long as the frenzy was raging, this had to be done at the sacrifice of life; and in every remaining instance they were retracted at a later time, when matters again were quiet. These facts dispose of a large portion of the confessions. To another portion belong a different class of considerations, equally conclusive as to their significance. The confessions were often extorted in such ways that the persons who made them were not in a state of mind to entitle their declarations to any confidence. They were subjected to appliances such as drive clear and robust minds to insanity. Kept day and night, day after day, night after night, in a state of high nervous excitement; plied perpetually by entreaties and reproaches; bewildered by the detestable legerdemain practised against them by the informers; frightened by their prison solitude, and weakened with their prison fare; worried while awake, and scared while asleep, by phantoms of the infernal world conjured up in the imaginations of others to be reflected into their own: one cannot wonder if many of them should become sufficiently distracted to think that they verily were what other people said they were, and to own that they had joined in Satan's sacrament, or set their names to his black book, or any other foolish thing that was asked of them. The following is a declaration of six women at Andover, who had confessed, and respecting whose character more than fifty of their most respectable neighbors testified that, "by their sober, godly, and exemplary conversation, they had obtained a good report in the place, where they had been well esteemed and approved in the church of which they were members." Relating first the circumstances of their apprehension, they go on to say: —

"After Mr. Barnard had been at prayer, we were blindfolded and our hands were laid upon the afflicted persons, they being in their fits, and falling into their fits at our coming into their presence, as they said; and some led us and laid our hands upon them, and then they said they were well, and that we were guilty of afflicting them. Whereupon we were all seized as prisoners, by a warrant from the justice of the peace, and forthwith carried to Salem. And by reason of that sudden surprisal, we knowing ourselves altogether innocent of that crime, we were all exceedingly astonished and amazed and consternated and affrighted, even out of our reason; and our nearest and dearest relations, seeing us in that dreadful condition, and knowing our great danger, apprehended there was no other way to save our lives, as the case was then circumstanced, but by our confessing ourselves to be such and such persons as the afflicted represented us to be. They out of tenderness and pity persuaded us to confess what we did confess. And, indeed, that confession that it is said we made was no other than what was suggested to us by some gentlemen, they telling us that we were witches, and they knew it, and we knew it, which made us think it was so; and our understanding, our reason, our faculties almost gone, we were not capable of judging of our condition; as also the hard measures they used with us rendered us incapable of making our defence, but said any thing and every thing which they desired, and most of what we said was but in effect a consenting to what they said. Some time after, when we were better composed, they telling us what we had confessed, we did profess that we were innocent and ignorant of such things; and we hearing that Samuel Wardwell had renounced his confession, and was quickly after condemned and executed, some of us were told that we were going after Wardwell."[1]

Perhaps the fictitious character of the charges would have been satisfactorily evinced to the persons conducting and otherwise present at the trials, if the accused had been defended by able counsel, learned in the laws of evidence and skilled in exposing falsehood by cross-examination. But there were no trained lawyers in the Province. The

[1] Calef, More Wonders, &c., 111; comp. Hist. Soc. Col., XIII. 221.

few persons who were in the habit of acting as counsel had had no regular education in the law. The alleged witches had no counsel whatever. Nor had their judges the competency which that station demands for instructing a jury on an intricate case of felony. Stoughton and Sewall had been educated for the pulpit; two of their five associates were physicians, and one was a merchant; not one was a lawyer. When such men did cruel injustice, it was partly from imperfect knowledge of the rules of proof, and partly because their minds were prepossessed with misleading imaginations. On the whole, the court represented the sense of that portion of the people, with whom a merciful incredulity or a mere natural relenting was least likely to prevail against the bewildering theory of the age. The court was not constituted by the people of Massachusetts, but, without their authority, by the Governor set over them by the King; and it was constituted, not of persons possessing the confidence of the people, but largely of former functionaries recently discharged by the popular vote. Stoughton was its head and soul, and he was a man so stubborn that, when his theory had been adopted, any humane reluctance was to him only an impertinence and a sin. The timid conscientiousness of Sewall precisely prepared him for the sway of his positive and grim associate. Wait Winthrop was rather a feeble person, and something of a courtier. Saltonstall was disgusted with the proceedings from the outset, and refused to sit. Bradstreet's heaviness was wiser than the mercurial temperament of some of his eminent contemporaries. He had steadfastly refused to order the execution of a convicted witch some years before the Salem tragedy; [1] he is not known to have done any thing to countenance the follies which had been rife in the last three months of his administration; and there is every probability that, had he continued to be Chief Magis-

Untrustworthiness of the investigation.

1680.

[1] Upham, Salem Witchcraft, I. 450.

trate, the misery and shame which inaugurated his successor's government would have been spared.

Precedents of popular fanaticism.

The transactions which have been described have been visited by the severe reprobation of later times. Yet epidemic delusions, and delusions having tragical issues, have not been so uncommon in history, as that their occurrence should excite surprise as monstrous deviations from the order of human things. Not fifteen years before the alarm of witchcraft in New England, large numbers of innocent men in England had fallen victims to a popular madness, excited by the flagitious fiction of the Popish plot; and in New York, half a century later than the tragedy at Salem, fifty persons were transported and sold, twenty-two were hanged, and eleven were burned to death, on regular legal conviction, for being concerned in a conspiracy, which no sane person has the slightest belief in at the present day, and the history of which only remains to confound the notions of those who desire to place confidence in the truth of testimony, the rectitude of magistrates, and the common sense of men.[1] No doubt, such delusions are especially contagious and dangerous when they are associated with religious superstition and with the mysteries of the invisible world; but it needs not they should have that association, to make them capable of interfering with the righteous administration of justice. Judges and juries in the witchcraft trials did not appear more passionately bent on preposterous mischief than did the English courts which fourteen years earlier made themselves the bloody instruments of Oates and Dangerfield, or the New York court which fifty years later transported, hanged, and burned the confederates in a plot that never was made, or the office-holders and citizens who, more than a century later yet, busied themselves in the Free States of America in replacing the fetters of the escaping bondman.

There is one class of thinkers entitled to take confidently

[1] Chandler, American Criminal Trials, 222, 252.

the ground that an allegation, in any case, of demoniacal agency in human affairs is mere fraud or folly. It consists of those who, reasoning from the attributes of God and his relations to his world, as made known by nature and by Christianity, have arrived at the conviction so wisely maintained in the work of Hugh Farmer, that "all effects produced in the system of nature, contrary to the general laws by which it is governed, are proper miracles, and that all miracles are works appropriate to God."[1] But this result of careful thought is certainly not the state of mind of the great majority of those who now are swift to reject as essentially incredible all accounts of diabolical intervention. At all events, it is to the last degree improbable that instances of that state of mind were to be found in the seventeenth century. That belief in a possible demoniacal agency which, partly by force of thought and reasoning, and much more by force of a vague prevailing scepticism,[2] has now to a large extent lost its hold on the popular mind, was the universal conviction of the earlier time. The person who, in a careless state of general distrust as to every thing but what he can see and touch, condemns the credulity

Theories of demoniacal agency.

[1] Farmer, Essay on the Demoniacs of the New Testament, Introduction, 1. — Reginald Scot, who, according to the title-page of his "Discovery of Witchcraft," "wrote and published in anno 1584," defined "witchmongers" as "such as attribute to witches the power which appertaineth to God only." (Prefatory Epistle to Sir Roger Manwood, 7.) He speaks of the "proofs brought against witches" as "incredible, consisting of guesses, presumptions, and impossibilities, contrary to reason, scripture, and nature." (Prefatory Epistle to Sir Thomas Scot.) "Is it not pity," he asks, "that that which is said to be done with the almighty power of the Most High God . . . . . should be referred to a baggage old woman's nod or wish?" (Prefatory Epistle to Archdeacon Readman.) "Our fancy," he says, "condemneth witches, and our reason acquitteth, our evidence against them consisting in impossibilities, our proofs in unwritten verities, and our whole proceedings in doubts and difficulties." (Prefatory Epistle to the Readers.) And much more to the same effect. — It is amazing to find such language used in the sixteenth century. The copy which I use of this extremely rare book belongs to James Russell Lowell.

[2] Lecky, History of Civilization, I. 35 *et seq.*

of believers in witchcraft, has certainly not as definite and respectable a foundation for his theory as they for theirs, however much nearer to the truth he may happen in this particular instance to be.

The estimation of witchcraft as a crime equally real as murder and more heinous, and the practice of punishing it accordingly, were much older than the Puritan occupation of New England. They were much older than the Protestant Reformation. Treatises had been written upon it, laws against it had been enacted, persons charged with it had been tortured and killed, through ages of Christian history and in distant parts of Christian Europe. It had been punished with a wide carnage as early as the century when the Roman empire became Christian.[1] The superstition had shown no symptoms of decline in the later ages.

Prevalence of the superstition of witchcraft in Christendom.

In the century of the Revival of Learning a Bull of Pope Innocent the Eighth proclaimed
1484. the wide prevalence of the crime, and enforced on all good Catholics their responsibility for its extirpation, — a measure which, as has been calculated, caused the death of not fewer than a hundred thousand persons in Germany alone. In the next century, in the district of Como in Lombardy, a thousand witches are related to have been
1524. slaughtered in one year, and one hundred in each
1615. of several years afterwards. In the next, five hundred persons charged with witchcraft were put to death in the home of Calvin, the enlightened republic of Geneva, which had then a population not more than half as great as was the population of Massachusetts at the time when the frenzy there cost twenty lives. Within twenty-five years of the popular infatuation in Massachusetts, Sweden had been the scene of a similar delusion and misery, brought about by a similar instrumentality of some unnaturally wicked children. Eighty-eight witches in one

[1] Gibbon, Decline and Fall, &c., III. 75; comp. V. 126; Milman, Latin Christianity, I. 542, VIII. 202.

neighborhood, including fifteen children, are said to have been executed; while large numbers, as has con- 1669.
tinually occurred elsewhere, saved their lives by 1670.
confessing themselves to be guilty of the imaginary crime.

As to the currency of the superstition among the British race, the executions for witchcraft in Scotland, in the reign of King James the Sixth, are believed to have been so numerous as to require to be reckoned by thousands.[1] The coming of that monarch to England as James the First gave an impulse there to the study of a department of learning and law in which especially he prided himself on his proficiency. His treatise on Demonology discusses the character and diagnostics of witchcraft, with just as absolute a conviction of the reality of the crime described as would be felt by the author of a treatise on poaching;[2] and in his reign an Act of Parliament was passed which gave vigor to the application of his theory.[3] Nor in this matter was commonwealth wiser than royalty, — the sage Justice Matthew Hale than the foolish King James Stuart.[4] In the days of the Long Parliament there were more than a hundred execu- 1645.
tions for witchcraft in the English shires of Essex 1646.
and Sussex, with the approbation of the ministers Baxter and Calamy, than whom there were no higher authorities for New England;[5] and in the year of the decapitation of King Charles fourteen witches were burned, in a "village consisting of but fourteen families."[6] The English statutes

Its prevalence in Great Britain.

[1] Howell's Familiar Letters, 405, 438.

[2] "Dæmonologie" in Workes, 94 *et seq.*

[3] The Act was of the second year of his reign. (Chap. XII.) There had been earlier Acts of Elizabeth (1562), of Henry the Seventh (1541), and of Henry the Sixth.

[4] State Trials, VI. 641; comp. Campbell, Lives of the Chief Justices, I. 566; II. 170.

[5] Baxter, Certainty of the World of Spirits, 52 *et seq.* — "I am so much taken with your History of Prodigies," wrote Richard Baxter to Increase Mather (in 1689?), "that I propose to put my scraps into your hands, so much as is not lost, ... for I see you have great skill in collecting and contracting." (MS. Letter in Dr. Williams's Library.)

[6] Whitelock, Memorials, &c., 450.

against witchcraft were repealed only forty years before the American Colonies ceased to be part of the British
1736. empire.[1] The popular commentary upon English law, which was published almost at the end of the seventeenth century, recognizes witchcraft as a real crime;[2] nor had the juridical science of the last half of the eighteenth century improved the theory.[3] When the course of proceeding in Massachusetts against witchcraft was brought to the notice of the Privy Council of King William the Third, they did not order their Governor to be instructed that it was all cruel nonsense, and that an immediate stop must be put to it. Nothing of the kind. They took on themselves no responsibility so rash. They paraded no such audacious eccentricity. They bade the King's Secre-
1693. tary of State to instruct the Governor "that in all
Jan. 26. proceedings for the future against persons accused for witchcraft, or being possessed by the Devil, the greatest moderation and all due circumspection be used, so far as the same may be without impediment to the ordinary course of justice."[4] At the board where this recognition

[1] Anno IX., George II., Chap. V. — In 1716 Mrs. Hicks and her daughter were hanged for witchcraft in Huntington. (Knight, History of England, V. 430.) An execution in Scotland for the crime took place in Sutherlandshire as late as 1722. (Weld's History of the Royal Society, 89.) The London "Spectator" for 1863 (p. 2514) relates a case of mobbing, on account of an alarm of it, only ten years before I write this note.

[2] Dalton's "Country Justice," which was the current law manual in New England, discusses witchcraft at large in Chap. CLX., "Felonies by Statute" (383). The principles and rules of judgment, and the methods of investigation, digested in this authoritative book, are those which were approved and used in Massachusetts. The commissions of justices recited therein made it the duty of any two or more of them "to inquire of all and all manner of felonies, witchcrafts, enchantments, sorceries, magic art," &c. (Page 18.) — Chief Justice Holt, whose sagacious eye may have seen the folly of the whole thing, managed to get off Hathaway, charged before him with witchcraft in 1702. But it was on a question about the evidence. He did not venture to deny the reality of witchcraft. (State Trials, XIV. 630.)

[3] "To deny the possibility, nay, actual existence of witchcraft and sorcery, is at once flatly to contradict the revealed Word of God, in various passages both of the Old and New Testament." (Blackstone, Commentaries on the Laws of England, Book IV., Chap. IV. § 6.)

[4] Privy Council Register, *sub die*.

of the reality of witchcraft was registered, was collected the ripest intelligence of England.[1]

It was not to be expected of the colonists of New England that they should be the first to see through a delusion which befooled the whole civilized world, and the gravest and most knowing persons in it. Men are not omniscient, nor is it common, any more than just, to blame them for not being so. We do not find fault with Aristotle for being ignorant of the law which directs the movements at once of an apple falling from a tree and of a comet in the distant fields of space. We do not pronounce Galileo incapable because he did not know the weight of the planet Jupiter, nor Franklin because he did not invent the magnetic telegraph. It is rash to say that men should rise above their age. They should strive to do it; but, after all, what more is it possible for them to seize than what is within their reach?[2]

[1] Of the numerous collections of facts relating to the prevalence and the consequences of the belief in witchcraft among the civilized nations, the reader may be referred to Lecky, History of the Rise and Influence of the Spirit of Rationalism in Europe, I. 28 *et seq.*, 117 *et seq.*; Francis Hutchinson (1718), Historical Essay concerning Witchcraft (Lecky, I. 120, note, says that the chronological table of facts in this work "is the most complete authority on this subject"); Walter Scott's Letters on Demonology, in the Family Library; Howell, Epistolæ Ho-Elianæ, 405, 438 *et seq.*; Charles Mackay, Popular Delusions, II. 167 *et seq.*; Chandler, Criminal Trials, 67 *et seq.*; Upham, Salem Witchcraft, I. 342 *et seq.*; and, *instar omnium*, Howard Williams, Superstitions of Witchcraft, a very learned, curious, and exhaustive work. — The literature of witchcraft is copious. Mr. Cutter, the learned librarian of the Boston Athenæum, has lent me a list of the titles of not fewer than four thousand treatises upon one or another of the various departments of the subject.

[2] "The arguments which convince us that witchcraft is a delusion . . . . . could not have convinced an ordinary man four centuries ago. Nay, paradoxical as the statement may seem, they ought not to have convinced him; for in themselves they were not so strong as they are now. In themselves, we repeat, they were not arguments, but statements of arguments, and behind them lay a hidden context which took for granted a myriad of propositions. But those propositions had not been proved to the satisfaction of the people; on the contrary, they seemed monstrous untruths. To us they seem truisms, because we have come under a host of influences that never acted on our forefathers." (North British Review, XLVII. 400.)

A sober consideration of the tenor of human affairs expects occasional disturbances of them, even in propitious circumstances, from "fears of the brave and follies of the wise." But the condition of the people of New England in the seventeenth century was deplorably unfavorable to that immunity from a superstitious panic and madness of the sort in question, which in the most advantageous state of things would then have been no easy attainment. If any may be specially excused for being led astray by gloomy superstitions, it is they who are surrounded by circumstances, and pressed by griefs and anxieties, such as incline to sad and unhealthy meditation. The experience of the three heroic generations of English exiles in Massachusetts had been hard and sorrowful. Of those who were living when the provincial charter came into effect, the memory of the oldest went back to the primitive times of want and misery; the middle-aged men had been out in arms in the most dreadful of the Indian wars, and the middle-aged women had passed years of mourning for the husbands, lovers, and brothers whom it had swept away. The generation just entered upon the stage had been born and reared in melancholy homes. The present was full of troubles and forebodings. The venerated charter had been lost. Social ties had been weakened. Social order was insecure. The paths of enterprise were obstructed. Industry had little impulse. Poverty was already felt. There was danger of destitution. A powerful foreign enemy threatened, and the capacity for defence was crippled by penury. A people in the mood to which such surroundings naturally lead could scarcely be expected to set the example of a release from gloomy visions which bewildered the rest of mankind. Nor would it be fanciful to ascribe some influence on the spirits and the imagination to the austere environments of the settlers, and the harsh aspects of the scenery amid which their temper had been

Predispositions in New England.

educated and their daily life was passed.[1] An ocean divided them from the old seats of civilized life. Almost in the primitive nakedness of existence, they were waging a contest with the awful elements. Their little settlements were isolated and unjoyous. The scene all around, — river, rock, covert, mountain, forest, — almost as wild and sombre as creation left it, invited to stern and melancholy musing. And if evil spirits anywhere had power, it might seem to be where savage men had kept their bestial rites, and where Sabbath bells, till the strangers brought them, had never knolled to church.

Fidelity to religious conviction.

But, with or without peculiar exposures to delusion, the people of New England believed what the wisest men of the world believed at the end of the seventeenth century; and never was a people in whom honest conviction, of whatever kind, was surer to shape itself in act. They read in the Bible the command, "Thou shalt not suffer a witch to live," and, instead of interpreting the Hebrew legislator as denouncing in these words a craft of juggling impostors, whose tricks were connected with that idolatry which in every form was a capital crime under the Mosaic polity,[2] they understood him to recognize the existence of practitioners really possessing supernatural powers derived from the Prince of the Power of the Air, and using them for purposes mischievous to men and hateful to God. Oracles of their faith from the other side of the water had taught that on the good Christians of New England God had peculiarly im-

1 Robert Walsh, Appeal, &c., 52.

2 See Palfrey, Lectures on the Jewish Scriptures and Antiquities, I. 451. — "Formerly there were witches; otherwise God's law had fought against a shadow. 'Thou shalt not suffer a witch to live.' Ex. xviii. 22." (Fuller, Holy and Profane State, 365.) Fuller's essay, entitled "The Witch," consists of paragraphs, each of which is headed with a general proposition: *e. g.*, "Formerly there were witches." "There are witches for the present, though those night-birds fly not so frequently in flocks, since the light of the gospel." The tone of the essay is, as might be expected of the writer, not savage. His genial spirit, in spite of his faith in witchcraft, is apparent.

posed the responsibility of defeating the Devil, in the place where he could "show most malice," because there "he is hated and hateth most."[1] Their ambition had been to build up in a new world a pure worship of Jehovah, and transmit churches "without spot or wrinkle, or any such thing, beautiful as Tirzah, comely as Jerusalem, and terrible as an army with banners." They easily believed that Satan would not permit such a conquest without a conflict, that he would bestir himself to corrupt and vanquish in its feeble state the church which in its spiritual manhood, should that be attained, was destined to be mighty through God to the pulling down of all his strongholds. That the Devil, with all the vast and malignant power which they ascribed to him, was their enemy, was an unquestioned fact which to them carried not an overmastering but an arousing terror. They must give him battle bravely, and abide the issue; for they were the Lord's soldiers, and since the adversary did not wear a bodily shape for them to strike at, they must make his nefarious instruments feel their unsparing blows.

Nor, as an independent influence, is the naked fact to be overlooked that witchcraft was a felony by statute.

Popular devotion to law.

There is no denying that a vital, constitutional, ingrained reverence for law as such, additional to and even irrespective of considerations of the equity or wisdom of any of its provisions in a given instance, has been in all times a characteristic of the people of New England; and the hanging of witches was partly the expression of a fanatical devotion to law in Essex County at the end of the seventeenth century. Witchcraft stood on the books as a capital offence; and when the

[1] Richard Baxter's Preface to C. Mather's Memorable Providences, 6; comp. Lawson's Sermon, as quoted by Upham, II. 85. Scottow, in his "Narrative of the Planting of the Massachusetts Colony" (1694), treats largely of the hostility of Satan to the transfer of the Gospel to New England (Mass. Hist. Col., XXXIV. 311 *et seq.*), and especially finds an instance of it in his proceedings at Salem. (Ibid., 315.)

authorized expounders of the law were seen to take part against the accused, the mighty conservative element in the community was summoned to the oppressor's side. In the judgment of an important and habitually venerated class, to interpose for the sufferers was to speak evil of dignities and associate one's self with those who sought to unsettle the foundations of society. In such circumstances, the more enlightened lovers of Law and Order — of Order, which can never be permanently dissociated from humanity — of Law, which justice always ought to underlie and inform — were forced into a false position. To manifest their loyalty many felt themselves bound, in conscience and duty, to do violence to their sentiments of justice, humanity, and honor. They were placed at a great disadvantage for any useful interference, when they could only attempt it at the cost of seeming to take a factious part, which in truth they loathed. When they echoed the maxims of Stoughton and his set, they were in much the same state of mind as were the loyal citizens of the same community who, a hundred and sixty years later, presented their thanks to the champion of the Fugitive-Slave Bill for refreshing their sense of obligation in respect to the demands of that enactment.[1]

[1] Robert Calef, whose work in controversy with Mather has been quoted from, was a trader in Boston, whose social position, scoffed at by Mather, did not particularly expose him to this class of influences. A sharp correspondence between him and Cotton Mather began as early as January, 1694; but Calef did not publish his protest till five years after the Salem tragedy was over, and till Mather had begun to make another stir with the adventures of Margaret Rule. A vindication of the Mathers against this book was published in 1701, under the names of eight of their parishioners and friends (John Goodwin among them), with the title, "A Few Remarks upon a Scandalous Book," &c. — An elaborate argument against the proceedings at Salem, while they were going on, was placed in the hands of Justice Corwin. But it was not published, and has remained in manuscript. It is subscribed with the initials R. P., under which is written in another hand the name of Robert Pain. But Mr. Upham (II. 449), with much plausibility, argues that Robert Pike, a man of consequence and a Counsellor, was the writer. If he was, it seems that he felt the embarrassments of his place, and shunned publicity and the appearance of officiousness and of faction. — Thomas Brattle

Happily for the present age, it understands the laws of the divine economy and of the human mind otherwise than as they were understood in the time of the Dutch King of England. By reason of opinions now outgrown, twenty innocent persons — not hundreds and thousands of innocent persons, as elsewhere under the same charge — were put to death in Massachusetts in that age. The madness of which they were the victims raged for about half a year in a part of that Province, mostly in a part of one county, instead of the long periods of time, and the large districts of country, in which it has done its dreadful work elsewhere. Unoffending men and women were put out of the pale of sympathy; were put in gaol, were put in chains, were put to death. And this was sad enough, and bad enough. But they were not burned to death, nor were they tortured upon the rack, nor in the boots, nor by the thumb-screw, as others by

Limitations of the cruelty.

was dissatisfied with the proceedings, and expressed his sentiments in a letter to a friend, in October, 1692. But his letter was confidential, and does not show even to whom it was addressed; and some expressions in it are full of meaning in their connection with the conservative cowardice of the time. "I should be very loath," Brattle writes, "to bring myself into any snare by my freedom with you, and therefore hope that you will put the best construction on what I write, and secure me from such as would interpret my lines otherwise than as they are designed. Obedience to lawful authority I ever accounted a great duty, and willingly I would not practise any thing that might thwart and contradict such a principle. Too many are ready to despise dominions, and speak evil of dignities; and I am sure the mischiefs which arise from a factious and rebellious spirit are very sad and notorious; insomuch that I would sooner bite my fingers' ends than willingly cast dirt on authority, or any way offer reproach to it. Far, therefore, be it from me to have any thing to do with those men your letter mentions, whom you acknowledge to be men of a factious spirit, and never more in their element than when they are declaiming against men in public place, and contriving methods that tend to the disturbance of the common peace. I never accounted it a credit to my cause to have the good liking of such men. 'My son,' says Solomon (Prov. xxiv. 21), 'fear thou the Lord and the King, and meddle not with them that are given to change.'" (Letter of Thomas Brattle, in Mass. Hist. Col., V. 61.) — The names, also, of Brattle's brother William, and of John Leverett (afterwards President), appear out of place appended to such a document as the Proposals of the President and Fellows of the College to the Ministers. (Magnalia, VI. 2.)

superior barbarity have been tortured and killed elsewhere. There is a difference — and this the deluded people of Massachusetts in the worst access of their frenzy knew — between doing what is thought needful for security, and making the agonies of the helpless feed the rage of the inhuman and strong. Nor among the many communities in which at different times this shocking infatuation has gained a foothold, is it possible to name one in which reason, courage, and humanity have so soon resumed their sway as in Massachusetts, and so well done their proper office. Nor can a thoughtful mind fail to consider of what stuff some men and women of that stock were made, when twenty of them went to the gallows rather than soil their consciences by the lie of a confession. Nor can even the conduct of the blinded Magistrates be set down as merely brutal fury, when they uniformly pardoned such as acknowledged their offence and promised blameless lives for the future.

CHAPTER V.

THE ship of state was spreading her sails for another venture with the elements. Massachusetts was entering on a new experience. Except during the three years of the despotisms of Dudley's Council and of Andros, that community, during its life of more than sixty years, had substantially made its own laws and conducted its own administration. During a third part of that time, — the period of the civil conflict in England, — the political subordination of the Colony to the parent country had been little more than nominal; and during the rest, though there had been repeated menaces on the part of the British ministry, there had been little practical obstruction. Massachusetts was henceforward unquestionably and distinctly a province of the British crown. Her chief executive authority now resided in the King of England, or in the Governor, his agent and representative. To no small extent a like transfer was made of her legislative power. One branch of her Legislature could not be constituted without the assent of the Governor, who, by the new charter, could reject the election of Counsellors by the General Court. Further, an Act of her Legislature did not become a law till it obtained the Governor's consent. Further yet, every law of hers might be repealed by the King within three years after its enactment. She could not depose the Governor; but she could obstruct him by legislation or by refusing to legislate, and she might hope to deter him from hostility by keeping him in dependence for his living. The struggle to this effect, soon to present itself, was long and arduously conducted, till at length it was crowned with victory to the Province.

Restricted freedom of Massachusetts.

Of the objects of the founders, civil and religious liberty, the latter seemed sufficiently attained under the dynasty which succeeded the bigoted Stuarts. As to the former, the people of Massachusetts were not ostensibly deprived of such securities as they had hitherto enjoyed for life, liberty, and property. On the contrary, the charter guarantied to them "all liberties and immunities of free and natural subjects, ... to all intents, constructions, and purposes whatsoever, as if they and every of them were within the realm of England." Nevertheless, it was undeniable that by the stipulations of that instrument they were henceforward living under laws which they had a very limited discretion in framing, and which would not be allowed to be such as to protect them against plausible schemes of oppression which might be conceived by some British ministry. The administrators of those laws, the judges, could not be commissioned without the Governor's assent. It was not impossible that the provision respecting a right of appeal to the English courts might be abused and made oppressive, though its limitation as to the litigated amount made it applicable only to cases not likely often to arise. It might be anticipated that usurpation on the part of the mother country would take the form of pecuniary imposition. An early movement to obtain security against this was unsuccessfully made, as will presently be seen. But, though express security was not to be had, this encroachment, as things turned out, was not seriously attempted till seventy years more had passed; and, when seriously attempted, then came resistance, revolution, and independence.

Internal condition of Massachusetts.

The Province of Massachusetts Bay, as constituted at the opening of this new chapter in her history, may have contained sixty thousand inhabitants.[1] These were distributed in seventy-five

[1] No certainty is to be had on this point, and there is great diversity in the estimates. Cotton Mather says (Magnalia, I. 23) that "in less than

towns, seventeen of which belonged to Plymouth; and the number of congregational churches was nearly the same, almost all the churches having one minister, and some being served by two. Boston had not far from a thousand houses and seven thousand inhabitants, being much the most considerable place on the continent. Other principal commercial and fishing towns were Salem, Charlestown, Ipswich, Newbury, and Scituate. The people were farmers, woodmen, fishermen, and merchants. With rare exceptions, all were poor. No kind of business was flourishing. Ten years had passed since the last despairing appeal had been made for the old charter. It was eight years since that instrument was cancelled. It was six years since King James had imposed the grinding tyranny of Andros. For three years a desolating Indian war had been going on, in the midst of which a disastrous military expedition on a large scale of cost had reduced the Colony

fifty years,"—that is, fifty years before 1680,—the population of New England "had increased into, they say, more than a hundred thousand;" a statement which would be worth more, if Mather had a better repute for accuracy. Holmes (Annals, &c., I. 459) puts the population of all New England at that number in 1696. But he has nothing better for his opinion than an estimate of President Stiles. Grahame (History, I. 429) quotes Sir William Petty as making the population of all New England one hundred and fifty thousand in 1691. A memorandum, of Feb. 14, 1700, represents "the freemen of sixteen years and upwards in New England [Massachusetts], Connecticut, and Rhode Island" as sixteen thousand in number. (British Colonial Papers.) What qualifications the author of this paper possessed for making a correct estimate does not appear. But it is indorsed by Lord Bellomont. The very judicious editor of the census of Massachusetts for 1865 says (Abstract, 173), "The population of Massachusetts, subsequently to the union of Plymouth therewith, is stated, in 1696, at sixty-three thousand;" which I reckon to be not far from the truth. In 1690, Sir Edmund Andros reported to the Board of Trade that the number of enrolled militia men was 7021 in Massachusetts proper, and 1392 in Plymouth. (British Colonial Papers.) And in sufficient accordance with this is the Board's information from Lord Bellomont, in 1700, that there were "9304 men in the several regiments in the government of Boston." (Ibid.)—In 1695, the ten richest towns in the new Province were the following, arranged in the order of their valuation: viz., Boston, Ipswich, Salem, Newbury, Charlestown, Dorchester, Watertown, Marblehead, Lynn, Cambridge. The richest town in the Old Colony was Scituate, taxed for £167. The tax levied on Boston was £1,666; on Ipswich, £466; on Cambridge, £180.—Comp. Williamson, II. 37.

to living on its deteriorated paper notes, imposed a crushing burden of taxation, destroyed confidence and killed enterprise in commercial transactions, and enforced that hard frugality which puts an end to the healthy relation between the need of being served and the capacity of service. Scarcely, it seemed, could there be a more disheartening state of things. It might be thought that there was absolutely no circumstance of encouragement, except that the discouraging prospect was spread before the eyes of a sort of people not apt to be unmanned and cast down. In fact, they addressed themselves with quiet resolution to the new business in hand, seeking carefully to do the best that circumstances and the times allowed. Debts and the war made imperative demands; but still there was attention to spare for permanent social interests, and provisions for the schools, for the College, and for the observances of religion had their place in the legislation of the first months of the newly instituted government.[1] And from the first moment the uses which the new constitution might be made to serve for the public benefit in future generations were deliberately and sagaciously inquired into and provided for.

First provincial General Court.

Except in matters rearranged by the new system, the internal administration of Massachusetts proceeded, throughout the time of Sir William Phips, in methods much the same as had been followed under the colonial governors. When the Court came together, which was convened by his writ, William Bond, on his presentation as Speaker of the Deputies, "prayed his Excellency, in their behalf, that there might be allowed unto them the accustomed privileges of an English assembly, which he expected as their due;" and he specified them as being liberty of debate, free access to the Governor, and security from arrest

1692. June 8-July 2.

[1] Acts and Resolves of the Province of the Massachusetts Bay, I. 38, 58, 62.

for themselves and their servants, except for felony and treason, during sessions of the General Court and journeys to and from the place of meeting.[1] A bill for the erecting of a Naval Office was passed,[2] another "for the holding of courts of justice," and another to incorporate the College; but all three were destined to be disallowed by the Privy Council. Overlooking the power vested in the Governor by the new charter to nominate civil officers, Phips allowed them to be chosen by the Council,[3] — an irregularity, however, which did not pass into precedent, being remarked and set right by his less careless successor. Some necessary financial arrangements were made; and the Governor was authorized, should a sufficient exigency occur, to march the militia of the Province into New York or any New England Colony. And the court adjourned after enacting that all such laws of Massachusetts and Plymouth, existing at the abrogation of the old charter, as were not inconsistent with the new charter or with English law, should be revived and be in force till the following autumn, when it was to meet again.

June 27. June 28. 1695. Aug. 22.

Early provincial legislation.

The legislation which followed was for the first few years prosecuted in embarrassing circumstances. While changes were unavoidable to meet the obligations of the new constitution, the Legislature was aiming to admit as few alterations as possible of the ancient system. The consequence was an unsettled condition of the law. Statutes would be enacted and sent to England for confirmation, going into effect meanwhile. At some

[1] Bond's prayer was modest; for, before this period, the privilege of Parliament extended much further.

[2] Acts and Resolves, &c., I. 34; comp. 30, 163, 269, 347.

[3] Provincial Council Records. — A Journal of the Proceedings of the Council of Massachusetts — begun May 25, 1686, with the Presidency of Dudley — had been discontinued at the time of the consolidation of New England at the end of Andros's first year (Dec. 29, 1687). A Council Journal, beginning May 16, 1692, with the administration under the new charter, was regularly kept thenceforwards.

In this year Sir John Trenchard succeeded Lord Sidney as Secretary of State.

time within three years a notice of their being disapproved would come back. The General Court would try some other way of disposing of the same question, and repeated attempts on their part were liable to meet a similar discomfiture.

The Legislature came together for its second session, with the task before it of conforming the inherited institutions to the new order of things, and of doing this in a manner to retain as much as might be of what had been valued in the past. The primitive provincial legislation was marked by comprehension of the circumstances, by foresight and good sense. The law-makers knew only too well that their action on the weightiest matters could be no more than tentative. But they saw no serious discouragement in the character of their Governor, nor in his relation to themselves. And, as to the further action of the King's Privy Council, they had only to do their own part bravely and discreetly, and await the issue with hopeful patience. The confidence with which the General Court was at first inclined to proceed is indicated by the first measure of its second session under the new charter. The thoughtful Legislature passed, and the easy Governor approved, an Act which provided that "no aid, tax, ... or imposition whatsoever" should be "levied on any of their Majesties' subjects or estates, on any pretence whatsoever, but by the act and consent of the Governor, Council, and Representatives of the people assembled in General Court."[1] If this had been confirmed, the cause of dispute which brought about the independence of the United States would have been taken away. But such proved to be not the will of the Privy Council of King William.

1692. Oct. 12.

Oct. 13.

[1] Provincial Acts and Resolves, I. 40. See Chalmers, Introduction to the History of the Revolt, &c., I. 236. According to Chalmers (Ibid., 234), Elisha Cooke, as early as this time, "gave warning to his constituents to establish no officer's salary, to perpetuate no public revenue."

Some features of the ancient criminal code were modified by Acts "for the Punishment of Criminal Offenders" and "for the Punishment of Capital Offenders." The recent insecurity of landed property under the government of Andros gave rise to a law which vested a title after an undisturbed possession of three years. Other laws provided for municipal regulation, for the support of ministers and schools, for the solemnizing of marriages by ministers or justices, for the observance of the Lord's day, and for various matters of ordinary administration.[1]

A revisal of the judicial system had become necessary. An Act "for the establishing of judicatories and courts of justice within the Province"[2] created a Superior Nov. 25. Court, Courts of Common Pleas, Courts of Sessions, and the office of Justice of the Peace, of which the duties had, under the old charter, been performed by the Assistants. The Superior Court, which was to consist of a Chief Justice and four associates, was vested with original jurisdiction in cases involving an amount not less than ten pounds; it heard appeals from the Dec. 14. inferior courts; and was authorized by a supplementary Act to issue writs of *habeas corpus*.[3] William Stoughton was the first Chief Justice, with Thomas Danforth, Wait Winthrop, John Richards, and Samuel Sewall for his associates; no one of the five having been bred a lawyer. Richards died within three years, and Elisha Cooke was appointed in his place.

The Act provided for a Court of Common Pleas for each of the eight counties, each court to consist of four judges. They were to have original jurisdiction in all civil actions, their judgments being subject to appeal; and they could entertain appeals from decisions of justices of the peace. The Courts of Sessions, of which also each county had one, were constituted of all the justices of the peace

[1] Provincial Acts and Resolves, I. 41, 51, 55, 58, 61, 62, 64.

[2] Ibid., 72.

[3] Ibid., 95.

within the county. They heard appeals from justices' courts in criminal matters; superintended houses of correction; licensed innholders and retailers of liquors; and performed various functions of the county commissioners of the present day. Justices of the peace were to have jurisdiction "in all manner of debts, trespasses, and other matters not exceeding the value of forty shillings, wherein the title of land was not concerned;" and they were to suppress quarrels and riots, "make out hue-and-cries," and punish "lying, libelling, and spreading false news," profanation of the Sabbath, gambling, drunkenness, profaneness, and other breaches of the public order.[1] A Chancery Court was to consist of the Governor, or such presiding officer as he should appoint, with eight or more Counsellors.[2] The probate of wills had, under the colonial charter, been a function of the courts of common law. The provincial charter transferred it to the Governor and Council, who proceeded to entertain questions of testaments and inheritances as a court of appeal, but devolved the original jurisdiction in each county on a judge of probate of their appointment.[3]

From the first moment of the operation of the new charter, the great question of a salary for the Governor, destined to be keenly discussed for nearly half a century, fixed the attention of the wary patriots of Massachusetts Bay. As the first year drew to a close, the General Court passed an Act with the cautiously worded title, 1693.
"An Act for ordering the sum of five hundred March 7.
pounds unto his Excellency the Governor, for his service and expense since his arrival."[4] Phips approved
April 3.
it, but he wrote to the Board of Trade that "no salary was settled," and he "desired it might be considered;" and, again, that "the General Assembly
Nov. 23.
had not yet appointed a salary," and that he "re-

[1] Provincial Acts and Resolves, 51, 53, 56, 57, 67.

[2] Ibid., 75, 144.

[3] Ibid., 43.

[4] Ibid., 109, 787.

quested his Majesty to nominate to said Assembly a salary sufficient for his support as Governor."[1] They not only paid no attention to his wish in this respect, but they 1694. June 8. suffered the second political year to expire before allowing him compensation for it; and then they gave him "for his great service in the government the last year the sum of five hundred pounds," and they Oct. 27. made the next grant "for this present year" in the same well-guarded language.[2]

At the first election of Counsellors for the new government, Election of Counsellors. the chronic party division reappeared; and the Governor made an ungracious use of his new authority in rejecting Elisha Cooke, who was elected into 1693. May. the Council by the General Court. A considerable change was at the same time made in the constitution of that body as it had been arranged by the King. Several places were vacated in favor of persons more favorable to the old order of things. Stoughton, however, was retained.[3] Obnoxious as he was to many, the clergy were on the whole kindly disposed to him; the forward part which he had taken in the Revolution was something to set off against his earlier and later ill-deserts; and his long and various experience of affairs was some security against the effects of his superior's incompetence. Danforth was one of those who were restored by the popular will to power. The omission of the old Governor, Bradstreet, was probably in accordance with his own wish.

In the second year of Phips's government, a not immaterial change was made in the qualifications of Nov. 28. members of the Lower House.[4] Hitherto a town

[1] British Colonial Papers.

[2] Acts and Resolves, &c., 174, 188.

[3] Through the previous year Stoughton had sat in the Council by virtue of his place as Lieutenant-Governor, there being twenty-eight Counsellors without him. But the authority for this was by no means clear, and it was now thought safer to elect him as one of the twenty-eight. (Comp. Hutch., II. 70.)

[4] In the year after the Revolution (Feb. 29, 1690), Boston, "upon consideration of the number of free-

might elect for its Deputy an inhabitant of some other town, being thus at liberty to engage in its service the best talent it might find in the Colony. Against the protest of the Speaker[1] and twenty-one other Deputies, it was now enacted that a Deputy must be an inhabitant of the town represented by him,[2] — a restriction continued as long as the representation of towns existed, and still in force as to the electing districts. The unavoidable effect has been to reduce the standard of ability in the Legislature. But if an electing district may not now, as in the early times, look wherever it will in Massachusetts for the man most fit to watch over its interests and do it credit in the Legislature of the Commonwealth, some compensation for the sacrifice is afforded by a degree of experience in the management of public business, which, under the system that connects representation with inhabitancy, is perpetually carried from the central government into every part of the territory. As so often happens with important changes, this was brought about by a merely incidental and temporary cause. Many representatives of country towns — friends to the old charter, or for other causes unfriendly to Governor Phips — were inhabitants of Boston. To get rid of them, advantage was taken of local pride, and of the interests of men in the rural districts who were impatient of obscurity.

New qualification of Deputies.

The hostility of the natives in the Eastern country was one of the matters that claimed the Governor's instant attention. It was in the next month after his arrival, that a party, five hundred in number, including with Indians several Frenchmen from Canada, attacked the post at Wells, held by some thirty English, who drove them off after a desperate fight, in

Indian hostilities.

1692. June 10.

holders," was allowed to send four Deputies to the General Court. This arrangement was ratified (Nov. 30, 1692) under the new charter. (Acts and Resolves, I. 88.)

[1] The Speaker was Nathaniel Byfield, a stirring person, at that time, in various ways.

[2] Acts and Resolves, &c., I. 147.

which women shared, and did good service.[1] Sir William had been instructed in England to build a fort in Maine, both for a security against the Indians and as a demonstration against the French; and, probably under the advice of Andros, who had a strange confidence in that position, Pemaquid was the designated spot.[2] Phips led four hundred and fifty men from Boston, and on the site of Sir Edmund's old fort proceeded to construct a work said to be more formidable than Castle William at Boston, or Cape Diamond at Quebec, or any other fortress in America.[3] Phips was joined at Pemaquid by Major Church, the veteran partisan of Philip's war, who had John Gorham of Barnstable for his second in command. The Governor consulted Church about the work he was erecting, but the unscientific campaigner retained his old prejudice against fortifications, and would take no interest in the matter. Church went in search of the Indian enemy to the Penobscot and the Kennebec, but they eluded him, and he accomplished nothing.[4]

September.

The next year there was for a time a better prospect. Major Converse, the officer who had so distinguished himself in the recent defence of Wells, scoured the country from the Piscataqua to the Kennebec with four or five hundred men, and returning built a stone fort on Saco River, a few miles from the sea, in the heart of the Indian country. Thereupon the Indians expressed their willingness to make peace; and accordingly thirteen chiefs, who represented themselves as

1693.

Aug. 11.

[1] See above, p. 87; comp. Niles's History in Mass. Hist. Col., XXVI. 228.

[2] For descriptions of Pemaquid, and many particulars of proceedings there, see Thornton's "Ancient Pemaquid," in Maine Hist. Col., V. 139 *et seq.*; comp. II. 238.

[3] Jeremiah Dummer (Defence of Charters, 31) describes it as it was built by Phips at this time. (Comp. Mather, Magnalia, VII. 81.) The French presently sent a couple of ships of war against the fort. But the commanders, having reconnoitred it, deemed it not prudent to persist. (Charlevoix, II. 122.)

[4] Church, Entertaining Passages, 82–86; see above, Vol. III. 156, note 6.

empowered by all the tribes as far east as to the Passamaquoddy, concluded at Pemaquid a treaty, in which they acknowledged themselves to be subjects of the crown of England, and promised future good behaviour.[1] This agreeable issue of the campaign did not obtain unqualified approbation for the Governor. Spending money at Pemaquid was already a distinctly unpopular proceeding, and the House could not venture to deny a vote which was proposed, declaring the recent erection of a costly fort there to be unauthorized and "a grievance."[2] Dec. 13.

Enterprise against Canada.

The ill-success of the recent expedition against Canada was so apparently due to mere accident, that it rather invited than discouraged a further attempt. The home government at last entered into the scheme with alacrity. There was an English fleet now in the West Indies, with two thousand seamen and about as many soldiers. It was arranged that this force should come to Boston in the spring, and, being joined there by some other ships and troops, should proceed to the conquest of Quebec. But the whole project miscarried. Information and orders sent from England in reference to it were five months on the passage over sea, so that when the fleet arrived in Boston no preparations had been made. Nor, if they had been, could the enterprise have been prosecuted, for an epidemic sickness had broken out in the ships, and carried off more than two-thirds of the crews. The Governor and Admiral could do no better than to concert a plan for the next year, which they proposed to have carried out by two thousand men to be sent from England, and as many more to be furnished by the Colonies.[3] The scheme was that the two forces

February-July.

[1] The treaty is in the Magnalia (Book VII. 85); comp. Charlevoix, Histoire, II. 143 *et seq.*, whose account of these transactions, however, is inexact. Comp. Williamson, Hist. of Maine, I. 640; Belknap's Hist. of New Hampshire (Farmer's edit.), 138.

[2] Prov. Rec., *sub die.*

[3] Phips wrote to the Lords of Trade (September 25) that he "was utterly ignorant of the King's reso-

should rendezvous at the obscure point of Canso, at the eastern end of Nova Scotia, so as not to attract observation; and that then, sailing up the St. Lawrence, one portion should proceed to Montreal, while the other remained to attack Quebec. By the despatch of the whole force by sea, it was expected to avoid some of the difficulties which had defeated the former expedition. But the project was
1694. April. not pursued. Probably the prosecution of it was discouraged by that financial pressure which led, in the next year, to the establishment of the Bank of England.

Decline of Phips's reputation.

Phips had entered on his administration with no great support of popular favor, and what there was of it fell off. There was not reason to complain of him for any such contemptuous conduct as that with which Dudley had inaugurated his unwelcome government, far less for any inclination towards such oppressive measures as had made odious the name of Andros. On the contrary, credit was not denied him for being an honest friend to the Colony, and for being unambitious to push to any extreme the prerogatives of his position. But, as he was more known, his capacity was less highly estimated. His expedition against the French had not only not prospered, but it had involved the Colony in well-nigh ruinous embarrassment; and every undefined feeling of discontent excited by the various troubles of the time tended to take the shape of dissatisfaction with the chief ruler. Further, he was weakened by qualities which repel respect. Though not intending to be unreasonable, and not constitutionally pertinacious, he was naturally sensitive and hasty, and had been used to the discipline of the quarter-deck, so that, when opposed, he easily lost his temper and forgot his

lution to attack Canada with squadron and land forces under Sir Charles Wheeler, ... until Wheeler's arrival. . . . . . It was then too late to prepare for Canada, the year too far spent. Had the King's commands arrived in time, nothing should have been wanting or omitted by him." (British Colonial Papers.)

dignity.[1] He very soon involved himself in quarrels which, equally when he was right as when he was wrong in respect to the matter of dispute, exposed him to just reproach for conduct unbecoming his high station, and which speedily deprived him of the confidence of his superiors in England.

His many quarrels

An officer named Short commanded the frigate (the "Nonsuch") which brought Sir William to America. On the passage the Governor took a dislike to him, — reasonably enough, as may be inferred from Short's later proceedings. He had been in Boston only a few weeks, when he committed the outrage of an assault upon two members of the General Court in their bedchambers; they appear to have incensed him by opposing his pretensions to impress men for sea service.[2] The colonial Governors had control of ships of war on their coasts. When Phips went to the eastward, he left an instruction for Short to follow him forthwith with his ship, and the order was not obeyed to his satisfaction, nor another order to cruise in the Bay after some French vessels. Meeting the captain in a street in Boston, Phips accosted him with reproaches, and a fight ensued, in which the Governor knocked down his antagonist and beat him with his cane. He then put him in gaol, and from gaol sent him first to the fort, and thence on board a vessel bound to England, to be conducted there to the Secretary of State.[3]

1692. June.

September.

1693. Jan. 4.

[1] See Brodhead, History of New York, II. 555, note.

[2] Jan. 15, 1693, the Board of Trade had before them a "complaint of John Tomson, Representative of General Assembly, against Captain Short, for coming to complainant's quarters at the Green Dragon, dragging him out of bed, and his men insulting and calling him names" (July 1, 1692), and a "complaint of Peter Woodbery," of the same tenor. (British Colonial Papers.)

[3] February 15, Phips wrote to Lord Nottingham an account of this transaction. He had suspended Short, and given his command to the gunner of the ship, Short's lieutenant being a coward. He says that Short had impressed men without a warrant, and that he "was heard the night

The provincial charter provided for an administration of admiralty powers by the King, but no court had yet been created. Jahleel Brenton, of Rhode Island, had under Randolph's patronage been made Collector of the Customs in Boston. This arrangement was not of unquestionable validity in point of law,[1] and was disagreeable to the merchants, who had been used to paying duties only to the colonial naval officer. Phips, who had lately appointed a naval officer, took their part. Brenton seized a vessel, which had arrived in Boston from the West Indies. The Governor caused it to be released, and, when Brenton remonstrated, offered him some personal violence, which was afterwards differently described by the parties. The occasion was such as could not fail to bring Sir William into disfavor in one of the most influential quarters in England. Brenton complained to the Lords of Trade, at whose instance the King in Council instructed the
Dec. 7. Lords of the Treasury to appoint commissioners to take evidence in New England respecting the facts
1694. alleged.[2] But this method of proceeding was
Feb. 8. soon superseded by an order to Phips to come to England.

He incurred scarcely less displeasure by another quarrel, which he followed up with great determination. His

before [the fray] to say he would go and huff the Governor the next morning." Two officers who were present sent to the Board of Trade their deposition in the Governor's favor. Officers of Short's ship reported him to the Admiralty as a drunkard. (British Colonial Papers.)

[1] "We do not find any Act of Parliament requiring the same, ... and the Governors of the several plantations are especially enjoined by law to take care that the Acts of Trade and Navigation be duly observed." (Letter to Sir Henry Ashurst and Constantine Phipps, of Feb. 21, 1693, in Hutch. Hist., II. 76, note; British Colonial Papers.)

[2] Privy Council Register for Dec. 7, 1693. — On the complaint of Brenton, the Lords of Trade represented that the Governor "had discouraged several masters of vessels arriving from England, &c., from clearing" with Brenton, or producing certificates to him, and had ordered them to apply for their clearances to a naval officer appointed by the Governor.

generosity of heart disposed him to feel for the cruel fate of Jacob Leisler, who — certainly not without rashness and imprudence, nor in ways altogether proof against censure — had undertaken to follow in New York the course pursued by the wiser Massachusetts patriots in ridding themselves of the despotism of Sir Edmund. Colonel Benjamin Fletcher, who associated himself with the ferocious party that had brought on the catastrophe, had now succeeded, as Governor of New York for the King, to Colonel Sloughter, who held that place for a year and a half after Leisler's deposition.

Mar. 1691 – Sept. 1692.

Fletcher was as irascible as Phips, and it did not take a long time to bring the two into a violent collision. By virtue of their respective commissions, both claimed the command of the militia of Connecticut. Fletcher pretended a right also to the jurisdiction of Martha's Vineyard, as a dependency of New York, and informed Phips that he was coming thither to assert it, — a message which Phips answered by a sort of challenge. A man named Abraham Gouverneur, son-in-law[1] of Leisler, and an underling in his ephemeral government, had been found guilty of murder in New York, but had been discharged by Governor Fletcher agreeably to instructions from England. Gouverneur went to Boston, and thence wrote a letter to his parents, giving an account of an interview of his with Phips, in the course of which, among other unfavorable remarks respecting the state of things at New York, Phips had said, "The Governor is a poor beggar, and seeks nothing but money, and not the good of the country." Fletcher intercepted the letter, and sent an officer to Phips to demand the surrender of the writer into his hands. This was refused

1692. Oct. 12.

1693. January.

[1] See Historical Record, 276. — Nine years after this (Aug. 19, 1701) Gouverneur was chosen to be Speaker of the House of Assembly of New York. (See Smith, History of New York, 137; also Documentary History of New York, II. 248; IV. 4–12.)

with insulting language, and with threats of violence to the messenger.[1]

Complaints of the Governor coming from such various
quarters demanded the attention of the government.
December. Phips sent an agent to England to vindicate him
against the representations of Short and Brenton, but the
Privy Council thought them so serious that they
His recall. 1694. despatched to him a peremptory order to come
Feb. 8. before them to clear himself, at the same time
instructing the Lieutenant-Governor to take depositions
to be used on his examination.[2] Accordingly,
July 12. after no little delay, which he excused on the
ground of a call for his presence in the Eastern country,
he sailed from Massachusetts, bringing to an end
Nov. 17. an unsatisfactory administration there of two years
and six months. In England he was not unkindly re-
1695. ceived, for in his guileless and genial temper there
January. seems to have been a fascination which won for
him more favor than he could fairly claim for any public
services. He carried with him an Address with the sig-
1694. natures of a bare majority of the House of Repre-
Oct. 31. sentatives, praying that he might not be removed.[3]

[1] This story is told in full, and with much repetition, in letters, of which I have copies, in the collection "America and West Indies," in the British State Paper Office. Usher and Dudley were Fletcher's friends. (Thomas Clarke's letter of January, 1693.) — "Your absurd and abusive letter plainly demonstrates that if (as you say) I have forgot my manners to gentlemen, I have forgot what you never had." (Letter of Phips to Fletcher, of Jan. 27, 1693, in O'Callaghan, IV. 5.) Phips means to go to Martha's Vineyard, and to assert his authority there, "which, if you think fit to dispute, I shall take such measures to defend as you may not like." (Ibid.) — Between Fletcher and Stoughton there was a correspondence in 1696 (Mass. Archives, XXX. 371), which shows them to have been on not unfriendly terms.

[2] Privy Council Register, *sub die;* British Colonial Papers. — March 15 of this year Lord Shrewsbury succeeded Lord Nottingham as Secretary of State.

[3] Hutchinson (II. 79, note) gives the following extract of a letter from Boston to London, Nov. 1, 1694: "It was very surprising to me to see the laborious methods taken to obtain an address from the General Assembly here for the continuance of Sir William in the government. The opposers were gentlemen, principally of Boston, who were too near Sir

But before any thing was decided he was seized with an illness, which perhaps was aggravated by prosecutions instituted against him in London by Dudley and Brenton, and which brought his life to an end within a few weeks after his arrival.

1695. Feb. 18.

Meanwhile the war with the savages had been disastrously renewed, being stimulated by the Catholic missionaries from Canada, of whom the most noted, Sebastian Rasle, had lately established himself at Norridgewock on the Kennebec. In the hamlet in Dover called Oyster River, there were now twelve garrison-houses. At dawn of a midsummer day, these were assailed at one moment by a party of Eastern savages, judged to be not far from two hundred and fifty in number, led by a French officer and a French priest. Four years having passed since their last invasion, and the treaty made the last summer at Pemaquid being in force, the occupants were off their guard and scantily supplied with ammunition, while most of the neighbors remained in their own dwellings; but, on the other hand, the signal of the Indians was prematurely given, and the

1693

Renewal of Indian hostilities.

1694. July 17.

William to think well of him, but served in the House for several towns and villages at some distance, where some of them were born, and others had their estates and improvements above any dwellers in the place for which they served. To be rid of them all at once, a bill was brought in, or rather a clause brought into a bill, that no man whatsoever should serve in the House of Commons for any town, unless where he did at that time live and dwell, which passed with the dissent of twenty-four, the whole House consisting of fifty, and with some heat in the Upper House. Sir William hereupon rushes into the House of Commons, and drives out the non-residents, and I am mistaken if either for estates or loyalty they left any of their equals in that House." — Jan. 12, 1694, Byfield wrote from Boston to Dudley in London an account of Phips's objecting, at the May meeting of the General Court, to certain Representatives, who, it appears, had been elected in violation of the law of the previous November. (See above, p. 143.) "Let not the Governor's treatment of the Assembly and abuse offered to the King's charter in refusing the five members die, but let us know how such things are resented at Whitehall." To Usher Byfield writes (July 12) of Phips's treatment of the Assembly the year before: "It has been such as I do think no place belonging to the English nation comparable." (British Colonial Papers.)

surprise was not complete. In one house were fourteen persons, who were all massacred, and all lie buried in one grave. Another garrison-house was surrendered on a promise, which was not kept, of security to life. Three were hastily abandoned, and most of the occupants escaped. The others were defended with success. In one of them a man sent off his family by water, and, remaining alone, changed his dress as he kept firing first from one window, then from another, and shouting as if he had companions. As the morning advanced, the invaders, fearful of being attacked from the neighboring settlements, retreated towards Lake Winnipiseogee, with several prisoners. They had burned five of the fortified houses and fifteen other dwellings, and the number of persons killed and captured by them amounted to nearly a hundred.[1]

Once, at least, the savages came to Portsmouth, where, at an outlying farm, they killed the widow of
July 21. President Cutt, and three of a party of haymakers whose work she was directing. Exeter and Dover, especially the latter settlement, were repeatedly ravaged. At
July 27. Groton twenty persons were killed and nearly as
Sept. 24. many made prisoners.[2] Kittery and Haverhill were the scene of more limited massacres.

The help of the more powerful natives in the Western country was always coveted by the English; and a short time before the departure of Phips, commissioners from New York, New Jersey, Massachusetts, and Connecticut met a delegation of the Five Nations at Albany.[3]
Aug. 15. The Five Nations had by no means abandoned their hostile attitude towards the French. But they were

[1] According to Charlevoix (II. 148), two hundred and thirty English were killed, and fifty or sixty houses burned, while the victors lost not one man, and had only one wounded. — I suppose that by "the fort near Boston" (Ibid.) Charlevoix, imperfectly informed, meant Groton.

[2] Butler, History of Groton, 93.

[3] A Journal kept by Wadsworth, one of the Commissioners for Massachusetts, is in Mass. Hist. Col., XXXI. 102, &c.

not without their jealousies of the rival people. The conference with them had no result beyond some general assurances of good-will on their part; and without actual intervention in arms they were too remote to exert a useful influence over the tribes which threatened Massachusetts.

The Lieutenant-Governor, on whose hands the war was left at Phips's departure, did not want resolution to conduct it.[1] New negotiations which were attempted proved delusive or fruitless. The scattered English posts at the East were exposed and feeble, and a fresh succession of massacres began in the spring. Near 1695. March.
Saco, near Pemaquid, and elsewhere, more than July 6. Sept. 9.
fifty Englishmen from the small population which had been recovering its ground were killed or carried away captive. In an opposite quarter the Indians broke up the fourteen years old settlement of French Protestants August.
in Worcester County; and the few Huguenot families, hopeless of a quiet residence on the exposed frontier, removed in a body to Boston. In the following winter, a party of savages presented themselves before Pemaquid, and proposed an exchange of prisoners. Yielding 1696.
culpably to a not unnatural resentment, Captain Feb. 16.
Chubb, the commander of the garrison, allowed an attack upon them, in which four were put to death and some others were taken prisoners. The exasperation which followed increased the activity of the enemy. At Dover they shot, close by his own house, an unwary person May 7.
who had once been their captive; and presently July 26.
after, as the townspeople were dispersing from their place of Sunday worship, a party of Indians fired upon them, killed three, wounded three, and laid hands on as many more, whom they carried into captivity.

[1] Chalmers (MS. Annals, II.) says that Stoughton "was chosen, not as a soldier, but as a scholar." But he was his father's son, and there was material for a soldier in him.

But the marauding movements which had been keeping the detached hamlets in terror, or reducing them to ruin, were presently succeeded by a victory on a different scale. The new fort at Pemaquid, with its strength in structure, armament, and ammunition, and its garrison of a hundred men, had been thought secure. The French Governor of Quebec resolved to attempt it. He despatched from that place two men-of-war and two companies of soldiers, who on their way were reinforced at Port Royal and at the mouth of the Penobscot by some four hundred Indians. The French squadron met and engaged two English armed vessels which were on the watch, and increased its strength by the capture of one of them. When summoned to surrender, Chubb returned a braggart reply; the French landed and invested the place; and Castine, who had accompanied the expedition, sent in a message to the effect, that if there was further delay, the garrison would receive no quarter. Chubb capitulated, with the condition that his command should be protected from harm and insult, and be sent to Boston. The French could not enforce their agreement. The Indians fell upon the English and put many to death, while the rest were withdrawn under a French guard to an island out of their reach. The victors dismantled and blew up the fortification, and set sail for Penobscot River.[1]

June.

July 14.

July 15.

July 18.

Chubb, tried for cowardice, was acquitted. The calami-

[1] Mather, Magnalia, VII. 84–90; Charlevoix, II. 121, 144, 178. The assault on the English prisoners I state on the authority of Williamson (I. 644). Charlevoix (II. 179) allows the reader to understand that the precautions for their safety proved sufficient. For the French official account of this important conquest, see O'Callaghan (IX. 657, 658). Villebon, Governor of Nova Scotia, had recommended the expedition two years before. "No conjuncture," he wrote to M. de Pontchartrain, Aug. 20, 1694, "can be more favorable than the present to attack Fort Pemaquid, inasmuch as the Indians are resolved to wage a more vigorous and a more cruel war than heretofore, as they have demonstrated in the last expedition [that to Oyster River], having spared neither women nor children." (Ibid., 514.)

tous news created consternation at Boston. Five hundred men were immediately enlisted for a campaign at the eastward, and the Lieutenant-Governor gave the command to Benjamin Church, who, if his capacity did not equal his zeal, retained the advantage of a traditional reputation. Four armed vessels were despatched from Boston to the Penobscot,[1] but did not arrive there till the French squadron had sailed for St. John. Church led his force up the Penobscot, finding some plunder, but no enemy. Returning he met the squadron, with Colonel Hathorne, who came to supersede him in the command. There seemed nothing to be done either by land or sea against an enemy by no means so hard to vanquish as to find, and both troops and ships came back to Boston.[2] In an Address to the King the General Court represented "the exhausted state of the Province through the languishing and wasting war with the French and Indians," and prayed for orders to the several colonial governments to contribute their assistance for the settlement and fortification of Port Royal and St. John; for a supply of ammunition, and the protection of a naval force; and for aid in the reduction of Canada, — "the unhappy fountain," they said, "from which issue all our miseries."[3]

Aug. 3.

Sept. 3.

Sept. 28.

Sept. 24.

[1] Sept. 16, the ministers of Boston and of several neighboring towns were invited to meet the General Court, then in session, to pray for "success to the forces then gone forth," and "the day was spent in religious exercise." (Mass. Prov. Rec., *sub die.*) September 18, the court voted to subscribe the "Association" for the security of the King's person. (Ibid.; comp. Macaulay, History of England, IV. 533.)

[2] Church, Entertaining Passages, &c., 86 *et seq.*

[3] September 16, John Nelson (of whom see above, Vol. III. 581, 584) presented himself to the Privy Council, "and said that he was taken by the French in '91 in attempting to settle Port Royal in Acadia, and that he had been prisoner either there or in France now almost five years." He represented Canada as powerless against a well-concerted invasion, being guarded, two years before, by no more than four hundred soldiers. (Journals of the Board of Trade, *sub die.*) The Board took his statements into consideration, and referred them (November 20) to the Privy Council, from which they do not appear to have received attention. — For fur-

The winter, keeping the savages inactive, gave to the borderers its usual repose, and the approach of warm weather brought its accustomed calamities. Early in the spring a band of marauders made a successful assault upon Haverhill. One of the captives whom they took thence was Hannah Dustin, who had borne a child only a week before. Her husband, with their other children, had escaped. Her captors dashed out the infant's brains. They proceeded a hundred and fifty miles on their retreat towards Canada, when they told her that, on their reaching one of their own camps, she would have to be stripped and run the gantlet. This inspired her with a desperate resolution. With the woman who had been nursing her, she was in the custody of an Indian party, consisting of two men, three women, and seven children, who had also in charge an English boy, taken prisoner a year or two before. She enlisted her companion and the boy in her scheme. When they were halted in a retired spot, they watched the opportunity of their keepers being sound asleep, and then, with rapid blows, despatched with their own hatchets all but two, — one of whom, a child who had been kind to them, they intentionally spared; while the other, a woman whom they supposed they had wounded mortally, revived and escaped. The heroine and her helpers found their way to her home before the end of spring, bringing the scalps of their ten victims. The General Court expressed their satisfaction with the deed by a present of fifty pounds.[1]

1697. March 15.

June 8.

Exeter owed to an accident its preservation from a well-laid plot for its destruction. A party of

June 10.

ther particulars of Nelson's transactions with the French, see Murdoch, History of Nova Scotia, 199 *et seq.*

[1] Mirick, History of Haverhill, 86 *et seq.* The grant of the General Court was made on a petition of the woman's husband, who represented himself as impoverished by the war. One half of the money was given to his wife; the other half was shared between Mary Neff and Samuel Lenerson, her companions. (Mass. Prov. Rec.) Aug. 30, 1739, the Court gave Mary Neff's son 200 acres of land.

Indians were lying about it in hiding-places one day, intending to fall upon it early the next morning, as was their habit. Some women, with their children, had gone a little way out of the town to gather strawberries. They had been told that it was imprudent, and some persons whose caution they had neglected fired alarm-guns to frighten them. This caused a muster of the men; and the Indians, supposing themselves to be discovered, decamped in haste. Major Frost of Kittery, a Counsellor of the Province, and formerly colonel of the militia of York County, was going home from the Sunday worship with his wife and a servant, when the three were fired upon and killed by Indians, who lay in ambush for him behind a log. At York, at Wells, and at Saco, the old experience of stealthy murders was again and again renewed.[1]

July.

But a greater anxiety of the time related to a different kind of operation. There was intelligence that the King of France was designing to send a strong fleet into Massachusetts Bay, and at the same time to bring fifteen hundred French and Indians into New England across the northern frontier. There was nothing improbable in the project, which was afterwards known to have been in fact entertained.[2] The King of England was so circumstanced that he could not do much for his Massachusetts lieges, even if he cared more about them than in truth he did care. He was pressing for a peace, and, as things stood with him, not a guinea nor an ounce of powder could be spared from his needs in Europe. If Massachusetts was now to be taken care of, it must be by herself. The forts were repaired, manned, and provisioned. Companies of minute-men were enrolled.[3] Five hundred men under Major March, an officer of the best reputation, were

Alarm of a French invasion.

[1] Mather, Magnalia, VII. 91, 92; Niles, in Mass. Hist. Col., XXVI. 240, &c.

[2] Charlevoix, II. 217; O'Callaghan, IX. 659 *et seq.*

[3] A letter of Stoughton to the Board of Trade, of Sept. 30, 1697, and a letter to John Nelson, of August 2, set forth the anxieties and the activity of the time. (British Colonial Papers.)

sent down to the Kennebec, which was thought likeliest of any place to be presently the seat of war. Landing at Damariscotta, he was attacked by a body of sava- Sept. 9. ges, whom he repulsed after a bloody fight, in which he lost twelve or thirteen men.[1]

This was a few days only before the conclusion Treaty of Ryswick. Sept. 20. of the treaty of Ryswick, which made peace between France and England. Intelligence of that event, which gave such relief to New England, came early in the winter. Dec. 10. But, though there were no more battles in this war, there was not yet a cessation of murders, pillages, and burnings. At Lancaster a party 1698. February. of Indians massacred twenty or thirty people, with their minister. Another party burned several houses at Andover, putting to death a number of the inhabitants, — among whom was Chubb, the recent commander at Pemaquid, — and carrying away others. One of the captives was the late Governor's son, Colonel Bradstreet, who, however, escaped when the marauders were closely pursued.[2]

But the Indians had been learning that, by reason of the peace lately made in Europe,[3] they could no longer rely on open support from their friends in Canada; and without it they could not venture to persevere in their rava- October. ges. Proposing to make a new submission, they sent delegates to Pejepscot on the Kennebec, between whom and commissioners from Massachusetts Pacification with the Indians. (Colonel Phillips and Major Converse) a treaty of peace was concluded, with stipulations such as they had been accustomed to make, and, as soon as 1699. Jan. 7. they dared, to violate.[4] If this treaty should prove more binding upon them than earlier ones, it would be because perfidy appeared less safe, or because French

[1] Mather, Magnalia, VII. 92.

[2] Ibid., 92, 93; Hutch., II. 106.

[3] Authentic intelligence of the peace was not received by the French in Canada till May, 1698, though a rumor of it had reached them in February. (Charlevoix, II. 225.)

[4] N. H. Prov. Rec., II. 299.

solicitation was less active. Beginning in the administration of Andros, this grievous war, waged by the tribes of the north-eastern wilderness, had lasted ten years. They had taken, and either held for a longer or shorter time, or destroyed, all the settlements in Maine, with three exceptions. More than seven hundred Englishmen were killed, and two hundred and fifty carried into captivity, — many of them never to return. The territory which Massachusetts had bought of the heir of Ferdinando Gorges, and been endowed with by King William, had as yet proved hers only to defend at heavy cost and with disastrous losses.

Revisal of the provincial legislation.

In the midst of the last distresses of the war, the time came for the King's government to consider of limits to be imposed on the legislation of provincial Massachusetts. In respect to the earliest enactments, the term of three years allowed by the charter for the rejection of laws was about to expire. Till now that provision had been suffered to remain inoperative; and, encouraged apparently by this inaction in the courtly circle, the provincial General Court proceeded with confidence in their new legislation. But Somers and his associates in King William's cabinet were men not less watchful than those who presumed upon their negligence. With well-judging prudence, they avoided interposing any new provocation till there had been time for the discontent to subside, which was produced by the burial of the old charter and the substitution for it of a system comprehending privileges so much less liberal. In good season the ministers took up that work, favored also not a little by the conditions of the time; for Massachusetts was enfeebled and dispirited by the calamities of the *woful decade*, and her shallow, but sometimes obstinate, Governor had yielded his place to a man pliant to prerogative, and as little loving as loved by his fellow-citizens.

The first enactment of the newly constituted Legislature 1692. June 15. had been in these words:[1] "That all the local laws respectively ordered and made by the late Governor and Company of the Massachusetts Bay and the late government of New Plymouth, being not repugnant to the laws of England, nor inconsistent with the present constitution and settlement by their Majesty's royal charter, do remain and continue in full force in the respective places for which they were made and used until the tenth of November next." Nov. 9. When that day arrived, the provision was renewed without limitation as to time. The enactments were duly certified to England; and, no opposition being for the present manifested there, the Province rejoiced in the quiet of its ancient administration, and looked for that conclusion of three years which would confirm it past danger of recall. But the Privy Council counted the months as attentively as the Province, and just before the end of the three years it broke its delusive silence. It disallowed the Act, and directed "that in any new law to be enacted for the said purpose the laws to be continued be therein expressed and particularly specified."[2]

This beginning was unequivocally significant of what was to follow. Of forty-five Acts passed at the first two 1695. Aug. 22. sessions of the provincial Legislature, fifteen were disallowed by the Privy Council in one busy day.[3] One "for the erecting of a naval office" was thought to encroach on the privileges of the "Commissioners of his

[1] Provincial Acts and Resolves, 27. — One observes here the change of the enacting clause from "It is ordered by the Governor and Company of Massachusetts Bay," the form hitherto used, to "Be it ordered and enacted by the Governor, Council, and Representatives convened in General Assembly."

[2] Ibid., 99, 100.

[3] Journal of the Privy Council, *sub die.* Somers, as Attorney-General, had the business in hand from March 29 to June 4. (Journal of the Board of Trade; comp. Province Laws, I. 109, 110. The "Observations on the Laws of Massachusetts" smack strongly of Randolph.)

Majesty's Customs."[1] To another, "for incorporating of Harvard College," it was objected that "no power was reserved to his Majesty to appoint visitors."[2] The "Act setting forth General Privileges," in effect a Bill of Rights, declared an exemption from all taxes except those levied by the General Court; and it found no favor with the prescient wisdom of the King's advisers,[3] though the poor pretence for disallowing it was only an objection to some provisions of detail, and the great question was not faced. In what seems bold disregard of that provision of the

[1] Provincial Acts and Resolves, 34, 35.

[2] Ibid., 38, 39.

[3] Ibid., 40, 41. — The attempt was followed up by the passing, June 7, 1694, of an Act, providing "(1) that the House of Representatives of the people of this Province, being a part of the Great and General Court or Assembly, have, by their Majesties' most gracious charter, undoubted right to all the liberties and privileges of an English Assembly, and to have and use freedom of debate and suffrages in all matters proper to them as such; and the choice and appointment of all civil officers, not particularly directed to and enumerated in the charter, doth of right belong to the Great and General Court or Assembly; and that, when and so often as any motion is made to the House of Representatives for the granting of any money to be levied of the people of this Province, the said House of Representatives ought particularly to be advised what uses and improvement such money is to be raised for; (2) that the appointment and establishment of all salaries of any officers within this Province be and hereby is declared to belong to the said General Court or Assembly; and that no public money be or ought to be disposed of by His Excellency the Governor, and Council, but for the uses and intents of and according to the Acts by which the said money is raised; and that no money may or ought to be drawn or paid out of the public treasury of this Province, but by warrant or order of the Governor, with the advice and consent of the Council, for the time being, expressing particularly the Act by which the said money was raised, and for what particular service the same is designed, and to be applied pursuant to the said Act or Acts, other than contingent charges for the support of the government of this Province for the time being." (Ibid., 170.)

This was before the Privy Council had taken up the Act of October, 1692. It was immediately after the reception of Phips's recall to England, and when perhaps it was expected that Dudley would succeed him. This Act, too, was disallowed by the Privy Council (Dec. 10, 1696), for no better avowed reason than that the previous Act "for the setting forth of general privileges" had "already been repealed." (Provincial Acts, &c., 170.) But, though dead, it yet spoke, and continued to do substantial service. It was a *programme*, carefully prepared, for future action; and it was faithfully acted upon throughout the later years.

charter, which granted to Massachusetts men "all liberties and immunities of free and natural subjects, ... as if they and every of them were born within our realm of England," the "Act for the better securing the liberty of the subject, and for prevention of illegal imprisonment," was set aside, because the "privilege of the writ of *habeas corpus* had not as yet been granted in any of his Majesty's plantations."[1] This process of disallowance was repeatedly applied, though with diminishing frequency, to the provincial legislation of the first eight years.

At the end of this time, when Somers had gone out of office, either the ministers had become less wary or
1700.
less fastidious, or the people of Massachusetts had come to a better understanding of how much they might undertake for their own benefit, with a reasonable prospect of carrying it through. But it was not her internal legislation alone in respect to which Massachusetts was taken into training by the British government, at this important crisis. The whole subject of colonial management attracted renewed attention. It has been mentioned that colonial affairs, which, since the middle of the reign of Charles the Second, had been in the charge of a committee of the Privy Council, were now again intrusted to a special board, the title of which, "The Lords Commissioners for Trade and Plantations," painfully indicated the policy which was to regulate colonial government.[2] This authority addressed itself in earnest to the task of enforcing the Navigation Laws, which in New England had not hitherto had considerable effect. Randolph was at hand, maliciously anxious to furnish the board with suggestions helpful to carry out their design. It was at this time that the colonial system was

Rigor of commercial administration.

1696. May 15.

[1] Provincial Acts and Resolves, 95, 96.

[2] See above, Vol. IV. 21; comp. Anderson, History of Commerce, II. 214. — May 9, Sir William Trumbull (Pope's friend) succeeded Sir John Trenchard as Secretary of State.

reinforced by new Acts of Parliament, which, among other strict provisions, required the colonial governors to swear that they would use their utmost diligence to make the Navigation Laws effective, and gave to revenue officers in America the same powers with which they were clothed in England.[1] A little later was the hard law which forbade not only the exportation to foreign parts, but the conveying into any other plantation, of any "wool or manufacture made or mixed with wool, being the produce or manufacture of any of the English plantations in America."[2] A Windsor good-wife, crossing the line for a visit to her gossip at Springfield, could not lawfully take a ball of yarn for her afternoon's knitting. In Massachusetts (by a provision, now first made effective, of the new charter), as well as in the other Colonies, Vice-Admiralty courts were established, with prosecuting and executive officers.[3]

1697.

1698.

July 30.

It is probable that considerations incident to the commercial relations of the Colonies both dictated the delay in filling the place vacated by Governor Phips, and finally influenced the choice of his successor. As long as the war with France was on his hands, the King would prefer to avoid the risk of displeasing his subjects in New England, who were disposed to take so active a part in it; and the provisional administration

Question of Phips's successor.

[1] See above, Vol. IV. 19, notes 4, 5.

[2] Ibid., 20.

[3] Privy Council Register, *sub die.* — Douglas says (Summary, I. 483) that Wait Winthrop, appointed May 22, 1699, was the first Admiralty Judge. — "The beginning of the year 1697 is the era of a remarkable change in the colonial jurisprudence, by the erection of courts of Vice-Admiralty in the various plantations. In the reign of William, adjudications by judges of the civil law were substituted for the trial by jury, so favorable to the interests of justice and of freedom." (Chalmers, Annals, &c., II. 230. The volume, never published, is in manuscript, in Mr. Sparks's collection) "Prior to the statute of 7th and 8th of William the Third, there existed in the plantations no Admiralty courts. They were soon after created by the advice of the Peers, who considered the existence of the Acts of Navigation dependent on their establishment." (Chalmers's Letter to Lord Mansfield, 92, in manuscript in the Sparks collection.)

was well enough cared for by the loyal and punctilious Stoughton. When peace again brought the time for thinking of the succession, Dudley did not lose sight of it for himself, nor feel discouraged on account of his former misbehaviour; for that Andros and his friends had not incurred the King's permanent displeasure by the course which had made them hated in America, had been proved by their subsequent promotion.[1] Coming out as a Counsellor of New York, Dudley had been made Chief Justice of that Colony, and as such had presently the satisfaction of condemning Jacob Leisler to death,[2] for proceedings which, though less discreet, were, as to their general character, the same as those of the Massachusetts patriots who had put an end to the government of Andros. Even before Phips's recall, Dudley had intrigued in England for the appointment to return to Boston as Governor.[3] He was not without love for his home, and that arrangement would further have promised him opportunity to gratify his revenge, while its provocations were still recent. But the English statesmen could not but be aware that in a movement in which conciliation as well as authority must have a part, Dudley was not yet, at least, the proper person for their service. Besides, he had been accustomed to the old way of the Boston merchants in transacting business, and it could not be surely known how far he would be active in correcting it, notwithstanding his present position of sycophancy. Finding the prospect discouraging, — the more so from the resolute opposition of Constantine Phipps[4] and Sir Henry Ashurst, now agents for Massachusetts, — he contented himself for the present with the

[1] In February, 1692, Andros was appointed Governor of Virginia. (Privy Council Register for Feb. 11; Luttrell's Diary in Hist. Mag. for 1868, p. 289.)

[2] Chandler, Criminal Trials, 255 *et seq.*

[3] "Captain Dudley stands fairest to succeed Sir William Phips." (Luttrell's Diary, for March, 1695, in Hist. Mag. for 1868, p. 291.)

[4] Constantine Phipps, Attorney-General for Ireland, ancestor of the Marquesses of Normanby of the present day, was no relation of the American Sir William Phips.

appointment of Lieutenant-Governor of the Isle of Wight, which place he held under Lord Cutts, the dashing soldier of Marlborough's wars,[1] adding to it, after a while, a seat in Parliament.

The choice of a successor to Governor Phips fell on the Earl of Bellomont. As a member of the committee of the House of Commons, which had under consideration a reversal of the attainder of Leisler, he had imbibed a strong dislike of Dudley, and at the same time engaged for himself the friendship of Phips and Ashurst. In the autumn after the peace, he embarked for New York with a commission constituting him Governor of that Province, and of New Jersey and New Hampshire, as well as of Massachusetts.

1697. November.

Hitherto all the Governors of Massachusetts since the settlement had been either original immigrants or natives of the country. Just as its highest office was to be occupied for the first time by a person unconnected with it, Simon Bradstreet died, the last survivor of those founders who had been chosen to the magistracy before they came from England. When he emigrated, he was twenty-eight years old; he lived to complete his ninety-fifth year. The General Court voted to contribute a hundred pounds towards the expenses of his burial, "in consideration of his long and extraordinary service." He had been Secretary of the Colony; an Assistant forty-six years; a Commissioner of the Confederacy twenty-four times; Agent to England; Deputy-Governor and Governor; — a man hardly equal to the most difficult occasions, but patriotic, faithful, honest, and laborious, and always esteemed and trusted. Not often has a human memory been laden with experiences more diversified. A

March 27.

March 31.

1 "I had the honor to serve under my Lord Cutts as Lieutenant-Governor nine years and a half, which time he was in Flanders." (Letter of Dudley to John Usher, Nov. 28, 1703, in British Colonial Papers.) From this it appears that Dudley returned from New York to England as early as the autumn of 1692.

youth passed amidst the refinements of old civilization; the destitution of a wilderness, and conflicts with savage men; the growth of a virtuous and vigorous commonwealth; its subversion, resurrection, and reorganization under restricted but permanent conditions, — such was the outline of nearly a century's events, traced by the recollections of a leading actor in them.[1]

[1] "The only surviving antiquary of us Nov-Angles, the prime Secretary and Register of our civil and sacred records, and the bifronted Janus who saw the closure of the old, and the overture of this New-Albion world; one who, in your juvenile strength, engaged you all to raise and build up the arduous and hazardous structure of this then despised and despicable fabric: so as its observers said of it, 'What will these feeble men build? If a fox go up, he shall even break down the stone wall;' of which themselves, and all its spectators, must now say, 'Lo, what hath God done!'" (Scottow, Narrative of the Planting of the Massachusetts Colony, &c. (1694), Dedication to Bradstreet.) — The inscription over the Governor's grave at Salem commemorates him as having been "vir judicio Lynceario præditus, quem nec nummus, nec honos allexit; regis auctoritatem et populi libertatem, æquà lance libravit; religione cordatus, vitâ innocuus."

CHAPTER VI.

THE selection of Phips to be Governor of Massachusetts was expected to gratify the people of that Province, and so to facilitate the introduction of their new constitution of government. Even had his administration been much more satisfactory than it proved to be, the choice of his successor would not have been dictated by the same considerations. While the new system had settled itself, and was in quiet operation, the home supervision of the Colonies had been changed by the transfer of it from a committee of the Privy Council to the Board of Trade;[1] and the new functionaries naturally desired to justify and to signalize their advancement by some novelty in the energy and methods of their proceeding. Nor could it seem amiss to inaugurate their business by committing the administration of the principal Colony to a man of ability, of resolution, and of high social standing.

1696.

Two needs of the Colonies seemed to demand special attention at this moment. In the long war with France, private armed ships had been much employed. By their rude navigators the distinction between privateersman and pirate failed of being always observed; and it was said that there was some resort of freebooters to the American coast, where they had advantages for eluding detection and arrest. Again, the disappointments and disasters of the war in America had proved at what a great disadvantage the English were, notwithstanding their preponderance in numbers, by reason

Reasons for Lord Bellomont's appointment.

[1] See above, 21.

of their want of combination under one head. The management, by Nicholson and Fletcher, of affairs with the Indian tribes on the New York frontier, had not been satisfactory. The peace just made in fact lasted through the period of Lord Bellomont's service. But from the first it was understood to be of uncertain duration, and, against the time when hostilities should be renewed, it was prudent to provide for a better handling of colonial resources. The scheme of a general government, like that of Andros's rule, or even more comprehensive, was repeatedly entertained and pressed. But objections occurred, partly arising out of the charters; and it was thought that the nearest approach to a consolidation which could well be made for the present was by extending over New York and New Jersey the authority of the Governor of Massachusetts and New Hampshire, and by placing him in command of the military force of all the northern Colonies.[1]

It was indeed impossible, in the circumstances, that the peace of Ryswick should be more than a truce. It was a truce of undetermined length, and of imperfectly defined conditions. The parties did not mean to bury their quarrel; they but wanted respectively a resting-time to look about them to reorganize and to recruit. The cessation from arms probably lasted longer than any of them anticipated. That between French and English the strife was only adjourned, was manifest to both the late belligerents. An article of the

[1] For William Penn's "Scheme for a Union of the Colonies in America," see O'Callaghan, IV. 296; comp. Edmund Harrison, Representation to the Board of Trade, Feb. 1, 1697 (British Colonial Papers). He wrote, "The uniting the government of New England and New York is of the utmost necessity for the good of both." The project of a union was not without favor in high quarters in Massachusetts. "Many small governments: . . . . . these should be united under one government, or rather a viceroy sent over all." (Letter of Stephen Sewall to Edward Hull, of Nov. 2, 1696, Ibid.) Sir Henry Ashurst subscribed his name to a memorial to the Lords of Trade in favor of such a measure, but afterwards withdrew it. (Journals of the Board of Trade for Feb. 8, 1697.) For the final decision of this question by the Lords, see O'Callaghan, IV. 259. The plan of a union was discarded Feb. 25, 1697. (Ibid., 261.)

treaty provided for a mutual restitution of "all territories, islands, forts, and colonies, wherever situated," to the power which possessed them before the war. The limits of Acadia were not now described, and had never been defined. The French always held that that province, which now reverted to them, was bounded on the west by the Kennebec; the English maintained that their possession extended eastward to the St. Croix, and that accordingly all between the Kennebec and the St. Croix was now part of Massachusetts. The same contradictory interpretations included the right to the allegiance of the Indians within the disputed territory, and the right to take fish along its coast and among the neighboring islands. Villebon, the French Governor of Acadia, gave formal notice to the government of Massachusetts that he was instructed to assert by force his master's claim in these particulars.[1] It was especially with reference to this controversy that the home government was at different times so urgent with Massachusetts to keep up the fort at Pemaquid, so as to command the river Penobscot.

French pretensions.

1698. Sept. 5.

The new Governor of Massachusetts, Richard Coote, grandson of Sir Charles Coote, a soldier of Queen Elizabeth, was the second Baron Coloony, and the first Earl of Bellomont, in the peerage of Ireland.[2] He was now sixty-two years old. He had taken a serviceable part in the measures which led to the recent Revolution, but, as a member of the House of Commons in the new King's second Parliament, had incurred his displeasure by moving an impeachment of two law officers of the crown in Ireland.[3] From the consequences of this loss of favor he was relieved by the friendship of Lord Shrewsbury,[4]

[1] Letter of Stoughton of Oct. 24, 1698. (British Colonial Papers.)

[2] See Burke, Extinct Peerage, Art. Bellomont.

[3] Hansard, Parliamentary History, V. 816.

[4] "Compassion will not permit me to refuse seconding what my Lord Sunderland says he has writ to your Majesty in behalf of my Lord Bellomont, that he may have some forfeited lands in Ireland. His condition

who at this moment stood especially high in the royal graces, by reason of his having consented, after much 1694. solicitation, to resume office, for which acqui- April 30. escence he had been rewarded with a duke-dom; and the King's reconciliation with the offender must be presumed to have been cordial, since it 1696. was after the Duke's intervention that his client was raised a degree in the peerage.

1697. It was in the seventh month after his appoint- April 8. ment[1] that Lord Bellomont left England, and four or five months more passed before he landed at New York, adverse weather having driven him off to the West The Governor's arrival at New York. Indies.[2] He had doubted to which of his governments he should repair first. He had learned in 1698. London that "the merchants and others belonging April 2. to New England did little stomach the discourse that had been about the town of his going first to New York, as if the people of New England (who are the bigger body of people, and far more considerable than the others) were thereby slighted." "Therefore that they 1697. might not take it ill of me," he writes in a memo- Aug. 26. rial to the Board of Trade, "I think it absolutely necessary to have the direction of your Board, or of the Lords Justices, to which of those Provinces I am first to go. The reasons hinted to me by the Lords Justices for my repairing first to New York are chiefly two; namely,

I really believe is necessitous to a great degree, and there are several persons, members of Parliament, who lay great weight, and think his friends obliged to see him taken care of. He seems to the world to have been displaced for a reason that would do your Majesty great prejudice to have it believed that it sticks with you As to indiscretions, sir, I will not be answerable for him, but dare engage that no man living is more faithful and zealous to your Majesty and your government, even under these hardships, than he is." (The Duke of Shrewsbury to the King, June 11, 1694, in the Correspondence of Charles Talbot, &c., 40.)

[1] Privy Council Journal, *sub die.*

[2] Letter of Lord Bellomont to the Lords of Trade, in O'Callaghan, IV. 302. — At the end of the year (Dec. 18, 1697) of Lord Bellomont's appointment, James Vernon succeeded Sir William Trumbull as Secretary of State.

New York's being a frontier, and my being to supersede the present Governor thereof."[1]

Under the Lieutenant-Governor of Massachusetts, affairs proceeded in so satisfactory a train, that the superior magistrate did not consider his immediate presence there to be needed; and he remained at New York a full year, conducting meanwhile an active correspondence with Stoughton.[2] When at length, however, he came to Boston, where he was received with a warm and generous welcome, it was evident to what party his sympathies inclined. In England, while he was a member of the House of Commons, he had, as has been told, taken an active part in proceedings against Dudley for his malicious treatment of Leisler. Influenced more or less by this resentment, he was inclined to treat Stoughton with coldness as Dudley's partisan, and to confide in Elisha Cooke and his friends.[3]

His arrival in Boston. 1699. May 26.

[1] British Colonial Papers, Aug. 26, 1697; comp. Ibid., May 10.

[2] 1697, May 27, Stoughton announced the Governor's appointment (General Court Record *sub die*); and July 12 the court passed a vote providing for his reception. (Ibid.) Dec. 16, his arrival being then expected, two Magistrates (Wait Winthrop and Elisha Cooke) and the Speaker of the House (Penn Townshend) were sent to New York to greet him and carry an address. (Ibid.) They were accompanied by a chaplain (John Rogers), whom the court employed to take care of their spiritual health. — April 12, 1699, when Bellomont had at last given notice of his intention to come to Massachusetts from New York, Stoughton wrote to Sir Henry Ashurst that he should be glad to "be eased of the burdensome care and fatigue of government, which," he says, "I have been so long obliged to undergo, to the no little impairment of the health of my body." (British Colonial Papers.)

[3] Fletcher, of New York, — or perhaps it was Evans, a navy officer, one of Fletcher's satellites, that was meant, — came in for a share of the frank vehemence of the Earl's aristocratic contempt: "I serve the King in the station I am in honestly and with my endeavors, and 'tis hard that I must be so barbarously treated by such an upstart fellow, the son of a shoemaker in Ireland, and I expect from your Lordships justice." (Lord Bellomont to the Lords of the Admiralty, Sept. 7, 1699, in British Colonial Papers.) The Board of Trade had received charges against Fletcher of complicity with the pirates. (Journal of the Board for Sept. 15, 1698; comp. O'Callaghan, IV. 479 *et seq.*)

Legislation on the Judiciary.

The business of immediate interest in Massachusetts at the time of the arrival there of Lord Bellomont concerned the existing judicial system of the Province. It has been related that in the first year of the organization under the new charter an Act was passed by the General Court "for the Establishing of Judicatories and Courts of Justice within the Province." When, just before the expiration of the three years to which the King's right to abrogate the laws was limited by the charter, his Privy Council went to work on the early provincial legislation, among the thirteen Acts which its wakeful jealousy disallowed out of the thirty-five passed at the second session of the first provincial General Court, was the Act "for the Establishing of Judicatories." The objection to it was that, departing from the words of the charter, it restricted the right of appeals to the Privy Council to personal actions involving a sum exceeding three hundred pounds.[1]

1692. Nov. 25.

1695. Aug. 22.

Being informed of this, the General Court re-enacted their law, with the exception of the obnoxious clause, and of a provision for establishing a Court of Equity. This Act in turn was disapproved by the Privy Council, for an alleged reason which seems either not weighty or else not perspicuously expressed. It is not unnatural to think that what in fact influenced the Council was the peculiarity of the language in which the General Court had withdrawn the exceptionable enactment. The new law did not invest the suitor with an unlimited privilege of appeal, which was what the English Ministry wanted. It "declared void, and of none effect, the section or paragraph of the said Act providing for liberty of appeal unto his Majesty in Council," thus withdrawing the question of appeal under whatsoever condi-

1696. Oct. 3.

1698. Nov. 24.

[1] Provincial Acts and Resolves, I. 73, 76; comp. 217.

tions, and leaving the General Court unsustained indeed by the crown in the qualification which it had sought to obtain, but, on the other hand, uncommitted by any action on its own part to an abatement of its claim to complete exemption.[1]

The General Court tried again. They passed an "Act
for Establishing of Courts," which went more into 1697.
details, but was substantially the same as that of June 19.
five years before. It renewed the provision restricting appeals to England to cases of pecuniary importance. It was hoped, perhaps, that the Privy Council would rather on reflection have an express grant of appeals, though a limited one, than have the whole question remain open; and the Lieutenant-Governor and Council sent to the King
a "Representation and Address relating to appeals, 1698.
and praying to be continued in the enjoyment of May.
all those privileges granted in the royal charter."[2] This
Act too was, however, disallowed in England, for Nov. 24.
the alleged reason that, inasmuch as it granted the right of trial by jury in all cases, it took away the option given by English law to custom-house officers, respecting trial by an Admiralty Court, which has no jury, and so interfered with a vigorous enforcement of the Navigation Laws.[3] The Superior Court, which was engaged in a trial
when intelligence to this effect was received, im- 1699.
mediately dissolved itself.[4] It is likely that this April 26.
movement hastened Lord Bellomont's journey to Massachusetts, and that an anticipation of it was the cause of
the General Court's urgency when they sent to 1698.
New York an Address praying that he would "be Nov. 22.
pleased to favor the Province with his presence . . . . .

[1] Provincial Acts and Resolves, I. 248, 249.

[2] Privy Council Register for July 16, 1698.

[3] Provincial Acts and Resolves, I. 287.

[4] Washburn, Judicial History of Massachusetts (quoting from Sewall's Diary), 151. — "The courts of justice have fallen." (Bellomont's speech to the General Court, June 2, 1699.)

so soon as the season of the year might comfortably admit his undertaking so long and difficult a journey."[1]

He came accordingly, as has been mentioned, in the following spring, and in his first speech to the General Court[2] advised a re-enactment of the law for constituting courts, with an omission of the obnoxious provision; and that step was immediately taken, so far as that all reference to appeals was avoided, and that question was relegated to future consideration. Certain chancery powers were at the same time given to that court and to the Court of Common Pleas, and it was now declared that the Superior Court was to have jurisdiction "as fully and amply, to all intents and purposes whatsoever, as the Courts of King's Bench, Common Pleas, and Exchequer, within his Majesty's kingdom of England, have or ought to have." The British ministry made no further objection, and thus at length the judicial system of the Province was permanently established.[3] For the administration of Admiralty powers, which, exercised by the Assistants under the colonial charter, had, under the charter of King William, been reserved to the crown, the Lords Commissioners of the Admiralty proceeded to

1699. June 2.

June 26.

[1] Mass. Archives, CVI. 430.

[2] Lord Bellomont introduced the practice of speeches by the Governor to the General Court. In the exuberance of his zeal for King William, and in his confidence that the sentiment would be well received in Massachusetts, he made free to comment on preceding reigns, as the reigns of monarchs who had "plotted and contrived to undermine and subvert our religion, laws, and liberties." And in his speech the next year he recurred to the topic, declaring that "the parting with Canada to the French [by the treaty of Breda], and the eastern country, ... were most execrable treacheries to England, and intended, without doubt, to serve the ends of popery. It is too well known what interest that King favored, who parted with Nova Scotia, and of what religion he died." This was delicate ground for the courtiers of the Dutch King. Reflections on the policy of James the Second and his brother were reflections on not a few persons now sitting in high seats about the nephew of those monarchs. The Board of Trade sent the Governor a caution (April 11, 1700), which came too late to serve its purpose, "not to reflect on preceding reigns." (British Colonial Papers.)

[3] Provincial Acts and Resolves, I. 367–375; 465.

constitute a court of Vice-Admiralty for New England and New York, with a King's Advocate, a Registrar, and a Marshal. The common-law courts claimed a right as recognized by the charter, and confirmed by the law, to revise the decisions of the Admiralty Court, which had the important function of trying offences against the Laws of Tràde; and this conflict of jurisdiction finally led to important complications.

While affairs in Massachusetts were in loyal and competent hands, and could proceed satisfactorily without the Governor's personal attention, New York was torn by factions, and never free from danger from the excitable Indians on the western frontier, who were now also exasperated at having been deserted by the English in the late treaty, and left unaided to provide for their own protection against the French of Canada. Lord Bellomont remained in Massachusetts only fourteen months. While he was there, he used laudable diligence in preparing himself to make reports to his superiors on the condition of his Province; but, as was to have been expected from his own want of acquaintance with the country, and the little time at his disposal for inquiry, the information which he communicated was by no means exact.[1] He informed the Lords of Trade that the

1700. June.

Lord Bellomont's impressions of Massachusetts.

[1] Letter of Lord Bellomont to the Lords of Trade, of Aug. 28, 1699. (British Colonial Papers.) Comp. his letter to the Lords of April 20, 1700, in O'Callaghan, IV. 638: "I pretend to be able to demonstrate that if the Five Nations should at any time, in conjunction with the Eastern Indians and those that live within these plantations, revolt from the English to the French, they would in a short time drive us quite out of this continent; and the reason is plain, for their way of fight is not to come hand to hand, or to present their bodies to their enemies, but they lie skulking in the woods behind bushes, and flat on their bellies, and if those they shoot at drop, then they run and scalp them, but if they perceive they have missed their shot, they run away without being so much as seen (for the most part) by those they shoot at; and 'tis to as much purpose to pursue them in the thick woods as to pursue birds that are on the wing. They laugh at the English and French for exposing their bodies in fight, and call them fools. At my first coming hither, I used to ridicule the people here for suffering three or four hundred Indians to cut

eastern tribes had not above "three hundred fighting men," yet that they had broken up a thousand families of English settlers. He represented that "the Province of Maine, a noble country, had been destroyed in the late war," and that there were "no thoughts of repeopling it; the people were not public-spirited enough." He distinguished a portion of the Council as "the sour part." He reported them as saying that "they were too much cramped in their liberties already," and he complained that a bill relating to piracy, especially a clause punishing it with death, "would not go down with them by any means." He had had a sharp dispute with the Council about their alleged right to a share in the appointment of certain officers. Sir William Phips had been weak enough, he said, to yield that point to them; and Stoughton had done the same, though not without a protest. The Governor was honorable, frank, and sensitive, perhaps over-confident, perhaps not without arrogance. The sight of knavery in others enraged him, and he could not endure to be himself suspected of any indirection. He was genial and good-natured, and was esteemed to be not ungenerously disposed towards the people whom he came to rule. For his short service the General Court made him two grants of a thousand pounds each;[1] a greater liberality than was

off five times their number of them; but I was soon convinced that it was not altogether the want of courage and conduct in the English that gave the advantage to the Indians this last war, but chiefly the Indians' manner of birding (as I may call it) the English, and using the advantage of the woods and fastnesses for shooting, and then sheltering themselves.

[1] July 14, 1699, and July 4, 1700. (Provincial Laws and Resolves, I. 394, 437.) Each Act explicitly declares the grant to be "a present." From the first the ground assumed by the Province against a fixed salary for the Governor was steadily maintained. When, in 1694, the Court made a grant to Phips of five hundred pounds "for his great service in the government the last year," it was not till the day after they had passed the "Act for the setting forth of General Privileges," declaring such grants to be within their own unshared discretion. (Ibid., 170, 174.)

No grant was made to Stoughton while he was acting Governor, because in Bellomont's commission he was instructed during his absence from the seat of his government to allow half of his emoluments to the Lieutenant-

ever shown to a Governor of Massachusetts, before or since his time. They overrated the extent of his friendship for them. They might have been less liberal, had they known of his writing home that in his government he wanted persons, employed in the King's service in all ranks, "from the Governor to the meanest officer," to be "not men of the country, but Englishmen."[1]

Question of the Governor's support.

A present of a thousand pounds of the provincial currency, made to him by the General Court, Lord Bellomont said, was equivalent to no more than seven hundred pounds sterling, whereas, before leaving England, he had been led to expect a regular salary of twelve hundred pounds. "I never did," he writes, "nor ever will ask them any thing, and it troubles me that I am on so precarious a foot for a salary for this government."[2] This complaint being communicated by the Lords of Trade to the agent of Massachusetts, Sir Henry "said he believed the Council and the Assembly would not consent to settle a salary upon all Governors for the future; but that if his Majesty should be pleased to write to them, or if this Board should do it, he doubted not but that they might be persuaded to settle a suitable salary upon the Earl of Bellomont during his government."[3]

1700. Jan. 31.

Governor. (Journal of the Board of Trade for Oct. 1, 1695.)

[1] Letter of Lord Bellomont to the Lords of Trade, of April 23, 1700. (British Colonial Papers.) Again, he writes to the Lords of the Admiralty, Sept. 7, 1699, that he has appointed for King's Advocate in the Admiralty Courts of New Hampshire and Rhode Island "Thomas Newton, an Englishman born, which I confess is one quality I shall always desire to meet with in men that I recommend to employment in these plantations."

[2] Letter of Aug. 28, 1699, in British Colonial Papers. — He adds that he is "put to great inconvenience for want of a house, and obliged to pay £100 a year for one, besides the hire of a stable. There is a very good house-plot where Sir Edmund Andros had lived, standing on the best part of the town. £3000 would build a good house and offices, — not much, considering that building here is at least a third dearer than in London."

[3] Letter of Sir Henry Ashurst in British Colonial Papers. Perhaps, as the demand was not yet pressed, the Court was not averse to the agent's using this compliant language, as long as he did it on his own responsibility alone.

Thus early the dispute was announcing itself, which continued with intermissions for nearly half a century, and which was at last decided in favor of the Province by the parent government's desisting from its pretension. From the time of the conception of the arrangement for Lord Bellomont to go to America, before the institution of the Board of Trade, the project of a stated provision for the colonial Governors was in the contemplation of the British Ministry. The Lords Justices, during an absence of the King upon the continent, resolved "that the Governors in America should . . . . . not be left to depend solely on benevolence of assemblies for their support," while they did "not think that the charge should be laid on revenue in England; it might be an ill precedent."[1] Immediately on his appointment, he represented to the Lords of Trade the fitness "that a salary suitable to the dignity of those governments might be proposed for him to the King."[2] After two years' experience of his American governments, he wrote to the Lords that his "appointments were so very narrow that he could not live on them;" that he was the "pensioner" of the General Court of Massachusetts "just as long as they pleased."[3]

1695. July 16.

1697. April 15.

1700. July 15.

[1] British Colonial Papers. — Lord Bellomont's instructions were "the usual instructions given to Governors of Massachusetts, with the addition of the usual clause for restraining the Governor for accepting money given by the Assembly without the King's leave." (Journal of the Board of Trade for Oct. 1, 1695.) Accordingly this leave was expressly given in his case. (Provincial Laws and Resolves, I. 766, 777.)

[2] British Colonial Papers. Comp. Journal of the Board of Trade for July 4, 1695. — Writing to Popple, Secretary of the Board, April 14, 1697, Lord Bellomont specifies £1200 as a proper salary for Massachusetts to pay, and says, as to the style he should live in, that "it will be expected he should make somewhat a better figure than Sir Edmund Andros did." (Ibid.; comp. a Representation of the Lords of Trade to the King, in O'Callaghan, IV. 263.)

[3] British Colonial Papers.—Yet he found his government of Massachusetts the most comfortable of the three. Stoughton and Addington were "very assistant" to him, and he "would rather govern four such provinces as the Massachusetts Bay than New York."

The Board agreed with him that he was not made as independent of the Court as was desirable, and remarked on the contumacy of "the only Province depending immediately on the King which had not settled an allowance on the Governor," while it was "able the better to do that, and build a house for the Governor, because they were not in debt."[1]

One consideration known to have had weight in the selection of Lord Bellomont for the chief administration in America related to the piracies believed to have been committed by vessels equipped in or resorting to the ports of that country.[2] Already, before his lordship's arrival, Stoughton had instituted inquiries respecting these crimes. A ship of three or four hundred tons, called the "Adventure," came in suspicious circumstances into Narragansett Bay. Taking alarm at some circumstances of their reception, the crew landed and dispersed into the country. The captain, named Bradish, and ten others, were arrested in Massachusetts.[3] From them it was learned that the vessel, then mounting twenty-two guns, had a year before sailed from Gravesend for Borneo, on a trading voyage for some London merchants; and that, after they had been six months at sea, part of the company, twenty-five or twenty-six in number, conspired to seize the ship, left the master with the rest of the crew and passengers on an island, and chose the boatswain's mate to be their captain. After a division of the plunder, which yielded to each more than fifteen hundred dollars in money, besides a share in other valuable property, they sought a place

Quest for pirates in the northern Colonies.

1698. March 16.

[1] Journal of the Board of Trade for April 11, 1700; comp. Ibid. for June 12, 22.

[2] See *e.g.* the letter of the Lords of Trade, of March 21, 1698, to Lord Bellomont, in O'Callaghan, IV. 299; comp. his letters to the Lords of Trade, Ibid., 304, 307, 309.

[3] Bradish escaped, with the connivance, as was believed, of the gaoler (O'Callaghan, IV. 585), but was briskly hunted for and retaken. (Letter of Lord Bellomont of Oct. 24, 1699, in British Colonial Papers.) Feb. 16, 1700, he was sent to England with Kidd. (Sewall's Diary.)

where they might land and disperse without observation.

1699. March 19. At the end of a year from their going to sea, the rovers had made a port at the east end of Long Island, where they deposited some of their booty, while they should make further observations. Proceeding thence to Block Island, they took the alarm which occasioned their dispersion and flight.[1]

In respect to another criminal, the activity of Lord Bellomont was stimulated by a personal interest. William Kidd was the pirate whom he was especially desirous to get into his hands. Four or five years before, the Governor had become interested in an enterprise for clearing the eastern seas of piratical cruisers which were preying there on European commerce. In London he had formed an acquaintance with Colonel Robert Livingston, of New York, and took "occasion to mention to this gentleman the scandal which lay upon New York in respect to the encouragement and retreat which pirates found there." At a subsequent interview, Livingston "said he had spoke with one Captain William Kidd, lately come from New York in a sloop of his own upon the account of trade,[2] who told him that he knew most of the principal men who had been abroad roving, and divers who had lately gone out, and likewise had some knowledge of the places where they usually made their rendezvous, and that he would undertake to seize most of them, in case he might be employed in one of the King's ships, a good sailer of about thirty guns, and might have a hundred and fifty men. . . . . . Livingston affirmed that Kidd was a bold and honest man. . . . . . The King was

The pirate William Kidd.

[1] Stoughton's letter of April 12, 1699, to Vernon, Secretary of State. (Hutch. Hist., II. 116, note.)

[2] Kidd was known and well reputed in Massachusetts earlier than this time. June 8, 1691, within the year after Phips's disaster before Quebec, he and another shipmaster received commissions from Bradstreet and his Council, "for going forth on their Majesties' service, to suppress an enemy privateer now upon this coast." (Mass. Hist. Col., XXI. 122.)

made acquainted with the proposal by the Earl of Bellomont, which he was pleased to think very necessary to be immediately considered, because about that time divers informations upon oath had been sent to the Secretary of State of several vessels gone and a-going from Bermuda, New York, Rhode Island, etc., upon piratical designs. . . . . . His Majesty was pleased to consult the Admiralty on this occasion; but the war employing all the King's ships which were in a condition for service, and the great want of seamen, notwithstanding the press and all other means used, together with the remoteness of the voyage, and the uncertainty of meeting with the pirates, or taking them though they might be found out," occasioned after some deliberation the laying aside of this project as impracticable at that time.[1]

Lord Bellomont then proposed the fitting out of a privateer, which he insisted would prove a profitable speculation. This enterprise he succeeded in carrying into effect.[2] Several of the first men of the kingdom, the Earl of Oxford (first Lord of the Admiralty), Somers (Lord Chancellor), the Duke of Shrewsbury, the Earl of Romney, took shares, and the King was to have a tenth part of the profits 1696.
of the cruise. Kidd obtained a commission under April.
the Great Seal for his ship, and went to sea from Plymouth with a small crew. He crossed to New York,
whence, having there, with Governor Fletcher's September.
help, increased his company to the number of a 1697.
hundred and fifty men, he sailed for the eastern February.
seas.[3]

[1] "A Full Account of the Proceedings in relation to Captain Kidd, in two letters written by a Person of Quality," pp. 3, 4. — Livingston "affirmed to the Earl that Kidd was a settled inhabitant at New York, lived regularly, had a competent estate of his own, and had married at New York a wife with a considerable fortune, by whom he had a child." (Ibid.) He was a Scotsman by birth. (O'Callaghan, IV. 583.)

[2] The Articles of Agreement by Bellomont and Livingston with Kidd (Oct. 10, 1695) are in O'Callaghan, IV. 762 *et seq.*; comp. 815.

[3] Livingston afterwards told Lord

But either Kidd had been a rogue from the beginning, or the new temptations which he encountered were too much for his little virtue. The times of Drake and Hawkins were not distant, and the morals of the seas were far from being settled. Madagascar and Borneo were a great way from the country where English evil-doers might be called to account, and there were richer prizes along their coasts than the paltry vessels of their native thieves. Kidd was not long in seeing that his good ship would be less gainfully employed in hunting pirates than in piracy. At first he was timid, if he had ceased to be scrupulous, and he contented himself with taking the ships of Asiatics, whose sovereigns would not be likely to bring their complaints to the ear of his. But use lessens marvel. Presently he became the terror of the Indian commerce of the Portuguese. As he grew reckless, he grew savage. He landed with his brutes for expeditions of burning and massacre. He scourged his prisoners to make them reveal the hiding-places of their rupees. When the news of his doings came slowly to London, the merchants were con-

Bellomont that this successful enlistment was owing to a criminal arrangement between Kidd and Governor Fletcher of New York. "Kidd obliged himself to give Fletcher £10,000 if he made a voyage. . . . . . Colonel Fletcher suffered and countenanced Kidd's beating for volunteers in this town, and taking with him about a hundred able sailors." Fletcher was formally arraigned (Jan. 31, 1699) before the Board for his criminal practices with the pirates. (Extract from Luttrell's Diary in "Historical Magazine" for 1868, 292.) Lord Bellomont's agency in promoting Kidd was a subject to him of sore mortification and uneasiness. "I never saw him," he says [that is, in London], "above thrice. Mr. Livingston came with him every time to my house in Dover Street." (O'Callaghan, IV. 759, 760; comp. 815.) "If I have served the King and interest of England here, I am sure I have been strangely rewarded there." (Ibid., 725.) Nobody, however, was hostile to Lord Bellomont. It was Somers and his friends that he had to suffer for.

I am surprised at the inaccuracy of some of Lord Macaulay's statements respecting Lord Bellomont's connection with Kidd (History of England, V. 246 *et seq.*), when such good authorities were accessible to him as the reports of Kidd's trials (State Trials, XIV. 123 *et seq.*) and the "Account of the Proceedings," &c., above-quoted. This work, a warm vindication and panegyric of Lord Bellomont, breathes the vehement spirit of the time.

cerned for what had been done, and distressed by fear lest their turn should come next. The members of the East India Company were aghast in view of the retaliation to which such freedoms on an Englishman's part might expose their feeble factories.[1] The Lords of Trade sent orders to those in authority in the foreign possessions of England to keep a look-out for the ravager. Lord Bellomont's past agency in Kidd's promotion imposed on him a special responsibility. The matter had assumed a high political importance. The jealous mood of England, at the time when Parliament had refused the King's request to retain his Dutch guards, and was meditating an impeachment of Lord Somers, fastened upon Kidd's crimes as a means of bringing odium on the Whig leaders. In the House of Commons a resolve was proposed, and defeated by a majority of less than fifty votes, that the affixing by Somers of the Great Seal to Kidd's letters-patent was "dishonorable to the King, against the law of nations, contrary to the statutes of the realm, an invasion of property, and destructive of trade and commerce."[2] Even the King's august name was brought rudely into the question, as if he had been a stockholder in a pirate ship.

[1] The East India Company complained of Kidd to the Lords of Trade as early as the summer of 1698. (Journals of the Board of Trade for August 22 and September 15.) They produced as witnesses two men who had deserted from his service.

[2] Hansard, Parliamentary History, V. 1202. — "The Parliament . . . . . called some great persons in the highest offices in question for setting the great seal to the patent of an arch-pirate, who had turned pirate again, and brought pirates into the West Indies, suspected to be connived at on sharing the prey. But the prevailing part in the House, called courtiers, outvoted the complaints, not by being more in numbers, but by the counter party being negligent in attendance." (Evelyn, Memoirs, III. 376, for Dec. 3, 1699; comp. Rapin, History, &c., III. 396; Shrewsbury Correspondence, 599, 600.) — "I have been much troubled to find my name brought on the stage in the House of Commons about Kidd. 'Twas hard, I thought, I should be pushed at so vehemently, when it was known I had taken Kidd, and secured him in order to his punishment, which was a sure sign the noble Lords concerned with me, and myself, had no criminal design in sending out that ship." (Bellomont to the Lords of Trade, Oct. 17, 1700, in O'Callaghan, IV. 725.) Lord Bellomont was named in the preamble to the proposed Act.

With marvellous rashness, since he must have assured himself that there had been no talebearer, Kidd came back with some of his spoils to an English colony. He 1699. May. appeared in Delaware Bay with about forty comrades, and having taken in some supplies proceeded to Rhode Island,[1] whence he sent a messenger[2] to Lord Bellomont, who had then just arrived in Boston, to say that "he was come thither to make his terms in a sloop, which had on board goods to the value of ten thousand pounds, and was able to make his innocence appear by many witnesses." The Governor feared that the culprit might yet escape. With the advice of his Council, he sent a message to Kidd that, "if he would make his innocence appear, he might safely come to Boston." Thither, accordingly, Kidd came in his sloop. After an unsatisfac- June 1. tory examination before the Governor and Council, June 6. he was "committed close prisoner with divers of his crew." The Governor transmitted his minutes of the July 8. examination to the Lords of Trade,[3] and asked that a ship of war might be sent to convey the rover to

[1] Full Account, &c., 9. — "June 19, 1699. Last Thursday Captain Kidd came into Rhode Island harbor." (News-letter in Proceedings of Mass. Hist. Soc. for 1863, 422.)

[2] The messenger was one Emott, whom the Governor describes to the Lords of Trade (Letter of July 8, 1699, in British Colonial Papers; comp. letter of September 12, of the Lords of Trade to the Lords Justices, in O'Callaghan, IV. 583) as "a cunning Jacobite, a fast friend of Fletcher's, and my avowed enemy." (Comp. his letters to the Board, of July 26, August 28, in British Colonial Papers.)

[3] Kidd sent a present of some jewels to the Countess of Bellomont. The Governor informed his Council, who advised that they should be accepted, lest Kidd should be alarmed into reserve, while the examination was proceeding. He had further thrown out a hint of a present of a thousand pounds "in gold dust and ingots." (O'Callaghan, IV. 583, 584.) On the arrest of Kidd, the jewels were handed over to trustees. — "Captain Kidd sent the gaoler to me a fortnight ago to acquaint me that, if I would let him go to the place where he left the ship "Quedah Merchant," and to St. Thomas Island and Curaçoa, he would undertake to bring off fifty or three-score thousand pounds, which would otherwise be lost; that he would be satisfied to go a prisoner, to remove from me any jealousy of his designing to escape; but I sent him word he was the King's prisoner, and I could hearken to no such proposition, but I bade the gaoler to try if he could prevail with

England for trial, there being no provincial law for punishing piracy with death.[1] He was tried at the Old Bailey for murder and for piracy, found guilty under both indictments, and executed.[2] 1701. May 8.

In the latter part of the time of Lord Bellomont's short stay in Massachusetts,[3] the Indians divided his attention

Captain Kidd to discover where his treasure was hid by him, but he said nobody could find it but himself, and would not tell any further." (Letter of Lord Bellomont to the Lords of Trade, of June 5, 1699, in British Colonial Papers; comp. Full Account, &c., 11.)

1 Kidd continued to be a *bête noire* for more than a century. A broadside was still in circulation in my childhood, which purported to record his "Last Dying Words and Confession": —

"My name was Captain Kidd, as I sailed, as I sailed,
My name was Captain Kidd, as I sailed;
My sinful footsteps slid, — God's laws they did forbid,
But so wickedly I did, as I sailed."

2 The murder was that of one of his sailors, whom, provoked by rude language, he had struck with a mortal blow.

"I murdered William Moore, and left him in his gore,
Not many leagues from shore, as I sailed."

The piracies specified in the indictments were the capture and robbery of a ship named the "Quedah Merchant," owned by Armenians, commanded by an Englishman, and navigated by a Moorish crew; of three Moorish vessels, one of them having also an English and another a Dutch captain; and of a ship of Portugal. It appeared on the trial that, after the capture of the "Quedah Merchant," Kidd had transferred himself to her with part of his crew. On his return voyage, he had left her with some twenty of his men in the West Indies, and there had bought the sloop in which he came to New England.

The surgeon of the ship and a seaman became King's evidence. Kidd's defence was, as to some of his captures, that they were within his commission, the vessels being furnished with French passes; as to others, that he was not responsible for them, his men having mutinied and coerced him.

3 One of the last objects of Lord Bellomont's attention before he left Massachusetts was the condition of the French Huguenots, who, thirteen years before, in the time of Governor Andros, had been established in the town of Oxford. (See above, Vol. III. 546, note 4.) In 1695, three years before Lord Bellomont's arrival, the settlement was broken up by the Indians (see above, 153), and the fugitives came to Boston, where they established a church, which continued for several years, till domestic alliances formed with other inhabitants of the town drew off its supporters. There are numerous descendants of theirs in Boston and its vicinity, but mostly through females of the stock. Only a few names are continued, as Sigourney, Cazneau, and Johonnot. Others were distinguished within a recent time, as Bowdoin, Faneuil, and Chardon. There was a Boudinot at Oxford, but Philadelphia was the birthplace of Elias Boudinot, the New Jersey philanthropist. Gabriel Bernon was the principal man of the Huguenots who came from Oxford to Boston. Dec. 18, 1696, he was in London,

with the pirates. The recent peace with the Eastern tribes had inspired confidence, and the English who had fled from Maine were returning to reinstate their ravaged dwellings, when a report was spread that those tribes had made another conspiracy so extensive as to include even the Iroquois, and the remnants of the nations in the more compact English settlements.[1]

Agitation among the Indians.

1700. Jan. 29. The Governor of Connecticut wrote to Lord Bellomont that he had information to this effect on such authority as to justify vigilance.[2] At the same time, a rumor got into circulation among the Indians that the whites had resolved upon their extirpation, and were all but ready to strike the blow; and this apprehension of theirs lent probability to the story that they were preparing for new disorders. The Governor, believing the danger to be real, issued his proclamation, enjoining upon the people to abstain on the one hand from all offensive or questionable conduct, and on the other to observe their savage neighbors, and take precautions for defending themselves, in case of any outbreak.[3] He even proceeded to convene the General Court, which took prompt

March 13. measures of precaution. Laws were passed for raising and equipping troops, for punishing mutiny and desertion among them, and for marching them out of the

when he represented to the Lords of Trade that he had "spent seven years and large sums of money in bringing all sorts of naval stores to perfection," and "offered his services for supplying the King with these commodities." (British Colonial Papers.) He lived to be eighty years old. (Hist. Col., XXII. 29–33, 49–54, 59–70.) — In Lord Bellomont's speech to the General Court, May 30, 1700, he advises them to make a provision for the Huguenot clergyman, his congregation being reduced in numbers. "Let the present raging persecution of the French Protestants in France," he says, "stir up your zeal and compassion towards him." The people, he says, are ingenious and industrious, and deserving of encouragement. They were naturalized in April, 1731. (Provincial Laws, II. 586, 595.)

[1] See O'Callaghan, IV. 606–620; comp. Journal of the Board of Trade for April 19, 1700. — The Colonial Papers contain indications of renewals of the alarm from January to the autumn. Comp. N. H. Provincial Papers, III. 324 *et seq.*, 346.

[2] O'Callaghan, IV. 612–616.

[3] Letter of Bellomont to the Board of Trade. (O'Callaghan, IV. 636.)

Province at the Governor's discretion; and small garrisons were posted at three or four places in the western part of Maine. But either there had in fact been no danger, or these proceedings averted it. The natives remained quiet, and the alarm passed away, having continued through nearly all the year.[1]

The Governor gave various particulars of what he had observed of the condition of his Provinces, in a letter written to the Lords of Trade after his return to New York.[2] "'Tis demonstrable these plantations are capable of employing a thousand good ships of burden and twenty thousand seamen, more than are at present employed by England. . . . . By due encouragement to the two following articles of naval stores and cultivating vineyards, ... the proposed improvement and increase of shipping and seamen will be accomplished. Under the head of naval stores, I suppose tar, pitch, rosin, turpentine, oil of turpentine, ship timber of all sorts, as planks and compass timber, masts, bowsprits, and yards." "The staple in the Massachusetts Province," he said, "is the fishery. . . . . They compute at Boston that they ship off fifty thousand

1700. Nov. 28.

Statistics of Massachusetts.

[1] Hutchinson (Hist., II. 120) thought that the report which alarmed the New England Indians was a device of the Iroquois, who got presents as often as the English had occasion for a treaty with them.

[2] "Last April I examined the registers of all the vessels in the three Provinces of my government, and found there then belonged to the town of Boston 25 ships from 100 tons to 300; ships about 100 tons and under, 38; brigantines, 50; ketches, 13; sloops, 67: in all, 194 vessels. To other towns in that Province there belonged then about 70 vessels of all sorts, whereof 11 were ships of good burden. To New York there then belonged 6 ships above, and 8 under, 100 tons; 2 ketches; 27 brigantines, and 81 sloops. To New Hampshire at that time 11 ships of good burden, 5 brigantines, 4 ketches, and 4 sloops. I believe one may venture to say there are more good vessels belonging to the town of Boston than to all Scotland and Ireland, unless one should reckon the small craft, such as herring-boats. . . . . Some merchants at Boston, with whom I discoursed sometimes about the trade of that Province, ... computed that Boston had four times the trade of New York." (Lord Bellomont to the Lords of Trade, in O'Callaghan, IV. 787, 790, 791.)

quintals of dry fish every year, about three-quarters whereof is sent to Bilboa." There were sixty-three wharves in Boston, and fourteen in Charlestown. He had good hopes as to projects for "making salt and pot-ashes," and there seemed to him to be a fair prospect as to the production of silk and wines. But he had heard murmurs against the legal restrictions on commerce. "Some gentlemen of the Council . . . . . were very warm, and expressed great discontent at the Acts of Trade and Navigation that restrained them from an open free trade to all parts of the world. They alleged they were as much Englishmen as those in England, and thought they had a right to all the privileges that the people of England had; that the London merchants had procured those restraining laws to be made, on purpose to make the people of the plantations to go to market to them."[1]

In Massachusetts, and at the capital especially, what remained of the primitive religious strictness could not fail to be relaxed by the extension of commercial activity, as well as by the influence of that provision of King William's charter which detached the political franchise from church membership. The only place of worship of the English establishment had had a hard struggle for life against the passionate dislike of the people; its supporters had been dispersed, and its minister had gone home discouraged, at the time of the recent revolution; and it recovered with difficulty from the disrepute contracted by its connection with the usurpation of Andros. Lord Bellomont, the first Governor, except Andros, attached to its communion, attempted to revive it in Boston. He brought from England a present from the Bishop of London of a collection of books for the Boston church, and an assistant for Mr. Myles, the rector, who had succeeded to the place of Randolph's

The English church in Massachusetts.

[1] O'Callaghan, IV. 781 *et seq.*

friend, Ratcliffe.[1] The assistant, dying in the West Indies on the voyage, was followed by another, Mr. Bridge, who held the place some eight or nine years. The Governor, while in Boston, worshipped at King's Chapel on Sundays; but he did something by way of amends by a regular attendance at the weekly Thursday lecture of the First Church. He wrote to the Lords of Trade that some persons in New England desired "a Church-of-England minister," and expressed his hope that they would "patronize so good a design." In the temper of England, at that moment especially, the patronage of the Board for that good design did not need to be solicited, and they interested themselves with the Bishop of London to obtain for the colonists the advantage of ecclesiastical supervision.[2]

1699. Oct. 24.

A passage much more important than these in the religious history of the time related to an abatement of the ancient rigor of Congregational administration. A fourth Congregational church was established in Boston upon principles highly distasteful to the friends of the old order of the churches. Most, if not all, of the *undertakers*, as the associates in this enterprise were called, were persons of substance and of social

New phase of Congregational politics in Boston.

[1] Ratcliffe, the clergyman imported by Randolph (see above, III. 494), went back to England in three or four months after the Revolution. About the same time Mr. Samuel Myles came over and took his place. Myles went to England after a few years, and bespoke the favor of the sovereigns for his church; and William, after the Queen's death, made it a present of some furniture, and of some plate for the communion table. (Greenwood, History of King's Chapel, 50-67.)

[2] Journals of the Board of Trade for Feb. 2, 1700. — A notable publication of this year was that of a tract by Judge Sewall, entitled "The Selling of Joseph." It was an argument against slavery, with a refutation of reasonings in its favor, the same as have been current in our own day. It seems to have produced fruit, for in the following year (May 26, 1701) Boston instructed its Representatives in the General Court "to promote the encouraging of the bringing in of white servants, and to put a period to negroes being slaves." (Mass. Hist. Col., XVIII. 184.) — Thomas Danforth died Nov. 5 of this year, having lived to be seventy-six years old. He had long disappeared from public life.

consideration, though none were high in office. In their form of worship they proposed no deviation from the existing practice, except in respect to the reading of the Scriptures without comment, which — probably on account of its being prescribed in the English rubric — had hitherto not been practised in the churches of New England. But the great changes which, to the extreme displeasure of the leaders of religious opinion, they introduced into their own use, were such as struck at the foundation of the dignity of church-membership. Hitherto the usage was for a candidate for admission to the privileges of communion to give an account in public of his personal religious experiences; the terms of admission to baptism, though they had been modified, were still strict;[1] and the church (the body of communicants) invited and contracted with a minister, whom the body of worshippers was then compelled to support according to the terms which the church had made.[2] The projectors of the "Church in Brattle Square," in a "manifesto or declaration" which the clamor around induced them to publish, professed that they "dared not refuse baptism to any child offered by any professed Christian, upon his engagement to see it educated, if God gave life and ability, in the Christian religion. But this being a ministerial act," they thought it "the pastor's province to receive such professions and engagements. . . . . . We judge it fitting and expedient," they continue, "that whoever would be admitted to par-

1699. Nov. 17.

[1] See above, Vol. II. 491.

[2] Acts and Resolves, 102, 216. These Acts were passed to define and settle the respective rights of church and congregation. The claim of the churches to the right of appointing ministers had not been asserted, or, at least, not been submitted to, with absolute uniformity. As early as 1672 the church and congregation at Salem acted together in the choice of their pastor. In 1685, a minister was elected at Dedham, "the inhabitants voting together without distinction of communicants and non-communicants." In 1697, the church in Charlestown followed the same method. (Lamson, History of the First Church in Dedham, 40, 90; comp. Robbins, History of the Second Church, 41.) But such deviations had scarcely broken the continuity of the usage.

ke with us in the Holy Sacrament be accountable to the astor, to whom it belongs to inquire into their knowledge ad spiritual state, and to require the renewal of their aptismal covenant. But we assume not to ourselves to apose upon any a public relation of their experiences. . . . . Finally, we cannot confine the right of choosing minister to the communicants alone; but we think that very baptized adult person, who contributes to the maintenance, should have a vote in electing." At the same me they declare that they "approve and subscribe the onfession of Faith put forth by the Assembly of Divines Westminster;" that they "design only the true and ure worship of God, according to the rules plainly apearing to them in his word;" and that it is their "sinere desire and intention to hold communion with the aurches here, as true churches."[1]

[1] See Lothrop, History of the aurch in Brattle Street, Boston, -26. — The "Manifesto" was inted on a broadside, of which e present pastor has the only copy hich is known to be extant. It ave rise to a brisk controversy. In e following January, President ather attacked it in his "Epistle edicatory" to a pamphlet entitled The Order of the Gospel, professed ad practised by the Churches of hrist in New England, justified by e Scripture and by the Writings many Learned Men, both Anent and Modern Divines." He as answered in "Gospel Order evived, by Sundry Ministers of the ospel in New England," the authors which were understood to be the oung ministers John Woodbridge, Hartford, Simon Bradstreet, and enjamin Colman. This tract has o advertisement of the printer's ame or place of residence. It is refaced with a notice that "the ress in Boston is so much under the we of the reverend author whom we answer and his friends, that we could not obtain of the printer there to print the following sheets." The printer here referred to was Bartholomew Green, a man much respected, and then, or afterwards, a deacon of the Old South Church. He published his vindication in a handbill, dated Dec. 21, 1700, in which he affirms that when the work was brought to him he agreed to print it, until he was told that it must be done with secrecy, and then he declined, unless he should be allowed first to consult the Lieutenant-Governor (Stoughton), which condition was rejected. To this statement are appended a few vituperative periods, without an author's name, but charged upon Cotton Mather. (Thomas, History of Printing, II. 458–467.)

The following year appeared "A Collection of some of the many Offensive Matters contained in a Pamphlet entitled The Order of the Gospel Revived," attributed to Cotton Mather, with a preface of severe invective signed by his father. This

This movement — or rather, it may be said, the state and tendency of public opinion of which it was a symptom — increased the alarm already felt by the friends of the ancient order of things for the safety of the College, and urged them to measures for keeping it under their control. On the return of Increase Mather from England with the provincial charter, he had

Affairs of Harvard College.

tract, the declared purpose of which is to point out "some of the scandalous violations of the third, fifth, and ninth commandments" in the preceding work, is a specimen of the least tolerable style of controversy. The vocabulary, so long consecrated to assaults upon reformers, of "gross immorality," "impudence," "deep apostasy," "open impiety," "profaneness," and, finally, "tendency to atheism," is most liberally used. It appears from several allusions that the authors supposed Colman to be the principal writer of "Gospel Order Revived," though they do not name him. He had been a member of their church, and is accordingly rebuked for "vilifying his superiors, unto whom he owes a special reverence." The President calls him a "little thing," "a raw and unstudied youth, but also of a very unsanctified temper and spirit." He also speaks of "one that is of the same spirit with him, viz., T. B., who likewise in print scornfully styles his President a reverend scribbler. A moral heathen would not have done as he has done." These initials can denote no other than Thomas Brattle, who showed this disrespect to *his* President, being at that time Treasurer of the College.

In a sermon printed in 1702, called "Ichabod; or, A Discourse showing what cause there is to fear that the Glory of the Lord is departing from New England," the President recurs to the subject, though incidentally, and more covertly. "Some scandalous practices," he says, "which not only the Waldenses, but the reformed churches in France and in Holland have, in their discipline, declared to be censurable evils, are now indulged in some churches in New England;" which hint is explained when he comes to speak of "ministers, not like their predecessors, not principled, not spirited as they were," who "have in print mocked and scoffed at holy practices, which have been the glory of these churches of the Lord;" who "despise that glory which their fathers had such a value for," and "will part with truth and holiness, and yet at the same time, by new notions and practices, make divisions."

In their "Testimony to the Order of the Gospel in the Churches of New England, left in the Hands of the Churches by the two most aged Ministers of the Gospel yet surviving in the Country," Higginson and Hubbard allude to this controversy in terms expressive of a lively concern. The former had also, in 1699, written, jointly with Mr. Noyes, the other Salem minister, a letter of admonition and reproof to the *Undertakers*, which is preserved in Vol. Ha. XIX. of the Historical Society's manuscripts. It is severe, without being unkind or disrespectful; and while, in point of argument, it does not compare favorably with the writings of the Mathers, has greatly the advantage of them in its temper. Some of the points in this dispute are touched in "famous" Solomon Stoddard's "Doctrine of Instituted Churches," published in London, in

resumed his former position as President. The old charter of the institution was understood to have expired with that of the Colony by which it had been conferred.[1] It was at President Mather's instance that the Provincial General Court at its first session passed an Act incorporating the College anew, with an organization materially changed. Under the ancient system, the Corporation of that society consisted of a President, Treasurer, and five Fellows, who governed the institution under the supervision of a *Board of Overseers*, composed of the Governor, Deputy-Governor, and Assistants of the Colony, with the Congregational ministers of Boston and of the six adjoining towns. The present Act created a Corporation, consisting of ten persons, who were to exercise their trust without responsibility, no provision being made for any body of visitors.[2] The new Corporation organized itself, and discharged its functions for three years, at the end of which time came a notification that the King had disapproved the Act, on account of the absence from it of a provision for a Board of Visitors.[3] The institution was still dead in law. Governor Stoughton took the responsibility of making a provisional arrangement by reinstating the administration which had existed under the old charter. The General Court made a new

1692. June 27.

1695. Aug. 22.

Oct. 12.

1700. "A Soft Answer" to this work was furnished by President Mather. Stoddard rejoined, in his "Appeal to the Learned," in 1709.

[1] It was a year after the dissolution of the colonial charter of Massachusetts (see above, Vol. III. 556, note) that Increase Mather was elected "to take special care for the government of the College, and for that end to act as President until a further settlement be orderly made." His parochial charge in Boston was, however, not relinquished; and he continued to live there, discharging his function as President of the College only by occasional visits. When he went to England during Andros's government (Ibid., 555), he left it under the care of the Tutors, John Leverett and Thomas Brattle. (Quincy, History of Harvard University, I. 88.) Before he came to the Presidency, the College had educated two hundred and thirty-five young men.

[2] Increase and Cotton Mather, Samuel Willard, and the two Tutors, Leverett and Brattle, were five of the ten.

[3] Provincial Acts and Resolves, I. 39; comp. Oldmixon, British Empire in America, I. 212.

attempt. Under the influence perhaps of such as desired to make the most of the time when a zealous friend of the old ecclesiastical order was at the head of the Province, and when he might be superseded at any moment by a Governor differently disposed, they passed an Act[1] creating
1697. a corporation of sixteen (afterwards changed to
Jan. 4. seventeen) persons, including a Vice-President, — a new office, which the Reverend Mr. Morton was designated to fill. The official term of a Fellow was to expire at the end of ten years, and the Governor and his Council were to be Visitors. President Mather and his son (also a member of the new Corporation) were not pleased with this last arrangement, conceiving, as they did, that the power of the conservative school of clergy was not therein sufficiently secured.

After this Act had been adopted by the Council, the opposition of the President and his friends prevented its being sent down to the Representatives until it had received some modifications,[2] one of which allowed the President to have his residence out of Cambridge. In this shape it received the signature of Lieutenant-Governor Stoughton; but while the question was agitated of sending an agent to England to solicit the royal approbation, — a commission of which President Mather was earnestly ambitious, — Lord Bellomont, who had arrived in New York, discouraged that movement as offering no prospect of success. Accordingly the Act remained without the royal assent
1699. when the Governor came to Boston. He intro-
May 30. duced the subject in his first message to the General Court, recommending an application to the King for a charter. The King's scruple had been the provision for the exercise of the visitatorial function, which, unshared

[1] Provincial Acts and Resolves, I. 288.

[2] Jan. 6, 1697, the two Mathers, James Allen, and Samuel Willard gave written notice that, if the charter, as then projected, went into effect, they positively would not serve. (Quincy, Hist., &c., I. 489.)

with the Council, he chose to exercise himself through his Governor. The General Court yielded this point. By a new Act they gave the power of visitation "to his Majesty and his Governor and commander-in-chief July 13.
for the time being of this Province;" but they provided that five Fellows of the Corporation should always be persons elected from the Council. The influence of the President and his friends had also prevailed to introduce the novel provision "that no person shall be chosen and continued President, Vice-President, or Fellow of said Corporation, but such as shall declare and continue their adherence unto the principles of reformation which were espoused and intended by those who first settled this country and founded the College, and have hitherto been the profession and practice of the generality of the churches of Christ in New England." The Governor objected to this exclusion of members of the English establishment from the academical government. He arrested the Act, and "advised to address his Majesty for a royal charter of incorporation."[1] The suggestion having led to nothing, — for the General Court were reluctant to allow the necessity of committing every thing to the royal pleasure, — the Governor renewed it the next year. The Council 1700.
passed a vote to carry it into effect, but the Repre- June 11.
sentatives still preferred to frame a charter for the July 12.
King's consideration. At last the two branches agreed upon a "Draught of a Charter of Incorporation for Harvard College, ... to be humbly solicited for to his Majesty." The care of it was intrusted to Lord Bellomont, with a request for him to use his interest in England for its adoption, which one of his letters shows that he was entirely disposed to do.[2] But he did not live to bring July 15.

[1] He "would not be guilty," he wrote to the Lords of Trade, August 28 (British Colonial Papers), "of the absurdity of sending an Act for the royal approbation which he had twice refused before."

[2] "The settlement of it [the College] seems to involve the ardent de-

the matter to the notice of the King.[1] He died in New York before the end of the year after his return thither; happy, perhaps, to escape the unjust reception which was awaiting him in England,[2] on account of his connection with Lord Somers.

Death of Lord Bellomont. 1701. March 5.

Perhaps he died of sheer disappointment and mortification,[3] for he knew how he was maligned in England; and the King's ministers, who should have been his vindicators, had given him recently no sort of attention. A week before his departure from Boston, he wrote thence "in the anguish of his soul:" "There came hither two ships from London,[4] the last week in May, which brought me not a letter from any of the ministers, and another ship four days ago, but not a letter by that neither. What must the people here and in New York think, but that either the King and his ministers have no sort of care or value for these plantations, not minding whether they

1700. July 9.

sires and affections of these people beyond all other things in this world; for, as they have an extraordinary zeal and fondness for their religion, so any thing that disturbs them in that touches them in their tenderest part." (British Colonial Papers.)

[1] November 19, the Board of Trade considered a letter from Sir Henry Ashurst, "together with the draft of a charter, desired by that government of the Massachusetts Bay, for Harvard College, in New England." (Journal of the Board of Trade.) But no action on the subject is recorded.

[2] Randolph, who was hostile to Lord Bellomont, and who had come to Bermuda, was, as usual, making mischief. The Governor of that island had occasion to seize his papers, and among them found copies of letters to the Board of Trade, in which he wrote "very villanously and in a very scurrilous manner against Lord Bellomont," ascribing to him "no less than the character of a rogue." (Letter of Blake to Nanfan, of November 6, 1699, in British Colonial Papers.)

[3] One of his annoyances was his being straitened as to means of living. "I must be so free with your Lordship as to tell you that, unless care be taken to provide an honorable maintenance for me, and certain, I must go to Boston next spring to make sure of their annual present of £1600 their money. I were to blame if, because I am neglected at home, I should neglect myself here." (Letter to the Lords of Trade, of Nov. 28, 1700, in O'Callaghan, IV. 784.)

[4] Letter to Secretary Vernon, of July 9, in British Colonial Papers. — Nov. 22, 1700, Sir Charles Hodges succeeded Vernon as Secretary of State. May 26 of this year, Bellomont's friend, the Duke of Shrewsbury, had gone out of office, and been succeeded by the Earl of Jersey.

fall into French hands or no; or else that I am in disgrace with the King, and that all this neglect proceeds from a personal slight to me. I never in all my life was so vexed and ashamed as now; I put the best face I can on it, but I find other people take the liberty to judge of the present conduct of affairs in England."

After he went to New York, and still more completely after his death there in the next year, the local administration again devolved on Stoughton, as Lieutenant-Governor. Stoughton survived his superior by not many months. A token of popular approbation, of a kind to which he had not been used, came to cheer his last solitary days. The House — perhaps in a sudden access of good-will for an old servant often visited with the popular rebuke, perhaps from a really grateful sense of his recent commendable services, perhaps from no kinder motive than was supplied by an apprehension of having Dudley for their ruler — resolved to send a petition to the King, for the appointment of Stoughton to that office. But the Council refused to concur in the measure. Stoughton's health was failing. He presided at the opening of the next General Court; but, while its business was yet unfinished, was forced to prorogue it for a month, "being incapable, by reason of sickness, of further affording his presence in the Assembly, or of admitting of their going to him." Before the month was out, he died in Dorchester, where he had passed his joyless life, having been born there in the second year after the great immigration.

1701. April 18.

June 30.

Death of Stoughton. July 7.

1632. May.

He had filled many offices, and performed their duties with a surly assiduity, which commanded a certain sort of esteem. He perhaps loved nobody, though the winning as well as commanding powers of Dudley may have blended something of affection with the deference into which he was subdued by the genius of that highly endowed man.

On the other hand, if he was not loved, Stoughton was not of a temper to be made uncomfortable by isolation, while it was a pleasure to him to feel that he had some command of that confidence which men repose in such as they see to be indifferent to their good-will, and independent of it as coveting nothing which it has to bestow. When his constituents were angry at the result of his mission to England, he did not distress himself for their displeasure, but waited patiently for it to subside; and when they solicited him to go a second time on the same errand, he told them, with no warmth and no reflection on the past, that they could not have his services. While, like every landholder in Massachusetts, he was frightened at the excesses of Andros, he had little enthusiasm for the rising by which Andros was expelled. The prosecution of the witches was a proceeding quite to his mind; the "stern joy" of inflicting great misery under the coercion of an unflinching sense of duty was strangely congenial with his proud and narrow nature; he had a morbid relish for that class of duties which, bringing wretchedness on others, may be supposed to cost the doer a struggle against the pleadings of pity. When, sympathizing with the almost universal sorrow and remorse that succeeded the witchcraft madness, his gentle associate Sewall publicly bemoaned his sin, and in agony implored the Divine forgiveness, Stoughton professed that, whatever mistakes might have been made, he saw "no reason to repent of what he had done with the fear of God before his eyes." While, on the one hand, his habitual unconcern about popular favor generally gave him the command of as much of it as he cared for, he was helped, on the other, by the friendship of the clergy, which he took as much pains to secure as he ever thought it worth while to bestow for any amiable purpose. If the people did not want him, he could be content; at all events, he would not complain or solicit. If they did want him, he would serve them without fraud and without ambition, but it must be after his own grim fashion, — a fashion to be dictated, as the occasions arose, not only by his judgment and sense of duty, but by his prejudices and his temper. He meant to be excellently firm; he excelled in being churlish, morose, and obstinate, in a style of the most unimpeachable dignity.

The Board of Trade had not been satisfied with the recent conduct of Massachusetts. They had not been able to prevail upon that Province to undertake the expense of rebuilding the fort at Pemaquid, notwithstanding their having pressed it with urgent repetition. The General Court, resenting the renewed activity in enforcing the Acts of Navigation,[1] which they regarded as unjust and heavily oppressive, had refused to pass laws desired in England for the more rigorous execution of those Acts.[2] The Board were informed by an official person,[3] writing from New York, that he feared "the government at Boston might represent him as a warm man for publicly exposing the argument of one of their clergy, who maintained that they were not in conscience bound to obey the laws of England, having no

Displeasure of the Board of Trade.

1701. Dec. 29.

[1] It was at this time, too, that the excessive jealousy of colonial manufactures referred to above (IV. 20) was manifested.

[2] Chalmers, MS. Letter to Lord Mansfield, 86. — April 11, 1700, in anticipation of the business of the approaching session, the Board advised the Governor to consider "whether it would not be proper to reject those Counsellors who opposed passing a law [to make piracy a capital offence], and were averse to the laws of England." They "desired him to dispose the Assembly to build forts, especially at Pemaquid, because the Province of Maine was annexed to Massachusetts for maintaining that fort, which would secure the coast and the fishery." They commended him for his course in the "contest with the Council about the nomination of officers, and refusing to pass a bill about Harvard College." It was, they wrote (April 19), "strange that Massachusetts should pay so little regard to their own safety, with relation to the Eastern Indians," as to neglect the building of the fort; "they must be pressed to it; their obstinacy might oblige Parliament to provide some remedy." (British Colonial Papers.)

[3] Letter of William Atwood, in O'Callaghan, IV. 930. He was a Judge of Admiralty. (N. H. Rec., II. 359.)

representatives there of their choosing."[1] The Board wrote to Lord Bellomont: "The denial of appeals is a humor which prevails so much in proprietary and charter plantations, and the independency they thirst after is now so notorious, that it has been thought fit those considerations and other objections should be laid before the Parliament."[2]

April.

In fact this had been done, and the three New England charters were in serious danger.[3] The Lords of Trade had represented to the King that the chartered Colonies "had not only assumed the power of making by-laws repugnant to the laws of England and destructive to trade, but they refused to transmit their Acts, or to allow appeals, and continued to be the retreat of pirates and illegal traders, and the receptacle of contraband merchandise;" that "these irregularities, arising from the ill use they made of their charters, and the independency they pretended to, evinced how necessary it became, more and more every day, to introduce such a regulation of trade, and such an administration of government, as should make them duly subservient to England;" and that, "since the royal commands had not met with due obedience, it might be expedient to resume their charters, and to reduce them to the same dependency as other Colonies, which would be best effected by the legislative power of the kingdom." A bill was accordingly submitted to the House of Lords, pretending to annul the charters, and to invest the King with the same power in the chartered governments as in New Hampshire and the others which possessed no such security.[4] A similar measure

Threatenings against the charters.

March 1.

[1] 1701, Jan. 4, Charles, Earl of Manchester, was made Secretary of State, *vice* Lord Jersey.

[2] O'Callaghan, IV. 854.

[3] Chalmers, Revolt, II. 302, 307; Hutch., II. 130.

[4] "A bill has been brought into the House of Lords for resuming the right of government in those Colonies to the crown. (Letter of April 29, 1701, of the Lords of Trade to Lord Bellomont, in Mass. Archives, XX.

was urged upon the Commons. What would have followed, had it now come to a vote, can be only conjectured; but the exciting question of the impeachment of the King's friends was pending in Parliament, and the movement could not obtain attention. The King's death, and the new interests thereby presented, postponed the revival of it; but it was only two months before that event that the Board laid before him their opinion that "the national interest required that such independent administrations should be placed, by the legislative power of the kingdom, in the same state of dependency as the royal governments."[1]

1702. March 18.

After the death of the Governor and the Lieutenant-Governor, the Council, by a provision of the charter, became the chief executive authority of Massachusetts.[2] There now appeared a prospect that Joseph Dudley's ambition to govern there might be gratified. He had been industrious in endeavoring to remove those discouraging obstacles to his promotion which have been mentioned. New York was no sphere for him; and the satisfaction which he had had in bringing Leisler to the gallows, for proceedings bearing some resemblance to those of the Massachusetts patriots against himself and his friends, was more than balanced by the apprehensions which followed it when the party of Leisler revived. After a few months passed in New York as Chief Justice,[3] he returned to England, and there employed his rare powers of address to recommend himself on the one hand to men in power,

Intrigues of Joseph Dudley in England.

1692. September.

44; XL. 689.) October 18, the Board received from the General Court a remonstrance against the measure. (British Colonial Papers.)

[1] Chalmers, Revolt, II. 307; Journals of the Board of Trade for January 8.

[2] The Council Records show Winthrop to have been the presiding officer of that body, though he was not the oldest member.

[3] Dudley was made Chief Justice of New York, May 15, 1691. (Brodhead, New York, 646.) He was displaced by Governor Fletcher, in September, 1692. (Fletcher to Blathwait, in O'Callaghan, III. 848.)

and on the other to conciliate the dissenting ministers who might make peace for him in Massachusetts. Disappointed by the persistent opposition of Constantine Phipps and Ashurst, the agents, in his hope, first of displacing Sir William Phips, and then of succeeding him at his death, he became Lieutenant-Governor of the Isle of Wight, under Lord Cutts, whose valuable friendship he had secured. In Parliament, where at length he obtained a seat, his superior capacity, indefatigable diligence,
1701. and engaging manners, obtained for him no small consideration, and his obsequious officiousness in promoting the measures for the subversion of the colonial charters, alike with his local knowledge and experience, marked him for the kind of instrument now required by the British government.

Lord Bellomont's death revived his hopes. If his pride was enormous, still, unless when his violent passions were roused, he had a will strong enough to bridle his pride, if it threatened to obstruct his ambition. The Mathers had shared and stimulated the hot resentment which had driven him from power in Massachusetts. But the father was at the head of the clergy of the Province, and the son was the most active of men, whether as partisan or as foe. Their weaknesses were familiarly known to Dudley, and he managed with patient assiduity to bring them over to his side. The two agents in England understood him, and continued to loathe him in their hearts. But he showed to them at least no anger for their triumph over him in the appointment of Lord Bellomont, and by the time when the vacancy again occurred Ashurst had withdrawn from the agency,[1] and the Jacobite Phipps, who may have indulged in the hope of making Dudley his tool, professed

[1] May 20, 1701, the Lords of Trade wrote to Stoughton to present the case of John Champante, "a diligent and prudent person, who has acted as agent for the Massachusetts Bay since Sir Henry Ashurst ceased to act." He was "an entire stranger" to them, and had only a sort of appointment from the Lords. (British Colonial Papers.)

to have been brought to think that, among the untried candidates for the succession, the colonists might do worse than by favoring their able compatriot, upon whom, it might be hoped, so much hard experience would not prove to have been thrown away.[1] If no trust could be placed in his virtue, his selfishness might be confidently counted on, and in future it might prompt to better services. An active member of Parliament was not without opportunities to oblige, or at least to compliment and to encourage, the dissenting ministers, whose cause, throughout William's reign, was in a condition at once critical and hopeful. The judgment of the dissenting ministers of England was of the greatest weight with their brethren in Massachusetts, and Dudley at length got it in favor of his coveted advancement. He voted for Onslow, put forward by the court for the place of Speaker of the Commons, though he was under what are called obligations of gratitude to Harley, the opposing candidate. The King, knowing how he was hated in Massachusetts, was unwilling to appoint him. But Dudley produced a petition in his favor, purporting to be from Massachusetts men then in London, and from merchants trading with that Province. Finally he placed in the King's hands a letter from Cotton Mather, authorizing him to affirm that "there was not one minister nor one of the Assembly but were impatient for his coming," — a strong statement, which might be wondered at if it came from some other source.[2]

[1] April 17, 1702, Constantine Phipps, writing to Addington, says that Dudley, "in the opinion of all understanding men here, as well as with you, is the only person under whose administration you would be as easy as you are now like to be." (Mass. Archives, LI. 139.) "It was a very great satisfaction to me that I had an opportunity of giving him some small assistance." (Ibid.) Sir Henry, however, did not weary of his opposition to the persistent candidate. As late as November 13 of the same year, "Colonel Dudley acquainted the Board that, whilst his commission for the Governor of New England was passing the seals, Sir Henry Ashurst had presented a memorial against him to the Lords Justices." (Journals of the Board of Trade; comp. Hutch., II. 123.)

[2] Perhaps Cotton Mather did not know that the *ci-devant* Congregational preacher had turned Episcopalian.

The House of Representatives had resolved on sending a special agent to England. The ostensible object was to obtain a charter for the College, and to represent the uneasiness felt in Massachusetts on account of the French claim to the eastern country and the fisheries on the eastern coast. But there is no doubt that the immediately urgent motive was to obstruct the elevation of Dudley. Elisha Cooke, the opponent of President Mather in respect to the new charter, was now the most powerful man in the General Court. The President, who in England had been flattered with much attention in high circles, was extremely desirous to be employed in this agency.[1] Cooke's old grudge, or permanent distrust, or persuasion that the President was already Dudley's partisan, determined that the President should not be gratified. While Mather was urging and Cooke was counteracting, Dudley had convenient time for his operations in England. Wait Winthrop was at length appointed to be agent, but, just as this was done, news came of Dudley's appointment to be Governor. The vote which had been passed for instructions to Winthrop was then reconsidered, and the project of sending him was dismissed. The needs of the College and the apprehensions from the French were no longer thought so serious as to require immediate attention.

Frustrated plan of Increase Mather.

The King's sudden death before Dudley was prepared to leave England made it necessary for him to receive a new commission. But there was now no competition for the post, and the commission was issued on the second day of the new monarch's reign. Dudley was fifty-seven years old when, convoyed by two armed vessels,[2] he came back to the place associated in his memory with events of such various interest.

1702. March 10.

June 11.

[1] Scarcely is there more amusing reading than the extracts from the Diaries of the Mathers, relating to this subject, in Quincy's History of Harvard University, I. 475–484.

[2] Privy Council for Feb. 15, 1702.

CHAPTER VII.

The relation which had subsisted between Massachusetts and New Hampshire after their political separation was inconvenient and vexatious to both parties. The four feeble settlements which collectively were known by the latter name lay close to and between some of the towns of Massachusetts, but, forming another body politic, were beyond her protection or control when they were in danger or in disorder. When a band of Indian marauders was passing between the towns of Massachusetts on the Merrimac and her towns in Maine, she had to chase them through the territory of a different government; and her vessels going into the river Piscataqua were subject to be visited by the custom-house officers of a foreign jurisdiction. For New Hampshire this separation was still more disadvantageous. To her the connection with Massachusetts had been uniformly and unexceptionally beneficial. The sister Colony had afforded an effective defence, and its government had been honest and generous. There had been parties and cabals among the New Hampshire people; but, as often as there had been occasion for their deliberate sense to be expressed, it had always proved to be in favor of incorporation into the chief Colony of New England.

New Hampshire an independent government. 1679.

Two influences had all along more or less obstructed this arrangement, and both were in action at the time when King William gave to Massachusetts her second charter. From the earliest period of the importance of that Colony, the English statesmen, not excepting those of the Commonwealth, had been jealous of her growth. Occasionally it was unavoidable for them to allow weight to considerations which had another bearing. When they wanted the border towards New France to be watched, when they wanted garrisons in Nova Scotia and a fortress at Pemaquid, they had to choose between charging this expense upon the royal treasury, or devolving it upon Massachusetts by including within her territory the country which needed to be secured; and proceedings dictated by this calculation sometimes appeared to indicate sentiments more favorable to her than in truth were entertained. In general, whoever was in power in England, — whether it was Clarendon or Vane, Danby or Somers, — there was a disposition to disable and humble Massachusetts, as the representative and mainspring of a power which might grow in its pretensions as long as it should be suffered to mature in strength.

The influence of the first John Mason and of his successors and representatives was another obstacle. His claim, and that of his heirs and assigns, to lands on the Piscataqua, founded on alleged grants of the Council for New England, though always resisted by Massachusetts, had been regarded with some favor by the English courtiers and lawyers. It had been decided that Mason had a valid claim to more or less territory on that river, but it was not admitted that he, like Gorges, had received authority to govern the country which had been granted.[1] Mason's rights, whatever they were, had been inherited by his grandson, Robert Tufton, who took the name of Mason, and who died while one of the Counsellors of Andros.[2]

Claim of John Mason.

The expulsion of Andros deprived New Hampshire of a government. Fierce inroads of the Indians followed while the Colony was in this chaotic state,[3] and some of the principal men summoned a convention of delegates from the towns, to consult respecting the measures required by the necessity of the time.

Incorporation into Massachusetts. 1690. January.

[1] See above, Vol. III. 281, 307.

[2] Ibid., 534.

[3] See above, Vol. IV. 32–35, 47, 48.

At a second meeting the convention resolved to apply to Massachusetts to be received again into her jurisdiction. The request was complied with; and members for the New Hampshire towns sat in the General Court of Massachusetts, and civil and military officers, displaced under the recent order of things, were recalled to service.[1] Feb. 20.

Meanwhile the claim of Robert Mason had passed, by his death, into other hands. Two sons, who inherited his property, sold their interest in New Hampshire for seven hundred and fifty pounds, to Samuel Allen, a London merchant. A daughter of Allen was the wife of John Usher, who may be supposed to have advised the purchase.[2] It was he who, some years before, had bought Maine of Gorges for Massachusetts.[3] From his father, Hezekiah Usher, a man of moderate consequence in the colonial times, he had inherited some fortune, which he had increased by successful business, first as a bookseller and afterwards in foreign trade. He had been a Counsellor under the presidency of Dudley, and Counsellor and Treasurer under Andros, and since the Revolution he had been urgently pressing upon Massachusetts a settlement of his account as Treasurer, which, made up as it had been, the Colony refused to allow, notwithstanding repeated interpositions of the Privy Council. 1688. September. 1691. April 27.

Allen bought Mason's rights, whatever they might prove to be, in New Hampshire, while Mather and his colleagues were soliciting the charter of Massachusetts, and were urging the expediency of Government of Samuel Allen.

1 "The Humble Address of the Inhabitants and Train-Soldiers of the Province of New Hampshire," subscribed with 374 names, is in the Provincial Papers of New Hampshire, II. 34–39. The Governor and Council of Massachusetts promptly accepted the proposal of the sister Province (February 28), and their action was confirmed by the General Court (March 18) as soon as it came together. (Mass. Col. Rec., *sub die.*)

2 Usher had gone to England before July 23, 1689. (Letter of Randolph, of that date, to the Lord Privy Seal, in British Colonial Papers.)

3 See above, Vol. III. 312.

including New Hampshire within that jurisdiction. When their prayer was denied, and it was determined to set up New Hampshire again as a royal Province, Allen naturally aspired to be the Governor. He was accordingly appointed to that office,[1] with Usher for his Lieutenant, to administer the government in his absence; a trust which Usher presently assumed on the spot. The Chief Magistrate was to be assisted by fifteen Counsellors, of which number nine persons, residents of the towns, were nominated in the original commission; the Governor was to propose the others after obtaining further information. Usher understood that the people continued to be disinclined to acquiesce in the settlement which had been made, and were "presenting their petition to their Majesties that they may be joined to the Massachusetts government." But rather than this should be done, he advised the Lords of Trade that it would "be for their Majesties' interest and security of the people" to place the whole of New England under one general Governor. "Otherwise," he added, "I hope their Majesties will dismiss me from this little government, who by their poverty are not able honorably to support itself."[2]

1692. Feb. 21.

Aug. 13.

Oct. 29.

[1] N. H. Provincial Papers, II. 57; Privy Council Register, *sub die;* Journal of Board of Trade, for Jan. 11.

[2] Usher to the Lords of Trade, in British Colonial Papers. He repeated his recommendation of a consolidation of the New England Colonies under one government, in two letters of the 31st of the following January. (Ibid.) "I find the people are against kingly government, whatever else they pretend to. . . . . . If joined to the Massachusetts, then they are in hopes, when a favorable opportunity presents, the kingly government may be thrown off." Nor had he any thing more favorable to report of the loyalty of Massachusetts. "I see not," he wrote to the Lords (Feb. 28, 1693), "one person, excepting Mr. Stoughton, but endeavour what they can (as they judge) to act for the country and not for the King, and do what in them lies to hinder all matters relating to the same. Have only to add any of their proceedings on (*sic*) the Revolution time ['unhappy Revolution' is his phrase in another part of the letter] is encouraged, but any thing from the King it's against their minds to comply with." — He had "been round the Province [New Hampshire] and taken a strict muster of all the men, which from twenty to sixty are but 754 in number." There was no fort in the Province,

Their poverty was undeniable, but it was far from being their only distress. The reader wonders at the courage and hopefulness which, in those times of savage war, nerved the borderers of New Hampshire to bear their miserable life, while he perceives a reason of their earnest desire for that union with Massachusetts which would place them in a better position to look to her for relief. Their insecurity made their poverty all the more grievous. Their living was to be got from the fields, the rivers, and the forests. But they could not go out to cut timber, or to plough, or mow, or fish, with any confidence that they were not to be fired upon from the nearest thicket, or that their families would not be butchered before they came back.[1] There was almost no money, and every sort of commodity for food, clothing, or enjoyment was scarce and dear. Provisions were sometimes wanting even for soldiers in the field. The case was made harder when the unhappy people had to reflect that the homes they were defending at such cost and peril were not securely theirs. Throughout their short history their ancestors had been vexed by the claims and suits of a succession of English absentees, and now the last of the Masons had turned them over to another stranger, who, with fresh energy, was about to renew the annoying usurpation.

Poverty of New Hampshire.

Usher had a twofold office to fulfil in the interest of his master and father-in-law; he had to defend the domain on the one hand against the arms of savage invaders, and on the other hand against the claims of Englishmen who esteemed themselves proprietors, but whom, if the word had been then invented, he would have called *squatters*. In his discharge

Administration of Lieutenant-Governor Usher.

"except that at the mouth of the harbor. . . . . . Houses palisaded round to secure the indwellers." He had made amicable overtures to Phips, but "could, after tedious waiting, get no other answer but neglect, slights, and reproaches."

[1] Lord Bellomont's letter to the Lords of Trade, of April 20, 1700, in British Colonial Papers.

of the latter function, he had of course nothing but resentment and resistance to expect from the people whom he had been sent to rule.[1] As to the former, the interests of the two parties were the same, so that as often as there was apprehension of an Indian inroad, they had a good understanding together, and were able to act in harmony. Usher, though impetuous and quarrelsome, and soured by the recent issue of his connection with Andros, was not wanting in capacity or vigor, and the scanty resources which he possessed were used with activity for the defence of his Province, if not always with good judgment.

A wiser man, in his circumstances, would have cultivated a good understanding with the persons in power in Massachusetts. But while vigorous military movements should have been in progress, the administration of Usher was embarrassed by the dispute which he nursed with Phips, who on his part was not indisposed to make the most of it; his hatred of Andros, which was so strong as to vent itself in violent threats when he returned to Boston just after the Revolution, having a natural tendency to extend itself to Andros's adherents.[2]

Beginning with a collision as to their respective powers, the open feud between the Governor and Usher was aggravated by accidental causes. The merchant-ship in which Phips had provided a passage for Captain Short to England put into Portsmouth, in New Hampshire, the master's design being, as Phips understood, "to take in deserters from the 'Nonsuch,'" who had found their way to that Prov-

[1] Newcastle, the fifth town, was chartered in the first year of the Province, May 30, 1693. (N. H. Provincial Papers, II. 107.)

[2] Phips and Usher, alike in their frankness and impetuosity, however little their mutual resemblance in other qualities, had come into their governments all ready for a quarrel, as belonging respectively to the parties differently disposed towards Andros. As early as on his voyage from England in the spring of 1689, Sir William had "breathed out threatenings and slaughter" without stint against the despotic Governor. (O'Callaghan, III. 583, 587, 588; comp. Brodhead, History of New York, II. 555, note.)

ince. Phips came thither by land, and applied to Hinckes, President of the Council, and in Usher's temporary absence the head of the government, for a warrant to seize Short "as their Majesties' prisoner fled from justice;" but, with the approbation of the Council, it was refused. Phips summoned Hinckes to arrest Short on board the merchant-ship, which the latter declined to do. The Governor, with an armed party, went to the vessel, and demanded the surrender of Short, who, the master said, "was on shore and out of his power to deliver." Phips then took from the ship-master the warrant he had given him in Boston for the transportation of Short to England, and tearing from it his signature and seal, substituted another for the surrender of that officer to the purser of the "Nonsuch," who had come to New Hampshire to apprehend him and the deserters. Phips ended, if Short told the truth, by breaking open his chest, and seizing his papers. The ship-master, with vehement complaints, applied to the Council for advice and protection. But the Council, willing to be rid of the matter, advised him to find "his remedy at law," and concluded, as to Phips, that it might "be inconvenient to call him to account by this Board."[1]

His quarrel with Phips.

1693. March 28.

Phips's commission made him General and Admiral of the King's land and sea forces in the north-eastern Provinces. In this capacity he undertook to inspect the fort at Portsmouth, but Usher refused him admission to it, and when, notwithstanding this, he attempted an entrance, he was met by a corporal's guard which turned him back.

[1] Memorial (March 30, 1693) of Jeremiah Tay, commander of ship "Walter and Thomas," to the Council of the Province of New Hampshire; Letter (April 6) of Phips to the Lords of the Admiralty; and Letter (April 20) of Short to the Secretary of the Admiralty, in British Colonial Papers. — It is very hazardous to dissent from Dr. Belknap; but in details his narrative of these transactions (Hist. of New Hampshire, 136, 137) does not accord with the contemporaneous documents, which I follow. (Comp. N. H. Provincial Papers, II. 91, 99–102.)

He demanded assistance in vain to search for the deserters from the frigate. Finally, in resentment of the disrespect which had been shown him, Phips ordered back April. into Massachusetts a force which he had detached for the defence of the feebler Province.[1] In the last sum- 1694. mer of his administration, after that devastation July 18-30. at Dover which has been mentioned in connexion with the renewal of the Indian war,[2] there was a sharp correspondence between him and Usher, introduced by requisitions from the latter for military assistance.[3] With Stoughton, who had much disapproved Phips's conduct on this occasion, Usher transacted business more agreeably, after the Governor's retirement. In the last year but one 1695. of the war, the Lieutenant-Governor of Massachu- June. setts, at Usher's solicitation, sent a reinforcement of troops "for the security of the frontiers;" and the appli- 1696. cation was repeated in the following summer, when June 26. a party of Indians, landing from canoes, had murdered fourteen persons near Portsmouth.[4]

Except for the military operations, and for his strifes with the Governor of Massachusetts, Usher's administration was uneventful. He passed much of his time in Boston, attending to his private affairs,[5] though he liked to magnify his office by coming to New Hampshire and summoning meetings of the Council, with slight pretences of business to be done. When he asked the Assembly for money,[6] he was told too truly that the people were

1 N. H. Provincial Papers, II. 104, 105, note.

2 See above, Vol. IV. 151. — The havoc at Dover was frightful. (N. H. Provincial Papers, II. 125-130.)

3 Letters to and from Phips and Usher, in British Colonial Papers.

4 N. H. Provincial Papers, II. 158, 169, 189, 190, III. 37; comp. Mather, Magnalia, VII. 89.

5 "The Lieutenant-Governor declared to the Board that the reason for his not staying here was that the Province had not made provision for support of the honor of the King's government." (N. H. Provincial Papers, II. 115.)

6 "Having been two years with you, and not one penny received for support of the honor of the government, but instead thereof the Province, by their Representatives, have

poor;[1] and when he applied for troops, he was answered that the Province was overtasked, and could not hold its ground without the help of Massachusetts; which was not only very near the truth, but what they wished to have represented at court, that it might weigh in favor of that annexation which they never ceased to desire.[2] The government was parsimoniously supported by a duty on imported goods, and an excise on wine and spirits, levied from year to year by the Assembly. The Lieutenant-Governor moved them urgently to do something better. They replied that their means seemed exhausted in providing for their defence, but that, if possible, they would oblige him, "provided he and the Council would join with them in petitioning the King to annex the Province to Massachusetts." They made him no allowance. Allen had guarantied to him a salary of two hundred and fifty pounds a year, which, on Usher's application at the end of three years, he refused to pay. Usher then asked to be relieved, either by the Governor in person, or by the appointment of some successor in his own place. Without his knowledge, he had been anticipated in this request. An application, favored by the Governor,[3] had been made for the appointment of William Partridge, Treasurer of the Province, to be Lieutenant-Governor. Partridge, a ship-builder, who had large connexions

1695. Nov. 9.

Lieutenant-Governor Partridge.

put an affront upon the King's commission, as in that of fourteenth Luke, 28, 29, 30 verses. Have spent of cash out of my own estate about £300." (Letter of Usher to the Council, Aug. 11, 1694, in British Colonial Papers.) — "It being now about four years since I arrived with his Majesty's royal commission, and at the charge of the Province have not had a house provided to lie in, nor one meal's meat, nor one drop of drink." (Speech of Lieutenant-Governor Usher, Sept. 24, 1696, in N. H. Provincial Papers, III. 46.)

[1] Ibid., II. 120; III. 35.

[2] N. H. Provincial Papers, III. 47. — Feb. 16, 1697, Shadrach Walton, of New Hampshire, told the credulous Lords that "there were fifty thousand fighting men in the Massachusetts government," while there were "but between seven hundred and eight hundred in New Hampshire. The extent of New Hampshire," he said, "is about fifteen or sixteen miles square." (British Colonial Papers.)

[3] Privy Council Register for June 8, 1696.

in England with the dealers in masts and timber, went
1697. out to further the movement, and to Usher's
January surprise returned with a commission to succeed
1696. him, obtained six months before from the Lords
June 6. Justices, — the King being at that time on the continent. The newly-constituted Board of Trade had been influenced by Sir Henry Ashurst in favor of the appointment.

By this time Usher had changed his mind as to the attractiveness of his office. At all events, an involuntary retirement was distasteful to him. In consequence of having come out without his instructions, or from failure in some other preliminary, Partridge was not ready to take his official oath.[1] The Council and Assembly, however, held a meeting, and proceeded to some acts which Usher, writing of them from Boston to England, described as the
1697. "Piscataqua Rebellion."[2] The Lords of Trade
Aug. 3. instructed him to retain his place, till Partridge should take the oaths, or Lord Bellomont, who was to be Governor of New Hampshire, as well as of Massachusetts, should arrive in America.[3] Accordingly he went
Dec. 13. to Portsmouth, where he proclaimed the peace of Ryswick. But his resumed sway was short-lived. The next day his successor assumed the government,[4]
Dec. 14. and Usher went back, a private man, to his Boston counting-room.[5] The Assembly presently sent to the Lords
1698. of Trade their thanks to the King for the new
Feb. 3. appointment, and their assurance, as to Usher,

[1] N. H. Provincial Papers, I. 209.

[2] Ibid., III. 77, 78; British Colonial Papers, under the dates of Sept. 30, Oct. 8, 1696, Feb. 16, Feb. 18, June 8, 1697, and Dec. 9, 1701.

[3] N. H. Provincial Papers, II. 216, 217.

[4] Ibid., 259, 261.

[5] Dec. 31, 1692, a Committee of the Council of Massachusetts, with Stoughton at its head, reported that Usher's account, as Treasurer, extending from May 25, 1686, to July 6, 1690, charged the Province with over £5000, of which sum only £851 was rightly his due, the rest having been paid by him without authority to Sir Edmund Andros. (British Colonial Papers.)

that "there had been no disturbance but only what Mr. Usher had endeavored to give."[1]

While Lord Bellomont remained in New York,[2] his commission for New Hampshire not being yet published, Allen came over, and assumed the chief magistracy of New Hampshire. Usher also appeared there, and claimed to be admitted to a seat in the Council. This led to a dispute, which was terminated for the present by the Governor's dissolving the Assembly.[3] Every thing remained in suspense till Lord Bellomont, having inaugurated his government in Massachusetts, came to Portsmouth, where he confirmed Partridge in the place of Lieutenant-Governor, and made other arrangements which so recommended him to the people,[4]

Sept. 15.

Nov. 29.

1699. Jan. 7.

July 31. Lord Bellomont in New Hampshire.

[1] N. H. Provincial Papers, II. 267. — Usher's want of personal dignity provoked gross affronts. The Lieutenant-Governor acquainted the Board that "Richard Torlington, constable of New Castle, had offered a great contempt to himself in impressing his saddle, when he had noticed that it was the Lieutenant-Governor's." (Provincial Papers, II. 134; see 199 for another anecdote, not *transcribable*.) — His invariable style of speaking and writing had a ludicrous peculiarity, consisting partly in the omission of connecting words. The following is a specimen of his characteristic manner: "Acts of Parliament ought not to be laws for plantations, unless had representatives in Parliament, if may write plainly, are not for kingly but for commonwealth government, which pray *libera nos*." (Usher to Lords of Trade, Dec. 12, 1700, in British Colonial Papers; comp. N. H. Prov. Papers, II. 595, 675; III. 332, 598.)

[2] Oct. 17, 1697, the Council of New Hampshire sent a messenger to New York to wait on the Governor. "Take good advice," he was instructed, "how you demean yourself. If you find my Lord high and reserved, not easy of access, you must manage your business by some of the gentlemen about him. . . . . . The principal end in sending you on this message is to pay our respects and duty to his Lordship, and to prevent Mr. Usher or any other malcontent prepossessing him with any ill thing against us." (N. H. Provincial Papers, II. 264.) — For the Earl's commission for New Hampshire, see Ibid., 305.

[3] Ibid., 280-293.—The disappointed Governor was disturbed by the "irregular proceedings and growing insolence of the Lieutenant-Governor, W. Partridge, and three or four more of the Council," and thought that they should be sent for to England "to reward them according to their merits." (Letter of Allen, of Nov. 28, 1698, to the Lords of Trade, in British Colonial Papers; comp. letter of same to same, of Jan. 14, 1689.)

[4] Lord Bellomont wrote to the

that, in token of their good will, the Assembly gave him five hundred pounds.[1] He returned from New Hampshire to Boston after two or three weeks, leaving Partridge at the head of the administration, his own commission having superseded that of Allen. By letter he advised the Province to provide materials for a fort in Portsmouth Harbor, at a cost estimated at more than six thousand pounds, by an engineer whom he employed.[2] The Assembly replied that they had never, when the exigency was greatest, been able to raise more than a thousand pounds in a year, and that they were now especially disabled by reason of their debt incurred in defending themselves against the Indians, and of the insecurity of their property, occasioned by the claim of Allen; and they went on to complain that, after spending more money in the defence of the border than their estates were now worth, they should be called upon, as they had been, to send men to protect the frontier of New York, — a Colony in which, they said, their savage enemies found a refuge, and a market for their spoils.[3] They professed, however, their disposition to do any thing which he should esteem it reasonable to demand, when he should have acquainted himself with their poverty.[4]

1700. June 6.

The Lords of Trade looked to New Hampshire as a source of supply of naval stores for the use of the royal navy, and instructed the new Governor accordingly, who

Lords of Trade (September 9), expressing his satisfaction with his reception in New Hampshire, and giving an account of the factions which had there arisen. (British Colonial Papers.)

[1] The bilious Usher wrote to the Lords of Trade (September 21), "For a sin-offering they presented my Lord with £500, judging by it their crimes may be obliterated." (British Colonial Papers.)

[2] N. H. Provincial Papers, III. 96.

[3] Of a force of 1350 troops which the home government had ordered to be held in readiness against the Five Nations, the contingent of New Hampshire was 40 men. Massachusetts was to send 350, and Virginia 240. New York, which was to be protected, was to furnish but 200. (Farmer's Belknap, 157.)

[4] N. H. Provincial Papers, 101-103, 106-110.

entered into the scheme with his characteristic zeal. But he found himself "obstructed by some cross accidents,"[1] among which were the mismanagement of two agents of the Admiralty, the pending Indian war, and the "distractions" occasioned by Allen's proceedings in "turning people out of their properties without process of law." He refused to enter into the controversy with Allen respecting the proprietorship of the soil, referring it to the judicial courts which were instituted in conformity with his advice.[2] What he had seen of Allen had affected him with profound disgust. That adventurer had attempted to bribe him to "favor his cause." First he offered him, in general terms, "a handsome recompense." Then he proposed to "divide the Province" with him, and to match his daughter with a younger son of the Earl, endowing her with "ten thousand pounds in money. . . . . . But I told him," wrote Bellomont, "that I would not sell justice, if I might have all the world." Allen accompanied the Earl part of the way on his departure from New Hampshire to repeat the offer, and came to Boston to press it yet again "with more earnestness than ever," representing that the lands claimed by him were "worth twenty-two thousand pounds per annum at threepence per acre quit-rent."[3] Bellomont wrote to the Lords of Trade that "Usher, indulging his choleric temper," had refused to take his place in

His disgust with Allen.

Aug. 1.

Aug. 8.

Aug. 17.

1700. February.

June 11.

June 22.

[1] Letters of Bellomont to the Lords of Trade, of May 25 and Dec. 14, 1698, in N. H. Provincial Papers, II. 344, 345; comp. letter of the same to the same, of Jan. 22, 1700, Ibid., 348; comp. III. 116, 120; O'Callaghan, IV. 668.

[2] N. H. Provincial Papers, II. 316.

[3] Memorandum of Lord Bellomont, dated June 19, 1700, in British Colonial Papers. Three days after, he wrote letters to the same effect to the Lords of Trade (O'Callaghan, IV. 673), and to Secretary Vernon (British Colonial Papers). "I hope among you," he says, in this last letter, "Mr. Blathwayt will be cross-bit by this bargain of his with Allen. The seizing Colonel Allen's papers would discover this villanous bargain." "Colonel Allen's pretension to New Hampshire, and all other claims derived from Mason, are an abomination and mystery of iniquity."

the Council, and that Blathwayt,[1] formerly Secretary to
1699. Sept. 9. the Board, was corruptly concerned with Allen. Nor was he much better satisfied with Partridge, after some experience of that functionary. "I take it,"
1700. April 23. he wrote to the Lords of Trade, "to be the chiefest part of the trust and business of a Lieutenant-Governor of this Province to preserve the woods for the King's use, and that it was no more fit to commit that duty to a millwright than to set a wolf to keep sheep;"
April 22. and he refused to permit Partridge to load a ship with timber for Lisbon, and rebuked him for making the request.[2]

When Allen brought his business into the newly constituted courts, he expected to find a record of judgments obtained by Mason in Governor Cranfield's time.[3]
1700. Allen's unsuccessful litigation. But it was sought for in vain, while several leaves relating to the period appeared to have been abstracted from the books. Allen's case was thus at a disadvantage. He could get no verdict in his favor, and was mulcted in costs. He claimed the right of
Aug. 18. 1701. April. an appeal to England, but the court refused to allow it. The Assembly then passed laws, with
Sept. 13. Partridge's concurrence, confirming the titles which Allen had impeached, and directing surveys to determine the boundaries of the lands which had

[1] The attack upon the Secretary was a hazardous measure. The Earl's independence of character, together with his high rank, emboldened him to use great freedom in his correspondence with the home authorities.

[2] Letters of Lord Bellomont to the Lords of Trade, of May 25 and June 22, 1700, and Jan. 2, 1701, in N. H. Provincial Papers, II. 347, 354, 357. — "I remember I rebuked Sir Henry Ashurst in the privy garden at Whitehall for promoting Mr. Partridge to be made Lieutenant-Governor of New Hampshire, who is a carpenter by trade, and a sad, weak man. I told him his genius had a strong bias to carpenter-Governors, for it was he, with Mr. Mather, that got Sir William Phips made Governor of New England." — In defiance, or in evasion rather, of strict prohibitions of the Lords of Trade, there was an active transportation of ship timber from New Hampshire to Portugal. (O'Callaghan, IV. 794, 798.)

[3] See above, Vol. III. 413, 418; comp. Farmer's edition of Belknap, 157, note.

been in litigation. Allen petitioned the King in Council, who authorized an appeal, to be prosecuted within eight months.[1] The previous refusal of it by the New Hampshire courts occasioned great displeasure on the part of the Lords of Trade, who expressed their feeling with emphasis in letters to Lord Bellomont.[2] He died before they came to his hand. Allen sent Usher, and the Province sent William Vaughan, a Counsellor and a popular favorite, to represent them respectively in England.[3]

1702. May.

Connecticut after the Revolution.

Accordant as were the sentiments of the people of Massachusetts with those which in England brought about the Revolution, the proceeding of that Colony in the deposition of Andros was so irregular and bold that it could not have failed to raise serious questions in the minds of the prerogative-loving King William and his cautious ministers. And however wrongfully her charter had five years earlier been abrogated, it had been condemned with all legal formalities. In both these respects, as the reader knows, the position of Connecticut and Rhode Island was different. When their Governor and his Counsellors had been imprisoned in Boston, it was indispensable, if they would not have anarchy, that some other authority should be set up, and the most natural and most unexceptionable course was that which they adopted when they reinstated their charter governments. They could maintain that they had but submitted to duress when Andros threatened them; and if Connecticut had done this with reluctance and reserve, and Rhode Island with alacrity, the legal condition of the two Provinces was nevertheless the same. Accordingly, when the sentiments of one and the interests of both prompted them to seek a

1 Privy Council Register for Nov. 20, and Dec. 18, 1701.

2 N. H. Provincial Papers, II 341.

3 Ibid., III. 158.

good understanding with the new sovereign, and obtain his sanction for the restoration of their ancient governments, both found a favorable hearing.

1689. June 13. The Address in which Connecticut congratulated the King and Queen on their accession solicited a confirmation of her charter,[1] and four years later 1693. Sept. 1. Fitz-John Winthrop was sent to England to renew the suit.[2] The confirmation was never formally given, but the Colony had in England a serviceable friend in Increase Mather, as long as he remained there, and they felt safe in proceeding when he had obtained authoritative judgments in favor of their pretension. The law officers of the crown 1690. Aug. 2. gave their opinion "that the charter not being surrendered under the common seal, and that surrender duly enrolled of record, nor any judgment of record entered against it, the same remained good and valid in law."[3] Abortive schemes against her charter. Occasionally the home government would be seized with a fit of jealousy in respect to the charter, and take some step which created a temporary uneasiness. 1697. Jan. 25. Once, eight years after the Revolution, the newly instituted Board of Trade deliberated on a plan for uniting Connecticut and New York under the same government;[4] but the consultation ended in an instruction from the Privy Council to the Feb. 25. Attorney-General to "inspect the charters of Connecticut and Rhode Island in relation to the government and powers of constituting Governors of those Colonies, and report how he finds the same."[5] A step 1701. Jan. 14. equally without result was taken when the same officer was consulted by the Board of Trade respecting "the means by which the proprietors of the

[1] Conn. Col. Rec., III. 463–466.

[2] Ibid., IV. 103. — A full abstract of Winthrop's well-reasoned instructions is in Trumbull's History, I. 390–392. The tone of the Address is not confident. The chief anxiety at the moment related to the command of the militia.

[3] Trumbull, History, I. 387.

[4] Journal of the Board of Trade, *sub die*.

[5] Privy Council Register, *sub die*.

plantations might be obliged to present the names of their Governors to his Majesty for his approbation." [1]

New Hampshire was a royal Province, having the first branch of its Legislature, as well as its executive officers, appointed by the King, and subject to have its government remodelled by him at any time. In Massachusetts the chief executive officers were appointed by the crown, but the Council was elective, subject to the Governor's refusal. Neither Rhode Island nor Connecticut had any such close dependence upon the government at home, and those Colonies accordingly conducted their affairs with less apprehension of interference. In the *woful decade* in King William's reign, their people, enclosed within other English settlements where they did not border on the sea, were spared most of the calamities experienced by their neighbors of the two other Provinces. Connecticut, however, was active and generous in supporting the common cause. When, in the summer after the Revolution, she received an application from Governor Bradstreet to take part in the war with the Indians at the East, though devastated at the time by an epidemic sickness,[2] she immediately sent some of her considerable men to Boston, to consult on the exigency with commissioners from the other Colonies; and on their report that the war was, "on the part of the English, a defensive war, and just and lawful," two hundred of the militia of Connecticut were immediately sent into the field.[3] When the light-headed Jacob Leisler attempted to imitate in New York the revolution conducted by the Massachusetts patriots, Connecticut, wishing well to his cause, sent him a few men to hold his fort in the town of New York, and keep the uneasy people there in order, and a company to help guard the western frontier of his Province against the French

Her share in the war.

1689. July.

July.

1690. February.

[1] Journal of the Board of Trade, *sub die.*

[2] Conn. Col. Rec., IV. 1, note.

[3] Ibid., 2, 3, 4.

and their savage allies.[1] From the latter force, under the
1690. command of Captain Bull, a party was posted at
Feb. 8. Schenectady, at the time of the calamitous assault
on that place, and lost five men killed and five captured.[2]
A reinforcement of two hundred Connecticut sol-
April 11. diers was then marched to Albany; and on applications from Massachusetts, other troops were despatched
1697. to the seat of war in the Eastern country, and
May. three times at least to secure the upper towns on
the Connecticut River.[3] Contributions were made in the
churches of Connecticut to relieve the sufferers
1692. from the Indian ravages in New Hampshire and
Maine.[4] On an alarm of a landing of the French in Nar-
1691. ragansett Bay, troops were moved eastward, and
May. 1693. works were erected at Saybrook and New London.[5]
May. These operations were costly; and the share of
Connecticut in the expense of the ten years' war, to which she was not prominently a party, is believed to have exceeded the sum of twelve thousand pounds.[6]

The most important of her military movements during this period belonged to the expedition against Canada in the year after that of the Revolution. It has been related
that the plan of the campaign was for a force to
Her defeated expedition to Montreal. be operating against Montreal at the time when
the ships under Phips's command should appear
before Quebec, and that the miscarriage of the
former part of this scheme caused the discomfiture of the
latter. The plan of the expedition had been digested at
1690. a meeting held at New York, by commissioners
May. from that Colony and the Colonies of New Eng-

[1] Conn. Col. Rec., III. 255, IV. 15, 16; comp. O'Callaghan, III. 589; Documentary History of New York, II. 20, 43 *et seq.*

[2] Conn. Col. Rec., III. 463, note.

[3] Ibid., IV. 47, 67, 89, 149, 204, 205.

[4] Ibid., IV. 193.

[5] Trumbull, History, I. 387; Conn. Col. Rec., IV. 48, 97. For an account of a spirited movement in February, 1700 (see above, p. 186), when there was an alarm of discontent among the Indians, see Proceedings of the Mass. Hist. Soc. for 1867, 473 *et seq.*

[6] Trumbull, History, I. 397.

land. The land force was to consist of eight hundred Englishmen, with eighteen hundred Indians of the Five Nations. Fitz-John Winthrop of Connecticut was to have the chief command, and the Colony of New York was to take care for the supply of provisions. The place of rendezvous for the English and Indians was an inlet called Wood Creek, at the southern end of Lake Champlain. When the English arrived, they found only some seventy Indian allies; and a messenger sent to look for the missing warriors returned without satisfactory intelligence. What was much worse, the boats which the Indians had been relied upon to furnish for the passage of the lake had not been collected, and the provisions which it had been the business of Milborn, the New York commissary, to supply, were found to be inadequate to subsist the army while on its way towards the French plantations.[1]

August.

In these circumstances, whatever might have been done by officers of more enterprise and more resource, nothing seemed possible to Winthrop and his council of war but a precipitate retreat. Their resolution to this effect enraged Milborn and Leisler, on whom it threw an odious responsibility.[2] It is related that the latter, in virtue of his assumed authority as Governor of New York, went so far as to arrest Winthrop, and to keep him some days under guard, with the purpose of bringing him before a court-martial;[3] and that when his

[1] Winthrop's Journal of his "march from Albany to Wood Creek" is in O'Callaghan, IV. 193 *et seq.* He had found "no possibility of getting provisions to support the forces any longer, and that here was not canoes to transport half the Christians." (Comp. letter of Milborn to Winthrop, in Mass. Hist. Col., XLI. 439.) The disappointing news, as it first came to Boston, was published, Sept. 25, 1690, in a newspaper, which, under the title of "Public Occurrences, both Foreign and Domestic," was attempted thus early, but failed after the publication of two or three monthly numbers. (Hist. Mag., I. 229.) Comp. the circumstantial account of those transactions in Shea's translation of Charlevoix, II. 146, note.

[2] Leisler and his Council at New York presented their case to Lord Shrewsbury in a letter dated Oct. 20. 1690, for which see O'Callaghan, III. 751.

[3] I say "it is related," as it is on the excellent authority of Trumbull

trial was about to come on he was rescued by some Mohawks, "to the universal joy of the army."[1] It is certain that the magistrates of Connecticut had what they esteemed credible information of Winthrop's being confined by Leisler at Albany, and that they sent to that headstrong person a peremptory demand for the release of their officer.[2] On an examination of the case, the

Oct. 9.

colonial Assembly vindicated Winthrop's course, and commissioned two of the Magistrates to "thank the general for his good services to their Majesties and to this Colony, and to assure him that, on all seasonable occasions, they would be ready to manifest their good sentiments of his fidelity, valor, and prudence."[3]

The home government was too busy elsewhere to bestow much attention on the affairs of Connecticut, unless

Her resistance to judicial appeals.

some special occurrence called for its notice. An occasion arose for it to declare its judgment on the right to entertain appeals from the colonial courts. On a representation from the Board of Trade that the courts

1699. March 9.

of Connecticut had refused to allow an appeal to England, the Privy Council had made an order "that it is the inherent right of his Majesty to receive and determine appeals from all his Majesty's Colonies in America."[4] A suitor in the Court of Assistants of Connecticut

(Hist., I. 384). But there are parts of the story that especially perplex me. I cannot understand how Leisler, inconsiderate as he was, could have supposed himself entitled to assume such a power; nor how, if he was, Winthrop should have allowed himself to be rescued by an Indian rabble; nor how any number of Mohawks should have got up their courage to the point of taking a prisoner out of the hands of a European guard who were on the look-out for them; nor how Connecticut troops should have been willing to leave to such agents to do for their commander what it was to their "universal joy" to have done. There is a letter on the subject from Secretary Allyn, of Sept. 9, 1690, in Mass. Archives, XXXVI. 177. But it rather stimulates than satisfies curiosity.

1 Trumbull, History, I. 385, 540; Conn. Col. Rec., IV. 38. — The reader cannot but observe that Winthrop's Journal of his "March from Albany to Wood Creek" does not allude to this transaction.

2 See their letter in Trumbull, I. 540.

3 Conn. Col. Rec., IV. 38; Documentary History of New York, II. 162.

4 Privy Council Register, *sub die*.

claimed this privilege, and was denied. He petitioned the
Privy Council, who referred his case to the Board 1700.
of Trade.[1] The Privy Council finally directed Dec. 5.
that the appeal should be heard; but the order 1702.
was not obeyed, and forty years passed before the Feb. 12.
question was disposed of. Then the claim of the Colony
was allowed.[2]

A question arose respecting the chartered right of Connecticut to dispose of her military force.[3] Successive instructions given to Phips, Governor of Massachusetts, and
to Fletcher, Governor of New York, authorized 1693.
them to command the Connecticut militia.[4] Phips Feb. 23.
was not disposed to assert the authority, and it was before
long withdrawn; Fletcher was less forbearing.
The Magistrates sent one of their number to New Command of her militia.
York,[5] to engage him to suspend his claim till they
should have had a hearing in England; but he refused to
delay, and, coming to Hartford while the Assembly
was in session, demanded an acquiescence in his Oct. 26.
pretension, at the same time promising to place the troops
under the immediate command of the Governor as his

[1] Privy Council Register, *sub die*.

[2] "In full view of the possible consequences of their decision, the colonial court unhesitatingly affirmed the supremacy of colonial law, and denied to the statutes or common law of England any force except such as was given them by the explicit action of the General Assembly. From this decision they never deviated in any of the numerous cases in which the same issue was subsequently presented for adjudication. And it happens, curiously enough, that not a single appeal taken from the Connecticut courts to the King in Council was ultimately successful, however great the discrepancy between the Act of Assembly under which judgment had been rendered and the laws of England. Once only in such case a law of the Colony was declared null and void. It cost the Colony some thousands of pounds and some twenty years of unremitted effort to procure a reversal of this decision, and place the annulled law again upon the statute-book; but the work was accomplished, and the legal advisers of the crown concurred in approving the restoration." (Letter of J. H. Trumbull to the author; see below, p. 578.)

[3] Conn. Col. Rec., IV. 77, 102.

[4] R. I. Rec., III. 296; Privy Council Register for Feb. 23, 1693. For Fletcher's commission, see O'Callaghan, III. 827.

[5] Conn. Col. Rec., IV. 105.

lieutenant. There is a more than doubtful tradition that, the train-bands of Hartford being paraded, by his command or request, before the place where the Assembly was in session, he ordered his commission and instructions to be read; that upon this, Captain Wadsworth, of Charter Oak memory, ordered the drums to be beat along the line; that when the drummers ceased, Fletcher's secretary began again, and again his voice was drowned by the noisy music; that Fletcher would have stopped it, but Wadsworth threatened to *make the sun shine through him*, if he interfered again; whereupon, the temper of the crowd of townspeople who stood around being manifest, the baffled Governor thought it prudent to withdraw.[1] However erroneously or imperfectly the details of the transaction have been reported, certain it is that Fletcher came to Hartford with the demand in question, and that he met with such resistance as induced him to desist from urging it for the present. He went away in an angry state of mind. Two days after his repulse he wrote to the Secretary of State:[2] "I have gone so far to assert their
Oct. 28. Majesties' commission to me for the lieutenancy of this Colony as I could without force. . . . . . I never saw magistracy so prostituted as here. . . . . . The laws of

[1] Trumbull, History, I. 393. I do not think it credible that, in the relation in which Connecticut then stood to the King, she should have countenanced her officer in precisely these proceedings. Trumbull, with all his gravity, had a tenderness for sensational traditions, of which his narrative of the hiding of the charter is another example. (Ibid., 371.) When I came to entertain a distrust of this story, I did not know that it was questioned in Connecticut. But Mr. Hoadly says (Conn. Col. Rec., IV. Pref. vi.), "The story of how he [Fletcher] was foiled by Captain Wadsworth does not rest on any good foundation." (Comp. Ibid., 111–117.) In his letter of October 28 to Lord Sunderland, Fletcher wrote: "I expected no opposition, came with a few servants, found these people sat in a General Court. I went up to them, caused my commission to be read, gave their chief a memorial requiring obedience to the King's command, and so left them to debate. Two days after they sent me a paper insisting on their charter, and refusing obedience. By much ado I got some of them to a conference. To all appearance they went away convinced and satisfied; but I quickly found them resolved and positive."

[2] British Colonial Papers.

England have no force in this Colony. . . . . . They set up for a free State."

On being apprised of Fletcher's offensive claim, the government of Connecticut resolved to send Fitz-John Winthrop to England with a remonstrance, September. having first, as in their judgment befitted the solemnity of the occasion, taken the sense of the freemen, who approved that proceeding by a heavy majority of their votes.[1] The Address represented with abundant specification the insecurity which would follow, both in respect Oct. 4. to external enemies and to domestic tumult, if the Colony should lose the power to use promptly its military arm according to its own discretion; setting forth, Her address to the King. at the same time, its willingness to continue and enlarge the voluntary exertions which it had liberally made for the military protection of the King's other dominions in America. The question was readily and not unreasonably disposed of by the Privy Council. At the present moment it was not entirely, if indeed it could be said to be mainly, a question of power. What the government wanted was to avail itself effectively of the military strength of all the Colonies in hostilities against the French and their allies. Therefore, to carry on the war at the North and East, they proposed to place the militia of Rhode Island under the Governor of Massachusetts, and to place the militia of Connecticut under that command which it was supposed would make them most useful at the West. Within a few weeks after Winthrop presented his Address, the Council, in pursuance of the advice of the 1694. Jan. 29. Board of Trade, limited Fletcher's right over Con- April 19. necticut troops to that of including in his command a force of a hundred and twenty men, to be furnished to him by that Colony "at all times during the war."[2] Win- May 5. throp further obtained from the Board of Trade

[1] Conn. Col. Rec., IV. 102.

[2] Privy Council Register, *sub die;* comp. Trumbull, I. 541-545.

an instruction to Fletcher "in relation to the quota to be furnished by Connecticut, that he shall not demand a greater number than in proportion to the adjacent Colonies respectively." Lord Bellomont's commission, like those of Phips and of Fletcher, included a grant of the command of the militia of Connecticut,[1] but he made no attempt to put it in force.

The internal administration of the Colony proceeded in the same quiet course as heretofore. Treat and Bishop continued to be made Governor and Deputy-Governor from year to year, till Bishop's death (when he was succeeded by William Jones, formerly Deputy-Governor of New Haven),[2] and till Treat grew so old that, taking the second place, he was glad to yield the first to Fitz-John Winthrop, when Winthrop returned from serving the Colony four years in England.[3] In the first year of Winthrop's administration the important change was made in the constitution of the Legislature, of dividing it into two branches, each with a negative on the other's action, thus assimilating it to the Legislatures of the parent country and of Massachusetts.[4] Three years after, a rule was made for the autumnal meetings of the General Court to be holden at New Haven, instead of, like the spring meetings, at Hartford, as had been the practice since the union of the two Colonies.[5] The government sought to secure Lord Bellomont's good-will by sending a formal deputation to New York to welcome his arrival at that city.[6]

1691. June. Her internal administration.

1698. May 12.

Oct. 13.

1701. May 8.

1698. May.

Enjoying, unlike New Hampshire and Massachusetts,

[1] N. H. Provincial Papers, II. 343.

[2] Conn. Col. Rec., IV. 384. — John Allyn, the famous Secretary of Connecticut for thirty-three years, died Nov. 6, 1696. (Conn. Col. Rec., IV. 190.)

[3] The Colony placed extraordinary confidence in Winthrop, of which from time to time it gave liberal proof. (See Conn. Col. Rec., IV. 240, 280.)

[4] Ibid., 267.

[5] Ibid., 343.

[6] Ibid., 238.

both a government strictly her own, and immunity from the ravages of French and savage war, — unlike Rhode Island, the tranquil order of a religious population, — Connecticut was the happiest of the Colonies of New England. Her thirty towns had each its church and educated minister. Her free schools raised all her children above the hardships and the temptations of poverty, and prepared them for the discharge of the duties of virtuous citizens. The agricultural industry which mostly employed her people was favorable to health, frugality, content, and love of freedom. Her prudence,[1] and the less urgent demands upon her for costly military operations,[2] had saved her from incurring heavy debt, and she had little share in the financial embarrassment which weighed so heavily on the more powerful Colony. Her relations with the mother-country brought little occasion for conflict or solicitude.

Her happy condition.

Encouraged by the prospect of permanent self-government as the danger of interference from England appeared to diminish, Connecticut addressed herself with a wise assiduity to measures for the improvement of her institutions and the well-being of her people. In the year of the Revolution, the franchise was extended to "all and every person and persons of peaceable, orderly, and good conversation, being in possession of freehold estate to the value of forty shilling in country pay per annum, and being twenty-one years of age."[3] Two years later the taxable property of the Colony amounted to one hundred and eighty-four thousand pounds, divided among three thousand and one hundred persons. In ten years the number of tax-payers had risen to three thousand eight hundred and fifty, and the aggre-

1689. October.

1691. October.

1701. October.

[1] For the cautious dealing with questions of finance, see *e.g.* Conn. Col. Rec., IV. 166, 176, 180, 198.

[2] A letter from Mr. Ripley, of Windham, to Governor Winthrop (Mass. Hist. Col., XLI. 449), illustrates one of the alarms occasioned by an alleged plot of the Indians. (See above, 186.)

[3] Conn. Col. Rec., IV. 11.

gate amount of their property to two hundred and ten thousand pounds.[1] Towards the close of every year, grants were regularly made to the principal officers of government, ranging between eighty and a hundred and forty pounds to the Governor, and between ten and seventy pounds to the Deputy-Governor. Assistants had each a salary of ten pounds, besides fees for suits brought before them on appeal. Deputies were paid three shillings for each day of official service, besides the expenses of their travel.[2] The roll of their House was called every morning, and an absentee lost his pay for the day, besides being liable to a fine of ten shillings.[3] Any person who, at the
1698. annual General Court for Elections, should "take
October. it upon him to speak without liberty first prayed and granted to him by the honored Governor, or in his absence by the Deputy-Governor," was fined "a shilling
1694. in silver."[4] Ferries were made free to persons
May. employed by the King's Postmaster-General in the conveyance of letters and parcels.[5] All purchases of
1702. lands from the Indians were declared illegal and
October. void, except such as were made by towns under grants from the General Court.[6] The office of Justice of
1698. the Peace was instituted; "three or four at least
Jan. 22. of the most able and judicious freemen" to be annually appointed to it for each county by the General Court, with judicial powers similar to what had been hitherto exercised by Assistants.[7] In each county two
October. justices, with the judge of their county court, had the charge of the probate of wills, and of the business of wards and guardians.[8] After long and painstaking deliberation, a revised edition of the laws

[1] Conn. Col. Rec., IV. 56, 360.
[2] Ibid., 84, 152, 175, 179, 181, 223, 225, 259, 266, 268, 281, 302, 305, 329, 361, 400.
[3] Ibid., 269.
[4] Ibid., 266.
[5] Ibid., 123.
[6] Ibid., III. 52, 54, IV. 397.
[7] Ibid., IV. 235, 260, 324, 376; comp. 94, III. 412, 414.
[8] Ibid., IV. 268.

was published by authority.[1] Eight ports of entry were established, each to be superintended by a Naval Officer.[2]

1702. October.

Prominent among the cares of the government was that of securing for all its people the instructions of a learned ministry, and for all its children opportunities for acquiring knowledge. No church could be founded without permission from the General Court, and every citizen was obliged to pay in proportion to his means towards the support of the minister of the geographical parish of his residence. Ministers were exempt from taxation of every kind.[3] "For the satisfaction of such as were conscientiously desirous to be married by the ministers of their plantations," that function, hitherto vested in lay magistrates only, was extended to the pastors.[4] Towns consisting of fewer than seventy families were obliged to keep up schools through half the year for the tuition of their children, "with able and sufficient schoolmasters;" towns of seventy families and upwards had to continue their school through the year; in the capital town of each of the four counties, a free "grammar school" with a public endowment of land was established, where young men might be prepared for college;[5] and an Act was passed, which was to bear rich fruit, "for the founding and suitably endowing and ordering a collegiate school, ... wherein youth may be instructed in the arts and sciences, who, through the blessing of Almighty God, may be fitted for public employments both in church and civil state."[6] Physicians might not practise their art without a license from the General Court, which was generally obtained on the recommendation of the minister of a place where med-

Religion and knowledge.

1694. October.

1700. October.

1701. October.

[1] Conn. Col. Rec., IV. 182, 201, 282, 332, 343, 362, 396.

[2] Ibid., 374, 397.

[3] Ibid., 198, 287, 316, 335, 405.

[4] Ibid., 136.

[5] Ibid., 331, 375, 402.

[6] Ibid., 363.

ical help was wanted.[1] Of professional lawyers there is perhaps no trace to be found in the public record of those times, except so far as they should fall under the censure of the statute which, along with rioters, scolds, keepers and frequenters of houses of ill-fame, night-walkers, drunkards, and such like evil-doers, provides that "common barrators, which frequently move, stir up, and maintain suits of law in court or quarrels and parts in the country," shall give security for their good behavior or by any Assistant be sent to the common gaol.[2]

1698. January.

The inland boundaries of Connecticut on all sides remained undetermined. Massachusetts insisted on the correctness of her survey made by Woodward and Saffery in the early times, to ascertain the line of latitude, three miles south of the southernmost part of Charles River, which, according to her charter, made her southern boundary.[3] Connecticut judged the surveyors to have erroneously marked that line of latitude by a line

1642.

Boundaries.

[1] Conn. Col. Rec., IV. 139, 256.

[2] Ibid., 236.—I am indebted to my learned friend, Mr. Trumbull, for the following memoranda relating to the state of the legal profession in Connecticut in early times:

"It was not until many years of the eighteenth century had passed that Connecticut lawyers began to look to their profession as their only way of getting a living. But appearance "by attorney" had been common, and there were several well-read lawyers in the Colony. They appeared "by leave of court," and usually—perhaps always—by special authorization as attorneys. William Pitkin was employed in nearly all important cases tried by the Court of Assistants, or heard by the General Court on appeal, for twenty years, or more, after 1662. See his first appointment as "Attorney for the General Court," October, 1662 (Conn. Col. Rec., I. 388); and again, May, 1664 (Ibid., 426, 436); and his appearance in actions between private parties is frequently mentioned, as in Conn. Col. Rec., III. 22, 67, 127, and particularly, 165, and the note. Richard Edwards, of Hartford, was a good lawyer, and had a considerable practice in the higher courts, though his principal business was that of a merchant. He appeared as attorney as early as 1680. In 1684 he was employed in the action of Steele & Stanley *v.* Griswold (Conn. Col. Rec., III. 161, 167), Mr. Pitkin being on the other side. (Ibid., 176.) In 1702–3 he was one of the attorneys in the "fugitive slave" case, having for his opponent Gurdon Saltonstall. Captain Daniel Clarke "took the attorney's oath," before Andros's Court of Sessions for Hartford County, in March, 1687–88.

[3] See above, Vol. III. 119; comp. Mass. Prov. Rec. for June 13, 1696.

diverging towards the south from the true direction, when it came to reach her territory. Repeated proposals from her to unite in another survey were declined 1693. 1694. by the other party. It was urged by Connecticut 1695. 1700. that the new towns of Enfield and Suffield lay south of the legal border of Massachusetts and within her own. On the other part, the correctness of the ancient survey was insisted on; and it was further urged that, even if it should prove to be incorrect as to the disputed line of latitude, still it was understood to be correct at the time when King Charles gave Connecticut her charter, and must be considered as the line which was had in view when, in the charter, the northern boundary line of that Colony was described as being coincident with the southern boundary line of Massachusetts. For the present, it was found impossible to effect an agreement on the subject.[1] Nor for the present was there any better success in establishing the western boundary. The line on the New York 1683. side had, many years before, been settled on paper; Nov. 28. and King William's confirmation of it, which it had been thought prudent to solicit, was obtained.[2] But the 1700. running of it and erecting monuments was still March 14. delayed.

The question of the eastern boundary of Connecticut, again revived, still seemed insoluble, if it was to be discussed as a question of interpretation.[3] Nothing could well be plainer than that two successive royal charters gave the country between Narragansett Bay and Pawtucket River, the first to one Colony, the second to another. The decision of the commissioners who, towards the end of the reign of King Charles the Second, had reported adversely to the pretensions of Rhode Island by reason of the pri-

[1] Conn. Col. Rec., IV. 95, 136, 146, 155, 301, 319, 400.

[2] O'Callaghan, IV. 627 *et seq.*, comp. Privy Council Register, *sub die;* Conn. Col. Rec., IV. 335. See above, III. 440, note 3.

[3] Conn. Col. Rec., IV. 238, 243, 299, 399; see above, Vol. III. 428.

ority of the adverse title, had, it seems, not been acted upon by the Privy Council, and was not regarded as binding by that Colony. The strife accordingly was renewed, and was prosecuted as formerly, sometimes by mutual violence, sometimes by ineffectual negotiation. The Board
1697. Aug. 26. of Trade recommended a further attempt at an amicable settlement, and directed Lord Bellomont to use his endeavors to promote it.[1] He did so, but with-
1699. Sept. 26. out avail; and nothing remained for him but to advise the parties to send their agents to England to present their case to the Board.[2]

Though, when the despotism of Andros was subverted by the rising in Massachusetts, it became necessary for Rhode Island to organize some common government over her nine unquiet towns, the Revolution was by no means so joyful an event to her people as to those of the other Colonies of New England. Rhode Island had never been

Rhode Island after the Revolution.

a place so little disorderly, and so little disagreeable to live in, as under Andros's absolute sway; nor was he subject, within her bounds, to the same motives to act with rigor as those which dictated his course in Massachusetts.

Rhode Island had with little reluctance yielded her charter, and with it her liberty, to King James; and to many of her most considerable citizens even that little reluctance was offensive.[3] Of course Andros's hatred of Massachusetts did not harm his popularity in the sister Colony.
1689. Aug. 2. When the deposed Governor broke gaol and ran away, it was to Rhode Island that he directed his steps. He was stopped and delivered to officers sent after him from Massachusetts,[4] and his captors made a merit of

[1] Journal of the Board of Trade, *sub die.*

[2] R. I. Rec., III. 327, 354, 379, 380.

[3] See above, Vol. III. 506.

[4] O'Callaghan, III. 614–617; comp. Mass. Arch., XCVII. 248–256.

his arrest; but it is not unreasonable to doubt whether this would have been, had circumstances been such as to admit of his being suffered to pass without their being called to account. Letters written to London by influential citizens of the little Colony bewailed his removal as bringing them into a condition hard to be endured;[1] and, on the other hand, he stood by them in England in that important controversy which they were maintaining against Connecticut. The lapse of eight months had given them opportunity to form a judgment respecting the probability that the new order of things would prove stable, before they were prepared to report to the King what they had been doing.[2] 1690. Jan. 30.

Unsettled state of the government.

When, "under a sense of their deplorable and unsettled condition," after the fall of Andros, they determined to have a Governor of their own as of old, it was only on a third election that they found a candidate who would consent to attempt to rule them. The Quaker, Walter Clarke, the last Governor under the charter, having refused to resume his place, John Coggeshall, the last Deputy-Governor, remained at the head of the administration for several months, at the end of which time, Clarke persisting in his preference for retirement, and Christopher Almy also declining the unattractive honor of the chief magistracy, it was conferred on the Quaker, Henry Bull, who, how- Feb. 27.

[1] R. I. Rec., III. 259.

[2] They prayed (R. I. Rec., III. 258) that the King "would please, being *Pater Patrio nostro*, to extend his fatherly care," &c. When the freemen reconstituted the ancient government in May, 1689, they, "with all due and humble submission, made their humble address to the present supreme power of England," whatever that might turn out to be. They were "not only ignorant," they said, of what titles should be given in this venture, but also "not so rhetorical as becomes such personages." They had resumed their charter government, being "certainly informed" that the Boston people had imprisoned Andros and his Counsellors, "for what cause best known to themselves." (Ibid., 266.) "Rhetorical" accomplishments were clearly not all that had declined in Rhode Island since the days of Coddington, Williams, and John Clarke.

ever, after a single year's service, resigned it, as did also John Coggeshall, who had filled the second place.[1]

May 7. The next Governor was another Quaker, John Easton, from the time of whose election the records contain no information on the subject for five years.[2] That Easton's administration was not satisfactory or prosperous 1691. may be partly inferred from his reporting to the Nov. 19. King that he could not furnish his Colony's contingent of troops, because he could not raise the necessary money.[3] In the last year of this interval Caleb Carr was Governor,[4] and he was succeeded by Walter Clarke, during 1696. whose administration the Legislature of Rhode May 6. Island was assimilated to those of the other Colonies of New England by a division into two branches, each with a negative on the other.[5] When, in the next 1697. year, the office fell to Samuel Cranston, who afterwards was constantly re-elected to it for nearly thirty years till his death, the proper Quaker dynasty in Rhode Island may be said to have come to an end, though the Board of Trade was informed that "Mr. Cranston was one of the demi-Quakers only put in to serve the Quakers."[6] The Governor had an annual salary of from ten to thirty pounds, to which gratuities were occasionally added; the Deputy-Governor, of six pounds; and each Assistant, of four. Deputies in the General Assembly received three shillings for each day of service.[7]

Difficulty and disturbances occurred in the collection of taxes.[8] It was represented to the Board of Trade that the 1698. laws were "so meanly kept, and in such blotted March 8. and defaced books (having never yet any of them

[1] R. I. Rec., III. 260, 261, 268, 271.

[2] Ibid., 288.—From October, 1690, to July, 1695, there is only one record of a General Assembly, that of August, 1692, when Phips's claim to command the militia was considered.

[3] R. I. Rec., III. 289.

[4] Ibid., 304.

[5] Ibid., 313.

[6] Journal of the Board of Trade for Aug. 8, 1699.

[7] R. I. Rec., III. 309, 345, 430.

[8] See, *e.g.*, Ibid., 34, 324, 348.

been printed), that few of his Majesty's subjects were able to know what they were."[1] Randolph, who had no personal bias against the Rhode-Islanders, reported that "neither judges, juries, nor witnesses were under any obligation;"[2] his explanation of this unpleasant fact being that the management of the government (such as it was) was in the hands of Quakers and Anabaptists, who would take no oath.[3] There was no public provision for schools. Like Connecticut, Rhode Island encouraged the post-office

[1] R. I. Rec., III. 331, 339, 340, 376.

[2] Randolph played no important part in New England after his discharge by the Privy Council (see above, p. 67). Feb. 25, 1691, he was appointed to be "Searcher of their Majesties' duty of 4½ per cent at Bridgetown, Barbadoes." (Customs Minute Books, Vol. VI., in the Public Record Office, London.) Oct. 12 of the same year, he was made "Surveyor to visit the several Colonies upon the coast of America, at the salary of £200 *per annum*." (Ibid.) The first mention which I find of him in New England after 1689 is in a passing notice by Judge Sewall in his Diary for Sept. 4, 1692: "Mr. Randolph came to town last Friday." In 1694 he was in New Hampshire, being appointed by the Council, May 21st of that year, "to oversee the work at the fort." (N. H. Provincial Papers, II. 119.) Jan. 13, 1696, on the institution of the new Board of Trade, the Privy Council received from him a memorial as "Surveyor-General of his Majesty's Customs upon the northern coasts of America." (Privy Council Register, *sub die*.) Dec. 16, 1697, he arrived in Maryland from England. (See his letter of April 26, 1698, to the Lords of Trade, in O'Callaghan, IV. 300; comp. 311.) Jan. 3, 1698, Partridge wrote to the Lords that he was expecting Randolph to come to New Hampshire, with authority to administer the official oath to him. (British Colonial Papers; comp. N. H. Provincial Papers, II. 312.) May 21st of the same year, Randolph wrote to Blathwayt from New York (British Colonial Papers), and Sept. 19 the Board of Trade read a letter from him, "dated at Boston, in New England, the 30th of May last, about pirates and illegal traders in Rhode Island." July 13, 1699, the Privy Council passed an order (Register, *sub die*) that "Edward Randolph be discharged from his imprisonment in Bermudas, who was imprisoned by order of Governor and Council there." Nanfan, Lieutenant-Governor of New York, was informed by the Governor of Bermuda, Nov. 6, 1699, that "he had for some misdemeanor clapped Randolph in prison, and seized his papers, amongst which were copies of letters to the Lords of Trade, wherein he very villanously and in a very scurrilous manner writes against Lord Bellomont, who should have notice of this, for he gives him no less than the character of a rogue in the government that belongs to him." (British Colonial Papers.) In the biographical dictionaries of both Allen and Eliot it is said, I know not on what authority, that Randolph ended his bustling life in the West Indies. (Parentator, 107.)

[3] R. I. Rec., III. 339.

by a free carriage of mails across the ferries,[1] — a privilege which she also granted to magistrates, representatives, and jurymen. The Governor and Deputy-Governor, by virtue of their assumed admiralty powers, issued commissions to armed vessels. Peleg Sandford, commissioned by the English Admiralty to be Admiralty Judge in Rhode Island, complained to the Board of Trade that Governor Clarke had not only refused to administer to him the oath of office, but had taken away his commission and declined to restore it.[2]

Jan. 31.

Rhode Island, at this period, had not bettered the terms on which she had generally lived with the Governors of Massachusetts. Nor were her relations with New York altogether amicable. The ministers of King William, unable, as long as the charters of Rhode Island and Connecticut were respected, to appoint Governors over these Colonies, aimed to accomplish something in the way of military subordination by vesting the command of their military force in the King's Governors of Massachusetts and New York, for which arrangement they had a fair pretence in the necessity of a vigorous combination of forces in the colonial wars. One of Phips's first acts, after his arrival in Boston, was to write to the Governor and Council of Rhode Island that he was "commissionated from their Majesties with the power of lieutenant and commander-in-chief of the militia, and of all the forces by sea and land, within their Majesties' several Colonies of Connecticut, Rhode Island, and Providence Plantation, the Narragansett country or King's Province, and the Province of New Hampshire." And he acquainted them "that he desired and expected that some fit persons should be instructed and speedily sent to attend him at Boston with an account of the militia, and what

Command of the militia.

1692. May. June 2.

[1] R. I. Rec., III. 373.

[2] Ibid., 329, 331, 375; Journal of the Board of Trade for April 20 and Oct. 20, 1698.

further might appear necessary for their Majesties' service."

The Governor sent two commissioners to confer with Phips. They "attended about five days before they could have any treaty," and then they could get no satisfaction, nor so much as a sight of Phips's commission, while, on the other hand, he sent into Rhode Island a number of new commissions, "endeavoring thereby," as the local authorities phrased it, "to put the militia into the hands of most of them that disclaim their Majesties' authority here."[1] The Governor convoked the Assembly, who enjoined it upon their own officers to retain their commands, and prepared an Address to the King, setting forth their claim under the charter, and making an application for redress. They professed their belief that the movement of the Governor of Massachusetts to disable the military arm of Rhode Island had been "occasioned by private interest, some of the principal persons of his Excellency, Sir William Phips his counsellors, claiming interest to all the Narragansett country."[2] Christopher Almy carried this Address to England, where it was referred by the Privy Council to the Lords of Trade,[3] and by them to the Attorney-General and Solicitor-General; and those officers reported "that the power given by the charter to the government of the Colony to train and exercise the inhabitants of the Colony in martial affairs, as also the rest of the charter, was still in force;" but "that their Majesties might constitute a chief commander, who might have authority at all times to command or order such proportion of the forces of each Colony or plantation as their Majesties might see fit."[4]

Aug. 2.

1693. Aug. 24. Sept. 15.

1694. April 2.

[1] R. I. Rec., III. 285, 286.

[2] Ibid., 288.

[3] Almy's "Paper about the Militia of Rhode Island," among the Board of Trade Papers, is headed as follows, viz.: "Resuns that sum ill consequents may follow if the millshsha Bee taken out of our hands."

[4] R. I. Rec., III. 294, 297; British

This opinion was the basis of subsequent arrangements, the same as those made for Connecticut. The Queen (the King being then in the Netherlands) communi-
Aug. 21. cated it as such in a letter, instructing the Colony to place a force of forty-eight men for the present under the command of the Governor of New York, to whom, in
1693. the previous year, the power of commanding the
June 10. militia of Rhode Island had been transferred from Governor Phips, and with it the pending dispute respecting that authority.[1] Almy further moved the question respect-
1694. ing the eastern boundary of his Colony, claiming
May 15. that, rightly drawn, it would include a strip of territory, three miles wide, extending from north to south along the eastern shore of Narragansett Bay. The Privy
July 11. Council, by the advice of the Attorney-General,
Aug. 4. referred this question to "a commission of indifferent and unconcerned persons inhabiting near the places to inquire and certify the truth."[2]

But it was with Lord Bellomont more than with any other royal Governor that Rhode Island was on unsatisfactory terms. Narragansett Bay was a place of particularly convenient resort for the buccaneering vessels which
Disagreements with Lord Bellomont. so infested at that time the ports of North America, and which he had express charge to hunt down.[3] Rhode Island was especially implicated in the criminal transactions complained of, by reason of the use which had been made of commissions issued by her Governors to private armed vessels during the seven years' war with France.[4] Lord Bellomont received peremptory and minute
1699. instructions from the new Board of Trade to in-
March 9. vestigate these "disorders and irregularities," and

Colonial Papers for July 11 and 18, 1694, and Oct. 28, 1696.

[1] R. I. Rec., III. 296, 304.

[2] Ibid., 298.

[3] Journal of the Board of Trade for April 20, Sept. 15, and Oct. 20, 1698, and Aug. 8, 1699. — Testimony given to the Board implicated Governor Fletcher in complicity with the pirates.

[4] R. I. Rec., III. 319, 322, 328, 335–342, 351, 373–377, 400.

others related to them.[1] These were soon followed by a severe reprimand to the Colony from the Board. The Board rebuked them for "shuffling" in their correspondence. "Your answers are so contrary to truth and to your duty, that we wonder how you could write them. . . . . . You know better. But . . . . . if it were really so [that the Deputy-Governor had erred through ignorance], you ought to have taken better care that such an ignorant person had not been put in such an office."[2] Lord Bellomont wrote to the Secretary of the Board that this reproof of the Rhode Island people had "been a mortification to them." An agent was sent to England to accommodate affairs. He was disliked by Lord Bellomont, who describes him by saying that he "is one of their Council, yet keeps a little blind rum-house where the Indians are his best customers."[3]

Aug. 11.

Nov. 21.

Lord Bellomont passed a week in Rhode Island, employed in the investigation with which he was charged,[4] and as its result reported to the Lords of Trade the existence of a desperately bad state of things in that Colony. Under more than twenty heads he specified departures by its government and people from the provisions of their charter. Their rulers, he said, were incompetent and ill-conditioned persons. "A brutish man, of very corrupt or no principles in religion, and generally known to be so by the people, is . . . . . in the place of

Sept. 18-27.

[1] R. I. Rec., 363, 364; comp. Journal of the Board of Trade for Feb. 14, 1699.

[2] R. I. Rec., III. 376, 377.

[3] Letter from Lord Bellomont to the Lords of Trade, of May 7, 1700, in British Colonial Papers.

[4] "I stayed in that island a week, and collected matter enough in that time to prove that government the most irregular and illegal in their administration that ever any English government was." (Lord Bellomont to Popple, Secretary of the Board of Trade, of Nov. 6, 1699, in British Colonial Papers.) During his visit to Newport at this time he received a petition from sixteen persons for the allowance of a salary for a minister of the Church of England in that place. Bernon (see above, 185, note) and another Huguenot were among the petitioners. Trinity Church, Newport, was the fruit of this movement. (Arnold, History of Rhode Island, I. 559; comp. 498, 556.)

Deputy-Governor," and as such had given commissions to "private men-of-war," which sailed on piratical expeditions "to Madagaska, and the seas of India;" and "the place has been greatly enriched" by the spoils of these adventures. "The Assistants, or Counsellors, who are also Justices of the Peace, and Judges of their Courts, are generally Quakers and sectaries, ... illiterate, and of little or no capacity, several of them not able to write their names. . . . . . Their General-Attorney is a poor illiterate mechanic, very ignorant." No reliance was to be placed on the correctness of the copy of their laws, which, agreeably to a demand of the Board of Trade, had been transmitted to England. "Government have taken all this time to prune and polish them, yet I believe the world never saw such a parcel of fustian. . . . . . They have never erected nor encouraged any schools of learning, or had the means of instruction by a learned orthodox ministry. . . . . . The generality of the people are shamefully ignorant, and all manner of licentiousness and profaneness does greatly abound, and is indulged."[1] Sanford informed him that persons arrested under a charge of piracy found no difficulty in getting their bail-bonds filled to the amount of two or three thousand pounds.[2] In letters of profuse and awkward compliment to Lord Bellomont, after his return to Boston, the Governor and Clarke endeavored to appease the "displeasure" and "disgust" which he had conceived against what they meekly called "an ignorant and contemptible" people.[3]

Agents in England. Oct. 25. Nov. 21.

In their strait they desired to make interest in England, and to this end chose successively six different persons to be their agents there. But all refused to accept the place, for want of confidence, prob-

[1] Report of Lord Bellomont to the Lords of Trade, in R. I. Rec., III. 385–388; comp. Report of Jahleen Brenton, to the same, Ibid., 331.

[2] Lord Bellomont's Journal, in R. I. Rec., III. 388–393. The original is in Mass. Archives, II. 100–117.

[3] R. I. Rec., III. 394, 395, 396.

ably, that they would obtain compensation.[1] Jahleel Brenton, who had already been employed by them in London, though previously he had represented 1700.
them unfavorably to the government, was con- May 4.
firmed for the present in the agency.[2] An ostensible compliance was made with the Navigation Laws by an 1701.
"Act for supporting the Governor in the perform- May 6.
ance of his engagement to the Acts of Navigation."[3]

[1] R. I. Rec., III., 379–382, 403, 410.

[2] Ibid., 409.

[3] Ibid., 437.

CHAPTER VIII.

THE government of King William had contemplated three objects in respect to New England: 1, To reduce that dependency to greater subordination, which purpose it had advanced in the principal Colony by the stinted grants in the new charter, and by rigorous interferences with the provincial legislation; 2, To enforce more strictly the commercial regulations of the empire, in which undertaking there had been small success; 3, To gain an advantage over France by a conquest of her chief colony, but this hope had been grievously disappointed.

The government of Joseph Dudley in Massachusetts ran parallel with the reign of Queen Anne. That sovereign was a devotee to High Church principles; rather, she was governed by High Church prejudices and passions; and the religious tone of her reign was as bigoted and as hostile to nonconformists as the state of parties and other circum-
1711. stances would permit.[1] But the Occasional Conformity Act,[2] the restriction to churchmen of the
1713. right to teach youth, and other severities and insults to dissenters which dishonored her government, when, at a late period of it, the Tories came into power, were not measures of a character to be extended to the

[1] "If the Queen's life had preserved the Tory government for a few years, every vestige of the toleration would have been effaced." (Hallam, Constitutional History, &c., 627.) — "Through their influence [the influence of the nonjuring clergy] the Acts against Schism and Occasional Conformity were passed for the annoyance of Dissenters." (John James Tayler, Retrospect of the Religious Life of England, 27.)

[2] "Thus, after fifty years' exclusion from the public churches, ... are the poor dissenters excluded the service of the State." (Calamy, Abridgment of Baxter's Life and Times, I. 725.)

Colonies. It was in the renewal of a calamitous war, and in the endeavors of her ministers to fasten a stronger hold upon the foreign dependencies of the crown, — endeavors which happily the exigences of that war did something to embarrass and enfeeble, — that in her reign of twelve years the people of New England experienced most of the uncomfortable consequences of their political subordination.

Neither the administration of Phips, nor even that of Bellomont, had been satisfactory to their English masters. Dudley promised much better for their purposes. Besides his great abilities and industry, — his determination on the one part and address on the other, — he thoroughly knew the people he was to rule, and the men who led in their counsels; and that he would not lean to their side might be reckoned on as certain, from the indignities which they had put upon him, and the fury which their treatment had excited on his part.

Dudley's arrival in Boston.

It was a proud day for Joseph Dudley, when, after ten years of uneasy absence from his home, he landed from the "Centurion" man-of-war, under a salute which shook the town, and went up King Street to the Province House of Massachusetts to assume the government for Queen Anne. The last time that he left Boston with any observance, he went from a prison where he had lain five months. Since his last ramble through the once familiar streets, he had been a successful courtier in England, and a member of the imperial Parliament.[1] The

[1] Hutchinson says (Hist., II. 134) that Dudley was received with marks of respect. But he had only hearsay for this, and such marks must have been equivocal. A bitter letter of John Cotton, of Plymouth, written at the time of Dudley's return from England after his transportation, indicates that prevailing state of feeling towards him which he never overcame. (Hist. Soc. Col., XXI. 118, 119.)

After his discharge by the English Privy Council (see above, 67), Dudley, besides his appointment to be a Counsellor of New York, received (Dec. 5, 1690) a commission as Deputy-Governor of New Jersey (Hist. Soc.'s Proceedings for 1870, p. 204). But I have

native country which he revisited was changed since he had known it so well. With the loss of that charter to which he had been treacherous, the dream of self-government was for the present dispelled from the minds of the people of Massachusetts. If there was discontent among them, there was not concert in any endeavor for a change. They had been learning to regard themselves as, in another sense than in earlier times, the subjects of the British crown. And so far he might promise himself that in his communications with them he had the less impracticableness to apprehend at their hands.[1] On the other hand, he had good reason to count upon a vigorous support from the government which he came to serve. The inauguration of the last ministry of King William had dismissed

seen no evidence of his ever acting in that capacity. Accompanied by Brenton, who bore a commission as "Collector, Surveyor, and Searcher," he arrived in Boston from Cowes, in the Isle of Wight, Jan. 24, 1691. (Sewall's Diary, *sub die.*) In the autumn of that year, having done execution upon Leisler at New York in the spring, he was at his home in Roxbury (Ibid., November 20 and December 27), as he was in the autumn of 1692, at the time of the witchcraft excitement (O'Callaghan, III. 847, 848; IV. 2, 3), and in the spring of the following year (Sewall's Diary, for March 17, 1693). It was on account of his "living in Boston, four hundred miles from hence" (New York), that Fletcher, in September, 1692, "suspended" him from his judicial office. (Smith, History of New York, 129). It must have been in 1693 or 1694 that he returned to England; for, Nov. 28, 1703, he wrote to John Usher, "I had the honor to serve under my Lord Cutts as Lieutenant-Governor nine years and a half, while he was in Flanders." (British Colonial Papers.) In the last Parliament of King William the Third, he sat for Newtown, the borough which had been represented before his time by the Duke of Marlborough, while still a commoner, and which introduced George Canning into Parliament in 1793.

[1] March 18, 1702, Dudley presented a "memorial for removing one of the four foot companies at New York to New England." (Privy Council Register; comp. Journal of the Board of Trade for March 24.) Possibly he was timid about his reception, and wanted these troops for security. Certainly he could not have expected a cordial welcome. According to a letter of the time (George Larkin to the Lords of Trade, Oct. 14, 1701, in British Colonial Papers), "some declare publickly that they will oppose the landing of Colonel Dudley." But perhaps nothing more was in his mind than to keep up the state to which he had been used in the Isle of Wight, during the years while his superior was in Flanders.

the patrons of Lord Bellomont, and placed his own friends in power.

Dudley met the Court on the day of his arrival, and adjourned it for five days, after publishing his commission and that of the Lieutenant-Governor, Thomas Povey. The latter, who, when he took his place at the adjourned meeting, was a stranger in America, is believed to have been a brother of the new Secretary to the Board of Trade.[1] The Council for the year had been chosen a fortnight before, on the day prescribed by the charter. Of its members, several had been active opponents of the Governor in his earlier career, and some had taken a part both in the severities used towards him when the government of Andros was overthrown, and in the influence exerted in England to obstruct his advancement to the place which now rewarded his intrigues.

1702. June 11.

It is not to be assumed that Dudley was absolutely without good-will for Massachusetts. His own interest being first cared for, he was not unwilling to promote hers, and to promote it earnestly when the two might be advanced together. He would rather than not have her prosper, when no object personal to himself interfered. But, when he most desired her prosperity, it was in the spirit of an arrogant and jealous patron. It must be such as England, and as he, her ruler for England, should allow. He scouted the thought of having her judge for herself of her rights or of her wants; what she enjoyed, she was to receive and be thankful for as a boon. The opposite theory in her politics was held by the persons against whom he was also enraged by a sense of personal wrong; and the displeasure with which for both reasons he regarded them he disguised only till opportuni-

Policy of his government.

[1] Thomas Povey, at the time of this appointment, was a "captain in the Queen's own regiment of foot-guards." (British Colonial Papers.) The Queen had deviated from the order of business by appointing him without communication with the Board of Trade. (Journal of the Board for April 21, 1702.)

ties should come for its more effectual expression. As to them and to all opponents, he too well knew the conditions of successful ambition to allow himself to be ruled by more impulsive passions. To persist in any gratification of his pride which might incommode a serviceable friend, or confirm or give advantage to an inconvenient enemy, was no part of his plan or practice. He schooled himself to humiliations which won the favor of Randolph, and at an easier cost of professions and compliments he subdued the hostility of Cotton Mather. His tenacious resentments waited to do their work till the time should arrive when his interests no longer demanded their repression.

His meeting with the General Court. June 16.

The formal language of his manifesto (so to call it) when, following the example set by Lord Bellomont, he addressed the Legislature, at its meeting, in a set speech, disclosed the rancor which former events had inspired. Some of his hearers must have found it hard to listen with composure to the language of easy superiority in which he announced the proposed system of his government, and his views of the relations and duty of the Province to the parent country. "Not being," he told the Court, "so profitable to the crown in customs as the southern Colonies, Massachusetts ought to make up the deficiency by falling into such other articles of trade to supply the kingdom of England with naval stores, and other commodities there wanting, of which the Province was capable, as might remove this objection, and cause it to be less chargeable to the crown, at the same time keeping within the strictest bounds of all Acts of Parliament." Lofty insolence to be used to men who had sat by his side in council with Endicott and Danforth, and to whom he had been a suppliant in the former years of his merited defeat and helplessness! Galling insolence especially from the lips of the son of the stout Puritan who had left England behind for other objects than that of contributing to her supply of naval stores! The Governor announced that he was expressly instructed to urge the rebuilding by the Province of the fort at Pemaquid, the provision of a house for his residence, and the establishment of regular and sufficient salaries for the Governor, Lieutenant-Governor, and Judges.[1] He said it was remarked in England that Massachusetts was the only Province in which such provision was not made.[2]

Four days afterwards arrived intelligence from the Queen's Secretary of State[3] of her declaration of war against France. Thinking his presence immediately necessary in the eastern country, where trouble was now to be apprehended from the Indians, the Governor prorogued the General Court with some expressions of disappointment at their neglect of the matters of business he had laid before them. They had taken no action upon either of his proposals; but in place of the consent to one of them, which he had promised himself, they pursued the usual course. The scantiness of the grant which they made him of five

War with France. June 20.

June 27.

June 24.

[1] Hutchinson (History, II. 152) understood that Dudley had led the ministry to expect that he would be able to carry this point, and that accordingly his urgency in respect to it, and his mortification when he failed, were the greater.

[2] "Colonel Dudley desiring that some method may be taken for disposing the Assembly of Massachusetts Bay to settle a salary upon her Majesty's Governor of that Province, directions were given for preparing an article for that purpose to be inserted in the instructions to be given him." (Journal of the Board of Trade for June 24, 1702.) For Dudley's instructions, see Mass. Hist. Col., XXIX. 100.

In Governor Burnet's time, in the year 1729, when the controversy about stated salaries was at its height, the House of Representatives published a volume entitled "A Collection of the Proceedings of the Great and General Court or Assembly of his Majesty's Province of the Massachusetts Bay, in New England, containing several instructions from the crown to the Council and Assembly of that Province for fixing a salary on the Governor, and their Determinations thereon, as also the Measures taken by the Court for supporting the several Governors, since the Arrival of the Present Charter." Beginning with a recital of grants to Phips, Bellomont, and Stoughton, it exhibits in detail the transactions relating to this subject down to an advanced stage of the struggle with Burnet. I shall refer to it under the title of "Collection of Proceedings."

[3] 1702, May 15, Lord Nottingham became Secretary of State, *vice* Manchester. War was declared May 4.

hundred pounds,[1] when compared with their recent liberality to Lord Bellomont, was an indication both of their unfriendly sentiments towards himself, and of their determination to keep the question of the Governor's maintenance in their own hands.

The Governor, accompanied by a party of friends for whom he did not see fit to procure any authority from the General Court, proceeded into the eastern country, going as far as to Pemaquid. There he met some representatives of the native tribes, whom he persuaded to renew their assurances of pacific intentions. Congratulating the Court, when it came together again in the autumn, on this happy result of his journey, he renewed, but with no better success, his application for fixed salaries for himself and the Judges, and for the restoring of the fort at Pemaquid. He said that, on his late visit to that work, he had found that the foundation was still good; that a quantity of the materials of the old structure, demolished six years before by the French, was on the spot in a condition to be used again, and that there was abundance of lime close at hand. The Representatives could not be brought to view the proposal with favor. At this time, as well as earlier and later, they insisted that Pemaquid, remote from the vicinity of the settlements, was no fit place for a fort intended to give them security; that its position on the coast was such as to render it incapable of being made tenable against an enemy, except by a heavy outlay; and that in no view would a fortification there be useful to the Province in a degree proportioned to the inevitable cost. They judged that the pertinacity with which the matter was urged by the English government was due, not, as was pretended, to considerations of their interest, but to an exaggerated opinion of the importance of a work at Pemaquid in maintaining an English possession of that territory between the Kennebec and the Penobscot, which

Oct. 27.

Fortification of Pemaquid.

[1] Mass. Province Laws, I. 498.

belonged by treaty to the English or to the French according to the interpretation which should be given to the disputed name *Acadie*.

The House had no mind to discuss the question with the Governor. It preferred to hold its ground by silence and inaction. The Council, which, if not favoring his plan, desired at all events to have him conciliated by respect, proposed a conference, which the House took the strong and unusual step of refusing. Nov. 3. The Council, by a unanimous vote, declared this to be a breach of its privileges. The House yielded so far as to retract its refusal to go into a conference, but, after it had been held, persisted in its denial of the appropriation required. Nov. 11. It made an allowance to the Governor of six hundred pounds, "for the present year," including the five hundred pounds granted to him just after his arrival. This sum the Council voted to be insufficient. The House added a hundred pounds. The Council repeated its vote, but finding that here the Deputies intended to make a stand, they at length advised the Governor to accept the grant.[1]

Differences between the Representatives and the Council.

In considering the differences which throughout the provincial history occasionally, as now, arose between the two branches of the Legislature, the diversity in the constitution of the two bodies should be borne in mind. The House of Representatives, coming directly from the people, most naturally reflected the popular feeling of the day. The Counsellors, who were commonly men of property and advanced in life, might be supposed to be averse to novel and disturbing measures. Nominated from year to year as they were by

[1] General Court and Council Records. — Feb. 16, 1703, "ordered, that a representation be prepared to her Majesty upon the subject of the presents made to Colonel Dudley by the Massachusetts Bay Assembly since his arrival in those parts, and to set forth their neglect of making any settled provision for his salary." (Journal of the Board of Trade.)

the General Court, and on each nomination subject to be set aside by the Governor, the honor attached to the place made it an object of ambition, and so far disinclined the candidate to incur the displeasure of either of the parties who had it in their gift.

In view of the hostilities which were to be apprehended, the House voted to send aid to the neighboring Colonies, with the careful exception of New York, whose alleged cowardly alliance with the Indians and mischievous traffic with the French had awakened warm displeasure. Nov. 19. But, on a reconsideration of the subject, the exception was withdrawn. The Governor, conceiving that it was 1703. time for a Court to sit convened under writs bear- March 11. ing the name of Queen Anne, dissolved the existing Court, as he had power to do by the charter, though its legal year had not expired; and the parties separated with little mutual satisfaction.[1] The Governor vented his spleen in a letter to the Lords of Trade. Dudley's dissatisfaction with Massachusetts. Secure, as he supposed, against the exposure of his communications, he wrote: 1702. Dec. 10. "The figure this government makes is by no means so good as an ordinary head-borough in the kingdom of England, while they are a very important Province, and have the best harbors and outlets to the sea in all North America. The major part of the people by far would rejoice to be annexed, and brought under her Majesty's immediate commission, if her Majesty please so to command. . . . . . The Council being of the people's election, many of the most loyal people and of the best estates are not employed, and those that are so, many of them are Commonwealth's men, and all do so absolutely depend for their station upon the people that they dare not offend them, and so her Majesty has no manner of service from them."[2] Colonel Robert Quarry was at that time Judge of Admiralty in New York and

[1] Mass. Prov. Rec.

[2] British Colonial Papers.

Pennsylvania. He "thought himself obliged to make some remarks upon the government of New England" to the Lords of Trade. "Colonel Dudley," he wrote, "hath been forced already to dissolve two Assemblies, nor will the third any ways answer his expectation. . . . . . They say that he hath given several instances of his remembering the old quarrel, and they resolve on their parts never to forget it; so that it is generally believed he will never gain any point from them." Quarry thought that, towards a correction of a dangerous restlessness, nothing would "so effectually answer as reducing all the Provinces on the main of America to one standard rule and constitution of government."[1]

1703. June 16.

Having had his former knowledge revived of the intractableness of Massachusetts legislatures, the Governor prepared a less supercilious reception for the new Court. He congratulated them in courteous terms on their freedom hitherto from those inroads of French and Indians which there had been so much reason to dread, and he renewed his application for the construction of the fort at Pemaquid as a judicious measure of precaution. But on that point the Deputies were immovable.

The time had come for the confident Governor to assert himself by more than language. Giving effect to the provision in the charter that the nomination of Counsellors by the two Houses should be subject to the Governor's approval, Sir William Phips had set aside the election of Cooke, who had opposed him in England when the new charter was in progress. In no other instance as yet had this invidious power of the King's representative been exerted. When the first list of Counsellors chosen after his coming to the government was presented, Dudley "sent for Mr. Speaker and the House forthwith to attend him in the Council Chamber," and told them "he took notice that there were

His rejection of Counsellors. May 27.

[1] Mass. Hist. Col., XXVII. 230.

several gentlemen left out that were of the Council last year, who were of good ability, for estate and otherwise, to serve her Majesty, and well disposed thereto, and that some others who were new elected were not so well qualified, some of them being of little or mean estate." Accordingly he struck off five names from the list, those of Elisha Cooke and Thomas Oakes (the agents for the Colony in England twelve years before), Peter Sargent (husband of Governor Phips's widow), John Saffin, a leading citizen of Bristol, and John Bradford, grandson of the Governor of Plymouth. The reasons which he alleged had little application to these men. No one of them appears to have been "of little or mean estate," any more than, in a just estimate, "not well qualified." Cooke, at least, was a richer man than the Governor. Besides John Pynchon, who had died since the last election, the Court had left out from the last year's Board John Appleton, Barnabas Lothrop, Nathaniel Thomas, Nathaniel Byfield, and Samuel Partridge, and had substituted for them Edward Bromfield, Samuel Hayman, John Walley, John Saffin, John Bradford, and Thomas Oakes; the last three, rejected by the Governor, being one-half of the newly chosen Counsellors. This measure of his was taken with deliberation, the occasion for it having come seasonably to his knowledge. On the eve of the assembling of the Court, he wrote to the Lords of Trade: "The choice of her Majesty's Counsellors here is within a few days, and the Assembly already chosen for that purpose. There has been apparent methods taken in the choice of Assembly-men, that no such should be chosen as had shown their obedience to her Majesty's command for the rebuilding of Pemaquid, or for the settling of a salary for the support of the government."[1] His reflection

May 10.

[1] "As to the Province of the Massachusetts Bay, which is a charter government, the inhabitants have been always averse to any compliance with the directions that have been frequently sent from hence for set-

n the whole was: "It is every day more apparent that nothing will proceed well here till her Majesty will please o name her own Council. The best men in the Province an have no share in the civil government till then."[1] His ction naturally increased the coldness between him and he General Court, and a proposal which he made or the appointment of a Surveyor-General of ands granted by the Province was bluntly rejected.[2]

June 8.

Lord Cornbury, the Queen's cousin, who had now sueeeded Lord Bellomont as Governor of New York, informed Dudley of his having intelligence from Albany of meditated attack upon the settlement at Deerfield by a orce of French and Indians.[3] For the present this proved false alarm; but there was only too much reason to exect trouble along the whole northern frontier. Dudley

ling a fixed revenue for the support f that government or the Governor; nd upon application made to the Council and Assembly by Colonel Dudley, your Majesty's present Govrnor, pursuant to your Majesty's nstructions to him, they have wholly leclined the same, persisting in their usual way of making only temporary provisions for the charge of the govrnment, whereby they have kept your Majesty's Governors there in a continual dependence upon them for voluntary presents, which to the present Governor have been as yet very inconsiderable.

"Whereupon we humbly offer that your Majesty would be pleased, by a letter under your royal sign manual, directed to the Council of that Province, to be communicated likewise to the Assembly, to require them that, in consideration of the great privileges they enjoy, they do settle a constant allowance, suitable to the character and dignity of that government, without limitation of time, upon the Governor, together with a fitting provision for the Lieutenant-Governor or Commander-in-chief for the time being; in which letter it may be intimated to them that, if they neglect this opportunity of complying with your Majesty's just expectations, your Majesty will be obliged to have recourse to such remedies as may be proper and effectual in order to a due provision herein." (Representation of the Lords of Trade, April 2, 1703.)

"This representation is approved, and the letters and instructions abovesaid ordered to be written." (Register of Privy Council, April 10, 1703.)

1 Letter to the Lords of Trade, of Sept. 15, 1703, in British Colonial Papers.

2 July 21, 1703, "the Board was informed that Nathaniel Byfield is appointed Judge of the Admiralty, and Paul Dudley [the Governor's son] Attorney-General of the Massachusetts Bay." (Journal of the Board of Trade, *sub die.*)

3 Mass. Prov. Rec., for May 27, 1703; comp. letter of Solomon Stoddard to Governor Dudley, of Oct. 22, 1703, in Mass. Hist. Col., XXXII. 235.

invited the eastern chiefs to a conference, which, accompanied by several considerable men of Massachusetts and New Hampshire, he held with them at Casco, then the most remote English settlement that was recovering itself from the devastations of King William's war. The savages made the most friendly professions. "As high as the sun is above the earth," protested their chief spokesman, "so far distant shall our designs be of making the least breach between each other"[1] Another said that some French priests had been endeavoring to engage them in hostilities against the English, but that they were "as firm as the mountains, and should continue so as long as the sun and moon endured."[2] Some

Conference with the Indians. June 20.

[1] Folsom, History of Saco and Biddeford, 198 *et seq.*

[2] Penhallow, History of the Wars of New England, &c., 2–4; comp. Niles's History of the Indian and French Wars, in Mass. Hist. Col., XXVI. 247. The former work, of which there is a reprint in N. H. Col., I. 14 *et seq.*, is the great English contemporary authority for the events of this second *woful decade*. Its title-page bears the fit motto:—

"Nescio tu quibus es, lector, lecturus ocellis;
Hoc scio, quod siccis scribere non potui."

Samuel Penhallow was an Englishman, a pupil, with Daniel Defoe (see above, Vol. III. 547), of the Rev. Charles Morton, with whom he came to New England in 1686 (extract from Penhallow's Diary, in Mass. Hist. Col., XI. 161), being then twenty-one years old. He became a member of Morton's church at Charlestown, but before long established himself in trade at Portsmouth, where he married a daughter of President Cutt, and accumulated what was then thought a large property. When New Hampshire annexed itself to Massachusetts, after the deposition of Andros, he served as Treasurer of the Province (N.H. Provincial Papers, II. 41), and at the accession of Governor Dudley he became a Counsellor (Ibid., 376), in which capacity he was personally cognizant of much of that course of events which he relates. His narrative terminates with the pacification in August, 1726, and he died four months after that time. — Samuel Niles graduated at our Cambridge in 1699, the first native Rhode Islander ever bred at a college. ("I was the first that came to college from Rhode Island government." Mass. Hist. Col., XXVI. 274.) He was settled as minister of Braintree in 1711, and died there in 1762. A little time before his death he spoke of his historical compilation to John Adams; but it continued in manuscript, and was lost sight of, till some time after the year 1830 it was found in a box of papers belonging to the Massachusetts Historical Society, who published it in the twenty-sixth and thirty-fifth volumes of their Collections. The treatise, of which the design is announced to be "to give a narrative of the wars in the land from the year 1634 to this present year, 1760," is, as to all the period down to 1745, of extremely little original value, bearing the

suspicious circumstances were observed, but the parties separated in apparent friendship, and Dudley returned to congratulate the Court on the happy result of the expedition. The House made a grant to him of three hundred pounds "towards his support in the management of the government." The Council returned the vote, with a request to have it reconsidered. The House sent it back unaltered. The Council returned it a second time, with the inquiry "whether it was a gratuity, or payment for service, and for what time." The House refused to depart from the ground which it had taken. On the advice of the Council the Governor accepted the grant, and the Court was prorogued.[1]

July 8.

July 23.

July 27.

July 31.

Before it met again in the autumn, the Indians had committed outrages, which turned out to be the beginning of another terrible ten years' war. No act of the colonists provoked it. A party of English vagabonds on the Penobscot plundered a house belonging to a half-breed son of the Baron de Castine, who was now in France; but the action of the government of Massachusetts on the son's complaint was such that he expressed himself fully satisfied,[2] and it was not pretended that this incident had any connection with more serious disorders

Beginning of a new war.

same relation to Morton's Memorial, Church's Entertaining Passages, Hubbard's Indian Wars, Mather's Magnalia, and Penhallow's History, as that which exists between the Histories of Hubbard and Winthrop. The reader who will compare Niles's account of the *woful decade* in King William's time (Hist. Col., XXVI. 206–245) with Mather's of the same events (Magnalia, VII. 64–93) will find the former to be to a great extent a mere transcript of the latter, with occasionally an interpolation (Hist. Col., XXVI. 220–224); a strain of reflection (Ibid., 233, 234); a condensation (Ibid., 231, 232; comp. Magnalia, VII. 82–84); or an omission (Ibid., 85, 86). And the same was his treatment of Penhallow's narrative, not only of the second ten years' war in Queen Anne's time, but of the disturbances (1719–1726) in the next reign (Penhallow, 81–135; comp. Hist. Soc. Col., XXXV. 337–365), when he might seem to have reached an age to be capable of better work than that of a mere copyist.

[1] Collection of Proceedings, 10.

[2] Williamson, History of Maine, II. 42.

which broke out in the eastern country about the same time.

The calamities which were impending had a quite different source. Neither at the French court, nor by its military or ecclesiastical servants in Canada, had it been supposed that the war between New England and New France had been any thing more than suspended by the treaty of Ryswick. In the five years that had since elapsed, preparations for the renewal of hostilities had at no time been remitted by the soldiers and priests at Quebec and Montreal. "In the present juncture," thought the Count de Frontenac, when he had had six months to reflect on the news of peace, "there is nothing better to be done than to inspire the Iroquois with distrust of the New-Englanders."[1] Villebon, Governor of Nova Scotia, wrote home to the French ministry that he had not force enough to obstruct the restoration by the English of the fort at Pemaquid, and of the settlements along the Kennebec, but that he hoped to accomplish that object by means of the neighboring savages.[2] Frontenac died, and the inconstant Iroquois, relieved from the terror of his name, showed a disposition to withdraw from engagements which they had made with him.[3] De Callières, his successor, pursued with scarcely less skill his method of alternate intimidation and caresses. He piqued the savages with the assurance that the English claimed them as subjects, while the French respected them as voluntary allies.[4] He invited some of their chiefs to Montreal, and obtained their consent to a sort of treaty which he persuaded them need not disturb their friendly relations with the English.[5] He lost no opportunity for establishing priests and missionary stations among them,

French intrigues with the Indians.

1698. August.

Oct. 3.

Nov. 28.

1700. Sept. 8.

[1] Charlevoix, II. 229.
[2] Ibid., 235.
[3] Ibid., 237.
[4] Ibid., 242, 247, 364.
[5] Ibid., 252.

"not so much because they appeared disposed for religious instruction," but because of the utility of having persons among them "who should inform the Governor-General of their movements, and disconcert the intrigues of the English, who were little to be feared in that part of the country, unless they had the Five Nations for allies."[1] De Callières died, and again the advantage of the personal influence of an able statesman was lost. The most that could be done by his successor, De Vaudreuil, lately Governor of Montreal, was to obtain an engagement from the Iroquois of neutrality in the existing war.[2]

1703. May 26.

With the Abenaquis on the north of New England the solicitations of the French had been more successful, and a close friendship had been established. Some families of these savages, converts to Romanism, were collected in two villages, called Beçancour and St. François, on the south side of the river St. Lawrence, near to the town of Three Rivers.[3] At Norridgewock, on the Kennebec, close to the old English settlements, only thirty miles from the present capital of Maine, was another station, an important centre of communication and influence, superintended by the Jesuit, Sebastian Rasle.

Relieved for the present from anxiety about the Iroquois, the new French Governor turned his attention towards the northern frontier of New England. Two months had not passed since the treaty of Casco, when on one day six or seven bands of savages, some of them led by French officers, fell upon the scattered settlements. "They committed," says the calm French historian, Charlevoix, "some ravages of little consequence. They killed about three hundred men. But the essential point was to engage the Abenaquis in such a manner that

Hostilities in the eastern country. Aug. 10.

[1] Charlevoix, II. 285.
[2] Ibid., 289.
[3] Williamson, History of Maine, II. 40.

it would not be possible for them to retract."[1] At Wells thirty-nine persons, at Winter Harbor thirty-five, and at Spurwink twenty-two, were either killed or carried away prisoners. Cape Porpoise (now Kennebunk Port) was wholly desolated. The little fort at Scarborough maintained itself, but with the loss of several men. At Saco the marauders killed eleven persons, and carried off twenty-four captives. At the settlement of Perpooduck, consisting of nine families, twenty-five persons were murdered, and eight led away. Major March, at Casco, on the eastern border, was threatened by a force of five hundred French and Indians, and after a skirmish was only saved by the arrival of a reinforcement from Boston, having been by a flag of truce enticed out of his fort into an ambush, whence he was with difficulty extricated by a sally of some of his men. The party came as far west as Hampton, "where they slew four, besides the Widow Mussey, who was a remarkable speaking Quaker, and much lamented by that sect." The massacres were attended with every aggravation of cruelty. "As the milk-white brows of the grave and ancient had no respect shown, so neither had the mournful cries of tender infants the least pity; for they triumphed at their misery, and applauded such as the skilfullest artists who were most dexterous in contriving the greatest tortures."[2]

Sept. 1. The Governor called the Court together, to consult on the state of affairs. He informed them that he had marched four hundred troops into Maine, a

[1] These movements were directed by the Marquis de Vaudreuil, just appointed Governor-General of Canada, on the death of the Chevalier de Callières. "M. de Vaudreuil forma un parti de ces sauvages, auquel il joignit quelques Français sous la conduite du Sieur de Beaubussin, lieutenant, et il les envoya dans la Nouvelle Angleterre. Ils y firent quelques ravages de peu de conséquence, mais ils tuèrent environ trois cent hommes. D'ailleurs le point essentiel était d'engager les Abénaquis de manière qu'il ne fut plus en leur pouvoir de reculer." (Charlevoix, II. 289, 290; comp. 428.)

[2] Penhallow, 5–8; Niles, in Mass. Hist. Soc., XXVI. 248–250.

sufficient force, as he hoped, to secure tranquillity. But he was too sanguine. After a short pause, perhaps used to get a supply of ammunition, the ravages were renewed. At Blackpoint, twenty men, at work in the fields, were set upon by two hundred Indians, and all Oct. 6. but one were killed or made prisoners. A similar fate befell some twelve or fifteen persons at York and Berwick. At the latter place, in revenge for their repulse on a first assault, the savages burned to death one of their captives. In the winter they took a garrison- 1704. house at Haverhill by surprise, and made several Feb. 8. prisoners. Dudley sent two strong parties into the eastern country. But the distance at which the Indians kept themselves was such that before they could be reached, though extraordinary forced marches were made, the provisions which, over a country impassable by horses, the English carried in their knapsacks, were exhausted, and they were obliged to turn back for fear of starving.[1]

The alarm for an assault upon Deerfield had been only premature.[2] This village, slowly recovering from the ravages of the last war, was still so poor that the General Court had lately made a grant for the support of its minister. In the service of the Governor-General of Canada, the partisan soldier, Hertel de Rouville, " worthily filled,"

[1] Niles, in Mass. Hist. Soc., XXVI. 250–252; Penhallow, 9–11. —" February 8, Joseph Bradlee's garrison of Haverhill was unhappily surprised by a small scout. . . . . . The housewife, perceiving the misery that was attending her, and having boiling soap on the fire, scalded one of them to death. The sentinel within was slain, and she with several others were taken, which was the second time of her captivity. But that which heightened her affliction was being with child, and yet obliged to travel in a deep snow, under a heavy burden, and many days together without subsistence, excepting a few bits of skin, ground nuts, bark of trees, wild onions, and lily roots. Nevertheless, she was wonderfully supported, and at last safely delivered. But the babe soon perished for want of nourishment and by the cruelty of the Indians, who, as it cried, threw hot embers in its mouth."

[2] " From Deerfield in the west to Wells in the east is the frontier to the inland of both the Provinces." (Letter of Dudley to the Lords of Trade, of April 8, 1712, in British Colonial Papers.)

writes Charlevoix, "the place of his father, whose age and infirmities no longer allowed him to go on distant expeditions."[1] With four brothers, he led a party of two hundred and fifty French and Indians from Montreal to the north-western frontier of Massachusetts. The drifts which they traversed on snow-shoes lay deep around the little hamlet, and buried the palisades which had been set for its protection. Approaching stealthily, the enemy lay around it on a cold winter's night. "Not long before break of day," observing that the sentries had left their posts, they climbed over the snow-banks, and fell upon the sleeping inhabitants. They slaughtered sixty, and took a hundred prisoners; twenty-four hours they "spent in plundering, burning, and destroying," and then, to escape pursuit, "withdrew into the woods, carrying with them their plunder and captives." They were followed to some distance by as many armed men as could be suddenly collected from the lower towns; but, for want of snow-shoes, the pursuit was ineffectual, and the marauders, with their booty and their captives, reached Quebec and St. François by a march of twenty-five days.[2]

Sack of Deerfield. Feb. 29.

Mr. John Williams, minister of Deerfield, published an account of this tragedy, three years afterwards, when he had been ransomed and had come back to Boston.[3] He says he was roused from sleep by the sound of axes and hatchets plied against his doors and windows. Leaping from his bed, he found that the house was already entered, and by the time he could seize his arms, twenty of the enemy, as he judged,

Captivity of the minister of Deerfield.

[1] Charlevoix, II. 290.

[2] Penhallow, 11–13; comp. Niles, in Mass. Hist. Col., 252, 253; Charlevoix, II. 290.

[3] "The Redeemed Captive returning to Zion: A Faithful History of Remarkable Occurrences in the Captivity and the Deliverance of Mr. John Williams," &c., 1707. The book is dedicated to Governor Dudley, and commemorates gratefully his sending of William Dudley to Quebec to obtain a surrender of prisoners.

"brake into the room, with painted faces and hideous acclamations." A pistol, which he "put to the breast of the first Indian who came up," missed fire, and he was seized and bound. After nearly an hour, during which time they often threatened his life, "holding hatchets over his head," he and his family were allowed to put on some clothes, and, "about sun an hour high, they were all carried out of the house for a march, and saw many of the houses of the neighbors in flames." The snow was as high as their knees. His wife was feeble, having within a few weeks become a mother. He begged "to walk with her, to help her in her journey." She "told him that her strength of her body began to fail, and that he must expect to part with her," but "never spake any discontented word as to what had befallen, but with suitable expressions glorified God." The second day she was taken from him, and before the end of that day, having fallen from weariness in crossing a brook, "the cruel and bloodthirsty salvage who took her slew her with his hatchet." It was a great comfort to him afterwards to learn that "God had put it into the hearts of his neighbors to come out as far as she lay, to take up her corpse, recarry it into the town, and decently to bury it."

During the march Williams's captors often threatened his life. Nineteen of his fellow-prisoners were "murdered by the way, and two starved to death." His "feet were so tender, swollen, bruised, and full of pain, that he could scarce stand upon them;" yet he was forced to travel in snow-shoes twenty-five miles a day. One day he "judged that they went forty or forty-five miles. God wonderfully supported him, and so far renewed his strength, that in the afternoon he was stronger to travel than in the forenoon." He was distressed by vermin, which infested the rags given him in place of his own clothes. It was eight weeks after the catastrophe at Deerfield when he reached Montreal, where the Governor-General took him

from the Indians, and treated him with kindness.[1] After two years and a half more, his friends in Massachusetts having succeeded in obtaining an exchange of prisoners,
1706. he sailed from Quebec on his return, accompanied
Oct. 25. by fifty-seven partners in captivity, two of whom were his children. Another child was earlier ransomed. A son, who was absent from home at the time of the inroad, he found pursuing his studies at college at the expense of some friends. A young daughter, who was still detained, eventually became a Roman Catholic, and gave herself to an Indian husband. She came to Deerfield several years after, but she had become wedded to the wild life of the woods, and could not be wooed back to the scenes and friends of her early years. Such was one of the distressful passages which the Jesuit Charlevoix despatches in the sentence: "De Rouville, in his turn, surprised the English, killed many of them, and took a hundred and fifty prisoners."[2]

Under French officers and French priests, the war continued to be conducted with cruelty as aimless as it was brutal. Expeditions like those from Massachusetts against Quebec had a substantial purpose. If successful, they would establish the empire of New England, and terminate the chronic strife on this continent. For the French in America, so much less numerous than their rivals, conquest was out of the question, unless with the aid of such large forces from the parent country as they were not in the least likely to obtain. The war they waged was simply a succession of isolated barbarities, accomplishing nothing whatever

Aimless barbarities of the war.

[1] Williams, Redeemed Captive, 27. — Williams's house at Deerfield was standing till within twenty or thirty years, with the notches made by the Indian hatchets visible on the front door, and the beams perforated by their bullets.

[2] Charlevoix, II. 290. — A contemporary memorandum of the names of the slain and captives, with the amount of their respective losses in property, is in Proceedings of the Mass. Hist. Soc. for 1867, 481; comp. 478; Ibid. for 1870, 311; Hoyt, Indian Wars, 184–195; John Schuyler's letter in Mass. Arch. LXXII. 13–15.

towards a solution of the question of power.[1] A band of sanguinary savages was led hundreds of miles over the snow to an assault upon some hamlet, where a few poor people had made an opening in the forest, and were beginning to get a hard living. Watching for a time when it reposed in unsuspecting helplessness, they fell upon it by night, burned the dwellings, tortured and massacred some of the inhabitants, and then fled, carrying with them the rest. Of the spoils, they consumed the food and drink, as long as their fear of pursuit allowed. But they found little or no money to carry away, and for more cumbrous booty they had no means of conveyance. They gained nothing except the gratification of their monstrous appetite for mischief, and what they might be paid by their French employers for the prisoners whom they brought in. Nor does this latter kind of profit seem to have entered much into their account, if one may judge by the lavish butchering of their captives on the way.

At sea, there was occasional good fortune for the English. A French privateer, fitted out to intercept 1704.
the spring supplies shipped to New England from April 7.
the West Indies, was wrecked in Massachusetts Bay. A frigate, conveying two thousand muskets to Quebec, was captured by an English squadron.[2]

As warm weather approached, the Indians showed themselves at Wells and at Dover, in quest, at the latter place, of Colonel Waldron, who was fortunately absent April 25.
from home, and so escaped paying another penalty

[1] "Their lying in wait to kill and scalp single persons on our frontiers, their surprising and cutting off families, their stealing of captives, torturing and making slaves of them, and such like murders and cruelties, is what they call carrying on the war. All which is frequently done by their skulking parties, in conjunction with the Indians in their interest, whose bloody and barbarous manners they have imbibed and long practised. And these are mischiefs which nothing can give us so good hope of security from as that removal of this enemy which your Majesty designs." (Conn. Col. Rec., V. 246.)

[2] Penhallow, 13; Niles, in Mass. Hist. Col., XXVI. 254.

of the hoarded vengeance against his race.[1] Similar in-
June 1. vasions of the same place were repeated during
Aug. 11. the year. Even Portsmouth, though less exposed, had to be fortified. In the west, a garrison-house
May 13. on the edge of Northampton was attacked by such a surprise, and with such numbers, that a prompt surrender was the only resource. Of thirty-three persons who were led away, only three reached Canada; nineteen were put to death on the journey, eight were rescued by a pursuing party, and three contrived to effect their escape.[2] There is no variety in these transactions, to constitute the material of a narrative. The whole exposed northern border of Massachusetts, from Casco Bay to Connecticut River, was watched from hiding-places affording every facility for sudden invasion and safe retreat. "Under all these sufferings from a cruel enemy, little or no impression could ever be made upon them, by reason of their retiring into inaccessible swamps and mountains." Terrible distress was the lot of numbers, and, for all the dwellers along the wide border, life was insecure and miserable.[3]

A succession of disconnected inroads on the frontier towns took place during the summer, — as at Amesbury, Haverhill, Exeter, Dover, and York.[4] An abortive assault
Oct. 25. on Lancaster was made disastrous by the fate of Mr. Gardiner, minister of that place, who in

[1] Niles, in Mass. Hist. Col., XXVI. 254; Penhallow, 14, 15.—At this time, May 20, Robert Harley succeeded Lord Nottingham as Secretary of State.

[2] Ibid., 15, 16; Niles, in Mass. Hist. Col., XXVI. 255.

[3] In July of this year, Dudley sent one Captain Cary to England, to represent to Lord Nottingham the state of things in Massachusetts, and procure arms and stores. "Keep a good courage and temper," — so Dudley instructed him (July 20), — "and be loath to return without some favorable provision for us from her Majesty, and represent the government and its present state with the Indian enemy justly and honorably, as you ought." Cary obtained, Jan. 11, 1705, a grant of twenty cannon for Castle William. (British Colonial Papers; comp. Journal of the Board of Trade, for Jan. 26, 1705, Jan. 23, 1706.)

[4] Niles, in Mass. Hist. Col., XXVI. 259; Penhallow, 20.

the dark was accidentally shot by a sentinel.[1] In the winter, Captain Hilton, of Exeter,[2] led a force of two hundred and seventy men against the Jesuit post at Norridgewock. They marched through snow three feet deep, carrying provisions for twenty days. They found the settlement deserted, and had no reward for their enterprise, except the burning of the chapel.[3] 1705. February.

A messenger, sent to Canada to negotiate for an exchange and ransom of prisoners, learned that there were a hundred and eighty-seven in the hands of the French and their allies. The French Governor was with difficulty prevailed upon to consent to the liberation of one-third of this number, to whom, in the following year, were added nearly as many more.[4] A delusive period of comparative quiet had lasted through more than a year,[5] when at Oyster River a garrison-house was attacked. It happened at the moment to be occupied by none but women. "They put on hats, with their hair hanging down, and fired so briskly that they struck a terror in the enemy, and they withdrew."[6] Two days after, near Kittery, two men, a father and son, fell in the way of a party of savages. They killed the father, May 4. 1706. April 27.

[1] Niles, in Mass. Hist. Col., XXVI. 261; comp. Penhallow, 27.

[2] Dexter's edition of Church's Entertaining Passages, 146, note. There is a biographical notice of Hilton in the Historical Collections of Farmer and Moore, I. 241.

[3] Penhallow, 28; Mass. Hist. Col., XXVI. 260. A copy of a journal kept by Hilton on this expedition is in the collection of British Colonial Papers. On one day, January 17, his command marched thirty miles, and on some other days twenty-five miles. In a note at the end Dudley writes: "This march was made upon the snow a yard deep, every man on snow-shoes, with twenty days' provisions upon small hand-sleds carrying each four men's provisions, and of three hundred men in the expedition no man returned sick." (Comp. N. H. Provincial Papers, II. 453.)

[4] Niles, in Mass. Hist. Col., XXVI. 262, 278; Penhallow, 29, 30.

[5] "The English, by this time becoming skilful in wearing snow-shoes, terrified the Indians to such a degree that they came no more in the winter." (Mass. Hist. Col., XXVI. 275.) — "Since my coming hither, the people have got the skill of snow-shoes, to the terror of Indians." (Dudley to the Lords of Trade, April 8, 1712, in British Colonial Papers.)

[6] Niles, in Mass. Hist. Col., XXVI. 275; Penhallow, 32.

and took the son along with them. "In their march they were so inhumanly cruel that they bit off the tops of his fingers, and to stanch the blood seared them with hot tobacco-pipes."[1] In the excitement that existed, the government offered a reward to regular soldiers of ten pounds for every Indian scalp they should bring in, of twenty pounds to volunteers in the service, and of fifty pounds to volunteers not under pay.[2] Yet so difficult was the pursuit of these cunning enemies, that, according to the computation of the time, "every Indian we had killed or taken cost the country at least a thousand pounds. While they continued in great bodies, they did not commit the like spoil and rapine, in proportion as they did in smaller."[3]

This desultory and harassing conflict had been going on but a little time before the people of Massachusetts came to understand at what a disadvantage they were conducting it. Their superiority to the French in numbers and strength gave very partial protection, while, standing on the defensive, they presented to their enemy an extended frontier, which he could choose his own time and place for assailing. The actual distress in Massachusetts and New Hampshire was grievous. By special commissioners
1704. Dudley applied to Rhode Island and Connecticut,
November. for reinforcements of troops. It was still hoped that the Five Nations might be persuaded to undertake hostilities against the native adherents of the French, and a joint commission from Massachusetts and Connecticut was sent to endeavor to engage them in such a movement. "They promised to take up the hatchet whenever the Governor of New York should desire it."[4] Lord Cornbury could not be brought to interest himself in behalf of the suffering New-Englanders, being apprehensive, as was

[1] Penhallow, 33.

[2] March 7, 1707, a bounty of a hundred pounds for each scalp was voted to volunteers without pay. (General Court Record, *sub die.*)

[3] Penhallow, 39, 40.

[4] N. H. Provincial Papers, II. 260; Penhallow, 25.

thought, of a disturbance of "the vast trade between the Dutch and Indians." Yet under all these discouragements, when Vaudreuil, apprehensive, perhaps, that the fickle Iroquois might be brought into closer relations with the English, proposed a peace,[1] the General Court advised the Governor against the measure. 1705. Nov. 30.

When the English undertook to conduct the war on a system better according with their own position, it was still generally with more courage than good management, and rarely with good success. It was rightly thought that to attack the Indians, and yet more rightly that to attack the French, in their strongholds, was the true way to obtain tranquillity. But some fatality seemed to attend the conduct of expeditions of this sort.

Ineffective expedition of Major Church. 1704. May.

The spirited veteran, Major Church, not thought to be yet too old for effective service, was placed in command of an expedition expected to operate vigorously in the eastern country. Three ships of war convoyed thirty-six whale-boats, besides fourteen transports, which conveyed five hundred and fifty men. John Gorham, son of the officer of the same name who led one of the two Plymouth companies in Philip's war, was second in command, and had charge of the whale-boats.

Church, with abilities not equal to his self-confidence, accomplished but little towards the main object of the

[1] A paper in the British Colonial Office, dated at Quebec, Oct. 20, 1705, bears the title "Proposals of a Treaty to be made between the two Colonies of New France and New England, according to proposals made by Mr. Veech [Vetch?] in behalf of Mr. Dudley, General-Governor of New England, to M. de Vaudreuil, General-Governor of New France." The terms of pacification proposed by the French Governor are so moderate as to make it seem probable that he distrusted his ability to maintain himself. He proposed that he and Dudley should reciprocally bind themselves to "hinder all acts of hostility" on the part of the savages as well as of their own countrymen; to allow and promote commerce between their respective governments; to surrender all prisoners "taken as well by sea as land;" and "to do all that is possible to get" prisoners "out of the hands of the savages, and afterwards to send them to their countries."

war. He landed on the banks of the Penobscot and of Passamaquoddy Bay; but the natives kept out of his way, and he only took some prisoners, and brought away a quantity of "goods and stores," burning what he had not the means to carry off. Next he crossed the Bay of Fundy, and destroyed a little town called Menis, near Port Royal, in Nova Scotia. He had wished to attack Port Royal; but the Governor, to whom before leaving Boston he had proposed that step, had forbidden it, on the ground that it was under consideration in England, and had not as yet been authorized. Church, however, submitted it to the consideration of a council of war, who determined that the country had been so widely alarmed that it could not be attempted with a prospect of success. The expensive expedition had no important consequence. The people of Massachusetts were disappointed and angry. Dudley was suspected of having played false. Church's reception at home was cold, though, both to save appearances to the public, and avoid mortifying a well-intentioned and on the whole well-deserving man, the General Court judged it expedient to gratify him by a formal vote of thanks and approbation.[1]

June 20.

July 4.

Not so soon as might have been expected, offensive operations were resumed. The government of Massachusetts resolved to make a descent on Nova Scotia, and

[1] Penhallow, 16–19; Niles, in Hist. Soc. Col., XXVI. 253, 255–257; Church, Entertaining Passages, 99–120. — In January, 1707, under Dudley's orders, Colonel Hilton conducted a second expedition, of two hundred and fifty men, to Norridgewock. It had no further success than the killing of sixteen Indians. On this occasion one of those marvels is related to have occurred which have occasionally found a place in other histories. "This happened at break of day on the 21st of January, and in the morning of the same day the story of the exploit was told at Portsmouth, a distance of sixty miles from the scene of action." (N. H. Provincial Papers, II. 492; comp. Penhallow, 40, 41; Niles, in Mass. Hist. Col., XXXV. 312.) If the writers had had a smattering of Greek history, they might have referred to Herodotus (X. 100) for a parallel case.

solicited help from the other Colonies for that purpose.[1] New Hampshire[2] and Rhode Island engaged in the enterprise, in the measure of their small ability. Connecticut, little annoyed by the continuance of the existing state of things, did not see reason to take a part.[3] Under the convoy of a frigate of the royal navy, and an armed vessel belonging to the Province, a thousand men commanded by Colonel March sailed from Boston and landed before Port Royal. After a skirmish, the French shut themselves up in their fort, which was well provided. They kept up a constant fire upon the besiegers, who were at the same time attacked on the other side by a force of Indians from the interior. The English made regular investments and approaches, and feebly attempted an assault. But, except personal courage and some experience in a small way, March appears to have had no qualification for command. He became bewildered, and his troops fell into discouragement and disorder. A council of war resolved "that the enemy's well-disciplined garrison in a strong fort was more than a match for our raw, undisciplined army," and, in less than two weeks from the time of landing, the troops were re-embarked on board the transports.[4] The fleet came to Casco Bay, whence a message was sent to Boston for further orders. Boston was thrown into a rage, in which the characters of the commanders received ungentle treatment. Dudley, reluctant to acquiesce in so discreditable a

Fruitless expedition against Port Royal.

1707. May 13.

May 26.

May 29.

June 6, 7.

[1] General Court Records, for March 10–22, 1706.

[2] N. H. Provincial Papers, II. 497, 498.

[3] Conn. Col. Rec., V. 17.

[4] Penhallow (42, 43) and Niles (Hist. Soc. Col., XXXV. 313, 314) tell this mortifying story very briefly. They lay the blame on the commander of the British frigate. Hutchinson (II. 169 *et seq.*), from authentic sources, supplies many interesting facts. — "Three transport ships, five brigantines, and fifteen sloops, with whale-boats answerable," were employed. (Penhallow, 42; comp. N. H. Provincial Papers, II. 504–513.)

termination of his undertaking, sent a message to March to await further orders where he was.

To supersede him by a superior officer would have been imprudent, for he was a favorite with the soldiers, and, if he had not acquitted himself well in this instance, there was no reason to suppose that he had failed to do his best.

July. Three members of the Council were despatched, with a reinforcement of a hundred men, and with authority to represent the Governor. After acquainting themselves with the state of things in the camp, they wrote back that they only persisted because such were the Governor's positive commands. They reported that the force in officers and soldiers did not amount to so many as seven hundred and fifty, "sick and well," and that these were "so extremely dispirited" as not to be "equal to three hundred effective men." Before the expedition returned to Port Royal, there was a mutiny which had to be quelled. March was no longer himself, and at his instance the command was transferred to Wainwright, who was next to him in rank.

Wainwright, though "much disordered in health by a great cold," tried "to keep up a good heart," but there was nothing to inspirit him. His troops were ailing and demoralized. What with dysentery and "mighty swellings in their throats," they were, he wrote from Aug. 14. before Port Royal, "filled with terror at the consideration of a fatal event of the expedition, concluding that, in a short time, there would not be enough to carry off the sick." The enemy were receiving "additional strength every day." They had with diligence and skill been strengthening their fortifications, and were becoming more aggressive, so that it was now "unsafe to proceed on any service without a company of at least one hundred men." Wainwright was uneasy about his Indian auxiliaries, who were intractable and insolent. The captain of the nglish man-of-war attached to the expedition had been elied upon for the help of a hundred men, but he had nade up his mind that it would be exposing them for no ise, and had withdrawn them. "In fine," Wainwright vrites, "most of the forces are in a distressed state, some n body and some in mind; and the longer they are kept iere on the cold ground, the longer it will grow upon hem, and, I fear, the further we proceed the worse the vent. God help us." Within a week the camp vas broken up. The troops were attacked while getting on board the transports, and were only too happy o effect the embarkation without much loss. The miscar-iage, and all its circumstances, were deeply mortifying. A court-martial was ordered, but was never held, perhaps because too great numbers would have come under its scrutiny, and forgetfulness, as speedy as could be had, was better than punishment or amnesty, and better than any attempt at discrimination.[1] Aug. 20.

Dudley's chagrin must have been bitter. But he was not a man to increase his humiliation by avowing it. He met his enraged General Court with no expression of a discomposed mind.[2] "Though," he said, "we have not obtained all that we desired against the enemy, yet we are to acknowledge the favor of God in preserving our forces in the expedition, and prospering them so far as the destruction of the French settlements and estates in and about Port Royal, to a great value, which must needs distress the enemy to a very great degree."

While the expedition which thus disastrously failed was in progress, the savages were more than ever at liberty to

[1] General Court Journal for Oct. 29. When the Governor had ordered a court-martial, officers enough to compose it were not to be found. — The Representatives had desired Dudley to demolish the fort at Port Royal if it should be taken. (Comp. Charlevoix, II. 314–321; Haliburton, Account of Nova Scotia, I. 84.)

[2] Hutchinson, II. 169. — Dudley told the Representatives (General Court Record for August 13) "the forces left Port Royal without any direction from me."

prosecute their devastations along the northern frontier; May–October. and the exposed settlements at Dover, Groton, Kittery, Exeter, Kingston, Casco, York, Wells, Marlborough, Winter Harbor (Biddeford), and Berwick again suffered from their ravages.[1]

Renewal of Indian inroads. It was the usage of these barbarians to disperse with their booty after a hasty invasion, and they left New England to a degree of repose through the next winter. As summer came on, they, with their friends the French, were again on the alert. Two parties, attached to one of which was Hertel de Rouville, who had led the expedition to Deerfield four years before, started from Quebec for the settlements, — one by the way of the river St. Francis, the other by Lake Champlain, — intending to meet near the English border. From cowardice or from whim, most of the Indian auxiliaries fell off, but a party not less than a hundred and fifty in number surprised the score or two of dwellings which made the town of Haverhill, on the Merrimac. Coming upon it just before 1708. Aug. 29. daylight, they fired several houses, plundered others, and killed some thirty or forty of the inhabitants, among whom were the minister, Mr. Rolf, and Captain Wainwright, lately the commander at Port Royal. The towns-people rallied, and after an hour's fighting drove 1709. May 6. them away.[2] Amesbury, Brookfield, and Kittery were again beset, but without much damage. Exeter, near one end of the border line, and Deerfield, near the June 23. other, were invaded anew. One of four men whom the Indians carried off from Exeter, they roasted to death. From Deerfield, though they attempted it with a force of nearly two hundred men, they were this time repulsed with little loss to the conquerors.[3] Dudley in-

[1] Penhallow, 44–46; Niles, in Mass. Hist. Col., XXXV. 314.

[2] Penhallow, 47; Niles, in Mass. Hist. Col., XXXV. 317; comp. Charlevoix, II. 325, 326; Chase, History of Haverhill, 218–225.

[3] Niles, in Mass. Hist. Col., XXXV. 317, 318; Penhallow, 48, 49.

formed the General Court of the arrival of Lord Lovelace as Governor of New York, and advised that he should be desired "to let loose the Maquas and dependencies;" and messengers (Wait Winthrop and John Leverett) were accordingly sent by the Court to New York to confer with him.[1]

Feb. 16.

The plan of attacking the French at the central point of their power, and so cutting off the source of the continually recurring miseries, was so obviously the correct one that it could not fail to be revived as often as from adverse accidents it miscarried; though, more or less, it was embarrassed all along by the sense which prevailed in Massachusetts, and was expressed by her at this time to Lord Dartmouth, Secretary of State, of "the criminal neutrality maintained by New York with the French Indians."[2] The General Court sent an address to the Queen, praying for aid to an expedition, towards which they professed a desire themselves to do their utmost, for the conquest of Nova Scotia and Canada. The proposal was favorably received at Court, and operations on a larger scale were concerted.[3] Colonel Vetch, who, two years before, had been in disgrace in Boston, as will hereafter be related, brought information from England that it was determined to despatch what was thought a sufficient naval force, and five regiments of the regular army; and by him Lord Sunderland sent instructions to Dudley respecting the action of the Colonies. Twelve hundred men were to be enlisted and equipped by Massachusetts and Rhode Island. These united forces were to attempt Quebec, while fifteen hundred men from the Colonies further west were to make a movement by land against Montreal.[4]

Plan for the conquest of New France.

March 31.

April 28.

[1] General Court Record, *sub die.*

[2] Memorial of Massachusetts to Lord Dartmouth, of March 11, 1711. (British Colonial Papers.)

[3] Charlevoix, II. 335 *et seq.*

[4] Letter of Lord Sunderland to Dudley, of April 28, 1709, in British Colonial Papers. — Aug. 14, 1709,

May 20. The Massachusetts troops were promptly mustered at Boston before the end of spring, in consequence of partial intelligence which had preceded the full development of the plan.[1] The western contingent proceeded towards Lake Champlain, and lay encamped at Wood Creek, awaiting information of the arrival at Boston of the English fleet. Month passed after month of anxiety and expense, and the fleet did not appear. At length, General Stanhope having lost the battle of Almanza, intelligence came that the troops expected in Boston were wanted in Portugal, and had been sent thither; and the ministers directed a consideration of the question, whether the preparations which had been made in Massachusetts might not be serviceable against Port Royal. The plan was approved at a consultation between the New England Governors. But the officers in command of the few King's ships which had come to Boston declared that their orders would not justify them in affording assistance, and they took the responsibility of sailing away at once.[2] There was now no convoy for the troops, and, on a request from the General Court, the Governor disbanded them, to put an end to the oppressive expense.[3] The army at Wood Creek, under the command of Nicholson, Lieutenant-Governor of New York,

Postponement of operations. Oct. 11.

Dudley wrote to Lord Sunderland: "I have these seven years last past represented to her Majesty, by all the offices proper, the unspeakable benefit to the British nation to have all the North America in her Majesty's hands, of which there is now a fair prospect, by the favor of Almighty God." (British Colonial Papers.)

[1] As early as March 1, 1709, Vetch received instructions on the subject, which recognized him in a manner as the originator of the scheme. (Papers in the British Colonial Office.) Writing from New York, May 18, he reported that vessels which had been despatched from Portsmouth, March 11, had reached Boston, April 28.—May 26, in his speech at the opening of the General Court for elections, Dudley announced the Queen's purpose, and recommended the utmost expedition and diligence on the part of the Province in carrying out the project.

[2] See letter (dated Boston, Oct. 24, 1709) of Dudley, Vetch, Nicholson, and Moody to Lord Sunderland, in British Colonial Papers.

[3] Dudley put the best face upon the matter in a speech to the General Court, October 26.

was distressed by an epidemic sickness, occasioned, as was afterwards believed, by the perfidy of their native allies, who threw putrid skins into a stream which supplied the English camp.[1] That force also, threatened by a movement of the French, precipitately withdrew, and the whole costly expedition came to nothing.

The project was renewed in the next year as to the less important of its objects, — the conquest of Nova Scotia. Nicholson, who had gone to England for the purpose of urging it, returned to Boston with a fleet of small vessels,[2] which was increased during the summer, by ships of the four New England Colonies and of the royal navy, to the number of thirty-six. These conveyed to Port Royal a force, under his command, consisting of four regiments from New England, and a regiment of royal marines. The garrison, under the command of the officer, Subercase, who had foiled Captain Wainwright three years before, consisted of only two hundred and fifty men, and was too feeble to oppose the landing. At the end of a week, some mortar batteries having been erected, a summons was sent into the fort, and it capitulated the following day on favorable terms. The garrison was to march out with the honors of war, and be conveyed to a French post. Persons dwelling within three miles of the fort (who turned out to be four hundred and eighty-one in number) had liberty to remain for two years at their homes, with their farm-stock, provisions, and furniture, on taking the oaths of allegiance and fidelity to the Queen.[3] The fort was out of repair, and the siege cost the English the lives of only fourteen or fifteen men. But the French were dissatisfied with their officer's conduct.[4] Agreeably

1710. July 15.

Sept. 24.

Conquest of Nova Scotia. Oct. 1.

[1] Charlevoix, II. 337, 339.

[2] Charlevoix (II. 341) relates that this was learned by the French from English prisoners. — Jeremiah Dummer, in England, had solicited the appointment of Judge-Advocate to this expedition. (British Colonial Papers for July 15.)

[3] Haliburton, Nova Scotia, I. 85.

[4] Charlevoix, II. 343.

to a promise from Lord Sunderland, Vetch was "left in command there."[1] It was also intended that he should be Governor of Canada, when further projected operations should have succeeded.[2] Nova Scotia has remained ever since a possession of the British crown.

The summer had brought its accustomed sorrows along the line of the outlying settlements. At Exeter three men were killed, among them Colonel Hilton, of Norridgewock memory. At York, Biddeford, Berwick, Chelmsford, Brookfield, and other places, some murders were committed. The savages went as far as Connecticut, where they entered the towns of Simsbury and Waterbury.[3]

Lord Bolingbroke's project for the conquest of Quebec.

In England the Tory statesmen, Harley and St. John, were now in full power, from whom the people of Massachusetts did not presume to expect proofs of friendship for themselves, or of hostility to France. The surprise was great when Nicholson, who, before the change in the English minis-

1 Penhallow, 49-56; Niles, in Mass. Hist. Col., XXXV. 319-323; comp. letter of Dudley to the Secretary of State, of Nov. 15, 1710, in British Colonial Papers.

2 "The charge last year, when we did nothing, and the reduction of Port Royal this year, have cost this Province forty thousand pounds, which, added to their debts for the defence of the frontiers, will leave them greatly in arrears, while Virginia, Maryland, Pennsylvania, Jersey, and New York are covered by these northern Provinces, and sit quiet from losses or charges." (Letter of Dudley to the Secretary of State, of Nov. 15, 1710, in British Colonial Papers.) — March 21, 1711, "Governor Vetch" drew, in favor of his friend "John Borland, her Majesty's agent," for £2115, "for one hundred and twenty days' victualling of five hundred and sixty-four men," serving "in her Majesty's garrison of Annapolis Royal, in Nova Scotia." (British Colonial Papers.) — Dec. 31, 1712, three months before the peace, the Massachusetts House of Deputies refused to make a grant for supplies to Port Royal. (General Court Records, *sub die.*) — Hutchinson mentions (II. 185) a message sent at this time to Quebec, by the way of Penobscot River, to acquaint Vaudreuil with the conquest of Acadia, and demand the restoration of his prisoners (comp. Penhallow, 56); and he says that the journal of Major Livingstone, who conducted the expedition, was in his hands. After being lost sight of for a century, it has come a few years ago into the possession of the Chicago Historical Society. (Proceedings of the Mass. Hist. Soc. for 1861, 230.)

3 Mass. Hist. Col., XXXV. 325, 326; Penhallow, 58, 59.

try, had gone to England to solicit aid in another expedition,[1] returned with two frigates and two transports, 1711.
bringing orders to proceed in the plan on a large June 8.
scale. His representations had been seconded by Jan. 3.
those of the very able Jeremiah Dummer,[2] who,
the autumn before, had been charged by the General 1710.
Court of the Province with the agency in Nov. 11.
England, Sir Henry Ashurst being now dead, and his brother, Sir William, having declined to succeed him.[3] A fleet was promised, and the engagement was presently made good by its appearance in Boston Harbor, 1711.
after a seven weeks' voyage, to the number of June 24.
fifteen men-of-war of different sizes, and forty transports, conveying more than five thousand troops. As one of the methods to conceal its destination, it was not provisioned in England, but supplies for it for ten weeks were to be procured in Boston.

The extreme difficulty, which might prove to be an impossibility, of making this provision, led to a suspicion that the home government was not sincere, but intended to impute to the Colony the failure which would ensue. The jealousy was not unnatural, considering what had occurred in the last year; but in this instance it was without foundation. Letters of the Secretary, St. John[4] (soon to be Lord Bolingbroke), admit no doubt of his having

[1] Letter of Dudley to Lord Dartmouth, of May 22, 1711, in British Colonial Papers.

[2] Memorial of Jeremiah Dummer, of Sept. 10, 1709, in Mass. Hist. Col., XXI. 231, and of Jan. 3, 1711, in British Colonial Papers.

[3] June 6, 1710, Jeremiah Dummer informed the Board of Trade that the government of Massachusetts had appointed Sir William Ashurst to be their agent, but that he, being incapacitated by ill-health, had devolved the trust upon himself (Dummer). November 11, Dudley unwillingly signed Dummer's commission as agent. (Journal of Board of Trade for June 6, 1710, and Feb. 5, 1711.)

[4] In the year 1706, Charles, Earl of Sunderland, had succeeded Sir Charles Hodges as Secretary of State; in the following year Henry Boyle succeeded Harley; June 14, 1710, Lord Sunderland gave place to William Lord Dartmouth; in September of the same year, Henry Boyle to Henry St. John; in 1713, Lord Dartmouth to William Bromley.

been in impatient earnest as to this business.[1] Apparently the Tory ministers, who had been scheming to arrest Marlborough's great series of victories in Europe, and withdrawing his troops, wished to compensate this proceeding, and protect their popularity, by so striking an exploit of their own as would have been the conquest of New France; and it would have been a special satisfaction to the Queen's new favorite, Mrs. Masham, if at the same time that she distressed her discarded rival by the recall of the great Duke from his triumphs on the continent, she could have raised her brother to consequence as the winner of a new empire for England in America, and gratified Harley, her kinsman, by the glory which that conquest would have shed upon his administration.

February-August. St. John's mind seems to have been filled with this scheme during half of the first year of his official life, till it failed. No one was informed of it,— Feb. 6. so he writes to Hunter, Governor of New York, in a letter of which he sent a copy to Dudley,— except the Queen, himself, and his colleague, Lord Dartmouth. "It is my favorite project," he says, "which I have been driving on ever since I came last into business, what will be an immense and lasting advantage to our country, if it succeeds, and what, if it fails, will perhaps be particularly prejudicial to me." Those who were to be employed in the expedition were made to understand that it was destined for a landing in the south of France. Sealed instructions were prepared for the naval commander, not to be examined by him till he should reach the fortieth April 10. degree of latitude. When, after some delay, at which St. John constantly and passionately ex-

[1] Yet it seems a very different view of St. John's object was entertained, according to Grahame, who does not give his authority for the statement. "Harley . . . . . subsequently affirmed, in a memorial to the Queen, that the whole affair was a contrivance of Lord Bolingbroke and the Lord Chancellor Harcourt to defraud the public of twenty thousand pounds." (Comp. Smith, History of New York, 131.)

presses his vexation, Nicholson sailed with the instructions to Dudley and Hunter to hasten their preparations, the Secretary's nerves were somewhat quieted, but his irritability returned as the preparations for so great an expedition proved to require no little time. He "must be forgiven," he writes to the General, "if more uneasy than ordinary upon this account. But the Queen is so herself." They "earnestly contemplate the several vanes."[1]

May 1.

The British statesman's impetuosity was responded to with genuine animation on the other side of the water. A Congress of six officers, over which Dudley presided, was held at New London to arrange the details of the enterprise.[2] To raise money, the General Court of Massachusetts, which was in session when the fleet arrived, resolved on borrowing, for two years, on bills of credit to the amount of forty thousand pounds. An immediate levy of nine hundred "effective men" was ordered.[3] A price was established for provisions; and when this caused them to be con-

June 21.

Zeal of Massachusetts.

June 12.

[1] I take these facts and extracts from a series of nearly a hundred letters, which, down to the present time, have remained unobserved in the Letter Book of the Secretary of the Home Department. The first paper consists of twenty closely written pages of instructions to Governor Hunter, bearing the date of Feb. 6, 1711: the last, dated November 2 of the same year, consists of "directions for landing and taking a strict survey of the remainder of her Majesty's stores now on board the several transports in the Thames, from North America," returned from the ill-fated expedition. The papers exhibit an extraordinary amount of care and anxiety expended in the preparations for the enterprise. The Secretary's extreme eagerness to push it forward, his repeated and urgent appeals to all departments of the government to bestir themselves actively in carrying out the secret service proposed, his impatience of all red-tape routine, and his nervous irritability at every delay, at once correspond to the domineering impetuosity of his character, and express his intense interest in what he hoped to make the crowning exploit of his administration, and a title to his permanent supremacy in the national councils.

[2] British Colonial Papers.

[3] A proclamation of Dudley, June 12, promised to every officer and soldier "a coat, breeches, stockings, shoes with buckles, two colored shirts, colored neck-cloths, and hat, gratis," and "booty, houses, lands," &c., to all who should "distinguish themselves."

cealed, a law was passed, commanding the seizure of them and authorizing forcible entry for the purpose.[1]
July 7. An embargo was laid to suppress intelligence of the design, and secure a supply of seamen.[2] An order was issued "to impress all bakers, brewers, coopers, &c., who cannot or will not supply the public in their way at the stated prices." A proclamation of the Governor re-
July 3. quired the selectmen of towns to send every day meat and vegetables to be bought by the commissaries for six thousand men encamped on Noddle's Island.[3] There was a voluntary agreement among the citizens to eat no fresh meat till the fleet should be supplied. Three
July 22. Iroquois sachems came to Boston to consult respecting the plan of the campaign. A day for
July 16. fasting and prayer was appointed. The enact-
July 18. ment of a severe law against harboring deserters did not prevent the admiral from complaining, with an arrogance which has sometimes been observed in the English naval service, and demanding that there should be a press of seamen to make up his loss, — a demand, however, with which it was not thought prudent to attempt to comply. The admiral could not himself impress seamen
1696. in New England, by reason of a standing prohibi-
Dec. 3. tion of the Privy Council to this effect.[4]

1 "This [July 8] being Sunday, nobody would do any work, although the troops were in want of bread." (King, Journal of the Expedition.)

2 Dudley's proclamation of the embargo is in the Proceedings of the Mass. Hist. Soc. for 1870, 206.

3 Colonel King thinks it worth while to relate (Journal, &c.) that, July 4, "the Brigadier was invited to a Commencement at the College at Cambridge, near Boston, where he assisted for no other reason than to put the people of the Colony in humor to comply with the present necessary demands of the troops."

4 Records of the General Court, *sub dieb.*; comp. letters of Dudley to St. John, of July 11, July 25, and Sept. 3, 1711, in British Colonial Papers. On the same day (July 25), when Dudley wrote to the minister of the happy prospects with which "three days will despatch the fleet and forces in good health and vigor," Richard King, "Colonel of her Majesty's train of artillery," sent him a very different report. In his judgment, expressed in a full "Journal of the Expedition," the prospect was not flattering, and this was owing not only to "the misfortune that the

The provisioning was done with extraordinary celerity, and the fleet left Boston Harbor, conveying seven thousand well-appointed troops, regular and provincial. General (soon to be Lord) Hill, brother of the lady of the bedchamber to the weak Queen, was the incompetent commander. In three weeks the fleet was at the mouth of the St. Lawrence. Proceeding up that river, it lost its way in a fog, and then a high wind began to set the ships towards the northern bank. The pilots, New England ship-masters, had undertaken their task unwillingly, not pretending to much knowledge of the eddies and soundings of the stream. When they were some thirty miles up the river, the admiral gave orders for the ships to lie to, heading towards the south. The pilots afterwards insisted that this was contrary to their judgment. The fate of the superb expedition was settled without much delay. It did not come within many leagues of Quebec, nor come near enough to the settlements to be attacked from them, nor to distribute among them the printed proclamation in the French language, which the General had prepared to tempt their loyalty with the usual promises and threats. By midnight of the second day after entering the river, ten or eleven ships had drifted upon ledges of rock, where they went to pieces, and nearly a thousand persons were drowned, among whom were thirty-one com-

1711. July 30.

Aug. 20.

Disastrous failure of the expedition.

Aug. 22.

Colonies were not informed of our coming two months sooner," which to an unprejudiced person might have seemed a sufficient cause, but to "the interestedness, ill-nature, and sourness of these people, whose government, doctrine, and manners, whose hypocrisy and canting, are insupportable. 'Tis easy," he thought, "to determine the respect and obedience her Majesty may reasonably expect from them for the future; and how absolutely necessary it is, and with what great truth one may affirm that, till all their charters are resumed by the Crown, or taken away by an Act of Parliament, till they are all settled under one government, with an entire liberty of conscience, and an invitation to all nations to settle here, they will grow every day more stiff and disobedient, more burthensome than advantageous, to Great Britain." (British Colonial Papers.)

missioned officers of various rank, and thirty-five women.[1]

Aug. 25. With the vessels which escaped, including all that belonged to the royal navy, the disheartened admiral sailed down to the mouth of the river.[2]

He and his captains still hoped to cover their disgrace by an attempt upon Placentia in Newfoundland; but on a reconsideration they determined unanimously in a Sept. 8. council of war of nine navy officers and nine colonels, with the general and admiral, that this scheme also must be given up, for lack of a sufficiency of provisions.[3] What remained of the provincial force sailed for Sept. 16. Boston, to excite loud complaints of the admiral's mismanagement; while he and the general went to England to excuse themselves by representing that the Massachusetts people had been tardy and penurious in fitting out the fleet.

Nicholson, who, in accordance with the strategy before adopted on the like occasion, had led a force from Connecticut and New York towards Lake Champlain to operate against Montreal,[4] received intelligence of the disaster which had taken place lower down the river, in season to withdraw out of reach of the attack which Vaudreuil was preparing to make upon him with his undivided force, as

1 Charlevoix (II. 357) erroneously puts the number of drowned at nearly three thousand. He inserts a copy of Hill's proclamation.

2 Aug. 25, 1811, a Council of War, consisting of the Admiral (Sir Hovenden Walker) and eight of his captains, decided unanimously "that, by reason of the ignorance of the pilots, it is wholly impracticable to go up the River St. Lawrence with the men-of-war and transports as far as Quebec, as also the uncertainty and rapidity of the currents, as by fatal experience we have found." (British Colonial Papers.)

3 This Council was held on board the fleet, "in the Spanish River." (Ibid.)

The sad story is told by Penhallow, 62–67, and by Niles, in Mass. Hist. Col., XXXV. 328–331; comp. Journal of Colonel King, in British Colonial Papers; Letter of Sept. 12, 1711, from George Lee, "Lieutenant-Colonel, commanding the Royal Irish contingents," to St. John. (Ibid.)

4 It had been arranged that, on the same day when the fleet sailed, Nicholson should leave Boston for New York on his way to Albany, "where his troops were assembling to make the diversion." (King, Journal, &c.)

soon as the danger at Quebec should be over. The ship-masters who acted as pilots had been impressed by Dudley in Boston and other ports.[1] This coercion was necessary, because they felt themselves to be incompetent, by reason of their little acquaintance with the river. Three of them were sent to England, where, however, they were not examined; perhaps because the Ministry thought they might tell what it was as well for those in power that the people of England should not know, and especially it might not be agreeable to the sovereign that in the circumstances they should draw attention to the commander of the land forces.[2]

In Massachusetts the consternation, as well as the disappointment, was extreme. The expedition having so miserably failed, the cost of it appeared all but ruinous. The General Court, however, never giving way to despair, sent an Address to the Queen, praying for a further renewal of the repeatedly frustrated enterprise. As to their own capacity for contributions to it,

Oct. 17.

[1] In a letter of Nov. 13, 1711 (in British Colonial Papers), Dudley tells St. John that formerly, "being long in hopes of such a day as this," he had sent twice up the river of St. Lawrence to Quebec for the exchange of prisoners to make pilots and see the place, till Mr. Voderil (*sic*) forbade my coming that way about five years since." At one of these times his son, William Dudley, and Colonel Vetch "were brought thither, and tarried there twenty days, and made all the advantageous observation they could."

[2] Penhallow, 66; Niles, in Mass. Hist. Col., XXXV. 330. — The naval commander, Sir Hovenden Walker, was charged by the Admiralty not only with incompetency, but with peculation, and was left off from the list of half-pay officers. After nine years' silence, part of which time he passed in seeking his fortune in Carolina (Introduction to Journal, 7), he published a vindication, prefixing it to a journal of the expedition which he had written, covering the time from April 6, 1711, when he received his commission, to October 10, when he got back to Plymouth. He does not impute the defeat of his expedition, so confidently as some of his officers had done, to dilatoriness on the part of the government of Massachusetts; but unfounded reports to that effect had been carefully spread in England by the mortified English soldiers and seamen, and had made such an impression as to make Dummer think it worth his while to refute them in a publication which he entitled "Letter to a noble Lord concerning the late expedition to Canada."

they prayed for some forbearance, "because of their enfeebled and impoverished state." As one proof that it was not zeal in which they were wanting, they represented that one man out of every five in their jurisdiction, capable of bearing arms, had been doing military service in the past year.[1] While their agent in England was "to vindicate and justify the government," they magnanimously or prudently instructed him not to "fault or impeach others for want of doing their duty, or for their conduct in that affair." Some little consolation was derived from the knowledge that a plan entertained by the French for the retaking of Port Royal had been disconcerted by the necessity of concentrating their forces for the strengthening of Quebec.[2]

Oct. 24.

In the following year some of the customary inroads of Indians, varied by no novel circumstances, took place along the north-eastern border.[3] On the whole, in the discouragement which prevailed, the intelligence of the discreditable peace of Utrecht was received with welcome in Massachusetts.[4] The Indians proposed to the officer command-

1712.

Peace of Utrecht.

1713. March 31.

[1] British Colonial Papers.

[2] "Letter read [June 8, 1713] from Mr. Harley, referring to the Board petition of officers who served in the late war, and now disbanded, to the Queen, praying a grant of a great tract of land in North America, uninhabited, between New England and Nova Scotia, in order to their settling and planting there." (Journal of the Board of Trade, *sub die.*) Mr. Dummer, as agent for Massachusetts, appeared before the Board, June 11, and expressed his approval of the project. A negotiation followed (July 6, 9, 10, 21) respecting the expenses of their transportation. An "estimate of the charges" was "sent [April 8, 1714] to Sir Isaac Newton, master worker of her Majesty's mint, for his opinion and observations thereon." The Queen died a few months after this, and the scheme, though not yet abandoned, came to nothing.

[3] Niles, in Mass. Hist. Col., XXXV. 333–335; Penhallow, 71–74; comp. N. H. Provincial Papers, III. 543–546.

[4] May 4, 1713, the Privy Council "ordered that the Lords of Trade forthwith cause the proclamation for publishing the treaties of peace and commerce lately concluded between her Majesty and the French king to be sent to the Governors of her Majesty's plantations, with directions to cause the same to be solemnly published." (Register of the Privy Council.)

ing at Casco to make a treaty on their own account.[1] Dudley kept up his dignity by answering that they must come to him at Portsmouth; and there accordingly they made another of their untrustworthy pacifications, professing themselves loyal subjects of the British Queen, and imploring forgiveness for their past misdeeds and perfidies. It was estimated that the eastern tribes had lost one-third part of the whole number of their warriors during the past ten years, and an equal proportion of women and children, and that the proportion of lives sacrificed had been little, if at all, less among the English population of Maine. While some families were extinct, others mourned parents, brothers, children, murdered or torn from them to hopeless captivity. The settlements were reduced to miserable poverty; their trade was ruined; their houses were burned; their fields were devastated. More than a hundred miles of sea-coast, lately the seat of prosperous life, bore no longer a trace of civilized humanity.

July 11.

[1] Mass. Archives, XXIX. 22-29, 30-32.

CHAPTER IX.

THE renewal of the Indian war at the beginning of Dudley's administration, while it invited harmonious action between him and the General Court, did not suspend their jealousy of one another. He called the Court together to consult on the state of affairs, informing them that he had already sent succors into Maine, in sufficient force, as he still hoped, to restore tranquillity. It was not unnatural that he should regard a moment when he felt his importance to the people to be great, as being a favorable one for the enforcement of measures which he knew to be disrelished by them; and he read a letter from the Queen urging anew the matter of stated salaries for the high officials. The House replied that, in the absence of many of its members, kept at home by the existing alarm, they could not prudently proceed to consider a subject of such moment.[1] The importance of a stated and permanent salary for the Governors had been as clearly seen by themselves as by their masters from the institution of the provincial government, — by the Ministry, because it so materially affected the power of their representatives to serve them; by the Governors, both for that reason and for their private comfort and ease. Sir William Phips was not long in seeing the expediency of praying the King to "nominate to said Assembly a salary

Discord between the Governor and the General Court. 1703. Sept. 1.

April 8.

1693. November.

[1] Nor did the Governor find the Council pliant. "Till the Queen appoints the Council, the best men can have no share in the government." (Dudley to the Board of Trade, in September, 1703, in British Colonial Papers.)

sufficient for his support."[1] Lord Bellomont, before he left England, applied to have "such a salary fixed on him as might be suitable to the government;" an application of which the unsatisfactory result has been seen in the reply of the agent of Massachusetts to the message of the Lords of Trade.[2] 1695. July 4.

At the Governor's next opportunity for communication with the Court, his urgency for action in respect to established salaries and the restoration of the eastern fort was such as to bring the House to a formal defence of that policy, which it had adopted at the beginning of the provincial history, and in which it persisted to the end.[3] There was now discord between the two branches of the Legislature, the Council siding with the Governor on questions of form and of his prerogative. The Representatives had sent an Address to the Queen, without consultation with the Council. The Council desired to see it. The Representatives replied that their Journal, in which it was recorded, was open to the Council's inspection, but they refused to send their clerk up with the Journal, or to furnish a copy of the paper. Dudley summoned the House to come to the Council Chamber with their Journal. They came, but did not bring it. At length they were prevailed upon to furnish a copy of the Address, and the altercation came to nothing except as manifesting the jealous temper which prevailed.[4] 1703. Nov. 16.

[1] See above, p. 142.

[2] Ibid., p. 177.

[3] "It hath been the privilege from Henry the Third, and confirmed by Edward the First, and in all reigns unto this day granted, and is now allowed to be the first and unquestionable right of the subject, to raise when and dispose of how they see cause, any sums of money by consent of Parliament, the which privilege we, her Majesty's loyal and dutiful subjects, have lived in the enjoyment of, and do hope always to enjoy the same, under our most gracious Queen Anne and successors." (Mass. Prov. Rec., Nov. 16, 1703.) Before the Governor obtained this answer, he had to send twice to remind the House of the application he had made. (Comp. Ibid., for Nov. 4 and 15.)

[4] Ibid., for November 15, 16, 17, and 18.

The House made a grant to Constantine Phipps, as agent for the Colony. Dudley held that, with his be- Nov. 23. coming Governor, Phipps's agency, being unauthorized by him, had ceased. The House voted that Nov. 26. the Governor's appropriation to other uses of moneys granted by them for the fortification of Boston Harbor was a "grievance." They presented a Dec. 2. list of other complaints relating to his military administration, and were about to extend it still further when he prorogued them, after a rebuke accompanied with lofty assertions of his prerogative as "her Majesty's commander-in-chief in Massachusetts." They parted in mutual ill-humor, and Dudley wrote to Lord Not- Dec. 19. tingham that he had communicated the Queen's requisitions to the Assembly, but though he had "for a month's time used all possible methods with them," he found it "impossible to move that sort of men, who love not the crown and government of England, to any manner of obedience." They meant, he said, to "put a slight upon her Majesty's government, of whose just rights I will not abate the least point to save my life, it being so very necessary to watch to support it amongst a people that would destroy it, if possible."[1]

The Governor's first speech to the General Court after the sack of Deerfield was occupied with that sub- Provisions for the war. ject to the exclusion of the commonplaces of the 1704. March 8. salaries and of the eastern fort. The Court called for six hundred volunteers, offered a premium of a hundred pounds for scalps, and sent to solicit military aid from Rhode Island and Connecticut. A large supply of money was wanted. Bills of credit were issued to the amount of ten thousand pounds, and a tax was laid for their redemption.

The Representatives never overlooked the importance

[1] Letter of Dudley, in British Colonial Papers.

of the pending question of provision for the Governor's support. They made him a grant of two hundred pounds. The Council sent down a message, recommending an increase of the allowance and a grant besides to the Lieutenant-Governor. The House replied that they had "resolved not to raise any further money this session," and were presently prorogued.[1] They came together again for a few days in the following month, but attended to nothing beyond some arrangements for the prosecution of the war. At the annual meeting for the election of Counsellors, the Governor again refrained from pressing the measures which were most upon his mind. But, on the other hand, he again resorted to an offensive exercise of his prerogative by setting aside the choice of the popular favorites, Elisha Cooke and Peter Sargent, to be Counsellors.[2] The Speaker "addressed his Excellency in the name of the House for his favor to accept the two gentlemen to be of the Council, whom he had disallowed of." The House had compromised its dignity in vain. "His Excellency returned answer to that motion, and dismissed the House to their business." After a fortnight's delay, and not without being prompted by a message from the Council, the House consented to go into an election to supply the vacancies; and Simeon Stoddard and Samuel Hayman, who were now chosen Counsellors, were admitted

March 25.

April 18-27.

Rejection of Counsellors by the Governor.

May 31.

June 14.

[1] "I am sorry nothing that could be said would move them from a stubborn resolved temper, which has possessed the Assembly, that they will agree to nothing wherein they may show their obedience to her Majesty." (Letter of Dudley to Lord Nottingham, April 21, 1704, in British Colonial Papers.)

[2] Sir Henry Ashurst took umbrage at a repetition of this strong measure, and, July 3, 1705, presented to the Board of Trade "a memorial that Colonel Dudley had refused to admit his cousin, Peter Sargent, into the Council of the Massachusetts Bay, though annually chosen for that place, and desiring the Board to write to Colonel Dudley to admit him. Letter ordered to be written to know the reason of his constant refusal." (Journal of the Board of Trade.) Dudley probably gave heed to this, for he admitted Sargent to the Council in 1707.

by the Governor. "The election of Counsellors," wrote Dudley to the Lords of Trade, "is scandalously used . . . . . to affront every loyal and good man that loves the Church of England and dependence on her Majesty's government."[1]

July 13.

The disagreement with him on the essential points of policy went on for the present without check, notwithstanding the general good understanding which united the two parties in the conduct of the war. The House granted forty pounds to each Judge of the Superior Court for his service for the year, and the same sum to the lieutenant of the castle. To Povey, Lieutenant-Governor, as captain of the castle, to which place Dudley had advanced him over Hutchinson, they voted a hundred and twenty pounds as a year's pay; but it was on onerous conditions, one of which was that, except for special reasons, he should not fail to be at the castle three days in every week. The Council gave him fifty pounds more for the first half of the year, at which proceeding the House took high offence, and voted that it was "arbitrary and illegal, and a violation of our English and charter privileges and rights." The Council sent down a message asking for "a grant for the support of the Governor and the Secretary, and to know what consideration they had had of the memorial presented by the Judges," complaining of the insufficient provision for them. A list of grants was laid before the Council, in which they in vain informed the House that they found none for the Governor. "I humbly ask," he wrote to the Secretary of State, "your Honor's favor and patronage for me in my difficult part with an angry people that can hardly bear the government nor Church of England amongst them, and, while my care is to keep them steady to Acts of Parliament, will make me as uneasy as they can."[2]

Disputed question of salaries. June 30.

Nov. 10.

Nov. 18.

Nov. 27.

[1] British Colonial Papers. [2] Ibid.

Nor did any thing more satisfactory follow, when at the beginning of another session the Council formally solicited "a just and honorable supply to the Governor for his support in the remaining part of the year." He had been too peremptory for prudence in his opening speech. In that harangue he had declared that the Commissioners of Trade had instructed him to express their regret for the refractory temper of the Assembly (referring to her Majesty's commands for the rebuilding of Pemaquid), and to say that it was "very unfit Assemblies should make representations to her Majesty without the consent and knowledge of her Majesty's Governor," and that it was unreasonable for the people of Massachusetts to "expect that they should be furnished with stores of war at her Majesty's expense, while they, of all the Colonies of America, did alone refuse to settle a salary on her Majesty's Governor and other officers there." And he added a lofty assertion of his acquaintance with the interests of the Province, his desire to promote them, and his persuasion that "their affairs would proceed better when they should think so of their Governor, and accept his service well."[1] On the other hand, in his message at the close of this session, he said he should report to the Queen that he "had asked nothing referring to the war of the Assembly, but that it had been very easily complied with."[2] The Queen had just repeated her instructions on both those points, and had added, "If they do not forthwith comply with our just expectation herein, they will appear to us undeserving of our royal favor and bounty towards them on the like occasion."[3] But either that communication had not yet reached him, or he considered that prudence required it to be withheld till he had obtained the money which was urgently needed for the war.

Dec. 29.

Dec. 27.

1705.
Feb. 21.

Jan. 11.

[1] Mass. Prov. Rec.
[2] Ibid.
[3] British Colonial Papers.

Depreciation of paper money. June 30, 1704–Feb. 27, 1705.

The financial difficulties created by the war pressed heavily. Within two-thirds of a year, successive issues of bills of credit amounted to no less a sum than twenty thousand pounds. With a supply so inflated, a provision that they should be received in payments into the treasury at an advance of five per cent did not save them from continued depreciation. Nor was this the only trouble which attended on them. They were freely counterfeited; and the scrupulous rulers, while they labored to stop the forgeries by penal laws, thought it their duty to make good the loss occasioned by them to innocent private holders.

Control of the Speakership by the Governor. 1693. Nov. 21.

The Governor put forward a new pretension. As early as the second year of the provincial charter, the question of "the power of the Governor to dismiss the Speaker" had come before the Board of Trade;[1] but for the time it passed by without serious discussion. In the organization of the third General Court constituted since Dudley's arrival, the House chose Thomas Oakes for its Speaker, the agent who in England had opposed the charter. The Governor

1705. May 30.

pronounced his disapproval, and directed them to proceed to a new election. The House voted that it was "not in the Governor's power to refuse the election of a Speaker." The Governor hesitated to take the responsibility of arresting the public business. He needed a grant of twenty-two thousand pounds, which the House was ready to make, when he should cease to interfere with its organization. He proposed to the House to "put another person in the chair, with a *salvo jure*, till Counsellors should have been chosen," an election which, by the provision in the charter, could not be delayed. Without paying regard to the suggestion, they proceeded to the election of Counsellors; and the Governor, yielding to

[1] British Colonial Papers.

the inconvenience of further pressing the question, consented to the whole list.[1] He wrote to the Lords of Trade, that Oakes, to whom he had objected as Speaker, was "a known Commonwealth's man, never quiet, nor satisfied with the government, but particularly very poor."[2] It was at this General Court that Lieutenant-Governor Povey appeared for the last time.

July 25.

Sept. 15.

The Governor had accepted a grant of two hundred pounds made to him by the General Court now expired.[3] Taking care to keep his claim alive, with however little prospect of present success, he sent a message "to move the new House for a suitable and honorable allowance for the support of the Governor." For answer they gave him another three hundred pounds, whereupon he prorogued them for two months, expecting, before the expiration of that time, to be prepared for a more vigorous movement. Accordingly, when they came together again, he told them of the letter which he had received from the Queen, expressing in positive terms her Majesty's expectation that they would rebuild the fort at Pemaquid, contribute to the repair of the work at the mouth of the Piscataqua, and establish regular salaries for the Governor and Lieutenant-Governor; and he added that he was instructed to represent that "the neglect of these commands would show the General Assembly undeserving of her Majesty's royal favor and bounty towards them." The Representatives replied that, since the date of the Queen's letter, which was several months old, they had, in an Address, explained

March 2.

Persistent claim of the Governor for a fixed salary.

June 22.

June 30.

Sept. 5.

Jan. 25.

1 Mass. Prov. Rec.

2 British Colonial Papers.

3 "I have received her Majesty's picture and coat-of-arms. The arms were the next day fixed in the Council Chamber of this Province. . . . . . Her Majesty's picture I have set up in my own house, where it is always in the view of all masters of sea, strangers, and others who are bound to make their attendance, and where the Counsellors and gentlemen of the country frequently are." (Letter of Dudley to the Lords of Trade, of March 10, 1705, in British Colonial Papers.)

themselves to her Majesty on the subject of fortifying Pemaquid; and they desired that the two other matters might be deferred to the next session, and then "debated and answered by a full House," which now, on account of "the affairs of husbandry," could not be obtained, "the members of three counties being absent."

The Governor still insisted, and the House, having probably first ascertained that they might promise themselves support in the other branch, sent up a resolute
Sept. 11. message presenting their whole case. They said, 1. That, while the fortifying of Pemaquid would occasion a great outlay, which they were in no condition to meet, — for the war had already cost them "not less than eighty thousand pounds, the greatest part whereof was still unpaid," — it would be simply useless when done, for the fort on Casco Bay, fifty miles west of Pemaquid, was "seated near the extent of the former settlements and plantations of the English within the Province, and considerably beyond any of the present English dwellings;" 2. That the cost to New Hampshire of the fort on the Piscataqua would not equal the sum expended in the war by many single towns in Massachusetts; that Massachusetts vessels passing in and out of the river paid toll at that fort; and that forts built by Massachusetts without aid from New Hampshire were as useful for the defence of New Hampshire as of the sister Colony; and, 3. That as to the establishment of permanent salaries, their circumstances and ability were different at different times, and it was "the native privilege and right of English subjects to raise and dispose of money according to the present exigency of affairs." The great principle of the question, still evaded, was not presented till some years later. The Governor was ill-advised enough to bring the sub-
Sept. 12. ject before the Council, on which it may be presumed that he still relied for support. But the Council, being brought to a vote as to the three proposals which

the House had put aside, determined that they could not give their advice in favor of any one. An Address to the Queen, framed by a joint committee of the two branches, was debated in the Council, "the Governor and Lieutenant-Governor withdrawing." It was adopted with some amendments; the Secretary was directed to sign and forward it; and the Court was prorogued the same day.[1]

Sept. 15.

The discontent with Dudley, so rife in Massachusetts, was seeking a hearing in England.[2] John Nelson, who had taken a prominent part with the patriots in the deposition of Andros, but who had since changed his side, wrote to the Secretary of the Board of Trade, urging the continuance of the Governor in his place. He was "informed of the endeavors of a faction who are busy to reinstate themselves into the government." There was no reasonable "complaint against him [Dudley]; but that which displeases is his care and attendance on the Church of England,"[3] his

Endeavors to displace the Governor.

1706. Feb. 11.

[1] Mass. Prov. Rec. and Council Rec., at the dates. — "It is the native right and privilege of English subjects," said the Council and Representatives in this joint Address, "by consent of Parliament from time to time to raise and dispose such sum and sums of money as the present exigency of affairs calls for. The which privileges we, your Majesty's loyal and dutiful subjects, humbly crave leave to plead our right unto, not only as subjects of the crown of England, but also as privileges by the royal charter granted to this Province by their late Majesties," &c.

[2] Interest had already been making to supersede him by the appointment of Sir Charles Hobby. (Hutch., II. 153.) Hobby is represented as being a man of loose life, though Cotton Mather was one of his zealous partisans. He was a native of Boston, who, says Hutchinson, "had been knighted, as some said, for fortitude and resolution at the time of the earthquake in Jamaica; others, for the further consideration of £800 sterling." (Comp. Provincial Papers of New Hampshire, III. 631, note.) Dec. 10, 1706, he presented a Memorial to the Board of Trade, "desiring copies of such complaints as Colonel Dudley has or shall transmit over against him." (Journal of the Board of Trade.)

[3] "He [Dudley] joined himself to the congregation of *Queen's Chapel*, as it was now called, on the accession of Queen Anne, and his name . . . . . constantly appears on the list of vestry-men." (Greenwood, History of King's Chapel, 61.) It stands also at the head of the names of subscribers to a letter addressed, Dec.

urging action relating to the building of an eastern fort and the establishment of salaries, and his "care of the Acts of Trade."[1] As one of the wardens of Queen's Chapel, Nelson at the same time joined with the clergyman and "chief of the church" in representing to the Bishop of London that Dudley had "been very successful in his government;" that "his constant attendance and care for the peace of the church and support and honor thereof was apparent to all men, as well as his example of justice and virtue;" and that "his continu-

23, 1703, by "the members of the Church at Boston" to the Archbishop of Canterbury, in which they solicit his favor for Mr. Bridge, their minister (Hist. Mag., for December, 1868, 268), and of subscribers to a letter to the "Society for the Propagation of the Gospel," Dec. 8, 1713, representing that "nothing can contribute more to the flourishing state of religion among us" than the scheme for settling bishops in these American parts. (Greenwood, History of King's Chapel, 167.) But Dr. Colman, in his funeral sermon, says ("Ossa Josephi," 35): "He was in principle a Calvinist, according to the manifest doctrine of the Church of England in her Articles. He preferred the way of worship in our churches, and was wont frequently to say that he loved a great deal of ceremony in the government, but as little as might be in the church." It seems that the Episcopalians claimed or disclaimed him according to their exigencies, as these presented themselves from time to time; and this equivocal position entirely comported with his own policy, enabling him to call on one or another set of champions, as his occasions made convenient.

Directly on the heels of the letter of Dudley and others soliciting the appointment of Bishops, went another, of Feb. 17, 1714, from Myles, the minister, representing that "the Church here, and also in other parts of this Province, would increase much more under a Governor that was a constant communicant thereof, from whom we might reasonably expect all requisite protection and encouragement. The present Governor, Joseph Dudley, Esq., is a member of an Independent Church at Roxbury, where his dwelling is, and has communicated there from his first coming to be Governor, and never communicated with us . . . . . only this 25th of December last past." (Mass. Hist. Col., VII. 217.)

Sewall was much disturbed by the encouragement given by Dudley to the setting up of an Episcopal congregation in Newburyport in 1712. (Proceedings of Mass. Hist. Soc. for 1873, 374–378.)

[1] Letter of Nelson to Popple, in British Colonial Papers. He says that before leaving England Dudley had "paid £1300 sterling for seals, equipment, &c.;" that in four years of administration he had received from Massachusetts "£1400 sterling, and no more, which will not pay him his advance, and find him a stable to put his horses in;" and that during these four years "his expense, house-rent, servants, horses, and a table, amounts to £700 per annum, his own proper cost."

ance in the government would be most acceptable to all her Majesty's good subjects, merchants and planters, that have their dependence on the government of England as well as the church here."[1] It may have been from an unpopularity like his superior's that the Lieutenant-Governor, too, found his position uncomfortable. He had lately gone home; and a memorial from members of the Church of England in Boston prayed that he might be sent back, "with a good establishment, both for the Governor and himself, to put them beyond the power of a difficult and ungrateful people."[2]

Feb. 4.

At the next election of Counsellors, the Governor rejected two, Joseph Hammond and Elisha Cooke, his old antagonist. Events had now been providing an occasion for the deep-seated animosity against him to break out with violence. A vessel, under the command of one William Rouse, had been sent twice to Nova Scotia to bring back some of the prisoners of the war.[3] He had little success in his proper errand, and was charged with using his opportunity to trade with the enemy and provide them with military stores. The House entertained the accusation, extending it to Samuel Vetch as an accomplice,[4] and presently to John Borland and Roger Lawson, merchants of Boston.[5]

May 29.

Alleged treacherous correspondence with the French.

June 14.

June 24.

As the offence alleged had been committed, if at all, in Nova Scotia, a doubt arose whether it could be investigated by the judicial tribunals of Massachusetts; and the

[1] Greenwood, History of King's Chapel, 164.

[2] British Colonial Papers.

[3] See above, 246; comp. Niles, in Mass. Hist. Col., XXVI. 276.

[4] It was on this occasion that Samuel Vetch, who afterwards acted so important a part, made his first appearance in New England history. I have learned nothing of his antecedents.

[5] Borland was an Englishman. (Shurtleff, Description of Boston, 686). I know nothing of Rouse or Lawson, except from their concern in this transaction. The six prisoners applied to Judge Sewall for a writ of *habeas corpus*, on the plea that they were entitled to be enlarged on giving bail; but he refused it. (Mass. Hist. Col., XVIII. 240–242.)

House, inclining to a process of impeachment, sent up a message to the Council, asking "that such pro- June 25. ceedings, examinations, trials, and judgments might be had and used, upon and relating to the said persons, as were agreeable to law and justice." Already it was whispered that the Governor had been a sharer in the crime and its profits, and the House thought July 9. themselves called upon to send up their denial of a report that they had begun their examination of the suspected men with the question whether the Governor was concerned with them; and they went so far as to add that his alacrity in pursuing the scrutiny "had removed all color for such vile suspicion." The session being about to close, the House sent a message to desire that the July 12. prisoners, to whom John Phillips of Charlestown, and Ebenezer Coffin, were now added, might be kept in close confinement, "in order to their being brought to their trial before the Great and General Court." The Council determined that they should be proceeded against at the next session by a bill of attainder, and the Court was then prorogued.

In his speech at the opening of the next session, the Governor enlarged upon the gravity of the crime Aug. 7. which was alleged, but urged upon the Court its duty to pursue the prosecution with caution and good temper. In a conference between the two Houses, Aug. 10. the form of a bill of attainder was determined. The Judges and the Attorney-General (the Gov- Aug. 13. ernor's son Paul), being directed by the Council to consult together on the conduct of the trial, advised that a copy of the charges should be delivered to the prisoners, and that they should be successively arraigned before the whole Court, beginning on the following day. Aug. 15. Counsel having been assigned them, Vetch was Aug. 16, 17. tried on one day, Borland and Lawson on another, Aug. 19, 20. Rouse and Phillips on a third, and then Coffin.

A vote of the whole Court convicted them all, Aug. 21.
and a joint committee reported on the punishments Aug. 24.
to be assigned to each. The Council objected to the sentences as being on the whole too severe, and the House was persuaded to a partial relaxation. The conclusion was that the penalty of imprisonment, which, as well as that of fines, had been proposed for all the convicts except Coffin, was remitted in every case; that Rouse was excused from "sitting an hour upon the gallows with a rope about his neck;" and that he was fined twelve hundred pounds, besides being declared incapable of sustaining any public trust. The fine of Borland was fixed at eleven hundred pounds; that of Lawson, at three hundred; of Vetch, at two hundred; of Phillips, at one hundred; and of Coffin, at sixty. And a separate Act was passed, disposing of each case. The House voted a grant of fifty pounds to the Governor "for his extraordinary Sept. 3.
trouble," and other allowances to the members of the Court, to be paid from the fines. But he refused his consent to these gratuities, and immediately Sept. 4.
prorogued the Court.[1] He wrote to the Lords of Trade that he thought the fines imposed — espe- Oct. 8.
cially that laid on Rouse — to be excessive, and hoped that the Queen might be advised to remit them. The members of the Assembly, he said, had proceeded unadvisedly and harshly, because they were "of less education and knowledge in the law," and "in a very great displeasure against traders with the enemy."[2]

Whatever was the Governor's opinion of the illegality of these proceedings, and whatever might be his personal interest in them, it was hard for him to place any impediment in their way, so jealously was he watched, and so unfavorable would have been the inferences drawn from

[1] Mass. Prov. Rec., and Records of the Provincial Council, at the dates entered in the margin.
[2] British Colonial Papers.

any action of his on the side of lenity. The Acts were
1707. Sept. 24. submitted to the consideration of the Queen in Council, by which authority they were annulled. The Queen was advised that "the crimes in the said several acts mentioned" were "in no wise cognizable before the General Assembly [of Massachusetts], in regard they have no power to proceed against criminals, such proceedings being left to the courts of the law there." And it was accordingly ordered that the fines should be repaid. The convicts were to give bonds to stand a trial at law, which bonds were to be void, unless prosecution took place within a year.[1]

Their case could not fail, in existing circumstances, to involve the character of the Governor, and to inflame whatever there was of long-hoarded hostility against him.

The Governor charged with treachery. June 12.

Before that action of the Privy Council which has just been related, some twenty men of New England, most of them then resident in London, had addressed to the Queen a formal petition for the removal of Dudley from his government.[2] Professing to pass over "divers unheard-of corruptions and oppressions, and unjust and partial practices of the said Dudley, on which they might ground many complaints," and of which they were "certainly informed," they alleged that he had "countenanced a private trade and correspondence with the French of Canada and the Indians in their interest, and furnished them with ammunitions and provisions;" that he embarrassed the prosecution of the persons concerned with him in this crime, till they brought on the Colony a loss of not less than thirty thousand pounds; that having thinned the House of Representatives by artful delays of their business, "he prevailed with those that

[1] Register of the Privy Council for Feb. 20, March 13, Sept. 24; Journal of the Board of Trade for Feb. 25, Feb. 27, April 3, April 7, May 23, June 19, 1707.

[2] Register of the Privy Council.

remained, who were scarce a number to make a House, that the accusation against his agents should be changed from treason to misdemeanor, and, they being convicted, he labored to mitigate their fines."[1] The name which stands first among the signatures to this memorial is that of Nathaniel Higginson, a highly respected merchant of Salem; the second, that of William Partridge, formerly Lieutenant-Governor of New Hampshire; the third, that of Stephen Mason, a Counsellor named in the charter.

A copy of the memorial came to Dudley. He laid it before his Council, and demanded that they should vindicate him without delay. They did so, by what was represented as a unanimous vote, which they sent down to the House. The House paused, perhaps embarrassed between a disposition to be civil and misgivings about the truth. The Council sent to inquire whether any action was in progress. Two days later they repeated the question in a message conveyed by the Secretary and eight Counsellors. Still obtaining no satisfaction, they proposed a conference; and here they somehow prevailed; for the House, now echoing the Council's words, voted that the charge against the Governor was "a scandalous and wicked accusation." Thomas Newton, one of the subscribers to the memorial, being "convented before the Council," said that he had signed it "under provocation," that he knew nothing of the truth of the charge, that he was sorry for what he had done, and that he had asked the Governor's pardon. As to action in the General Court, the business was finished by an order of the Council[2] for printing the exculpatory votes of the two Houses in the "Boston News-Letter," — the weekly newspaper just then established.[3]

Nov. 1.

Nov. 5.

Nov. 7.

Nov. 20.

Nov. 21.

[1] For the memorial, see "Deplorable State of New England," &c., 38 *et seq.*; comp. Hutchinson, Hist., II., 158, 159.

[2] Mass. Prov. Rec., and Records of the Provincial Council, at the dates named in the margin.

[3] "The Boston News-Letter, published by authority," was the first American newspaper which can

But the dispute was no further at an end than as it was discharged from legislative cognizance. Presently
1708. there appeared in London a pamphlet of some

be said to have been established, though a similar enterprise had been undertaken fourteen years earlier. In the collection of British Colonial Papers is a single copy of a newspaper, designed to be published in Boston once a month, bearing the title, "Publick Occurrences, both Foreign and Domestick," and the date of Sept. 25, 1600. Among its contents was an account of the retreat of Winthrop's force from Lake Champlain. Phips's disaster had not yet occurred. No second number was published, the General Court having forbidden its continuance. (See Hist. Mag., I. 228–231.)

The first number of the "News-Letter" bears the date of April 24, 1704. It was issued every Monday. The printer was Bartholomew Green, son of Samuel, printer to the College, a person commended to posterity, in his epitaph, for his "caution of publishing any thing offensive, light, or hurtful." The proprietor, however, for the first eighteen years, was John Campbell, the postmaster of the town, whose office naturally gave him access to intelligence useful to his work.

The earliest numbers were printed on a half sheet of *pot* paper. Afterwards, when there was a special press of matter, like what now calls forth a *supplement*, a whole sheet was used. In the first number there was one advertisement, and two in the second. The paper introduced itself to the public as follows: "This 'News-Letter' is to be continued weekly, and all persons who have any houses, lands, tenements, farms, ships, vessels, goods, wares, or merchandizes, &c., to be sold or let, or servants run away, or goods stole or lost, may have the same inserted, at a reasonable rate from twelve pence to five shillings, and not to exceed, who may agree with Nicholas Bowne for the same at his shop, next door to Major Davis's, apothecary in Boston, near the old meeting-house." The "News-Letter" was continued till the evacuation of Boston by the British troops in 1776, being in its latest years the organ of the Tory party.

Newspapers in the parent country were not a century before those in the Colony. The first English newspaper has been supposed to have appeared when the Spanish Armada was in the channel in 1588. Some numbers of what purports to be such a publication are in the British Museum, the title being "The English Mercury." (For an account of what has been pretended to be the earliest number that has been preserved, No. 50, see Nichols, Literary Anecdotes, IV. 34, note.) But it has been proved by the late Mr. Watt, of the Museum, to be a forgery. (See Quarterly Review, IX. 97, 184; Westminster Review, LXIV. 496.) The first ascertained publication of the kind was the "Weekly Newes," published in London in 1622. Newspapers began to multiply from the assembling of the Long Parliament, and in the year 1742 as many as twenty were established. "Mercuries," with all sorts of epithets; "The Scots' Dove," "The Parliament Kite," "The Secret Owl," "The Smoking Nocturnal," were some of the fanciful titles. A daily paper, "The Courant," was established in March, 1702, three days after the accession of Queen Anne. In the year of the Restoration of Charles the Second had appeared "A Perfect Diurnal of the Daily Proceedings in Parliament, published according to Order;" but this was

forty pages, arraigning Dudley with unbounded severity.[1] "Colonel Dudley," says the writer, "in King Charles the Second's reign, was intrusted with the precious depositum — their greatest treasure, their religious privileges and civil liberties, which were conveyed to them by charter, but were both betrayed by him." "This is the third time that he has been trusted with power from the crown in America, and he has constantly abused it, to the dishonor of the government, and almost ruin of the people he was sent to govern."[2] The treatise reviews, in five sections, the career of Dudley in Massachusetts, from the time of his presidency of the Council after the dissolution of the colonial charter, to that of the censure passed upon his accusers by the votes of the Council and of the Representatives. The following is an abstract of its contents: —

Deplorable state of New England.

Colonel Dudley, having been trusted by the Colony as its agent in England, "joined with the instruments that overthrew the charter;" then "accepted an illegal and arbitrary commission from King James;" and next became "a chief tool of all the ensuing barbarous and infamous administration" of Andros. The abuses of that outrageous administration are described in detail. "Judge Dudley

not what is understood by a newspaper.

There was as yet small encouragement in New England for such an enterprise as that of the "News-Letter." Seven years after it was established, Campbell told the General Court that he could not "vend two hundred and fifty copies of one impression;" and fifteen years passed before the "Boston Gazette," the second publication of the same kind, was set up. (Comp. Hist. Soc. Col., V. 208.)

[1] It was entitled "The Deplorable State of New England, by reason of a Covetous and Treacherous Governor and Pusillanimous Counsellors, with a Vindication of the Honorable Mr. Higginson, Mr. Mason, and several other gentlemen, from the scandalous and wicked accusation of the votes ordered by them to be published in their 'Boston News-Letter,' to which is added an account of the Shameful Miscarriage of the late Expedition against Port Royal."

[2] The words are quoted from the Epistle Dedicatory addressed to Lord Sunderland, principal Secretary of State, and subscribed with the letters A. H. Perhaps they indicate Alexander Holmes, who was one of the subscribers to the Memorial to the Queen. (Deplorable State, 39.)

was a principal actor in all this wickedness. . . . . . All things were going to wreck, but yet Colonel Dudley was like to enrich himself and his family in the general shipwreck; there lies the mystery! . . . . . The world has heard how narrowly Colonel Dudley escaped a *De Witting* for these his follies, from the enraged people in the Revolution." Sent over to England as a prisoner, he next appeared as Chief Justice in New York, where he did that "bloody business" of the condemnation and execution of Leisler and Milbourne, which was presently denounced in Parliament as "a barbarous murder." Notwithstanding, "by many fair promises," he prevailed to be made successor to Lord Bellomont in Massachusetts. "He had not been long in that government" before a memorial was sent to London asking for his removal, on the grounds that he had refused to approve acts of the General Court, till he had been bought over by bribes; that "merely to gratify his own arbitrary will and pleasure," he had left vacancies in the judicial offices, "by which means the courts dropped, and the course of justice was obstructed;" that he had sold indulgences to a company of pirates who were in prison; that, by cheating the troops employed in the expedition to Acadia out of nearly one half of the booty that had been promised them, he had discouraged for the future the engagement of volunteers;[1] and that he was as hostile to the existing provincial, as he had been to the colonial, charter of Massachusetts, and as he was known to be to the charter of Connecticut. In confirmation of this last charge, a letter was produced, which had been addressed to a friend in London, by the Attorney-General of Massachusetts, the Governor's son. "If there

[1] It seems that Dudley was not so reserved in his conversation upon such matters as would have become a prudent man. "On some one's saying that bribes were given to the Duke and Duchess of Marlborough for military offices, Dudley said that 'there had not been any admitted these thousand years, but in a way like that,' mentioning his own experience in the Isle of Wight." (Sewall's Journal, for Feb. 2, 1708.)

should be any occasion," wrote Paul Dudley, a year and a half after the Governor's return to Massa- 1704. chusetts, "you must be sure to stir yourself and Jan. 12. friends, and show your affection and respect to my father, who loves you well, and bid me tell you so. . . . . . This country will never be worth living in, for lawyers and gentlemen, till the charter is taken away. My father and I sometimes talk of the Queen's establishing a Court of Chancery in this country. I have wrote about it to Mr. Blathwayt."

The writer proceeds to treat at length of the "blanching business" of Dudley's vindication by the General Court. He says it was in the hurried moment of 1707. October the breaking up of a meeting of the Governor's and November. Council on a Saturday that he produced to them the memorial of Higginson and others to the Queen, and required them "immediately to clear him from these imputations. . . . . . Three or four of the Council . . . . . prayed that, since the thing was both new and weighty, it might be put off till Monday." The Governor, with a boisterous fury, required them to do it immediately, and they did it immediately. One of the Counsellors, Judge Sewall, reflecting that he had acted with precipita- Nov 25. tion, withdrew his vote, and caused his reasons for so doing to be entered on the Council's record. They were, that his motion for the postponement of a matter of such great concern had been unreasonably disregarded; that a vote so affecting "the Governor's personal interest . . . . . ought to have been debated and framed by the members of the Council, apart by themselves, in his absence;" that, on mature consideration, he did "not firmly believe that the Governor did no way allow Mr. Borland and Captain Vetch their trading voyage to her Majesty's enemies, the French." Finally Sewall said: "I have been acquainted with Mr. Nathaniel Higginson these forty years, and I cannot judge the offering of this Address to her Majesty to be in him a scandalous and wicked accusation, unless I know his inducements. And I fear this censure may be of ill consequence to the Province in time to come, by discouraging persons of worth and interest to venture in appearing for them, though the necessity should be never so great."[1] While Sewall had thus cleared himself, the pliancy of others of the Council was imputed to their dependence on the Governor for their places. "We advise you that you would not be so monstrously afraid of the Governor's putting his negative upon you, the last Wednesday of May. Should you be negatived out of the Council for your fidelity to your country, it would be a much greater honor to you than to be there, and no great honor to them that are left behind."

The writer next deals with that vindication of the Governor, which was at last, though slowly, obtained from the Representatives. He professes to account for it on the authority of two letters which had been received by Sir

[1] "1707, Nov. 1, just about noon, the Governor produces the petition signed by Mr. Higginson and others for his removal, and urges the Council to vote an abhorrence of it. I prayed that it might be considered of on Monday, which the Governor would not hear of, but ordered Mr. Secretary to draw up a vote, which, with some alteration, was passed. Said he had no gall. After coming from Council, I read the book printed against the Governor in London. I had not seen it before." (Journal of Judge Sewall; comp. Hutch. Hist., II. 160, note, and Proceedings of Mass. Hist. Soc. for 1873, p. 367, 368.)

November 22, Sewall had a conversation with Borland, who convinced him that "the Governor did connive at the trading with the French, which," he says, "has opened a tragical scene, that I know not when we shall see the close of it." (Sewall's Journal.)

November 25, Sewall, in the Council, addressing the Governor in reference to the Governor's having told the House "that every one of the Council remained steady to their vote, and every word of it," said, "This screwing the strings of your lute to that height has broken one of them, and I find myself under a necessity of withdrawing my vote; and I do withdraw it, and desire the Secretary may be directed to enter it in the minutes of the Council." (Ibid.)

In an entry in his Journal for November 20, Sewall says that, in a speech to the General Court, Dudley pronounced himself "the first Governor born in New England." If he did so, he must have flattered himself that the Court had forgotten Sir William Phips. But I have observed no other report of such a declaration of his.

Henry Ashurst, one of them signed by some twenty members of the House. When the first direct action was had on the Governor's case, "about forty-five members, more than two to one of the House, voted that they could not clear him." In a second trial, he fared no better. "The Governor's friends were now at their wits' ends, and in humble wise besought the House that they would confine their vote unto the particular trade of Vetch, Borland, and Lawson [thus avoiding the question of his connection with Rouse, which was thought to be more certainly made out]; and it was urged that Borland and Lawson had cleared the Governor. . . . . Hereupon the flexible honest men, perfectly worried and wearied out of their lives by three weeks' altercations, did so many go over, as to make a sort of a vote of it." Appliances in which Dudley was skilful were said to have assisted the operation. "Besides the caresses of the table, which are enough to dazzle an honest countryman, who thinks every man means what he speaks, the influence which preferments and commissions have upon little men is inexpressible. It must needs be a mortal sin to disoblige a Governor that has enabled a man to command a whole country town, and to strut among his neighbors with the illustrious titles of *our Major*, *the Captain*, or *his Worship*. Such magnificent grandeurs make many to stagger egregiously!"

Finally, the misconduct of the discomfited expedition against Port Royal is alleged as special matter of reproach. It is said that that post might have been easily carried at the beginning of the war, but that Dudley could not be persuaded to authorize a movement against it; and that afterwards, when Church was despatched to the eastern country, he "not only had the taking of the fort left out of his orders, but was positively forbidden to meddle with it." The disappointments and disgrace which followed are elaborately laid to the Governor's charge; and the conclusion is, "Under his admirable conduct an impoverished country has, as we are credibly informed, been put to above two-and-twenty thousand pounds' charge, only to be laughed at by their enemies and pitied by their friends."[1]

Contrary to the expectation of both friend and foe,[2] Dudley succeeded in some way to evade or allay the storm which had been raised against him. No presumption in his favor in this controversy arises from his general character. He was certainly not a man whom conscientious scruples alone would restrain from shameful conduct. But in respect to a crime, needing, if really committed, to be covered up with all sorts of disguises, it is not unlikely that the justly strong feeling of dislike to Dudley dictated suspicions of more than was true. From some of the

[1] "The Deplorable State of New England," though published in London, bears indications of having been written in Massachusetts. There is throughout the tract a constant effort to intimate the contrary, which awakens more than suspicion. An intimate acquaintance is disclosed with transactions in the Province, while "we hear," "we likewise hear," are expressions used in respect to them with needless repetition, as if for a blind. "You will do well to resolve that you will never sign addresses of this nature till you have had opportunity in some Convention, *if you have such things*, for we are strangers to your methods." (Deplorable State, 2, 29.) I doubt very little that Cotton Mather was more or less concerned in the composition. It has no little of his smartness and pedantry in its style. "If you'll permit such as are no clergymen to address you with stories out of old councils, we could tell you that the First Council of Orleans, A. D. 52, made a strange decree," &c. (Ibid.) The spite against Leverett is suggestive of his unsuccessful and mortified rival. "It is reported by some now in London . . . . . that Dudley has made that Tory lawyer to be President of their College. No question but the lawyer will bring up hopeful young divines, to be sent hither for my Lord of London to ordain them. We hear that they have sung the *Gloria Patri* in their College hall already, and that several of their clergy stood up at it. An auspicious beginning under their lawyer President, who, we also hear, was chosen a lieutenant of their artillery company at Boston, the last summer. Such reports as these make their friends here think that the people in New England are running mad." (24, 25, 29.)

[2] Povey wrote to him from London that he must expect to be superseded; and Sir Henry Ashurst, in a letter of May 10, 1707, said, "Though he may meet with some with you that will sacrifice their country and consciences to his interests, I can assure you he will not meet with any such here. I doubt not but in a little time he will be succeeded by a more worthy person, and the country freed from his oppressions." (Hutch., II. 161.)

crimes alleged, his prudence would have been likely to deter him. It is plausibly argued by Governor Hutchinson that, if his connection with the shipment of goods to be sold to the French by Rouse and others had amounted to any thing more than connivance, the accomplices would scarcely have failed to denounce him when he approved those Acts of the General Court which condemned them to imprisonment and fines.[1] Yet his inclination to protect Rouse is suspicious; and so strong was the persuasion of his criminality and of his cunning, that there were those who believed it to have been by his management that the business had been submitted to the General Court, so as to keep it from the cognizance of the common-law courts, where the investigation would have been conducted with more method and vigor, and the verdict would have been more decisive.

[1] Hutch. Hist., II. 162.

CHAPTER X.

It has been told above, that, hostile as the Mathers had been to Dudley at the time of the Revolution, his arts and assiduities had won them over, and he was not without obligation to their good offices at court for his appointment to be Governor of Massachusetts.[1] It was impossible, however, that the friendship thus concerted should be lasting. Neither party could be content with any thing short of absolute control within its own province, yet neither could consent to refrain from interference with the province of the other. Personal considerations belonging to the settlement of the new charter united with motives of public spirit to incline the Mathers to a popular interpretation of that instrument, to which the arbitrary biases of Dudley were constantly opposed. The consequence and power of the former materially depended on the stability of the primitive ecclesiastical constitutions of New England. Dudley, in his ten years of English life, had probably passed for a member of the Established Church. After his return to Massachusetts, his relations with the small circle of adherents to it in Boston had at least been amicable, and his friendships with Congregation-

Dudley and the Mathers.

[1] There was still some shyness between the Dudley family and Cotton Mather. (Magnalia, II. 16.) But the Governor, on coming to Boston, paid him an early visit (June 16, 1702). "Mr Dudley hath been with the young Pope, who hath absolved him of whatever hath been amiss, so that now he is a very good man." (Letter to John Usher, in British Colonial Papers.) Mather availed himself of the interview to offer advice, which the Governor is not unlikely to have thought officious, against his coming under the influence of Mr. Byfield and Mr. Leverett. "The wretch went unto these men, and told them that I had advised him to be no ways advised by them, and inflamed them into an implacable rage against me." (Extract from Mather's Diary, in Mass. Hist. Col., III. 137.)

alists were with those leading men among them, — such as Colman, Leverett, and the Brattles, — who of late years had abandoned the ancient strictness. The unfriendliness which had thus grown up on the part of the ex- Harvard President and his son against the Governor proved College. of excellent service to the College in bringing about its re-establishment on the ancient basis.

It was understood on all hands that, since the abrogation of the Colonial charter, the College had been defunct in law.[1] Dudley, during the short term of his rule 1686. as President of the Colonial Council, made provisional arrangements for carrying on the institution,[2] which Andros, during his government, did not disturb, further than to offer the affront of placing an Episcopal 1688. clergyman in the pulpit with the presiding academical dignitary on the day of the annual Commencement.[3] Increase Mather, when in England on the business of the Colony, addressed himself successively to King James and to King William for favor to the College, but without result.[4] The legislative proceedings had with reference to the institution during the administrations of Phips, Stoughton, and Bellomont have been related in a former chapter.[5]

After Mather's return from England and resumption of the Presidency he continued to live in Boston, as minister of the Second Church. This arrangement gave increasing dissatisfaction, and the General Court very 1693. soon passed a vote "that the President of Harvard Dec. 2. College, for the time being, shall reside there, as hath been accustomed in time past."[6] When after a year and a half

[1] The phrase of the time was, *vitulus in ventre matris mortuus*, the college charter having been conferred by the Colony, and the Colony being extinct.

[2] Quincy, History of Harvard University, I. 58.

[3] Ibid.

[4] Sibley, Biographical Sketches, &c., 424.

[5] See above, 193–195.

[6] Mass. Prov. Rec.

he had taken no notice of this action, a vote of the House 1695. of Representatives expressed their "desire for Mr. June 5. Mather to go and settle at the College, that the College may not be destitute any longer of a settled President; . . . . . but, if Mr. Mather do not settle there, then that the Corporation do propose some other meet person to the General Court, who may be treated with to settle there, that the College may no longer be destitute of a settled President." There is no record of a concurrence in this vote by the Council, and it did not move the President to a change of his purpose. Soon came intelligence of the rejection by the Privy Council of that new Oct. 12. charter of the College under which Mather was acting. Under the provisional arrangement made by Stoughton, he was confirmed in office,[1] and so continued till the end of the administration of Lord Bellomont. The 1698. General Court renewed their protestations against Dec. 8. his absence from Cambridge, and sent a committee to urge in a personal interview their impatience for his 1699. removal thither.[2] He threatened to resign; but, Feb. 6. on reflection, resolved to refer the question to his Boston church, who refused to part with him.[3]

Contemporaneously with their solicitation to the King 1700. through Lord Bellomont, the General Court ex- July 11. pressed to the President with so much peremptoriness their determination that he should reside at the College, that he obtained the consent of his church, and removed accordingly. But, after a residence of only three months, he returned to Boston, and sent a letter to Oct. 17. Stoughton, "containing the reasons of his removal from Cambridge, as not having his health there, and desiring that another President may be thought of."[4] After due 1701. deliberation, the General Court, recognizing that March 14. "the constitution requires that the President reside

[1] See above, 193.
[2] Quincy, Harvard University, I. 480.
[3] Ibid., 97.
[4] Ibid., 111.

at Cambridge, which is now altered by his removal from thence, and to the intent that a present necessary oversight be taken of the College," proceeded to vote "that in case of Mr. Mather's refusal, absence, sickness, or death, Mr. Samuel Willard is nominated to be Vice-President, and . . . . . invested with like powers and authority in all respects."[1] Upon this the President again removed to Cambridge, but after three months went back a second time to Boston. He wrote a letter for the Assembly, announcing his purpose not to return "when the College is in such an unsettled state," and expressing his "earnest desire that the General Court would, as soon as may be, think of another President."

June 30.

The House was still unwilling to part with Mather, or to consider it hopeless that he should revise his decision; and, after some ineffectual negotiation with Willard, minister of the South Church in Boston, who was found to be also unwilling to transfer his residence to Cambridge, they sent up to the Council a Resolve "that Mr. Increase Mather be desired to take care of and reside at the College." The Council, in which Elisha Cooke, Mather's ancient antagonist, was now the leading spirit, refused to concur. By a Resolve which they substituted, and which was concurred in by the House, "Mr. Samuel Willard, nominated Vice-President of the College, ... was desired to take the oversight of the College and the students there, ... and to manage the affairs thereof as he has proposed in his answer to the Court; namely, to reside there one or two days and nights in a week, and to perform prayers and expositions in the Hall."[2] Willard continued to administer the College six years, until his death; retaining the title of Vice-President, and residing through the whole time in Boston.[3]

Sept. 6.

[1] Quincy, Harvard University, I. 111.

[2] Ibid., 116.

[3] President Quincy entertained the opinion that "the avowed were not the prevailing motives for the

When Dudley came to his government, Samuel Willard was in the second year of his official service, and Cotton Mather was aspiring to succeed him at the head of the College, when the time for his retirement should come. The wives of Dudley and Willard were sisters, and this affinity may have done something to quicken the new Governor's interest in the management of the institution.
1703. March 11. He took an early opportunity to say to the General Court that he should "very freely" lay before the Queen any thing that might appear to concern its welfare. "I am sorry," he said, "for the mistake of this government, at any time, in that affair;" and when the House asked an explanation of that stricture, he replied that "the mistakes he referred to were a first, second, and third draft of a charter of incorporation for the College, sent to England, and there refused."[1]

The ancient influence of the Mathers in the affairs of the College was never recovered.[2] Cotton Mather, who

exclusion of Dr. Mather" from the Presidency. The opinion is corroborated by language of Cotton Mather in his memoir of his father (Parentator, 173); and it is especially remarkable that the condition of residence, so insisted on in the case of Mather, was dispensed with as to his successor. But it is to be remembered that the state of the College was such as did not encourage an eminent clergyman to connect himself permanently with it at the cost of leaving his parochial charge, and that the votes which had been passed relating to the Vice-Presidency of Willard admitted of a choice of Mather, Willard, or any other person to be President, whenever the existing objections to a residence at Cambridge should cease.

During Mather's Presidency of sixteen years the College sent out 210 graduates.

[1] Mass. Prov. Rec.

[2] It was not, however, yet by any means extinct. Owing to causes which it is in vain to conjecture (though possibly it may have been a mere expression of resentment of Dudley's freedom of speech five days before), only a year and a half of Willard's administration as Vice-President had passed, when the Representatives voted *unanimously* (March 16, 1703) "that the Rev. Mr. Cotton Mather be treated with, in order to be obtained for a resident President of Harvard College." The Council returned the vote non-concurred, "with the message that the Board could not accept a President named by that House." (Mass. Prov. Rec.) This transaction confirms the suggestion made above, that the arrangement with Willard was understood all along to be only temporary, and subject to be superseded at any time by the election of a President.

had not attended a meeting of the Corporation since the accession of Vice-President Willard, was regarded as having "abdicated," and his place at that Board was given to one of the Brattles, a favorer of the recent religious movement which had led to the establishment of the Fourth Congregational Church of Boston. Two years passed before the question of a charter for the College was resumed. Then "his Excellency intimated to the Council that, by letters from England, there was encouragement to hope that a charter of incorporation might be obtained, ... if proper application was made; and the draft proposed in his late Majesty's reign was ordered to be laid on the table to be read." Again the question slept. Probably no satisfactory compromise could be arranged between the religious party which represented the primitive ideas of New England and that which had recently risen into importance by the maintenance of more liberal views; besides which, it must have been believed by both these parties that the Queen would not consent to such provisions as both desired for the exclusion of the Church of England from interference in the concerns of the institution.

1705. Jan. 2.

The death of Vice-President Willard revived attention to the question.[1] To the infinite disgust

1707. Sept. 12.

[1] Sixty-six young men were educated at the College during Willard's uneventful administration. In matters of church doctrine and discipline he sympathized with the Mathers; but their arrogance offended and repelled him, and in personal relations he was constantly drawn closer to the party of Leverett, Colman, and the Brattles.

The reader curious about such details of ancient manners may see in the published Proceedings of the Massachusetts Historical Society for 1861 (160, 161) the bills of fare for a Commencement dinner in Willard's time, and for the dinner at Leverett's installation. For that of 1703, the "hens and chickens" cost £2 7*s.*; the beef, £5 9*s.* 6*d.*; lamb, £2 6*s.* 8*d.*; bacon, 2*s.* 6*d.*; four geese and four tongues, £1 2*s.* 8*d.*; and eighteen gallons of wine were provided, at the cost of £2 18*s.* 7*d.*, besides four barrels of beer and one of cider. There was a supply of carrots and turnips, apples, oranges, and cherries, but of no other vegetable or fruit. A charge of candles indicates that the festivity extended into the evening. For the like provision in 1708 (comp. Quincy, I. 493), when the whole cost was only

of Cotton Mather, the Corporation elected John Leverett to be President. The Representatives, after considerable delay and opposition, — for the party of the Mathers was still potent, — granted him a salary; and the
Dec. 6. two branches concurred in a vote which, referring to the ancient charter now suspended for more than twenty years, directed "the President and Fellows of the said College from time to time to regulate themselves according to the rules of the constitution by the Act prescribed, and to exercise the powers and authorities thereby granted for the government of the House and support thereof."[1] The Governor, whether expecting to escape the observation of the government at home, or to satisfy it of the expediency of such action, approved the bill.[2] The English Ministry never took steps to disturb the arrangement; and the College charter, confirmed by an article in the Consti-
1780. tution of the Commonwealth at the time of the separation from Great Britain, has remained in undisputed force to this day.

The Governor's approbation — if we are not rather to say, his active promotion — of the choice of President Leverett, together with the establishment of the President's friends in the College Corporation, put an end to any thing that remained of simulated courtesy in the intercourse

£10 6*s*. 6*d*., whereas on the former occasion it had been £26 14*s*. 10*d*., the Steward charges 1*s*. for parsnips, 8*d*. for cranberries, 8*d*. for potatoes (which had been but lately introduced), and 6*d*. for onions. For this feast the cider disappears, and only 5*s*. 8*d*. was spent for beer. There was now a new outlay of 2*s*. for two pounds of tobacco, and 2*s*. 8*d*. for four dozen pipes. Sewall notes, in his Journal, that neither of the Mathers was present on this occasion. — The speeches of Dudley and Leverett are preserved. (See Proceedings of the Mass. Hist. Soc. for 1867, 502, 504; comp. Pierce, History of Harvard University, 80, 81.)

1 Mass. Prov. Rec.

2 Is it possible that the Governor, now in desperate trouble with the local government (see above, p. 302), hoped to make friends by doing an act which would be extremely acceptable to them; which he could take time to excuse or palliate to his superiors across the water; and which, in the last resort, it was in their power to disavow and undo, so that in no case eventual harm to them need result?

between him and the Mathers, father and son.[1] Henceforward there was no course for the latter party but war to the knife. The circumstances of the moment favored them; for it was the moment of intense exasperation against Dudley on account of his alleged malpractices in Nova Scotia. Increase Mather wrote him a frank letter, charging him with "bribery and unright- 1708.
eousness" in arresting a process in the Admiralty, Jan. 20.
till satisfied with a sum of money; with plotting against the liberties of the Province, a crime proved by a letter of his son Paul; with "hypocrisy and falseness in the affairs of the College," shown by his consent to the revival of that charter, which for a long time he had declared to be dead; with "the guilt of innocent blood" in the cases of Leisler and Milburn; and with "ordinarily forsaking the worship of God," and spending his Sunday afternoons "with some persons reputed very ungodly." Two considerations, said the ex-President, prompted him to "discharge his conscience with these rebukes. One is, in that you have sometimes said, that if ever you had a spiritual father, I was the man; and there was a time when I encouraged the church, with whom I have been laboring in the work of the Lord these forty-six years and more, to call you to be my assistant in the ministry. The other is, that a letter thought to have been written by me induced the late King William to give you a commission for the government here."

The ex-President's son wrote to the Governor on the same day, in a yet more animated strain. Having hitherto "in divers letters sought out acceptable words," he says, "your Excellency now compels me to see that the schemes

[1] Nov. 25, 1707, the Council sent four of its members to Cotton Mather to inquire respecting a letter which he was said to have addressed, Oct. 2, 1706, to Sir Charles Hobby, animadverting upon Dudley, and respecting other letters of his to Dudley himself. The next day the Committee reported to the Board that they had had a conference with him. (Council Record.)

of speaking and modes of addressing used among persons of the most polite education will not answer the expectation I have had of them." Adopting accordingly a different method of address, he tells the Governor that his letter, erroneously ascribed to his father, favoring Dudley's appointment, had been written when he "weakly believed that the wicked and horrid things done before the righteous Revolution had been heartily repented of, and that the rueful business at New York, which many illustrious persons of both Houses of Parliament often called a barbarous murder, ... had been considered with such a repentance as might save him and his family from any further storms of heaven for the revenging of it. . . . . . Your snare," he writes, "has been that thing, the hatred whereof is most expressedly required of the ruler, namely covetousness;" and he largely repeats and expatiates on the charges of the Governor's evil conduct in the voyages to Nova Scotia; in his obstruction of the capture of Port Royal; in his appointments to office; in his management of meetings of the Council; in his arresting the course of justice; and in "the horrible trade carried on at the castle," where the Governor was said to have misapplied certain funds specially appropriated by the Representatives.

The astute and well-poised Governor was more than a match for men enfeebled by passion. After a fortnight's interval, which perhaps he found useful to get the better of his own choler, he replied in what is on the whole a tone of calmness and dignity, though the reader may think he also observes signs of a timidity indicative of a conscience ill at ease, and the consciousness of an insecure position. Dudley gives back Scripture in abundance, and turns the tables upon his correspondents in the way of edifying recommendations of self-scrutiny. He knew, he says, what was the root of their bitterness. "Every one can see through the pretence, and is able

Feb. 8.

to account for the spring of these letters, and how they would have been prevented, without easing any grievances you complain of. . . . . . I desire you will keep your station, and let fifty or sixty good ministers, your equals in the Province, have a share in the government of the College, and advise thereabouts as well as yourselves, and I hope all will be well. I am an honest man, and have lived religiously these forty years to the satisfaction of the ministers in New England, and your wrath against me is cruel, and will not be justified. . . . . . The College must be disposed against the opinion of all the ministers in New England except yourselves, or the Governor torn in pieces. This is the view I have of your inclination."[1]

Discord between the Governor and the Representatives.

The elections of the next General Court after that at which Dudley had obtained an ostensible acquittal, and its proceedings as soon as it came together, showed the strength of the popular feeling against him. Along with the Queen's disallowance of the penalties which had been imposed upon Vetch (May 30.) and the persons charged with having been concerned with him, the Governor laid before the Court a communication "declaring the royal style upon the union of the two kingdoms of England and Scotland." The occasion rendered proper an Address to her Majesty, and the Representatives drew up minutes for such a paper, and desired the concurrence of the Council. (May 31.) The minutes proposed did not please that body, and, after a delay which they may have hoped would tend to allay the existing irritation, as well as afford time for reasoning and management, they proposed on their part to intrust to a joint committee the preparation of the heads of an Address. (June 24.) The Representatives at first "insisted upon the heads offered by that House" (which probably embraced the

[1] For this spirited correspondence, see Mass. Hist. Col., III. 126 *et seq.*; comp. Pierce, History of Harvard University, 80 *et seq.*

question as to the prosecution of Vetch and his partners), but gave their consent to a memorial congratulat- June 26. ing the Queen on the consummation of the union of the kingdoms. The House sent up a list of "grievances," most of which related to unauthorized July 1. uses by the Governor of moneys granted by them for specific objects, though there was also a complaint that Leverett, now President of the College, still retained the office of Judge of Probate. The House granted to the Governor the sum of two hundred pounds, instead July 3. of the three hundred usually voted at the spring session. There was also a deviation from past usage in the language of the vote. The Council sent messengers "to observe the same to the House," but it "was afterwards sent up again without alteration." The Council proposed to the House an enlargement of the grant to the Governor; but, "finding that they could prevail nothing therein," they consented to it as it stood, and the July 5. Governor relieved himself from further opposition for the present by a prorogation of the Court.[1] He complained to the Board of Trade that there had been July 10. "considerable alterations, more than usual, in the House, and . . . . . they showed their temper, and left out three principal gentlemen of the Council, of approved loyalty and of the best estates in the country."[2] He now

[1] Mass. Prov. Rec. and Council Records, at the dates.

[2] The "three principal gentlemen" were Joseph Lynde, Eliakim Hutchinson, and Penn Townsend. (Mass. Prov. Rec.) — "Our present General Assembly have acted like men. They have turned out of the Council several of D—'s creatures, and the country has chosen better Representatives than they had the last year. The present House of Commons here has voted an Address to the Queen, in which they declare that they declined sending a former Address, because there was an article in it applauding the Governor's conduct, and praying his continuance," &c. (Extract from a letter from Boston, of July 17, 1708, in Deplorable State, &c., p. 4). — July 19, the Board of Trade received from Dudley his "defence against a representation presented to her Majesty at Windsor, June 23, 1707." (Journal of the Board of Trade.)

gave up in discouragement the contest for his favorite object. He desisted thenceforward from pressing the desperate claim for a fixed salary; and the House, on its part, made him grants from year to year, of five hundred pounds for each remaining year of his administration, giving him half of that sum at each of the two sessions.

The next session began with a dispute about the "grievances." The Council was disposed to justify the Governor. The House maintained its position. The Council again requested a reconsideration; a conference took place; and, partly by explanations of the past and partly by promises for the future, a truce of that dispute was effected; and by a grant of three hundred pounds instead of two hundred, which latter sum was the usual autumnal allowance to the Governor, the recent reduction from his accustomed pay was made up. He asked for a small allowance to defray the charge of a journey which he proposed to make into the eastern country, to acquaint himself with the progress of the war there. The House "prayed him not to expose his person in a journey eastward at this season, but to command the officers of the forces there to attend him at Boston to receive his commands." But he urged the advantages of his own plan, and they gave him twenty pounds to enable him to carry it out, "in consideration of the extraordinary occasion."[1]

Oct. 26.

Nov. 3.

Nov. 5.

Nov. 6.

Vetch, at the time fixed for his trial, was still in England, detained there by solicitations which he had gone to make for an enterprise against Quebec.[2] When the next General Court came together, he had returned, bearing the Queen's commission as Colonel, and invested with a high command in the expedition which was on foot. His present importance overbalanced his former delinquency; the legal acquittal of one of his partners, who had been tried during his absence,

Remission of Vetch's fine. 1709. April.

[1] Mass. Prov. Rec., at the dates.

[2] See above, p. 302.

relieved the Court from the embarrassment of retracing its steps against him; and a vote was passed for remitting the fine and costs to which he had been condemned in the former proceedings.

June 2.

Comparative quiet of Dudley's later administration.

In the last half of Dudley's administration, the collisions between him and the elected government of Massachusetts were to a great degree suspended by the cares incident, first to the war, and then to its calamitous consequences. He had been hopelessly defeated as to the objects which in entering on his office he had obstinately insisted on. The General Court would not build a fort at Pemaquid; they would not contribute to the cost of the fort at Portsmouth; and, above all, they would not fix salaries for the Governor and Judges. The grant of five hundred pounds, which in the latter years of Dudley's service they made him annually, was a much smaller allowance than they had given to his predecessor, Lord Bellomont; and he had made up his mind to approve the votes, and take the money without remonstrance. He no longer indulged himself in obstructing the Representatives' choice of a Speaker, and they no longer complained when he gratified his grudges by rejecting Counsellors of their choice. Resentments do not last for ever in their full fierceness, when the mutually angry parties come to have interests in common; and, though the elder contemporaries of Dudley could not be expected to forget the character of his important career sufficiently to extend to him respect or confidence, yet it was not a time for them to seek or use occasions for quarrel, when, distressed by a French and Indian war, they found him conducting their military affairs with activity, and, on the whole, not without good judgment, if with indifferent success. They were assured by some of their English friends that if they got rid of him they would be likely to fare worse, and that they would do well to reconcile themselves to his rule on the principle enforced in the ancient fable, that half-gorged bloodsuckers are more tolerable than a fresh and more hungry swarm. And if at present it was for his interest to practise those arts of insinuation of which he was a master, on the other hand nothing is more depressing to the pride and spirit of a community than the financial difficulties which were now weighing more heavily every day; and to Dudley's boldness and resource men willingly looked for such means of extrication as might be possible.

Loyalty in Massachusetts.

Nor was Massachusetts now in the same restless mood as at some other times. In the quarter-century which had passed since the abrogation of the old charter, a generation had come upon the stage of active life, not trained in the maxims of independence so dear to her in earlier days. In their minds, the foreign sovereign was recognized with a reality with which he had not been conceived in the minds of the fathers since English Massachusetts had a being. When the Charleses had claimed and threatened, she had denied, "avoided," and kept quiet, waiting her time. When Cromwell had attempted to cajole, she had excused herself with a decision which he had sense and sympathy to understand. But now English Puritanism had been, after a feeble fashion, indulged and conciliated by the crown; and Massachusetts Puritanism — as to its antagonistic attitude, at least — had lost its powerful backing in the parent country. It was not the time for Puritan Massachusetts to be contumacious and impracticable when the Protestant sovereigns, William and Anne, had come to hold the British throne by election against the legitimate Popish monarchs of the Stuart line, and the Act of Settlement which gave the crown to the House of Hanover had made a still wider departure from the hereditary principle. In the new circumstances, loyalty had become a virtue and a genuine sentiment; and if the object of such loyalty turned it to advantage by putting hard tasks upon it and summoning it to inconvenient submission, that was no new experience in the history of sovereigns and of sentimental subjects. King William and Queen Anne, and the ministers of both, had as little positive liking for Massachusetts as the line of tyrants which they superseded; and practically Massachusetts had the less power of self-defence against them because of their being in theory less unfavorably disposed to her and to her well-wishers in England.

Governor Hutchinson entertained the opinion that at the time of the Treaty of Utrecht "there was not
1713.
double the number of inhabitants in the Massachusetts Province, which the Colonies of which it was formed contained fifty years before," while the people of the other Colonies had quadrupled their numbers in the same time; and he ascribes this slow growth to the wars which, with only two short intermissions, had been going on through the forty years since the outbreak under Philip of Pokanoket. Within that time he calculates that "five or six thousand of the youth of the country had perished by the enemy, or by distempers contracted in the service." He supposes that the expenses of Massachusetts in this, called Queen Anne's War, "were beyond those of any other ten years from the first settlement," and that the military operations "added to the support of civil government, without any relief or compensation from the crown, certainly must have occasioned such an annual burden as was not felt by any other subjects of Great Britain."[1]

Population, industry, and trade.

In the seventh year of his administration Dudley reported to the Lords of Trade: "I judge this Province to contain, when I arrived, fifty thousand souls. These are all freemen and their children, besides the blacks. . . . . . This number is increased by a thousand every year, ... the wars and troubles with the Indians

[1] Hutch. Hist., II. 201. — Supposing my estimates of the population of Massachusetts and Plymouth in 1665 (see above, Vols. III. 35, IV. 135) to be correct, the estimates of Dudley for 1702, and of Hutchinson for 1713, would agree sufficiently well with them and with one another.

notwithstanding. . . . . . The people here clothe themselves with their own wool. New English goods are here sold at less than a hundred and fifty pounds per cent advance; most goods more. . . . . . They are proud enough to wear the best cloth of England, if chopping, sawing, and building of ships would pay for their clothes, and this method would double the sale of English woollen manufactory presently. . . . . . There is no trade to the coast of Guinea."[1] Massachusetts, he reported, had twenty ships of over a hundred tons' burden; sixty of between fifty and a hundred; and a hundred and twenty smaller vessels for trade to the West Indies, "which must demand a thousand sailors, as near as I can set it, besides a like number of all sorts built every two years for merchants of London and elsewhere." "This Province has all sorts of manufactures settled that belong to iron, leather, linen, though to no degree capable to serve the inhabitants as yet." There was an exportation of codfish to Spain and elsewhere to the amount of £30,000 annually, and of mackerel to the West Indies to the amount of £5,000. Three years later he wrote: "The revenue of both the Provinces [Massachusetts and New Hampshire] consists of an impost for goods and merchandise brought in, an excise upon taverns and retailers of wines and liquors, and a land and poll tax laid once a year."[2]

1712. April 8.

In Governor Dudley's time, an Act of Parliament was passed, of which the important political bearing does not seem to have been weighed either by the government at home or by the colonists. It provided for erecting a General Post-Office in all the Queen's dominions, and for settling a weekly sum out of it for the service of the war and other occasions.[3]

1710.

Post-office arrangements.

[1] Various particulars of the commerce of Boston in 1709 are contained in an account by an English visitor to that place, published in the Historical Magazine for 1866, Supplement, II. 119; comp. N. H. Hist. Col., III. 140.

[2] British Colonial Papers.

[3] Statutes at Large; Act of the 9th of Anne, Chap. X. Those times

Some rude arrangements had been early made in New England for the transmission of correspondence. When 1639. Nov. 5. a few years had passed after the first settlement in Massachusetts, the General Court appointed Richard Fairbanks of Boston to take care of letters "brought from beyond the seas or to be sent thither," and to receive a penny for each, "provided that no man be compelled to bring his letters thither except he please."[1] After thirty years, as communications improved, arrangements were made for a mail to leave New York 1672. for Boston the first Monday of every month.[2] A little later, on a petition from merchants and others, who 1677. May 23. complained that their letters were "many times imposted and thrown upon the Exchange, so that who will may take them up, ... whereby merchants especially, with their friends and employers in foreign parts, were greatly damnified," the General Court made choice of a postmaster "to take in and convey letters according to their direction."[3] At the Revolution, Ran- 1689. June 11. dolph's function having ceased, the General Court appointed Mr. Richard Wilkins "for postmaster, to receive all letters and deliver them out; to receive one penny for each single letter."[4] When William and Mary 1691. Feb. 17. had been two years on the throne, they gave by patent under the great seal, "unto Thomas Neale, Esq., his executors, administrators, and assigns, full power and authority to erect, settle, and establish within the chief ports of their Majesties' Colonies and Plantations in America an office or offices for the receiving and despatching letters and packets;" to be paid, however, for his services by "such rates and sums of money as the planters should agree to give."[5]

are not commonly thought to have been scrupulous; yet the last section of this Act forbids the interference of postmasters in elections.

1 Mass. Prov. Rec.

2 Brodhead, New York, II. 196.

3 Mass. Prov. Rec.

4 Ibid.

5 Mass. Hist. Col., XXVII. 50.

Neale appointed Andrew Hamilton his deputy, and Hamilton applied to each of the Colonial legislatures to "ascertain and establish such rates and sums" payable for the conveyance of posted matter, as, affording him sufficient compensation, should tend to "the quicker maintenance of mutual correspondence amongst all the neighboring Colonies and Plantations, and that trade and commerce might be the better preserved." The governments of New England received the proposal favorably, and gave the mail-carriers free passage over their ferries. Massachusetts established a "General Letter Office" in 1693.
Boston, and fixed the rates of postage. The June 9.
smallest charge was two pence "for every single letter from Europe, the West Indies, or other parts beyond the seas;" the largest, for a single letter carried between Boston and Maryland or Virginia, was two shillings. The conveyance of a letter from Boston to Salem cost threepence; to Ipswich, fourpence; to Portsmouth, sixpence. The carrying of letters or packets for hire by any but the servants of the Postmaster-General was prohibited under a penalty of forty pounds. The Postmaster-General and his servants were made liable to fines for negligence in their duty.[1] Under the authority given by the General Court, Hamilton appointed Duncan Campbell, a 1694.
Scotsman, to be his deputy in Boston. On a rep- June 20.
resentation from Campbell that his receipts did not equal his expenditures, the Court granted him for several years an annual allowance of about twenty-five pounds, sometimes exceeding and sometimes coming short of that sum.[2]

[1] This Act was disallowed by the Privy Council as being "prejudicial to the office of the Postmaster-General, ... and inconsistent with the patent granted in the year 1691 to Thomas Neale, Esq." (Mass. Prov. Laws, 117; comp. 123, 263, 420.) Sir Thomas Trevor, the Attorney-General, had represented to the Board of Trade that to the Massachusetts Act "a clause should be added reserving certain powers and authorities to Thomas Neale." (British Colonial Papers.) "On consultation with him [Feb. 3, 1697], some little alterations" were made at his suggestion. (Journal of the Board of Trade.)

[2] Mass. Hist. Col., XXVII. 55–

Neale's patent was for twenty-one years. Two years before it was to expire, the House of Commons, deliberat-
1710. Feb. 14. ing on the "ways and means for raising the supply granted to her Majesty," resolved that "towards the raising the supply, her Majesty's revenues, both inland and foreign, to arise in the General Letter-Office or Post-Office, or the office of Postmaster-General, be increased;" and the series of Resolves went on to specify higher rates of postage, which were to be demanded in every part of the Queen's dominions for inland or foreign correspondence. The postage of a single letter between New York and London, for example, or between New York and Boston, was fixed at a shilling; between New York and

70. "The public letters I have passed free yearly, upon the usual allowance, was to a great deal more than was paid me; besides the charge of weekly sending your Excellency's letters to Roxbury in times of snow or rain." (Campbell to Dudley, Nov. 18, 1709.) — Oct. 19, 1711, a petition of his, "with an account of the charge of forwarding the public letters for five years, amounting to £142 3*s.* 11*d.*, was read." March 21, 1712, the Court granted him £50 "in full to date." (General Court Records, Mass. Hist. Col., XXVII. 69.) So enterprising was this functionary that in 1714 he established a post to carry letters once a fortnight to New York during the three winter months, his carrier "to go alternately from Boston to Saybrook and Hartford, to exchange the mail of letters with the New York rider." (Ibid., 82.)

"A new and exact map of the Dominions of the King of Great Britain on the continent of North America, ... according to the newest and most exact observations, by Herman Moss, geographer," bears the date of the year 1715. In a corner of it is the following note: —

"An account of the posts of North America, as they are regulated by the Postmasters-General of the Post-House. The western post sets out from Philadelphia every Friday, leaving letters at Burlington and Perth Amboy, and arrives at New York on Sunday night; the distance between Philadelphia and New York being one hundred and six miles. The post goes out eastward every Monday morning from New York, and arrives at Seabrook Thursday noon, being one hundred and fifty miles, where the post from Boston sets out at the same time; the New York post returning with the eastern letters, and the Boston post with the western. Bags are dropped at New London, Stommington, Rhode Island, and Bristol. The post from Boston to Piscataway, being seventy miles, leaves letters at Ipswich, Salem, Marblehead, and Newberry.

"There are offices kept at Burlington, Perth Amboy, in New Jersey, New London and Stommington in Connecticut, at Rhode Island, Bristol, Ipswich, Salem, Marblehead, and Newberry; and the three great offices are at Boston, New York, and Philadelphia."

Salem, at a shilling and threepence; between Boston and any place not more than sixty miles distant from it, at fourpence.[1] The Act which was passed in pursuance of the plan of these Resolves was entitled "An Act for erecting a General Post-Office in all her Majesty's dominions, and for settling a weekly sum out of it for the service of the war and other occasions;" and one section of it required a weekly payment of seven hundred pounds to be made "into the Queen's Exchequer, in order to a supply of money for carrying on the war, and other her Majesty's most necessary occasions."[2]

In fact, from the first institution of a regular post-office in England, which was in the time of King Charles the First, the income from that source, sometimes 1635. obtained by a lease to a private party, had always been treated as a part of the royal revenue. It may excite surprise that while, by its English promoters, the character of this Act, as a measure for raising revenue, was not only not concealed, but was formally avowed, it does not appear to have raised in New England any resistance or animadversion on that account. The truth is, there was nothing in the Act, except the language of its title, to awaken jealousy as to its being a scheme for taxation by the Parliament of the mother country. Men in New England had been all along accustomed to look upon what they paid for the conveyance of their letters just as they looked upon payments for any other service rendered. It was no novelty that the persons who had rendered this service for them were appointed under authority from the crown; and

[1] In Douglas's "Summary," &c., I. 466–471, is a curious "account of the general and frequent travelling roads from Penobscot Bay . . . . . to St. Juan or St. John's River, in Florida," as they existed in 1755. — "From Boston there is a post by which we [at New York] can hear once a week in the summer time, and once a fortnight in winter. . . . . . Sometimes a letter is six weeks coming from Virginia; sometimes longer." (Letter of Lord Cornbury to the Lords of Trade, of July 1, 1708, in O'Callaghan, V. 55.)

[2] Mass. Hist. Col., XXVII. 72–79.

the service, so far as it included communications with England, could hardly have been well rendered otherwise. The people had been assured by their Boston postmaster, and had reason to believe, that the English post-office conducted their business for them at a cost greater than it was reimbursed for by the postage which it received; and the new arrangement promised a still better transaction of the business than that which had been experienced heretofore. In these circumstances, it would have been hard for them to make out a grievance from an Act which required useful work to be done for them at little cost, solely on the ground that the new Act, relating to all parts of the Queen's empire, called itself an Act for raising revenue.[1]

The post-office department complained to the Board of Trade that it failed to get its dues because payments were made to it in the depreciated colonial currencies.[2] It shared this loss with public creditors of every description. During the first half of the eighteenth century, the prosperity of Massachusetts was kept down by her use of a vicious substitute for money. Even before the disastrous result of the late expedition against Canada,[3] the Province was in arrears to the amount of a hundred and twenty thousand pounds, and

1711.

Financial difficulties.

[1] Dr. Franklin, in his examination before the House of Commons, in 1766, was reminded of the long acquiescence of the Colonies in the post-office system, and his answer was, "The money paid for the postage of a letter is not of the nature of a tax. It is merely a *quantum meruit* for a service done. No person is compellable to pay the money if he does not choose to receive the service. A man may still, as before the Act, send his letter by a servant, a special messenger, or a friend, if he thinks it cheaper and safer." (Sparks's Franklin, IV. 180; comp. 198.)

[2] Journal of the Board of Trade, for June 25, 1713.

[3] Just before the very inopportune time of the arrival of this doleful news, occurred a destructive conflagration in Boston, called *the great fire* till the more destructive one in 1760. It broke out on the evening of Oct. 2, 1711, in the narrow avenue then as now called *Williams Court*. According to Cotton Mather's reckoning (Sermon preached Oct. 4), "near about a hundred" buildings were consumed. Among them was the town-house, and the place of worship of the First Church. And several lives were lost. The Council Record of October 7 states that that body "met the House in its chamber."

this though a tax of twenty-two thousand pounds had just been levied, and more than four thousand pounds were annually received from imposts and excise.[1] Measures of retrenchment had been repeatedly resorted to or advised; but the difficulties of the time obstructed them, and in fact extremely little relief was obtained in that way.[2]

Nor was by any means the whole difficulty experienced by the public creditor and the tax-payer. There was no sound currency for the transactions of commerce. Nearly down to the close of Dudley's administration, though in twenty years the amount of paper money had been largely increased, driving almost all the coin abroad, the precautions taken against a depreciation of it had had a considerable degree of success;[3] but it broke down under the failure of the second costly expedition to Quebec. The embarrassments and discontents usual in such circumstances followed, and the devices, a thousand times conceived and as often defeated, for paying debts with something different from money. The brilliant prospect of Harley's South Sea Company in England gave

Financial expedients.

[1] In 1706 (Nov. 2), the General Court had ordered the "imprinting" of £10,000 of paper money; in 1707 (March 22, June 12, and Nov. 28), of £22,000; in 1708 (Oct. 29), of £10,000; in 1709 (June 18 and Nov. 8), of £60,000; in 1710 (June 29 and July 28), of £40,000; in 1711 (June 13 and July 6 and 21), of £65,000. As early as 1708 (May 27) the Governor had found occasion to move the General Court for laws to "prevent the bills of credit from being undersold, and thereby defamed." Even Dudley had yet to learn that laws will not stop the depreciation of inconvertible paper money; in other words, of unpayable promises to pay. — A bill was brought into the House (Nov. 16, 1709) to make the counterfeiting of bills of credit a capital offence.

[2] According to a letter from Boston of the year 1712, in the British Colonial Papers, "the standard yearly charges of the Province of Massachusetts to maintain their barrier against the enemy" were then "£30,000 *communibus annis*."

[3] Till the year 1707 the Province's bills were all made redeemable within two years. In that year paper was issued to run for three years; in 1709, for four years; in 1710, for five years; and in 1711, for six. The amount of bills of credit paid into the Treasury of the Province between May, 1703, and May, 1714, was £194,950. (Felt, Historical Account of Massachusetts Currency, 63, 66; comp. Proceedings of the American Antiquarian Society, April 25, 1866, pp. 44–51.)

encouragement to schemers. Some merchants of Boston
1712. presented a memorial praying "to have bills of
Oct. 29. credit made current to answer debt by laws," which was received with favor by the House. The wiser Council replied by asking a conference. But their scruples did not prevail. The urgency of the universal need was considered to be irresistible, and an "Act to
Nov. 8. prevent the Oppression of Debtors" was passed, making the Province's bills of credit a legal tender in payment of debts contracted within the seven preceding years, and within three years subsequent to the enactment of the law.[1]

The Governor proposed a plan for extrication from this dismal financial embarrassment, which, after a
1714. Oct. 20. sharp debate, obtained legal sanction. A *public*
Nov. 5. *bank*, as it was called, was instituted, with a capital provided for it by the General Court, consisting of fifty thousand pounds in bills of credit. Its management was committed to five trustees, who were authorized to lend the bills for periods not to exceed five years, for an interest of five *per centum* annually, and a payment each year of one fifth part of the principal sum, the payments to be secured by mortgages of real property.[2] The principal opposition to this plan proceeded from friends of the project of what was called a *private bank*. They proposed to form a company which should issue and lend its own notes, or bills of credit, the payment to be secured by mortgages on their estates. Their scheme was frustrated when the General Court, preferring the plan of the public
Aug. 20. bank, refused them an act of incorporation.[3] But

1 Provincial Laws, I 700.—"Nov. 3, 1712, Mr. Jonathan Belcher comes to me, and speaks very freely for passing the Act about bills of credit; said I should do well to be out of the way, rather than hinder so great a good." (Sewall's Journal.)

2 Mass. Prov. Rec.; comp. Felt, History of the Currency, 68.

3 Ibid., 66; Mass. Prov. Rec.—August 20, Paul Dudley, as Attorney-General, presented to the Governor in Council a memorial against the private bank, which produced a prohi-

they did not despair, and the controversy which they kept alive made for some years the prominent question in the politics of the Province.[1] A few judicious persons were in favor of making strenuously the exertions and sacrifices necessary for a speedy return to a solid currency. But in the difficulties of the time they could obtain little hearing; and, as a choice between evils, they generally favored the public bank.[2]

Sir Henry Ashurst, head of the dissenting interest in Parliament, and Constantine Phipps, ancestor of the Marquesses of Normanby of the present time, had for many years been agents of Massachusetts in England. Phipps, attaching himself to the Tory Ministry which, after the blunder of the Whigs in the proceedings against Dr. Sacheverel, held power in the last years of Queen Anne, became thereby unacceptable to the people and General Court of Massachusetts; and about the same time Ashurst died. Sir William, his brother, equally respected for his worth, and regarded as a person of more ability and influence, was elected to be agent, against Dudley's strenuous opposition. But it was no object of ambition to him, the less so as he thought the agents had not been liberally treated; and he declined to serve, pleading ill health, and recommending Jeremiah Dummer for the place.[3] Dummer, grand-

1710.

Appointment of Dummer to be agent.

bition to the projectors (among whom were persons so considerable as Nathaniel Byfield, Peter Faneuil, and Hezekiah Usher) to issue bills, or print their scheme, till they had laid it before the General Court. (Council Record.)

[1] For a list of publications in this controversy, see Proceedings of the American Antiquarian Society, April 25, 1866, p. 88.

[2] Aug. 8, 1715, Dummer informed the Lords of Trade that he had been directed by the Province, if a project of a bank should be submitted to the Lords, to pray that, before any action was taken, they might have opportunity to examine it; and he asked that all action might be suspended till the new Governor should arrive in Massachusetts. (British Colonial Papers.) Again, August 24, he laid before them an argument against the proposed bank, maintaining that the bills of credit of the last quarter-century afforded a better circulating medium, and that if a profit was to be made the public ought to have it. (Ibid.)

[3] Journal of the Board of Trade.

son of a former Assistant of Massachusetts, and a graduate of Harvard College, was chosen to be agent, also against Dudley's recommendation of another person.[1] After leaving Cambridge, Dummer had studied at the University of Utrecht for some years. (1699.) Then, after a short visit to his home, he went to England, where he obtained the notice and engaged in the service of Henry St. John; and a prospect of advancement opened before him, which was closed by the Queen's death.

This appointment, especially after his opposition to it, made Dudley anxious. He feared that the failure at Quebec would be used to his prejudice. (1712. Oct. 29.) He wrote to Lord Dartmouth, protesting that every thing possible had been done by him to promote the ill-fated expedition. (Dudley's insecure position.) "If after all my sincere endeavors in that affair," he said, "I should lose my reputation with the people here, and her Majesty's favor, I should be the most unfortunate man living. I have served her Majesty here faithfully these ten years. . . . . . I have left nothing undone, ... and have had but a mean support, and yet am not willing to lose my station."[2] As

for June 6, 1710; comp. Ibid., for Feb. 5, 1711. — Oct. 26, 1711, the General Court revived the matter of the executions for witchcraft twenty years before. All the attainders, twenty-two in number, were reversed; and pecuniary damages were awarded to the amount of £578. (Mass. Prov. Rec.)

[1] "1709, Feb. 7. — Council Meeting. The Governor spake against the thing [choice of an agent] largely and earnestly. . . . . . To choose Sir William was to cut him down. . . . . . Sir Henry had injuriously pursued him these twenty years. Sometimes nobody followed him save Sir William. Could they procure no one else? . . . . . Would none serve but Sir William Ashurst?" "February 8, at a meeting of the Council, sixteen were present, and fifteen voted for the appointment, in concurrence with the Deputies." But, February 9, the Governor refused his assent. "July 27, 1710. This day the Deputies sent in a bill [Sir William Ashurst having declined the agency] to choose Mr. Jeremiah Dummer for their agent. Governor says he will be drawn asunder with wild horses, before he will be thrust upon, as last year." (Sewall's Journal.) — June 6, 1710, Dummer informed the Board of Trade that Sir William declined to accept the agency. Feb. 5, 1711, he presented his own commission, signed by Dudley the preceding November 10. (Journal of the Board of Trade.)

[2] Letter in British Colonial Papers.

to his mean support, Usher, on the other hand, whom Dudley (moved perhaps by the memory of their ancient participation in Andros's councils) had usefully befriended, but who had now quarrelled with him, affirmed that Dudley, though always complaining, had been saving money out of his pay. There is some reason to think that, at this time, Vetch was intriguing in England to supplant the Governor. But he not long after fell into discredit. Nicholson wrote of him from Boston to Lord Bolingbroke: "He hath, I think, acted very arbitrarily and illegally, and hath defrauded her Majesty very considerably, ... and hath gone away."[1] 1714. April 23.

[1] Letter in British Colonial Papers. But Dummer, sustained by several other persons who were examined by the Board of Trade, gave a very different character of Vetch. Dummer said that "Colonel Vetch was a man of good sense, well affected to the government, and a good soldier; that he had heard of no complaint against him but what had been made by Colonel Nicholson." (Journal of the Board of Trade, for Jan. 17, 1715.) Nicholson appears to have espoused in this case the cause of Sir Charles Hobby, who had made interest to supersede him as Governor of Nova Scotia. The rivals were reconciled, and with Vetch's acquiescence Hobby was "made Lieutenant-Governor of Annapolis Royal." (Ibid., for February 4.)

As late as 1724, Vetch was hoping to succeed Shute as Governor of Massachusetts. In a letter to the Duke of Newcastle, of June 22 of that year, he set forth his former services in the expeditions against Canada and Nova Scotia. He says that, after the Treaty of Utrecht, he was removed from the government of the latter Province, "only for his zeal for his present Majesty's royal family and interest." He thinks it "next to impossible Mr. Shute should go back, considering the vast breach that is now between him and the whole body of the people and government there," and he "dares without vanity affirm that no person is more capable [than himself] of serving the interest of the crown in that country, and no person can be more acceptable to the whole people there." (British Colonial Papers.)

Colonel Nicholson, while in Massachusetts, was by no means modest in his assumptions of authority, and Dudley stood his friend. In conferences with the Council, it was his custom to place himself at the head of the table, by the Governor's side. On one occasion, Sewall and another justice sent his secretary to gaol for some noisy joviality on a Saturday night. Nicholson complained, and the Governor obtained the Council's consent for the offender's discharge. (Sewall's Journal, for Feb. 14, 1711.)

June 8, 1713, "Letter read from Mr. Harley, referring to the Board petition of officers and soldiers who served in the late war, and now disbanded, to the Queen, praying a grant of land in North America uninhabited between New England and Nova Scotia, in order to their settling and planting there." (Journal of the Board of Trade.) A negotia-

The Governor, as usual, set himself to conciliate those whom he found himself unable to break down. Sir William Ashurst was induced to write out to Massachusetts, Aug. 10. that, if Dudley should be displaced, the Province might prove to be the loser.[1] Phipps, who at first had pursued him with acrimony, had still earlier been won over. The agent and the Governor, both devoted clients of the new Tory Ministry, were naturally brought together by this sympathy. Dudley never stood so strong in England as he did just before Queen Anne died and Lord Bolingbroke fled.[2]

His last days of office.

But though his desisting from the offensive demands with which he had begun his administration had removed the principal immediate cause of contention between him and the people of Massachusetts, and though the advantage to them of his activity and capacity in the conduct of the war did not fail to be appreciated, yet it would be an error to suppose that he ever reinstated himself in their confidence or good-will, after the treacheries of his earlier public life. When Sept. 29. he had made a speech to the General Court, an-

tion followed respecting the terms of the grant, and provision for the expenses of the enterprise. (Ibid., for June 12, July 6, 9, and 10, August 14, 19, 21.) But the demands of the petitioners were thought to be "so high that their Lordships could not represent any thing to my Lord Treasurer in their favor." The project was subsequently revived, but still fruitlessly. (Privy Council Register, for December 6, and Journal of the Board of Trade, for Dec. 30, 1714, and Feb. 15, 1715.)

On the night of May 20, a mob in Boston "broke into and entered a warehouse," and "broke the windows of a gentleman of her Majesty's Council." The Council took notice of it the next day (Council Records), and, May 28, the Governor made a speech upon it to the House. (Mass. Prov. Rec.) He said that his doing so was not for want of power of his own to suppress disorders; and the House seem to have agreed with him, for they took no action. I do not know who was the Counsellor, or what provocation he had given.

[1] Letter of Sir William Ashurst to Increase Mather, in Hutch., II. 211, note.

[2] In 1714, the fifth Congregational Church, called the *New North* Church, was established in Boston. It was dedicated May 5, and John Webb became its pastor. (John Eliot, Sermon preached May 2, 1804; Francis Parkman, Sermon preached Nov. 27, 1814; Mass. Hist. Col., XXV. 215.)

nouncing the Queen's death, the Council followed it up by a vote for a joint committee of the two Houses to prepare an Address to the King, praying a renewal of the commissions of the Governor and Lieutenant-Governor. The Representatives refused to concur in it; they refused, when solicited by the Council, to reconsider their vote of non-concurrence; and the Court was prorogued without further discussion of the matter. The Governor continued to execute his office for the present by virtue of an Act of Parliament, which was understood to extend such authority for a period of six months from the sovereign's death.[1] At the end of that time he withdrew, and the Council assumed the chief executive authority conformably to a provision of the charter. In a few weeks, however, came a royal proclamation, reinstating him in his place in time to preside at the next General Court.[2]

Oct. 1.

Oct. 2.

1715. Feb. 4.

March 21.

[1] It may be thought to betoken the weakness of Dudley's last days of office, that the General Court (Mass. Prov. Rec. for Nov. 5, 1714), averse to the continued expense of defending a great extent of frontier, ordered that no person should thenceforward, unless by special license, settle anywhere in Maine, except at York, Berwick, Arrowsick, Kittery, and Wells. A garrison at Pemaquid would be of no use to any of these plantations.

[2] Addington showed to Sewall an order from the Queen, of May 3, 1707, constituting the oldest Counsellor Governor in case of the Governor's death or absence. (Sewall's Journal, for Jan. 1, 1715.) But this was not the provision of the charter.

Jan. 27, 1715, the Governor presided in the Council as usual. Feb. 1, the Council sent a committee to him to inquire whether, six months having expired since the sovereign's death, he had received any order to continue the government. He replied that he had received no orders. Those of the Counsellors who were then in town called a meeting of the Council for the second following day. Feb. 4, that body "published by beat of drum" a proclamation making known that a "Devolution had taken place," and that they had assumed the government; and sent a committee to acquaint the Governor with this. Lieutenant-Governor Tailer made his claim to preside in the Council; but it was disallowed, and Wait Winthrop was made its presiding officer. (Council Records; Sewall's Diary; Letter of the Council to the Lords of Trade, of March 2, 1715, in Mass. Arch., LI. 271). — March 16, the Council made inquisition respecting an unsigned printed sheet, entitled "The Case of the Governor and Council of Massachusetts Bay." Thomas Fleet, whom they examined,

One of the Counsellors chosen by the new Court was Nathaniel Byfield, whom again the Governor gratified his ill-humor by rejecting, whether on account of an unkindness of long standing, or because of Byfield's position as to the proposed bank.[1] On the other hand, at this last moment of his power, he relented towards Elisha Cooke, and consented to his introduction into the Council.[2] Soon came intelligence that one Colonel Burgess, who had served in Spain under General Stanhope, had by his favor received the royal appointment to be Governor,[3] and the Council voted to raise a joint committee to attend to "the reception of the Governor speedily to be expected." But the House would not consent. On the day to which, for the

May 26.

Appointment of Burgess to be Governor.

April 21.

said that he had printed "a quire" of copies secretly, and delivered them to Paul Dudley. Jonathan Belcher said he had received three copies, of which he had sent two to England.

When the Governor proclaimed his restoration, he came to town for the purpose at the head of four troops of horse. (Sewall's Journal, for March 21.) A few days after (April 1), he proposed his son Paul for Judge of Probate. But the Council rejected the nomination by a vote of ten to eight. Paul Dudley had refused the Council's commission to be Sheriff, saying that he already had the Governor's. The Council then made another appointment, but Paul Dudley was made Sheriff again on his father's restoration. (Council Record; comp. Sewall's Journal.)

[1] Nathaniel Byfield (see above, Vol. III. 579, note, 583, note 2), who was a person of some importance at this period, was son of a member of the Westminster Assembly of Divines, and nephew of Bishop Juxon. He came from England in 1674, and settled at Bristol. In 1693, he was Speaker of the House, and Judge of Probate for his county. In 1703, he was appointed Judge of Admiralty, and held the office through the whole of Dudley's administration. Dudley, when he came over as Governor, found him in office as a Counsellor, but they soon fell out, and the breach was never reconciled. (Whitmore, Andros Tracts, I. 3, 4.) In England, Byfield quarrelled with Dummer, who took Dudley's part, though between himself and the Governor there was still no good will. (See letters of Dummer to Colman, of Jan. 15, 1714, in Mass. Hist. Col., V. 197, and to Tutor Flint, of March, 1715, in Mass. Hist. Col., VI. 78.)

[2] Perhaps Cooke was now in failing health. He died October 31 of this year.

[3] "News comes that Colonel Burgess is to be our Governor. . . . . . This news will damp my daughter of Brookline her triumph." (Sewall's Journal.) Sewall's son had married a daughter of Dudley, and the young couple did not agree any better than their parents.

last time, Dudley prorogued the Court,[1] Lieutenant-Governor William Tailer met them as chief magistrate in the absence of Colonel Burgess, who still loitered in England, and whose appointment he announced. He said nothing of the late Governor's withdrawal. Tailer, a connection of Stoughton by marriage, and one of his heirs, had brought over his own commission as successor to Povey four years before, having probably owed his advancement to approved military service at the capture of Port Royal.[2] Nicholson in person,[3] and the Governor by letter, had introduced him favorably in England.

Accession of Lieutenant-Governor Tailer. Nov. 23.

1711.

1710. Nov 20.

Dudley was now sixty-eight years old. He lived five years longer, but took no further part in public business. When he died, he was commemorated by the Boston newspaper, as "a singular honor to his country, and in many respects the glory of it; early its darling, always its ornament, and in his age its crown."[4] It is happy for bad men of ability that injured

Retirement and death of Dudley. 1720. April 2.

[1] September 22, Addington being now dead, Secretary Woodward arrived, and produced his commission.

[2] "June 18, 1711. Heard that Colonel Tayler was made Lieutenant-Governor. Dr. Mather said 'twas impossible." (Sewall's Journal.)

[3] Letter of Tayler to Lord Dartmouth, of Feb. 27, 1710; Letter of Dudley to the same, of Nov. 20, 1711, in British Colonial Papers.

[4] "Boston News-Letter," of April 11, 1720. — This is what would be called in our day the testimony of "the press" to Dudley's merit. More precisely stated, it is the testimony of the Scottish adventurer, John Campbell, postmaster, to the official friend who had done serving him, and whom he had done serving; and it evinced a more generous gratitude than what is a mere sense of benefits expected. — What is more painful than this is to see how Dudley's character is treated by so good a man as Dr. Colman, who, as far as I have found, preached the only funeral sermon on the Governor. Colman might feel biassed towards him, by reason of his services to the College, to which Colman was so zealous a friend. And the Attorney-General (the Governor's son) had been eighteen years a member of Colman's church (Sermon, Præf. iv.). But, after all, he is so far from commending the Governor without caution, that the most unpleasant feature of the composition is the ill-disguised slyness with which he attempts to compromise between his desire to please and his sense of truth (Sermon, 10, 32). In his exhibition of the virtues of the patriarch Joseph he abounds in flattering insinuations, but he is observably reserved about

communities are forgiving, that power and shining qualities confuse the moral judgment, and that apologists are so easily enlisted from among the interested and the ignorant, the good-natured, the reckless, and the insincere.

It is needless to multiply words on the character of Dudley. It was not a mystery, nor was he a monster of turpitude. There is no necessity to regard him as having been destitute of all moral sense, nor even to set down his religious professions as merely hypocritical and false. Many a transgressor feels the presence of a conscience which has power enough to rebuke and distress, but not enough to arrest and reform him; and religious conviction and sensibility have been often known to exist in the absence of upright conduct. For aught man can know, this man, like many others more famous and many less famous than he, had tampered with his better mind till the distinctions which make the world's security were obscured to his own view; and with a certain sort of sincerity he could call evil good, and good evil, as often as only evil would suit his domineering aim. At all events, he had no purpose to be true and useful. He meant to get power, and all that power brings with it, and with gay arrogance placed his unimportant self above the rights and the welfare of the community, which with honest affection had empowered him to do it grievous harm.

Mentally and morally, Dudley belonged to a class of actors who again and again have strutted their hour on the busy stage, applauded to the echo by the throngs who admire cleverness and "idolize success." A sordid ambition does not begin its career with revelations of its character. It makes public services its earliest stepping-stones. Public good-will in free States is the card essential to the

making applications of them to that other Joseph whom the occasion summoned him to commemorate, thus offering less provocation to the criticism of a discerning public. Funeral sermons are a grievous snare to the historian, till he has read a sufficient number of them to be reasonably upon his guard.

playing of the game of self-advancement. The confidence and gratitude which follow good behavior in early life make the stock-in-trade of the unscrupulous aspirant for place and fortune. With them he enlists partisans; makes adverse judgment distrust itself, and utter timid protests; buys an indulgent silence respecting his misdeeds, or a reluctant and forbearing condemnation; defies criticism with insolent boasts of injured merit. The Greek Themistocles earned at Salamis the power to treat with Persia for the sale of Greece. The Roman Manlius, if from his youth he meditated treason, could not have done a better thing for his object than by repelling the Gauls from the assaulted citadel. Benedict Arnold, when he rendered brilliant service to his country at Quebec and Saratoga, was placing himself in a position to concert his country's ruin at West Point.

Dudley united rich intellectual attributes with a grovelling soul. To his mean nature personal aggrandizement was the prime necessity. He had paid one price for it by dutiful behavior in his early years, and another by useful conduct in middle life, as often as such conduct would not thwart, and especially as often as it would further, the aims of his cupidity. The first price bought him the popularity which was sure to prove a gainful instrument: the second secured the toleration which would permit him to proceed with less obstruction in his ulterior schemes.

From his early awakening to the consciousness of uncommon powers, he seems to have considered with a confident disdain what an unwise part his father had chosen when he undertook to be a witness and a sufferer for liberty and right. Though he never knew his father, who died in his early childhood, he had heard from his nursery-days of the hardships which Christian heroism had brought on that lofty-minded, if narrow-minded, man; and in his own bosom he found nothing that promised compensation for the sacrifices of such a career. The father's associates, with an easy faith, assuming the son to be the heir of ancestral virtue, loaded him with their honorable trusts; and while the business of the hour was to acquire a reputation to be used for future profit, he applied himself to that acquisition with a diligence which commanded an unsuspecting trust. While he was rendering himself eminently capable of effective treachery, the British court had been informing itself how much his treachery would be worth. When his power to wrong and distress the native country which had confided and taken pride in him had been well ascertained, he had no reluctance to this more lucrative service; for the lust of gain had silenced all misgivings, and by constitution he had sufficient courage to be not only without scruples, but without shame. Thomas Hutchinson, two generations later, was so like him as to be quite unconscious of the condemnation which he was pronouncing when he said of Dudley that "he had as many virtues as can consist with so great a thirst for honor and power."

When the world grows wiser, great mental faculties and great personal achievements will less dazzle its judgment, and it will be less easily deluded to regard useful acts done for an aspirant's own advantage as compensation for unworthy acts done as soon as his own advancement demands a sacrifice of his honor and of the general welfare. It will come to see that the devotion of great powers to base uses is only worthy of scorn and loathing.

CHAPTER XI.

In New Hampshire Dudley was not unwillingly received as Governor, when he came thither soon after returning to America from his service in the British Parliament.[1] In that Province such causes for resentment as had made him unwelcome in Massachusetts had been little operative at the time of their occurrence, and had been lost sight of in the lapse of years. In a letter to the Lords of Trade he commended in warm terms the liberality of the Province, "which bore the proportion but of the eleventh part to Massachusetts," yet had voted "five hundred pounds to begin the reform of their fortification" at the mouth of the Piscataqua, and had granted him an annual salary, for the whole period of his commission, of a hundred and sixty pounds,[2] which he said was as much as they could

Dudley in New Hampshire. 1702. July 13.

1703. Dec. 19.

[1] For Dudley's commission for New Hampshire, see N. H. Provincial Papers, II. 366 *et seq.* — Partridge, in a letter of April 17, 1702, informed the Lords of Trade that the Province was grateful for the appointment. (British Colonial Papers.) — Joseph Smith, of Hampton, a pragmatical person (N. H. Provincial Papers, II. 207, 263, 265, 591), was a friend of Dudley, and in the following year was recommended by him for the post of Counsellor of the Province. Sept. 22, 1701, Smith wrote to John Usher in London: "As for the old Revolution pillars among us, they begin to shake and tremble at the news of Colonel Dudley's coming Governor, and some of our little justices, I hear, with eyes lifted up, cry, 'Poor New England hath seen its best days; now, now Popery will be brought into this land of uprightness;' and yet we shall find these Shimeis with a dog's heart will be the first that congratulate his happy arrival." (British Colonial Papers.)

[2] Sept. 3, 1703, a letter from the Queen, of the preceding April 20, was read to the Assembly, in which her Majesty, declaring that "several inconveniences have arisen to our government in the Plantations by gifts, presents, and temporary salaries made or assigned to our Governors by the General Assemblies,"

afford, and as much for them as ten times the amount would be for Massachusetts.[1] In other respects they satisfied him less, as he informed the Lords of Trade with much explicitness. The courts disappointed him by not condemning goods seized for alleged violation of the Navigation Laws. "So it is, my Lords, that the judges are ignorant and the juries stubborn, that it is a very hard thing to obtain their just service to the crown, all which will be prevented if your Lordships please to let me have a judge of Admiralty settled here."[2]

1704. Feb. 11.

Next to the exposure to inroads from the French and Indian enemy, already described, the main subject of concern to the people of New Hampshire was the pending controversy for their lands with Allen, the assign of John Mason. It was now about to be brought to an issue. Dudley was not unfavorable to the claim of the settlers; and the liberality of the Assembly, at the same time that it reciprocated his good-will, bespoke his future favor.

Claim of Samuel Allen to lands.

Allen's son-in-law, Usher, succeeded in obtaining a re-appointment to be Lieutenant-Governor of New Hampshire, notwithstanding the opposition of the agent of that Province;[3] and Partridge withdrew from public affairs to attend to the increase of his fortune

Lieutenant-Governor Usher.

signified her "expectation that, in regard of our receiving our good subjects of that Province [New Hampshire] under our immediate protection and government, they do forthwith settle a constant and fixed allowance on our Governor and Lieutenant-Governor of our said Province for the time being, and that the same be done without limitation of time." (N. H. Provincial Papers, III. 251.) Accordingly the vote above referred to was passed October 6. (Ibid., 230; comp. 305, 308.)

[1] Dudley's letter, in British Colonial Papers.

[2] Ibid.

[3] His commission, dated June 10, 1703, is in N. H. Provincial Papers, II. 406.—In April, 1703, William Vaughan, the agent, presented to the Lords of Trade a memorial against the appointment of Usher. "Mr. Usher," he said, "hath got himself universally hated in the Province by managing a suit against the interest of all the people of the whole Province." He asserted that Usher had impressed members of the Assembly, and sent them to do garrison duty. (British Colonial Papers.)

at Newbury, where, after some years, he died.[1] Partridge had written to thank the Lords for appointing Dudley to be Governor of New Hampshire, and Dudley had expressed himself to the same authority in terms of commendation of his subordinate in office;[2] but, on the other hand, he declared himself pleased with the reappointment of Usher, and rendered to him a service which, as the parties then stood, was more material, by pronouncing a claim which he was urging on Massachusetts for a sum due in the settlement of his accounts, as former Treasurer of that Province, to be "very plain and just."[3] Usher did his duty not ill in respect to the conduct of the war; but his antagonistic position in the controversy about the lands was fatal to his good standing with the Assembly, and they would do no more for him than to pay the rent of two rooms for his official residence when he came to New Hampshire, and provide penuriously for the cost of his journeys to and from Boston, where for the most part he continued to reside.[4]

1702. April 17.

1703. Aug. 5.

1704. Feb. 29.

1705.

Before the Queen's Privy Council, to which he had appealed, Allen failed to make out his case, for want of being prepared to show that Mason, whose rights he represented as assign, had ever been in legal possession of the lands in dispute. The Council referred him back to the courts of New Hampshire, where accordingly, as a test question, he presented his claim by a writ of ejectment against Richard Waldron, for lands held by the latter in the town of Exeter. The people

Litigation of Allen's claim.

1 He went to England meanwhile. (N. H. Provincial Papers, II. 408, where his name is on the memorial against Dudley. See above, 303.)

2 "He [Partridge] is very sincere and industrious, in my observation, in every thing that imports her Majesty's service, since my arrival, however it was before." (Letter of Dudley to the Lords, in British Colonial Papers.)

3 Letters in British Colonial Papers.

4 N. H. Provincial Papers, II. 440, 441, 459. — "I must say the provision made for my lodging worse than my negro servants', both as to room and lodging." (Ibid., 589.)

raised no question with Allen as to the property of lands lying beyond the bounds of their townships. But this concession would not satisfy him; he coveted the towns which they had labored and suffered in cultivating and defending for two-thirds of a century. Dudley had orders to demand from the jury a special verdict on some points, to the end of facilitating an appeal to the Privy Council, if the verdict should be against the claimant. But, when the Governor was expected at the trial, he was detained (not unwillingly, it was thought), first by an alarm of an Indian inroad, and then by illness.[1] The jury decided against Allen, and gave no special verdict. To avoid another troublesome appeal, the Assembly proposed a compromise. They offered to Allen that they would relinquish all pretension to any lands except such as were included in their four towns, and in Newcastle and Kingston, which were in progress of settlement; and that they would set off to him five thousand acres within those six districts in consideration of a quitclaim to be given by him of the rest, and pay him two thousand pounds "current money of New England" in two yearly instalments.[2]

May 3.

He died before this agreement, so advantageous for him, could be concluded,[3] and the controversy was inherited by his son, who received permission from

May 5.

1 "Colonel Dudley went so far as Newbury, where, being seized with a violent fit of the gravel, did not proceed further." (Short Narrative, &c.)

2 N. H. Provincial Papers, III. 274-276.

3 Allen died the day after Dudley communicated the proposal to him; "and so the appeal and trial and compromise all ended." (Dudley to the Lords of Trade, July 25, 1705, in British Colonial Papers.) — The transactions relating to Allen's claim, from the alleged grant to John Mason by the Council of Plymouth to the death of Thomas Allen, son of Samuel, in 1715, are related in a pamphlet, published in Boston in 1728, entitled "A Short Narrative of the Claim, Title, and Right of the Heirs of the Hon. Samuel Allen, to the Province of New Hampshire in New England, transmitted from a gentlewoman in London to her friend in New England." The writer expresses the hope (p. 1) that "the heir, in a little time, will be of age, and capable to prosecute his right."

the Queen in Council to have a new trial, with the same instruction to the jury for a special verdict as had been disregarded the year before. At the trial the counsel for Allen rested his case on the alleged grants of the Council for New England to John Mason, whose rights, such as they were, they had no difficulty in proving to have descended to their client; and they produced depositions given twenty years before by several persons, then aged, to the effect that Mason had taken actual possession. The material points of the argument on Waldron's part were that the Council for New England never made a legally valid grant to John Mason of the lands in question, and that, on the other hand, Waldron's family had been settled seventy years on those lands with a title derived from four Indian chiefs, whose formal deed of conveyance to the minister Wheelwright and others was produced in court. The jury returned a general verdict in Waldron's favor. They refused a special verdict, declaring that the occasion for it arose only when there was doubt as to law or fact, and that they had no doubt in respect to either. Before Allen's appeal to the Queen in Council was brought to any issue, his son and heir also died. The son's heirs were minors, and the claim was not renewed in their behalf; and so a quarrel which had subsisted since the foundation of the Province seemed to be at an end. The question of the genuineness of the alleged Indian deed to Wheelwright has been largely discussed by modern antiquaries. That it was a forgery, must be now pronounced to be past dispute.[1] At the time of the trial Usher denounced it as such, charging

1706.

1629.

1715.

Forged Indian deed.

[1] The character of this deed escaped the sharp discernment of Dr. Belknap. (History, I. 164.) Mr. James Savage, the distinguished editor of Winthrop's Journal, detected the fraud, and his acute and learned argument may now be confidently said to leave no room for doubt. (Winthrop's History, edit. Savage, I. 486 *et seq.*) A full account of the trial is in N. H. Provincial Papers, II. 514–562.

the act upon Richard Waldron.[1] He argued, as has been done recently, that Englishmen whose names are on the instrument as grantees and witnesses were not in America so early.

The friendship between Usher and the Governor was
1703. Oct. 22. not lasting. Usher, who came to the government the year after his superior, professed to find that Dudley had not been devoted enough to the sovereign. "It is high time," he wrote to the Lords, "to have
Quarrel between Dudley and Usher. a Governor who will assert her Majesty's prerogative, and curb the anti-monarchial principles."
Dec. 30. And he added that of the subordinate officers commissioned by Bellomont, and still employed by Dudley, "many were disaffected to crown government."[2] The truth was that Dudley befriended the local party with which in the late administration Usher had been at feud, and that he did not mean to be incommoded by interference on the part of his lieutenant. Usher undertook to
December. restore Jefferys, who had been removed from the post of Secretary by his predecessor. He complained that Waldron and Partridge had "misapplied the public money," and that Dudley wrongfully continued Hincks as commander of the fort, one reason for this favoritism being that "Hincks is a Churchman." "I must say Partridge and Waldron governs; nothing to be done but what they are for."[3]

The Lieutenant-Governor's dissatisfaction cast off all re-
1704. Jan. 19. serve as time passed on. "The country," he wrote to the Lords of Trade, "is universally against

[1] "On hearing Mr. Allen's case, Waldron produced a pretended deed to one Wheelwright. . . . . . Upon inquiry, Mr. Wheelwright came into the country many years after date of said deed. Waldron, being producer, judged to be the author." (Letter of Usher to the Lords of Trade, in British Colonial Papers; comp. Hist. Mag. for 1857, 57.)

[2] British Colonial Papers.

[3] N. H. Provincial Papers, II. 395–399; Letters in British Colonial Papers.

him [Dudley], and he does not find one that gives him a good word; if we have not a change by having a new Governor, we shall in a short time be ruined. . . . . . We want a good soldier to manage the war. . . . . . Nothing like a viceroy over all." It is not likely that Dudley was acquainted with these letters, but the breach went on widening. Usher wrote to the Lords, "His Excellency 1709.
is pleased to tell me, when I go into the Province Aug. 5.
I put all in a flame." Dudley, on his part, informed them, "Mr. Usher has been very unfortunate in putting Nov. 15.
himself into Mr. Allen's affair, the delay of which has made him poor and angry, and particularly with Mr. Waldron." In a letter to Dudley, Waldron calls Usher "an envious, malicious liar." Dudley encloses it to the Secretary of State, and acquaints him that though Waldron's language is "too harsh," the statement which it clothes "is true."[1]

Dudley ordered by letter that Waldron should be received into the Council, over which, in the Governor's absence, Usher was presiding. Usher asked the Secretary whether he had received the warrant with the 1710.
royal sign-manual appointing Waldron, and being Nov. 21.
informed that it had not come he refused to allow Waldron to be sworn, who, on his part, "said he should not take notice, but wait the Governor's instructions," and then "parted sourly with his hat on." "When at any time," so Usher wrote, "I come into the Council, if Waldron is there before me, with disdain has his back some time to me, and at a distance says, 'Your servant,' with insulting deportment, affronts many and great, with disrespect to the Queen's commission." Such were the official amenities of that place and time.[2]

[1] Letters in British Colonial Papers.

[2] "Robert Ellott, Esq., one of the members of her Majesty's Council, exhibited a complaint against Major Shadrach Walton, for abusing him, and calling him a knave, and threatening him, &c., as upon file.

"An account of the circumstances and state of New Hampshire," drawn up by George Vaughan, who had succeeded his father as agent of the Province in England, represents it as containing "six towns; viz., Portsmouth, Dover, Exeter, Hampton, Newcastle, and Kingstown, — the two last very small and extraordinary poor; drove to great straits by reason of the war, ... there not being a thousand men in the whole government." Dudley wrote to the Lords, "I account New Hampshire is in value of men, towns, and acres of improvement just a tenth part of the Massachusetts, and I believe I do not misreckon to a hundredth part, their trade excepted, which will not make much more than the thirtieth part of Boston and dependencies." "Our poverty is such," the Representatives replied to the Governor's application for aid to the expedition against Canada, "that one-third of the inhabitants have not bread to eat, nor wherewithal to procure it, there being a seventeen hundred pound tax forthwith to be paid, which we fear will be very hard and difficult for the poor people."[1]

Condition of New Hampshire. 1708. July 6.

1709. March 1.

June 27.

Major Walton appeared and acknowledged before this Board that he did call Robert Ellott, Esq., knave, and that he did say if Mr. Ellott took those persons' parts, which the said Walton called rogues and rascals, and said he would cut their ears and split their noses, he would do the same to him, the said Ellott; and, further, the said Walton did declare that he was sorry that he should use such language to Mr. Ellott; upon which Mr. Ellott declared himself satisfied for the abuse used to his person." The Council cautioned Walton against such intemperance in future, and discharged him on the payment of a fine of £2 16*s*. 6*d*. (Record of the Council of New Hampshire, for June 20, 1707, in N. H. Provincial Papers, II. 508, 509; comp. Journal of the House, in Ibid., IV. 433.)

[1] N. H. Provincial Papers, III. 386. — "One half of our men are employed against the daily insults of a barbarous enemy, which renders us very poor and feeble." (Address to the Queen, Oct. 30, 1711, in Ibid., 507.) — In such a state of things it is very noticeable that the Province turned its attention to a quite different interest, and made as a Province its first provision for free schools. A "Latin School" was established in Portsmouth. The master, to "be appointed by his Excellency, Council, and settled minister of the town," was to "be paid after the rate of fifty pounds per annum, besides what the

At the time of Dudley's special straits, the government of New Hampshire sustained him by addressing the Queen with earnest representations in his behalf.[1] Similar representations were made after the death of Queen Anne, but without effect.[2] Usher obtained no more favor with the new home government. William Vaughan and five other Counsellors wrote to George Vaughan, still agent in London, "We pray Lieutenant-Governor Usher may have his quietus, which he said he had often written to England for. He complains his office is a burden to him, and the people think it is a burden to them, and so 't is a pity but both were eased."[3] Usher was displaced, and George Vaughan was made Lieutenant-Governor. Usher withdrew to his stately home at Medford, in Massachusetts, where he died when nearly eighty years old.

1706. July 25. 1707. Oct. 22.

1715. March 18.

Retirement of Usher.

1726. Sept. 25.

The commission of Dudley empowered him to command the militia of Rhode Island; but that chaotic community did not afford a hopeful sphere for the application of his arbitrary principles. Soon after his return from his early visit to the eastern country, he went to Newport, attended from Boston by several members of his Council and others, and in form presented his claim to the Governor and Council of Rhode

Visit of Dudley to Rhode Island. 1702. Sept. 3.

selectmen of Portsmouth shall order to be paid by each of their inhabitants that sends his child to learn Latin." Portsmouth was to pay twenty-eight pounds of this salary, Hampton eight, Exeter and Dover each six, and Newcastle two. (Ibid., 364, 365; comp. 570.) While New Hampshire belonged to Massachusetts, there was, under the law of that Colony, a free school in Dover, at least as early as 1658. (Ibid., I. 312.)

[1] N. H. Provincial Papers, III. 328, 350. On the latter occasion he was also extolled in an Address from the six ministers (Ibid., 351), and from numerous civil and military officers and others. (Ibid., 839.)

[2] Ibid., 576; comp. 547.

[3] British Colonial Papers.

Island. They referred him to the grant of the control over its militia made to the Colony in the charter
Sept. 4. of King Charles the Second, and said they could take no step in compliance with his demand, except under authority from the General Assembly, which would not be in session till the next month. Dudley ordered the major of "the Island regiment" to parade his command on the following day. The major excused himself, say-
Sept. 5. ing he was sworn to serve the colonial government; and nothing could be done in that way. In the Narragansett country, to which Dudley passed on, he
Sept. 7. succeeded better. The militia officer there in command made no trouble. "The whole body of the soldiers in arms" took the oath which the Governor proposed; and, having "treated the soldiers as the time and place would allow," he went home. The Governor and Council of Rhode Island came to the Narragansett country, and there "used all methods to bring back the people to confusion." The General Assembly, meeting soon
Sept. 17. after, voted to send an agent with an Address to the Queen on the important subject in dispute.[1]

Another matter of scarcely less interest was Dudley's claim, justified by a similar order in his commission, to exercise jurisdiction in Rhode Island as Vice-Admiral. The Governor of that Colony had issued commissions to armed vessels. Dudley held that Cranston had no authority for so doing, and that such commissions were void. Nathaniel Byfield, Judge of Admiralty, refused on this
1705. ground to condemn a French prize brought in by
June. a Rhode Island privateer, and thereby gave such offence that, when he adjourned his court in Newport, he "was hooted down the street, without any notice being taken by any in the government."[2]

[1] R. I. Rec., III. 458–463.

[2] Ibid., 539; comp. 508–510, 536–538, 540.

Reporting these transactions to the Board of Trade, Dudley wrote that, when he published his instructions in Rhode Island, "the Quakers raged indecently, saying that they were ensnared and injured." He "could obtain nothing of them but stubborn refusal, saying they would lose all at once, and not by pieces." "I do my duty," he said, "to acquaint your Lordships that the government of Rhode Island, in the present hands, is a scandal to her Majesty's government. It is a very good settlement, with about two thousand armed men in it, and no man in the government of any estate or education, though in the Province there be men of very good estates, ability, and loyalty; but the Quakers will by no means admit them to any trust, nor would they now accept it, in hopes of a dissolution of that misrule, and that they may be brought under her Majesty's immediate government in all things, which the major part by much of the whole people would pray for, but dare not, for fear of the oppression and affront of the Quakers' part making a noise of their charter." In his passionate disgust against the Colony, he called it "a perfect receptacle of rogues and pirates." He complained that not only would the Rhode-Islanders, with Massachusetts between them and harm, contribute neither men nor money to the war, but that they harbored and hid deserters from the camps. "While I am here [in Massachusetts] at twenty-two hundred pounds per month charge, the Colony of Rhode Island hath not had a tax of one penny in the pound this seven years, which makes her Majesty's subjects of this Province very uneasy under their charge and service in the field, while other of her Majesty's subjects sleep in security, and smile at our losses and charge, which are an equal service to themselves."[1]

His low opinion of that Colony. 1702. Sept. 17.

1703. May 10.

Dec. 19.

[1] British Colonial Papers. — Dudley held even a more unfavorable opinion of "the Gerizzim of New England" than Cotton Mather pleased himself with expressing at length. (Magnalia, VII. 20.)

The Board of Trade, under instructions from the Privy Council, drew up charges, partly founded upon these complaints, and sent them to Dudley, who caused them to be served upon the authorities of Rhode Island, and proceeded to furnish to the Board a large mass of proof in support of the several specifications.[1] The Board repeated and adopted his representations in a Memorial to the Queen.[2] At the same time they both made similar complaints against the Colony of Connecticut, and reported the contumacy of Massachusetts in refusing to rebuild the fort at Pemaquid, to contribute towards the erection of a fort at Piscataqua, and to settle salaries on the Governor, Lieutenant-Governor, and Judges. And the Attorney-General and Solicitor-General advised the Queen that in such a state of things as then appeared to exist in Connecticut and Rhode Island, or, as they phrased it, "upon an extraordinary exigency, happening through the default or neglect of a proprietor, or of those appointed by him, or their inability to protect or defend the Province under their government, and for the protection and preservation thereof," it was lawful for the Queen to "constitute a Governor of such Province or Colony."[3] But matters of more importance claimed the attention of the home government, and nothing of the kind proposed was undertaken.

Complaints against the Colony in England. 1705. Nov. 2.

1706. Jan. 10.

The question so long and pugnaciously contested between Rhode Island and Connecticut about their boundary was brought at last, as was thought, to a settlement — as if of little importance to the stronger party — by an agreement between commissioners appointed by those Colonies respectively. The construction of the charters always maintained by Rhode Island was now assented to, so as that the line should run northerly from the Sound along "the middle channel of

Boundaries of the Colony. 1703. May 12.

[1] R. I. Rec., III. 543, 544.
[2] Journal of the Board of Trade.
[3] R. I. Rec., IV. 12–16.

Pawcatuck River, *alias* Narragansett River," leaving the town of Westerly, and all east of it, on the Rhode Island side.[1]

The northern boundary also now came under debate. Dudley gave notice to the government of Rhode Island that questions of title to land had arisen between citizens respectively of Mendon in Massachusetts, and Providence in Rhode Island, making it desirable "to renew the ancient line of their Province, settled sixty-four years since." As Connecticut was equally concerned with Rhode Island in the southern line of Massachusetts, commissioners appointed by Rhode Island were instructed to communicate with the government of the other Colony, "that they likewise may come, if they please, and see the departure, so that they may have no wrong, as well as us." Several committees were subsequently appointed to make this settlement, but for the present their negotiations "proved to no effect."[2]

1707. Feb. 25.

In answer to a requisition from the Board of Trade, the General Assembly of Rhode Island passed a law for taking a census of the inhabitants. It was found that the total number was seven thousand one hundred and eighty-one, of whom one thousand and fifteen were freemen, and one thousand three hundred and sixty-two were enrolled in the militia.[3] There were four hundred and eighty-two servants, of whom four hundred and twenty-six were blacks, twenty or thirty being brought every year from Barbadoes, but none directly from the coast of Africa.[4] There were nine towns, in which

Population and employments. 1708. April. August.

[1] R. I. Rec., III. 474, 480; IV. 175.

[2] Ibid., III. 302, 528, 529; IV. 4, 63, 83, 85, 94, 110; Arnold, History, II. 26, 27.

[3] R. I. Rec., IV. 32, 45.

[4] Ibid., IV. 53-60. — Governor Cranston wrote to the Board of Trade (Dec. 5, 1708): "We have never had any vessels from the coast of Africa to this Colony. . . . . . The whole and only supply of negroes to this Colony is from the island of Barbadoes, from whence is imported, one year with another, betwixt twenty and thirty, and, if those arrive well and sound, the general price is from £30 to £40 per head." One vessel, in May, 1696, had brought forty-seven slaves from the coast of Africa,

it is observable that Newport, with twenty-two hundred and three inhabitants, had but a hundred and ninety freemen; Providence, two hundred and forty-one freemen, with fourteen hundred and forty-six inhabitants; and Kingston, two hundred freemen, with just six times as many people. Of shipping, there were two brigantines and twenty-seven sloops, navigated by a hundred and forty seamen. They carried on a commerce with the other Anglo-American Colonies, with Madeira and Fayal, the West India Islands, and the Spanish Main. They were freighted with horses, lumber, and provisions, and some candles and iron, and brought back sugar, molasses, rum, cotton, ginger, indigo, rice, English manufactured goods of wool and linen, peltry, wheat, tar, pitch, resin, turpentine, wines, and some "pieces of eight," or Spanish dollars. In eight years there had been built in the Colony two ships, eleven brigan-
1698-1708. tines, and eighty-four sloops, but of these all but two brigantines and twenty-seven sloops had been sold abroad.[1]

The Board of Trade were dissatisfied with the condition of this commerce. They sent a circular letter to Rhode
1708. Island and other Colonies, complaining that pro-
July 3. hibited articles, "such as rice and molasses, are produced and made in the said plantations, and carried to divers foreign markets in Europe, without being first

and three vessels had sailed from Newport for the Slave Coast in 1700, but they had disposed of their return cargoes at Barbadoes. The Board had informed him that they desired the slave-trade to "be carried on to the greatest advantage," as "so beneficial to the Kingdom." He replied that he could afford "but small encouragement for that trade to this Colony, since, by the best computation we can make, there would not be disposed in this Colony above twenty or thirty at the most, annually, the reasons of which are chiefly to be attributed to the general dislike our planters have for them, by reason of their turbulent and unruly tempers." — Some Indian prisoners, taken in the war, having been brought into the Colony, "on pretence of being brought up as servants," a law was passed (R. I. Rec., III. 482, 483) prohibiting such importations for the future.

[1] This seems but a small number, when compared with Governor Cranston's statement to the Board of Trade (R. I. Rec., IV. 58), that the young people's "inclinations being mostly to navigation, the greater part betake themselves to that employment."

brought into this kingdom, dominion of Wales, and town of Berwick-upon-Tweed, contrary to the true intent and meaning of the foresaid laws [the Navigation Laws], to the great prejudice of the trade of this kingdom, and the lessening the correspondence and relation between this kingdom and the aforesaid Plantations."[1] But it does not appear that this remonstrance led immediately to any legislation in Rhode Island. The expedition to Canada engrossed the attention of the time.

The Colony was divided into two counties, called respectively by the names of Providence Plantations and Rhode Island.[2] For every day of the session of a General Court that an Assistant was absent from his place, he was fined six shillings.[3] The Governor and his Council had not proper accommodations, and it was "enacted, that there shall be a room built on the side of the Colony House, of about sixteen feet square, and about eight to nine feet stud, for his Honor and Council to sit in."[4] There was not yet, nor for many years after, a Colonial provision for the instruction of youth, though a school was somehow kept up at Newport.[5] Samuel Niles, who took his first degree at Cambridge sixty years after the founding of his Colony, appears to have been the first young Rhode-Islander educated at a college.

Municipal arrangements. 1703. June.

1712. Feb. 27.

1699.

The backwardness of the Colonies not immediately in danger from the French and Indians to take their fair part in the war was a constant subject of complaint in Massachusetts and in England, and as constantly strengthened the wish to transfer the command of their militia to the royal Governors of Massachusetts and New York. Rhode Island made some contributions from time to time to the common cause, but not without much haggling, and strong representations of her

Participation of Rhode Island in the war.

[1] R. I. Rec., IV. 91; comp. III. 437.
[2] Ibid., III. 478, 479.
[3] Ibid., III. 495.
[4] Ibid., IV. 139.
[5] Arnold, II. 41.

own exposure to invasion by sea, requiring all her attention and means for defence.[1] After the attack on Deerfield,
1704. some volunteers from Rhode Island took the field
May 3. under Colonel Church, and the Colony made provision for paying them.[2] When the war had raged a year
1705. and a half, the Assembly, at Dudley's urgent re-
Feb. 14. quest for assistance, raised a company of forty-eight men, which they authorized the Governor to march into the "neighboring governments, as necessity might require."[3]

Two years later, under a similar requisition from Mas-
1707. sachusetts with reference to the proposed expedi-
Feb. 25. tion against Nova Scotia, Rhode Island called out eighty volunteers, and bought a vessel to convey them.[4]
1709. She placed under the command of Colonel Nichol-
June 27. son an auxiliary force of two hundred men for the abortive expedition against Canada.[5] When the project
1711. was renewed, the Colony contributed from its eight
May 2. towns a hundred and seventy-nine men, of which
June 28. number forty-seven were taken from Newport,
1710. and from Providence and Kingston thirty-five
July 30. each.[6] The heavy expense was met, as in Mas-
Oct. 25. sachusetts, by issues of bills of credit, which it
Nov. 27. proved necessary to protect by severe laws against counterfeiting.[7] Rhode Island was much longer than her sister Colonies in extricating herself from the embarrassment entailed by this miserable system of unfounded credit.[8]

Two years before Dudley's retirement from office, he
1712. was "of opinion that Rhode Island had twenty-
April 8. five hundred fighting men, and Connecticut seven

[1] R. I. Rec., III. 468. This charge against Rhode Island and Connecticut of backwardness in the common cause constantly reappears as often as attacks were made upon their charters. (Comp. Ibid., 543-546.)

[2] Ibid., III. 500. — I do not find that these volunteers had been called out by the government of Rhode Island. But perhaps they had been. The record is defective.

[3] Ibid., III. 497, 518.

[4] Ibid., IV. 5.

[5] Ibid., 70-82.

[6] Ibid., 93, 98, 99, 121.

[7] Ibid., 96, 102, 105, 106, 117.

[8] Arnold, II. 39.

thousand."[1] The military organization of the former Colony appears to have been falling at that time into an unsatisfactory state, partly perhaps by reason of the Quaker element in the government. "The Assembly, having been credibly informed of the irregular proceedings of the soldiers in their election of military officers," passed a law continuing in their commands the officers then holding commissions, till there should be time for a mature consideration of plans for a more efficient system. The existing law, making military offices elective, being found to be repugnant to provisions of the charter, was repealed, and the power of appointment was vested in the Governor, Council, and Assembly, to be used annually on the first Monday of May. But the proceeding was too arbitrary to meet the approbation of the voters, and the next year the old disorder was restored.[2]

1713. May 6.

June 16.

1714. June 15.

Connecticut, at a safe distance from the seat of the eastern war, perhaps somewhat affected by the apathy of the Governor of New York, and at the same time offended by his claim to command her militia, took no part in the early conflicts of Massachusetts with the French and Indians in Queen Anne's reign.[3] The Colony declined a proposal from Governor Dudley to assist the expedition against Acadia.[4] Fitz-John Winthrop was Governor for ten successive years, till his death.[5] He was succeeded by a clergyman, Gurdon Saltonstall, of New London.

Relation of Connecticut to the war.

1707. April 2.

Nov. 27.

Dec. 17.

[1] Letter of Dudley to the Lords of Trade, in British Colonial Papers.

[2] R. I. Rec., IV. 149, 155, 156; comp. 173.

[3] "In this present war with the eastern Indians this Province doth wholly cover both the Colonies of Rhode Island and Connecticut, to whom I have made all possible application for a quota of men for the service. I can obtain nothing." (Letter of Dudley to the Lords of Trade, of Dec. 19, 1703, in British Colonial Papers.)

[4] Conn. Col. Rec., V. 17, 18; comp. IV. 443, 444, 462, 483.

[5] John (Fitz-John) Winthrop, second Governor of Connecticut of that name, was a second dilution of the vigor of his race. As there was some decline, in respect to the highest qualities, between his grandfather

After the election of this very able Magistrate, which was renewed through seventeen successive years, the Colony 1709. May. assumed a more spirited attitude. Connecticut raised with alacrity her proportion of troops for that expedition against Canada, which never got so far as June. the border;[1] and, like her sister Colonies of New England, supplied or rather simulated the means by bills of credit.[2] When the military operations were 1710. August. renewed in the next year, the zeal of Connecticut again appeared, and she sent three hundred men in five transports to the capture of Port Royal.[3] In the 1711. June. following summer, the Governors met at New London to consult upon the larger enterprise which was now contemplated. Connecticut raised three hundred and sixty men for it, to be employed in the diversion by Lake Champlain,[4] while the fleet and army, under August. the command of Walker and Hill, should go up the St. Lawrence to Quebec;[5] and Governor Saltonstall himself led them as far as Albany.[6] The great disaster which followed has already been described.

Connecticut, happier than the two northern Colonies, had never been invaded during this war, though once the danger of an inroad appeared such that the General Court ordered the fortification of four border towns.[7] 1709-1713. In four years the Colony issued bills of credit

and his father, so there was a much wider between his father and himself. He was, however, a blameless person, and a painstaking public officer. On the resumption of the charter, after the fall of Andros, he was chosen a Magistrate. The following year he led the unfortunate land expedition against Canada. He went to England, as agent for the Colony, in 1694. He was chosen Governor in 1698. He died in Boston, where, after a week, he was buried from the Council Chamber. (Sewall's Journal.)

[1] Conn. Col. Rec., V. 91, 122.

[2] Ibid., 111.

[3] Ibid., 163.

[4] Ibid., 249.

[5] Ibid., V. 245 *et seq.* — The journal of one of the two Connecticut chaplains, Thomas Buckingham (Ibid., 265, 287), erroneously named *John* by his editor, has been preserved, and was printed at New York in 1825. It contains nothing of value.

[6] He left them there August 29. On his return to New Haven, he heard that the fleet was in the St. Lawrence, August 13. (Letter of Saltonstall to St. John, of September 10, in British Colonial Papers.)

[7] Conn. Col. Rec., V. 15.

to the amount of thirty-three thousand five hundred pounds, but so judicious were the arrangements for their redemption, that they appear to have been scarcely at all depreciated, before the final extinction of the debt.[1] The Act of Parliament which made arrangements "for erecting a General Post-Office in all her Majesty's dominions, and for settling a weekly sum out of it for the service of the war and other occasions," caused no more uneasiness in Connecticut than in Massachusetts.[2] The establishment of posts under an authority common to all the Colonies was a great practical convenience, and the political significance of the measure attracted little notice. But it was a faint prelude to Mr. George Grenville's Stamp Act.

The Post-Office in Connecticut. 1710.

The agreement respecting the eastern boundary line of Connecticut, adopting the construction maintained from the first by Rhode Island, has already been mentioned. Connecticut was tired out by her pertinacious neighbor, and the territory in question was not worth the trouble of a prolonged and, after all, uncertain contest. Connecticut renewed the question upon the correctness of her northern line, coincident with the southern line of Massachusetts, which had been laid down agreeably to a survey made by the ship-masters, Woodward and Saffery, sixty-six years before.[3] The dispute respected the line of latitude which bounded Massachusetts on the south, three miles south of the most southerly part of Charles River. Massachusetts insisted that it had been correctly drawn; that if it had not been correctly drawn, it had been recognized and ratified in the royal charter to Connecticut; and that, at all events, possession for two-thirds of a century ought to be held to give a title. Massachusetts, however, at length consented to have a new survey, under the superintendence of commissioners

Boundaries of the Colony.

1708. May.

[1] Conn. Col. Rec., V. 407.

[2] Ibid., 318.

[3] Ibid., V. 58; comp. IV. 400, 443; Trumbull, I. 395, 401, 402, 432, 446.

of the two Colonies, it being first stipulated that, in the event of any readjustment of the boundary, towns should continue under the jurisdiction of the Colony to which they had hitherto belonged, and that compensation should be made by equivalent grants of other land. The result was an agreement that, by the divergence of the erroneous line of latitude, Massachusetts had encroached upon Connecticut to the extent of about a hundred and six thousand acres. Massachusetts accordingly made a transfer of other land to that amount, which was presently sold by Connecticut for six hundred and eighty-three pounds in currency,[1] a price amounting to about six farthings an acre; such was the value of land in that day. The proceeds, after some years, were given to the infant College.[2] When in the same year commissioners from Connecticut and from New York erected monuments to mark the line agreed upon thirteen years before,[3] the domain of the former Colony appeared to be defined on all sides, except for the space of a few miles of the northerly portion of the western border.

1713.

The Colony was involved in another controversy with the remnant of the Mohegan Indians. Major John Mason, conqueror of the Pequots, had, in behalf of the Colony, bought of the Sachem Uncas certain lands, which the Colony, in its turn, had conveyed to English proprietors. His grandson, of the same name, associating with himself some other disaffected persons, pretended that both the Mohegans and Major Mason's heirs had been overreached and wronged by the colonial authorities, who, as they alleged, had occupied more land of the former than they had bought, and had taken to themselves the benefit of a purchase made by Major Mason on his private account.[4] For the sake

1659.

The Mohegan Indians.

[1] Conn. Col. Rec., V. 528, 529; comp. 361, 376, 386, 390, 391, 399, 403, 413, 418, 467, 480, 488.

[2] Ibid., VII. 412.

[3] Ibid., V. 401; comp. 184.

[4] In 1698, the Court had consented

of peace and the credit of magnanimity, the government offered to the chief Owaneco, who represented the Indians, to pay them again for the land. But Mason and his friends interfered, resolved to obstruct any accommodation.

Mason went to England, with a complaint against the Colony for extortion from the natives,[1] and the Queen appointed a commission of twelve persons, two of whom were the Governor and Lieutenant-Governor of Massachusetts, to investigate the affair.[2] Messengers from the Governor of Connecticut appeared before this Court, and questioned its jurisdiction. They were ready, they said, to show the injustice of the complaints against their Colony, if the object of the commissioners was only to obtain a knowledge of the facts, with a view to a report to the Queen; but if the commissioners claimed power to decide the question judicially, they had no duty except to protest against that pretension. The commissioners assumed the right to decide as to the property of the territory in dispute, and adjudged it to the Mohegans and their friends, at the same time mulcting the Colony in costs to the amount of nearly six hundred pounds. Dudley represented to the Lords of Trade that he and his associates were treated on this occasion

1704. July 19.

1705. Aug. 24.

Nov. 1.

to a request of the remains of the Pequots to be placed under the guardianship of Governor Winthrop. (Ibid., IV. 280.)

[1] He took with him young Mahomet, the anti-Sachem, to push his claim to the inheritance of Owaneco, and both died in England, of small-pox, in 1736. (Caulkins, New London, 410, and Norwich, 268.)

Mr. J. Hammond Trumbull has a letter written by Captain Thomas Coram, in September, 1738, to "Augh Quant Johnson, otherwise Cato, of the Mohegan tribe of Indians, a young man who came over to England with Mr. Mason in the beginning of the year 1736. He is in some part of Connecticut." Captain Coram warmly espoused the cause of Mahomet and Mason. He writes to "Honest Cato, ... Let me advise you and some of the chiefe of them, to write a respectfull letter to the Tribe's great good friend, the Right Honourable Sir Charles Wager, to testify the Tribe's thankfulness to that great man for his kind offices of Friendship for their sakes. . . . . . My wife remembers her love to you very kindly," &c. (For Coram, see below, 567.)

[2] Register of the Privy Council for March 23, 1704.

with rudeness and insult.[1] Sir Henry Ashurst, by a petition to the Queen in Council, succeeded in arresting further proceedings; but it was not till more than sixty years later that the question was put to rest, when it was decided in favor of the Colony.[2]

1771.

The representations made by Dudley upon this subject refreshed and strengthened the unfavorable impression made upon the royal Privy Council by his hostile statements relating to a variety of other matters.[3] Never without some disturbing ambition,

Plots against the charter.

[1] Towards the execution of the award of the commissioners, "I am well assured," he says, "that nothing will be done. Their managers read a protest against my repeated commands, and then drew off at a distance, and with their officers clamorously commanded all persons to withdraw, and not to attend us nor give evidence, and some of them boisterously pulled down the hand of a witness swearing, and drew him out of the court, and the people spoke freely among themselves of seizing us at the Board." (Letter in British Colonial Papers; comp. Book of Proceedings, &c., 61–63.)

[2] See, for this story, Trumbull, History, I. 410–413, 421–427. It could be but very imperfectly gathered from the public records, though in this I find nothing but what accords with his account. (See Conn. Col. Rec., IV. 108; V. 26.) Besides John Mason, Nicholas Hallam represented the disaffected party in England. As early as Dec. 2, 1703, the business was before the Board of Trade (Journal of the Board), which proceeded forthwith to the appointment of the commission for investigating the dispute. (Ibid., for Jan. 28, March 22, 23, 31, 1704.) For an account of the termination of it, four years before the War of Independence, see Stuart, Life of Jonathan Trumbull, 139. — Down to the year 1743, the course of proceedings in the case is minutely related in the volume quoted above, entitled: "Governor and Company of Connecticut and Mohegan Indians, by their Guardians. Certified Copy of Book of Proceedings before Commissioners of Review, 1743." It was published in London in 1769, just before the final hearing. — Owing to Sir Henry Ashurst's appeal (Book of Proceedings, 153), the judgment of Dudley and his associates (Ibid., 26–29) remained unconfirmed (Ibid., 5). In 1737, the Queen appointed a new commission (Ibid.), which was superseded by another appointed in 1743 (Ibid., 3). A majority of these commissioners (three out of five) reversed the finding of Dudley's commission, and decreed in favor of the Colony (Ibid., 137–142). But the Indians again appealed (Ibid., 280), and one of the dissentient commissioners protested (Ibid., 281), and the final action of the Privy Council was once more deferred.

[3] Register of the Privy Council, for Aug. 3, 1704; Feb. 12, 1705. — "Sir Henry Ashurst, agent for the Colony, writing from Kensington, Feb. 15, 1704–5, says: "There's one Mr. Buckley, all by Mr. D[udley]'s contrivance, has sent a large folio book, which he calls per the name of

he was now haunted by the dream of a promotion to the extensive government which had been enjoyed by Andros. The colonial charters stood in his way. If they could be cancelled, the sovereign might appoint a Governor or Governors at pleasure. Though not overlooked in his plan of revolution, the charter of Massachusetts, as the most recent, offered the least encouragement to an assault. Those of Rhode Island and Connecticut belonged to a former reign, which was now in no good credit; and no living English statesman could be supposed to have an interest in them, or any objection to their being overthrown in law. Lord Cornbury, besides his despotic impulses, had plans of his own, which disposed him to be Dudley's ally; and his private influence, which was great, especially from his near relationship to the Queen, was given to the Governor of Massachusetts. Like Rhode Island, Connecticut was charged with a maladministration in various particulars justly punishable by a loss of the charter; — with violations of the Acts of Trade and 1705.
Navigation; with encouraging maritime disorders, Nov 26.
liable to be qualified as piracy; with refusing or neglecting, when lawfully summoned, to furnish military levies; with executing capital punishment without authority from the charter; with denying justice in its courts to the Queen's subjects, not inhabitants; with disallowing appeals to the Queen in Council; with refusing to commit its militia to Governors of neighboring Colonies, holding the Queen's commission for that command; and with obstructing members of the Church of England as to their

'Will and Doom, or History of the Miseries of Connecticut under the Arbitrary Power of the Present Government,' wherein he mightily commends Sir Edmund Andros's government, and says all the malicious things he possibly can invent, with great cunning and art." (Introduction to C. J. Hoadly's edition of Gershom Bulkeley's "Will and Doom.") This book, which failed of its purpose at the time of its original publication (see above, Vol. III. 544, note), had probably passed out of memory in the next ten years, till it was revived by Dudley in furtherance of his schemes.

freedom of worship:[1] to all which charges was now added 1706. that of contumacy in the recent denial of the Jan. 10. authority of the royal commissioners to pass upon the complaint of the Mohegan Indians.

This last proceeding occurred at a time which made it especially serviceable for the purposes of the plotters against the colonial governments. Their unfriendly representations had already so far prevailed that again[2] 1704. a bill was brought into Parliament, declaring the charters of various Colonies in America, and among them all the charters for New England, to "be utterly void and of none effect," and vesting all their powers and privileges in the crown. At a hearing before the Privy Council, Sir 1705. Henry Ashurst, appearing with legal counsel for Feb. 12. Connecticut, argued in respect to some of the proceedings complained of, that they had not in fact taken place; in respect to others, that they were justified by the charter. And he obtained leave for copies of the charges to be sent to the Governor of Connecticut, and for time to be allowed him for further reply. At this critical moment the transactions with the commissioners on the claim of the Mohegan Indians intervened.[3] The Privy Council directed the Board of Trade "to lay before the Dec. 20. 1706. Queen the misfeasances of the proprieties, and the Jan. 2. advantages that may arise by reducing them," which was accordingly done.[4] The Privy Council ordered Feb. 7. that, "in regard the matter contained in said rep-

[1] R. I. Rec., IV. 12–16; comp. Trumbull, I. 411.

[2] See above, p. 200; comp. Hutch. II. 130.

[3] This was the time too when the English Quakers were bestirring themselves. (See below, 449.) At their instance, the Lords of Trade called the attention of the Privy Council to an old Connecticut law against their sect; and, agreeably to a decree of the Council (Oct. 11, 1705), the General Court of Connecticut repealed the Act (May, 1706). Sir Henry Ashurst wrote that he considered this act of the Queen's Council "to be a very extraordinary order, considering you were in possession of your own charter. But," he continues, "the hand of Joab is in it. I mean D." [Dudley]. (Conn. Col. Rec., IV. 546.)

[4] Register of the Privy Council; Journal of the Board of Trade.

resentation is proper for the consideration of the legislature of this kingdom, said representation be sent to Secretary Hodges to receive her Majesty's further pleasure therein."[1] There is extant a draft, belonging to this period, of an Act of Parliament declaring that "the sole power and authority of governing the said [the American] Plantations and Colonies, and every of them," and "of appointing Governors and all other officers," is "forever united to the imperial crown of Great Britain."[2] A bill passed through the House of Commons "for the better regulation of the charter governments, and for the encouragement of the trade of the Plantations."[3] But it failed of obtaining the concurrence of the Lords. There were legal embarrassments, opinions differed as to the relative expediency of different methods of restraining the Colonies, and the war raging upon the continent of Europe demanded the attention of English statesmen; so that again, for the present, the question went by.

February.

A material change was made in the ecclesiastical constitutions of Connecticut. Throughout the settlements and the history of New England there had been a succession of departures from the original theory of the mutual independence of the churches. In Connecticut the opinion now prevailed that a more energetic system of church government had become necessary than at present existed, or was consistent with the theoretical independence of the several congregations. The Legislature convoked a Synod of ministers and lay delegates to deliberate upon the subject.[4] Twelve ministers and four delegates, deputed by ministers and messengers of the churches in the several counties, came together at the town of Saybrook, from which circumstance the result of their deliberations derived the name of the *Saybrook Platform.* Having adopted for

Saybrook synod and platform. 1708. May 13.

Sept. 9.

[1] Register of the Privy Council.
[2] British Colonial Papers.
[3] Chalmers, I. 342.
[4] Conn. Col. Rec., V. 51.

their constitution the Confession of Faith of the *Reforming Synod* held at Boston twenty-eight years before,[1] and the "Heads of Agreement assented to by the United Ministers [in England], formerly called Presbyterian and Congregational,"[2] they proceeded to arrange a system which made some partial approximation of Congregational to Presbyterian usages. It provided that "the particular pastors and churches, within the respective counties in this government," should "be one consociation, or more, if they should judge meet, for mutual affording to each other such assistance as may be requisite, upon all occasions ecclesiastical;" and the authority hitherto exercised by councils formed by voluntary selection by individuals or churches was vested in permanent councils appointed by these bodies. Disobedience to the decree of a council so constituted was to be punished by excommunication of the contumacious pastor or church. A council might invite a council from a neighboring consociation to aid in its deliberations, and a church might designate permanent representatives to appear for it in councils convened from time to time. And it was recommended that a General Association of representatives of all the churches in the Colony should be held every year at the time of the civil election.[3]

1692.

The plan became law by the action of the General Court, who attached to it, however, a prudent provision, "that nothing herein shall be intended or construed to hinder or prevent any society or church that is or shall be allowed by the laws of this government, who soberly differ or dissent from the united churches hereby established, from exercising worship and discipline, in their own way, according to their consciences."[4] One consociation was organized in each of the four counties,

1708. Oct. 14.

[1] See above, Vol. III. 330, 331, note.

[2] The "Heads of Agreement" are in Mather's Magnalia, V. 59.

[3] The Proceedings and *Result* are in Trumbull's History of Connecticut, I. 482–488.

[4] Conn. Col. Rec., V. 87.

except in the county of Hartford, which had two; and the same organization has been continued to the present day. The General Court ordered the printing of an edition of "The Confession of Faith, the Articles of Agreement between the United Brethren in England, formerly called Presbyterian and Congregational, together with the Discipline agreed upon by the General Council of the reverend elders and churches assembled at Saybrook."[1] It was thought that the ratification of the Articles of Agreement, which allowed greater latitude in faith and administration, helped to disarm opposition to the new Discipline.[2]

1709. May 12.

Another important movement of this period was the establishment of the venerable institution now so widely and honorably known by the name of *Yale College*. For sixty years the only school for higher education in New England had been Harvard College, at Cambridge. The people, and especially the clergy, of Connecticut naturally desired the benefit of a similar establishment nearer home. The three ministers of New Haven, Milford, and Branford first moved in the enterprise. Ten ministers, nine of them being graduates of Harvard College, met at Branford, and made a contribution from their libraries of about forty volumes in folio "for the founding of a college."[3] Other donations presently came in. An Act of Incorporation was granted by the General Court. It created a body of trustees, not to be more than eleven in number nor fewer than seven, all to be clergymen and at least forty years of age. The Court endowed the College with an annual grant, subject to be discontinued at pleasure, of one hundred and twenty pounds in "country pay," — equivalent to sixty pounds sterling. The College might

Yale College.

1700.

1701. Oct. 9.

[1] Conn. Col. Rec., V. 97.

[2] Trumbull, I. 487.

[3] Ibid., 473; Bacon, Thirteen Historical Discourses, 188; Kingsley, in American Quarterly Register, VIII. 14, 16.

hold property "not exceeding the value of five hundred pounds per annum;"[1] its students were exempted from
1703. the payment of taxes and from military service;[2]
Oct. 14. and the Governor and his Council gave a formal
Oct. 21. approval of its application to the citizens for pecuniary aid.[3] Judge Sewall, of Massachusetts, and Addington, Secretary of that Province, concerned for what to their sensitive vigilance seemed the declining orthodoxy of Harvard College, which they would gladly compensate
1701. elsewhere, furnished to the clergymen interested
Oct. 6. in the project the draft of a charter for their institution.[4] But whether it was that the arrangements had been already matured, or that a different judgment prevailed, their proposals do not appear to have influenced the projectors or the law-makers.[5]

The first President was Abraham Pierson, minister of Killingworth, at which place he continued to reside, though the designated seat of the College was at Saybrook. Eight students were admitted, and arranged in classes.
1702.
1703. At each of the first two annual commencements
1704. one person, at the third three persons, received the degree of Bachelor of Arts. President Pierson was suc-
1707. ceeded, at his death, by Mr. Andrew, minister at
March 5. Milford, to which place the elder pupils were accordingly transferred, while the rest went to Saybrook, where two tutors had been provided to assist their studies.[6]

1714. In the last year of Queen Anne's life the people of Connecticut were probably between twenty-five

[1] Conn. Col. Rec., IV. 363.

[2] Ibid., 440.

[3] Ibid., 454.

[4] Quincy, History of Harvard University, I. 519.

[5] Ibid., I. 197, 226, II. 462 *et seq.*; Kingsley's Review of the same, in American Biblical Repository, VI. 177, 384, VII. 175 *et seq.*; Kingsley's Sketch of the History of Yale College, in American Quarterly Register, VIII. 13 *et seq.*

[6] See Beardsley, Life and Correspondence of Samuel Johnson, D.D., 5–15, for some interesting particulars relating to the early history of Yale College.

thousand and thirty thousand in number.[1] The Colony had twenty or thirty vessels, mostly sloops, and not more than a hundred and twenty sailors.[2] Grain and other provisions were sent from it to Boston and New York; masts and naval stores to England; and horses, provisions, and cattle to the West Indies, whence returns came in rum, sugar, and molasses.[3] "For the preservation of timber" the exportation of it was restricted.[4] In a temporary scarcity of grain in Massachusetts and Rhode Island, the exportation of it from Connecticut was forbidden, except to those Colonies.[5] Of the bills of credit which had been issued to the amount of thirty-three thousand and five hundred pounds, all but twenty thousand had now been redeemed.[6] The valuation of estates in Connecticut amounted to three hundred and one thousand pounds.[7] There were thirty-eight towns,[8] and forty-three ministers, or one minister to about eighty families.[9] Ministers were exempt from taxes of every kind.[10] The right to vote in their election was not limited to communicants, but belonged equally to every person qualified "to vote in all other town affairs."[11] Only travellers might "drink any strong drink . . . . . in any tavern or house of public entertainment."[12] "Liberty of worshipping God" was guaranteed on the same terms as those specified by an Act of Parliament of the first year of King William and

Internal condition of Connecticut.

[1] Trumbull (I. 451) says 17,000, and Chalmers (II. 7) 47,000. But certainly they both were far wrong. In 1708 and 1709, a statement of the number of taxable males is appended to the list of taxes assessed upon the towns. (Conn. Col. Rec., VI. 71, 88, 115, 140.) They were then about 4,600 in number, which, supposing each to be the representative of a family consisting of five persons, would give a population of 23,000 in 1709. But this, which would probably be somewhat too large for that date, would probably be exceeded, through the natural increase, in 1714.

[2] Trumbull, I. 451.

[3] Ibid., 428, 453; comp. Conn. Col. Rec., IV. 524.

[4] Ibid., V. 499.

[5] Ibid., 417.

[6] Trumbull, I. 450.

[7] Conn. Col. Rec., V. 409.

[8] Ibid., 451.

[9] Trumbull, 491.

[10] Conn. Col. Rec., V. 2.

[11] Ibid., 48.

[12] Ibid., 502.

Queen Mary.[1] The observance of the Lord's Day was guarded with rigor; a vessel in Connecticut River within two miles of a meeting-house might not change her moorings on Sunday, except to approach the place of worship.[2]

During recesses of the General Court, a permanent Council, consisting of the Governor, two Assistants, and "three or five judicious freemen" invited by the Governor, had charge of the public affairs.[3] The salary of the Governor, to which from time to time were added gratuities, was raised in a series of years from a hundred and
1703-1715. twenty pounds a year to two hundred pounds.[4] Editions of the Laws were printed and circulated in the towns.[5] The reception of illegal votes was held to cancel elections.[6] The government was as firm as lenient, and
1715. easily repressed any petulance even of its highest
May 12. men, as was shown in an instance when Captain Wadsworth gave offence.[7] The public attended with thoughtful humanity to the misfortunes of the insane, of idiots, of soldiers returned from captivity.[8] With a parental care it provided, from time to time, for the wants of the poor and sick, and the protection of injured persons in circumstances not contemplated by the general laws.[9] Even the unwary receiver of counterfeits of its bills it "saved harmless."[10] It was unwearied in providing for the comfort of the Indians, and for their protection against the rapacity of their neighbors. On the other hand, it guarded against their being practised upon to their own

[1] Conn. Col. Rec., V. 50.

[2] Ibid., 525.

[3] Ibid., III. 505; IV. 287, 468.

[4] Ibid., 441; V. 7, 96, 144, 220, 349, 399, 526.

[5] Ibid., IV. 396; V. 477, 479.

[6] Ibid., 484, 486.

[7] Ibid., V. 492. — To this same Captain Wadsworth the Assembly, at the same session (Ibid., 507), made a grant of twenty shillings "as a token of their grateful resentment of his faithful and good service in securing the duplicate charter of this Colony in a very troublesome season, when our constitution was struck at, and in safely keeping and preserving the same ever since unto this day. (See above, Vol. III. 453; and Conn. Col. Rec., III. 464, 465.)

[8] Ibid., V. 358, 361, 400, 429, 432.

[9] Ibid., 342, 344, 386, 420, 479, 489.

[10] Ibid., 475.

harm and that of the Colony, by a strict order against the admission of Indians made prisoners in the war then waging in South Carolina.[1]

A condition of society so happy as that enjoyed by Connecticut at this period, especially during the long administration of Governor Saltonstall, has been rare in the experience of mankind. If from time to time the charter of her liberties was threatened, the danger of a repetition of such misgovernment as that of Andros was too remote to excite serious solicitude. A prevailing mutual respect and confidence softened the intercourse among citizens, and between citizens and rulers. The friendly sentiments inspired by religious faith were promoted by a general harmony of religious opinion. To the youth of every family was offered at the public cost, near its own door, an education sufficient for the advantageous transaction of business, for the enjoyment of leisure, and for a measure of refinement of mind. Frugality and industry, friends to rectitude and content, secured a comfortable living, and a comfortable living was not to be had without them. A steady but unoppressive force of public opinion rendered a life of blameless morals easy and attractive, and assured to a public-spirited and religious life a career of dignity and honor. A remarkable approach to an equal distribution of property prevented the assumptions and resentments of caste, and the jealousy of disproportioned privileges. The people of Connecticut enjoyed to a singular degree a fulfilment of their prayer "that peace and unity might be continued among them, and that they might have the blessings of the God of peace upon them."[2]

Prosperity of the Colony.

[1] Conn. Col. Rec., V. 516.

[2] Ibid., 491. — A Journal of a "Madam Knight," who in 1704 went to New York from Boston on a matter of business, was printed in 1825 from the original manuscript. Mrs. Knight was a woman of good connections, who taught a school in Boston. She tells her story with rude vivacity. She made her journey through Connecticut on horseback, with guides. She found the roads

1714. Aug. 1. Intelligence of the death of the Queen, and of the accession of the Elector of Hanover to the throne of Great Britain, having been received in a letter from Jeremiah Dummer, orders were given for Oct. 13. noticing both events with due solemnity; and an Address of congratulation was despatched to the new sovereign.[1] A vessel in which a more formal com- Aug. 5. munication had been sent out by the Ministry was wrecked; but the document was picked up and brought to its destination; and, out of scrupulous regard for form, or of exuberant joy at the renewed security of the Protestant succession, a second proclamation of the new Dec. 3. reign was made with more pompous ceremony.[2]

rough. She mentions no bridges; she crossed the Connecticut at Saybrook by a ferry, but her horse had to wade or swim over several streams and inlets. She fared but ill at the country hostelries, but enjoyed sumptuous hospitality at New London, at the houses of Governor Winthrop and the Reverend Mr. (afterwards Governor) Saltonstall. Connecticut, she says (p. 65), "is a plentiful country for provisions of all sorts, and is generally healthy. No one that can and will be diligent in this place need fear poverty, nor the want of food and raiment." New York she found "a pleasant, well-compacted place, ... the buildings brick generally, very stately and high, though not altogether like ours in Boston."

[1] Conn. Col. Rec., V. 450.

[2] Ibid., 478, 480.

BOOK V.

PROGRESS UNDER THE HANOVERIAN KINGS.

BOOK V.

PROGRESS UNDER THE HANOVERIAN KINGS.

CHAPTER I.

THE difference made by the course of events through two generations in the relations between the Colonies of New England and the parent country had become distinctly manifest. The Great Rebellion, though defeated by its own excesses, had made a permanent change in the system of English politics. The principles that excited that movement had reappeared in sufficient force to drive into banishment the odious dynasty which had provoked it. The spell of hereditary succession had been effectually broken, when two elected monarchs had occupied the throne with reigns of no short duration and now a third was holding it in a peaceable tenure the security of which was only illustrated by the issue of a feeble insurrection. The last serious danger of usurpation on the part of the Church of Rome might well be considered to have passed away, when the plots of Queen Anne and her last Ministry in her brother's favor had been foiled, and the people of England had bravely preferred the unwelcome expedient of taking for their King the head of a moderate German principality, a man advanced in years, ignorant of their institutions and even of their language, of unattractive presence and coarse manners, of private habits no better than those of the last Stuart monarch, and even avowedly

Security of Colonial freedom.

1715.

taking little interest in the affairs of the kingdom to which he had so strangely been promoted.

If the Protestant Church establishment of England continued to be arrogant, still under such prelates as Tillotson and Tenison, Patrick, Burnet, and Hoadly, there was little reason to apprehend that it would reassume a distinctly persecuting attitude. The tolerance of William the Third, whether proceeding from magnanimity or policy or indifference, had exerted to some extent a wholesome influence on the national habits of thought, and in the recent political complications the place of the dissenting body had been such as enabled them to command a degree of respect, and to act with some efficiency for their own protection. The Toleration Act of William the Third[1] had given to non-conformity a recognized legal position, and the restraints which ostensibly the law continued to impose were in a great measure forgotten or disused. In the Tory ascendency of the last four years of Queen Anne's reign, there was a reaction of church bigotry under the lead of the infidel Lord Bolingbroke; and the Act against Occasional Conformity,[2] and what was called the Schism Act,[3] insulted and embarrassed dissenters anew. But, in the divided and fluctuating condition of public sentiment, it was reasonably hoped that these would prove to be only spasmodic movements; and the event speedily justified that
1719. expectation, for the repeal of the obnoxious laws
Jan. 7. was an early proceeding of the next reign.[4] The plot of Queen Anne's latest favorite to set aside the Protestant succession at her death was not known at the time, as it has since been exhibited by the disclosure of contemporary documents. But the moment when, if the legal settlement was to prevail, the crown of the Stuarts was to

[1] Act of the first year of William and Mary, Chap. VIII.

[2] Act of the tenth year of Anne, Chap. II.

[3] Act of the twelfth year of Anne, Chap. VII.

[4] Act of the fifth year of George I., Chap. IV.

pass to a German stranger from a princess, who, however slight her claim of regular inheritance, was native-born, was reasonably regarded as extremely critical; and when the Elector of Hanover had been quietly proclaimed and received as King of England, a heavy weight was lifted from the minds of English friends of freedom.

The people of Massachusetts had their full share in this relief, and in the grateful sense of it. Had the sovereign who was just dead been succeeded by her Romanist brother, the fear of what had been suffered and threatened during the earlier rule of their infatuated family would reasonably have revived. Had her life been prolonged, no little trouble seemed in store from the arbitrary policy of the counsellors to whose direction she had yielded her feeble mind. In either case Joseph Dudley would be likely to be continued in his government, and his ancient offensiveness would be not unlikely to be renewed under superiors of similar character and views. As things turned out, the conspiracy in the midst of which she died, foiled as it was, was of vast service to English liberties.

King George the First knew nothing about English liberties, and may be presumed to have cared as little, besides being too old to begin to learn. In his own insignificant realm he had been a despot, though in a benevolent way. But it was easy for him to be informed who it was that had schemed against his succession to the throne of England, and accordingly the doors of his council chamber were shut close against the Tory statesmen. The Duke of Marlborough (Whig and Tory by turns) was slighted. Bolingbroke and the Duke of Ormond fled to France, to which country Bishop Atterbury too was banished. Oxford was sent to the Tower, to await his trial for high treason. The administration was committed to Lord Townshend, General Stanhope, and other men disposed, on the whole, by their sentiments and connections, to a liberal policy in religious affairs. The Whig party of England was not what it had been; it had lost no little of the courage and disinterestedness which had assured to it the love and confidence of the people of New England. But the selection which was presently made of a new Governor for Massachusetts might seem to authorize the expectation that her religious position would not be unkindly regarded in the new reign.

Policy of Massachusetts.

During the greater part of the quarter-century since the provincial charter of Massachusetts went into effect, the necessities of war had chiefly attracted the public attention; though in the provincial administration there had been unmistakable manifestations of a policy of self-defence against the home government, in the reluctance to submit to instructions which respected military service, and especially in the steady resistance to instructions which related to permanent provision for officers of the crown. There was now to be a peace between England and France of no less than thirty years' duration, giving to the settlements of New England a long-desired respite from the calamities inflicted on them by the French in Canada, and to a great extent from the invasions of the savages whom the French had stimulated, trained, and led. And this pause from martial conflict and its miseries gave opportunity for the canvassing of political questions, which hitherto had been more or less suspended by reason of the necessary attention to more pressing concerns.

While the provincial charter had divested the colonists of very important ancient privileges and powers, it had left the King's Governor dependent on the provincial Legislature for his support, for which the government at home made no provision. In this prerogative of a legislative body, chosen by the people directly in one branch, and nominated by them indirectly in the other, and in its other prerogative of originating laws, consisted the protection of the people against arbitrary designs of the Governor, and of the monarch or court whom he represented. The future was to show what occasions would present themselves for the use of these powers, and how effectual they would prove. The powers themselves were created by the charter, a withdrawal of which instrument, if that were possible, would annihilate them; and they were further liable, in cases which might arise, to receive a more or less favorable interpretation in the English courts.

Such were facts which demanded cautious consideration, and a policy at once firm and inoffensive, on the part of a people who had not strength to maintain themselves in arms against the hostility of England, and who had no longer, as they had had in their early history, the alliance of an array of powerful sympathizers in Parliament and about the throne. Though no great question was now at issue between the British government and its dependency of Massachusetts, like that which had bred disagreements during the period of the first charter, and though the charter of William and Mary had aimed to fix with precision the limitations of power on both sides, there still remained, in its construction and application, large room for dispute. The British Ministry could restrain Massachusetts by means of the high powers vested by the charter in the Governor whom they appointed, and by the authority which the charter gave them to rescind even such Colonial laws as had received the Governor's assent. Massachusetts could resist the Ministry by distressing the Governor as to his means of living, and by refusing to accommodate to their wishes the character of her Legislature and her legislation.

Massachusetts was not factious nor disloyal. It could not be but that the lustre of Queen Anne's reign in letters and arms should make any reflecting dweller in New England more proud than ever of the name of

Englishman.[1] And the prospect of a degree of freedom, civil and religious, assured by the succession of the house of Hanover to the throne, could not fail at once to attach the colonist to the government, and to quicken his sympathies with his fellow-subjects at home. But it does not follow that, as he became more devoted to his prince, he became less tenacious of his own rights; nor that, while his English sense of self-respect was exalted,

[1] It is natural to inquire how far the literary activity of Queen Anne's time in England attracted attention in the Colonies. In 1723, the old library of Harvard College appears, from its catalogue published in that year, not to have contained any work of the wits of Queen Anne's time, — of Addison, Atterbury, Bolingbroke, Gay, Pope, Prior, Steele, Swift, Young. It had writings of Bacon, Barrow, Baxter, Boyle, Burnet, Chillingworth, Clarendon, S. Clarke, Cudworth, Hales, Harrington, Lord Herbert, Holinshed, Thomas Hooker, Lightfoot, Henry More, Newton, Raleigh, Selden, Sherlock, Stillingfleet, Stow, Jeremy Taylor, Sir William Temple, and Usher. There was nothing of Locke, nor of Dryden, nor of South, nor of Tillotson; and Shakespeare and Milton had been recent accessions, for the copy of the former was of an edition of 1709, and of the latter of an edition of 1720. — In only a few instances do the advertisements in the "News-Letter" of books on sale contain the titles of books, and then they throw no light on this question. The few titles are mostly of theological treatises of home production. The small number of other books of which the subject is specified are works of history, geography, and such like, and the writers are not named. — "A Catalogue of Books on all Arts and Sciences, to be sold at the Shop of T. Cox, Bookseller, at the Lamb, on the South Side of the Town House at Boston," was published in 1734. It contains eight hundred and fifty-six titles, embracing, with a variety of miscellaneous matter, classical books, and books of divinity, geography, medicine, history, and mathematics. No copy appears of Shakespeare or of Milton. There are copies of Dryden's translation of the Æneid, and of his Plays and Miscellanies; of Pope's translation of the Iliad, but of no other of his works; of Locke's and Addison's collected writings; of Butler's Hudibras; of several works of Steele; of the Tatler and Guardian, but not of the Spectator; of Swift's Miscellanies, and of his "Tale of a Tub." Among the divines are Patrick, Barrow, South, and Sherlock; among the historians, Kennett, Clarendon, and Burnet; among the poets and dramatic writers, Prior, Roscommon, Rowe, Otway, Shadwell, Southern, Vanbrough, Wharton, Garth, Hughes, and — writers of whom especially a small supply might be supposed to suffice for such a market — Congreve, Wycherley, and Mrs. Behn. — I have observed that Colman once quotes Steele (Election Sermon of 1718, p. 25), and I think I have met with other instances. He also quotes Barrow (Ibid., 20). He was a friend and correspondent of Bishop Kennett, Dr. Watts, and Mrs. Rowe.

his jealousy of invasions of English rights should abate. Through all the time when the greatness of the King of France was declining, and naturally and rightfully there was fascination in the thought of sharing in the glory associated with the name of Englishman, the colonists had kept a watchful eye upon the securities of their freedom, and continued to repel such attempts as were made upon its integrity. If they took pride in the thought of belonging to the nation which had exhibited the highest type of humanity, this sentiment did not tempt them to abandon for themselves, by any unworthy concessions to their fellow-subjects, the manliness which illustrated the race.

Almost the first act of Lieutenant-Governor Tailer was to approve an allowance which had been made by the General Court to the heirs of Dudley's enemy, Elisha Cooke, of three hundred pounds, for services rendered by him in his agency in England. The Court voted an Address to the King,[1] praying, first, a continuance of the privileges granted by the charter; secondly, encouragement to the production of naval stores; and, thirdly, precautions against the enlarging settlements of the French in Cape Breton, to which island they had betaken themselves in considerable numbers, after their loss of Nova Scotia. John Usher thought that now was his chance, if ever it was to be, to get a favorable hearing for his often-repeated claim as former Treasurer of the Colony. He represented that the Province owed him more than a thousand pounds, besides sixteen hundred pounds for interest for the twenty-six years since the Revolution. The Court resolved that they owed him nothing, and thenceforward he ceased

1715. Nov. 26.

Dec. 3.

Legislation of Massachusetts.

Dec. 21.

[1] The ministers had been beforehand with the General Court. April 13, on the reception of the royal proclamation (see above, 339), they sent an Address, drawn up by Increase Mather. The New Hampshire ministers joined in it. (British Colonial Papers.)

to urge the suit. Colonel Church, the partisan of the
1716. Indian wars, was regarded by them with different
June 18. feelings. They provided for the comfort of his old age with a gratuity of sixty pounds.[1] They sent
June 2. to the King an Address of congratulation on the success of his arms against the Popish pretender, and voted to set apart a day for Thanksgiving for the suppression of "the late horrid and unnatural rebellion."[2]

In the hot dispute which arose out of the financial question of the day in Massachusetts, Colonel Burgess was understood to be partial to what was called the *private bank* party, and his appointment was accordingly unwelcome to many of the most important persons in the Province. Their views, urged in England by one of the most active of them, Jonathan Belcher of Cambridge, were also maintained by Jeremiah Dummer, the new agent, and by Sir William Ashurst, who, though he had refused the agency, never ceased to interest himself in the affairs of the Province. To Burgess the government of Massachusetts was nothing but a job; and for the consideration of a thousand pounds, furnished by Dummer and Belcher, he agreed to decline the promotion. The choice next fell upon Samuel Shute, also a colonel in the army, a brother of John Shute, afterward Lord Barrington in the peerage of Ireland. John Shute, though at a later time expelled from Parliament for alleged dishonesty in some lottery transactions, was now a person of political importance, especially in the non-conformist circles. The maternal grandfather of the brothers was the famous Presbyterian minister, Joseph Caryl. The Governor had been a pupil of Charles Morton, the bold minister of Charlestown in the time of Andros.

Appointment of Governor Shute.

[1] In the second following year, Church was killed by a fall from his horse. (Hutchinson, II. 223, note.)

[2] June 20, an Act was passed, offering a bounty of two pounds each for the importation of male servants between the ages of twelve and sixteen.

Under the same influences, Lieutenant-Governor Tailer was superseded, and his place was given to William Dummer, son-in-law of Governor Dudley, a native of New England, but for some years resident in the parent country. Dudley was much gratified by this arrangement, which he professed to regard "as a mark of the King's favor for his thirteen years' successful service to the crown," though, had the benefit been withholden, his "loyalty and good behavior to the government should have been equally apparent to everybody. The King," he added, "has for ever endeared the hearts of his loyal subjects in these Provinces by appointing so prudent and good a man as Colonel Shute to rule over them. I am now grown old, and having lived to see his Majesty triumph over his enemies, and the administration of the kingdom settled in a wise and faithful ministry, I think I have lived long enough."[1]

Appointment of Lieutenant-Governor Dummer.

Nov. 16.

More than two years had passed since the death of Queen Anne when the new Governor of Massachusetts came to Boston, though his appointment had been known there for four months.[2] The Board of Trade had been informed, with heedless exaggeration, that in Massachusetts there were then ninety-four thousand white people, besides two thousand negroes, and twelve hundred Christian Indians. The commerce of the people of that Colony was not so inconsiderable as might be inferred from the embarrassing disorder of the currency. They dealt with some profit in timber and cured fish, in horses, furs, pitch, tar, turpentine, whale oil, and

Arrival of Shute in Massachusetts.

Oct. 4.

[1] Letter of Dudley, in Mass. Hist. Col., XXXII. 308.

[2] General Court Record, for June 5, 1716. — Hutchinson says (Hist. II. 19) that "he was received with usual parade." I should think, at all events, that it was not with any parade that was unusual. It cost the sum of £36. (General Court Record, for November 13.) — "Certain news is brought that Colonel Samuel Shute is made our Governor, to our great joy." (Sewall's Diary, for June 4.) — It was as late as April 21, 1716, that Stanhope directed the Board of Trade to make out Shute's commission. (British Colonial Papers.)

staves; their ship-building amounted to six thousand tons annually; and their manufactures supplied a large part of their demand for shoes and for the coarser kinds of linen and woollen cloth. Some iron works had been erected, and "some hatters had lately set up their trade."[1]

Prospects of his administration.

With all the advantages incident to the loyal and tractable temper of the people, it was impossible that the task which lay before the new Governor should prove to be an easy one. The generation on the stage of active life had been living under strong excitements, and questions of grave interest between them and their foreign rulers were still pending. With a few short interruptions, the war with the Indians which had just been closed had harassed the people of Massachusetts, and made constant demands on their energies, for forty years. Of this period twenty-five years had passed under that new constitution of government, which took away some material powers and privileges enjoyed under the colonial charter. Though the passion for self-government, thus restrained, had been delayed by the troubles of the times in marking out a definite course of opposition, the traditions of freedom were still venerated and cherished. In the time of the able and resolute Governor Dudley, the people had made experiments on their strength, the result of which, if not conspicuous, had not been discouraging. Not only was his successor an antagonist less formidable in proportion to his greatly inferior abilities, but the state of affairs more easily admitted of a contest with him without prejudice to other interests. It was a dangerous as well as a thankless operation to embarrass Dudley while he was conducting the common defence against the Indians. When the public enemy was quieted, internal dissension became safe; there was always least probability of collision between the two parties of freedom and prerogative in times of peril from

[1] Chalmers, History of the Revolt, II. 7, 12.

abroad. As often as her borders were invaded by the allied French and Indians, the policy of Massachusetts leaned towards conciliation and deference to the government whose assistance was so desirable; while the Ministry, on the other hand, was interested to keep Massachusetts favorably disposed. When peace was restored, the domestic quarrel was ready to break out afresh.

Thus, when the pacification of Utrecht, binding the French to refrain from hostility, had just deprived the Indians of that alliance which was their main stimulus and strength, the people were less liable than in the past years to be incommoded by a quarrel with their Governor and his masters. Shute, indeed, came into his office with one personal advantage in respect of favorable prepossessions on the part of those whom he was to govern. He was a dissenter from the Church of England, which Lord Bellomont never was, and which the facile courtier Dudley had ceased to be.[1] But religious sympathy was no longer

[1] There is extant, in a half-sheet folio, "A Speech made unto His Excellency, Samuel Shute, Esq., Captain-General [&c.]. By the Reverend Dr. Cotton Mather, Attended with the Ministers of the Massachusetts-Province, New England, May 30, 1717. Printed and sold by B. Green, in Newbury-Street." Mather outdid himself in extravagance of eulogy. Shute's appointment was "An Happiness whereinto we have been indeed most agreeably Surprized, by the Providence of our Glorious LORD, who has with most Remarkable Circumstances herein testified His Tender Care of His Flocks in the Wilderness. . . . . . Your EXCELLENCY having honourably spent your Younger Years in the Armies which bravely fought for the Glorious Cause of Rescuing the Liberties of *Europe* and of Mankind, ... you have been generously Willing to devote your later Years to the Publick Service in a Care for the Good of Others. And our Gracious GOD has ordered it, that This His People shall have the Felicity of being made the Objects whom your Care shall be employed upon. — *Felices nimium, sua si bona norint.*" And so on.

Barrington comes in for a good word, near the end: "And we promise ourselves, that whilst your Incomparable BROTHER is a Patron of so much consequence unto our United Brethren on the other side of the *Atlantick*, your EXCELLENCY will vouchsafe us [the Ministers] our part in your most auspicious Patronage."

"His Excellency's Answer," in six lines, assures the addressors that he "takes this Address very kindly, and especially because it comes from a Great and Good Body of Men, for

the bond of union that it had been between the non-conformists of England and of the Colonies. There was no longer a common ambition, or a sense of common danger. Nothing could be more different than were the persecuted non-conformist ministers of the times of the Charleses, and the easy non-conformist ministers of the time of Anne, husbands of the daughters, of whom Shute's mother was one, of London citizens magnificent on the exchange. The legislation in England during the reign of King William, while it had given to dissenters in England all the privileges which at present they could hope for, had given to dissenters in Massachusetts most of what they desired. The national church, it is true, had set up its worship among them; but that was an annoyance from which they could no longer have any expectation of escaping, and to which, in the course of thirty years, they had become accustomed, if not reconciled. Of the new Governor, in other respects, they could have scarcely heard any thing, except that he was a person who possessed some interest with the new managers of England, and who had coveted some office that would enrich or maintain him. There was no reason why they should welcome him with ardor; he came not to gratify or benefit them, but to get a living and to execute his orders; and he came at a moment when they were in no humor to be well pleased with any thing. Year after year they had been fighting the French, with all but ruinous ill-success, with no useful help from England, and through a succession of quarrels with the incompetent and overbearing English officers, who had misused their money, wasted their force, and protected themselves by maligning their character. Their sturdy industry did not so prosper but that they were very poor; and, in two par-

whom I have always had a great Esteem, and this will increase it," &c.

After more than a year's further trial of the Governor, Mather wrote again to Lord Barrington, Nov. 4, 1718, in exuberant praise of him. (Mass. Hist. Col., I. 105.)

ties about equal in strength, they were angrily discussing the cause and the remedy of their poverty.

Such was the state of things in Massachusetts to which Shute was to accommodate his administration. His abilities, without being contemptible, were not such as to fit him to confront a resolute and able opposition. He was good-natured and fair; but at the same time was capable of taking hasty offence, and of being impelled by it to imprudent action. Without jealousy of prerogative, or personal pride, he was alive to the soldier's point of honor in obedience to orders; and, while to many of the subjects of his government the mere thwarting of the Ministry had become a sufficient motive for persisting in a measure, the Governor found sufficient justification of a measure or a pretension in the fact that it suited the Ministry's will. It was impossible that in the circumstances the provincial government constituted by King William's charter should work smoothly. The Governor considered it to be his business to promote the wishes of the British courtiers, and the interest of the British traders. The Representatives considered it to be theirs to look after the well-being of their constituents, which they assumed that they better understood than it could possibly be understood by a Spanish campaigner, — a stipendiary and creature of General Stanhope. His ear had been instructed by Dummer and Belcher, and he took the right side as to the most troublesome question of the time. But, even in so doing, he exposed himself to the displeasure of some of the most considerable men about him, and threw them into an acrimonious opposition to his government; while the party with which he allied himself, having already substantially won the day, had not much need of service from him, and did not much care for his patronage.[1]

Occasions of opposition to him.

[1] The question of public or private bank was discussed in Shute's time with vehement passion. Pamphlets of that period agree in describ-

Shute's commission was in the same terms as that of his predecessor, not excepting even the authority to command the militia of Rhode Island. His instructions were digested in seventy-eight articles. Among other things, he was directed to transmit to England a copy of the laws of his Province within three months from their enactment, or by the first opportunity, "upon pain of the King's highest displeasure, and of the forfeiture of the first year's salary." He was "to propose to the General Assembly, and accordingly to use his best endeavors with them, that an Act be passed for the settling and establishing fixed salaries" upon the Governor, Lieutenant-Governor, and Judges for the time being, and "for the building of a fit and convenient house" for the Governor. He was to persuade the Province to rebuild "that important fort at Pemaquid, which they too easily suffered to be taken and demolished by the French during the former war." He was "to provide, by all necessary orders, that no person have any press for printing, nor that any book, pamphlet, or other matters whatsoever, be printed without his special leave and license first obtained."[1]

His instructions from the Ministry.

The Legislature of Massachusetts was to have come together in a few days after his arrival. His first act was to prorogue it, that he might have opportunity for some inquiry and consultation. It was unavoidable that he should be at once beset with gloomy representations respecting the condition of the currency, and consequently of trade, and with discordant representations as to a remedy. In his first speech he

His disagreements with the General Court.

ing the state of things as distressing, for want of a circulating medium. The author of "The Distressed State of the Town of Boston" (1720) urged the necessity of enlarging the currency by the expedient of a private bank. "Silver," he says (p. 3), "there is not a penny passing;" which statement, however, is not to be taken strictly to the letter, for Judge Sewall, in his Diary, mentions his giving away hard money now and then. The panacea of the author of "The Present Melancholy Circumstance of the Province" (1719) is domestic industry, and abstinence from importation.

[1] British Colonial Papers.

urgently called the attention of the General Court to that ungrateful but inevitable subject. And he went on to inform them that he was instructed to revive the subject of a stated salary for himself, and to say that "Massachusetts was the only Province in America under the crown of Great Britain which did not settle a salary on its Governor and Lieutenant-Governor;" to complain of the unlawful "cutting down of trees proper for the royal navy;" and to repeat the applications heretofore made in vain for the building of a fort at or near Pemaquid.

Nov. 7.

The Court disposed of the first matter by resolving on a further issue of paper money, to twice the amount of that authorized two years before. The form of the measure had been that of a loan of fifty thousand pounds in bills for five years, at an interest of five per cent, with an engagement for a repayment annually of twenty per cent of the principal. One hundred thousand pounds more were now issued, to be repaid in ten years. On the other points proposed, the Representatives were more sensitive than the Governor had probably been prepared to find them. After awaiting their action for what he thought a sufficient time, he sent a message to inquire "whether the Governor might expect a further answer to his speech." They replied the same day that "they had already answered all that was proper or necessary." He sent again to ask "whether the House had *done* all that was proper or necessary in answer to his speech." They replied that they had, "having passed an Act to prevent cutting and carrying off timber." Not being inclined at present to pursue the discussion, he contented himself with proroguing the Court.[1] Such a beginning did not promise mutual confidence or harmony for the future.

Dec. 4.

It might be guessed that Shute was no master of the science of finance. But the emotion with which he speaks

[1] General Court Records.

of the depreciation of the Province's hundred and fifty thousand pounds of irredeemable paper money indicates that it occasioned him both surprise and dismay. When 1717. April 10. he next met the General Court, it was to implore them to make some provision against the "intolerable discount" upon their bills, as well as to renew the requests for a fort at Pemaquid, for an establishment of stated salaries, and the security of the Queen's rights in timber proper for her navy.[1]

This last had become a prominent matter of attention. 1666. As long ago as fifty years before this time, Massachusetts had brought the wealth of her woods to the notice of England by a present to King Charles of ship-timber, which was thought to have contributed not a little to the success of his operations against France; and about the same time the Colony recognized the importance of this interest to

Projects for supplies of naval stores.

[1] British Colonial Papers. — In a former volume (II. 30, note), remarking on the conditions of slavery in Massachusetts, I said that "no person was ever born into legal slavery" within her jurisdiction. My statement was of the law. I have not affirmed that uniformly, through all the generations, popular opinion was accordant with, or observant of, the law. I give to such as would impugn my representation of it the benefit of a fact which I do not know that they have observed. Nov. 10, 1716, William Brown, "son of a freeman by a servant woman," was sold as a slave; his master wished to manumit him; and the Representatives agreed that the master should be released from liability for his support. (Mass. Prov. Rec.) Perhaps they thought that he was not legally a slave; that question was not now brought up, and nothing is better settled than that even the express *dictum* of a judicial court is unauthoritative when it relates to a point not in issue. In the instance now referred to, it may be presumed that neither man nor master understood his legal rights. But, nevertheless, the legislative will of Massachusetts, the directory of judicial action, was expressed in that provision respecting slavery in the "Body of Liberties," — the foundation of the Colonial Statute Laws, — which had never been abrogated. So, again and again, under a mistaken construction of the unamended Federal Constitution, slaves brought into the Free States by their masters, and there absconding, were reclaimed, hunted, and surrendered. But at length the point was raised in Massachusetts; and the decision, never since disputed, was that the slave was not liable to recapture when he had come into a Free State by his master's will. (Pickering's Reports, XVIII. 209; comp. Reports of Cases by Josiah Quincy, Jr., 29, note 2.)

herself by a law which "reserved for the public all pine-trees fit for masts which are twenty-four inches 1668. diameter and upwards within three foot of the May 27. ground, that grow above three miles from the meeting-house." The capacity of producing other naval stores was not overlooked. The General Court granted 1671. "a privilege to Mr. Richard Wharton, etc., to May 31. make pitch, rosin, turpentine, etc."[1] In the ill-conditioned times after the charter of Massachusetts was vacated, Randolph obtained a "commission to be surveyor of 1685. all the woods and timber growing within ten or October. twelve miles of any navigable river, creek, or harbor within the Province of Maine."[2] When Allen solicited

[1] General Court Records.

[2] British Colonial Papers. — As early as the year of the Revolution there was a movement in England "for a grant of mines in New England" to a trading company. Among the English partners were Sir Matthew Dudley and others, and among those in Massachusetts appear the names of Stoughton, Wait Winthrop, Hezekiah Usher, and other leading citizens. The Attorney-General advised the Board of Trade "that their Majesties may erect such a corporation, and enable them to purchase lands and exercise government of the same." (Ibid., for Aug. 10, 1688, and Sept. 10, 1690.) July 7, 1692, an order was passed accordingly. (Register of the Privy Council.) But the measure was arrested, for, June 15, 1692, the Board had had before them a memorial from the government of Massachusetts to the Privy Council, representing "the inconveniences which might attend the passing of a charter of incorporation for raising copper and other minerals in New England, to plant flax, &c., and provide naval stores, and to purchase lands of Indians or others in America." The memorial set forth "the inconsistencies of the grant with the royal charters already granted to the Provinces in New England," and the ill consequences of "the petitioners making any settlements, and thereby acquiring large tracts of land." "All, either singly, or in joint stock companies, have always had free liberty to trade and raise commodities." "Trade will be engrossed, and all commodities advanced in price." (British Colonial Papers; comp. Ibid., for Sept. 12 and 19, 1692, April 6 and Dec. 13, 1693, Jan. 18, Jan. 27, and Feb. 22, 1694, July 22, 1696, July 5, 1697; Register of the Privy Council, for April 6 and Oct. 5, 1693, and Jan. 11 and 18, 1694.) The Province repeated its protest, June 20, 1694. (Mass. Prov. Rec.) July 31, 1696, Sir Henry Ashurst presented it again. (Ibid.; comp. Ibid., under dates of Dec. 21 and 30, 1696, and April 5, May 7, Sept. 18, and Oct. 2, 1697.) Oct. 8, 1697, "their Lordships resolved not to make any further concessions to the petitioners for that patent [Sir Matthew Dudley's], but let that matter lie as it now does." (Journal of the Board of Trade; comp. Ibid., under the dates of July 31 and

the government of New Hampshire, he informed the Privy
1691. Council that he had "contracted with the Navy
March 30. Board to supply their Majesties' navy with masts, yards, bowsprits, and other timber, during the term of seven years."[1]

The ship-builder, Sir William Phips, well understood the value of ship-timber, and, in the provincial charter which he helped to negotiate, the last article,
1692. appended in the last stage of the transaction, reserved for the King's use all trees which measured two feet in diameter at the height of a foot above the ground.[2]

1695. The General Court of Massachusetts reported to
June 25. the Privy Council that their Province could furnish for the royal navy an annual supply of a hundred and fifty tons of rosin, a hundred and fifty tons of pitch and tar, two thousand tons of timber, and a hundred thousand feet of oak planks.

On a recommendation from the Admiralty, the Privy
1696. Council commissioned Benjamin Furzer and John
Sept. 3. Bridger to go to New England, "to inspect and survey and give advice of the naval productions those

Dec. 21, 1696.) But the scheme revived at the beginning of the next reign. Sir Matthew Dudley and his associates again presented their petition to be incorporated; and it was approved, after certain modifications of the plan. (Journal of the Board of Trade, for Dec. 17, 23, and 30, 1702, and Jan. 5, 8, 18, and 20, 1703.) Again it was opposed by the agent of the Province (Jan. 29, 1703), and both sides were heard at length. (Ibid., for Feb. 9, 18, 22, and 26, March 3 and 4, April 5, 13, 14, 19, and 30, May 6, June 15, Aug. 4 and 10.) The Board judged that there was now a "final obstruction of that design by the undertakers refusing to comply with a clause against stock-jobbing." (Ibid., Nov. 6, 1703.)

In a letter to Secretary Willard (from London, Sept. 9, 1719) Dummer says that Sir Matthew Dudley was executor on Governor Allen's estate. (Mass. Arch. LI. 328.) The letter, sixteen pages long, communicates important particulars of the movements of Usher, Byfield, the Quakers, and others at the English court.

[1] Privy Council Register.

[2] "He had a new scene of action opened unto him in an opportunity to supply the crown with all naval stores at most easy rates, from those eastern parts of the Massachusetts Province, which, through the conquest that he had made thereof, came to be inserted in the Massachusetts charter." (Mather, Magnalia, II. 71.)

places did produce, and what improvements might be there made for the future."[1] In no less than three points of view the object contemplated by the English Ministry was important. They looked to this country for abundant and secure supplies, not only of timber, but of naval stores, pitch, tar, and turpentine for their military and commercial marine. They desired to encourage the industry of New England in this department, to the end that its profits might support large demands for English manufactured goods. And they wished, by confining the attention of the people to these pursuits, to keep them from creating a supply of woollen fabrics for themselves. "I am glad," wrote Dudley to the Board of Trade, "to be ad- 1704.
vised your Lordships have been pleased to encour- Oct. 10.
age the trade of tar, rosin, and other naval stores and commodities of this Province, without which it is impossible to prevent this Province to run into the woollen manufacture to that degree that in a few years they will demand very little supply of that sort from the kingdom of England, which if I should not inform of and labor to prevent, I should be wanting in my duty. The inhabitants of this Province are proud enough to wear the best cloth of England;[2] but, without they be employed upon tar, hemp, iron, spars, masts, and building of ships, they have no returns to make, and of those things there might be enough, if proper methods were settled and taken, and persons sent to take care and encourage so to do."[3]

[1] Privy Council Register; Letter of Bridger read to the Board of Trade, March 31, 1704.

[2] Aug. 16, 1720, John Jekyll, a revenue officer, wrote from Boston to the Lords of Trade, that camblets, druggets, and serges were manufactured, which were "worn by the meanest sort of people. As for the tradesmen and mechanical part, they are very ambitious," he says, "of appearing above themselves," and dressed only in the fabrics of Europe. He adds, as pertinent to the topic, that the Council "have their dear idol, the charter, much at heart, and great love for independency." (British Colonial Papers.)

[3] Ibid. — This was not long after the House refused to appoint a Surveyor-General at the Governor's request (see above, 255), though the Council approved the measure.

The war of Sweden against the other Baltic powers, and especially the signs which her erratic sovereign, now courting the friendship of the King of France, had given of an inclination to befriend the Pretender, at once increased the importance to England of an ample supply of naval stores, and the uncertainty of obtaining it from the hitherto customary sources. Furzer, the surveyor, having died on his way to America,[1] the omnivorous Randolph aspired to be his successor, but was defeated by the opposition of Ashurst.[2] Bridger arrived at his destination, having followed Lord Bellomont from the West Indies. He easily embroiled himself with the inhabitants of the forest tracts, and his conflicts with the rough people whose interests he had to invade took for years a considerable place in the action of the government. New Hampshire, especially, without contesting the sovereign's right, showed no zeal in protecting it against the trespassers, to whom the plunder of timber on the banks of distant and solitary navigable waters was at once so safe and so lucrative.

1700.

Resistance to the Surveyor-General of Woods.

Lord Bellomont informed the Lords of Trade that there had been "a prodigious havoc of the woods in New Hampshire within four years," so that he feared that "in two or three years all trees that are near water carriage will be cut up." He complained of the "trade of sending ship-timber to Portugal, still carried on," and desired "an Act of Parliament to hinder transporting of ship-timber."[3] Bridger wrote to him that he had been "for two years preparing trees in the woods near Piscataway to the number of several thousands, for the making of tar for his Majesty's service, but found

April 23.

April 9.

[1] "Mr. Furzer and Bridger fell sick of the fever three or four days before I left Barbadoes, contracted by a debauch they made. Mr. Furzer died, who, I believe, was the best of the two." (Letter of Lord Bellomont, of May 25, 1698, in N. H. Provincial Papers, II. 344.)

[2] Letter of Randolph to W. Blathwayt, of May 21, 1698, in British Colonial Papers.

[3] British Colonial Papers.

them in May last nearly all burnt, to the loss of nearly a thousand barrels of tar."[1]

Bridger had been but a short time in New England, when the Lords of Admiralty advised his recall on Nov. 14. account of the expensiveness of his service.[2] But either he or his business had steady and powerful friends, and early in Dudley's administration he received 1705. the Queen's commission "to be Surveyor-General Dec. 24. of Woods in America, and to instruct the inhabitants in making pitch and tar, curing hemp, etc."[3] He wrote to Secretary Godolphin that the tar, pitch, rosin, and 1706. turpentine were not yet very good, but he would Oct. 18. "engage in two years' time the stores that is raised here . . . . . shall be equally as good as any imported into England. . . . . . I hope," he said, "to divert and turn their labor and thoughts from working up their own wool, which they have made a very great progress in, to the raising of naval stores." If this hope should fail, "the effect would be the loss of the exportation of a hundred and fifty thousand pounds per annum of the manufactures of England to this place only, — I mean Boston." The prospect was, however, uncertain; for soon he had to report a large decrease in the exportation of naval 1708. stores, of which, he said, one reason was that "the March 13. country people and planters had entered so far into making their own woollens that not one in forty but wears his own carding, spinning, etc."[4] When he appealed to 1709. the courts, he "could not get a judgment against July. the people for cutting trees." An Act of Parliament was passed "for preserving white-pine trees," which 1710. punished all persons who should destroy them, except the owner, with a fine of a hundred pounds.[5]

[1] British Colonial Papers.

[2] Privy Council Register.

[3] The Queen's commission is in N. H. Provincial Papers, III. 334; comp. 337.

[4] Letters of Bridger to Godolphin and Blathwayt, in British Colonial Papers.

[5] Act of the ninth year of Anne, Chap. XVII.

Bridger wrote that prosecutions under it were useless,
1711. and that "her Majesty could never hope of any
May 21. justice here, where judge and juries are offenders, for they plead their charter. . . . . . They adore it, equal, if not preferable, to their schismatical doctrine." And his inference was: "Were this charter gone, her Majesty's prerogative would shine bright and influence the whole, so that they would be more obedient to her Majesty's commands, and civil to her interest and officers; and, were they more dependent, they would be much more serviceable."[1]

In the last year of Dudley's administration, Bridger went
1714. to England, having appointed deputies to act for
December. him during his absence. He had probably learned that his presence there was necessary to counteract a movement which was on foot for his removal. Dudley wrote
1715. home in his favor; but Colonel Burgess, while
Jan. 15. expecting to go out as Dudley's successor, had objected to Bridger's continuance in office, having been satisfied, by the evidence of Vaughan and others
June 15. of New Hampshire, that he had made corrupt use of its opportunities.[2] Bridger succeeded in clearing himself to the satisfaction of General Stanhope, and came
Aug. 11. back with a new commission. He was to meet with more vigorous opposition than ever. Elisha Cooke, son of the lately deceased Counsellor, and his successor in the popular regard, charged Bridger with exceeding his authority in forbidding proprietors to cut timber on their own land, and with receiving bribes for permitting the spoliation of timber on the public domain. Bridger justified himself, and Governor Shute took his part, showing
1718. his displeasure against Cooke by excluding him
May. from this time from the Council, to which, however, he continued to be elected by the Court from year to

[1] Letter of Bridger to "My Lord," in British Colonial Papers.
[2] British Colonial Papers.

year, while he found a better sphere for agitating, in his place in the House of Representatives, of which he was a member for Boston. In the ardor of his antagonism, Cooke went so far as to urge that Maine having been granted by the crown to Gorges, and by his heirs sold to Massachusetts, "no reserve was to be made of any woods or trees thereon to the use of the crown."[1] It does not appear that that view had any other open defenders, though it is very likely to have prevailed so far as to prevent vigorous legislation for the security of the royal rights.

Bridger wrote to the Secretary of State that, at Exeter, of seventy trees which had been marked with the 1717.
Queen's broad arrow, only one remained standing.[2] Dec. 30.
The outrage was committed, he says, while Vaughan was Lieutenant-Governor of New Hampshire, "who put out those persons I had deputed for deputies, and put in creatures of his own, which suffered any thing to be done as would please the people; for, as long as there are New England persons Governors,[3] the King must not expect any justice as to the woods; for all the people on the frontiers depend on the woods for their livelihood, and say the King has no woods here, and they will cut what and where they please, as long as the charter's good." Dummer, agent for Massachusetts in England, interested himself successfully against the forester. "I have read," wrote Bridger to the Lords of Trade, "the sur- 1718.
prising and unwelcome news that I am superseded. Oct. 24.
. . . . . My letters informs me that I was removed by the insinuations and malicious contrivances of Mr. Dummer, ... whom I know to be a false and cunning person. . . . . . I have been here but one year and a month since I renewed my commission. . . . . . After twenty-two years'

[1] Mass. Prov. Rec., for June 14, 1718.

[2] This was after Shute's representation on the subject had been disregarded by the General Court. (See above, 393.)

[3] This was a kick at the dead lion Dudley.

faithful service to this country, I am turned out and obliged to beg my bread."[1]

The General Court which Shute found in office, now drawing near to the term of its legal existence, may have thought proper to adopt toward a new Governor a course of action to be a precedent for its successors. The Representatives gave the Governor no satisfaction as to the trespasses upon the woods, and, with unmistakable distinctness they informed him that they declined to restore the fort at Pemaquid, or to establish salaries for the King's officers. "In consideration of his assurances of friendly behavior," they made him a grant of three hundred pounds, and he dismissed them to their spring husbandry, after thanking them for their present, which, he said, "will help the defraying the charge of my transportation." Their six months' acquaintance had not tended to ripen into friendship.

1717. April 11.

Unfriendliness between the Governor and the Representatives.

Referring to the defeat of the Pretender's enterprise, the

[1] British Colonial Papers. — Jan. 13, 1719, "a long discussion arises at the Board in reference to the premiums paid on the importation of naval stores from the Plantations, which amounted the last year to upwards of fifty thousand pounds; and complaint is made by the Board of the very inferior quality of the pitch and tar so imported, whereby it seemed the makers depended on the premiums more than the goodness of these commodities. Among those examined was Mr. Astell, who said he knew not whether it would be safe for him to give his opinion in this affair, for he had been very much abused and insulted upon the Royal Exchange by two persons present, Mr. Baron and Mr. Dummer, for having given his thoughts to the Board in relation to said importation of naval stores. Examination into this matter follows, and the Board agreed that it would be necessary to express some resentment of Mr. Baron's behavior, to prevent the like for the future; and, as to Mr. Dummer, their Lordships resolved to receive no application from him after the Governor of the Massachusetts Bay shall have had another opportunity to choose another agent, and that the Governor should be writ to that they appoint one accordingly." January 22, Astell informed the Board that Baron and Dummer had made him a satisfactory apology, and accordingly the Board "countermanded the direction given for writing to Colonel Shute relating to Mr. Dummer." (Journal of the Board of Trade.) Shute interested himself in Bridger's behalf. (Ibid., for Sept. 22.)

Governor told the next General Court, that their meeting must be "so much the pleasanter by the removal of some fears they had lately had of being deprived of so valuable a privilege. God Almighty long continue," he said, "your religious and civil rights and liberties, with wisdom so to improve them that they may never be forfeited!" And instead of provoking for the present a renewal of the dispute respecting naval supplies, he informed the Court that Parliament was "deliberating on measures for the encouragement of the trade" in those commodities, and "the rather, at this present juncture, by reason of the unjust and surprising intended invasion from Sweden."[1] The Court made him a grant of five hundred pounds for his services in the first half of the civil year. In acknowledging it, he desired "to be told if he had not rendered faithful service." The sum given, he says, referring to the state of the currency, "is in reality but two hundred and fifty pounds." He wished but to be supported with dignity. "I think I may say, without much vanity, I have deserved it." In the next year he received the nominal sum of six hundred pounds. But the depreciation of the notes in which payments were made was an oppressive and a continually growing evil.[2]

May 30.

Nov. 22.

1718. Dec. 4.

The Governor had lately called attention to it again, but all in vain.[3] The subject had become one of mutual irritation between him and the Represen-

May 29.

[1] At this session, the Court (June 20) passed a vote from which something is gathered as to the church architecture of the time. The sum of £150 was granted for the erection of a house of worship at Provincetown, to be "thirty-two feet long, twenty-eight feet wide, fifteen feet studs, with galleries on three sides."

[2] "What we call a hundred pounds is really but as seventy, if so much; and in effect proves the same injury to the receiver as the unjust steward's treachery did to his lord, who, when he asked the debtor, 'How much owest thou unto my lord?' and he said, 'An hundred measures of oil,' he said unto him, 'Take thy bill, and sit down quickly, and write fifty.'" (Benjamin Colman, Sermon preached before his Excellency, Samuel Shute, Esq., &c., 1718, p. 40.)

[3] "If you would reflect a little

tatives. The General Court, as one of its financial expedients, imposed for the year a duty of one per cent on the value of goods imported from England. The Governor, with the advice of the Council, inconsiderately
June 22. consented to the bill. But when there was a movement to re-enact it the following year, he appealed to his instructions, which restrained him from approving it, on the ground of its being in violation of the charter provision, which forbade the Court to make laws contrary to the laws of England. In a vote which followed, the
1719. House was so bold as to express a doubt whether
June 19-30. "his Majesty's instruction to his Excellency the Governor was entirely agreeable to the liberties and privileges granted in the royal charter." This alarmed the Council, who requested that the clause might be stricken out. The Representatives refused, and presently after expressed their indignation by a vote in which they called the Council "the Upper House," — a name which did not belong to it, and against the use of which the Council protested.[1]

At a special meeting of the Court the Governor communicated to them an extract from a letter of the
November. Lords Justices of England, — the King being now

upon the miserable state of our neighbors at Carolina, it would awake you." In 1712, the Colony of South Carolina issued bills of credit to the amount of £48,000, to pay for its war with the Tuscaroras. In the first year this currency fell off one third, in the second one half. (Felt, Historical Account of Massachusetts Currency, 70.)

[1] For a complete summary of the three weeks' transaction between the Council and the House on this occasion, see Province Laws, II. 158-161. May 26, 1719, the Privy Council passed an order, "on representation of Lords of Trade of 24th April last, approving the same, and directing Secretary Craggs to write to the Governor of Massachusetts Bay, in conformity to said report, and to give him a severe reprimand for consenting to the passing an Act [that of June, 1718] so contrary to his instructions, and to the laws and interests of England." (Register of the Privy Council.)

The aurora borealis was first observed in New England in the year 1719. (Mass. Hist. Col., II. 17.) It is said to have been first observed in England only three years before. (Ibid., 14.)

upon the Continent, — threatening them with the loss of their charter for presuming to lay a tax on English goods and merchandise. And he told them that the Board of Trade desired them to take measures for a strict inspection of pitch and tar, for the protection of the King's masts, for respectful treatment of the Surveyor-General of the Woods, and for preventing the unlawful exportation of ship-timber to Spain, with which country England was now at war.[1] The House refused to strike out the provision for a duty on English merchandise from their bill "for making and emitting one hundred thousand pounds in bills of credit on the Province," and so prevented that assent of the Governor which was necessary to its becoming a law. The Governor repeatedly requested, and the House repeatedly refused, the withholding from the press of an "Additional Answer to his Speech," relating to a charge made against the provincial government by the Lords Commissioners of having "hindered the Surveyor-General of the lands in the execution of his office." He declared that, having "the power of the press," he would prevent the publication which they designed. But the Attorney-General advised him that there was no law investing him with that authority, notwithstanding the article in his instructions which presumed it to exist. He could not maintain the pretension; the Answer was published in the "News-Letter;" and the liberty of printing was thenceforward established in Massachusetts.

Imposition of a duty on English merchandise.

[1] He had announced to the Court the declaration of the war against Spain, May 28, 1719. (Mass. Prov. Rec.)

CHAPTER II.

Antagonism between Massachusetts and the Governor.

THREE years of more and more angry fencing had brought the Governor and the people of Massachusetts into an attitude of obstinate antagonism to one another; and whether or not it should prove that a permanent system had been marked out for opposition of the Colony to the crown, at all events it seemed probable that between the Colony and the present Governor there could no more be genuine good-will.[1] Besides the special objects which the Ministry had pressed, they aimed in general to exercise, confirm, and extend their authority. Besides the aversion of the people to special measures pressed upon them, they desired to obstruct and defeat the Governor and his masters, and to keep and accumulate as much power as possible in their

[1] An Act passed by the General Court in December, 1719 (Province Laws, II. 153), required officers of the Province, on assuming their trusts, and all persons when required by two justices, to take the oaths prescribed in Chap. XIII. of the Act of the first year of King George the First, "for the further security of his Majesty's person and government, and the succession of the crown in the heirs of the late Princess Sophia, being Protestants." (Statutes at Large, V. 31, 32.)

The Declaration against transubstantiation belongs to the twenty-fifth year of King Charles the Second. (Ibid., III. 377.) The Oaths of Allegiance and Supremacy were prescribed in Chap. VIII. of the first year of William and Mary (Ibid., III. 417); and, again, in Chap. IV. of the last year of King William; and in Chap. XXII. of the first year, and Chaps. VII. and XIV. of the sixth year, of Queen Anne. (Comp. Ibid., IV. 82, 106, 277, 289.)

The provision in the Act of Parliament referred to in the provincial Act did not expressly embrace the Colonies. The law of Massachusetts was intended to insure the loyalty of public officers within her limits, "and also to discourage and prevent all persons disaffected to his Majesty's rightful and happy government, and the Protestant succession as by law established, from coming into, or residing within, this Province." (Comp. Conn. Col. Rec., VI. 466.)

wn hands. Since self-government, as it had been enjoyed nder the covenants of the old charter, was no longer to e had, it was now their aim to secure as much self-govrnment as could any way be asserted under the provisions f the new charter, without encountering the risk of its eing annulled, as the old had been, on the charge of a surpation of powers not granted by it. Whether a power btained would be for the present beneficial or fruitless vas not, practically, a final question. If not effective now, ccasion might come for it to be reduced to some useful pplication. And a corresponding apprehension was as aturally entertained on the other side. Nothing immeliately depended on the question whether the Houses of egislature or the Governor should appoint a day for fastng; little seemed immediately to depend on the higherounding question whether the Representatives' choice of heir Speaker should be subject to the Governor's approval. 3ut such pretensions on the part of the Representatives vere regarded by the Governor as "continual encroachnents on the few prerogatives left to the crown." And he Board of Trade, to whom he soon after told his story, hought "it was apparent from recent transactions that the nhabitants were endeavoring to wrest the small remains of ower out of the hands of the crown, and to become indeendent of the mother country."[1]

[1] Memorial of Shute to the King, August, 1723, and action of the Board hereupon, August 27–September 3, n British Colonial Papers.

"They fancy us," wrote the agent Dummer, April 8, 1720, "to be a ittle kind of sovereign state, and onclude for certain that we shall be o in time to come, and that the rown will not be able to reduce us t so great a distance from the hrone. . . . . . I have therefore ver found, since I have had the onor of serving the Province, that our greatest prudence is to lie quiet and as unobserved as we can, and that, the less show we make to the world, the safer we are from the stroke of public as well as private envy." (Hist. Soc. Col., XXI. 145.)

In "the memorable year 1720," says Hutchinson (II. 231), "the contests and dissensions in the government rose to a greater height than they had done since the religious feuds in the year 1636 and 1637." But this is merely an exaggeration. The times were any thing but tran-

After the death of Elisha Cooke, the antagonist of Mather and of Dudley, his policy was prosecuted by his son, who succeeded to his great popularity. The gentleman who had been Speaker of the House in the last years, John Burrill of Lynn, had been much esteemed in that capacity. But, as the temper which now possessed the Representatives required a bolder leadership, he was promoted to the Council, and Cooke was elected to fill his place. The transactions which followed illustrate the unfriendly relation between the parties.

1715.

1720. May.

A committee of the Representatives went to the Governor's house and informed him of their choice of Cooke. According to their report, he said, "Very well," and they took their leave. The same afternoon he came to the Council Chamber, and informed the Representatives by a message that he was now ready to hear from them respecting the election of a Speaker. They replied that he had already been acquainted with it, and that his answer had been recorded in their journal; and they proceeded to desire the Council, as usual, to go into convention with them for the choice of Counsellors for the coming year. The Governor said that no such convention could be held before he was informed how the House was organized. The Representatives sent up a committee to communicate that information anew. The Governor refused to approve Mr. Cooke, and desired them to proceed to another choice. This they declined to do, and renewed the proposal to the Council to go into an election of Counsellors. A doubt whether, by the charter provision, this election could be legally made on any subsequent day, induced the Governor to desist from opposition to the choice of a Speaker, after acquainting the House by a message that the power which he claimed was

Oppugnation of the Legislature.

quil; but they were not so stormy as during the presidency of Dudley, the despotism of Andros, or the interval between the Revolution of 1689 and the new charter.

conferred by the English Constitution and by the charter, and, as he was told, had been exercised by Governor Dudley. An election was accordingly made of Counsellors, of whom he rejected two, Nathaniel Byfield[1] and John Clark, known as friends of Cooke. This done, he sent a message to the House, avowing his reasons for preventing the elevation of Cooke, who, he said, had invaded the royal rights in the woods of Maine, and had offered him personal ill-treatment[2] He advised them to choose another Speaker, with a reservation of their asserted right till the authorities in England should be consulted. Without a dissenting voice they refused to do so, and he immediately dissolved the Court, and issued writs for another to meet in six weeks.[3] May 30.

[1] Byfield had been in England, where Jeremiah Dummer, in a letter to Secretary Willard, of Sept. 9, 1719, represents him as associated with John Usher in machinations against the Province. (Mass. Arch., LI. 319.)

[2] A letter from Shute to Penhallow, in N. H. Provincial Papers, III. 752, throws light on the disagreeable relations between the Governor and Cooke.

[3] In the interval Cooke published two editions of a pamphlet, entitled "Mr. Cooke's Just and Seasonable Vindication respecting some affairs transacted in the late General Assembly at Boston, 1720." The Governor's right to set aside the House's choice of its Speaker is extremely well argued, though with a warmth belonging alike to his personal temperament and to the excitement which prevailed. (Comp. the "Boston News-Letter," for June 6, 1720.)

It was about the time of these transactions, which so stimulated the public mind, that the second and third Boston newspapers were set up, — the "Boston Gazette," established Dec. 21, 1719, by William Brooker, Campbell's successor in the post-office; and the "New England Courant," by James Franklin, Aug. 17, 1721. Franklin took up a strain of offensive comment on the respected men and opinions of the day. He was aided in his editorial labors by a society variously qualified as the "free-thinkers" and the "hell-fire club." But the master-spirit in the "Courant's" better days was Franklin's brother Benjamin, then a boy apprenticed in the office. The appearance of the "Courant" provoked the "News-Letter" to speak of it as "a third newspaper in this town, ... by *homo non unius negotii* [Franklin's motto], or Jack-at-all-trades, and it would seem good at none, giving some very, very frothy, fulsome account of himself." Increase Mather published his opinion of it as follows, in the "Boston Gazette:" "Whereas a wicked libel, called the 'New England Courant,' has represented me as one among the supporters of it, I do hereby declare that, although I had paid for two or three of them, I then, before the last 'Courant' was published, sent him word I was extremely

It was composed of nearly the same members as the last. But, as another dissolution would have much embarrassed the public business, the House did not persist in a re-election of Cooke, but contented themselves for the present with remonstrance and protest as having acted under duress. Their surly session lasted only ten days. They denied the Governor's request for a small sum of money to gratify the Penobscot Indians. They set up a new claim to choose notaries-public, in concurrence with the Council. They refused the money to pay for the

July 13.

offended with it. In special, because in one of his vile 'Courants' he insinuated that, if the ministers approve of a thing, it is a sign it is of the devil, — which is a horrid thing to be related. . . . . . And he doth frequently abuse the ministers of religion, and many other worthy persons, in a manner which is intolerable. For these and such like reasons I signified to the printer that I would have no more of their wicked 'Courants.' . . . . . I can well remember when the civil government would have taken an effectual course to suppress such a cursed libel. Which if it be not done, I am afraid that some awful judgment will come upon this land, and that the wrath of God will arise, and there will be no remedy. I cannot but pity poor Franklin, ... and I cannot but advise the supporters of the 'Courant' to consider the consequences of being partakers in other men's sins, and no more countenance such a wicked paper."

This was the clerical way of dealing with strictures. The "Great and General Court" could do more than rail back; and (Jan. 14, 1723) a committee "appointed to consider of the paper called the 'New England Courant'" reported that they were "humbly of opinion that the tendency of the said paper is to mock religion and bring it into contempt; that the holy Scriptures are therein profanely abused; that the faithful ministers of the gospel are injuriously reflected upon; his Majesty's government insulted; and the peace and good order of his Majesty's subjects of this Province disturbed, by the said 'Courant:' and, for the prevention of the like offence in future, the said committee humbly propose that James Franklin, the printer and publisher thereof, be strictly forbidden to print or publish the 'New England Courant,' or any pamphlet or paper of the like nature, except it be first supervised by the Secretary of this Province; and the Justices of his Majesty's sessions of the peace for the County of Suffolk, at their next adjournment, are directed to take sufficient bonds of the said Franklin for his good behavior for twelve months' time." To evade this order, the name of James Franklin was removed from the imprint of the paper, and that of Benjamin substituted, though the brother was then only seventeen years old. James quarrelled with his precocious apprentice, who, in October, 1723, ran away, and went to distant Philadelphia. (Mass. Hist. Col., VI. 64–66; Thomas, History of Printing, &c., II. 199, 200, 214–223; Sparks, Works of Franklin, I. 22–28.) Such was the unpromising prelude to the career of the since world-renowned Dr. Franklin.

customary celebration of public holidays, such as the anniversary of the King's birthday.[1] After an unusual delay, they made a grant to the Governor of five hundred pounds, in the depreciated currency, for a half-year's compensation, instead of the six hundred pounds which had been their allowance in the three preceding years of his administration. To the Lieutenant-Governor, instead of the accustomed fifty pounds or more, they voted thirty-five pounds, which he refused to receive, at the same time informing them that his office had cost him more than fifty pounds a year. Their whole legislation seemed but an expression of their dissatisfaction and ill-will. The most favorable interpretation to be put on it is, that they designed to show that they had power to make terms for themselves by obstructing and retaliating.

Dispute respecting the royal claim to timber.

The matter of the reservation of pine-trees for masts and spars for the royal navy was a standing subject of contention. The House maintained that, though, by the charter, trees fit for this use, while standing upon land which had not become private property at the date of that instrument,[2] belonged to the King, yet, after they had been felled, the property of the timber was in the owner of the land. And Cooke per-

[1] That this was not much of a money-saving operation, appears from the memoranda of earlier expenses of this kind. Sept. 23, 1715, Captain Edward Brattle presented his "account of powder expended in his Majesty's fort at Marblehead," viz.: thirty-five pounds in firing eight guns "in condolence of the death of the Queen;" forty pounds in nine guns on the proclamation of King George; twenty-three pounds in five guns on the anniversary of the "gunpowder treason;" thirty pounds in seven guns on the anniversary of the King's birthday; twenty-three pounds in five guns on the anniversary of the Restoration of King Charles the Second. (British Colonial Papers.)

[2] 1718, Nov. 12, the Board of Trade were advised by Richard West, their solicitor, that the crown was entitled to all trees of the prescribed size, in Maine and other parts of Massachusetts, "except only those trees situated on lands which were legally granted to private persons before the charter of 4 Caroli I. was reversed." Solicitor Eyre further instructed the Board, May 12, that bodies politic (as towns) were among the private persons on whose land the crown could not claim trees.

sisted in his argument that the whole claim was wrongful, Massachusetts having bought Maine of Gorges, free from any such encumbrance. The House raised a committee to seize for the use of the Province such timber as had been cut under the Commissioner's license, alleging that it had not been devoted to the King's use, but had been converted by that officer to his own profit. When Bridger had lost the confidence of his English masters, one Burniston, appointed to succeed him, sent John Armstrong to New
1719. England as his deputy; a man, writes the angry
June 13. ex-official, who was "bred a kind of clerk to a country attorney in Cumberland, or that way. He knows not an oak from a pine, nor one pine from another." Bridger repeated his complaint of the hardship of being displaced, when, as he wrote to the Lords of Trade, he
1721. had been nearly twenty-five years in office, and
March 10. when he had "made the first tar, and sowed and cured the first hemp, that ever was made or raised in New England fit for the service of the navy."[1]

Revolutions in Nova Scotia.

At this time Nova Scotia received a permanent organization as a British Province. It had been
1667. ceded to France by the Treaty of Breda, and subsequently was occupied to some extent by a French
1690. population. Having, a year after the Revolution,
May 20. been successfully invaded by a Massachusetts force under Sir William Phips, it was presently included
1692. in that Province by the charter of William and Mary. The petition of Massachusetts to the crown, pray-
1696. ing it to garrison Port Royal,[2] must be interpreted
Sept. 24. as expressive of a desire to be rid of a possession which was merely a burden and a charge. In the next year, by the Treaty of Ryswick, Nova Scotia was again handed back to France.[3] The surrender to Gov-
1710. ernor Nicholson gave it once more to Great Britain,

[1] British Colonial Papers.

[2] Ibid.

[3] Sept. 10, 1709, the always vigilant agent for Massachusetts ad-

of which it has since remained a permanent possession, being confirmed as such by an article of the Treaty of Utrecht. 1713. April 11.

Nicholson, placed in the charge of it after Vetch, administered it as simply a military government. Colonel Phillips, who succeeded him at the end of five years, was instructed to surround himself with a Council, to be selected from among the principal English inhabitants. An officer, sent by Governor Shute to warn the French from fishing in the Nova Scotia waters, captured two French vessels, "took what fish he found on shore, and pulled down their huts."[1] The Board of Trade reported to King George the First: "Although Nova Scotia is expressly included in this charter [the provincial charter of Massachusetts], yet the same being, at the time the charter was granted, in possession of the French by virtue of the Treaty of Breda, this part of the grant has always been esteemed of no effect, and the people of New England do not pretend any right thereunto."[2]

1714. Settlement of Nova Scotia. 1719. 1718. November. 1721.

The charter of Massachusetts vested in the Governor the power of adjourning, as well as of summoning and dissolving, the General Court. The Representatives, wishing to be at their homes to keep a Fast day, desired the Governor to adjourn them for that purpose. He refused, important business being under consideration; and they adjourned themselves for six days. When they came back, he insisted upon an avowal of their fault before they should resume the session, which they accordingly made, so far as to allow that they should have informed him of their inten-

Continued disputes in Massachusetts. July 12.

dressed the Lord Treasurer and the Secretaries of State with a memorial in favor of reclaiming the territory. (Hist. Soc. Col., XXI. 234.)

[1] Letter of Shute to the Board of Trade, in British Colonial Papers.

[2] O'Callaghan, Documents, &c., V. 596. — June 26, 1716, the territory belonging to the Province, east of the District of Maine, had been annexed to the County of York. (Mass. Prov. Rec.)

tion; but at the same time they attempted a distinction between his power by the charter to adjourn the General Court and their assumed right to adjourn their own House. This did not satisfy the Governor, as indeed there was no reason why it should, and after rebuking them he dissolved the Court. When it met again, the small-pox was Aug. 23. raging in Boston.[1] The House voted to transfer the session to Cambridge. The Governor replied, that, while he had no objection to that arrangement, it was

[1] At this time there was a prodigious excitement in Boston over the question of inoculating for the small-pox. At five different times before this (Douglas, Summary, II. 395), the malady had spread in that town, causing grievous mortality and distress. In 1721, according to Douglas (Ibid., 396; comp. Mass. Hist. Col., XXXII. 168; V. 207), there were 5,989 cases of it, of which one in seven proved fatal. Dr. Zabdiel Boylston, against great opposition, undertook to introduce that safeguard against the disease, which he affirmed to have been found in the method of inoculation (or *ingrafting*, as it was also called). This practice had but just been introduced into England by Lady Mary Wortley Montagu, who had become acquainted with it in the east, and who caused her daughter to be inoculated in London in April, 1721; though eight years earlier it had been made known by a Greek physician of Constantinople to Dr. Woodward, who communicated it to the Royal Society of London, in whose Transactions an account of it was published. Cotton Mather received a copy of the paper, and he and his father consulted upon it with Dr. Boylston. This gentleman caused it to be reprinted, and felt such confidence in the method, that he proceeded to make the experiment on his own children and servants. This occasioned a great outcry; and not only did a hot war of pamphlets follow, but there were threats of personal violence against the champions of the novelty. Among the writers on this side, besides Dr. Boylston ("Abridgment of Two Accounts," &c.; "Historical Account of the Small-Pox," &c.), Dr. Colman was prominent, arguing the case with courtesy and moderation, though with confidence and boldness, and the Mathers, Increase and Cotton, with the acerbity characteristic of them, especially of the son. On the other side were two masters of ribaldry, the Scotsman, Dr. William Douglas, author of the Summary; and John Williams, whom I find mentioned sometimes as a medical man, sometimes as a tobacconist. A sermon by Mr. Mussey, of London, was reprinted in Boston, and met with great favor; its text was from Job ii. 7, and its doctrine that Satan was the first inoculator.

The year of President Mather's participation in this controversy was the last of his public activity. There is a tract of his, bearing the date of Nov. 20, 1721, and the title, "Several Reasons proving that inoculating or transplanting the Small-Pox is a Lawful Practice, and that it has been blessed by God." (Mass. Hist. Col., IX. 275.) He died Aug. 23, 1723, having entered on the eighty-fifth year of his age.

within his official discretion, and to request him so to order was the proper method of proceeding. The House rejoined, that by law Boston was the place for meetings of the General Court, and that the law could be suspended only by a joint act of Governor, Council, and Representatives. Both parties persisted. Notwithstanding the danger in Boston, the House refused to ask the Governor's permission to go to Cambridge. They again expressed their resentment by voting him for half a year's service the sum of five hundred pounds in paper, which was now worth little more than one half of the nominal sum.[1]

The House imagined that frauds had been practised in the muster-rolls which were presented when the pay of soldiers was to be voted; and they proposed to inspect the garrisons by a committee of their own, before whom the commanders should be obliged to parade their men. The Governor refused to consent to this interference with his military authority. In reply to a renewal of his application for a fixed salary, the House said that "they humbly conceived what was granted him was an honorable allowance, and the affair of settling salaries being a matter of great weight and wholly new to the House, and many of the members absent, they did not think it proper to enter into the consideration of it, but desired the Court might rise." To another of his recommendations, that they should adopt some expedient to keep up the credit of their bills, they replied that "they had passed a bill for issuing one hundred thousand pounds more in bills of credit;" the surest way possible to increase the depreciation which he lamented, notwithstanding the

March.

[1] "The Lord Barrington . . . . . represented to the Board the undutiful behavior of the Lower House of Assembly in perversely refusing to comply with every proposal to them from his brother the Governor; . . . . . that, by the riotous and insulting carriage of the populace in the said Province towards their Governor, it is to be apprehended there will soon be a dissolution of all government, if he be not supported and encouraged from home." (Journal of the Board of Trade, for Aug. 18, 1721.)

always illusory measure, which at the same time they had taken, of prohibiting "the buying, selling, and bartering silver at any higher rates than set by Act of Parliament."

July 19. Shute wrote home that the Assembly went so far as to disavow all responsibility to the Board of Trade.[1]

Cabals in the College. The innocent College shared in the trouble resulting from this long series of altercations. The stricter Calvinists of the period, countenanced by the aged Ex-President Mather, and stimulated by his disappointed and angry son, had all along viewed with displeasure the administration of the College by President Leverett. The struggle as to which influence should prevail had for the present been determined, about the time of Shute's 1717. arrival, by the election into the College Corporation of Benjamin Colman, minister of the church in Brattle Square, Boston, and his friend Nathaniel Appleton, minister of Cambridge, both of whom sympathized with President Leverett and with the less rigorous sectarian methods of the time, while the prevailing sentiment in the House of Representatives was very decidedly the other way. The better qualities of Shute's character led him to take a friendly interest in the College;[2] and to Colman, who, after the President, was the leading spirit of its government, he was naturally attracted by the excellent qualities of that distinguished divine, whom, in cultivation and manners, he found to be a fair representative of the class of dissenters to whose society he had been used in England, and of some of whom Colman was a personal friend and correspondent.

[1] British Colonial Papers.

[2] He bespoke for the College, though without effect, the good-will of his other Province. "It will tend greatly to the reputation of this Province to show their grateful acknowledgment of the benefits their children receive there, by making some handsome present for the augmentation of the library." (Message to the Assembly of New Hampshire, Sept. 24, 1719, in N. H. Provincial Papers, III. 764; comp. 766.)

A graduate of the College, named Pierpont, was refused admission to the degree of Master of Arts, for having used language disrespectful to the academical authorities. He prosecuted a tutor, who had reported his offence, for slander. The late Governor, and his son Paul, Attorney-General, who was said to be chagrined in consequence of failure to be appointed Treasurer of the College, took his part. The Overseers, summoned by Shute, advised Pierpont to acknowledge his error, which he refused to do. He carried his claim into the courts, where it was dismissed, as legitimately belonging to the jurisdiction of the College by its charter. The matter seems trivial, but under the treatment of the Mathers and the Dudleys it assumed so much importance as, in the judgment of President Leverett, to threaten the dissolution of the College.[1]

1718. Oct. 31.

Two tutors had set up a claim to be members of the Corporation of the College, on the ground that it was the sense and intention of the charter that resident instructors, being not more than five in number, should be members of that body. The House of Representatives passed a vote sustaining this construction.[2] The Council concurred in the vote, but the Governor would give only a conditional approval. "I consent," he said, "provided the Reverend Mr. Benjamin Wadsworth and the Reverend Mr. Benjamin Colman and the Reverend Mr. Appleton are not removed by said orders, but still remain Fellows of the Corporation." The House sent up their vote again, with a message "to desire his Excellency to pass absolutely thereupon, according to the constant

1722. June.

[1] Quincy, History of Harvard University, I. 219. — President Quincy prints (Ibid., 523) a delightful letter of Cotton Mather in relation to this dispute.

[2] The question was revived, and again fully argued, in the year 1824, when Professor Norton and Professor Everett, on the part of the resident officers, presented the case to the Overseers. Like their predecessors in 1721, they failed in establishing the claim.

usage and practice ever since the present happy constitution." The Governor said that his decision was not to be changed; and another appeal from the House failed to move him. 1719. It was happy for the College that, before the hottest of the dispute between him and the Representatives began, he had obtained from them the money to erect at Cambridge an expensive building, which, under the name of Massachusetts Hall, commemorates the liberality of the Province to this day.

Shute's reputation for military spirit and experience constituted his best means of influence with the people of his government. The conflict with the Indians of Maine, which had had few intermissions since the time of Philip's War, had been no more than suspended by the pacification at Utrecht. The French of Canada could no longer openly counsel or assist the barbarities of their Indian friends, but in secret they were scarcely less busy than before.

Indian settlement at Norridgewock.

On a bend of the river Kennebec, a few miles above the present town of Augusta, the Jesuit priest, Sebastian Rasle, had collected a company of Indian converts, and erected a chapel and some cabins. The place still bears its ancient name of Norridgewock. Rasle was a capable and accomplished man, and resolute and self-sacrificing in his bigotry. At the age of thirty-two 1689. he had established a mission for the Abenaquis in the neighborhood of Quebec. Thence, after two or three years, he followed the steps of Marquette and other explorers to the upper lakes and the river Illinois. 1693. From this experience, which lasted about as much longer, he was recalled by his superiors to be stationed at Norridgewock, on the extreme western border of the country claimed by the French under their interpretation of the name *Acadie*. There, before and during the war in Queen Anne's reign, he confirmed and extended his authority over the Indians, under instructions from the Governors and ecclesiastics at Quebec. The nature of his labors was not misunderstood in Boston; and, in his absence, Colonel Hilton, sent by Dudley on winter expeditions against the hostile tribes, burned his chapel to the ground, and killed a few of his people.[1] In no wise discouraged, he hastened, after the Treaty of Utrecht, to restore the chapel, and returned with new vigor to his troublesome operations.

1705. 1707.

Shute, in the next summer after his arrival at Boston, invited the eastern tribes to a conference at Arrowsick Island, on the Kennebec, desiring to secure their peaceable behavior towards the immigrants who were now setting their faces towards that region. Rasle was understood to have accompanied the chiefs, but he kept himself out of sight. Shute, giving the sachems an English flag, and a Bible in the English with another in the native language, reminded them that they were subjects of the King of England, and offered them the services of a schoolmaster to instruct their children, and of one of his companions, the Reverend Mr. Baxter, to teach them the English religion. He assured them of just treatment from the English, and of favorable attention to any complaints they might from time to time have to make. They desired to defer their answer to the next day; and then replied, that they had no objection to being King George's subjects if they were not molested in the occupation of their lands, but that they were "not capable to make any judgment about religion," and were attached to their present teachers. As to their lands,

Treaty with the eastern Indians. 1717. Aug. 9.

[1] See above, pp. 267, 270, note. According to the biographical sketch of Colonel Winthrop Hilton in the "Collections" of Farmer and Moore, I. 240, he was a descendant from the family of that name, early settlers on the Piscataqua (see above, Vol. I. 205), and was born at Exeter, in or about the year 1671. He was an active commander during the war in the time of Dudley, who, in their correspondence, calls him his "kinsman," but does not always refrain from treating him with arrogance. He was with the unfortunate expedition against Port Royal in 1707, when he had the good fortune to please the Governor, while other officers fell under his displeasure. (Ibid., 249.) He was killed by a party of Indians in 1710.

they said that they claimed none on the west side of the Kennebec, but "were sure they had sold none on the east side;" and they produced a letter from Rasle, in which he affirmed that he had it from Vaudreuil that the King of France had assured him that he had not ceded any country east of the Kennebec to the English, but, on the contrary, would maintain the Indian right to it. At this Governor Shute took offence, and was
Aug. 11. about to break up the conference, when the Indians, alarmed, begged for another interview. The result
1713. was that the treaty made four years before with
July. Dudley at Portsmouth was renewed, with its stipulations that the natives should demean themselves as faithful subjects of the crown of Great Britain, and that the English might without molestation reoccupy their former settlements.[1]

Renewed Indian hostilities. A year and a half had passed, when some threatening demonstrations on the part of the eastern
1719. savages caused the Governor to convene the General
March 11. Court. The Court immediately ordered the raising of a company for service against the tribes, and the Governor was able to report that the move-
May 28. ment was quelled without bloodshed. The next
1720. year there was another alarm. The Indians sur-
Aug. 7. prised some English at Canseau, in Nova Scotia, killing three or four and robbing the rest. Further disorders followed in the same quarter, occasioning a destruction of property to the amount, as was said, of not less than twenty thousand pounds; and the French Governor of Cape Breton, to whom application was made, declined

[1] A full account of this treaty, called the "Treaty of Georgetown," was printed at Boston in a pamphlet, by B. Green. A reprint is in N. H. Provincial Papers, III. 693–701; comp. Niles, in Mass. Hist. Col., XXXV. 338, 339; Penhallow, Indian Wars, 83; Francis, Life of Sebastian Rasle, in Sparks's American Biography, XVII. 246 *et seq.*; Shute, Letter to Rasle, of Feb. 21, 1718, in Mass. Hist. Col., V. 112; Mass. Arch., LI. 306.

to interfere.[1] Shute, hoping that a general war might be avoided, instructed the commander of the troops in Maine to propose a conference. The Indians agreed. But the Representatives in the General Court preferred a different way of proceeding. They passed a resolve for sending a force of a hundred and fifty men to Norridgewock, to demand of the Indians there and thereabouts "full satisfaction for the damage they had done the English," and, if they should refuse to give up Father Rasle to be brought to Boston, then to bring thither a sufficient number of them to be pledges for his surrender. The Governor disapproved this measure, both because he was averse to a new war, especially in the existing state of the finances, and because he properly considered the military administration as belonging to his own prerogative. The dissension thus originated between him and the Representatives proved to be the most irreconcilable of all.

Nov. 2.

The old chief of the Norridgewock Indians died, and a person less unfriendly to the English became his successor. Under his auspices, hostages for the quiet behavior of the tribe were sent to Boston. Rasle and his friends at Quebec were disturbed and displeased at this proceeding. The Governor, Vaudreuil, wrote to Rasle in terms of extreme dissatisfaction. He said that he had prevailed upon the natives in the vicinity of Quebec to send messengers to inform the English that if they continued their encroachments they would not have to deal with the Norridgewocks alone, and that another Jesuit father was despatched to encourage that tribe to behave with firmness, and to engage the Penobscot Indians in an alliance with them. And the Intendant-General of Canada (Bygon) wrote that the authorities there were waiting orders from the King as to whether they should

1721. June 15.

June 14.

[1] This autumn there was a general alarm as to the temper of the Indians, to which these movements at the east may have contributed. (See below, p. 480.)

give open assistance to the savages, or only continue to supply them with ammunition, as already they were freely doing. Your Indians, wrote Vaudreuil to Rasle, "if they have taken a sincere resolution not to suffer the English on their land, ought not to defer chasing them out as soon as possible. Your people ought not to fear the want of ammunition, since I send them a sufficiency."[1]

Sept. 25.

But the English had not the information contained in these letters, which fell into their hands at a later time. Whether other trustworthy intelligence came to Massachusetts of the French intrigues and the Indian ill-temper, or whether only an indefinite suspicion was entertained, the General Court considered energetic measures to be necessary. They renewed a vote that a force, now to consist of "three hundred men, should be sent to the head-quarters of the Indians," to require the surrender of "the Jesuits and the other heads and promoters of their rebellion," and "satisfaction for the damage they had done;" in default of which some of their principal men, "together with Rasle or any other Jesuit," were to be seized and sent to Boston. The Governor, though he gave his consent to this measure, which was taken just before the Court adjourned, delayed to carry it into effect. This was new cause of offence. At the next session the House again pressed the subject, and the Governor despatched a party to Norridgewock under the command of Colonel Westbrooke. The advance of these troops was watched by two of Rasle's Indians, who gave notice in season for him to escape. Among his papers, of which the English possessed themselves, were the letters which have just been quoted.[2]

August.

Nov. 3.

[1] Letters in British Colonial Papers.

[2] Charlevoix, Histoire, III. 381; comp. Farmer and Moore, Hist. Col., II. 108 *et seq.;* Mass. Hist. Col., XVIII. 250 *et seq.* — Among the papers was also a MS. glossary of the Abenaqui language, of Rasle's

Another person, of consequence in these hostilities, fell into the hands of the English. The young Baron de St. Castine was on the Kennebec when they came thither, — it was naturally supposed for no good purpose. He was brought to Boston, where he was examined by a committee of the Court. Whether he was honest, or they were credulous or distrustful of the good judgment of pushing matters to extremity, he succeeded in satisfying them that his design in coming among the Kennebec Indians was to persuade them to peace, and he was accordingly discharged. Shute wrote to Vaudreuil: "I suppose Mr. Rasle, who has been the great incendiary in all this affair, has acquainted you with his narrow escape. He will do well to take warning by it, and return to his own country." And again: "Norridgewock is within the territory of his Majesty King George, and it is contrary to an Act of Parliament of Great Britain, and to a law of this Province, for a Jesuit or Romish priest to preach or even reside in any part of the British dominions."[1]

March 14.

April 23.

There was to be further proof of the necessity of vigor-

composition, which is now in the Library of Harvard College. For an account of it, by the late Mr. John Pickering, see Memoirs of the American Academy, IV. 358 *et seq.*; comp. Francis, *ubi supra*, 293 *et seq.*

[1] Letters in British Colonial Papers. — May 25, 1722, the Board of Trade read letters from Shute of March 13, informing that Vaudreuil "did underhand stir up the neighboring Indians to maltreat his Majesty's liege subjects," and communicating copies of letters from him, which he says were found in Rasle's house. He wrote that he was well acquainted with the handwriting of Vaudreuil, and knew that these letters, purporting to be his, were genuine. "In a piece of a letter," he says, "where the name and date were cut out, there is mention made of one Charlevoix, who comes from the Court of France in the quality of an inspector, to make memoirs on Acadia and Mississippi, and the other countries round about."

The population of Canada at this period was probably not far from 25,000. (See above, 36, note 3.) In 1714, Vaudreuil estimated the number of the militia at 4,480. ("Importance of Cape Breton," 102; comp. Charlevoix, IV. 150.) The not altogether trustworthy census, made by the government in 1721, reported the population to be 24,511. In 1719, the Intendant-General represented it to be 22,530. (O'Callaghan, Documents, &c., IX. 897.)

ous measures of protection against these unreasoning and inconstant savages and their crafty and indefatigable prompters. Sixty warriors came into Merrimeeting Bay, on the Kennebec, and carried away prisoners to be security for their own hostages still detained at Boston. Three fishing-sloops were attacked in as many eastern harbors, several prisoners were carried off, and one vessel was burned. Next came intelligence of the burning of the town of Brunswick by a marauding party, and a letter was received from the Governor of New France, in which, as Shute informed the Lords of Trade, "he openly declared that he had and would assist the Indians, and that he had orders from the Court of France so to do."[1] There was no possibility of further forbearance. War against the tribes was resolved upon, at a juncture most unfortunate by reason of the mutual jealousies between the Governor and the House. The Governor, when he convoked the Court to make the necessary preparations, said: "One thing I would particularly remark to you, which is, that if my hands and the Council's be not left at a much greater liberty than of late they have been, I fear our affairs will be carried on with little or no spirit."

1722. June.

July 25.

Aug. 8.

A committee of the Court reported a liberal plan for enlistments, pay, and supplies, but they proceeded to lay out a detailed project for the disposition of the troops and the conduct of the campaign. The Governor replied, that he, by the charter and the King's commission, was commander-in-chief, and that he was bound to be governed by his own judgment as to military movements. The House passed a vote requesting him to discharge Major Moody, who was in command on the eastern frontier. The Governor replied that an officer was not to be displaced without reason shown. He asked for the enactment

Assumption of military authority by the General Court.

Aug. 17.

Aug. 18.

[1] British Colonial Papers.

of a law to punish mutiny and desertion. The House proposed first to inquire whether the frequency of these offences was not occasioned by reasonable dissatisfaction with the commanding officers; and it raised committees to visit the forces, and make investigation on the spot. When some delegates from the Iroquois, whose good offices it was hoped to engage against the eastern Indians, came to Boston by invitation, the House voted to have the Governor's speech to them prepared by a committee of the Court; and he finally yielded to their demand that he should adopt the novel method of addressing the Indians in the name of the Court, and not in his own, as official head of the Province.[1] These are but specimens of the perpetual jarring at this time between the executive and legislative powers.

Consenting to the wishes of the House, the Governor had directed an advance of troops towards the Penobscot, and they were already on their march when an alarm on the Kennebec caused them to be recalled by the officer who commanded in that quarter. The occasion justified that measure. Four or five hundred savages attacked Arrowsick Island, near the mouth of the Kennebec, in what is now Georgetown, where was a fort. Sept. 10. The assault was unsuccessful, and, after slaughtering the cattle without the fort, and sacking and burning twenty-six houses, they withdrew to refresh themselves at Norridgewock. The House judged that a disingenuous use had been made of the alarm thus occasioned, and that the alleged necessity for countermanding the eastward movement of the troops was a subterfuge to evade the execution of their wishes; and they desired the Governor to send an express messenger to the commander, Colonel Walton, with orders to him "to appear forthwith before the House to give a reason wherefore the orders relating to the expedition had not

Displeasure of the House against the Governor's commanding officer. Nov 30.

[1] Mass. Prov. Rec.

been executed." The Governor said to the committee who brought him this vote, that it was expressed in such terms as forbade him to take notice of it. The House sent another message, inquiring whether he intended to relieve Walton, as they had desired. He told the House's committee that he should take his own time to answer this question. The House came to a vote, that this conduct of his "extremely discouraged them in projecting any schemes for the future carrying on of the war;" and, "with the greatest sincerity and concern for their country's good," they repeated their request for the recall of Colonel Walton. When a copy of this vote was offered to the Governor, he refused to receive it, and, as the committee reported to the House, "went his way;" and when another committee, consisting of the Speaker and some other dignified persons, was sent to him, he refused to admit them to his presence.

Dec. 1.

The House, as intent as ever on their main purpose, but finding that they were not prospering in this peremptory invasion of the Governor's military prerogative, approached him next with a vote "that his Excellency the Governor be desired to express Colonel Walton that he forthwith repair to Boston, and when he hath attended upon his Excellency that he would please to direct him to wait on this House, that they may examine him concerning his late conduct in prosecuting the war." The Governor, who was willing to be conciliated, the rather as he might suspect himself of some appearance of passion in the last transactions, sent for Walton, and informed the House that he had done so. They followed up their advantage by a vote to raise a committee, to consist of four Counsellors and seven Representatives, to have, in effect, the management of the war during the recess of the Court. This proposal was so extraordinary, that it was rejected by a unanimous vote of the Council.

Dec. 1.

Dec. 4.

Dec. 11.

The committee which the House had sent to the eastern camp returned. Agreeably to the request of the House, the Governor had forwarded to the commander an order for their respectful reception; but, in his recognition of their mission, he expressed his expectation "that they would lay first before him their report as Captain-General, and afterwards, upon the desire of the House of Representatives, it shall be laid before them." The committee, however, on their return, reported directly to the House. Being informed of this, the Governor sent to the House to ask for the original of his order, which was in the possession of the committee. The House, disinclined to part with what might be used as evidence against themselves, would take no step to reclaim it. The Governor then demanded it of the Chairman of the committee; but the Chairman said he was instructed by the House not to let it go out of his hands.

Nov. 17.

On Walton's arrival in Boston, the House desired the Governor to order him to appear immediately before them. The Governor replied, that, if his subordinate was to undergo any legislative examination, it must be before the whole Court, and not before one branch of it. The House then sent its messenger to Walton, to command his presence. He came, accordingly, but declared that he had nothing to say without the Governor's commands. The Governor ordered him to present himself before the whole Court, and sent a message to the Representatives, that, on his appearance in that position, they should have opportunity to interrogate him. The next day he informed them by another message that Walton was then before the Council, with his journal, and subject to any examination which the House might wish to institute.[1] But the Representatives declined

Dec. 19.

Dec. 22.

[1] Walton's journal is in the office of the Secretary of Massachusetts. (Hutch. MSS., II. 440.)

the invitation, and insisted on their privilege of taking cognizance, in their sole capacity, of the conduct of all persons in the public service and pay.

The Governor had, some time before, privately obtained
1720. July 4. permission to go to England, ostensibly "to settle some private affairs."[1] By this time all hope of a good understanding between him and the local authorities seemed to be at an end, at least until the questions which had arisen between them should be settled by an authority superior to both; and nothing could be more disagreeable to a person of his disposition than the social relations into which circumstances had brought him. Imparting his purpose only to two or three servants, he went on board of a man-of-war, which lay at Nantasket bound to the West Indies, intending to take another passage thence for England. But, while he was detained a few days by bad weather, a merchant-vessel came down from the town, in which he sailed direct for London.[2]

The Governor's departure from the Province. 1722. Dec. 27. 1723. Jan. 1.

In the year before Shute's departure from his govern-
1721. Sept. 8. ment, the Board of Trade made an elaborate report to the King, describing the condition of his several

[1] April 8 of this year Sir William Ashurst died. (Dummer's letter, in Mass. Hist. Col., XXI. 146.) In him the Colony lost a most discreet, faithful, and valuable friend.

[2] The treatment of Shute by the Province displeased Dummer, who wrote from London, April 23, 1721: "Colonel Shute is known at court and at the offices of state under the character of a very worthy gentleman, and one of a singular good temper, fitted to make any people happy that are under his command. When, therefore, they find the contrary in New England, they conclude from it that we would have no Governor at all from hence, but want to be independent of the crown. Now, though this be a strained and most injurious inference, yet they can't easily be persuaded out of it." (Hutch. Hist., II. 290, note.) The Reverend Mr. Neale wrote: "The cry of the city here [London] runs exceedingly against you, and they revive the story of 1641." (Ibid.) When Neale wrote, Shute was in London, making his complaints in all companies. This freedom of Dummer so displeased the House, that it voted to dismiss him from the agency. The Council non-concurred in this vote, but the House had its way by refusing to make him an allowance.

dependencies in America. As to the Province of Massachusetts, they represented that it had a militia force consisting of sixteen thousand men; that within its limits were about twelve hundred converted Indians; that, of "products proper for the consumption of Great Britain," it had "timber, turpentine, tar and pitch, masts, pipes, and hogshead staves, whale fins and oil, and some furs;" that it had a trade to "the foreign plantations in America, consisting chiefly in the exportation of horses to Surinam and to Martinico and the other French islands," whence came in return sugar, molasses, and rum, which was "a very great discouragement to the sugar-planters in the British islands;" that the people had "all sorts of common manufactures," spinning and weaving "their own wool into coarse cloths, druggets, and serges," besides making "homespun linen, which was generally half cotton;" but that "the branch of trade which was of the greatest importance to them, and which they were best enabled to carry on, was the building of ships, sloops, etc.;" that about a hundred and fifty vessels were built in a year, measuring six thousand tons; that most of these were built for sale abroad, but that there belonged to the Province "about a hundred and ninety sail, which might contain six thousand tons, and were navigated with about eleven hundred men, besides a hundred and fifty boats, with six hundred men, employed in the fisheries on their own coast." "The certain annual charge of the government was about eleven thousand pounds" over and above "what was applied for discharging their former debts."[1]

Condition of the Province.

[1] O'Callaghan, Documents, &c., V. 596, 599, 615, 627–629; comp. above, 397. — According to information which the historian Neale professed to have obtained from the King's custom-house, 24,000 tons of shipping cleared annually from Boston about the year 1719. He estimated the population of that town at 20,000. (Shurtleff, Description of Boston, 62, 63.) William Douglas, on the spot, reckoned it at no more than 12,000. (Summary, I. 530.)

Alleged turbulence of the charter governments.

The Board of Trade found that the Province "on all occasions affected too great an independence on the mother kingdom." They represented that "the charter governments would be more effectively restrained if they were all of them under his Majesty's immediate government, and were by proper laws compelled to follow the commands sent them by his Majesty;" and they recommended proceedings "to put the whole under the government of one Lord-Lieutenant, or Captain-General, from whom other Governors of particular Provinces should receive their orders in all cases for the King's service. By this means," they added, "a general contribution of men or money may be raised upon the several Colonies in proportion to their respective abilities." By projectors capable of conceiving a scheme like this, the counsellors of King George were disinclined to be guided in administering the Colonies of England; and the historian Chalmers thought them blameworthy for this want of confidence.[1]

[1] Revolt, &c., II. 4. — Horace Walpole anticipated Chalmers in thinking that his father was wrong in not giving to the Board of Trade more respect and confidence. "The Board of Trade, ... during Sir Robert Walpole's administration, had very faultily been suffered to lapse almost into a sinecure." (Memoirs of the Reign of King George the Second, I. 396.)

CHAPTER III.

The Lieutenant-Governor, William Dummer, was a native of New England, but he had been much out of the country, and had held office abroad. Though by no means an earnest New England patriot, he was a man of integrity, moderation, and good sense. In an unimpassioned way he had generally given his support to the Governor; and, when the House on that account forbore to make him the allowance heretofore never withheld from the person holding his position, he had not betrayed any impatient displeasure, though on one occasion he declined a grant of theirs which was so small that it might seem intended for an affront.[1]

[1] Dummer, appointed Lieutenant-Governor after the annual election in 1716, took his place immediately in the Council. The General Court elected him a Counsellor the next spring (May 30), and thenceforward year by year. His predecessor, Tailer, also sat in the Council by successive yearly elections, though he took his place (Oct. 17, 1711) before he was elected. Povey, from the time of his appointment in 1702, appeared at the Board irregularly, but it must have been in supposed virtue of his office as Lieutenant-Governor, for the Court never elected him. Lieutenant-Governor Stoughton was brought into the Council at the first election under the new charter, and so continued to his death.

When Dummer met the Council as Chief Magistrate, Sewall, the only survivor of the Counsellors who had been in the government under the first charter, addressed him as follows:—

"If your honor and the honorable Board please to give me leave, I would speak a word or two upon this solemn occasion. Although the unerring providence of God has brought your honor to the chair of government in a cloudy and tempestuous season, yet you have this for your encouragement, that the people you have to do with are a part of the Israel of God, and you may expect to have of the prudence and patience of Moses communicated to you for your conduct. It is evident that our Almighty Saviour counselled the first planters to remove hither and settle here, and they dutifully followed his advice, and therefore he will never leave nor forsake them nor theirs; so that your honor must needs be happy in sincerely seeking their

Intractableness of the Representatives. 1722. Dec. 28.

In their long strife with the Governor, the House had taken grounds which consistency obliged them to maintain, and their position of antagonism to the chief magistrate was not relinquished at Shute's departure. They appointed a committee, to be joined by a committee of the Council, to concert measures for the conduct of the war, which, not much more than threatened as yet, was thenceforward to be vigorously carried on. The Council refused to concur in the measure, continuing to regard it as an encroachment on the authority of the Commander-in-Chief. The House resolved that the war ought not to be proceeded in, till Colonel Walton and Major Moody, the commanders, should be removed. Yielding to the storm, those officers proposed to the Lieutenant-Governor to resign, on receiving the arrears of their pay. The House was indisposed to grant them even this justice, and insisted on their unconditional dismission. The Council not acquiescing in so harsh a measure, the House came to a Resolve, — of which they sent a copy, not to the Lieutenant-Governor, but to the Council, — that, unless they were gratified, they should have to discontinue their provision for part of the troops in the field. The Lieutenant-Governor reminded them that the disposal of the troops was a function of his

happiness and welfare, which your birth and education will incline you to do. *Difficilia quæ pulchra.* I promise myself that they who sit at this Board will yield their faithful advice to your honor, according to the duty of their place." He adds, in his record of this harangue: "The Lieutenant-Governor and Council would stand up all the while, and then expressed a handsome acceptance of what I had said. *Laus Deo!*" (Diary, for Jan. 2, 1723.)

"The Governor [Shute] mentioned how ill it would appear to have votes passed on December 25; but his Excellency need not have been present, nor have signed any bill that day. I said the dissenters came a great way for their liberties, and now the Church had theirs; yet they could not be contented, except they might tread all others down. The Governor said he was of the Church of England. I told Mr. Belcher of his letter to me. He answered, he thought he had been a dissenter then." (Ibid., for Dec. 21, 1722.) Perhaps Shute had been soured into Church-of-Englandism by his experiences in Massachusetts.

office only, rebuking, at the same time, the disrespectful manner of their communication. Upon this they withdrew their Resolve, but adhered to their purpose, not only of withholding the pay of the obnoxious officers, but of refusing to vote further supplies till they should be superseded.[1] The Lieutenant-Governor submitted to the mortification, which seemed unavoidable unless he could take the responsibility of leaving the Province undefended.

When he had appointed Thomas Westbrooke to be commander in Walton's place,[2] the House proceeded with alacrity in making arrangements for the prosecution of the war. What had helped to disarm the Governor was a practice which had grown up of making payments from the treasury on the authority of a vote of the House after services had been performed, even if the services had been directed by a previous vote;[3] whereas by the charter the warrant of the Governor, drawn with the advice and consent of the Council, was a sufficient voucher to the Treasurer. The practice which the House had succeeded in establishing afforded them the opportunity of passing judgment on the manner in which services directed by them had been executed; a judgment which was at the same time liable to be biassed by prejudice and passion, and to be expressed in offensive criticism of the conduct of the executive. Walton accordingly remained unpaid, because he had obeyed the Governor's orders in disregard of those of the Representatives.

The next House did not communicate to the Lieutenant-Governor its choice of a Speaker, and 1723. May.

1 Mass. Prov. Rec.

2 Westbrooke, as well as Walton, was a New Hampshire man, and both were members of the Council of that Province.

3 This method of proceeding had been inaugurated by the House of Representatives of 1721-1722. To prevent obstruction of their scheme through disallowances by the Privy Council, they made their conditional grants thenceforward in the form of Resolves, which did not, like Acts, come under the revision of the King's Ministers. (Mass. Prov. Laws, II. 219-222; comp. 574.)

he submitted to the omission. It claimed to be consulted respecting the management of the war and respecting any negotiation for peace. It proposed, but, as before, without gaining the assent of the Council, to raise a joint committee of war to act during the recess of the Court. The Lieutenant-Governor had hoped to engage the assistance of the Six Nations,[1] and more than sixty representatives of those tribes came to Boston for a conference. But nothing could be obtained from them beyond a permission to such of their warriors as might so incline to enter the English service. They said, truly enough, that the war in the eastern country was no affair of theirs. The occasion furnished the House with another topic of complaint. They found fault with the Lieutenant-Governor for affixing his private seal to a present made to the Indian delegation, and ordered that an impression of the Province seal should be substituted for it; and, when desired by the Council to withdraw the offensive vote, they not only did not consent to do so, but went on to resolve that the Lieutenant-Governor's proceeding had been an affront to them, and that they expected to be informed who it was that had ventured to advise it.[2] The Lieutenant-Governor contented himself with silence.

Aug. 21.

But the necessity of uniting all resources and energies for the common defence suspended domestic faction. It would be unprofitable to attempt to relate in detail the miseries which followed. Indian warfare was always the same. The long frontier could not fail to lie exposed to brutal savages, who issued from their woods at their own choice of season, weather, and hour, and with a good knowledge of the doomed English homes where they had received hospitality, and of the refuges to which they might make their cowardly retreat as soon as

Renewal of Indian hostilities.

[1] The accession of the Tuscarora fugitives from South Carolina had lately brought the confederated Iroquois nations to that number.

[2] Mass. Prov. Rec.

their work of havoc and butchery was done. There could be no quiet sleep in a border settlement, unless it was at the same time a garrison. The wretchedness of constant apprehension was universal, when no one could guess better than another where the next sudden blow would be struck. And to whatsoever place the remorseless enemy did come in sufficient strength, that place was sure to be ravaged with fire and sword, and its inhabitants to share among them the woes of captivity, widowhood, orphanage, and death in all its forms of agony. Father Rasle sat in his chapelry at Norridgewock, and, himself directed by his ecclesiastical and lay superiors at Quebec, kept the tribes in motion against the villages of Massachusetts.[1]

The St. François Indians came down from the banks of the St. Lawrence. The Penobscot Indians moved westward towards the English settlements. The Indians further east undertook to deal with the Massachusetts fishermen resorting to Nova Scotia. One of Dummer's first acts had been to despatch Westbrooke to the Penobscot with two hundred and thirty men. He went up the river to an Indian fort, believed to have been at what is now Oldtown, above Bangor. Within the fort, which was now deserted, was a "chapel, in compass sixty feet by thirty, handsomely and well finished, both within and on the outside. A little further south was the dwelling-house of the priest, which was very commodious." The troops burned the buildings and withdrew. Another expedition, directed against Norridgewock, had less success. The winter had been warm, and copious rains had so saturated the land that the march was difficult. There was an epidemic sickness in the camp; and under these discouragements the undertaking had to be abandoned.

February.

March.

February.

[1] Specimens of Rasle's exulting representations of his exploits are in Mass. Hist. Col., XVIII. 245, 266. The former is a letter written on the day of his death.

With the advancing season, the war moved westward. April-August. Murders were perpetrated successively at Falmouth, Berwick, Wells, York, Scarborough, Saco, and Dover, and at the distant western village of Aug. 13. Oct. 11. Northfield, which in the summer and autumn was twice attacked, with a loss, however, in the two invasions, of only six or seven men. Sixty Indians made an unsuccessful attempt upon a little English fortifi- Dec. 25. cation at Muscongus, on the St. George. Captain Moulton was sent in search of Rasle to Norridgewock. He reached the place, but found it deserted. He brought away some books and papers, but, willing perhaps at the unfavorable season to avoid provoking a vigorous muster of the enemy, he left the buildings unharmed.[1]

In the early part of the following year there was little to diversify the familiar record of depredations on 1724. exposed outposts. In the settlements of Maine, during the spring, more than thirty persons were killed, badly wounded, or carried into captivity; and at this time, as well as during the following summer, some murders were committed about the villages on the Merrimack and the Connecticut. Fort Dummer, in what is now Brattleborough, Vermont, was built this year, at a point more northerly than had hitherto been occupied on Connecticut River. Captain Josiah Winslow, a young man only three years out of college, grandson of Josiah, and great-grandson of Edward, Governors of Plymouth, was in command of the fort on the St. George. He was attacked May 1. while outside of the walls with thirteen of his company, and every one of them was killed. The Indians seized and manned several fishing-vessels, with which they cruised with some success, killing, it is said, more than twenty men employed in the coasters, and making prison-

[1] Penhallow, 96–99; Niles, in Mass. Hist. Col., XXXV. 345–348; Williamson, II. 120–124.

ers of a larger number. They committed depre- May 16.
dations at Kingston and Chester. At Dover they June 2.
killed the children of a Quaker family, and carried
away the older persons, while the head of the house- Aug. 26.
hold was attending a meeting for worship. At Oxford some of them attempted to enter a house where a woman
was alone; but she was provided with two mus- Aug. 3.
kets and two pistols; she shot one of the assailants, and the rest hastily made off.[1]

The nuisance was intolerable. It had to be abated at its source. From Fort Richmond, on the lower waters of the Kennebec, two hundred men, under Captain Moulton and Captain Harman, were despatched to Norridgewock. Leaving their boats on the river, at the distance of one or two days' march below that place, they came near to it without being observed. As it was the middle of the day, and it was thought that some of the Indians might be in their cornfields, the troops were distributed into two parties, one to proceed directly into the village, the other to intercept such as should attempt to return. Moulton, who led the former party, saw no one stirring as he entered the hamlet at about three hours after noon. The men, who marched in silence, were already among the wigwams when an Indian came out of one of them and gave the alarm. The old men, women, and children fled. The warriors, sixty in number, tried to make a stand. The English, according to their orders, held their fire till the Indians had discharged their guns in a hurried and harmless volley. The English then fired with fatal effect. After a second discharge of their pieces, the Indians fled to the river, which was there about sixty feet wide, and at the time some six feet deep. After shooting some fugitives, as they paddled or swam across, the English returned to

Expedition to Norridgewock.

Aug. 12.

[1] Penhallow, 99–104; Niles, in Mass. Hist. Col., XXXV. 348–352.

the town. Orders had been given to spare Rasle, but a lieutenant burst in the door of his wigwam, and shot him dead. He said, for his justification, that Rasle came on loading and firing, and refused to accept quarter. Harman declared, under oath, that during the action the priest stabbed and shot an English boy, who had been brought to him as a prisoner.

An Indian village afforded but little plunder. The plate of the chapel was brought away, and those *properties* which were not worth transportation were destroyed. Harman's detachment came in, having found little service to do, and the party remained together that night. The next morning twenty-seven dead bodies of the enemy were counted, including that of Rasle. Bomazeen and Mogg, chiefs who had been of importance in the recent movements, were among them. When the return march had been begun, a friendly Indian was sent back to set fire to the church and the village. After an absence of only four days, the party, having suffered no loss, came back to Fort Richmond.[1] The pernicious Popish mission

[1] Francis, Life of Sebastian Rasle, in Sparks's American Biography, XVII. 309–320; Penhallow, 104–106; Niles, in Mass. Hist. Col., XXXV. 352, 353; Lettres Edifiantes, XVII. 327; New England Courant, for Aug. 24, 1724. Hutch., II. 311–314, repeats the account given by Harman in writing, and by Morton orally. — Rasle had been "slain in fight, making actual resistance, at the same time attempting to kill an English captive in his hands, and refusing to give or take quarter, to which account . . . . . Colonel Harman made solemn oath before me in council." (Letter of Lieutenant-Governor Dummer to the Lords of Trade, of March 31, 1725, in British Colonial Papers.) The Jesuit had "marched at the head of two hundred armed savages through one of the frontier towns of the Province before the war was declared." (Ibid.)

Rasle, at his death, was nearly seventy years old. He had been thirty years a missionary, twenty-six of which he passed at Norridgewock. His death was a great relief to the border settlements. Men of this century, not in danger from the tomahawk which his zeal lifted against the wives and children of a hundred and fifty years ago, can afford to be just to his good qualities, such as they were, and to be sentimental over his grave. It is not worth while to question that he obeyed his conscience; but not the less, if his conscience dictated brutal butchery, humanity required its instructions to be silenced. Fifty years ago, on

was not renewed, and we read scarcely any thing more of the Norridgewocks in the history of the tribes.

The story of this transaction has been told here as it is related in the English records of the time. The extravagant statement in the narrative of Father Charlevoix, that the invading force consisted of eleven hundred men, prepares the reader for the exaggerated and dramatic character of the rest of his recital. According to that account, the approach of the English was first made known by "a general discharge of their muskets, by which all the wigwams were pierced. There were then only fifty warriors in the village. . . . . . Father Rasle, informed by the shouts and tumult of the danger of his converts, went boldly to present himself to the assailants, in hopes to draw their attention upon himself, and so to protect his flock at the peril of his own life. His hope was not vain. No sooner was he seen than the English uttered a loud cry, followed by a volley of musketry. He fell dead near a cross which he had set up in the middle of the village. Seven Indians who were with him, and who wished to make a rampart for him with their bodies, were killed by his side. . . . . . The English, seeing no more show of resistance, fell to plundering and burning the cabins, not sparing the church, which they set on fire, after having desecrated the sacred vessels and the adorable body of Jesus Christ. They then withdrew with a precipitancy like flight, as if they had been smitten with a panic terror. The Indians immediately returned to their village, where their first care, while the women were looking for herbs and plants for the cure of the wounded, was to weep over the body of their holy missionary. They found it

the anniversary of the fatal day, a monument was erected over his grave, with appropriate solemnities, in which Catholics and Protestants took part, in the presence of delegations from the Indian remains of Penobscot, Passamaquoddy, and Canada. It is of stone, surmounted with an iron cross, and bears, on the face fronting the river, a Latin monumental inscription.

pierced with a thousand wounds, the scalp torn off, the skull broken by hatchets, and the mouth and eyes filled with mud, the legs broken, and all the members mutilated a hundred ways."[1]

As winter approached, which was the season of the most frequent devastations, Colonel Westbrooke, with three hundred men, scoured the country between the Kennebec and the Penobscot, meeting with no obstruction. An attempt was made to arrange affairs through the French Governor at Quebec. The General Court sent to him a commission of three persons to threaten that, if he did not discontinue his intrigues in Maine, his countrymen in Nova Scotia should pay the forfeit. He pretended ignorance of what had been going on, till his letters to Rasle, taken at Norridgewock, were produced. Whatever prisoners were held by the Indians, he said, were in no way subject to his disposal, but he agreed to a ransom for some sixteen persons who were in the hands of the French.[2]

To engage volunteers, the government had been in the habit, through these wars, of paying a bounty for Indian enemies killed or made captive. At this time the bounty for the scalp, which was the evidence of an Indian slain, was as high as a hundred pounds. One of the enterprising partisans whom patriotism or a less elevated motive enlisted was John Lovewell of Dunstable, on Merrimack River, son of a soldier of Cromwell, who emigrated to that place, and who was said to have reached the age of a hundred and twenty, when he died there. John Lovewell came to Boston for his money with a prisoner and a scalp, brought as far as from the region of the White Mountains. Trying his fortune again, he came with his party upon ten Indians asleep round a fire, by a solitary pond in what is now Fryeburg,

1725. Jan. 5.

Adventures of rangers.

[1] Charlevoix, II. 382-384.

[2] Niles, in Mass. Hist. Col., XXXV. 255; Williamson, II. 133; Penhallow, 108, 109.

next to Conway, sixty miles above Dover. His men killed them all, and their scalps too were brought to the Treasurer at Boston. Lovewell trusted too much to the facilities of his hunting-ground. The enemy, too, was good at ambuscades. On a third expedition, in which he was accompanied by forty-six men, he reached the scene of his recent good fortune, where, in a "small fortification," which he halted a day or two to build, he left his surgeon, a sergeant, and seven men in charge of supplies for future need, and of three of the party who had fallen sick or lame, thus reducing the effective force to thirty-four. The following day, "while they were at prayers, very early in the morning, they heard a gun, and some time after spied an Indian on a point that ran into Saco Pond. They now concluded that the design of the gun, and of the Indian's discovering himself, was to draw them that way; and, expecting without fail to be attacked, it was now proposed, whether it were prudent to venture an engagement with the enemy, who they perceived were now sufficiently alarmed, or endeavor a speedy retreat. The men generally and boldly answered, 'We came out to meet the enemy; we have all along prayed God we might find 'em; and we had rather trust Providence with our lives, yea, die for our country, than try to return without seeing them, if we may, and be called cowards for our pains.'"[1]

March 9.

Lovewell's fight. May 7.

Proceeding accordingly, they fell into an ambuscade, and a murderous conflict ensued, with fearful odds on the side of the savages. Lovewell and an ensign, a sergeant, and six men were killed, and two lieutenants and another man wounded, at the first onset, — twelve men out of thirty-four. The survivors fell back to secure a more favorable position, and the conflict was continued, with intervals, till sunset, when the Indians drew off, without having

[1] Symmes, Historical Memoirs of the Late Fight at Piggwacket, with a Sermon occasioned by the fall of the brave Captain Lovewell, &c., v.

scalped the dead. Ensign Wyman had commanded through the day, after the fall of his superiors. At its close he found that only nine remained unwounded. At midnight they began their retreat, helping on their suffering companions as best they could. Three were left on the ground, in a condition making it impossible for them to be removed, one of them begging it as a last favor to have his gun loaded again, to be discharged should the Indians return before he died. A lieutenant and the chaplain, a recent graduate of Harvard College, gave out by the way; and, unwilling to retard the march of their companions, begged to be left to perish in the woods. The remnant dispersed, and by-and-bye, after great suffering, came into the settlements separately, or by two and three. One of the men, miserably wounded, crept to Wyman, and begged to be only helped to the shore of the pond, where his body might be hidden and secure against the scalping-knife. He, however, recovered strength to roll himself into a canoe, which the wind and water wafted on till they brought him unconscious to a place of safety. His name was Kiss, and he lived to command a company in the next war. The little lake which was the scene of the action is now called Lovell's Pond, and the name of the town in which it lies commemorates the valiant chaplain.[1]

[1] Penhallow, 107; Niles, in Mass. Hist. Col., XXXV. 255–360; Davies, Address on the Centennial Celebration; Bouton's "Lovewell's Great Fight;" Symmes, Historical Memoirs of the Late Fight at Piggwacket; Kidder, Expeditions of Captain John Lovewell, &c. (The two last tracts contain lists of the names of the men engaged in the action of May 8.) Williamson, II. 135; N. H. Provincial Papers, IV. 168, 169; Fox, History of the old Township of Dunstable, 111–131; Farmer and Moore, N. H. Hist. Col., I. 25–36, III. 64, &c., 94, &c.

Lovewell's Fight was in its day as famous as Chevy Chase, and, like it, was the subject of a ballad, which continued to be familiar to our fathers to the end of our Colonial history. A few stanzas may serve for a taste of its quality: —

"Of worthy Captain Lovewell I purpose now to sing,
How valiantly he served his country and his king;
He and his valiant soldiers did range the woods full wide,
And hardships they enduréd, to quell the Indians' pride.

'T was nigh unto Pigwacket, on the eighth day of May,
They spied a rebel Indian soon after break of day;

The irresolute red men had again become tired of the war, and the death of Rasle had relieved them from the mischievous French influence. The Penobscots, who had always been the most tractable of the eastern tribes, professed friendly dispositions. They sent a delegation to St. George's River, where they were met by other Indians and by commissioners from Boston; an agreement was made for a time with a view to further negotiations; and some Penobscot chiefs came to Boston, where, in the Council chamber, they ratified this compact with the Lieutenant-Governor. A treaty of peace was consequently arranged in Boston, which was put into shape under the title of a

July 2.

July 28-31.

Nov. 16.

Dec. 15.

He on a bank was walking, upon a neck of land
Which leads into a pond, as we're made to understand.

Our men resolved to have him, and travelled two miles round,
Until they met the Indian, who boldly stood his ground;
Then speaks up Captain Lovewell: 'Take you good heed,' says he;
'This rogue is to decoy us, I very plainly see.'

. . . .

Then spoke up Captain Lovewell, when first the fight began,
'Fight on, my valiant heroes, you see they fall like rain!'
For, as we are informèd, the Indians were so thick,
A man could scarcely fire a gun, and not some of them hit.

. . . .

Our worthy Captain Lovewell among them there did die;
They killed Lieutenant Robbins, and wounded good young Frye,
Who was our English chaplain: he many Indians slew,
And some of them he scalpèd, when bullets round him flew.

Young Fullam, too, I'll mention, because he fought so well, —
Endeavoring to save a man, a sacrifice he fell;
But yet our valiant Englishmen in fight were ne'er dismayed,
But still they kept their motion, and Wyman captain made,

Who shot the old chief Paugus, which did the foe defeat,
Then set his men in order, and brought off the retreat;
And, braving many dangers and hardships in the way,
They safe arrivèd at Dunstable, the thirteenth day of May."

The chaplain was specially lamented, as thus, in the exordium to a long copy of verses, ascribed to his betrothed bride:—

"Assist, ye Muses, help my quill,
While floods of tears does down distil,
Not from mine eyes alone, but all
That hears the sad and doleful fall
Of that young student, Mr. Frye,
Who in his blooming youth did die."

Another ballad on the same subject, of more recent composition, concludes as follows:—

"Ah! many a wife shall rend her hair,
And many a child cry, 'Woe is me!'
When messengers the news shall bear
Of Lovewell's dear-bought victory.

With footsteps slow shall travellers go,
Where Lovewell's pond shines clear and bright,
And mark the place where those are laid
Who fell in Lovewell's bloody fight.

Old men shall shake their heads, and say,
'Sad was the hour and terrible,
When Lovewell brave 'gainst Paugus went,
With fifty men from Dunstable.'"

"Submission and Agreement of the Delegates of the Eastern Indians, namely, the Penobscot, Norridgewock, St. John, Cape Sables, and other tribes inhabiting within his Majesty's Territories of New England and Nova Scotia."[1]

Probably some doubt was entertained as to the authority of the Indian delegates to bind all these tribes. In the following summer the chief magistrates of Massachusetts and of New Hampshire came to Falmouth to obtain a ratification with circumstances of due solemnity. The chiefs who appeared proposed the transfer of the conference to Pemaquid. But to this the Governors would not consent; and at length a ratification was obtained, as sufficient as the circumstances admitted. It does not appear that any representatives of the Norridgewock tribe, or indeed of any tribe except the Penobscot, were parties to it.[2] The treaty now made accomplished its object better than earlier pacifications, not so much by virtue of any more binding character in its pledges, or of any new provisions, as because the French influence was for the present in great part suspended, and because the prudence of Lieutenant-Governor Dummer provided for the judicious management of the trading-houses, which he had engaged to keep up among the natives, and which, when well conducted, gave them important accommodation for their purchases and sales.[3] Till, after nearly twenty years, war again broke out between England and France, New England was little disturbed by Indian disorders.[4]

1726. July 16. Peace with the Indians. Aug. 6.

[1] Niles, in Mass. Hist. Col., XXXV. 360-364; Penhallow, 117-127.

[2] Ibid., 129, 132.

[3] Colman, Memoirs, &c., in Mass. Hist. Col., VI. 109. This little tract relates incidents occurring within the year after the treaty of Falmouth, showing the good management of Dummer, and the continued danger from French intrigues.

[4] In July, 1738, Governor Belcher held a *talk* with some representatives of the remnants of the Penobscot and Norridgewock tribes. "Governor: 'You must take care of one another,

Two hundred Englishmen are believed to have been killed or carried off by the Indians during the four years of this war. The cost of it has been estimated at two hundred and forty thousand pounds.[1] This large expense increased the long-existing financial difficulties, and renewed one chief occasion of dispute between the Chief Magistrate and the Representatives. A bill for the issue of notes of credit to the amount of fifty thousand pounds obtained the reluctant concurrence of the Council. The Lieutenant-Governor laid before the Council the King's instruction to approve no such bill. They agreed with him that his approval must be withheld, and the measure fell through accordingly. The House used its power and manifested its displeasure by forbearing to make grants for salaries; and the Lieutenant-Governor complained that he was left without a maintenance, because he declined to violate his instructions.

Financial arrangements.

The prohibition, however, made an exception for such sums as were wanted "for defraying the necessary charges of government," and for this clause a singular interpretation was proposed. To defray the annual necessary charges of government, the sum of twenty-four hundred pounds was necessary, — the interest, at four per cent, of sixty thousand pounds. It was urged, accordingly, upon the Lieutenant-Governor, that he would not violate his instructions if he consented to the issuing and lending of that sum in order to secure an income from the loan to pay for carrying on the government. He proposed the question to the Council, who declined to give advice, but expressed their judgment that, if the Lieutenant-Governor should find it consistent with his obligations to give his assent, it would be

1727. Feb. 17.

Feb. 19.

and see that you don't get drunk, for the English despise you when you get drunk.' Indians: 'We desire two quarts of wine and some cider at every meal, and three drams a day.'" (British Colonial Papers; comp. Williamson, History, II. 200.)

[1] Penhallow, 128; Niles, in Mass. Hist. Col., XXXV. 365; Williamson, II. 151.

"for the good and welfare of the Province." He signed the bill, and immediately the usual allowances were voted by the House.[1]

The Representatives were disposed to enlarge their power by encroachment on the prerogatives of the Council, as well as of the King's representative. While for purposes of legislation the two Houses, much unequal in numbers, acted separately and concurrently, each equal in power to the other, it had been their practice, in the election of civil officers, to vote in a convention, in which a Counsellor's suffrage counted for no more than that of a Representative. The Representatives were for extending this abnormal jurisdiction so as to embrace judicial action, and voted "that, when a hearing shall be had on any private cause before both Houses together, the subject-matter shall be determined by both Houses conjunctly." The Council unanimously refused its concurrence in this action.[2]

Meanwhile, Shute was in England, in no good humor with Massachusetts. When time enough had passed after

1723. Aug. 22. his arrival to give opportunity for consultation with his friends, he submitted to the King a memorial, with a formal complaint of the misconduct of the House of Representatives in the following particulars:

Shute's complaints in England.

namely, in respect to the ship-timber belonging to the King; to their claim to choose a Speaker, and to adjourn themselves without obtaining the Governor's consent; to their appointment of Fast days and Thanksgiving days; to their interferences with the care of the castle, the disposal of officers, and arrangements of the eastern war, represented as being so many usurpations of the Governor's rights, as commander-in-chief of the military force; to their persistence in crippling him as to his maintenance, and delaying their grants to him till he had met their wishes as to giving his signature to their

[1] Council Records. [2] Ibid.

bills; and, in short, to their perpetual invasions of "the few prerogatives that had been reserved by the crown." "The House of Representatives," he wrote, "are in a manner the whole legislative, and in a good measure the executive power of the Province. . . . . The greatest part of them are of small fortunes and mean education, men of the best sense and circumstances generally residing at or near Boston. . . . . Were it not for this Act,[1] the Assembly would certainly consist of men of much better sense, temper, and fortunes than they do at present," though even the people of Boston, he had to add, "supposed to contain about eighteen thousand inhabitants," were "too much disposed to a levelling spirit, too apt to be mutinous and disorderly."[2]

On being informed of these complaints by their agent, the House passed a vote appropriating a hundred pounds for the employment of counsel to make a defence. But

[1] The reference is to the Act of Nov. 28, 1693, requiring the Representatives of towns to be residents therein. (See above, p. 143.)

[2] British Colonial Papers; comp. Journal of the Board of Trade, for August 22.

A letter of four closely written pages, written from Boston, May 16, 1723, by one Thomas More to Lord Carteret, is preserved in the collection of British Colonial Papers. Its style puts the reader on his guard against receiving its statements without large qualification. But a few periods, as a specimen, will be found entertaining, at least. "I have," says the writer, "heard more treason here in one day than in all my life before, such as 'his Majesty has no business in this country; he is our nominal King, but has not one foot of ground among us; neither he or his Deputies or Governors have any thing to do here; the country is ours, not his.' While their frenzies run so high as to deny his Majesty's right here, what wonder his Governor is called blockhead, and has dead dogs and cats thrown into his coach, as to all which I refer you to Colonel Shute, our Governor, now at London. . . . . My Lord, sure the ship of this government has sprung so many leaks, your Lordship, as a master carpenter, ought to stop them, and I, as your mate, have made good plugs for you to drive in, not doubting but his Majesty, as captain of the ship, will be well pleased to have her tighted." [More was sent out with his Lordship's "passport, given me last summer to discover all things new and strange in his Majesty's Plantations of America."] "As I have been sworn at Highgate not to court the maid while I was welcome to the mistress, so I address to the head, leaving underling addresses to creeping spirits and designers that smell of the earth."

the Council, itself dissatisfied with many of those proceedings of the Representatives which were complained of, unanimously refused to assent to this measure. An answer to the complaints and an Address to the King were then prepared by the House; and, though the Council thought both of them ill-considered and imprudent, and again refused to concur, the House ordered that they should be transmitted to the agent. The House proceeded to resolve that, "in consequence of Governor Shute's memorial to his Majesty, it was their duty as well as interest to send some suitable person or persons from hence to use the best method that may be to defend the constitution and charter privileges." The Council proposed to substitute a vote intrusting the business to Jeremiah Dummer, who two years before had published his "Defence of the Charters."[1] An agreement was finally made for Mr.
1724. Jan. 18. Cooke to be joined with Mr. Dummer in the agency in England, and he sailed without delay. His arrival there stimulated the Governor to new activity.
March 5. In a second memorial, he complained of the House of Representatives for objecting to payments legally made by the Governor and Council; for refusing necessary supplies to the treasury; and for extending to the custody of the castle their usurping pretensions to the disposal of the militia. He represented various misdeeds of the House since his departure, — that they had affronted the Lieutenant-Governor by interfering with his right to command the troops, and to use what seal he pleased in transactions with the Indians; that Mr. Cooke, whom they had chosen to be their agent, was disaffected to the crown, and had been at the head of the factious movements; that the House had made no grant for his

[1] Council Records. — In the same year in which Dummer published that important work, his advocacy of Shute had so lost him the favor of the Representatives, that they voted to dismiss him from the agency; and, that measure failing for want of the concurrence of the Council, they for a while refused to make him compensation.

[o]wn pay since he left the Province; that they had "been [a]ll along endeavoring to intimidate the Council, and to [w]eaken the credit of the Council with the people;" and [th]at, in short, they steadily pursued their policy of aggran[di]zement and usurpation. The House of Representatives, [h]e said, had "in a manner got the whole legislative and [e]xecutive power into their own hands," obtained the con[tr]ol of the military force, and "overborne the Council, to [th]e giving up the only remaining security of the few and [u]ndoubted prerogatives of the crown."[1] He refused so [m]uch as to see Mr. Cooke, and Dummer's persistence in [th]e endeavor to bring them together had even the effect [o]f alienating his associate from himself. Cooke presented [a] memorial to the Duke of Newcastle, praying for [a] postponement of action on Shute's complaint till [h]e should have time to obtain further instructions from [h]ome.[2]

April 11.

[1] John Colman, of Boston, who [w]as in London at the time, wrote [(]May 18, 1724) a very interesting [ac]count of the hearing of Shute and [C]ooke before the Privy Council. [(]Mass. Hist. Col., II. 32.) Colman [w]as much alarmed by the appear[a]nce of things, and thought the [ch]arter would be vacated.

[2] British Colonial Papers; comp. [J]ournal of the Board of Trade, for [M]arch 10; April 28.

This year a dispute of long stand[in]g with the Quakers was brought [t]o an issue. It had existed, break[in]g out at intervals, as far back as [th]e second year of Queen Anne, [w]hen the Quakers complained "that [i]n New England there were some [s]evere laws of a long standing not [r]epealed, though not of late rigor[o]usly put in execution against per[s]ons of their character;" and "sev[e]ral of the other three denominations [o]f dissenters" wrote to their New Eng[l]and friends on the subject. (Calamy, [A]dditions, &c., to Baxter's Life, I. 670. — Oct. 11, 1705, the Queen in Council annulled a Connecticut law, "entituled Heretics" (comp. Conn. Col. Rec., IV. 546), in which Quakers are especially referred to. In Dudley's controversy with the General Court in 1706, he was placed at disadvantage by the representations of the English Quakers to the home government of wrong done to their friends under his rule. October 2 of that year, Campbell, editor of the "News-Letter," wrote to the Lords of Trade, excusing himself for having published a statement that the Quakers had complained of ill-treatment in Massachusetts, and communicating a letter from the London Quakers to the English Independent ministers, and a warning, occasioned by it, addressed by the latter to President Mather. (British Colonial Papers; comp. Journal of the Board of Trade, for Jan. 22, 1706, and Feb. 28, 1707.) The same day Dudley, who had no tenderness for the Quakers (see above, p. 355), wrote: "There

It may well be doubted whether any advantageous effect would have followed on such a zealous joint action of the

is no law in being that reflects upon the Quakers, or is grievous, saving the military laws, which demand fines for want of service," and this "has been used as moderately as I can bring to pass. . . . . . I pray your Lordships that I may not be a sacrifice to Connecticut and Rhode Island." (British Colonial Papers.) Campbell's apology was occasioned by a complaint made to the Lords, Jan. 22, 1706, that in "a 'News-Letter' published at Boston, 29th October last, there are some reflections against the proceedings of the Quakers here." (Journal of the Board of Trade.) Toleration of the Quakers had by this time made such progress that in 1706 they had a meeting-house in Boston. (Mass. Hist. Col., III. 260.) The disallowance and repeal by the Privy Council (Oct. 11, 1705) of the law banishing them from Connecticut, "I took," wrote Sir Henry Ashurst, "to be a very extraordinary order, considering you were in possession of your own charter; but the hand of Joab is in it; I mean D. [Dudley]." (Conn. Col. Rec., IV. 546.)

May 26, 1719, the Privy Council referred to the Lords of Trade a "petition of Walter Newberry, William Wilkinson, and Richard Partridge, of New England, in behalf of themselves and their suffering friends, the people called Quakers in Massachusetts Bay, setting forth the great hardships they suffer by not paying the demands of the priests there, and praying that, in regard the charter granted by William and Mary allows a free exercise and liberty of conscience to all subjects that should settle there except papists, that his Majesty will commiserate their case, and direct the Governor of said Province to relieve them herein." (Register of the Privy Council.) But for the present the movement seems to have been fruitless of consequences. The next year (July 21, 1720) certain Quakers of Massachusetts represented to the General Court "that the said people for years past had suffered the distraint and loss of their goods for the support of the Presbyterian or Independent ministers, and also for the building of their meeting-houses, and that too often with much extortion." (Comp. the Act of May 28, 1718, in Mass. Prov. Laws, II. 99; also, the letter of Samuel Danforth, of Taunton, of Aug. 8, 1720, in Mass. Hist. Col., XXXI. 255.) Two years later the General Court voted to establish Congregational ministers at Dartmouth and Tiverton, where the Quaker interest prevailed, and, in assessing the taxes on those towns, imposed an additional amount for the support of the ministers. Here began a stubborn contest. The towns, having Quaker selectmen, refused to collect the additional tax from their inhabitants; the General Court persisted, and the town officers who had refused to collect the assessment were prosecuted and sent to prison. Oct. 22, 1723, a petition in their behalf came before the King's Privy Council, which, after argument by counsel for the towns and for the Province at length (June 2, 1724), decreed that the taxes in question must be remitted, and the delinquent assessors released. (Mass. Prov. Laws, II. 269–277; Register of the Privy Council, for Oct. 22, 24, 1723, Jan. 14, 22, May 12, 15, 21, and June 2, 1724; Journal of the Board of Trade, for Nov. 14, 20, Dec. 12, 19, 1723, March 10, and April 1, 28, 30, 1724.) From this time Quakerism in Massachusetts was unmolested and insignificant.

agents of Massachusetts as was at all events prevented by their private jealousies. On a report of the law officers of the crown,[1] to whom, at Cooke's request, a reply to Shute which had reached the agent from Massachusetts, and a memorial of his own, founded upon it, had been referred, the House was condemned by the Privy Council as to all the points in issue. The Council represented to the King that Shute had "acted with great zeal 1725. and fidelity," and had "made good his charge of May 29. invading and encroaching upon your Majesty's prerogative. . . . . . The conduct of the said House of Representatives tends greatly to weaken the subordination and dependence of this Colony upon the crown of Great Britain, and may be of evil example in other Plantations." Therefore "all proper legal measures should be taken to assert your Majesty's royal authority and prosecute all such as have contemned the same, unless a due obedience be paid to your Majesty for the future."[2] The agents were accordingly charged to stop the irregularities of their constituents in respect to encroachments on the forests and on the em-

[1] The Attorney-General and Solicitor-General reported that Shute's charge against the Representatives of invading the King's right in the matter of the woods was well sustained; that the right of the Governor to interfere in the choice of a Speaker was an open question, the Speaker not being an officer of the General Court, but of the House, and that accordingly the action of the House on that subject could not be construed into a contempt, though, on the other hand, Shute's conduct had not been blamable; and that there were precedents for the appointment by the House of a day of fasting, but that it had no right to issue a proclamation to that effect.

[2] Register of the Privy Council, for March 3, April 30, May 4, 29, 1725. — The question of a royal charter for the College had not yet been lost sight of. Nov. 15, 1725, Henry Newman, of counsel for the Province, wrote to Delafaye, Secretary of the Privy Council: "If the government here should think fit to grant them [Harvard College] a royal charter now, I am persuaded they would thankfully accept it, and it would be a means to attach the students there to the King's interest, who, even now that they are dependent upon the orders of the Assembly, have dared to dedicate their theses to the Governor in his absence, as a mark of respect to the King's representative, and to pray for him publicly, while others are afraid of showing him so small a respect, for fear of incurring the displeasure of the mighty Lower House." (Proceedings of Mass. Hist. Soc. for 1868, 350.)

ployment of the troops. But no further formal measure of repression was adopted, except the recommendation to the King to grant what was called an Explanatory Charter, in which the necessity of the Governor's consent in the choice of a Speaker for the House, and in its adjourning itself for more than two days, was expressly affirmed.[1]

Explanatory Charter.

That the advantage was not pursued in an attempt to vacate the charter in the courts may occasion surprise.[2] Perhaps the Ministry thought that the pear was surely

[1] Dec. 9, 1724, "the several petitioners, shipwrights, attending their Lordships, had some discourse with them, who said that since the late war the number of workmen was reduced to half; that there were not at present a thousand men employed in building or repairing ships for the use of the merchants; that great numbers were gone to Muscovy, Sweden, or the Plantations; that in eight years, ending 1720, they were informed there were seven hundred sail of ships built in New England, and in the years since as many, if not more; that this New England trade had drawn over so many working shipwrights that there are not enough left here to carry on the work; that there were now twelve ships building in the Thames for the Greenland trade, but they were obliged to ask a longer time for want of men. Resolved to consider further thereof at another opportunity."

1725, Jan. 21, "the shipwrights attending, as desired, their Lordships, after some discourse with them, desired they would inform the Board what proposals they had to make to prevent the inconveniences complained of in their petition. To which they answered that, if the ships built in the Plantations were confined to trade only from one Plantation to another, or to Great Britain, it would answer the end proposed; or, if they were allowed to trade to foreign parts, that then they should be obliged to pay a duty of 5*d.* per ton each voyage they should make, and that they should also be restrained as to the bigness of such ships or vessels as should be built in the Plantations. (Journal of the Board of Trade.) — April 6, 1724, Governor Wentworth of New Hampshire wrote to the Lords of Trade: "In Massachusetts a ship is building of a thousand tons, to mount seventy guns. I suppose she is designed to carry timber and plank to Lisbon or Cadiz." (British Colonial Papers.)

[2] Samuel Vetch pleased himself with the hope of succeeding to Shute's place. June 22, 1724, he wrote to the Duke of Newcastle that, since it was not to be expected that Shute, in the unpopularity which he had incurred in Massachusetts, should be sent back to that government, he hoped that his own claims would be considered. He reminded the Minister that he had planned the expedition against Canada in 1708; that in 1710 he had been made Governor of Port Royal, the conquest of which he claimed to have been his own achievement; and that he had "continued to serve all the war till after the treaty of Utrecht." (British Colonial Papers.)

maturing, but was not yet quite ripe. Should the Explanatory Charter be rejected, should the plunder of the masts and the interference with the control of the troops be continued after this warning, each of which results might seem extremely probable from the past contumacy of the provincial authorities, a clearer case would be made against them, and a legal process, or a proceeding in Parliament, which was threatened, would be facilitated.[1] On the other hand, should the Province yield without further struggle the other points now contested, this would be an augury of more quiet and submission on its part for the future. The House seems to have become convinced that for the present it had gone as far in opposition as prudence would allow, and in concurrence with the Council it voted to accept the Explanatory Charter, though not till after a warm debate. Dummer informed the Duke of Newcastle how "dutifully" the House had in this instance behaved.[2] It may be believed that for some friends the measure was indebted to its provisions implying a waiver and condonation of some causes of complaint, and expressly confirming the existing charter, for which no little anxiety might well be felt. But, at all events, the compliance now practised was politic, and in skilful accordance with the plan of self-protection which had been conceived. In the first years after the inauguration of the second charter, in the administrations of Phips and Bellomont, the effort of Massachusetts to secure as much liberty as was attainable under the new order of things had been put forth in bold legislation, which had been overruled and fruitless; under Dudley it had been

1726. Jan. 15.

Jan. 18.

[1] "If such Explanatory Charter shall not be accepted, and a just regard showed to your Majesty's royal prerogative by the House of Representatives for the future in all the particulars aforesaid, it may be proper for the consideration of the Legislature what further provision may be necessary to support and preserve your Majesty's just authority in the said Province, and prevent such presumptuous invasion for the future." (Register of the Privy Council, for May 29, 1725.)

[2] Letter in British Colonial Papers.

shown in resistance and impracticableness. Under Shute it had again adopted, with more skill, the method of encroachment, and for pursuing this it gained an advantage for future aggression, when, as in the case of the Explanatory Charter, which required no material sacrifice, it won, by a cheerful assent, the praise of moderation.

While these transactions were in progress, the King's Ministers were displeased by intelligence of what they were especially sensitive upon, — a religious movement in

Project of a synod.

Massachusetts. No synod had ever been held there since four years before the abrogation of the old Colonial charter. The ministers, under the lead of Cotton Mather, now proposed to have one, "considering," they

1725. May 27.

said in their memorial to the General Court, "the great and visible decay of piety in the country, and the growth of many miscarriages, which we fear may have provoked the glorious Lord in a series of various judgments wonderfully to distress us."

June 3.

The Council gave its approbation to the scheme. The Episcopal clergymen of Boston, Cutler and Miles, remonstrated.[1] Both branches of the Court rebuked the remonstrance, but the House referred the further consideration of the subject to the next session.[2]

Meantime the Bishop of London, Dr. Gibson, apprised by his clergymen in Boston,[3] laid information of what was

Aug. 17.

going on before the Lords Justices administering the government while the King was in Hanover, and expressed his "fear lest it should give a fresh handle of complaint among the clergy here, who are apt to clamor for a sitting convocation."

Aug. 21.

He "thought it might be a doubt, upon the Act of Union between Eng-

[1] The Duke of Newcastle was informed in an anonymous letter from Boston, of Jan. 30, 1727, that Episcopal ministers have been mobbed here, and bonfires made near their houses; mocked and insulted, and forced to keep within doors." (British Colonial Papers.)

[2] Mass. Prov. Rec.

[3] Proceedings of the Mass. Hist. Soc. for 1865, 226, and 1866, 342.

land and Scotland, whether the Independents in New England are any thing more than a tolerated ministry and people. The clergy established here," he added, "may think it hard to be debarred of a liberty which is indulged in the tolerated ministers there, and the tolerated ministers here may think it equitable that their privileges should not be less than those of their brethren in New England."[1] Yorke and Wearg, Attorney-General and Solicitor-General, gave to the Lords Justices their opinion: 1, That synods cannot lawfully be held without the royal license; 2, That an application to the provincial legislature was a contempt of the sovereign, which Dummer should have reproved; and, 3, That if notice of this should find them (the synod) in session, the Lieutenant-Governor should "signify to them . . . . . that they do forbear to meet any more;" and, if they persevere, "that the principal actors therein be prosecuted by information for a misdemeanor." This prohibition was too serious to be matched by any attachment to the measure, and it was not persisted in. "Their excellencies," Jeremiah Dummer wrote home, "are very much displeased. It is thought here that the clergy should not meet in so public and authoritative a manner without the King's consent as head of the church; and that it would be a bad precedent for Dissenters here to ask the same privilege, which, if granted, would be a sort of vying with the Established Church. It has also been insinuated that the clergy would have come to some resolutions to the prejudice of the Church of England, if they had been permitted to convene."[2] The Lieutenant-Governor excused himself to the Board of Trade for his degree of complicity in the offence. A similar proceeding, he said, had passed without censure ten years before.[3] On the

Sept. 29.

1726. March.

[1] Letters of the Bishop of London to the Duke of Newcastle, in British Colonial Papers.

[2] Hutch. Hist., II. 323, note.

[3] June 1, 1715, at the instance of the ministers, the House authorized

present occasion the scheme had been no further approved than to be referred for consideration to the next session of the Court, and he had not thought himself under obligation to object to it at that stage, as his expectation had been that it would pass by without coming up again; an expectation which the fact had justified.[1]

March 15. Shute presented a memorial for an allowance of the arrears of his pay, and for "settling a certain salary on the Governor."[2] The Privy Council advised the King to "signify his royal pleasure to the said Mr. Shute by his sign-manual, commanding him to acquaint the General Assembly of those Provinces [Massachusetts and New Hampshire] that, if they hope to recommend themselves to the continuance of your Majesty's royal grace

1727. Feb. 22. March 28. and favor, it must be by an immediate compliance with what has been so often recommended to them" as to "a fixed and honorable salary." If they do not comply, it is added, "the committee do humbly apprehend that it may be worthy the consideration of the Legislature."[3] Governor Shute may have hoped that the coercion of this threat would secure to him a more satisfactory administration of his Province.

Death of King George the First. June 11. He had all but embarked on his return thither, when the sudden death of the King vacated his commission.[4]

a Synod. But the Council withheld its concurrence, and the movement fell through.

[1] Dr. Colman had promoted the measure, and defended it in a letter to the Bishop of Peterborough. (Turell, Life of Colman, 81, 137.)

[2] He represented that he had been urging these matters "three years, at great expense, besides the expense of a hazardous winter voyage, and kept a family in New England without receiving any salary." (British Colonial Papers.)

[3] Register of the Privy Council; comp. Journal of the Board of Trade, for July 6, 26, 27, 1726.

[4] Williamson says (History, II. 110), that Shute lived in England, "upon a liberal pension, to the advanced age of fourscore years."

CHAPTER IV.

At the time of the arrival of Governor Shute in New England, the population of New Hampshire was computed at "nine thousand persons, of which number there were fifteen hundred men, very few white servants, and a hundred and fifty blacks." The principal productions of the Province were ships, "lumber, fish, masts for the royal navy, and turpentine," the annual value of the whole "seldom exceeding fifty thousand pounds per annum of New England money." The lumber and some of the fish were exported to the West Indies and to the Western Islands in exchange for sugar, molasses, rum, and wine. Lumber, tar, and turpentine, sent to England and Ireland, brought back linen and woollen manufactured goods. The proceeds of fish shipped to Portugal and Italy were returned in salt, or remitted to England for purchases there. Twenty vessels made foreign voyages, and about a hundred were engaged in fishing. The Province had some four hundred seamen. There were no manufactures of any kind.[1]

Population and industry of New Hampshire. 1716.

[1] O'Callaghan, Documents, &c., V. 595. — 1721, April 12, Henry Newman, of the Middle Temple, who had been agent for New Hampshire since May of the preceding year (N. H. Provincial Papers, III. 779), furnished the Lords of Trade with a memorandum, entitled "Queries relating to New Hampshire answered." The following are entries therein: "Shipping are about 20 sail, from 50 to 100 tons each. . . . . . Trade is wholly lumber, fish, and masts for the royal navy. . . . . . Annual produce of fish, lumber, &c., is all £40,000. . . . . . The number of inhabitants are about 9000, of which about 150 blacks." (British Colonial Papers.) Joshua Gee, in 1729, says: "Those commodities [of New England production] fall very short of purchasing their clothing in England, and therefore what other necessaries they want they are forced to

While the litigation with Allen was going on in England, George Vaughan, son of the former Counsellor, William Vaughan, was employed there in maintaining the claim of the occupants of the soil. His own activity and his father's position recommended him to the favor of men in power, and, when Burgess was made Governor of Massachusetts and New Hampshire, Vaughan, at his instance,[1] was appointed his Lieutenant for the latter Province.[2] He came over immediately, and claimed the place. Usher contested his right to act before the arrival of his principal. But the Assembly allowed Vaughan's title, and Usher did not persist in his opposition.[3]

Lieutenant-Governor Vaughan. 1715. Oct. 12.

The Board of Trade, who, as usual, thought they were too little consulted by the Ministry, were displeased with Vaughan's appointment. They considered it liable to the same objection as had formerly been made against Partridge's, and that "there would be as much propriety in appointing a wolf to preserve the flocks of England, as to nominate a man concerned in saw-mills to guard from waste the masts reserved for the navy of Britain." And their dissatisfaction was not lessened when the difficulties he experienced from the contumacy of the provincials were such as to cause him to represent that their divisions were "so great as hardly to be expressed." [4]

Dudley was now looking forward to an early surrender of the office of Governor, and he came no more into New Hampshire. Vaughan lost no time in calling an Assembly, which failed to come up to his wishes

Nov. 8.

manufacture for themselves." (Trade and Navigation of England, p. 25.) But if he had kept close to the Report to the Board of Trade, he would have confined the statement to Massachusetts. (O'Callaghan, Documents, &c., V. 598.)

[1] N. H. Provincial Papers, II. 677.

[2] By Burgess's advice several changes were also made in the Council of New Hampshire (British Colonial Papers), which occasioned dissatisfaction in the Province. (N. H. Provincial Papers, III. 677–679.)

[3] Ibid., II. 678, 679; III. 603.

[4] Chalmers, Revolt, II. 35, 36.

in respect to grants of money, and was dissolved after a six months' session.[1] He urged his demand on the next Assembly,[2] which not only took no measures towards acceding to it, but resolved to defer all further consideration of the matter till the Governor should arrive.

May 19.

1716. Aug. 21.

When Shute came in that character, his first pressing business in the Province related to the scarcity of money, occasioned by the same causes as in Massachusetts. He began with giving offence to the House by ordering them to hold a conference with the Council on a question which he refused to announce beforehand; and when it turned out to be the question whether the issue of bills of credit should be to the amount which they had consented to, or to a larger amount proposed by the Council, they proved to be impracticable, and the Assembly was dissolved.[3] A new House came together in a better mood, and satisfied the Governor by agreeing to issue bills of credit to the amount of fifteen thousand pounds, to be lent for fifteen years, at ten per cent interest.[4]

Governor Shute in New Hampshire. Oct. 18.

1717. Jan. 24.

May 18.

A quarrel followed between the Governor and his second in authority. Vaughan, made arrogant by the consequence of his family and his personal hold on the popular party in his Province, proved a troublesome subordinate. According to Shute's interpretation of his commission, he was always Governor of New Hampshire, whether present or not within its borders. Vaughan held that in the Governor's absence the chief executive authority resided in himself.[5] Shute sent him an order to proclaim a day of fasting in New Hampshire, and it was not done. He instructed Vaughan to prorogue

Dispute between Shute and Vaughan.

[1] N. H. Provincial Papers, III. 599, 647.

[2] Ibid., II. 649.

[3] Ibid., III. 679.

[4] Ibid., 688.

[5] Ibid., II. 697, 698, 703–706.

the Assembly, and Vaughan dissolved it.[1] Vaughan suspended a Counsellor who reproved his insubordination.[2] Shute came to Portsmouth, restored the Counsellor, and suspended Vaughan.[3] The House declared its disapprobation of Vaughan's course.[4] The Representatives of one town, Hampton, expressed the opposite view in language so warm that the Governor called it libellous, and, with the Council's concurrence, he put them under heavy bonds for their good behavior.[5] In England, Shute's interest prevailed, with the aid of Sir William Ashurst, who, though not now official agent for any of the Colonies, was much consulted on their affairs, and who had been displeased by a proposal of Vaughan, while in England, to raise a tax in New Hampshire to be paid to officers of the crown.[6] Vaughan was accordingly displaced, and was succeeded by John Wentworth, of New Hampshire lineage and birth, formerly a sea-captain, now an opulent merchant, and for the last five years a Counsellor of the Province.[7] He abstained from making Vaughan's claim to execute the chief magistracy in the Governor's absence.

Sept. 30.

Sept. 24.

Sept. 12.

Lieutenant-Governor Wentworth.

[1] N. H. Provincial Papers, III. 704, 705.

[2] Ibid., 702, 703. This was Samuel Penhallow, author of the "History of the Wars of New England." For a sketch of his life and character, see Ibid., IV. 18.

[3] N. H. Provincial Papers, II. 710.

[4] Ibid., III. 709.

[5] Ibid., 710-713.—"May 10, 1718, Voted that any member of this House that shall neglect to wear his sword, or be found without it during sessions of General Assembly, from this day, shall pay a fine of five shillings to clark, for the use of the House." (Ibid., 732.)

[6] Belknap, Farmer's edition, 184, 187.

[7] Wentworth's commission (N. H. Provincial Papers, II. 711, 712) is countersigned by the great name of Joseph Addison, who had been Secretary of State since April 16, 1717. Addison succeeded Lord Townshend, who had taken Lord Bolingbroke's place, Sept. 17, 1714. (Comp. Ibid., IV. 587.) In 1714, Lord Stanhope succeeded Secretary Bromley. (See above, p. 279.) The later Secretaries of State in this reign were the Duke of Montrose (1714), Mr. Methuen (1716), the Duke of Roxburgh (1717), the Earl of Sunderland (1717), Mr. Craggs (who succeeded Addison in 1718), Lord Townshend (1721), Lord Carteret (1721), Robert Walpole (1723), and the Duke of Newcastle (1724).

He retained the office for thirteen years, administering it with conscientiousness and good judgment, and rarely giving cause of offence.

New Hampshire began to extend its narrow limits, which hitherto — such had been the terror of Indian invasions — had embraced only a space of some fifteen miles about the mouth of the Piscataqua.[1] The town of Stratham, within that radius, had been set off from Exeter with a separate incorporation, just before Shute's arrival.[2] The settlement of Londonderry was of greater importance. A hundred families from the town of that name in Ireland, famous for its heroic defence against the troops of King James the Second, resolved, with their four ministers, to establish themselves in America. Sixteen of these families, to whom numbers of others were soon added, received permission from the General Court of Massachusetts to occupy a tract of land on the left bank of the Merrimack, which, from the character of the growth upon it, was then known by the name of Nutfield. A few miles below the point where that river now turns the vast wheels of the mills of Manchester, they established a manufactory of linen, spinning and weaving their flax by hand labor.[3]

1716. March 20.

Extension of New Hampshire.

1719. April 11.

A question arose about the acquisition of a good title to their lands. In the old controversy with Allen, Mason's assign, it had been allowed on the other side that all of New Hampshire belonged to him except the portion already settled. But his heirs were minors; Usher, with them, had his undefined claims; and all parties, probably, were tired enough of the question to be willing to abstain from pressing it. Lieutenant-Governor Wentworth undertook to cut the knot. The jurisdiction, at all events, belonged to the King, whoever might prove to have the

1 See above, pp. 30, 352.

2 N. H. Provincial Papers, II. 691.

3 From their arrival in this country is to be dated the culture of the potato.

property of the soil. Wentworth gave to the Irish Presbyterians a qualified permission to establish them-
1719.
selves on the tract on the Merrimack,[1] which with a natural feeling they called *Londonderry*.[2] He proceeded to make grants for the towns of Rochester, Bar-
1722.
rington, Nottingham, and Chester, enclosing the old towns within an arc of a circle of thirty miles' radius, extending from the Piscataqua to Londonderry. Twelve years later, Massachusetts, still holding to her original
1734. claim in respect to her chartered limits, incorpo-
March 4. rated the town of Rumford, now Concord, still higher up on the Merrimack.[3] The grants which have just been mentioned of the four towns were made on the condition, "as far as in us lies," with reference to possible claims of Mason's assigns. The transaction was completed on the eve of Shute's departure for England, which left Wentworth at the head of the government of New Hampshire.[4]

Supplies of naval stores.

The same causes that had excited the people of New Hampshire against the deposed Surveyor of the Woods prepared an unfriendly reception for John Armstrong, the deputy of Burniston,[5] who had been appointed to that office after Bridger's recall.[6]
1706. Armstrong had first come to America ostensibly

[1] Parker, History of Londonderry, 53–57.

[2] Comp. N. H. Hist. Col., V. 206.

[3] Mass. Prov. Laws, II. 697.

[4] On further experience, the Scottish-Irish emigrants were not satisfied with the arrangements made for them in New Hampshire. In a letter of Jan. 22, 1727, more than three hundred of them represented that they were not allowed to settle "to the eastward of North Yarmouth." They said "the New England antipathy is very great against all Presbyterians and Church people." Mr. McGregor, of Nutfield, had been excommunicated "only for ordaining a Presbyterian minister. . . . . . If the King don't take this country and South Carolina under his more immediate government, we utterly despair of seeing this or that a thriving Colony." (British Colonial Papers.) — For an account of the experiences of the Scottish-Irish Presbyterians in this country, by the accomplished President of the Maine Historical Society, see Maine Hist. Col., VI. 1, &c.

[5] N. H. Provincial Papers, II. 727.

[6] See above, p. 401.

as Secretary to Lord Bellomont, but having for his more important employment an agency from Blathwayt, Secretary to the Board of Trade, who had formed a company with Sir Matthew Dudley and others for the exploration of mines in New England, and for a traffic in naval stores.[1] Shute professed himself "satisfied with Armstrong's good services" as Deputy-Surveyor of the Woods; but a memorial from the other side represented him to the 1722.
Board of Trade as guilty of "extortion, taking Nov. 13.
bribes, negligence, perjury, and disaffection to the King."[2]
He was consequently recalled, but the Lieutenant- 1725.
Governor and Council took his part,[3] and event- Nov. 2.
ually he succeeded in exculpating himself, and came back to resume his invidious duties.[4]

In Governor Shute's last year in New England, the Representatives of New Hampshire complained to 1722.
him of the grievance that their House had been May 1.
continued for five years, without being reconstituted by new elections. He expressed his surprise at the interference, but said he would take the matter into consideration, and that in the mean time it would be well for them to attend to the discharge of the Province's debts.[5] The result was that, when a new issue of bills of credit for that purpose had been authorized, the Assembly was May 9, 10.

[1] See above, p. 395, note 2. — In a memorandum entitled "The case of Robert Armstrong," he is said to have "prepared" this scheme, and to have been employed in the prosecution of it for fourteen years, before he was made Burniston's deputy. (British Colonial Papers.) — Among other offences, Armstrong was charged with being "a noted Irish Jacobite," and with having said, "Is it not a shame we should be governed by Germans and Dutch, and have such a fine English prince of our own? But I hope I shall yet live to see the right king upon the throne." Armstrong protested that he had never so much as been in Ireland. (Ibid.)

[2] Journal of the Board of Trade, for Nov. 7, 13, 16, 20, and 21, 1722.

[3] N. H. Provincial Papers, IV. 5.

[4] Letter of Armstrong to Burniston, in British Colonial Papers. — Wentworth was well disposed towards Armstrong. June 5, 1724, he wrote to Burniston that he would be very glad to see his "good friend, Mr. Armstrong, in New Hampshire again." (Ibid.)

[5] N. H. Provincial Papers, IV. 24, 25.

dissolved,[1] having been continued from the first year of Shute's administration.

From the time of the Governor's departure for England, New Hampshire was for six years a separate government, with Lieutenant-Governor Wentworth at its head, while Dummer filled the same office in Massachusetts. The two temporary Chief Magistrates were on friendly terms with each other, and conducted affairs of common interest with good mutual intelligence. New Hampshire, as usual, had to bear the worst miseries of the Indian war. By the convenient way of Lake Winnipiseogee, parties of savages came as far as Dover, and what is since Durham, murdering some half-dozen persons at each place.[2] The next year, still travelling by that route, they again infested the same region, eluding the armed men, and confining themselves, for the most part, to the slaughter of women and children, and of some Quaker borderers, whose scruples as to resistance had become known to them.[3] After Lovewell's battle, and the breaking up of Rasle's hold, they were for a while more quiet; and a commission sent on the part of Massachusetts and New Hampshire to remonstrate with Vaudreuil on his complicity, or at least forbearance, with these transactions,[4] had so much success (aided by the production of his letters to Rasle, captured at Norridgewock) as to obtain from him an engagement to discountenance and discourage the like proceedings for the future, and the restitution, for a ransom, of some twenty or thirty prisoners who had passed from the Indian marauders into the hands of the French. Dummer's treaty at Falmouth[5] soon followed, putting an end for the present to the long distresses and anxieties.[6]

Indian incursions.

1723.

1724.

March 16–June 10.

1725.

Dec. 12.

[1] N. H. Provincial Papers, IV. 36, 39, 44.

[2] Penhallow, 96, 97; Niles, in Mass. Hist. Col., XXXV. 346.

[3] Penhallow, 100–104, 106.

[4] N. H. Provincial Papers, IV. 163.

[5] Ibid., 188.

[6] In all the discouragements of these troublesome times, it is pleas-

The new Assembly of New Hampshire was not in session at the time of Shute's departure for England. When it came together again according to its prorogation, Wentworth announced the absence of his superior, which he expected would not last many months, and courteously bespoke the aid of the Council and Representatives in carrying on the public business.[1] For the most part the relations between him and the Legislature continued friendly throughout his administration, though he was confronted in his sphere by the two questions which had excited so much feeling in Massachusetts. While Shute was in New England, no salary had been settled upon him by New Hampshire. The Province generally granted him two hundred pounds a year in two payments.[2] The Assembly instructed their agent in England "to make all possible remonstrance against having any recommendation or direction sent to this government to settle a salary on a Commander-in-Chief, if any such design should be on foot, the Province being . . . . . ever cheerful in making an honorable allowance for the support of his Majesty's government here even much beyond its capacity, and the same good inclinations and loyal disposition still continuing in all his Majesty's dutiful subjects here."[3] At almost the last moment of Wentworth's independent government, he "disallowed" the House's choice of a Speaker. The House, in respectful terms, desired him to produce his authority for that proceeding, and he sent two Counsellors to read to them a clause in his commission. By a message in writing, they prayed him not

Administration of Wentworth. 1723. Feb. 18.

1727. May 19.

1728. April 9.

April 10.

ant to see that the people of New Hampshire did not overlook the need of education for their children. (N. H. Provincial Papers, III. 364, 365, 570, 646, 718, 799, 802; IV. 154, 268, 391.)

[1] Ibid., 81, 82, 88, 107, 128.

[2] Ibid., III. 690, 691; IV. 40. Shute thought his pay ought to be continued while he was in England (Ibid., 149); but the Assembly was of a different mind (156).

[3] Ibid., 249; comp. 156.

to "insist upon his disallowance of the choice;" and he replied "that, if they would add to their request that they did not question his Honor's right of negativing a Speaker, his Honor would then take their desire under consideration." The House did nothing for three days, and was prorogued till the following week, and then for another day, "the Lieutenant-Governor being out of town." The House saw itself to be at a disadvantage in the contest, and gave it up, proceeding to another choice, though "with a preamble in justification of the late Speaker." Whereupon "his Honor signified his allowance of the choice, but utter disapprobation of the preamble."[1] There was indeed no chance from the first for the claim which had been set up. The question had been settled four years before in the "Explanatory Charter" of Massachusetts.

April 13. April 17. April 18.

Rhode Island. 1715. In the first year of the reign of King George the First, the population of Rhode Island was estimated at nine thousand persons, of whom five hundred were negroes.[2] Colonel Samuel Cranston, who died in office, was Governor through the whole of that reign, as he had been through the reign of Queen Anne and the four last years of King William. Nine towns, namely, Newport, Providence, Portsmouth, Warwick, Westerly, Kingston, New Shoreham, Jamestown, and Greenwich, sent delegates to the General Assembly.

1727.

The Board of Trade represented to the King that "since neither . . . . . Connecticut nor Rhode Island were obliged to submit their laws to royal revision, an Act of Parliament was necessary to compel them to do

1714.

[1] N. H. Provincial Papers, IV. 283–286.

[2] Chalmers, Revolt, II. 7, note. Chalmers's estimate of the population of the Colonies in 1715, attributed by him to one Stephen Goden, a London merchant, though wide of the truth in some parts, is apparently correct in respect to Rhode Island. (Comp. above, 358, 359.)

that, without which it was impossible to enforce their submission." A bill was accordingly brought into the House of Commons for amending the charters of those Colonies.[1] It was on that occasion that Jeremiah Dummer wrote his able Defence of the American Charters. But the measure was dropped in Parliament, and it was not till seven years later that a new alarm occasioned the publication of the treatise. It will be referred to more particularly hereafter.

The charter in danger. 1715.

1722.

The Board of Trade had charged the people of Rhode Island with "numerous misfeasances," of which one was their way of eluding a law of the reign of King William requiring that "all propriety Governors shall be allowed and approved of by the King, before they enter upon the government. But by choosing the Governor annually, though it is generally the same person, his turn is expired before any such approbation can be had, if they did apply for it pursuant to the above Act, which hitherto they never have done."[2] At the same time a committee of the Privy Council, instructed to advise that body concerning the long-disputed boundary between Rhode Island and Connecticut, reported that "it were to be wished that they would both voluntarily submit themselves to his Majesty's immediate government, as some other Colonies have done, and that they might be annexed to New Hampshire.[3] It was not to be expected that either Connecticut or Rhode Island would willingly come into such an arrangement, even had there been no other objection than that New Hampshire, being merely a royal unchartered Province, was subject to whatever regulations the King might from time to time be disposed to make for its administration, — a liability which would have equally attached to the other governments, had the annex-

1706. Jan. 10.

[1] Chalmers, II. 5.
[2] O'Callaghan, Documents, &c., V. 599, 600.
[3] R. I. Rec., IV. 12, 308, 334.

ation which was proposed taken place. The true method of promoting the welfare of all the parties concerned, had the British Court had no other object, and had circumstances admitted of its being taken, would have been to replace New Hampshire under the authority and protection of Massachusetts, and to give to the turbulent towns of Rhode Island the benefit of the orderly administration of Connecticut, by an obliteration of the disputed eastern boundary of the latter Colony, similar to what had taken place when New Haven, sixty years before, had been annexed to it on the west.

When the trouble with the eastern Indians became seri-
1722. October. ous, the Assembly of Rhode Island, on a request from Governor Shute for assistance in men and money, raised a committee to inquire into the merits of the case. Having entertained the question somewhat
Neutrality in the Indian war. 1724. Dec. 29. over two years, the Assembly decided that "although the said Indian rebels deserved nothing but a total extirpation from the face of the earth for their continual and repeated rebellions, hostilities, and perfidiousness, yet that it would be by no means justifiable in the Colony of Rhode Island to join with the Province of Massachusetts in the prosecution of said war, as things were at present circumstanced," for the reasons, — that Rhode Island did its part towards the common defence by maintaining the maritime frontier; that the King's pleasure ought first to be ascertained, "who in his great wisdom might find out and prescribe ways to make those wild and inaccessible subjects of his come in and tamely submit to his government;" that "Rhode Island was never advised with by the Province of Massachusetts" in making war or peace with the Indians; that in treaties Massachusetts had secured to herself the advantages of Indian trade; and that it was not for Rhode Island to "buy for the Massachusetts this privilege with the blood of their young and strong." But they took the spirited measure of ordering a

letter to be addressed to the Governor of Canada, threatening him that, if he did not desist from his intrigues with the savages, Rhode Island would take part in the war.[1] The menace failed to deter the obstinate Vaudreuil.

Rhode Island was suffering from the great financial error of the time. Following with less excuse, but not till after some years, the unfortunate example of Massachusetts, she had undertaken to pay her war expenses by promises to pay, to which, so far as law could do it, she gave the character of money. There was some intelligent distrust, and a short suspension of the process; but it was presently revived,[2] and paper money continued to be made in Rhode Island down to the year of the framing of the Constitution of the United States. It must be owned that this easy command of funds did not tempt the Colony to extravagant expense. On the contrary, its creditors, whether individuals or neighboring Colonies, had occasional reason to complain of an unfavorable reception of their claims.[3]

Financial disorder.

1710. Oct. 25.

1711. May 2.

1715. July 5.

The laws of the Colony, such as they were, were observed to "lie in a very disordered condition, and only in the hands of some few persons;" and two Deputies were empowered to collect and transcribe them for the press.[4] A difficulty occurred, relating to that engagement under oath which is thought to contribute to the safe administration of justice. "Several persons, who were of this body politic, scrupled to take an engagement where the words 'as in the presence of God' is in, whereby the corporation was much hurt for want of their service in the same;" and, to relieve their scrupulous conscience, the simple solemnity was dispensed with.[5] Some of the citizens were less fastidious in their

Colonial legislation.

July 5.

[1] R. I. Rec., IV. 320, 351–353.

[2] Ibid., 102, 106, 117, 190; comp. Staples, Annals of Providence, 188, 189.

[3] *E.g.*, R. I. Rec., IV. 231, 257, 263, 302, 313.

[4] Ibid., 194, 195.

[5] Ibid., 271.

notions of political duty, and had to be restrained by law, under a penalty of fine, whipping, or imprisonment, from their practice of "putting or delivering into the hat two, three, or more votes for one officer, at the general elections, and other town elections."[1] In one thing the expenditure of the Colony was liberal. From the magnitude of the bounties offered for their destruction it must be inferred that wolves still abounded in Rhode Island.[2] The extirpation of crows, blackbirds, squirrels, and rats was also a subject of legislation.[3]

The same people needed to be withheld from meeting one another in engagements, susceptible of being enforced by law, for the maintenance of religious worship. With the wisdom of those who see the evil afar off and hide themselves, the Assembly of Rhode Island "enacted that what maintenance or salary may be thought needful or necessary by any of the churches, congregations, or societies of people, now inhabiting, or that may hereafter inhabit, within any part of this government, for the support of their or either of their minister or ministers, may be raised by a free contribution, and no other ways."[4] Perhaps the precaution was suggested by movements for setting up Episcopal churches in Rhode Island; for the worship of that denomination was instituted in Providence soon after, and an Episcopal congregation had been organized in Newport not long before.[5] This church was eminently loyal. In a memorial of its ministry, church-wardens, and vestry, they assured the King: "The religious and loyal principles of passive obedience and non-resistance are upon all suitable occasions strongly asserted and inculcated upon

1716. May 2.

Religions. 1720.

1724. June 1.

1 R. I. Rec., IV. 195, 196.
2 Ibid., 186.
3 Arnold, History, II. 55.
4 R. I. Rec., IV. 206.
5 Arnold, History, II. 76; Staples, Annals of Providence, 443 *et seq.* Bernon, the Oxford Huguenot, was one of the principal Episcopalian confessors. (Mass. Hist. Col., XXII. 70; comp. above, 185, note 3.)

your Majesty's good subjects of this church."[1] Observing the anomalous state of society which existed in Rhode Island, it was not unnatural for the Episcopal Church to identify the institution of its own worship with the introduction of Christianity into that Colony. "The people were negligent of all religion," says its historian, "till about the year 1722; the very best were such as called themselves Baptists or Quakers."[2]

Even the people of Rhode Island sometimes found that there was inconvenience in unlimited freedom, and that there was wisdom in the rule for every one so to use his own as not to harm his neighbor. The pet freak of some inhabitants of the town of Westerly, who called Sabbatarians.
themselves *Sabbatarians*, was to set apart the seventh day of the week as holy time. "Repeated informations" having been brought in against them, that 1725. May.
they "made a continual practice of doing servile labor on the first day of the week, and that they very publicly and otherwise profaned said day, which the law of the realm as well as of the Colony appoint to be kept as a sabbath, which is a great offence to the rest of the inhabitants of said Colony, and brings an odium upon the whole government as well as themselves," the General Assembly of the Colony "therefore advised and cautioned said inhabitants of Westerly in particular, and of the whole Colony in general, that for the future they reform their aforesaid vicious practices, and conform to the law; considering that, though the ordinances of men may not square with their private principles, yet they must be subject to them, for the Lord's sake; and that, lest they incur the further displeasure of this Assembly, and put them upon a more rigorous method of suppressing the aforesaid enormities."[3]

[1] British Colonial Papers.
[2] Humfries, in Staples, Annals, 444; comp. Arnold, II. 86.
[3] R. I. Rec., IV. 362.

A law excluding Roman Catholics from the franchise,
Disfranchisement of Romanists. and from competency to hold office, appears in
a collection of the statutes extant in a manu-
1705. script of the third year of Queen Anne. It is
1719. also in the collection printed in consequence
of the vote just mentioned. In the imperfection of the
records, the date of the enactment of that law, embodying
so wide a departure from the primitive principle of Rhode
Island, remains uncertain. In the Act of Repeal
1783. passed after the emancipation from England, it is
1663. referred to the same year as the grant of the charter.[1] The recent historian of the Colony supposes that it
never went through the forms of legislation, but was without authority interpolated by a committee which
1699. was charged to make a compilation of the laws in
the time of the Earl of Bellomont, — a supposition which
could not be entertained in respect to a community possessing the usual guaranties for the public order and safety,
but which is not in itself incredible in respect to Rhode
Island. The motive suggested in explanation of it, namely,
that it was "in order that their privileges, then threatened
by the powerful influence of Bellomont, might not be
taken from them," is also the less improbable, as it accords
with the usual unworthy policy of Rhode Island in its relations to the parent country.[2]

It has been told how the extreme disinclination to control, which signalized this peculiar people, asserted
Militia and franchise laws. itself in military affairs, where it is attended with
especial danger.[3] After four years' experience of
1718. the chaos which had been introduced, the influ-
Jan. 17. ence of the Governor and his friends prevailed
to have the elective system for military offices abolished.

[1] R. I. Rec., IX. 674; comp. Mass. Hist. Col., XXV. 244.
[2] Arnold, History, II. 492, 493; comp. Walsh, Appeal, &c., 427–434.
[3] See above, p. 361.
[4] Ibid., p. 238; comp. Arnold, II. 61.

After eight more years, the popular discontent compelled another trial of elected commanders of troops,[1] 1726.
but in a shorter time a renewed observation of the June 14.
"ill consequence" of the incongruous method oc- 1730.
casioned it to be again abandoned.[2] On the other May.
hand, the franchise of the Colony, originally so freely conferred, was subjected to rigorous limitation. A law was made establishing the possession of a freehold of 1724.
the value of a hundred pounds, or an annual in- Feb. 18.
come from real estate of not less than two pounds, as a qualification of a voter. But the eldest son of a freeman shared in his father's privilege.[3] This arrangement, so peculiar in a community otherwise so democratic, continued in force till nearly the middle of the present century.

After the return of the agent, Jahleel Brenton, Agencies in
William Penn had had the charge in England of England.
the affairs of the Colony. On the alarm for the charter at the beginning of the reign of King George the 1715.
First, Richard Partridge, described as "of Lon- June 13.
don," was appointed to be agent.[4] His principal business proved to be, at first, to pacify the Lords of Trade and Plantations in respect to the charges made against the Colony for illicit commerce. But presently the old question of the limits of the Colony on the side of Connecticut assumed more importance, and Lieutenant-Governor Joseph Jenckes was sent over to be associated with him in the agency.[5] The further progress and termination of this long-standing controversy will be related further on.

At the beginning of the reign of King George Condition and indus-
the First, the Colony of Connecticut is believed try of Con- necticut.
to have contained twenty-seven thousand five 1715.

[1] R. I. Rec., IV. 377.
[2] Ibid., 437.
[3] Arnold, II. 77.
[4] R. I. Rec., IV. 187; comp. 200.
[5] Ibid., 285.

hundred people, of whom fifteen hundred were negroes. There were fifty towns, and about the same number of churches and of ministers, — the number of towns having nearly doubled since the Revolution.[1] The occupations of the people were mostly agricultural, though Hartford and Wethersfield on the river, and New London, Stonington, New Haven, and other towns along the Sound, had vessels engaged in fishing, and carried on a considerable business with the West India Islands; and ships were built in all the inlets on the southern shore. There was for a time a delusive hope of profit from certain mines, — one in the town of Simsbury, the other in what afterwards became Wallingford, — which it was thought would yield copper, at least, in abundance, if not more valuable ores.
1718. October. The General Assembly encouraged the exploration of them by granting certain privileges to the proprietors and their workmen;[2] and not a little money was spent in the enterprise by capitalists of Massachusetts and New York. But it did not prove remunerative, and was abandoned after a few years. The excavated mine at Simsbury was afterwards turned to account as a State prison.

1708. Religious condition. The system of consociation of churches, which had been organized by the synod convened at Saybrook,[3] gave no little additional power to the clergy; and from an early period of the eighteenth century a

[1] Trumbull, I. 476. — At the time of the deposition of Governor Andros, Connecticut had twenty-eight towns. Between that time and the death of George the First twenty-two were added, viz.: Danbury (1693), Lebanon (1697), Colchester and Durham (1699), Voluntown (1700), Mansfield and Canterbury (1703), Hebron (1704), Killingly (1708), Coventry and Ridgefield (1709), Newtown (1711), East Haddam, Pomfret, and New Milford (1713), Ashford (1714), Tolland (1715), Stafford (1719), Litchfield (1721), Willington and Bolton (1720), and Somers (1726). In 1726, a new county by the name of *Windham* was formed of the eleven towns in the north-eastern corner of the Colony. The counties before this time had been Fairfield, New Haven, Hartford, and New London.

[2] Conn. Col. Rec., VI. 84–87.

[3] See above, p. 369.

severer religious rule began to prevail in Connecticut than in Massachusetts. The war in the time of Queen Anne was regarded by many good people of Connecticut as having unfavorably affected the character of the soldiers, and through them of the community at large. The Assembly "took into their serious consideration the many evident tokens that the glory is departed, that the providences of God are plainly telling us that our ways do not please him;" and they recommended "to the reverend elders to inquire and report respecting the state of religion in each parish," and particularly "how and whether catechising were duly attended, and whether there were a suitable number of Bibles in the various families in the respective parishes, and also if there were found in any parishes any that neglected attendance on the public worship on the Lord's Day; . . . . . and likewise, which and what are the sins and evils that provoke the just Majesty of Heaven to walk contrary unto us in the ways of his providence."[1] The Assembly laid a formal injunction upon all judicial officers, constables, and grand jurors, to give their strictest attention to the laws for the education of children, and against profaneness, Sabbath-breaking, lying, swearing, and intemperance.[2] Laws "for preventing and punishing the profanation of the Sabbath, or the Lord's Day," visited with pecuniary penalties absence from public worship, "rude behavior" on Sundays, and travelling on that day, except to and from the meeting-house.[3] Masters and mistresses were to be fined by Magistrates at discretion, not exceeding forty shillings, for neglect to teach and catechise, and instruct in Christianity, Indian children "put out" to them by their parents.[4]

1714. May.

1715. October.

1721. May. October.

1727. May 11.

Some annoyance was occasioned by a sect known by the

[1] Conn. Col. Rec., VI. 436.
[2] Ibid., 530, 531.
[3] Ibid., 248; comp. 277; V. 525.
[4] Ibid., VII. 103.

name of *Rogerenes*, disciples of John Rogers of New London, who had adopted and improved upon the scheme of his Rhode Island neighbors, the *Seventh-Day Baptists* of Westerly.[1] Differing from the Quakers in their esteem for the ordinances of baptism and the Lord's Supper, in other of their practices the Rogerenes imitated that extraordinary people. They came into the churches during Sunday worship in objectionably scanty dress, and with violent vociferations, "charging the ministers with lies and false doctrine." When they were brought into court, the judges and officers fared no better at their hands. The contest between them and the law was brought to an earlier termination, by reason, it is said, of the discovery of some gross immoralities of the leader, which tended to discredit him with his friends, and to cool their enthusiasm for his methods. Their irregularities probably occasioned
1723. the law by which persons absenting themselves
May. from their "lawful congregation," and assembling for worship in private houses, were made punishable by a fine of twenty shillings for each transgression, and "whatsoever person, not being a lawfully allowed minister of the gospel, should presume to profane the holy sacraments by administering or making a show of administering them," was to "incur the penalty of ten pounds, and suffer corporal punishment by whipping, not exceeding thirty stripes for each offence."[2] In Andros's time the Church of England had gained a foothold in Connecticut, especially in the western part of the Province. Its followers obtained from the government a fair recognition of their wishes.
1727. They were allowed to reclaim for their separate use
May. as much money as was levied on them in the town

[1] For a sufficient account of this short-lived sect, see Gillett's "Historical Sketch," &c., in Hist. Mag., XIV. 5-7. Comp. above, p. 471.

[2] Conn. Col. Rec., VI. 401. — Various gross particulars of Rogers's misconduct are related by Trumbull. (Hist., II. 30, note.)

rates for the support of the ministry, and to tax themselves for as much more as was requisite for the maintaining of their worship.[1]

Yale College.

For nearly twenty years the College of Connecticut had continued to be an unsatisfactory experiment. While the rector taught some youth at Milford, and two tutors had other pupils at Saybrook, and the few scores of books which had been obtained for a library were divided between the two places, there was small prospect of the results for which institutions of learning are created. Notwithstanding the general agreement that whatever facilities for the higher education could be commanded should be brought together and combined, the choice of the place was embarrassed by various considerations, some having reference to the public good alone, others more or less to the interest of property holders, who calculated on being benefited by the proximity of a literary colony. Saybrook, Wethersfield, Hartford, and New Haven competed with each other for the preference, offering such contributions as they were able towards the erection of a college building. The offer from New Haven, larger than that of any other town, was seven hundred pounds sterling. The plan of fixing the College there, promoted by the great influence of Governor Saltonstall, was adopted by the trustees; and with money obtained by private gifts, and two hundred and fifty pounds accruing from a sale of land given by the General Assembly, a building was begun, which finally cost a thousand pounds sterling.

1716. Oct. 17.

But the permanent site of the College was not yet absolutely determined. A remonstrance was presented to the Trustees, setting forth that there had been illegality in the proceedings; and it was not till after much debate in the lower House of Assembly that this clamor was disposed of by a vote "advising the reverend Trustees to proceed."[2] From that time, though opinions were

1717. October.

[1] Conn. Col. Rec., VII. 107. [2] Ibid., VI. 30.

not yet fully reconciled, affairs went on more prosperously.[1] The Assembly gave the College a hundred pounds.[2] Jeremiah Dummer sent from England a substantial present of books. Governor Saltonstall contributed fifty pounds sterling, and the same sum was presented by Jahleel Brenton, of Newport, in Rhode Island. But the chief patronage came from Elihu Yale, — a native of New Haven, but long resident in the East Indies, where he had been Governor of Fort St. George. He was now a citizen of London, and Governor of the East India Company. His contribu-
1711-1718. tions, continued through seven years, amounted to some four hundred pounds sterling; and he
1719. May. was understood to have made arrangements for a further bounty of five hundred pounds, which, however, through unfortunate accidents, never came to its destination.[3] The Province made a grant of forty pounds annually for seven years.[4] Mr. Andrew being unwilling
March. to remove to New Haven, Mr. Timothy Cutler, minister of Stratford, was made rector. But here occurred a mortifying disappointment. After a successful administration of the College of less than four years' duration, Cutler announced that he had conformed to the Church of England, a step which had also been taken at the same time by one of the tutors, and by the ministers
1722. Oct. 17. of West Haven and North Haven.[5] He was accordingly dismissed, and it was not till after four

[1] Conn. Col. Rec., VI. 30; comp. Ibid., 37, 83, 91–100, 256, 267, 340. — "The removal, however, was not effected without strong opposition. Forcible resistance was made at Saybrook to the transfer of the library, and the Governor and Council thought it necessary to assemble at that place, to aid the Sheriff in the execution of his duty. Besides other disorders, the carts provided for transporting the books were destroyed at night; the bridges between Saybrook and New Haven were broken down; and in the scramble many valuable books and papers were lost. The library was about a week on the road. (Kingsley, Sketch of the History of Yale College, &c., in American Quarterly Register, VIII. 17.)

[2] Conn. Col. Rec., VI. 38.

[3] Trumbull, II. 35.

[4] Conn. Col. Rec., VI. 125.

[5] This apostasy of Cutler, says Sewall in a letter to Governor Saltonstall, of Oct. 15, 1722, "quickly

years that his place was supplied by the induction of Mr. Elisha Williams, one of the ministers of Wethersfield. At this time the College had fifty-seven students.[1] 1726. September.

The condition of the Mohegan Indians, of whom a considerable remnant, always persisting in their rejection of the faith of their Christian neighbors, still kept together on the ancient site of their tribe, occasionally called on the Province for measures both of protection and of restraint. "Cæsar, sachem of Mohegan, Ben Uncas, and several other Indians," complained to Governor Saltonstall that two English neighbors had "set up the frame of a house within the land of the Mohegan country." The Englishmen were men of consequence, but such considerations were not apt to weigh with the straightforward Governor. Without a day's delay he arrested the trespassers, and placed them under bonds for future good behavior.[2] It was, on the other

The Mohegan Indians.

1714. March 4.

brought to my mind Rev. xvi. 15. I apprehend that, in this extraordinary and unexpected alarm, we have a demonstration that the drying up of the great river Euphrates is near at hand. . . . . . I am fully of Mr. Cotton's mind that Episcopacy is that upon which the fifth vial is poured out, and he will have hard work that shall endeavor to control that angel." (Proceedings of the Mass. Hist. Soc., for 1871–1873, p. 378.) A number of letters which passed on this exciting occasion are printed in Mass. Hist. Col., XII. 128 *et seq.*; XIV. 297 *et seq.*

The conversion of Cutler and his friends renewed an activity of the Episcopalians in New England, which had been suspended since the time of Andros. Cutler, transferred to a cure in Boston, claimed, though unavailingly, a right to a seat among the Overseers of Harvard College. (Quincy, History, I. 366.) Before long, Dec. 12, 1727, was sent from Newport to the new King, "The Humble Address of Several of the Clergy of New England," representing "the great necessity of a Bishop resident in these parts." It reached the Board of Trade with an indorsement that "the Bishop of London desired it might not be inserted in the Gazette." (British Colonial Papers.)

[1] I count this number on the Triennial Catalogue. — In the interval between Cutler's administration and Williams's, by provisions of an Act passed Oct. 10, 1723, the Legislature changed the restriction as to the age of Trustees from forty to thirty years, and constituted the Rector a Trustee *ex officio*. (Conn. Col. Rec., VI. 416.)

[2] Ibid., V. 421, 422; comp. 398, 431, 448, 518.

hand, in respect to the Mohegans that the suspicions were first entertained which at this late time spread through Connecticut an apprehension of a conspiracy
1720. June 18- Oct. 3. among what remained of the tribes.[1] The Governor questioned the Mohegan, Pequod, and Niantic chiefs, who resolutely protested that they knew nothing of any hostile plot; and the result of a searching investigation rendered it probable that they had been maligned by persons who coveted their lands, but that disorderly behavior on the part of the Indians had given some real cause for suspicion; and they were accordingly admonished "to remove all the occasions of it, and particularly to abstain from drink, which puts men upon saying and doing things that are provoking."[2] Intelligence of a
1723. Aug. 19. savage inroad, which was marked by the destruction of Rutland, led to measures for securing the frontier towns of Simsbury and Litchfield, and to a direction to all the Indians in the Colony to limit their hunting excursions within certain bounds.[3] The government complimented the Mohegans by sending representatives, "who understood well the language and manner of the Indians," to be present at their "convention . . . . . to install as their sachem Major Ben Uncas, the only surviving son of Uncas, formerly their sachem."[4] "John
October. Mason, of Stonington, in consideration of the respect justly due to the name of his ancestors, and the great trust the Mohegan Indians have had in them, as they now have in him, who has a great acquaintance with their language and manners, and may in that respect, as well as others, be of great use and service in endeavoring both to civilize and Christianize them," was authorized by the General Court to occupy any land among them which they might assign, and "to protect them from wrongs, to

[1] See above, p. 421, note.
[2] Conn. Col. Rec., VI. 109–205.
[3] Ibid., VII. 407.
[4] Ibid., VI. 407–409.

set up a school among them, and acquaint them in the Christian religion."[1] Three years later, in accordance with a petition of "Ben Uncas . . . . . with others" of the tribe, James Wadsworth and John Hall, both of them prominent citizens, were appointed to be their supervisors, and Ben Uncas was "established" as their sachem.[2]

1726. October.

It has been seen that Governor Shute considered the General Court of Massachusetts to be precipitate in its hostile measures against the eastern savages.[3] The government of Connecticut were of the same opinion. When applied to by Massachusetts for a contribution of men and munitions, the Legislature of the sister Colony declined to afford such aid, though it placed some small garrisons in its own western settlements, and sent a detachment of troops to aid in the defence of the Massachusetts towns on Connecticut River.[4] As time passed, and the savage invasions grew more annoying, Connecticut desired the Governor to obtain precise information from the authorities of Massachusetts respecting the occasion, the objects, and plans of the war, and made arrangements for maintaining a small force as high up the river as the most northerly English settlements.[5] The Indians committed now and then a murder in that quarter, but they did not come in force, and they eluded pursuit. The application from Massachusetts, more urgently repeated, met with no better success than before.[6] Connecticut professed to be dissatisfied as to the justice of the war, and as to her not having been consulted before it was entered upon.[7] Her historian thinks that this expression on her part expedited the peace which soon fol-

Share of Connecticut in the Indian war.

1722. Oct. 11.

1723. October.

1724. June.

July.

October.

[1] Conn. Col. Rec., VI. 429.
[2] Ibid., VII. 75.
[3] See above, p. 421.
[4] Conn. Col. Rec., VI. 334–336.
[5] Ibid., 426.
[6] Ibid., 474.
[7] Ibid., 503.

lowed.[1] This is not probable. It was enough that, without reckoning the wounds, the abductions, and the losses of property by fire and rapine, Massachusetts had lost some two hundred men killed, and that there was no longer any thing to fight for, for the Indians appeared to be tired out for the time, and to be willing to be peaceable, if they could have some trading facilities, which it was not difficult to afford. No Connecticut men lost their lives in this war, though it caused the Colony an expenditure of some thousands of pounds.

But Connecticut managed her money affairs with a
Financial condition. prudence which shamed her neighbors. In consequence of the disastrous attempt upon Canada,
1709. June 8. under Nicholson, the Colony found itself compelled to issue bills of credit; but the amount was only eight thousand pounds.[2] Four years later, just after the
1713. October. pacification of Utrecht, there was an order for a further issue of twenty thousand pounds;[3] but only a part of that sum was to be put in circulation from year to year, and the provisions for redemption were so judicious and so well enforced, that many years passed before the paper obligations of Connecticut ceased to have the whole value represented by them; and the depreciation never became considerable.

Even the normal sobriety of Connecticut did not absolutely avert the danger of popular tumults. One which
Mob at Hartford. took place in the time of Governor Saltonstall was of such violence as to call for an exercise of all his unfailing promptness and energy for its suppression. The right to a tract of land in and about what is now the town of Coventry was in dispute. A judicial decision dis-
1722. March. missed the claim of Jeremiah Fitch, who was a Deputy in the General Court, and otherwise a man of consequence. For resisting the execution, Fitch

[1] Trumbull, II. 78.
[2] Conn. Col. Rec., V. 111.
[3] Ibid., 379; comp. 381.

was committed to gaol in Hartford. His case was that of a number of his neighbors, who thought that injustice had been done, and that their own turn would be coming next. Their resentment got the better of their discretion. Some fifty of them went in procession to the gaol, and demanded the discharge of Fitch, which being refused by the keeper, they battered down the door with a heavy piece of timber and released him and his fellow-prisoners. The Sheriff, with such help as he could suddenly collect, pursued the party, but was defied and worsted by them. Oct. 22.

The Sheriff made his report of these doings to the General Assembly, which at the time was in session at New Haven. The Assembly proceeded to its deliberation with closed doors, and with an injunction of secrecy upon its members. An Act was passed, declaring a riot to consist in the assembling of three or more persons for an unlawful purpose, and making it punishable by a fine of ten pounds, or imprisonment for not longer than six months, or whipping, or any two or all of these inflictions, at the discretion of the court. A special session of the Superior Court was ordered to be held forthwith for the trial of the recent offenders, who were indicted for burglary, the gaol being under the same roof with the keeper's dwelling. Fifteen persons were arraigned and convicted. Fitch escaped unpleasant consequences, it being held to be no evidence of complicity in the crime of beating down the door that he walked out of it when he found the way clear. The sheriffs were invested with new power to call out the *posse comitatus* and the militia, and it was especially enjoined "that the sheriffs no more return that they cannot do execution."[1] Oct. 24. Oct 28. 1723. May.

[1] Conn. Col. Rec., VI. 332, 341, 345, 346, 353, 375, 387. By some extraordinary inadvertence, Dr. Trumbull has wholly misconceived this transaction. (Comp. Hist., II. 95–98.)

1683. Nov. 28. Western boundary. The agreement made in the time of King Charles the Second respecting the boundary line of Connecticut on the side of New York still remained unexecuted as to its northwardly extension.[1] 1718. May. Connecticut appointed commissioners to join with others from the sister Colony in marking the line and erecting monuments, "for the quieting the complaints and disorders of the borderers."[2] "Difficulties," which are not described, having "prevented the execution of the order of the Assembly," Dec. 3. its next step was to ascertain the line by a surveyor of its own.[3] The consent of a joint commission, however, being 1719. May. still considered as "of great consequence to the peace of his Majesty's subjects bordering on said line," 1720. January. Connecticut made the experiment again, but again was disappointed.[4] Well-nigh disheartened 1723. May. in her endeavors after joint action, Connecticut resolved, if one more proposal of it should prove fruitless, to solicit from the King an "order for the running and fixing said line, that the improvement of the lands bordering thereon may no longer remain under such discouragement."[5] The chance of a settlement, except by royal intervention, seemed desperate when a October. committee of the New York Legislature accused the government of Connecticut of having defaced former monuments, and the latter retorted the charge, pronouncing it, as against themselves, to be "very unreasonable and even monstrous."[6]

Nothing can be more wearisome than the recital of the Eastern boundary. long strife about the boundary between Connecticut and Rhode Island. The reader will be relieved to know that it is approaching its end. The circumstances

[1] See above, III. 440, note 3.
[2] Conn. Col. Rec., VI. 57, 71.
[3] Ibid., 96.
[4] Ibid., 126.
[5] Ibid., 382–386.
[6] Ibid., 418–422.

of an agreement which had been made respecting 1703. May 12.
this line have been related.[1] But it had never
been run, though under instructions from the As- June 22.
sembly the Governor of Rhode Island had twice 1714.
appointed commissioners to meet commissioners June 15.
from Connecticut for that purpose.[2] The question was reopened by an order from England to send over 1719.
a map of the contested territory; and commission- October.
ers were appointed by both Colonies.[3] Again they failed to agree, and again Rhode Island appealed to the King, sending over her Deputy-Governor, Jenckes, to urge her claim, and charging treacherous conduct upon John Winthrop in obtaining the charter for his Colony.[4] 1721.
The King in Council referred the matter to the June 19.
Board of Trade. The Board reported that the case of Rhode Island was not good in law, though they 1723.
thought it probable "that King Charles the Second March 22.
was surprised in his grant to Connecticut;" and they concluded that, as a convenient end to the dispute, it would be well for them to be annexed to New Hampshire.[5]

The Privy Council communicated this judgment July 17.
to Partridge, agent for Rhode Island, and to Dummer, agent for Connecticut, who both, after a time sufficient to communicate with America, reported the disinclination of their respective constituents to the proposal.[6] Again commissioners were appointed by the two Colonies 1724.
to establish the boundary by mutual agreement, October.
but no account of proceedings of theirs has been preserved.[7] Connecticut, perhaps alarmed by the scheme of union with

[1] See above, pp. 234, 356; comp. R. I. Rec., III. 474; IV. 175, 251, 273–285, 291.

[2] R. I. Rec., III. 476; comp. 480; IV. 175; Conn. Col. Rec., V. 443, 468.

[3] R. I. Rec., IV. 263; Conn. Col. Rec., VI. 188, 196, 197, 203, 219, 227.

[4] See above, p. 474; comp. R. I. Rec., IV. 277.

[5] See above, p. 468; comp. R. I. Rec., IV. 303–308.

[6] Ibid., 333, 334.

[7] Ibid., 346, 354; Conn. Col. Rec., VI. 538.

New Hampshire, had resolved to agree to any settlement, rather than have the dispute prolonged. That Colony 1723. Oct. 28. wrote to the Board of Trade, "notwithstanding the priority of our charter to that of Rhode Island, his Majesty's determination will, on our part, put a perpetual end to the controversy, and confirm that peace between us and them which your Lordships have been pleased to express such a regard for."[1] An order in 1726. Feb. 8. Council accordingly determined the boundary to be "a line drawn from the mouth of Ashaway River, where it falls into the Pawcatuck River, and thence extending north to the south line of the Massachusetts Bay."[2] The boundary thus established has been continued to this day. King's Province, included within 1729. June. Rhode Island, took the name of King's County,[3] the other counties of the Colony being called respectively Newport and Providence.

The charter in danger.

The settlement of the eastern boundary of Connecticut by the Privy Council might seem to be a confirmation of the charter of that Colony from the highest authority, and a relinquishment of the long-cherished scheme to make Connecticut a royal estate. But the permanent jealousy in England of Connecticut as well as of Massachusetts, as aspiring to be independent, and as failing to enforce the English laws for the regulation of commerce, was constantly stimulated by the selfishness of English merchants. As long ago as before the death of King William, Joseph Dudley, then in Parliament, had been concerned in the preparation of a bill for vacating the three New England charters, as well as those of New Jersey, Pennsylvania, Maryland, and some of the West India governments.[4] The bill was defeated, when proposed

[1] Conn. Col. Rec., VI. 373.

[2] Ibid.

[3] In October, 1781, the name was changed to that of Washington County.

[4] See above, pp. 164, 200.

early in the next reign, — a result which was largely due to the exertions of Sir Henry Ashurst. Dudley and Lord Cornbury[1] next presented complaints to the Privy Council, which after a hearing were dismissed. 1705. A similar attempt, by the same parties, some years later, met with no better success. 1713. After Dudley's retirement it was renewed in England by the mercantile interest; and a bill brought into Parliament for the "regulation" of the charter governments[2] 1715. caused Jeremiah Dummer, then agent in England for Connecticut, to write his famous treatise entitled "Defence of the American Charters."[3] Again the project miscarried, and again it was revived. The quarrel in Massachusetts between Shute and the Representatives 1721. renewed the dissatisfaction in England against Colonial privileges, and a resolute movement for their overthrow was reasonably feared.

The damage was averted for the time by the publication of Dummer's book, which he dedicated to Lord Carteret (afterwards Earl of Granville, Pope's "Granville the polite"), then newly made Secretary of State for the Colonies.[4] His argument was disposed under four heads: 1. "That the charter governments have a good and undoubted right to their respective charters;" Dummer's defence of the charters. which he urged by showing not only that they were grants from the sovereign, who had a right to make an irrevocable grant, but, further, "that the

[1] One may read noticeable things of this cousin of royalty in the Hist. Mag., XIII. 71.

[2] Chalmers, Revolt, II. 6.

[3] Defence, &c., 10.

[4] May, 1713, the General Court of Connecticut had "advice of complaints and endeavors against the charter governments, and ours in particular," and desired the Governor and Council to "use such measures" as might counteract them. (Conn. Col. Rec., IV. 376.) Aug. 1, 1713, Dummer wrote to them that there was "a design to obtain a new modelling the Plantations, and make alterations in their civil government." (Ibid., 410.) In 1715 (Ibid., 522, 523) the business had grown serious, and the Assembly supplied the agent, through Governor Saltonstall, with money for "extraordinary charges."

American charters were of a higher nature, and stood on a better foot, than the corporations in England," because "the former were given as premiums for services to be performed, and therefore were to be considered as grants upon a valuable consideration." 2. "That these governments have by no misbehavior forfeited their charters;" under which head he showed that they had at much cost and with great valor and constancy defended their people and assailed the common enemy;[1] that they had treated the natives equitably and humanely; that their administration of justice had been efficient and blameless; that they had observed and executed the laws of trade; that their legislation had not been "repugnant to the laws of Great Britain;" and that there was no good ground for the apprehension which had been expressed "that their increasing numbers and wealth, joined to their great distance from Great Britain, will give them an opportunity, in the course of some years, to throw off their dependence on the nation, ... if not curbed in time, by being made entirely subject to the crown."[2] 3. "That it was

[1] Dummer claimed credit for the Colonies for various works of supererogation. "When, in the year 1703, or about that time, Jamaica was in fear of an invasion, and desired some help from the government of the Massachusetts, they, notwithstanding the length of the voyage, which is often eight or nine weeks, sent them two companies of foot. . . . . . The companies arrived safe, and served there two years. . . . . . In 1705, when Nevis was plundered and ruined by Iberville, New England charitably, and of their own accord, raised £2000 for their relief, which they sent in two vessels, having each £1000 on board in flour and salt provisions for their subsistence, and in materials for rebuilding their houses and mills. This they did generously, neither desiring nor receiving any returns, when that island came into more prosperous circumstances. And now lately, when Carolina was engaged in a war with the Spanish Indians, and wanted arms and ammunition, they were supplied with both from Boston." (Defence, &c., 41, 42.)

[2] "I may say, without being ludicrous, that it would not be more absurd to place two of his Majesty's beef-eaters to watch an infant in the cradle, that it don't rise to cut its father's throat, than to guard these weak infant Colonies, to prevent their shaking off the British yoke. Besides, they are so distinct from one another in their forms of government, in their religious rites, in their emulation of trade, and, consequently, in their affections, that they never can be supposed to unite in so

not for the interest of the crown to resume the charters, if forfeited;" for such a resumption would impair colonial prosperity, and "whatever injures the trade of the Plantations must in proportion affect Great Britain, the source and centre of their commerce, from whence they have their manufactures, whither they make their returns, and where all their superlucration is lodged." 4. "That it seemed inconsistent with justice to disfranchise the charter Colonies by an Act of Parliament" instead of by a prosecution in the lower courts.

It was in the second year after Shute's return to England that a fit of apoplexy put an end to the life of 1724.
Governor Saltonstall, when he had administered Sept. 20.
the government of Connecticut for sixteen successive years.[1] A clergyman in the chief magistracy was a new thing in New England; but the experiment was in this instance grandly justified by the event. Winthrop, whom Saltonstall succeeded, was not equal to the demands of a time when the rigor of ancient opinions and manners was unavoidably abating. There was some danger that the pendulum would swing back too far. The receding tide threatened to pass into the region of extravagance and turbulence. The perpetual example of contiguous Rhode Island was unfavorable to good order; and that this influence was not unfelt may be inferred from the factious con-

dangerous an enterprise. It is for this reason I have often wondered to hear some great men profess their belief of the feasibleness of it, and the probability of its some time or other actually coming to pass, who yet with the same breath advise that all the governments on the continent be formed into one, by being brought under one viceroy, and into one Assembly. For surely, if we in earnest believed that there was, or would be hereafter, a disposition in the Provinces to rebel and declare themselves independent, it would be good policy to keep them disunited; because, if it were possible they could contrive so wild and rash an undertaking, yet they would not be hardy enough to put it in execution, unless they could first strengthen themselves by a confederacy of all the parts." (Defence, &c., 72, 73.)

[1] Miss Caulkins (New London, 382) has preserved the contemporary accounts of the imposing ceremonial of the Governor's interment.

duct of Mason and his friends, neighbors of that Colony, in their dispute with the people of New London about the Mohegan lands, and of Fitch and his Coventry friends in
the gaol-breaking riot. Saltonstall became Gov-
1708. ernor in the year of the synod which arranged the
Consociation of the churches. He forwarded that measure with all his great influence, and it was said that in return the clergy had no little agency in promoting his elevation to civil office. His hand upon the helm of state proved to be muscular and firm. To some it seemed to be even rough and heavy. But his abilities, energy, and various accomplishments were universally allowed, even when his enlightened public spirit sometimes failed to secure its just estimation.

Governor The reader remembers Sir Richard Saltonstall,
Saltonstall. the early Assistant of the Massachusetts Company,
1633. and head of the party of emigrants which estab-
October. lished itself at Watertown.[1] His eldest son, Richard, afterwards also an Assistant, married Mariel
1637. Gurdon, of Assington, in the English county of
1639. Suffolk; and their eldest son, Nathaniel, born at
1659. Ipswich, in Massachusetts, and graduated at Har-
1679-1686. vard College, was, like his forefathers, an Assistant
1666. of the Colony. Nathaniel's eldest son, born in
March 27. Haverhill, received the name of Gurdon. He
1684. graduated at Harvard College, and, devoting him-
1691. self to the clerical profession, became the minister
Nov. 25. of New London, and accordingly the pastor of the
Winthrops.

A local occasion engaged him in business, which led, by unanticipated consequences, to his large subsequent participation in the management of the affairs of the Colony.
1689. One John Liveen, of New London, had devised
Oct. 19. property to "the ministry" of that town. John
Winthrop and Edward Palmes, husband of Winthrop's

[1] See above, Vol. I. 317.

sister, were executors of the will. Winthrop would have proceeded in the honest discharge of the trust. But Palmes, an ancient friend of Andros, refused to convey the property, holding that the devise was void, as being in violation of the English statute of mortmain, and that, if not void, the "ministry" contemplated by it must be construed to be the ministry recognized by the laws of England; that is, the ministry of the Episcopal Church. The colonial courts decided against him; but on the death of Liveen's widow, John and Nicholas Hallam, her sons by a former marriage, revived the question, and resorted 1698.
to the alarming measure of an appeal respecting it to the King's Privy Council.[1] It was a question of radical importance, for it involved the goodness of the title to large amounts of property held by the towns for the maintenance of their pastors. And other questions, started at the same time by Major Palmes in connection with his inheritance from his father-in-law,[2] touched the validity of the laws of Connecticut in respect to the distribution of intestate estates, and would have unsettled titles deemed secure since the beginning of her history.

John Winthrop became Governor at this time. In his best estate he was scarcely equal to such a conflict. In the last years of his life he was much disabled by gout, and an embarrassment to his action arose from his being himself a party to one division of the controversy which was pending. It was natural that he should have recourse to a neighbor and friend, whose masterly talents he knew how to estimate, and who was already prompted to vigilance and activity by reasons partly personal. Saltonstall was, or in these circumstances became, by far the most learned lawyer in the Colony. In the last years of Winthrop's administration it was scarcely in any thing but name that Saltonstall was not Governor. The correspond-

[1] See above, p. 225; comp. Conn. Col. Rec., VII. 571-579.

[2] Register of Privy Council, for Feb. 14, 1706.

ence of the Colony with its agents and other friends in England was conducted by his pen. The parties in the Colony felt in every movement his commanding influence. As his habit of acting in the public business was strengthened, the objects of his attention in that sphere were multiplied. In addition to the dispute which first brought him into the political field, the claims of the Mohegan Indians, as they have been described, and the *location* of Yale College, furnished the most exciting questions of the period, and in all of them he had a hand, which was felt more and more to be weighty, if not controlling.

Meanwhile he had been pursuing his professional work at New London, entirely unexpectant, as far as appears or may be guessed, of a transfer to any civil post. Winthrop died, and the Assembly, in joint ballot, passing over the superannuated Lieutenant-Governor, Treat, chose Saltonstall to be Governor till the time of the next popular election. The people elected him the next spring, and continued to do so every year to the close of his life. That he received these repeated tokens of their confidence was not because he was popular, as that attribute is commonly conceived of. As far as scorn was possible to his grave and placid mind, he loathed the arts which are resorted to by base natures for the winning of popular adulation. Not only did his lofty sense of right forbid and disdain all deference to the prejudices and passions alike of "the little vulgar and the great;" his personal dignity dictated abstinence from professions of his always generous devotion to the public welfare.

1707. Dec. 17.

The element, in the western counties, of pretentious loyalty and taste for the Church of England, the disputes about Indian lands in the eastern counties, and the division of opinion respecting the *location* of Yale College, afforded a basis for parties which, united in a common disaffection, were capable of creating frequent embarrassments for the administration; and, especially during the early part of

Saltonstall's official term, he found the House of Deputies factious and intractable. So much had he been hampered and harassed that, after the experience of ten years in office,[1] he resolved to rid himself of the galling burden. At no other time did he descend so much to self-vindication, as when, declining to accept his tenth successive election to the place of Governor, he said to the Assembly, "I have, I thank God, this satisfaction in my own mind, that I was removed from a station of public service, to which I was (though unworthy) called in the Church, into this that I now am, without any the least secret projecting of it in my own breast. It was a real surprise to me. . . . . . I can with all assurance say that I endeavored in this affair not to go before, but to follow (and I hope I did sincerely follow) the conduct of Divine Providence, to which I would still be entirely resigned. . . . . . I am of opinion that it behooves any one who is intrusted as I am, to carry it in all management so as to deserve submission, and consequently to expect it. This I have endeavored to do, with all the condescension I could towards the peaceable and orderly. And when any persons behave themselves in an unruly and disorderly manner, I believe, too, they should be made sensible of their error. This also I have been solicitous to make my care, and this I am so firmly persuaded to be fit and necessary for upholding not only the honor but the usefulness and even being of government, that it's impossible for me to do otherwise. Now if this be like to beget and increase an uneasiness among the people, if the maintaining some

1717. May 10.

[1] Honored and beloved as he was, Saltonstall had not escaped paying, earlier than this time, his share of the penalty of distinguished merit. In 1715, the Assembly "made inquiry after and considered the representation which the Honorable Governor made of some scandalous report very grievous to his Honor." They could not "understand the least ground for any such reports," which they traced to "some ill-minded and seditious persons," and they "signified their earnest desire that his Honor would continue the service of God and his country in the office whereunto he was elected." (Conn. Col. Rec., V. 491.)

small degree of that respect due to government be not agreeable with our Constitution, it will be much better I should resign my charge, and never trouble others or myself any further with what in my opinion is so necessary and in theirs so grievous."[1]

[1] MS. speech *apud* J. H. Trumbull. — Feb. 19, 1717, the Governor and Council, on information of trespasses on some lands belonging to the Colony, "resolved, that a proclamation be issued out and published forthwith in those parts, signifying that such proceedings are without the privity of the government; that the land is still in the grant of the government; and that orders are given out for the apprehending of all persons who, in pursuance of such evil designs, shall commit any trespass thereon." Major Fitch, one of the trespassers, published a sort of counter proclamation, in which he says: "As to a kind of a proclamation lately come forth from the Honorable Governor and Council, in February last, I had thought to have taken it to pieces; and I think I could have done it, and cut it in as many pieces as the Protestant did the Popish wooden god;" and ends, "God save the King, and the Colony of Connecticut from self-defining and self-seeking men." "An information was exhibited against Mr. Fitch in the General Assembly, in May, 1717. He made a written acknowledgment that he had acted indiscreetly and disrespectfully to his Honor the Governor, asked pardon, and promised better behavior, whereupon he was discharged, though the Upper House wished to punish him." (Conn. Col. Rec., V. 586.) This transaction probably had its share in disgusting the Governor with public office.

The dignity of his character and conduct was unexceptionable. In the journal of the May session of 1724 it is recorded that "the question was put, whether this Colony be in arrears with his Honor the Governor in the payment of his Honor's salary for the years past. Resolved in the negative." (Ibid., VI. 443.) To this the editor appends the following note: "The Governor claimed that, by agreement, his salary should be £200 in, or as, money; and that, on account of the depreciation of the bills of credit, there was a considerable balance due to him. The claim had been in dispute between the Governor and the Assembly for several years; and the Governor at this time, in a speech delivered to the Assembly, May 19th, which, upon his desire, was entered in full on the Journal of the Upper House, said: 'I shall, in compliance with your desires, proceed to take the oaths, not doubting but when the present difficulties are over, and you can enter more fully into the consideration of the work and difficulties of my post, you will find them to bear a full proportion to all the recompense that I have ever insisted upon, and make no scruple to give order accordingly. In the mean time let us forget the debates we have had about it, and be as careful of husbanding our time in the public affairs as we seem to be of our money in this particular instance. It may be many of us may never live to another consideration of it; and, if this should be my lot, I shall presume you will not deny to mine what you have desired me, on public considerations, that I would insist no longer on at this juncture.'"

The House returned for the time to its better mind, and united with the other branch of the Assembly in entreating the Governor "with his wonted diligence and steadiness to proceed in the public business;" and he consented to retract his resignation. But as yet the favor of the Deputies was fickle. Two years more brought 1719. the crisis of the Governor's position. An attempt was made to supersede him in the chief magistracy by the nomination of Lieutenant-Governor Gold; and, apparently for the first time in her history, Connecticut witnessed a disputed election.[1] The attempt not only failed disgracefully, but brought a powerful reaction to the Governor's side. Hartford, angry with him for his influence in determining the place of the College, set aside her two Deputies to the General Court, and sent her two ministers in their place. One of them was not only not admitted May. to his seat, but was put on trial for "defaming his Majesty's government in this Colony," by charging the Governor "with the breach of the sixth and eighth commandments." And thenceforward the course of 1724. Saltonstall's administration was tranquil to its close. Its wisdom and vigor moulded the sentiments of a transition period, and no man memorable on the bright roll of Connecticut worthies did more to establish for her that character which was indicated by the name, appropriated to her through many generations, of "the land of steady habits."

We approach the period of the New England actors in the achievement of American Independence. When the first century of Massachusetts was coming to its end, simultaneously with the end of the reign of the first

[1] Professor Kingsley, in American Quarterly Register, VIII. 17; comp. "New Englander," II. 501.—I believe that Professor Kingsley found his authority in the manuscripts of President Stiles, in the library of Yale College. The public documents do not record the occurrence.

British monarch of the House of Hanover, James Otis, Samuel Adams, and Roger Sherman were children learning the alphabet; Israel Putnam was a school-boy; Jonathan Trumbull was a senior sophister of Harvard College; and the Boston-born printer, Benjamin Franklin, had just entered on man's estate.

CHAPTER V.

GILBERT BURNET, the famous Bishop of Salisbury, had several children. By his interest, one of them, who was named William after his royal godfather, and who had been bred to the legal profession, held in England a place in the treasury, from which he was transferred to be Governor of New York and New Jersey, being then just over thirty years of age. His administration of those Provinces was in general satisfactory to the people, though, towards the close of it, a faction was created against him on account of some regulation of the Indian trade which gave displeasure to the merchants of the town of New York.[1] Whether in consequence of their complaints, or because, as the historian Hutchinson had been informed,[2] the place, being lucrative, was coveted by a favorite of King George the Second, Burnet, on the accession of that prince to the throne, was transferred to the government of Massachusetts, a post then of more honor, but of uncertain pecuniary value. Though the government of New Hampshire was added, as had been the practice, except in Phips's case, ever since the Revolution, the profit from this was small. The change was disagreeable to Burnet, as he had lost largely in the South Sea speculation, and had a numerous family on his hands. The busy bishop was now dead, and his children had to rely on their own merits and fortune.[3]

Governor William Burnet. 1720.

[1] Smith, History of New York, 206 *et seq.*

[2] History, II. 325. — Chalmers (Revolt, II. 124) assigns a further reason for the arrangement.

[3] After Burnet's death, his brother

Governor Burnet possessed qualities imposing and attractive. His figure and manners were dignified and engaging. He was intelligent, witty, learned, accomplished, and experienced in business. He had a nice, if arrogant, sense of honor. In his youth he had been reputed to entertain doubts of the authority of revealed religion, but, under the influence of Sir Isaac Newton, he had come to a better state of mind, and while he was in New York he published a theological work, which had some reputation and currency.[1]

Question of a salary for the Governor.

The history of Burnet's fourteen months' administration of Massachusetts is little else than the record of a dispute with the House of Representatives about the settling of a stated salary upon the Governor.[2] The reader has seen that this question, largely

Thomas presented a memorial to the King in behalf of the Governor's children. In it he represented that King George the First, in recognition of the Bishop's services, had made William Burnet "Comptroller of the Treasury, being a patent place of £1200 a year;" that "having, by unfortunate dealing in public stocks, involved himself in considerable debts," he had, in 1720, been permitted by the late King to exchange places with Hunter, Governor of New York; that, had he retained the latter government, "he might have paid his debts, and made some provision for his destitute family;" but that, on the accession of his patron's son to the throne, it was found to be "for the King's service" to transfer him to Massachusetts, by which removal he "lost an income of £3000 a year." (British Colonial Papers.) — In the year of Burnet's appointment to be Governor of Massachusetts, Douglas wrote to Cadwallader Colden (Nov. 20, 1727): "Governor Shute did make of his government £3000 per annum. By management it may be doubled." (Mass. Hist. Col., XXXII. 176.) But Douglas is not a trustworthy witness as to facts; and what he meant by "management" is not explained.

[1] Sparks, Collection of Essays, I. 99. — In N. H. Hist. Col., VIII. 416–426, is a curious letter ascribed to Burnet, on the Romanist controversy. It was addressed to Christina Baker, who, at the sack of Dover in 1689, was carried by the Indians to Canada, and was there educated in the Romish religion.

[2] The currency question, urgent as it was, had to give place to the great dispute of the time, and was in abeyance during this administration. One of the royal instructions which Burnet brought out was not to give his "assent to or pass any Act . . . . . whereby bills of credit may be struck in lieu of money, without a clause inserted in such Act, declaring that the same shall not take effect" without a previous royal confirmation. (See Felt, Historical Account, &c., 85.)

The Episcopalians hoped to turn to account the occasion of a new

treated by Dudley and his successor, had been mostly lost sight of in the different concerns of the last years of the government of Shute, and in that of Lieutenant-Governor Dummer, which followed. For a short time, at the beginning of the new reign, the authority of the cautious Walpole was crippled, while the bustling imbecility of the Duke of Newcastle had much of the management of affairs. The crucial question as to the settling of a salary for the Governors of Massachusetts was now taken up with a zeal which looked like vigor. It was not brought to a determination in Governor Burnet's time, but it was then that the contest over it was most animated.

The lavish magnificence of his reception in Massachusetts,[1] so far as it expressed genuine enthusiasm, is to be ascribed to the veneration popularly entertained for the memory of his father. So far as it was dictated by prudence, its object may be naturally imagined to have been to conciliate the new ruler in respect to the matters upon which the Province had been at issue with his predecessors.

Losing no time in causing his position on the chief of these to be understood, he made it the sole theme

monarch's accession, and Cutler, Caner, and Miles, of Boston, Johnson, of Connecticut, and their associates, in an address of congratulation (Dec. 12, 1727), prayed the King to appoint a resident Bishop. (See above, p. 479.) I find no indication that this paper was ever before the Privy Council, and I strongly incline to think that the Board of Trade, perhaps under a *Walpolean* influence, suppressed it. A proceeding of Massachusetts churchmen a little earlier attracted more attention. July 14, when the movement for a synod had lately occasioned irritation (see above, p. 454), the Privy Council considered a petition from them, "praying the repeal of several laws passed in New England." (Register of Privy Council.) The petition was referred to the Board of Trade. The Board applied to "Mr. Attorney and Solicitor General for their opinion, whether the said Acts are repugnant to the charter of the Massachusetts Bay; and, if so, whether it be not in the King's power to repeal them." (Journal of the Board of Trade, for November 9, 10, 14.) The Massachusetts law of Dec. 19, 1727 (Province Laws, II. 459), was apparently the fruit of this movement.

[1] Some account of it is in Drake's History of Boston, 581, note.

The Governor's speech to the General Court. 1728. July 24.

of his first communication to the General Court. A few days after reaching Boston he addressed them in a speech, in the first sentence of which he not only declared peremptorily what he wanted, but cleverly turned the generosity of their reception of him into an argument in favor of his demand. "The commission," he said, "with which his Majesty has honored me, however unequal I am to it, has been received in so respectful and noble a manner, and the plenty and wealth of this great Province has appeared to me in such a strong light, as will not suffer me to doubt of your supporting his Majesty's government by an ample, honorable, and lasting settlement." He flattered their sense of importance by saying that they approached "the nearest of any of his Majesty's American dominions to the trade and numbers of people in his European kingdoms." He gave them notice of the King's pleasure respecting the salary, of his own immovable purpose to comply with it precisely, and of his confident expectation that they would do the same. "I shall lay before you his Majesty's instruction to me upon this subject, which, as it shall be an inviolable rule for my conduct, will without question have its due weight with you." Meanwhile he volunteered some suggestions of his argument in its support. "The three distinct branches of the Legislature," he said, "preserved in a due balance, form the excellency of the British Constitution. If any one of these branches should become the less able to support its own dignity and freedom, the whole must inevitably suffer by the operation. I need not draw the parallel at length. It speaks of itself. . . . . . The wisdom of parliaments has now made it an established custom to grant the civil list to the king for life. And as I am confident the representatives of the people here would be unwilling to own themselves outdone in duty to his Majesty by any of his subjects, I have reason to hope that they will not think such an example has any thing in it which they are not ready to imitate."

Next came a copy of the royal instruction, which justified the Governor's description of it.[1] After rebukes to the provincial authorities for their previous neglect of directions of the same tenor, it proceeded as follows: "Our will and pleasure therefore is, and we do hereby require and direct you to acquaint the Council and Assembly of our said Province of the Massachusetts Bay, that, as they hope to recommend themselves to the continuance of our royal grace and favor, they must manifest the same by an immediate compliance with what has been so often recommended to them in forthwith passing Acts to establish a fixed and honorable salary for the supporting and maintaining the dignity of our Governor and commander-in-chief for the time being; and we deem a competent sum for that purpose to be at least one thousand pounds sterling per annum from our said Province of the Massachusetts Bay. And in case the said Council and Assembly shall not pay a due and immediate regard to our royal will and pleasure hereby signified, we shall look upon it as a manifest mark of their undutiful behavior to us, and such as may require the consideration of the Legislature in what manner the honor and dignity of our government ought to be supported in our said Province for the future."[2]

Royal instruction concerning a salary.

This mandate was a usurpation. The King had no right to lay any injunctions on the colonists, except such as they were bound to obey either through their relation to him as his natural subjects or under the obligations of his charter. If an instruction from him claimed that which the charter left to their discretion, the instruction had no

[1] Mass. Prov. Rec. — The instruction had been maturely considered by the Privy Council. (Register, for Feb. 6 and 15, and March 26, 1728.)

[2] A Collection of the Proceedings of the Great and General Court or Assembly of his Majesty's Province of the Massachusetts Bay, &c., 41. For the occasion of this book, see below, p. 522.

validity. But this threat of a resort to the interference of Parliament was made significant by a remembrance of the measures which had from time to time been taken by the Ministry to engage Parliament in a scrutiny of the Colonial charters. The power of Parliament in respect to those charters was the more of a bugbear for having never been defined, nor so much as discussed. The Massachusetts patriots were confident that the reasons of their case were such as would sustain their pretensions in the courts of law, and they believed that a perception of this on the part of the courtiers would prevent them from proceeding to extreme measures. But a vague persuasion of the omnipotence of Parliament was a sort of English instinct. When the King said that he considered his authority as affronted, and that he might see fit to call on his Legislature to vindicate it, it was impossible that the Representatives of Massachusetts should not revert to those times, of which the memory was so recent, when the cancelling of their charter had placed them at the mercy of King James and his Governor. Nevertheless, their resolution was taken. Two days, morning and evening, they read over again and again the Governor's speech and the instructions referred to in it, "and spent some considerable time in debating thereon." The result was a simple Resolve "that the sum of seventeen hundred pounds be allowed and paid out of the public treasury to his Excellency William Burnet, Esquire, Captain-General and Governor-in-Chief of this his Majesty's Province, to enable him to manage the public affairs of the government, and defray the charge he hath been at in coming here."[1] The amount of the grant was unprecedentedly large. The Representatives were willing to be liberal, and gained some advantage by showing themselves to be so disposed. But the question of a greater or less

Resistance of the General Court. July 27.

[1] Collection of the Proceedings, &c., 42.

liberality, to be exercised at their own discretion, was one entirely different from that on which they had resolved to make their stand.

It is probable that the Governor was scarcely prepared for so prompt an exhibition of firmness on their part. On the third day after, the Council having meanwhile concurred in the action of the Representatives, the Governor sent a message to both Houses. The grant, he said, "is contrary to his Majesty's instruction communicated to you, inasmuch as that sum is allowed partly 'to enable me to manage the public affairs of the government,' which part of the application of that sum is the very thing against which the said instruction is levelled; for it recites that, 'instead of a salary, the Council and Assembly had from time to time made Governors such allowances and in such proportions as they themselves have thought his Majesty's Governors had deserved, in order thereby to make the said Governors the more dependent upon them,' which is by his Majesty termed a neglect of their duty; and an immediate compliance in settling a salary payable to the Governor is made a condition of his royal favor, and the contrary declared a manifest mark of undutiful behavior. For these reasons, I am utterly disabled from consenting to the said resolve, that I may not draw his Majesty's just displeasure upon myself; and I hope that when you have considered the whole matter with its consequences you will have the same thoughts with me."[1] July 30.

The issue was distinctly joined. A sharp dispute followed, which did not result in causing either party to abandon the position it had taken. The House, having meditated on the subject for a week, passed a Resolve dividing its former grant, and giving the Governor three hundred pounds "for defraying the charges" of his journey, and fourteen hundred pounds "to enable Aug. 6.

[1] Collection of the Proceedings, &c., 43.

him to manage the public affairs." And the two legislative branches joined in an Address praying him to accept this provision, and expressing their confidence "that this and succeeding Assemblies would at the usual times cheerfully afford a support suitable to the dignity of his person and station." They professed to "apprehend that his Majesty's service in the necessary defence and support of the government, and the protection and preservation of the inhabitants thereof, the two great ends proposed in the power granted to this Court for the raising taxes, will be best answered without establishing a fixed salary," and at the same time they "esteemed it a great unhappiness that his Majesty should think our method of supporting a Governor of this Province a design of making them dependent on the people."[1] This language seems carefully chosen. It does not affirm that such was not their design, but that they were sorry the King should so regard it. No doubt they regretted that his discernment was not more dull.

Progress of the dispute.

Aug. 9.

To this Address the Governor replied that "the privilege in the charter to raise money for the support of the government was therein expressed to be *by wholesome and reasonable laws and directions*, and consequently not by such as were hurtful . . . . . to the ends of government;" and that "a support given in such a precarious manner as had been usual here could not possibly be honorable, because it implied no sort of confidence in the government, and made the support of it depend visibly on an entire compliance with every thing demanded by the other branches of the Legislature." He made a telling point when he said, "I may appeal to the consciences of such gentlemen as have been concerned in the public affairs here, whether the allowance for the Governor's salary has not been kept back till other bills of

[1] Collection of the Proceedings, &c., 44, 45.

moment have been consented to, and whether it has not sometimes depended on the obtaining such consent. These matters, which are well known, leave no room to wonder why his Majesty thinks this method of supporting the Governors a design to make them dependent on the people. And as you have given me no reason at all against this opinion, I must believe it is the real view intended to be pursued."

To the Governor's message each branch of the Legislature prepared an answer, and neither would consent to adopt the form proposed by the other. The answer of the Council was brief, merely expressing in general terms their regret that a difference should have occurred at so early a period of the administration; their continued persuasion that the purpose for which the power to levy taxes had been conferred by the charter "would be best answered without establishing a fixed salary;" and their opinion that "an honorable allowance made by the General Court at the beginning of a session" could not "be justly looked upon as having a tendency to bring the Governor into a dependence on the people inconsistent with the dignity of his station, or his freedom of acting according to his judgment."

The House had come to deal more frankly with the policy of maintaining a control over the Governor by keeping him in dependence for his livelihood. "If," they said, "we resemble the British Constitution, as your Excellency has done us the honor to declare, we humbly apprehend that no part of the Legislature should be independent. We have ever conceived that it was the peculiar distinction and glory of the British Constitution, that every part of it had a mutual relation to and dependence on each other. . . . . . If your Excellency intends that we do not put so much confidence in the Governor as the Parliament do in our most gracious sovereign, to whom the civil list is granted for his life, (which God

Extension of the argument.

long preserve!) we freely acknowledge it. Is it reasonable or possible that we should confide in any Governor whatsoever so much as in our most gracious King, the common father of all his subjects, who is known to delight in nothing so much as their happiness, and whose interest and glory, and that of his royal progeny, are inseparable from the prosperity and welfare of his people, whereas it is most obvious that neither the prosperity nor adversity of a people affect a Governor's interest at all, when he has once left them?" They pointed out particulars in which both branches of the Legislature were dependent on the Governor, as constituting "vastly more than a counterbalance for any possible dependence of the Governor upon them. As to the past conduct of Assemblies in making the support of the government conditional, ... it is not easy," so they judged, "to say what men may have had or had not in their own views and thoughts; but this we can say, that to have done so, as the case might have been circumstanced, would not have been unreasonable in itself, nor without precedent from the Parliaments of England, when some of the greatest patriots and most wise and learned statesmen have been actors in them." And their unambiguously expressed conclusion was: "We are constrained in faithfulness to the people of this Province to say, that we cannot pass any Act to establish a fixed salary for the Governor, according to your Excellency's instruction from his Majesty."[1]

Persistency of the House.

[1] Collection of the Proceedings, &c., 46-50. — "The messages of the House, at first, were short, and are supposed to have been drawn by Mr. Cooke. . . . . . In the latter part of the controversy they were generally drawn by Mr. Wells, another member from Boston. . . . . . These were generally more prolix, and necessarily so from the length of the messages to which they were an answer." So says Governor Hutchinson (Hist., II. 348), who had opportunities to be well informed. He was an intelligent and inquisitive young man, already out of College in 1728, and his father was a Counsellor of the Province for many years, including those of Burnet's administration. Cooke was a Counsellor in the civil year 1728-1729. That fact does not contradict his being draughtsman of the papers of the House, especially of the later of

The Council entertained the opinion that "though it might prove of ill consequence to settle a salary upon the Governor for the time being, yet that a salary may be granted for a certain time to his Excellency, William Burnet, Esq., without danger to the Province;" and they passed a vote to that effect, with which the House refused to concur. Then the House asked the Governor for a prorogation, inasmuch as sitting all summer was inconvenient to them. He was as obstinate as they. "In answer," he said, "to your message of this afternoon, that the House is desirous to rise, I must observe to you that his Majesty expects an immediate regard from the Council and Assembly to his will and pleasure signified in his twenty-third instruction to me concerning the establishment of a fixed and honorable salary for the support of the government. If I should consent to your present desire, I should thereby make your immediate regard to his Majesty's pleasure impossible, which it is not as long as this present session continues; and therefore I cannot agree to a recess till you have finished this matter for which the Court is now met." The House renewed its request, and the Governor repeated his refusal, accompanying it with a threat. "I am persuaded," he said, "that you would be very sorry to have his Majesty's favor withdrawn from you on account of your undutiful behavior in not paying an immediate regard to this instruction; and you would be very much concerned to find the Legislature of Great Britain taking into consideration the support of this government, and perhaps something besides, which I for-

Aug. 20.

Aug. 28.

Persistency of the Governor.

Aug. 29.

them; nor does the circumstance that the Governor was a guest in Cooke's house for some time after his arrival. (Sept. 14, 1728, the Court allowed £60 to Elisha Cooke, "in consideration of his Excellency Governor Burnet and his family being at his house until his Excellency's removal into the Province House.") His name and that of Wells constantly appear on the committees charged by the House to conduct the dispute with Burnet in its last stage.

bear to name. When these things happen, as from your proceedings they naturally must, I am sure you will thank no person who has been instrumental in bringing matters to such a pass; and therefore for your own sakes, as well as out of duty to his Majesty, I declare to you my fixed resolution of doing nothing on my part that may put it out of your power to continue in your duty to the best of kings."[1]

To this message the House made a reply, into which were incorporated at length the reasonings of that paper of theirs which a fortnight before had failed to obtain the approbation of the Council.[2] The Governor answered it in a long argument which produced no other effect upon them than a repetition of the request for a prorogation, after the passing of two Resolves which took higher ground than ever. They were: 1. That they would not "take under consideration the settling a temporary salary upon the Governor or Commander-in-Chief for the time being;" 2. That they could not, "with safety to the people they represented, come into any other method for supporting the Governor or Commander-in-Chief for the time being, than what had heretofore been practised." When the committee of the House delivered their message to this effect, "And here," said the Governor, who had information of its purport, "is my answer thereto." It was as follows: "Gentlemen of the House of Representatives, I have already informed you that my duty to his Majesty will not permit me to agree to a recess till his instruction is complied with. I have given you my reasons why I think so, and I have answered all your objections. I can only assure you that unless his Majesty's pleasure has its due weight with you, your desires will have very little with me."[3]

Sept. 2.

1 Collection of the Proceedings, &c., 51–53.
2 Ibid., 54–56; Hutch. Hist., II. 337, note.
3 Ibid., 340, note; Collection, &c., 56–61.

Actuated, as they said, by "an earnest desire, by all just and proper ways consistent with the privileges of this people, to recommend them to the continuance of his Majesty's royal grace and favor, and to bring this session, which has been already so long and expensive, to a good conclusion," the Council "voted that it is expedient for this Court now to ascertain a sum as a salary for his Excellency's support, as also the term of time for the continuance of the same." The House refused so much as to consider this proposal. They turned to the people. They fortified themselves with an elaborate "Advice" to their constituents, recapitulating the transactions of the session, and explaining their own moderation, and the Governor's obstinacy. This was designed "to be transmitted to the several towns by their Representatives" on the rising of the Court, because, notwithstanding their confidence in the correctness of their proceedings, "several members had desired to know the minds of their principals."[1] But when the hope of a prorogation was disappointed, it was circulated at once.

Sept. 6.

Sept. 11.

Advice to the towns.

The Governor brought another influence to bear. He called the attention of the House to a letter written six years before by the Province's agent, Jeremiah Dummer, giving an account of a conversation between Dummer and Lord Carteret, Secretary of State. That Minister had advised Dummer "to write to the Assembly that they would so behave themselves for the future as not to provoke the government to bring the matter of their charter before the Parliament; for if they did, he said 't was his opinion that it would be dissolved without opposition." Lord Carteret had referred to a bill lately introduced into Parliament for the subjection of Ireland. "It was entitled, 'A Bill for better securing the Dependence of Ireland on the Crown of Great Britain;'

Sept. 12.

1722. March 10.

[1] Collection of the Proceedings, &c., 61–65.

and it passed without a division. This, his Lordship said, would be our fate on the like occasion." And complaining "that by several votes and resolutions of the lower House, printed in their journals, we showed an inclination to be independent of the administration here, and that we treated the King's commands as waste paper, particularly in not settling a proper salary on our Governors, he had recommended to them for their own sakes a more discreet conduct."[1] Governor Burnet did not serve his cause by this recollection. An unheeded and unexecuted threat has been divested of its terrors when it is six years old. Lord Carteret can scarcely be said to have been now in power. At all events, the new charm of his brilliancy, and with it a part of his consequence, was gone. To Robert Walpole's prudent policy it belonged not to touch the colonies as long as he could with decency leave them alone.

1728. Sept. 17. The Governor sent to the House a long and acrid stricture on their "Advice" to the towns, though he had received no formal communication of it. Sept. 20. The House promptly replied with a counter-criticism no less careful, but characterized by a calmness and dignity which rebuked his petulance; and the Sept. 21. next day they renewed the grant, which the Governor had declined, of fourteen hundred pounds "for his support in managing the affairs of the government," and added a grant of sixteen hundred pounds Sept. 23. more. Again he sent them an extended and peevish argument upon the case as they had last presented it. He resented as a grossly injurious imputation a suggestion which they had made of the reason why he refused them leave to separate. "What could be less decent or respectful, and more irritating, than directly to charge me with a design to keep you sitting in order to compel you to act contrary to your native freedom and

[1] Collection of the Proceedings, &c., 65–67.

declared judgment, and so betray the great trust and confidence your principals have reposed in you?" His reason for refusing to prorogue them was, as he tauntingly phrased it, "that I may do nothing on my part that may put it out of your power to continue in your duty to the best of kings." As to the three thousand pounds they had offered him, he would have none of their money except on his own terms. "As to your offer which you have now made, I see no difference between it and what I was obliged to decline before, but in the sum; that is to say, that you would give me still a higher reward for to take his Majesty's displeasure off from you and lay it upon myself, which I am by no means inclined to do." The House replied in a very few respectful words, merely affirming their continued conviction of the correctness of their views of the controverted question.[1]

Oct. 2.

The Governor was not at all discouraged. He owned to the Duke of Newcastle, that while he had "brought the Council into the measure of a fixed salary," he had found himself "contending with a stiff Assembly;" but at the same time he informed the Lords of Trade that he "intended to continue sitting with the Assembly till they comply, that the country, who pay about a thousand pounds a month to the Council and Representatives by way of wages during their attendance, may feel the inconvenience of their standing out." "I have now," he wrote, "reduced them to silence. . . . . . I am so far from desiring to have leave to depart from my instruction [so as to receive their grant of three thousand pounds], that I think his Majesty's authority in danger of being lost in this country, if it be given up in this point." [2]

Sept. 13.

Restraint of the General Court by the Governor.

Sept. 30.

The Governor tried yet another device. He informed the Houses in a formal speech that he

Oct. 1.

[1] Collection of the Proceedings, &c., 67–85, 87.
[2] British Colonial Papers.

had reason to believe that their Act for the issue of sixty thousand pounds in bills of credit, passed in the last year, would be disallowed by the King, a result which would be fruitful of embarrassments; and that the most likely way to save it would be to appropriate the interest which it would bring in to the salary which he was demanding.[1]

Oct. 5. The Council proposed to refer this communication to a joint committee. The House, refusing to make this disposal of it, referred it to a committee of their own, and sent out warrants to call in all the members for the more solemn deliberation on the subject. On the report of their committee, the House replied to the Governor's proposal: "If we should by such an Act settle the said four per cent, as your Excellency moves, it would be fixing a salary, which is concluded by this House to tend very much to the hurt of the people of this Province, as we have often declared, and in this opinion we still fully are." And they added, "As we have been very ready to show our honorable esteem and high respect for your Excellency at your arrival and till your settlement, and in adorning the Province House for your more pleasant entertainment, so we are very desirous that your Excellency may be still honorably supported, and therefore would again entreat you to accept of the fourteen and sixteen hundred pounds, which this Assembly have so cheerfully granted, and which is so far beyond any grants in this Province ever before; which if your Excellency should be pleased to do, we cannot doubt but that succeeding Assemblies, according to the ability of the Province, will be very ready to grant as ample a support. And if they should not, your Excellency will then have the opportunity of showing your resentments."

Oct. 24.

Removal of the Court from Boston.

The answer to this Address was an immediate adjournment of the Court by the Governor for a week, to meet at the end of that time at the Court

[1] Collection, &c., 85–87.

House in Salem. So bold an attempt at coercion did he deem expedient and becoming.[1] In justifying it to the Lords of Trade he wrote that, 1. Boston had instructed its Representatives to vote against the establishment of salaries; that, 2. "the people of the town were continually endeavoring to pervert the minds of the members who come from the country," while at Salem he was "informed the people were generally well inclined, as the members from that place were;" and that, 3. "the whole profit of the meeting of the Assembly was confined to the town of Boston, who deserve so ill at the hands of the government." He "begged leave to propose two expedients that he humbly apprehended would be necessary to bring this people to reason and their duty." One was "a disallowance of the Act for raising and settling a public revenue for and towards defraying the necessary charges of this government by an emission of sixty thousand pounds in bills of credit;" the other, "to lay before his Majesty the whole conduct of the Assembly, not only in refusing to comply with his Majesty's twenty-third instruction, but likewise in having the confidence to charge his Majesty with giving an instruction that has a direct tendency to weaken, if not to destroy, their happy Constitution." He "humbly submits if it is not absolutely necessary that his Majesty be moved to lay the matter before the Parliament." The action of Parliament which he desires "will be no final decision against their charter, but will give them just apprehensions of losing it, if they continue refractory." He begs the Board to "give all possible despatch to this affair, ... till which time this government is of no profit and has no authority." At the same time he informs the Duke of Newcastle that he has had "no subsistence at all but from perquisites from the shipping, which have amounted to about two hundred pounds sterling a

Oct. 26.

[1] Collection, &c., 88–90.

year, since they were raised to a par with those of New York."[1]

Oct. 31.

"You are, no doubt," he said, on meeting the Court in the unusual place for their assembling, "desirous of knowing my motives for removing the General Court from Boston, and I am as ready to satisfy you." He had, he said, "for some time had too much reason to think that the general inclination of the inhabitants of that town was against a compliance with his Majesty's twenty-third instruction, and that they used endeavors to work upon the minds of the Representatives to bring them into their own way of thinking." But, as he proceeded to explain, what had brought him to the determination to change the seat of government for the present, was "a public unanimous declaration, at a town-meeting [of Boston] called for the purpose, that they were against settling a salary." He had "therefore thought it proper to adjourn the Court to some place where prejudices had not taken root." In terms well adapted to exasperate the existing disagreement, he recommended "a harmony between the branches of the Legislature." He repeated his argument respecting the last emission of bills of credit; and as to their rejection of it he assured them that he could not "think without concern on the consequences it would have to their disadvantage, and therefore would earnestly persuade them, if possible, to reconsider with care what had perhaps been too suddenly resolved, that, before it was too late, they might avoid all the unhappy effects which those measures might bring upon them."[2]

The Governor's defence of the removal.

It was no time for intimidation when the Representatives and the capital were incensed by so violent a measure as the removal of the Court. Perhaps it was to show that they meant to do nothing in passion, that the House passed

[1] British Colonial Papers. [2] Collection, &c., 90–92.

a fortnight in the transaction of other business before uttering their sense on the great present grievance. There was then more gravity and calmness in their language than cogency in their argument. After expressing their grief at the Governor's imputation, "so very dishonorable to them," of being "influenced by the people in Boston," and declaring their persuasion that "the reasons that prevailed with them to determine as they had, would go with them, guide and influence them everywhere," they proceeded to complain of what was "so very grievous to them, and hurtful to the Province, as the removal of the Great and General Court from Boston."

The charter had given to "the Governor for the time being full power and authority from time to time to adjourn, prorogue, and dissolve all Great and General Courts and Assemblies;" and, besides the prescribed yearly General Court of Election, Courts were "to be held at such other times as the Governor should think fit and appoint." Nothing was said in the charter of the place of meeting; and the argument would have been plausible, at least, that no power short of that of the whole government could designate any place other than the ancient and customary one, where the public records were kept. But the Representatives went further. They urged that an Act, confirmed by the royal approbation, for "establishing the form of the writ and precept for calling a Great and General Court or Assembly" had "determined the town-house in Boston to be the only place for convening, holding, and keeping Great and General Courts or Assemblies;" and they represented that a few years
before, when Governor Shute, with the advice 1721.
of his Counsellors, had transferred the General Court to Cambridge, on account of the small-pox then raging in Boston, he had assented to votes of the whole Court giving validity to the proceeding in those new circumstances, and guarding against this act of the Governor being drawn

into precedent. They had now given the Governor an advantage. He told them very justly that the words in the writ were "to be understood by way of instance or example only," and no more determined Boston to be the only lawful place for holding General Courts than the appointed forms of precepts for the election of Representatives, which expressed the name of no other county but Suffolk, determined Suffolk to be the only county that could lawfully be represented. And he reminded them of the order in Council, passed in conformity with the opinion of the King's Attorney-General and Solicitor-General on the former occasion when the question was raised, to the effect "that the sole power of dissolving, proroguing, or adjourning the General Court or Assembly, either as to time or place, is in his Majesty's Governor."

Recurring to the main question, he asked, "If the settling of the salary of a Governor be not just and equitable, how came it to be just to settle the wages of the Council and Representatives, as had been lately done, by law? Would it not have been better to have waited till each session was over to see how much every member of either House might deserve by voting with the majority, and to allow them wages in that case only?" Their desire to return to Boston, and their persistence in the same views which they had entertained there, only satisfied him still more, he said, that Boston was not a safe place for him to trust them in. "If your thoughts are still the same that they were at Boston, it only proves how deep impressions were made upon you there, which I shall continue to hope will be removed in time."[1]

The Representatives, satisfied by this time that the Governor was inflexible, turned to the King.[2] In a respectful

[1] Proceedings, &c., 92–95.

[2] First, however, in consistency with their claim that the removal of the Legislature, without its consent, was illegal, they passed a Resolve (November 20) to legalize its proceedings, notwithstanding that irregularity.

Memorial, comprising a repetition of arguments grown familiar in this controversy, they justified their not having accommodated themselves to the royal instruction. They described the ample liberality of their grants to the Governor, and explained, on the other hand, that in the course of his administration they had had no encouragement to change their sentiments as to a permanent salary "from any grounds or reasons for special confidence in him; but the treatment they had met with in the methods that had been used to bring them into a stated salary had tended to confirm and abundantly strengthen them in their first determination." The Governor asked for a copy of this Memorial. The House, after debate, refused it. The House voted to instruct the Treasurer to remit a hundred pounds sterling to Francis Wilks of London, "to enable him to serve the interest of the Province in the affair of the humble Address the House have prepared." The Council unanimously declined to consent to this appropriation, "for that the Address of the House to his Majesty not having been communicated to this Board, they cannot judge whether it be for the interest of the Province or no," and also because Mr. Wilks was to be only the agent of the House. Mr. Jonathan Belcher, who was about to embark for England, was then desired by a vote of the House to co-operate with Mr. Wilks in endeavors to obtain the King's favorable reception of the Memorial.[1]

Appeal of the Representatives to the King. Nov. 22.

This movement had a good effect, which had probably been contemplated, though no purpose of the kind was avowed. It furnished the Governor with an excuse to himself for releasing the Legislature from its five months' imprisonment, persisted in hitherto from the moment of his arrival. For many successive days the only record on the Council's journal had been that there was "no business before the Board." The House would pre-

Nov. 16–28. Dec. 7–10.

[1] Proceedings, &c., 96–100.

pare none for them until the Council should concur in their protest against the Governor's removal of the Court to Salem, which the Council steadily refused to do. The Governor had offensively said that he could not be so unkind as to dismiss the Court, because a prorogation would put it out of their power to set themselves right by compliance with the King's instruction. But now that they had directly approached the King with the assurance that no such compliance was to be expected from them, there was an end to that pretence, and they were prorogued for three months, to meet again at Salem. The Governor wrote to England that he had been reluctantly "prevailed upon by friends in the Assembly, whose affairs suffered very much, to give them a recess before Christmas. As to the fixing of a salary," he said, "I have no expectation to succeed in it, till a censure of Parliament is passed."[1]

Prorogation of the Court. Dec. 22.

1729. Jan. 24.

He had kept the Board of Trade informed from time to time of his unsatisfactory relations to the Colony, and, on receiving from the Duke of Newcastle the Address to the King, the Board "resolved to take into consideration all the letters and papers received from Mr.

Jan. 31.

[1] British Colonial Papers. — Nov. 22, the House asked for a recess "for the space of three weeks or one month," because of "urgent affairs requiring their being at home for a short time to provide for their families during the winter season." "His Excellency answered that he did not think it proper to agree to an adjournment." — December 6, the House resolved they "could not but look on themselves in a sort of duress," "in a place never designed and no ways prepared for the House of Representatives, and where they could not, without great danger in this extreme season of the year to the lives or health of the members, attend to business with any application." — December 12, the House passed a vote expressing "their earnest desire to proceed to such business of the public only, the foregoing of which may disserve the public service, and that all who have demands on the public treasury may receive their just dues;" but the Council unanimously non-concurred, because it was accompanied with a proviso that it should not "be pleaded as a precedent for the time to come for the removal of any General Court from the place fixed and determined by law." The Governor sent the House a message that he gave them leave "to adjourn themselves to the Ship Tavern in this town for their convenient accommodation."—December

Burnet since his being appointed Governor of the Massachusetts Bay."[1] Mr. Wilks for Massachusetts, and Mr. Thomas Burnet for the Governor, were heard by counsel before the Board for the contending parties. The result was an absolute approval of the Governor's conduct, and an advice to the King to lay before Parliament the facts indicating the insubordination of Massachusetts.[2]

March 22.

13, the Council restated their usual argument against the House's view, and made warm complaint of the imputation of being less tender of the rights of their constituents.

[1] Journal of the Board of Trade, for Jan. 31 and Feb. 4, 1729; comp. Register of the Privy Council, for February 1.

[2] Journal of the Board of Trade, for March 22; comp. entries for February 5, 11, March 4, 14, 18. Sayer and Fitzakerly, of counsel for Massachusetts, boldly argued against the validity of the King's instruction respecting a salary. "As the twenty-third instruction had been obtained without the privity of the people, they had no opportunity of laying their reasons against it before his Majesty, which, had they done, they believed his Majesty would never have granted it, inasmuch as they conceived it was contrary to the charter granted to the Massachusetts Bay, which gave them a free liberty of passing laws for raising money for the defence and support of the government." The argument, a full report of which is entered on the Journal, is extremely able, and may well have alarmed the Duke into giving private instructions to the Governor, agreeably to Chalmers's statement (Revolt, II. 129), "to recede from his former demands of a standing salary." The counsel represented the adjournment of the Court to Salem as unreasonable and a hardship, but judiciously refrained from charging it with illegality. The counsel on the other side, the Attorney-General and the Solicitor-General, added nothing to the reasons which the Governor had all along skilfully presented. The conclusion, reported by the Board to the Privy Council (March 27), was that "his Majesty's twenty-third instruction . . . . . was proper to be enforced." The Privy Council raised a committee, which, after surveying again the whole ground, reported (April 22) "that the point contended for [by the Province] was to bring the Governor appointed by his Majesty over them to a dependence on their good-will for his subsistence, which would manifestly tend to the lessening of his authority, and consequently of that dependence which this Colony ought to have upon the crown of Great Britain;" that for this reason, and especially for "better securing a due execution of the laws for Trade and Navigation," it was "absolutely necessary . . . . . that a salary of £1000 sterling per annum should be settled upon the Governor;" and, finally, that in view of the refractoriness of the Province upon this subject, the King should be "humbly advised to order this whole matter to be laid before the Parliament of Great Britain." The report was approved (May 22), and it was "ordered that one of the principal Secretaries of State should receive the pleasure of the crown thereupon." (Register of the Privy Council.)

The Governor was much incensed. He wrote to the Duke of Newcastle: "I have seen so much of the temper of the people of this Province that I humbly conceive that some of his Majesty's forces upon the British establishment will be necessary to keep them within the bounds of their duty;" and he urged the expediency of sending over at least two companies of a hundred men each, and making him captain of one of them. The Privy Council considered the representation, but it does not appear to have led to any action.[1]

March 31.

May 14.

The Governor was all this while embarrassed for the means of living. He was resolved that he would not take the public money except on his own terms. The Representatives were resolved that he should not have it except on theirs. He resorted to a measure which would have occasioned much more outcry, if personally he had been less liked, and if the more material controversy which was pending had not absorbed attention. In his former government of New York he had been accustomed to receive fees for passes given to vessels cleared at the custom-house. It was complained of in England, and he was instructed to discontinue it. But it does not seem to have occasioned any violent crimination; and in Massachusetts he had resumed the practice, and had raised the fees till they yielded him a considerable revenue.[2]

Renewal of the dispute in a new session.

April 2.

His speech at the beginning of the session in the spring referred briefly to some matters of inconsiderable importance, but the topic with which it opened and closed was that which had caused the warm discussion of the preceding year. "All proposals to me," he said, "to deviate from my royal master's commands will be vain and fruitless, and, as I kept you together in the fall that you might avoid his Majesty's displeasure, till you put it out of my power to excuse you

[1] Register of the Privy Council. [2] See Hutch., II. 357.

by sending home a declaration that must have been highly offensive to him, so now I give you an opportunity which this House of Representatives will never have again, of retracting and retrieving so unhappy measures, and of showing that your professions of duty and loyalty to his Majesty are more than words."

April 4.

The House, after debate, voted that they would not "come into any further consideration of settling a salary on the Governor at this present session." They directed the Treasurer to remit three hundred pounds to Mr. Wilks and Mr. Belcher, to recompense their services in the matter of the Address. The Council refused, for the same reasons as before, to concur in this larger appropriation, and they complained that in the Address, of which they had only obtained a sight several months after its transmission, they found a statement, which they considered "partial, not to say unfair," that the House "had the concurrence of the Council in their conclusion, not to settle or fix a salary on the Governor." The failure to obtain money from the treasury for the purposes of the Address was made up by a voluntary contribution of merchants and others of Boston, whom the House engaged to "use their utmost endeavor" to reimburse "in all convenient time." In messages which passed between the two branches, vindicating with some asperity the proceedings had by them respectively, the House, by the citation of a precedent of Lieutenant-Governor Dummer's time, defended its course in respect to the appointment and remuneration of agents of its own, and to the withholding of their instructions from the knowledge of the Council, while the Council maintained that, inasmuch as they had "declared their readiness to come into a salary to the present Governor for a limited time, ... the Honorable House in their Address ought not to have represented the Council as concurring with them, ...

April 10.

April 11.

April 16.

April 17, 18.

but ought in justice either to have left the Board unmentioned, or . . . . . to have stated the matter in its true light."

Publication of earlier proceedings. April 17.

"For the more sure guidance and direction of his Majesty's good subjects here, if that affair should be brought for further consideration before the General Court," the House directed the members from Boston to compile and publish a collection of instructions from the crown to the Governors respecting the establishment of a salary, and of all proceedings which had been had upon that subject since the grant of the existing charter; and the volume was published in the same year.[1] The legal term of the Court was near to expiring.

April 18.

The Governor dissolved it without having given his approval to the Resolves which had been passed for its pay. "It may justly appear doubtful," he said, in his message, "whether the towns ought to bear an expense, the sole end of which was defeated; . . . . . and since you would not come into any further consideration of settling a salary on the Governor at this present session, I think you cannot wonder that I should defer the consideration of your allowances in the same manner." He communicated an extract from a letter from the Board of Trade, applauding his "prudence and integrity in declining to accept of money from the Assembly upon any terms different from those enjoined by the instructions;" and he concluded with an assurance of the satisfaction he had in thinking that in the approaching annual election "the country would have an opportunity, by a new choice, of showing their duty and loyalty to his Majesty, as well as their faithfulness to their own constitution."[2]

[1] This is the volume repeatedly quoted in the preceding notes, under the title of "Proceedings," &c. It consists of 112 pages, in small quarto size.

[2] Proceedings, &c., 101–112. — April 25, after the hearing before the Board of Trade, Wilks and Belcher wrote to the Speaker of the House of Massachusetts: "We can by no means think it prudent, just, or reasonable, but an infringement of the rights

Of course, the Governor did not expect this to be taken as sincere. At all events, the character of the new House, which also, agreeably to the writ, came together at Salem, was the same as that of the last. Its vote for Counsellors did not, however, express the resentment which would have been not unnatural. Only four new members were chosen to that Board, of whom two, Jonathan Belcher, the House's agent in England, and Isaac Little, were rejected by the Governor. The formal business of the opening of the legislative year having been transacted in two days, the Court was prorogued to the following month, when the House began the session by opening another question. It proposed to go into convention with the Council for the choice of an Attorney-General. The Council replied that it was not at liberty to do so, a royal instruction to the Governor having declared that that officer must be appointed by the executive department. The House appealed to a precedent of the time of Governor Shute, when the Council, after setting up this pretension, had on further reflection abandoned it.[1] But the Council now persisted;

New General Court. May 28.

June 25–July 10.

1715.

vested in the people by the royal charter, to fix a salary on a Governor by virtue of an instruction. Of what value is the charter, if an instruction shall at pleasure take away every valuable part of it? If we must be finally compelled to a fixed salary, ... if our liberties must be lost, much better they should be taken away, than we be in any measure accessary to our own ruin." The agents expressed their opinion that the Privy Council's threat of submitting the dispute to Parliament would be carried out. But it seems that the leaders in Massachusetts were otherwise and better informed. Either through communication with persons about Sir Robert Walpole, or from their own observations of his policy, they were satisfied that, in the last resort, the officious Board of Trade and the improvident Duke would be held back from making serious trouble.

[1] At an early period of the administration under the Provincial charter, the importance of the office of Attorney-General was perceived. Nov. 23, 1693, a memorial from "Thomas Newton, barrister, praying to be appointed Attorney-General for New England," was before the Lords of Trade. (British Colonial Papers.) Three years later (Sept. 10, 1696), the Privy Council directed the Attorney-General "to consider whether an Attorney-General may not be appointed for his Majesty in each of the several Colonies and

and with their advice and consent, Paul Dudley, who had held the office by annual elections of the Court, was reappointed to it by the Governor. The two Houses concurred
1729. July 3. in a vote to issue twenty thousand pounds in bills of credit to meet the current expenses of the government; but the Governor withheld his approval. He did "not think proper to consent to any form for supplying the treasury, but what was practised before the year 1721."[1]

The Representatives prayed him to issue his warrant for the payment of their predecessors who had served in the last House. The law, they said, prescribed no such condition of the remuneration of Representatives as that of "their being always of the same sentiments with the Governor." But they could get nothing from him beyond the answer that "he should lay the matter before the Lords of Trade, and take their directions therein." They were engaged in a discussion as to a grant to be made to the Governor, when, after a fortnight's session, he again prorogued the Court for six weeks, to meet again at Salem.[2] At neither of these sessions had he resumed the application for a salary. He was awaiting intelligence of the action of the King's Privy Council upon the Address which had been sent by the House. As soon as he had

Provinces." (Privy Council Register.) Randolph had recommended Thomas Newton for the post, representing "that Anthony Checkly, the present Attorney-General of the Massachusetts Bay, is not only ignorant of the laws of England, but has been himself an illegal trader." (British Colonial Papers.) To as late a time as the close of Dudley's administration, the Attorney-General had been appointed by the Governor, such being the construction of that Article of the charter which related to "officers belonging to the courts of justice." Lieutenant-Governor Tailer, in 1716, yielded the point to an assumption of the General Court; and the practice of election by that body, though excepted to by Governor Shute, was followed till Burnet revived the question.

[1] See Mass. Prov. Laws, II. 219-222; comp. above, p. 433; Hutch., II. 378.

[2] Mass. Prov. Rec. — In the morning of the day of the prorogation, the House had resolved to enter in the afternoon upon the consideration of an allowance for the Governor. But he was beforehand with them.

parted with the Court, he wrote to the Lords of Trade: "The principles of independency are too deeply rooted in them to be managed by any thing but the Legislature of Great Britain."[1] July 19.

He was ready, at the next meeting of the Court, to acquaint them with the action of the Privy Council, premising that, till he should be informed of it, he had purposely abstained from presenting the question respecting salaries to the present House, in order that they "might remain free and unconstrained from any share in the dispute." He now informed them that, after hearing the agents of the House by counsel and the law officers of the crown in reply, the Privy Council, with expressions of their high approbation of his perseverance, and with a reassertion of their judgment that the Governor of Massachusetts should have a permanent annual salary of a thousand pounds, had advised the King "to lay the whole matter before the Parliament of Great Britain." The House, however, at the same time, received information from the agents — which, to keep up the public spirit, they immediately published — to the effect that the reference to Parliament was not likely to be made.[2] The agents had probably discovered the resolute reluctance of the Prime Minister to meddle with the colonial administration. Aug. 20. May 22. Renewed demand for a salary.

The House again, in the same terms as before, passed its Resolve for the emission of bills of credit, to the amount of twenty thousand pounds, to meet the charges of the government. The Council amended the Resolve so as to clear it from that claim on the part of the House which had before been a Aug. 22. Aug. 23.

[1] British Colonial Papers.

[2] Ibid. — Jeremiah Dummer wrote from London, Aug. 10, 1729, urging strongly a compliance with the King's instructions: "I am afraid, if we don't do it willingly, we shall be compelled to do it unwillingly. The Ministers are determined to lay it before Parliament; and if they bring in the bill, who will undertake to get it thrown out?" (Barry, History of Massachusetts, II. 127, note 1.)

subject of dispute. The House refused to concur in the amendment, and again the measure fell to the ground. The Council by a unanimous vote refused to accede to a grant of five hundred pounds made by the House to its agents in England. In a calm and respectful message the House expressed to the Governor its approval of the position taken by the last House respecting the great question of salaries, and the Governor immediately resorted to another measure of coercion, adjourning the Court to meet after four days at Cambridge.

The further dispute was to be of no long duration. Of course the House met in no more manageable mood, when, for the gratification, as it seemed, of the Governor's passion, or for a harsher trial of his power, it found itself in a second unusual place. But it did not overlook the advantage of proceeding with dignity in a quarrel with an angry man. It now made a grant to him of six thousand pounds "for his support the last year, and further to enable him to manage the affairs of government." "If you will not comply," he said to the Representatives, "with his Majesty's instruction, you might at least forbear your endeavor to seduce one of his servants from his declared duty;" and in his ill-humor he warned them against adjourning themselves, as they had done, "from Saturday morning to Tuesday afternoon," and threatened to bring to the notice of Parliament this unauthorized extension of their right by charter to adjourn themselves for forty-eight hours. They answered his refusal of their money with an argument to which the frequent previous repetition of it now left nothing to be added.

Aug. 27.

Aug. 30.

The same day, as he came towards the ferry from Cambridge on his way to Boston, his carriage was overset, and he was thrown into the water. A fever followed, and he died at the end of a week,[1]

Governor Burnet's death. Sept. 7.

[1] New England Weekly Journal, for September 8.

[h]aving first, however, sent to the House from his sick-[ch]amber a very long vindication of his own proceedings [a]nd claims, accompanied with a strain of equally emphatic [co]ndemnation of the opposition which had distressed and [ba]ffled him.[1] The Court, which had little fault to find with [hi]m, except for his stubborn fidelity to a claim opposed by [th]emselves with as stubborn resistance, and which could [no]t be unimpressed by his generous qualities and [b]y his various accomplishments, honored him by a [su]mptuous funeral.[2] Sept. 12.

Appearing at the Council Board, from which he [h]ad been absent since the third day after Burnet [a]ssumed the government, Lieutenant-Governor [D]ummer adjourned the Court for a week. His [s]peech at its meeting briefly declared his good [in]tentions towards the Province, and referred to [th]e obligation which his instructions imposed to ask for a [st]ated salary. The House repeated, in the same [te]rms as before, its vote to supply the treasury by [a]n issue of twenty thousand pounds in bills of credit. [T]he Council amended the vote, with reference to the dis-[p]uted question of the liability of the money to be drawn [fr]om the treasury by the Governor's warrant. The House [r]efused to accept the amendment, and the Council to re-[c]ede from it. With the now familiar arguments, [th]e House replied to the Lieutenant-Governor's

Sept. 10.

Lieutenant-Governor Dummer.

Sept. 17.

Sept. 18.

Sept. 23.

[1] "It is not with so vain a hope [a]s to convince you that I take the [tr]ouble to answer your message, but, [if] possible, to open the eyes of the [d]eluded people whom you represent, [a]nd whom you are at so much pains [to] keep in ignorance of the true state [of] their affairs. . . . . . I am tied [u]p by my instructions on one hand, [a]nd meet with nothing but contradic-[ti]on and ill usage from you on the [o]ther." These are fair specimens of [th]e tone of the paper, which betrays [ra]ther the petulance of an invalid, than the haughty confidence of the general tenor of the Governor's career.

[2] It cost £1097 11*s.* 3*d.* (Mass. Prov. Rec., for September 6 and November 19.) Dr. Colman, as "the eldest minister of Boston," wrote to Thomas Burnet a letter of condolence on his brother's death, and took the opportunity to deprecate further persistence of the home government in the claim for a stated salary. (Turell's Colman, 195–197.)

demand for a salary; the Lieutenant-Governor justified it, and the House criticised his plea. But the other point, to
Sept. 24. which up to this time they had adhered with equal obstinacy, they now surrendered. The inconvenience of a suspension of payments from the treasury was too great to be longer borne; and the House had become discouraged as to carrying their point in respect to the form of the grant. The necessary supply was now granted in the manner which had been practised before the last year of Governor Shute; that is, it was made subject to be drawn from the treasury by the Governor's warrant without a subsequent action of the Legislature upon each
Sept. 26. payment. The Court, having sat a week, was prorogued to come together again at Boston, the Council having first repeated their refusal to make an allowance for the remuneration of the House's agents in England.[1]

Nov. 19–Dec. 20. In the next session, of a month's duration, the standing topics of dispute were again treated, but it was with no novelty of discussion, and nothing beyond
Dec. 19. routine business was accomplished, except that a law was passed relieving Baptists and Quakers from parish taxes.[2] The Lieutenant-Governor recommended to the House not to waste their time in deliberating about a grant to him, since he must adhere to the instruction to receive none except in a stated salary. To make good their own ground, they went through the form of granting him seven hundred and fifty pounds. The Council still refused to meet the House for the election of an Attorney-General, and to consent to its grants to its agents; and it refused, though earnestly urged, to have a

[1] Mass. Prov. Rec.

[2] Province Laws, II. 543. — Since the first year of King George the Second, the Baptists and Quakers had been excused from paying a poll-tax towards the support of ministers. The present Act exempted their estates. For some very suggestive views of the political relations in Massachusetts of the question concerning baptism, see Thomas Cobbet's letter, in Mass. Hist. Col., XXXVIII. 291; comp. above, II. 492.

conference with the House on those questions. The House voted to direct the Treasurer to place five hundred pounds at their disposal by paying it into their Speaker's hands; but the Council defeated this plan by an amendment directing the Treasurer to pay the money to Jeremiah Dummer, who in England represented the whole Court. The House, in a single vote, granted three thousand pounds to their agents, and two thousand pounds to the late Governor's children. Personally he had not been after their pattern; but they could not but respect his memory, for manliness is sure to command the respect of manly opponents. In another vote the Representatives attempted to get their agents paid as for services in calling Burnet to account before the Privy Council for taking illegal fees for the clearance of vessels. But against both devices they found the Council equally inflexible.

Dec. 9.

Grant to Governor Burnet's family. Dec. 13.

Dec. 15.

At the annual meeting for elections, the Lieutenant-Governor made no reference to the controverted questions. He told the Court that Burnet's practice as to taking fees had been disapproved by the Privy Council, and that Jonathan Belcher, one of the House's agents, was about to return to Massachusetts as Governor. The House, well knowing that it would not be accepted, made an allowance of nine hundred pounds to the Lieutenant-Governor, and then, on account of an alarm of the small-pox in Boston, and of the expectation of the speedy arrival of the new Governor, the Court at its request was prorogued for a month, to reassemble at the end of that time at Cambridge.

1730. May 27.

Appointment of Governor Belcher.

May 30.

CHAPTER VI.

At some time within the first nine years after the immigration of Winthrop's company, Andrew Belcher set up an inn in Cambridge. His son Andrew made a considerable fortune as a merchant, first of Hartford and then of Boston, and was a member of the Council of Massachusetts several years under the Provincial Charter.[1] He married a daughter of Deputy-Governor Danforth. His son Jonathan, after finishing the course of study at Harvard
1699. College, travelled abroad, both in England and on the Continent, and, according to a statement in one of his speeches, had an honorable reception at the court of the Elector of Hanover, and of his mother, the Princess Sophia, heiress presumptive to the British crown. Returning home, he followed in his father's steps, becoming a merchant, a Representative in the General Court, and a member of the Council.

Governor Jonathan Belcher.

He had not a generous nature, but in traits which attract popular good-will he was not wanting. His person and presence were graceful and pleasing. He had a cheerful countenance, a hearty voice, a demonstrative gesticulation, and an habitually affable address. He was a man of society and of the world. Though foolishly irritable, and prone to small resentments which he pursued without

[1] It was while he was a Counsellor that, the selectmen of Boston having objected to his sending corn to Curaçoa on account of a scarcity of that article, he was so public-spirited as to reply: "The hardest fend off; if you stop my vessels, I will hinder the coming in of three times as much." (Sewall's Diary, for May 20, 1713.)

dignity, he was not troubled, like his differently constituted and differently trained predecessor, with pride and obstinacy about points of honor. He loved intrigue and tortuous methods. The ways of thinking of his earlier profession kept their hold on his experienced mind. He brought into politics some habits of trade; when satisfied that he could not get what he wanted unless at an inconvenient price, he would accept with complacent good-nature as much as was to be had. If greedy in acquisition, he was no miser. He spent his money with an elegant liberality. Especially was his purse freely opened when it might buy large returns of praise and consequence.

A political manager, such as Massachusetts had not bred before, he anticipated, in forms less elaborate, some tactics of more recent times. For years he was known as a friend of high prerogative principles in the government. Great surprise was felt when, at the height of the quarrel with Burnet about a stated salary, it became known that Belcher had embraced the popular pretension. The House made him one of its agents to enforce that doctrine on the court, and in England he remained and persevered, though the provincial Council steadily refused its consent to his being paid. There the news of the death of Burnet found him, and another not less unexpected change in his position forthwith took place. Lord Townshend's quarrel with Walpole had more than begun, and each of the rivals wished to avoid strong measures which might offer an advantage to the other. Wilks, Belcher's colleague in the agency, persuaded Townshend that Belcher, if anybody, could manage the turbulent Representatives of Massachusetts. It was thought that the popular branch in the Legislature which had so lately chosen him to be agent could not fail to welcome him as Governor, and to be accessible to his persuasions; and, on the other hand, he volunteered satisfactory assurances to the Ministry of his determination to desert the popular cause. He assured 1729. Dec. 31. the Duke of Newcastle that there was no reason "to entertain a thought to his prejudice on the score of the station he lately sustained; no one," he said, "shall be more tender of the honor and dignity of the crown, nor more industrious to promote the interest of the mother kingdom."[1] Governor Shute, whose appointment Belcher had aided by a contribution of money fifteen years before, now repaid the boon by his good offices.

Lieutenant-Governor Tailer.

Dummer was not continued as Lieutenant-Governor. At the instance of the agent, Wilks, the place was restored to William Tailer, who fifteen years before had been superseded by Dummer. Tailer had lately held the Naval Office, a position of more emolument. Wilks, wanting it for a friend, made the other arrangement for Tailer, as a partial compensation for his loss. Belcher helped his associate in the agency in making this transfer. March 30. Avowing his preference for Tailer, he solicited of the Duke the "favor always allowed to the King's Governors, to be made easy in their Lieutenant-Governors."[2]

Tailer, who was on the spot, and who had received his 1730. June 30. commission, met the General Court at the time to which it was prorogued, before Belcher's arrival.[3] He told them that he should propose nothing but business

[1] British Colonial Papers. — Nov. 13, 1733, Belcher wrote to Delafaye, Under Secretary of State: "As I am a native of this country, and have been for fifteen years past concerned in the government, I do not suppose his Majesty could have committed the royal commission to any gentleman besides, that could have managed so stiff a people as these are. But I am so well knowing of their humor and circumstances, that they have not been able to impose upon me, or to make those evasions they might have done with a stranger." (Ibid.)

[2] Ibid.

[3] The House of Representatives began to print its journal just before the beginning of Belcher's administration, the first publication being of the proceedings of May 27, 1730. — Belcher met the Court at Cambridge, to which place it had been prorogued by Lieutenant-Governor Dummer for its meeting, by reason of the prevalence of small-pox in Boston (see above, 529), and the arrangement having been continued by the Lieutenant-Governor, by prorogations of June 30 and July 3 and 16.

of routine, but he did at once a graceful act by approving a grant made by the House to Dummer, from which Dummer, under the royal instruction, had withheld his approval, and which would otherwise have lapsed.[1] The Court sat but three days, and it was not till after four successive prorogations that they came into the presence of their new compatriot ruler.[2] July 3.

[1] Dummer lived to an old age, but was never again in public life, except for a short time (1738, 1739) as a member of the Council. (Hutch., II. 368.)

[2] After Burnet's death there had been much deliberation of the Board of Trade and the Privy Council on the result of the controversy between him and Massachusetts. Even before intelligence of that event reached England, his business, taken up where it had been left four months before, was again forced by the Duke of Newcastle before the Privy Council. At the Duke's instance the Board of Trade (October 6) summoned Wilks and Belcher to substantiate the charges of the Colony against the Governor, and Thomas Burnet to appear in his brother's defence. "As to the particular complaint of Mr. Burnet's adjourning the Assembly from Boston to Salem, ... they [the agents] did not dispute the Governor's power of doing it, but hoped they might have the liberty of remonstrating against the inconveniences and hardships which the Assembly suffered by that proceeding;" and they represented it as simply part of his plan for "harassing them" into a settlement of stated salaries, which the agents went on to argue that the Assembly was under no obligation to grant. They justified the claim set up by the Assembly to audit accounts before the issue of money from the Treasury, as having been acquiesced in by Governor Shute, and approved by the law officers of the crown, and they finished by complaining of the Governor's extortion of fees for the clearance of vessels going to sea. (Journal of the Board of Trade.) It was a fortnight after this hearing that news came of Burnet's death, and the agents represented to the Privy Council (October 23) that they withdrew "such parts of their petition as were altogether personal against him," and that they "insisted only on laying before their Lordships, ... as being of a public nature, and affecting the welfare of the Province," the charges that the Governor "had refused to consent to any form for supply of the Treasury but what was practised before the year 1721," and "that he had exacted extraordinary and illegal fees on the shipping." The Council approved the Governor's course in respect to the first point, and the agents promised to advise their constituents accordingly. As to the second, the Council disapproved the Governor's proceeding, and ordered an instruction to that officer "not to exact any such fees for the future, or to demand any other fees than what are legal, or have been customarily taken by Governors of that Province." (Register of the Privy Council.) Under an order of the Privy Council, the Board of Trade (November 6) inquired of Belcher and Wilks "what steps had been taken by said Assembly [of Massachusetts] in compliance with his Majesty's instruction for providing a fixed salary for their Governor,

Belcher's Inaugural Speech. Sept. 9.

In his inaugural speech he exhorted them to be watchful for the interests of religion, and tolerantly regardful of the rights of conscience; to attend to the condition of the Indians, of trade and currency, and of the fortifications, which were not to be neg-

or was intended to be taken for that purpose." The agents replied "that they knew not of any intention the said Assembly had to vary from their last resolution. Whereupon their Lordships told them that, as they were desirous that this dispute between the crown and the said Assembly might, if possible, be determined in an easy manner, and that his Majesty might not be under the necessity of laying their behavior before the Legislature of Great Britain, ... their Lordships would make them a proposal, wherein they would not insist upon forms, provided the substance might be obtained, and that the Governor might be made by any means independent of the people, and not lie under the temptation of retailing the prerogative of the crown or the interest of Great Britain to the said Assembly for his daily bread; which proposal was that, ... since the Assembly of the Massachusetts have already by several Acts provided stated salaries for their Council and Assembly men, that they should make like provision of one thousand pounds sterling per annum, in the same manner, for their Governor for the time being. To which the said agents at first answered, that without all doubt the Assembly would look upon this proposal as an act of great condescension and goodness in the government here, and would most certainly comply with it. But upon further discourse and explanation it appeared that what the said agents intended was, that as the Acts providing salaries for their Council and Assembly are near expiring, that when the same should expire the Assembly would for the future provide for the Council, Assembly, and Governor in the same manner, that is, by an annual Resolve every session only, and not by Act of Assembly, nor for any fixed term whatsoever; for to their knowledge Mr. Burnet had endeavored to persuade the people to come into a three years' provision only, which they had absolutely refused, and the said agents declared it to be their fixed and positive opinion that the Assembly would never make their Governor independent of them." After a few days (November 11), the agents "acquainted their Lordships that, having reflected upon what passed when they attended the Board the 6th instant, having reconsidered their letters, and apprehending that the death of Mr. Burnet might have abated the animosity of the dispute between him and the Assembly, and have made some alteration in the temper of that Province, they were ready to transmit any proposition to the Assembly that this Board should make to them, and would, as far as was compatible with their stations, enforce the success thereof, and were informed by the Board that they would apply to his Majesty for leave to make them a proposition in writing, and would humbly entreat his Majesty to suspend his just resentment against the Province until such time as the effect of the said proposition should be known." (Journal of the Board of Trade.) The Board of Trade reported its action to the Privy Council, who approved it (November 12), and (December 2)

lected, notwithstanding the peace lately made with Spain; to protect the King's rights in the woods and in naval munitions; and to maintain the contested boundary of Massachusetts on the side of New Hampshire. In the circumstances, his utterance on the subject of a settlement of the Governor's salary, which he had lately been employed to plead against in England, could not but be awaited with curiosity. He said that, according to the royal instruction which had been renewed to him, he must demand and expect from the Court a stated annual allowance of a thousand pounds. In his management of this delicate matter he probably gave himself credit for a dexterity which on the other part was not ascribed to it. He told the House that, having manifested, in their past course, the courage and persistence exemplified by Cato till the crisis at Utica, they certainly would not think of imitating the Roman further to the point of his self-destructive obstinacy. The Representatives thought the Governor's reasoning was the worse for this indulgence of his rhetoric. If their course hitherto had been as just and magnanimous as he implied it to have been, it was fit to be persevered in, at least till perseverance was shown to be attended with more danger than as yet appeared.

Demand for a salary for the Governor.

The instruction to Belcher was in terms more peremptory than had been before employed with respect to the same demand. If the salary should not "be forthwith fixed by law, his Majesty," it was said, "will find himself under a necessity of laying the undutiful behavior of the Province before the Leg-

advised the King to "order that no proceedings be had on the Order in Council made on 22d May last, until the effect of said proposition be known." (Register of the Privy Council.) As early as November 28 (Journal of the Board of Trade, for December 2), Belcher had been appointed Governor of Massachusetts and New Hampshire. May 8, 1730, he was sworn into office before the Council. (Register of the Privy Council.) He embarked for Boston in a ship of war a few weeks after, and landed in Boston, August 10, having put in at Funchal, whence he wrote home, June 29. (Letter to the Duke of Newcastle, of August 24, in British Colonial Papers.)

islature of Great Britain, not only in this single instance, but in many others of the same nature and tendency, whereby it manifestly appears that this Assembly, for some years last past, have attempted by unwarrantable practices to weaken, if not cast off, the obedience they owe to the crown, and the dependence which all colonies ought to have on their mother country." The demand was announced to be "the last signification of the royal pleasure to them upon this subject;" and, should it not be complied with, "it is our will and pleasure, and you are required," so wrote the Council in the King's name, "immediately to come over to this Kingdom of Great Britain, in order to give us an exact account of all that shall have passed upon this subject, that we may lay the same before our Parliament."[1]

But it was not the Governor alone who was attentive to what was passing in England. The popular leaders also had good sources of information, and on the whole their opinion was that, in the existing state of English parties, and of the mutual jealousies among great men, the danger of an attack in Parliament upon the Province was not imminent, and that the displeasure of the Privy Council might probably be exhausted in threats. They had reason to believe that by persons more powerful than those who constituted the well-informed and meddlesome Board of Trade the zeal of that body was rather feared than encouraged, and that the Privy Council, though it could do no less than echo the complaints of the Board, would not be disposed, or would not be suffered, to embarrass the existing party relations by forcing into Parliament a question susceptible of uses which could not be calculated. And in the last resort they judged that, if the question must be decided against them, it might be better that it should be so decided by Parliamentary usurpation than by their voluntary surrender.

[1] Hutch. Hist., II. 333.

In a message to the Council, the House made known its inflexible resolution on the subject. The Council, after taking time for consideration, proposed to the House to join them in an engagement to pay to the present Governor a fixed salary as long as he should fill the office. But neither to this arrangement would the House consent. A conference between the two branches effected nothing. The Governor made them a speech, and, quoting certain solicitations for action against the Province which seven years before had been addressed by the Board of Trade to the Lords Justices of England, warned them of the probability that the government would have recourse to the vigorous measures therein indicated.

Refusal of it by the Representatives. Sept. 21.

Oct. 1.

Oct. 2.

The House asked for an adjournment of the Court. The Governor refused it; adopting the pert language of his predecessor, he said that he could not do them such a wrong as to put it out of their power to show their duty to the King in the way which he had pointed out. Three or four weeks passed, and they showed no sign of yielding. The House made a grant to the Governor of a thousand pounds. The Council proposed to amend the vote so as to promise the same annual payment during Belcher's continuance in the office; but to this the House would not agree. He called on the Council to advise him, on their oaths, whether it would be for the King's interest that he should dissolve the Court. The Council unanimously advised against a dissolution, and he ordered a prorogation for seven weeks, to give the Representatives opportunity to take the better sense of their constituents.[1] When they next met, he touched the disputed question lightly, expressing

Oct. 3.

Oct. 28.

Dec. 16.

[1] In his speech on the prorogation of the General Court (October 28), Belcher said: "Although, after spinning out this session, you are come into something that has more the face of that duty and respect you owe to the King than you ever before manifested on this head, yet it does

little besides the hope that they had now come together "with good and dutiful inclinations to the King." At all events, they were not prepared to express those inclinations in the way that he desired. Again he treated the
Dec. 29. argument at large, adding that he "did not intend
1731. to give them any further trouble." They informed
Jan. 1. him in positive terms that their minds were made up upon the subject. He dissolved them with an
Jan. 2. angry rebuke, and ordered writs for a new election.

On the main question the new Court proved no more tractable than the old, and their constancy showed
Feb. 10. the way to a termination of the quarrel. The Governor was sorely incommoded by the want of money. The House desired that he should have it, but would give it him on none but their own conditions. The House proposed, and the Council agreed, that the two
April 1. bodies should unite in a Memorial to the King to permit the Governor to accept their temporary grants, as had been done by his predecessors.[1] That their course was not prompted by parsimonious considerations, they had taken care to show by generous gifts to the Governor (which there was no obstacle to his accepting) for his services as agent in England, and for defraying the expenses of his voyage.[2] The perseverance of the House prevailed

not answer his Majesty's expectation from you."—"The Assembly had passed an Act [Act of October 28] which, though it did not come up to the full terms of the instruction, yet it is going a great way further than they have ever yet done, and I think may be taken as a settlement during the present Governor's administration. . . . . . I have not signed the Act, but I have a reasonable prospect of their doing the matter still better at the approaching session." (Belcher to the Duke of Newcastle, Dec. 10, 1730, in British Colonial Papers.)

[1] The county of Worcester was created by an Act of April 2 of this year. (Provincial Laws, II. 584.)

[2] April 26, 1731, Belcher wrote to the Duke that he had dissolved the Assembly two days before; and, seeing "no reason to think they will ever do any thing further or nearer to" the instruction than they had done in the bill of October 28, he asks leave to sign it. "They are daily endeavoring," he says, "to encroach on the little power reserved to the crown in the royal charter. . . . . . I think they have too much already, unless they used it with more good manners to the King." (Ibid.)

to carry this all-important point so long and obstinately contested. For three successive years the Governor, on his urgent solicitations, received permission from England to accept the annual grant of the General Court. For a while this was accompanied with an order to urge the demand for a stated allowance. At length, however, the unavailing claim was disused, and the Governor was allowed permanently to take his money in the form in which the Court was willing to make the grant.[1] The Privy Council conceived that they partially preserved the point of honor by prescribing the condition that the Court's grant to the Governor, lest the prospect of it should appear to influence him, should be made at the beginning of its sessions; a condition which was observed through Belcher's administration.

Defeat of the claim. 1735. Nov. 5.

Politician as the Governor was by taste and practice, he

— From 1731 onward, Jonathan Belcher, Jr., appeared repeatedly before the Board of Trade to urge his father's suit for permission to accept the Colony's grants. The son was a graduate of Harvard College of the year 1728. The Governor wrote of him to the Duke (Nov. 7, 1731) that, "after spending the last seven years at our little University in Cambridge," he was then studying at the Temple; and that he needed indulgence, for he "was but the new production of the wilds of America." (Ibid.) At his death in 1776, he was Lieutenant-Governor and Chief-Justice of Nova Scotia.

[1] Register of the Privy Council, for Aug. 4 and 11, 1731; Aug. 10, 1732; Jan. 26, Oct. 4, Nov. 2, 1733; Nov. 5, 1735; Journal of the Board of Trade, for Aug. 5, 1731; Aug. 23, 1732; Feb. 2, June 19, Nov. 6, 1733; June 20, Aug. 22, 1734; June 12, Aug. 21, Oct. 31, Dec. 5, 1735; comp Mass. Provincial Laws, II. 632 *et seq.*, note. — Aug. 25, 1731, the agent, Wilks, wrote to Secretary Willard that Belcher had been permitted by the Privy Council to accept the grant of the General Court for that one year, and thenceforward to insist peremptorily on a fixed salary; and that the President of the Council (Lord Wilmington) earnestly advised the Province to oblige the King in this matter while he (the President) was in power, as afterwards they might not fare so well. (British Colonial Papers.) — 1733, June 28, Belcher wrote to the Duke: "There is not the least prospect of a Governor's ever being supported by an Assembly here in any other manner" but by grant. He hoped, in the last resort, "to be paid out of the royal exchequer." (British Colonial Papers; comp. Provincial Laws, II. 632–635.)

The question was revived for a moment ten years later. But it was now virtually settled.

addressed himself to the management of the parties, of which he had successively enjoyed and disappointed the confidence in past times. Unmindful of the maxim of the Great Monarch that every appointment to office makes one person ungrateful and ninety-nine angry, he sought to fortify himself by a new distribution of places, assuming that commissions needed to be renewed on each accession of a new Governor.[1] After the manner of his tribe, he thought it prudent to win opponents, and take for granted the continued support of friends. Cooke, the tribune of the time, was made a Judge of the Court of Common Pleas,[2] and, giving at last some signs of sycophancy, lost his popularity, and with it his power. The judicial courts had by law the appointment of their respective clerks. The Governor proposed a person whom he wished to advance as clerk for the county of York. The judges said they were satisfied with the present incumbent. The Governor superseded the judges, and so compassed his object.[3] This sort of proceeding was new in Massachusetts, except so far as precedents might be found for it in the administration of Andros. It was odious to the moral sense of the people, and presently fell again into disuse.

Belcher's political artifices.

[1] The pretension was never again allowed. It was put forward by Shirley, the next Governor, but was set aside by the Council after an argument by one of the Board, Mr. Read, a learned lawyer. (Hutch., II. 336, note.)

[2] In a letter to Delafaye, Under Secretary of State, John Pemberton complains (Oct. 8, 1733) that Belcher, contrary to instructions from England, had given to him, Pemberton, as clerk of the Naval Office, only a commission "such as should depend on his own pleasure," while he had promoted "a son of the famous Mr. Cooke, the New England Oliver Cromwell." (British Colonial Papers.) To make a place for Pemberton, as he had been instructed to do, Belcher had reluctantly cancelled his appointment to that office of Byfield Lyde, his daughter's husband. (Letter of Belcher to the Duke of Newcastle, of Oct. 4, 1733, in British Colonial Papers.) Cooke lived till 1737, but his consequence decreased in his last years, though he was not an old man.

[3] It is painful to record that William Pepperell came to the bench by this job.

An old controversy, revived for a moment by a vote of the House to adjourn itself for three days, brought a sharp rebuke from the Governor. The Explanatory Charter had settled that point, and it was impossible for the House to make good its pretension. Another dispute, which was in progress at the same time with that respecting a stated salary for the Governor, though pressed by the Representatives with scarcely less obstinacy, had a different issue. The House revived its old pretension to audit public charges before moneys which had been granted by them should be paid out. The Governor would not accede to it. The Court passed money-bills with that condition attached, and he rejected them. The laws for replenishing the treasury expired without renewal, and it was empty. This was a state of things which could not last, for government, to go on, must be paid for; and for the present, till the King's pleasure should be signified after a representation of the case, the House was prevailed upon to appropriate money for specific objects, to be drawn and paid on the Governor's warrant, without further action of that body. The Governor dissolved the Court on the day when this Act was passed.[1]

1731. July 13.

Claim of the Representatives to audit accounts.

1731. April 24.

But it seems that the constituencies were not pleased with this action of the Court, for the next House refused to repeat it. The Governor's speech at the beginning of the session was short, as was especially his reference to the vexed question respecting his salary. The reason was that he was expecting the royal consent to his departure from the instruction which he had so positively insisted on. At the prorogued session he announced that he had received permission to that effect for the present year.

May 27.

1731. Dec. 2.

The House again made appropriations with their cher-

[1] Provincial Laws, II. 593.

ished reservation of the right to audit the accounts which
were to be discharged, and now the Council acquiesced;
but the Governor, as before, refused to sign the
July 28. bill. A request of the House to be prorogued
Aug. 25–Sept. 22. was at first denied, but their importunity or their
Oct. 6–Nov. 3. inflexibility obtained for them three vacations in
Nov. 9–Dec. 1. the autumn, from neither of which did they bring
back any disposition to yield their point. Argument might seem to have been exhausted, but they had
not wearied of it. For the Representatives to withdraw
1732. their claim to see for themselves whether the
Jan. 20. specified charges defrayed from the treasury were
honest and reasonable and conformable to their appropriations, would be, they said, "to prostitute the money in the treasury to the unaccountable and consequently uncontrollable will and pleasure of the Governor and the major part of seven gentlemen of his Majesty's Council [seven Counsellors being the number prescribed in the charter for a quorum], which is four, and those such as the Governor shall pick and choose out of twenty-eight. . . . . . If his Majesty's instruction, and not what the General Court judges to be for the good and welfare of the Province, must be the rule, we dare not do it, being firmly of opinion that we shall act neither like Englishmen nor rational creatures, to comply with the instruction." The Governor replied
Feb. 2. with copious reasoning and reproof. He then
ordered a prorogation of the Court, and did not summon it again.

Emptiness of the Treasury.

He reminded the next Court that there had "not been any money in the treasury for more
June 1. than twelve months past," and he informed them
June 9. that the Privy Council had advised the King to
adhere to his sixteenth instruction, which forbade the issue of Massachusetts bills of credit, beyond the amount of thirty thousand pounds, without the King's express assent; and to his thirtieth instruction, which disallowed the pre-

tension of the House to audit the public accounts.[1] When the House again justified by an elaborate argument their perseverance in the latter claim, the Governor seems to have resolved to make a different experiment. He prorogued them for four months, perhaps thinking that if keeping them inconveniently away from their homes failed of its purpose, as it had done hitherto, the object might be accomplished by compelling them to see for a considerable time that discomfort and annoyance on the part of unpaid public officers, which for the time being they were deprived of the capacity to relieve.

June 30.

July 7.

But if such was the Governor's calculation, he had presumed too much. When he had made his customary complaint, with the specification that there had now "been no supply for eighteen months," only one Representative among fifty-seven was found opposed to a vote that a relinquishment of the ground which had been taken "would necessarily tend to destroy the powers and privileges granted to the General Court in and by the royal charter." Another exchange of long messages took place, and a positive refusal on the part of the House to give way. Trying another method, the Council joined with the House in an Address

Nov. 2.

Nov. 3.

Dec. 15.

[1] Register of Privy Council, for July 1, Aug. 11, Dec. 1, 1731; comp. Journal of the Board of Trade, for March 22, 1729.

Lieutenant-Governor Tailer died in March, 1732, and was succeeded by Spencer Phips, who had been several years a Counsellor. Hutchinson says (II. 383): "Mr. Belcher used his interest for Adam Winthrop, Esq." But there may have been some of Belcher's double-dealing here. April 18, 1732, a letter was "read from Governor Belcher, giving an account of the death of Colonel William Tailer, Lieutenant-Governor of Massachusetts Bay, and recommending Captain Paul Mascarene to succeed him." (Journal of the Board of Trade.) This was, I suppose, the engineer officer of that name, for whom, three years later (Journal of the Board of Trade, for Aug. 22, 1735; comp. Register of the Privy Council, for October 27), Belcher solicited a leave of absence from Nova Scotia, that he might "repair the fortifications in Massachusetts Bay."

to the King, praying for his indulgence in the matter, and in another to the House of Commons, soliciting their intercession. The latter measure gave displeasure to the Governor, as an insolent attempt at dictation to the crown,
1733. Jan. 4. and a prorogation followed for three months, which time nearly exhausted the political year.[1]

The next House persisted in its method of granting
June 6. supplies, attaching to them by a unanimous vote the condition that the Governor's warrant should not draw money from the treasury to satisfy any claims other than what the House should have examined and
June 14. approved; and the Governor assured them that he never would sign a supply bill to which that condition was attached. The House was at a disadvan-

[1] Belcher wrote to the Duke, July 26, 1731: "Since May 26, there has not been a shilling in the public treasury;" July 10, 1732: "There is not a shilling in the treasury of this Province, nor has been for fourteen months past. . . . . . £3000 is not, at this time, more than £850;" November 21: "There has not been a shilling in the treasury of this Province for eighteen months past;" December 26: "There has not been a shilling for nineteen months past, although there is now upwards of £40,000 due. . . . . . The Assembly here love to be clamorous and troublesome. . . . . . I take the single question on this head to be, whether the King shall appoint his own Governor, or whether the House of Representatives shall be Governor of the Province." With this letter he sent a long argument on the thirtieth instruction, entitled, "A Letter from one in Boston to his Friend in the Country, by a Lover of Government and Liberty." He was chafing under the laziness, dilatoriness, irresolution, and weakness of the Duke. Jan. 5, 1733, having prorogued the Court the day before, he wrote: "Your Grace will easily perceive that the House of Representatives of this Province are continually running wild, nor are their attempts for assuming in a manner the whole legislative as well as the executive part of the government into their own hands to be endured with honor to his Majesty. . . . . . Had they sat a few days longer, I should have expected they would have voted his Majesty's Council a useless part of the Legislature. . . . . . While I have been representing to your Grace for eighteen months past the great difficulty I am placed in, ... I have had no answer. But since the Province has come into the condition in which I now represent it, I must beg your Grace to be no longer silent;" and again, January 8, while petitions were flowing in from officers and soldiers, representing their destitution from want of their pay for "about twenty months:" "I beg your Grace to feel a little with me. . . . . . Can it be consonant to reason and justice, or the rules of honor?" &c. (British Colonial Papers.)

tage in the controversy. It was the Governor who was distressed, when, because a stated salary was denied, he refused to approve a bill granting money for his support; but it was the Province on whom the inconvenience fell, when, because of a condition which he would not admit, the Governor withheld his signature from a bill for providing the means to pay the salaries of subordinate officers and maintain the other provincial expenses. The last hope of opposition to him was lost when, the treasury having now been empty two years, intelligence came that the application for indulgence had been unfavorably received both by the King in Council and by the House of Commons.[1]

The House thereupon asked the Governor to issue his proclamation for a day of prayer and fasting, because of the Province being "under the manifest token of the Divine displeasure." But he did not see the exigency in that light. In fact, the House was helpless. There must be money in the treasury to meet current expenses, or the machinery of government would come to a stop. There was no way to place it there, except by the Governor's consent. It was clear that he had made up his mind not to yield to the conditions insisted on by the House, and that his superiors in England were equally determined. When the Court came together again in the autumn, the House first expressed its feelings, and then submitted to its defeat. The Representatives rejected by a vote of two to one a bill of supplies divested of the favorite condition, and on the afternoon of the same day, on a reconsideration, passed the same bill by a like

Defeat of the Representatives. Oct. 16.

[1] Register of the Privy Council, for Dec. 1, 1731, and March 28 and May 10, 1733. On the last of these days, "His Majesty doth declare and signify his high displeasure at these repeated applications upon points which have already been maturely considered and determined by his Majesty in Council;" and he renews the declaration of his pleasure that no alteration be made in the thirtieth article of Belcher's instructions.

majority.[1] Practically, the question was settled,[2] — a question not only fruitful of discord, but furnishing a two-edged sword, which cut deepest into the interests of the Province. And the other matter of dispute having also been put to rest by the consent of the Ministry to have their Governor maintained by grants from year to year, instead of a stated salary, there was a prospect of future harmony in the provincial administration. The prospect was realized;[3] and after a long continuance of harmony and quiet, which has bequeathed extremely little for a record,[4] the Governor

1737 found himself prompted to express to the Court

March 27. his satisfaction with their proceedings, in which,

May 28. he said, "they had so well conformed themselves to the directions of the royal charter, the effect whereof had been a general easiness and satisfaction through the Province."[5]

[1] Provincial Laws, II. 691–695, 701, 703.

[2] It was not, however, so absolutely put at rest but that once more a semblance of it appeared. (See below, 553.)

[3] Yet, with singular imprudence, the Governor soon after furnished to the House new materials for their argument. He overdrew the legislative appropriation, and provoked a remonstrance from the Representatives. (House Record, for Jan. 13, 16, 1736.)

[4] As early as the year 1737, news came to Boston that a forged letter, purporting to have been written there, had been received in London, in which it was declared that the ministers and others had been much rejoiced to hear that the King had "been most graciously pleased to appoint a new Governor for the Colony of the Massachusetts." Thereupon Colman, and with him the other ministers of Boston and Roxbury, wrote to the Duke of Newcastle, Sir Robert Walpole, and the Earl of Wilmington, expressing their confidence in Belcher, and contradicting the statement that there was any desire to have him superseded. (Mass. Hist. Soc., XXII. 271.)

[5] The Governor wrote to the Duke, June 11, 1734: The General Court "seem at present one of the best Assemblies that this Province has had since my coming into the government;" July 2: "The present Assembly seems to have a better sense of their duty to his Majesty than any other I have met since my arrival to this government;" November 26: "I think this Province is more quiet and easy than for near twenty years past;" Jan. 9, 1735: "The Assembly seem to be full of loyalty to his Majesty, and all things are become easy in this Province;" November 13: "At present the Assembly seems to be growing more dutiful to the King." (British Colonial Papers.) Such was the tranquillizing effect of the surrender by the Ministry of the question respecting the Governor's salary. While

But two other questions had meanwhile been acquiring a special importance,[1] — those of the redemption of the bills of credit, and of the boundaries of the Province, especially the boundary on the side of New Hampshire. When only five years remained before the latest time at which, agreeably to the instructions from England, the Province's bills were made payable, the House, after "a long while spent in debating," got so far as to resolve that they would lay proportionate taxes in the intervening years; at the same time, however, raising "a committee to prepare the draught of an humble Memorial to be presented to the King's most excellent Majesty in Council in the name of the Council and House of Representatives, setting forth the great inconveniences and difficulties his Majesty's good subjects here labor under on account of his Majesty's instruction to his Excellency our Governor, forbidding his consent in laying the funds for drawing in the public bills beyond the year 1741, and praying his Majesty of his great grace and favor would please to order the said instruction may be withdrawn."

Bills of credit.

1736. June 17. June 18.

This position of the question respecting supplies of the treasury by means of bills of credit forced into new prominence another question not now for the first time discussed. If the General Court passed a bill for the issue of notes redeemable later than the date determined by the King in Council, or causing the whole cir-

Question of royal instructions.

Belcher made such complimentary reports to the Ministry, to the Court itself, intent on a better bargain, he used the language of an injured man. He told them (Jan. 29, 1737) that, through the depreciation of the bills of credit in which they paid him £3000 a year (Provincial Laws, II. 661, 700, 741, &c.), he had been a loser by his office to the amount of £8000.

[1] In the year 1734 took place that expulsion of the Salzburg Protestants by the Austrian government, which, for its cruelty, gave wide offence in other countries. (Carlyle, Life of Frederick the Great, II. 314.) One would not expect it to become a subject of interest in a region so distant as New England; yet we find Dr. Colman, of Boston, exercising his Latinity in correspondence upon it with a German divine. (Turell's Life of Colman, 154, 156.)

culation at any one time to exceed the amount so determined, or if the bill was so framed as to go into effect without being first approved in England, the Governor disallowed it, pleading his instruction from the King. To the Governor, dependent on the King for his office, the King's instruction was conclusive. But not so with the Province. Their rights, as well as the King's authority, were sanctioned and maintained by the law of England. The Constitution of England in the first place, and in the second place their charter, defined and limited the King's power over them; and where was the King's remedy against them, if in disregarding a royal instruction they did no illegal act? The King, through the official action of his creature, the Governor, or otherwise, might embarrass and thwart them as to the exercise of their rights; but the mere fact that the King by his instructions set his Governor on work of this kind was no reason why they should not resist and protect themselves, as best they might, by taking care to keep their action within that law of England which was above even the King. Though, the Governor's continuance in office depending on the royal will, it might be supposed that he would not venture to violate the royal command, on the other hand, as long as the Governor's living depended on the people's will, it might be supposed that he would interest himself to prevent his instructions from oppressing them so much as to provoke them to starve him. And accordingly it had been with the best reason that they had adhered to that refusal to provide for the Governor otherwise than by annual grants which at last they had established in practice. It was the same policy that the Parliament of England had adopted towards King Charles the First.

Disorder of the finances.

Throughout the administration of Governor Belcher, the finances of the Province were in an extremely discouraging condition. The temptation to make a fictitious currency, and to defer the times for payment, was such as in like circumstances is always felt in prodigious strength. However doubtful the legal right of thė British government to interfere, there is no doubt of the disastrous tendency of the course which the Province was disposed to pursue.

To follow, step by step, the course of the dispute respecting financial affairs between the Governor and the Representatives, would be to weary the reader with a recital of intricate and dull details. The year of settlement, when a debt of thirty or forty thousand pounds was to be paid by the Province in sterling money,[1] was looked forward to with increasing dismay as it drew near. The flood of paper circulation in Massachusetts was increased to a deluge by the still more inconsiderate profuseness of a neighboring community. Rhode Island, with its little population and property, fancied that it enriched itself by the amount of a hundred and four thousand pounds, when it lent to its inhabitants its promises to pay that sum at the end of twenty years. The notes of Rhode Island came into circulation in Massachusetts. As a measure of partial protection, the merchants of Boston agreed together not to receive them, and formed a company, which issued bills to the amount of a hundred and ten thousand pounds, secured by their joint credit, and redeemable, one tenth part every year, in silver at the rate of nineteen shillings the ounce, or the equivalent in gold.[2] But the agreement not to receive the Rhode Island notes

1733.

[1] Hutch. Hist., II. 393. Chalmers (MS. Letter to Lord Mansfield, 106) states the amount of currency outstanding in 1739 at £191,500. In that year Belcher wrote to the Duke (Nov. 22) that the bills "issued here for many years past" were "not worth five shillings in the pound of the current silver money of this Province." (British Colonial Papers.)

[2] R. I. Rec., IV. 487. — "Upon a late emission of bills of credit by the Colony of Rhode Island of upwards of £100,000, ... a number of merchants and traders, as they say to prevent the depreciation of the bills of this Province, ... have met once and again, and are associated to circulate their notes in lieu of money to the amount of £110,000." (Belcher to the Duke of Newcastle, Nov. 13, 1735, in British Colonial Papers.)

was at first violated here and there, and then abandoned. Upon this, silver rose to twenty-seven paper shillings for the ounce; and the merchants' notes, payable at the rate of an ounce of silver for nineteen shillings, were withdrawn from circulation, and hoarded.

The chaotic condition of the finances suggested recurrence to an enterprise which had been defeated twenty-five years before.[1] A proposal of Thomas Hutchinson, then a Representative, afterwards Governor, to fund the debt by a loan in England, payable at distant periods, having been found not acceptable,[2] the plan of a *Land Bank* was again entertained.[3] A company, consisting of some seven hundred or eight hundred persons, was to issue its notes to the amount of a hundred and fifty thousand pounds. The security was to be a mortgage of real estate by each partner to an amount proportioned to the share taken by him in the stock, or a bond with two sufficient sureties; and each partner was to pay annually three per cent interest on the bills borrowed by him, and one twentieth part of the principal, in bills of the company, or in articles of the growth or manufacture of the Province at such rates as should be fixed by

Scheme of a *Land Bank.* 1739.

[1] See above, p. 334.

[2] Felt, Historical Account of Massachusetts Currency, p. 96; Hutch. Hist., II. 393. Hutchinson went to England, and a letter (of October, 1740) which he carried from Belcher represented to the Duke the need of an interference by Parliament to obstruct all schemes like that of the Land Bank. (British Colonial Papers; comp. Journal of the Board of Trade, for Dec. 9.)

[3] The scheme had been again canvassed as much as four years before this time. Aug. 15, 1735, the Board of Trade had information from Belcher to that effect, which they thought of consequence enough to refer to the Attorney-General "for his opinion thereon, and if, upon the whole, it appear improper, what may be done to prevent it taking place." (Journal of the Board.) Jan. 26, 1741, the Privy Council passed an "order on Report of Attorney and Solicitor General, relating to the Land Bank scheme at Boston, directing Lords of Trade to prepare draught of instructions to Governor of Massachusetts Bay to continue to give all possible discouragement to said Land Bank, as likewise to all other banks of the like nature, that may be attempted to be set up in that Province." (Privy Council Register; comp. Journal of the Board of Trade, for Feb. 12, 1741.)

the company's directors.[1] The project became a prominent political question, and, what with the numerous voters directly concerned in it and the much greater number who were induced to believe that it would advance their interests, a large majority favorable to it was secured in the House of Representatives.[2] 1740.

The Governor pronounced himself against it. He said truly that it was all delusive and mischievous, and he issued a proclamation, condemning it as "tending to defraud men of their substance, to disturb the peace and good order of the people, and to give great interruption and bring much confusion into their trade and business."[3] With a plausible plea of public advantage, he put in practice against it his system of administrative tactics. The elections of nearly half of the Council and of the Speaker of the House were set aside by him on account of the persons elected being officers and partners in the bank.[4] For the same reason, and

August.

1741. May.

[1] Felt, Historical Account, &c., 67, 68, 97; Hutch. Hist., II. 353.

[2] Oct. 23, 1740, the Privy Council received a petition from "merchants, traders, and inhabitants of Massachusetts Bay, complaining of a scheme lately projected and published at Boston, called the Land Bank," &c. Jan. 26, 1740, on a Report from the law officers of the crown, they ordered instructions to the Governor "to give all possible discouragement to said Land Bank, as likewise to all other banks of the like nature." (Register of the Privy Council.)

[3] Belcher's Proclamation, in Felt, Historical Account, &c., 99. — But there is some reason to believe that Belcher's course in this matter was but an instance of his characteristic duplicity. In 1744 was published in London a pamphlet entitled "An Account of the Rise, Progress, and Consequences of the Two Late Schemes, commonly called the Land Bank or Manufactory Scheme, and the Silver Scheme, in the Province of the Massachusetts Bay. . . . . . In a Letter from a Gentleman in Boston to his Friend in London." The writer was an admirer of Belcher's successor, Shirley, against whom he understood Belcher to be scheming in London. He was himself an enemy to the Land Bank, but he argues with a large induction of facts, and with much plausibility, that, in the early stages of the scheme, Belcher was interested in and for it; that he only shifted his ground when he saw the determined hostility with which it was regarded at the English court; and that, to the last, he was in secret complicity with Partridge, his brother-in-law, who was pleading for it before the King's Privy Council.

[4] "The General Court, when they came together, were so set upon

even for merely receiving or paying the bills, he displaced numerous office-holders, civil and military.[1] Notwithstanding this resistance of his, — or perhaps the more because of it, — the speculation forced its way, and it was said that paper professing to represent no less than fifty or sixty thousand pounds was issued by the company. On the other hand, some of the best men of the Province were so impressed with the dangerous nature of the scheme, that, despairing of protection from any nearer quarter, they went so far as to appeal to the authority of Parliament.[2] An Act of Parliament had been passed
1719. at the time of the explosion of the South Sea Company, which would be sufficient for the present purpose, if it should be held to be applicable to the Colonies;[3] and to settle that question a declaratory Act now affirmed the former law to have been in force in the Colonies from the time of its enactment. The Land Bank Company was caught in its own devices. For besides that, by force of this law, the company must desist from all further issue of its bills, each individual member of it was made liable, not only for the negotiable value of them, but for the sums at which, according to the stipulation on their face, they were redeemable in silver, with the further addition of interest from the time of their being put into circulation.

The ill-omened war between England and Spain, which

supporting the pernicious scheme called the Land Bank, by choosing persons into the Council of that way of thinking, ... I therefore disapproved of thirteen of the persons they chose, and then dissolved the Assembly." (Letter of Belcher to the Duke, of May 30, 1741, in British Colonial Papers.)

[1] Felt, Massachusetts Currency, &c., 100–110; Mass. Arch., CII. 92. — Nov. 10, 1740, on account of the Governor's proclamation of November 5, threatening to cashier military officers who should be concerned in the Land Bank, Samuel Adams (the elder) and other Justices of the Peace threw up their commissions. But, disregarding this act of theirs, he displaced them December 5.

[2] Register of Privy Council, for Oct. 23, 1740; comp. Journal of the Board of Trade, for Nov. 13, 1740, Feb. 12, June 11, 1741.

[3] Acts of the sixth year of George I., Chap. XVIII., and fourteenth year of George II., Chap. XXXVII.; Statutes at Large, V. 301, VI. 430.

1739. October. Recruiting for the war with Spain.

broke out at this time, involved the Governor of Massachusetts in another altercation with the General Court. A requisition was made upon the Province for a thousand men to serve in the expedition against Carthagena under Admiral Vernon. Both the Governor and the Court were honestly interested in the enterprise, but they were too much out of humor with each other to proceed harmoniously in means for its execution. The Court insisted that they should only be called upon to provide for the transportation of such troops as should be officered and armed before embarking. The Governor urged that the troops ought to sail in the expectation of having commissions and arms furnished when they should have joined the main force.[1] The Court, reviving their old pretension, that money granted by them should further await their own special sanction for its disposal, would not provide for the transportation of men without commanders and without equipments; and the consequence was that only four companies went to sea, of ten which had been enrolled.[2] It was well that any thing occurred to lessen the share of Massachusetts in the disaster which followed. Of five hundred of her troops who

[1] Sailing orders of Belcher to Captain Thomas Jenkins (Sept. 19, 1740), in Mass. Arch., LXIII. 620.

[2] September 6, the Governor published an order permitting "soldiers enlisted, who were not of the four companies which had received arms and commissions, to return home," but inviting them to enlist with the expectation of receiving arms and clothing in the West Indies. (British Colonial Papers.)

Franklin, before the House of Commons in 1766, made a merit of the forwardness of the colonists on this occasion. (Sparks, Works of Franklin, IV. 188.) The reader does not need to be reminded of the delineations of the miseries of this frightful campaign in Thomson's poetry and Smollett's novel.

July 9, 11, 1740, the Representatives voted a liberal supply for the repair of the works in Boston harbor. But they provided for associating their Speaker and a Committee with the Governor for expending the money, a restriction, however, which, on second thoughts, they made less rigorous. (Journal of the House.) He had written to the Duke, Nov. 22, 1739, that the Assembly would grant no money for the support of the government, without attaching conditions which his instructions forbade him to admit. (British Colonial Papers.) Oct. 29, 1740 (Ibid.), he expressed to the same Minister his hope that

went to Carthagena, only fifty ever came back to their homes.[1]

Boundary lines between Massachusetts and New Hampshire.

The settlement of the northern boundary line of Massachusetts was involved in endless perplexities. Did the charter of William and Mary renew the grant of territory contained in the charter of Charles the First? If it did not, what territory did it grant? If it did, at what point, on or near the river Merrimack, was the line to begin, which, produced westwardly as far as to the South Sea, or as far as to other possessions of the British Crown, was to make the northern boundary of Massachusetts through the greater part of its extent? The settlement of those questions would determine the southern boundary of New Hampshire. Where was the northern boundary line of that Province? This question also concerned Massachusetts, as determining the extent of her possessions in Maine. On the side of New Hampshire, the boundary of Maine, which Province Massachusetts had bought, was, by the grant of King Charles the First to Gorges,[2] a line "beginning at the entrance of Pascataway harbor, and so to pass up the same into the river Newichawocke [Salmon Falls], and through the same unto the furthest head thereof, and from thence northwestward till one hundred and twenty miles be finished," this line, a hundred and twenty miles long, making one side of an irregular square, of which it was intended that New Hampshire should consist. At what precise angle was it to run, the language of the patent being that the direction should be "northwesterly"?

Agreeably to advice of the crown law-officers to the

future acts of Parliament for governing the army might be made to "comprehend his Majesty's Plantations," since the Colonies would pass no such laws, and "without them there was no governing officers or men." Bladen, his special enemy on the Board of Trade, wrote to the Duke in the same month: "Massachusetts is a kind of commonwealth, where the King is hardly a stadtholder." (Ibid.)

1 Trumbull, II. 268.

2 Hazard, State Papers, I. 443.

Board of Trade, and of the Board of Trade to the Privy Council, a commission composed of twenty Counsellors of New York, New Jersey, Rhode Island, and Nova Scotia was appointed, after occasional spasmodic movements and much delay,[1] to adjudicate these questions; and to them the conflicting Colonies were directed to submit their respective claims.[2] The Colonies represented on the commission were all designated by the Privy Council on the nomination of the agent for New Hampshire. All but Rhode Island were royal governments. Rhode Island and New York had boundary disputes pending with Massachusetts. A proposal to include Connecticut failed, from an apprehension that Connecticut, from old associations, and from similarity of institutions and of character, would be partial to Massachusetts. On the day appointed for the hearing, eight commissioners, five coming from Rhode Island and three from Nova Scotia, met at Hampton, in New Hampshire. Waldron, Secretary of that Province, and Eleazar Russell, Sheriff of Rockingham County, appeared with the demand of New Hampshire, which was to the effect that a line running westward from a point on the Atlantic Ocean, three miles north of the middle of the channel of Merrimack River, should be established as the southern boundary of New Hampshire, and that the line defining the northern boundary of that Province should be drawn from the ocean up Piscataqua and Newichwannock Rivers, and from the head of the latter "northwestward, — that is, *north, less than a quarter of a point westwardly*, as far as the British dominion extends." On the part of Massachusetts, the claim was that the southern boundary of New Hampshire should be a line running from the sea parallel with the left bank of the Merrimack, and three miles distant from it to "the crotch or parting of the river" (where is now Franklin,

1737. Feb. 9.

Aug. 1.

[1] See below, p. 574.
[2] N. H. Provincial Papers, IV. 721, 732, 742.

and where, according to the use of the time, the name *Merrimack* ceased to be applied); thence to a point three miles north of the parting, and thence westerly to the South Sea; and that the line making the northern boundary of New Hampshire, and dividing it from the Massachusetts county of York, should run due northwest from "the furthest head" of the Newichwannock till it reached a point one hundred and twenty miles distant from the mouth of the Piscataqua. New Hampshire had hitherto been understood by the government and people of Massachusetts to be enclosed within and bounded by their territory (of which Maine was a part) on all sides, except at the point where the river Piscataqua flows into the sea.

While the commissioners, who had been joined by Philip Livingston, of New York, were sitting, the Legislatures of the two Provinces were brought by the Governor within five miles of each other, for the purpose of convenient conference, the one being adjourned to Hampton Falls, the other to Salisbury.[1] The boundary between New Hampshire and Maine the commissioners determined to be a line running up the Piscataqua and Salmon Falls Rivers, and in a direction "north, two degrees westerly," from the source of the latter till it had reached a distance of one hundred and twenty miles from the mouth of the Piscataqua. Whether the provincial charter granted all the lands conveyed by the charter of Charles the First, was a question which, finding themselves unable to resolve, they referred back to the King's Privy Council. If it was to be so construed, then they adjudged that the western direction of that southern line of New Hampshire, which ran towards the South Sea, was to begin at a point three miles north of the confluence of the Pemigewasset with the Winnipiseogee. If otherwise,

Award of commissioners. Oct. 14.

[1] The question respecting the Governor's right to determine the place of sessions of the Legislature appears now to have been suffered to subside.

then that line should be drawn due west from a point on the coast three miles north of the mouth of the river Merrimack.

As soon as there was time to digest their astonishment at this prodigiously capricious award, both parties took measures for an appeal to the King, the movement for New Hampshire, however, being made only by the Representatives, without the concurrence of the Council. Edmund Quincy, who was sent to England to prosecute the claim of Massachusetts, died presently after his arrival. Wilks, the agent of that Province, was no match in skill or activity for Tomlinson, who represented New Hampshire, and who was himself aided by a cunning and unscrupulous attorney of the name of Parris, whose papers contain curious developments of the way in which the business was conducted.[1] All sorts of influences were set to work to bias the decision. Belcher's private interest in it was dwelt upon, to destroy the effect of his official representations. The lands, the possession of which would be determined by the direction of the northern boundary line, were covered with valuable timber, which the government was concerned to withhold from the control of Massachusetts. Dunbar, who had lately come to England, increased the sensibility upon this subject by his stories of the obstructions he had met with in the execution of his office of Surveyor of the Woods.[2] Parris warmly represented the danger to which "the poor, little, loyal, distressed Province of New Hamp-

[1] Farmer, 250, 254.

[2] July 27, 1737, the Board of Trade presented to the Duke of Newcastle the case of Dunbar, who, they said, was "now in England," with a petition for relief against Belcher. He had been Lieutenant-Governor of New Hampshire "above six years, upwards of four whereof he actually resided within the same." He had "been for the most part forty years in his Majesty's service," and had been at expense in promoting a new settlement, which Belcher had done "all he could to destroy." (British Colonial Papers.) — The next year he asked to be appointed to succeed Colonel Cosby, deceased, as Lieutenant-Colonel of Governor Phillips's regiment, and Lieutenant-Governor of Annapolis Royal. He represented that he had been "bred in the army from ensign to Lieutenant-Colonel." (Ibid.; comp. below, 566.)

shire" was exposed from the rapacity of "the vast, opulent, overgrown Province of Massachusetts."[1] The Privy Council cut the knot by a decree of the most extraordinary kind, which, abandoning the interpretation of the charters, established an arbitrary line. For the northern boundary of New Hampshire the award of the commissioners was adopted; and it was determined that "the northern boundary of Massachusetts should be a curved line, pursuing the course of Merrimack River at three miles' distance, on the north side thereof, beginning at the Atlantic Ocean, and ending at a point due north of Pawtucket Falls (in what is now Lowell), and a straight line drawn from thence due west."[2] Thus not only was Massachusetts shorn of much more territory than the preposterous decree of the commissioners had taken from her; she had further to yield to New Hampshire both seven hundred square miles (much of it settled country), to no part of which had New Hampshire ever set up a pretension, and all the unexplored country lying west of the southern portion of New Hampshire towards the South Sea.

1740. March 10.

Decision of the Privy Council.

Governor Belcher's relation to this controversy had so brought him under the displeasure of excited parties as to become one of the main causes which rendered his position insecure and finally displaced him from it. An extraordinary grant of eight hundred pounds, made to him by the General Court of Massachusetts while the dispute was pending,[3] was construed into a corrupt arrangement for engaging him on their side, and was so represented to the

[1] Register of the Privy Council, for Feb. 6, July 20, Oct. 12, Nov. 12 and 30, 1738; Jan. 17 and 30, Aug. 29, Nov. 2, 9, and 21, and Dec. 27, 1739.

[2] Register of the Privy Council, for Feb. 26, March 5 and 10, and April 9, 1740; comp. Instruction to Governor Belcher, of Aug. 5, 1740, in N. H. Provincial Papers, VII. 224-226.

[3] The Governor had solicited this grant in consideration of the shrinking of his pay through the depreciation of the currency. (N. H. Provincial Papers, V. 84, 85.)

men in power in England.[1] Nor was it surprising that one who had so notoriously bribed others with office should be supposed capable of being himself bribed with money. But his removal was brought about by methods only so far connected with the policy of his administration, as it was this policy which set against him an honest opposition that at the same time encouraged the activity of unscrupulous partisans.[2] The First Lord of the Admiralty received a letter with the signatures, afterwards ascertained to be counterfeited, of five persons purporting to be inhabitants of Exeter, who informed him that the Governor had connived at the alienation of pine-trees fit for masts for the navy.[3] Another letter to Mr. Holden, head of the dissenters in England, charged Belcher with being engaged with the Episcopal interest in Boston in intrigues against the Congregational church. It had no signature, the writer pretending that this was withheld for fear of the Governor's resentment; but, from the style of the superscription, Holden believed it to have come from Dr. Colman.[4] A further unfavorable

Intrigues against Governor Belcher.

[1] Journal of the Board of Trade, for Aug. 8, 9, and 15, Sept. 4, 6, and 12, and Oct. 10, 1739; March 18 and Oct. 16, 1740.

[2] Belcher had been endeavoring to protect himself by favors rendered in various quarters. Nov. 22, 1740, he recommended to the General Court to make grants to the representatives of persons executed fifty years before for witchcraft, to adopt measures for the relief of Quakers, and to comply with an application from Horace Walpole for an allowance as "His Majesty's Auditor-General of all his revenues in America."

[3] Among the British Colonial Papers, under the date of Nov. 17, 1739, there is an affidavit of John Gilman, John Hall, and Peter Thing, three of the persons whose names were subscribed to this paper, declaring the signatures to be forged. They further swear, and with them the town-clerk of Exeter, that they know no such persons as Joseph Lord and George Gerrish, the other two names subscribed to the letter. The forged paper represented that Dunbar had restrained the signers from encroaching on the woods, but that Belcher stealthily encouraged them, and bade them "not to mind that Irish dog of a surveyor." It prayed that it might not be disclosed to Belcher; "for, were he to know it, he is of such an implacable temper that he would not stick at any thing to ruin us."

[4] The supposition was improbable, for Colman was Belcher's friend; but Holden was afterwards said to have been led into the mistake by the

impression was produced on Holden's mind by the representation of the agent for New Hampshire respecting that grant of eight hundred pounds, which certainly, however fairly due, Belcher ought not to have received at such a time.

The agent in London of the friends of the Land Bank was Richard Partridge,[1] who had married Belcher's sister, and was known to have been employed by him in England in his private affairs; and it was whispered in the ear of courtiers that Belcher's profession of hostility to the bank could not be honest, since a person so related to him was its champion. According to a story, said by Governor Hutchinson to have been told him by a person directly concerned, one Maltby, a zealous dissenter, who influenced the vote of Coventry, from which borough the Duke of Grafton desired to have his son returned to the House of Commons, was assured that Belcher was plotting with the Episcopalians against Congregationalism in Massachusetts, and that the Duke would obtain his removal on condition of Lord Euston's getting the seat in Parliament; and the bargain was made and carried out, to the great subsequent annoyance of Maltby, who presently heard the truth as to Belcher's steady adherence to the religion of his fathers.[2] At the same time also came the intelligence that Belcher had displaced several officers, civil and military, on account of their connection with the Land Bank, and had not only disallowed the election of no fewer than thirteen Counsel-

handwriting of the address on the envelope, which had been surreptitiously obtained. — Samuel Holden, Governor of the Bank of England, had lately declined an appointment to be agent of Massachusetts in England. (Letter to him, of Dec. 22, 1738, "in the name and by order of the Great and General Court, in Mass. Arch., VI. 31.) He corresponded during many years with Dr. Colman. Holden Chapel, at the College, was erected at the expense of his widow and daughters. (Quincy, History of Harvard University, II. 37, 38.)

[1] Partridge was son of the former Lieutenant-Governor of New Hampshire.

[2] Hutch., II. 357.

lors for the same reason, but had dissolved the Court almost immediately after its coming together, in resentment for its factious action in that matter. But this news arrived too late. The chalice of his brewing had been commended, with added ingredients, to his own lips.[1]

May 27.

His removal. 1741. May 6.

The general course of Belcher's administration had been not otherwise than advantageous to the Provinces which he governed. But his sense of duty was coarse, and his love of it was infirm. He easily yielded to the bad sophistry which teaches that a good end transfers its character to all means which promise to advance it, and had become stained with the baseness to which that doctrine leads. He had been a trickster in politics; and his enemies, as is natural and customary, followed his example against himself, and pushed it into applications reaching further than he might have been willing to go. Such is the normal retribution of men whose easy consciences so welcome artifice that nothing reveals to them the tortuousness of their course, till by the managers that come next it is fol-

[1] "The change in this Province was certainly the most surprising and unexpected to all my friends, being done soon after the most solemn and sacred promises to the contrary. But there is no faith in man, whose 'heart is deceitful above all things, and desperately wicked.' God alone is unchangeable, and there must thy trust be fixed," &c. So wrote the Governor to Sherburne, July 20, 1741. (Belcher's Letter-book, in the library of the Mass. Hist. Soc.) His correspondence at this period is even more enriched with Scriptural language than was Dudley's when he corresponded with the Mathers. There is in the same collection an edifying letter of his to Dr. Watts, of March 2, 1743: "If the late change that has passed over me from a glaring public station to an obscure private life may lead me to a more close communion with God, even to a life hid with Christ in God, happy, for ever happy and glorious, will be the exchange." The "Belcher Correspondence," in an Appendix to N. H. Provincial Papers (IV. 866–880), contains compositions amusingly illustrative of the writer's character.

Belcher was not altogether happy in his domestic relations. He fell out with his son Jonathan on account of the latter's extravagance and running in debt, and called him a "monster of ingratitude." (Letter-book; Letter to Partridge, of May 3, 1743.) He was scarcely on pleasanter terms with his other son, Andrew, whom he had placed in two offices, and who had been indolent and careless in them. (Ibid.; Letter to Andrew Belcher, of Jan. 20, 1743.)

lowed out and twisted further for their own defeat and overthrow.

When the injustice of some of the charges against Belcher had been shown, there was a disposition at court to compensate him,[1] and he was transferred to New Jersey, which Province he ruled with success, and with satisfaction to himself and the people, for sixteen years, till his death.[2] He remembered his early home with fondness, and directed that his remains should be brought to Cambridge for burial. It was a meagre life which was brought to an end. Belcher's old age was not cheered by the conscious satisfactions of generous endeavor, nor had he so much as attained, to a large extent, to such rewards as promise to gratify an ignoble ambition. It is not a pleasant thought that among the Governors of provincial Massachusetts those least entitled to her esteem

His death in New Jersey. 1757. Aug. 31.

[1] Jan. 29, 1739, when the movement for Belcher's removal was active, the English Quakers, influenced by his favor to their Massachusetts fellow-sectaries (Mass. Prov. Laws, II. 619, 876; comp. Register of Privy Council, for Feb. 2, 1736; Mass. Province Laws, II. 635), presented a memorial in his behalf. (British Colonial Papers.) — It was more than four years after his recall from Massachusetts before his appointment to New Jersey. The "Account of the Rise, Progress, and Consequences of the Two Late Schemes," &c., represents him (31, 39, 46, 82–91) as still in England in 1744, intriguing against Shirley. April 24, 1745, the Quakers sent another memorial to the Duke, praying for some appointment for him. His friend Partridge, who was a Quaker, was one of the petitioners. "Belcher has got the government of the Jerseys. It was done by Duke of Newcastle yesterday. . . . . . It is a shocking affair, and must destroy any favorable opinion entertained of the Duke of Newcastle by the people of the Colonies. . . . . . There is a very worthy set of people in the Jerseys that it will most fatally prejudice. . . . . . They will be in fine hands under Belcher, who is to be the tool of the Quakers. . . . . . The Duke, differing in this instance from every other circumstance of this sort during his administration, has fixed the thing in the greatest hurry." (Letter of Christopher Kilby to Thomas Hancock, of July 18, 1746, in Tuttle's Memoir of Kilby, 10.)

[2] Belcher succeeded as Governor of New Jersey to Louis Morris, who, formerly a popular favorite, had died in the midst of an altercation with the Assembly. The general tranquillity of Belcher's administration was not wholly undisturbed; but, on the whole, his dexterity in affairs availed him well in this new sphere, — the better, probably, on account of his enlarged experience. (Carpenter and Arthur, History of New Jersey, 117 *et seq.*)

were born upon her soil. The fact would have been her shame, as well as her misfortune, had they been of her own choice. But no doctrine of despotism is more familiar than that a community under foreign rule is most easily oppressed through the instrumentality of its own facile, corruptible, and capable citizens.

CHAPTER VII.

At the time of the death of King George the First, the Assembly of New Hampshire, owing to the absence of Governor Shute, had existed for the extraordinary term of five years. The least palpable of the objec-

Legislation in New Hampshire.

tions to such a duration of the Legislature without a recurrence to the sense of the people for new elections, was its inconsistency with the character of a popular government. An Act for limiting Assemblies to

1727. Dec. 15.

a term of three years received the royal assent, and in the absence of a charter was all that controlled the royal will in respect to the government of the Province. A Representative was, by the same law, required to have a freehold estate of three hundred pounds, and an elector an estate of fifty pounds, in the town in which the latter voted or the former was voted for, neither voter nor Representative of a town being required to be a resident.[1]

Some arrangements proposed by the new House, in relation to the judicial courts, led to disagreements between it and the other branch, which insisted on the continued allowance of appeals in certain cases from the ordinary courts to the Governor in Council, a process which had been established under instructions from the King.[2] The

1728. Jan. 27.

House persisted, and the Lieutenant-Governor dissolved the Assembly.[3] The breach was widened when a Speaker chosen by the next House was disallowed

[1] N. H. Provincial Papers, IV. 24, 25, 45, 114, 146, 263.

[2] Ibid., 269, 272, 273, 479.

[3] Ibid., 484.

by the Lieutenant-Governor, — an act which they maintained that he was not competent to do, though he pleaded a royal instruction for his authority.[1] After several days, they sent up the name of another Speaker, along with a vote in the nature of a protest. The Lieutenant-Governor adopted the second choice, and condemned the argument.[2] The session proceeded with mutual obstructions and provocations. The House voted an Address to the King, praying for an annexation of the Province to Massachusetts.[3] The arrival of the new Governor was expected, and it was agreed to send to Boston a joint committee of the two Houses, with the Lieutenant-Governor, to give him a respectful reception on behalf of the Province.[4]

After constituting for six years two distinct jurisdictions, each under its own Lieutenant-Governor, Massachusetts and New Hampshire were again placed under one executive authority. But during his short administration, Governor Burnet visited his Province of New Hampshire only twice.[5] For the latter government, as well as for that of Massachusetts, he was instructed to require a stated salary; and with little opposition the Assembly of New Hampshire passed a vote securing to him for "three years, or during his administration," an annual payment of two hundred pounds sterling, or its equivalent, six hundred pounds in bills of credit, from which amount, however, one third part was to be taken to be the compensation of the Lieutenant-Governor.[6]

Governor Burnet in New Hampshire.

1729. May 9.

[1] N. H. Provincial Papers, IV. 283–285. The Speaker chosen was Nathaniel Weare, of Hampton Falls, whose popular leadership was in New Hampshire not unlike that of Elisha Cooke in Massachusetts.

[2] Ibid., 286, 485–488.

[3] Ibid., 498. The attempt was repeated two years later, in Belcher's time. (Ibid., 613.)

[4] Ibid., 261, 277, 482, 491.

[5] November, 1728 (Ibid., 17), and April, 1729 (Ibid., 505).

[6] Ibid., 249, 513, 534, 536, 539, 543, 546. — "Our incomparable Governor Burnet died on the 5th. He meant to have settled the New Hampshire line, and was convinced of the Massachusetts unreasonableness." Though only "one twelfth part as

Governor Belcher in New Hampshire.

In the time of Governor Belcher the affairs of New Hampshire were more blended with those of Massachusetts than at any other period of their political separation. He was received in the former Province with the customary attentions,[1] but though it was a scene of small intrigue, which might seem to suit his genius, his connection with it proved signally unfortunate for him. The Council included some active men, who were his tools. But the best men of that body were opposed to him, and were in harmony with the Representatives,[2] who were not all intelligent patriots, but who, on the whole, had a just regard to the interests of their Province. He began his administration by taking offence against Wentworth, the Lieutenant-Governor, from whom, while the question of his appointment was pending, he had assurances of friendship and support, but who, he was told, had at the same time been making professions of a similar tenor to Shute. He required Wentworth to disavow all claim upon the Assembly for support, reducing him to dependence on his own liberality; and he removed the Lieutenant-Governor's son and his son-in-law from the Council.[3]

1730. Aug. 28.

Wentworth's death. Dec. 12.

Wentworth lived but a few months longer.[4] David Dunbar, an Irishman, who had been a colonel in the army, and had served in Spain, was appointed to succeed him, being already Sur-

1731. April.

big as the Massachusetts, we agreed to a settled salary cheerfully, because our King has given his Governor such an instruction. I hope our loyalty will be rewarded." — Men from Haverhill had driven away the "North Britain" settlers at Londonderry. (Wentworth to the Lords of Trade, Sept. 7, 1729, in British Colonial Papers.)

[1] N. H. Provincial Papers, IV. 531.

[2] Ibid., 836.

[3] Ibid., 665, 668, 794, 802, 833, 843, 846.

[4] Richard Waldron, scarcely a less considerable actor in public affairs through many years, died a fortnight before Wentworth. (Ibid., 587.) He was son of the Richard Waldron killed by the Indians in 1689. (See above, p. 33.) The son, a friend of Governor Belcher, was Secretary of the Province, and, at his death, his son succeeded to the place. (N. H. Provincial Papers, IV. 467.)

veyor-General of the King's woods.[1] Dunbar, who was a factious and determined man, had already made himself obnoxious in Massachusetts. Some years before this time, Thomas Coram, the London merchant,[2] who had been in New England, had set on foot a scheme for the settlement of lands between Nova Scotia and the Kennebec. Defeated for a while by the exertions of Jeremiah Dummer, agent for Massachusetts, who objected to certain restrictions sought to be imposed upon the fishery, the project was renewed just before the appointment of Belcher to be Governor,[3] and thirty men were sent from Nova Scotia to the Massachusetts post at Pemaquid. They were placed under the command of Dunbar. Belcher's appointment made him uneasy. He wrote to the Duke of Newcastle that the rumor of it occasioned much

Lieutenant-Governor Dunbar.

1718.

1729. Oct. 29.

1730 Feb. 4.

[1] Dunbar was made Surveyor of the Woods in the year 1728, and in the autumn of that year, being himself detained by sickness, sent out his brother and others as his Deputies. (Letter to Under-Secretary Delafaye, of Jan. 7, 1729, in British Colonial Papers.) "If," he wrote, "I could be admitted of the Council in New England [Massachusetts] particularly, it would give me authority among these people, who seem too regardless of any." (Ibid.) — There was no friendship between Dunbar and the government of Massachusetts. It was he that was meant (Chalmers, II. 123) when "Colonel Bladen acquainted the House how necessary it was to keep our Plantations in subjection to the mother country. He had an instance in his pocket, which made it appear the Assembly in New England had presumed to call a gentleman to account for giving evidence before a committee of that House two years past, and had censured him for it." (Francis Wilks to the Speaker of the Representatives of Massachusetts, Feb. 21, 1733, in Mass. Arch., LII. 423.)

[2] Thomas Coram, of philanthropic renown abroad, is first known to us of New England as master of a merchant ship, who lived some time at Taunton, in Massachusetts. (Baylies, Plymouth, Part IV., p. 82, and Drake's additions to Baylies, Part V., pp. 68–71.) The (revised) Biographia Britannica, and Chalmers's Biographical Dictionary, which borrows from it, record the incidents of his life in London. — In the library of Harvard College is what I take to be the original of a petition of Coram to Caroline, Princess of Wales, for facilities in the founding of his hospital.

[3] Register of the Privy Council, for April 19, Oct. 23, 1729; April 10, 15, Nov. 12, 17, 1730; Journal of the Board of Trade, for June 4, 19, 27, July 4, 1728; Dec. 2, 18, 1729; Aug. 27, Sept. 1, 1730.

apprehension and displeasure among the members of the Church of England, to which, he said, Belcher was a known enemy.[1]

At the instance of proprietors of land about Pemaquid, who had awaited his arrival for redress, Belcher issued his proclamation enjoining on all inhabitants of that region to remain in their allegiance to the Province. Dunbar maintained that "all the lands to the eastward of the river Kennebec were deemed to be Nova Scotia, when it was proposed to settle them, and had been included in Governor Philips's commission;" and he insisted that the cause of the complaints against him was his having rebuilt the fort at Pemaquid, which Massachusetts had disobediently refused to do. "The people's disowning his Majesty's sovereignty," he said, "is too notorious."[2] Belcher solicited the appointment of Henry Sherburne, of New Hampshire, to be Lieutenant-Governor of that Province, as successor to Wentworth.[3] The Board of Trade, after repeated applications, prevailed with the Minister to give the place to Dunbar. The objections to him, they said, were so many recommendations, for "every man who [in New England] does his duty to

Quarrels between Belcher and Dunbar.

1729. Dec. 3.

1730. Dec. 15.

1731. Feb. 10.

March 5.

[1] "Mr. Belcher some time since married a daughter to one Mr. Lloyd, a churchman, and obliged him to promise he would never more go to the Church of England, saying he would rather cut off his daughter's legs than marry her to a man of that church. This is a fact which he cannot deny." (Letter of Dunbar to the Duke of Newcastle, of Feb. 4, 1730, in British Colonial Papers.) In Dunbar's opinion "it would not be for his Majesty's service to have any native of this country appointed Governor, even though he were of the Church of England." (Ibid.)

[2] Letter of Dunbar, in British Colonial Papers.

[3] Jan. 11, 1731, Belcher wrote to the Duke of Newcastle that Dunbar had "written many palpable falsehoods to do him all the hurt in his power," and again, April 26, that he was distressed to learn that his enemy was made Lieutenant-Governor of New Hampshire. (British Colonial Papers.) Oct. 29, 1731, he applied again to the Duke and to the Board of Trade for an appointment of Henry Sherburne to supersede Dunbar. (MS. Letter of Belcher, in the Library of the Massachusetts Historical Society.)

the crown makes himself liable to the ill-will of the people, and therefore stands in need of all the support the government can give him from hence."[1] Dunbar came to Boston, where he demeaned himself with insolence. The question as to Pemaquid was settled by an order of the Privy Council, made on a representation of proprietors of the eastern lands.[2] The jurisdiction was declared to be in the Province.[3] Dunbar withdrew, and a Massachusetts garrison was placed in the fort.

When Dunbar came to New Hampshire, he did not delay to fan the flame which he found kindling against the Governor. He began his administration by setting up the claim, as old as Dudley's day, that the Lieutenant-Governor was Chief Magistrate of New Hampshire during the absence in Massachusetts of the Governor of both Provinces.[4] He was by this time so infuriated as to charge Belcher with intercepting his letters, and even with opening and publishing

July 10.

July 19.

[1] N. H. Provincial Papers, IV. 600; Letters of the Board of Trade to Dunbar, in British Colonial Papers.

[2] See Mass. Hist. Col., XXXIX. 195–203; comp. above, 462, note 4.

[3] Register of the Privy Council, for May 4, Aug. 2, 10, 1732.

[4] Register of the Privy Council, for Nov. 29, 1731; Journal of the Board of Trade, for Oct. 26, 1731, and Sept. 23, 1736. Dunbar's commission (for which see N. H. Hist. Col., VI. 82) authorized him to execute the functions of the Chief Magistrate, "in case of the death or absence" of the Governor, but it also required him to act "according to such instructions" as he should receive from the Governor. (Comp. Dunbar's letter to the Council of New Hampshire, of Dec. 6, 1733, in N. H. Hist. Col., I. 275.) — Sept. 20, 1731, Richard Wibird, of the Council, deposed to having heard Dunbar say, "I swear I will never take a commission under Governor Belcher." September 25, Shadrach Walton made affidavit that Dunbar claimed from him the command of the fort at Newcastle. "I told him I would admit him as Lieutenant-Governor, or as a private gentleman, but not as commander or captain of the fort, and . . . . . hindered him by shutting the gate." (British Colonial Papers; comp. N. H. Provincial Papers, IV. 624, 645, 730, 873.) Among those who adopted Dunbar's part with warmth, in opposition to the Governor, were Benning Wentworth and Theodore Atkinson, his brother-in-law, a man scarcely less considerable, both members of the Church of England. (Ibid., 629, 665, 668, 794, 802, 833, 836, 841.) The Secretary, Richard Waldron, was Belcher's most serviceable friend in the Province.

a letter to him from his wife.[1] In a memorial to which he obtained the signatures of fifteen persons, the July 10. King was solicited to discharge Belcher from his place. A counter-memorial followed, with no fewer than a hundred names.[2] Though the former failed to accomplish its specific design, it was not without effect to strengthen the party in opposition to the Governor, and to embarrass his administration. The Board of Trade brought persons disaffected to him into his Council, notwithstanding his remonstrances against them by name;[3] and his appointments to administrative offices were sometimes overruled, and other selections made, in England. There appeared reason to think that a jealousy of him had been created there which dictated the organization of a watch over him on the spot.

After three years' experience of uncomfortable association with Dunbar, the Governor made urgent but 1734. Feb. 18. fruitless request to the Minister for his dismissal.[4] Among other things, he said that the condition of May 5. the treasury of New Hampshire, which had been empty "near three years," was owing to Dunbar's perverseness.[5] Belcher went to New Hampshire, and dissolved the

1 "His Excellency has even handed copies about of one letter from my wife to me, the contents whereof is yet unknown to me." (Letter of Dunbar to the Duke, of July 19, 1731, in British Colonial Papers.)

2 N. H. Provincial Papers, IV. 614; comp. 584.

3 Register of the Privy Council, for July 7, 1738.

4 April 23 of this year, "a great number of ill-disposed persons assembled themselves together at Exeter, ... and in a riotous, tumultuous, and most violent manner . . . . . did fall upon, beat, wound, and terribly abused a number of men hired and employed by the Hon. David Dunbar, Esq., as Surveyor-General of his Majesty's Woods." After six months had passed, the House of Representatives desired the Council to make inquisition into the affair. (N. H. Provincial Papers, IV. 678.) The Governor accordingly issued a proclamation against the rioters, but Atkinson complained that he offered no reward for their discovery. (Ibid., 841; comp. 843, 845.) The Exeter people represented to Belcher (July 1) that the affair had been provoked by the misconduct of Dunbar, whose oppression had become intolerable. (British Colonial Papers; comp. Hist. Mag. for 1868, p. 190, and for 1870, p. 14.)

5 The character of their relations to each other appears from the Gov-

Assembly which Dunbar was holding. He found them still impracticable as to a supply of money, and "the source of it all," he wrote to the Duke, "is from the Lieutenant-Governor and his few adherents."[1]

Oct. 22.

Nov. 26.

At the end of the seventh year of his administration, he said to the Assembly: "There has been no supply of the treasury for five years past, and there is now due from this Province between four and five thousand pounds."[2] Dunbar had now gone to England, and thereupon Belcher went to New Hampshire,[3] where

1737. March 9.

ernor's informing his subordinate (May 2): "Had you not assumed in yours of September that the trembling in your hand did n't come by hard drinking, I should have thought yours of April had been wrote over a hearty bottle." Whoever is curious respecting Belcher's private epistolary style may find ample satisfaction in the Appendix to Vol. IV. of the New Hampshire Provincial Papers. See also the Historical Collections of Farmer and Moore, III. 90, 225, 254, 323.

[1] British Colonial Papers. — In May, 1735, the Governor claimed a right to judge of the election returns of Representatives. The House contested it, and the Governor did not persist. (N. H. Provincial Papers, IV. 681–684.) — May 25, 1736, Belcher wrote to the Duke that he was as well satisfied that Dunbar was the cause of the factious conduct of the Assembly of New Hampshire, as, equally without legal proof, he (the Duke) could be satisfied "that Mr. St. John and Mr. P—ltn—y help write the invectives in the 'Craftsman' against the royal family and the Ministry." (British Colonial Papers.)

[2] British Colonial Papers.—Whoever will be at sufficient pains to follow the long contest on this subject between Belcher and the Representatives of New Hampshire will find documents relating to the matter at different times within seven years, in N. H. Provincial Papers, IV. 616–618, 623, 641, 643, 644, 654, 657, 666, 673, 679, 685, 688, 697, 707, 711, 712. When, at the beginning of the discussion, the House took the ground (May 10, 1732) that an increase of taxes "would have a greater tendency to fill the public gaols than to supply the treasury," and the Governor replied (May 18): "I find, gentlemen, that the assurance you gave me at the beginning of the session of your doing every thing that might tend to his Majesty's service and the prosperity of his subjects were only words, of course, and on which there was to be no dependence," the prospect of a good understanding between the parties seemed faint.

[3] During this visit to New Hampshire, Belcher received intelligence of a riot in Boston. The butchers were incensed at a prohibition to sell meat about the streets; and a mob of their friends — disguised as clergymen — set the market-house on fire and destroyed it in the night of March 24. Three weeks after, Belcher, having returned to Boston, issued a proclamation offering a reward of

he found the Assembly in a more wholesome state of mind. 1738. Jan. 1. He wrote to the Minister that "after an obstinate refusal for six years" they had resolved to raise money for the public charges; adding that the public business would always have been carried on "with decency and good order . . . . . had the Province been so happy as never to have seen Colonel Dunbar." May 13. And he renewed the request for Henry Sherburne to succeed to the place. The question as to salary, which claimed so much of his attention in his other Province, gave him no trouble in New Hampshire. The Assembly complied 1730. Sept. 1. at once with the King's demand by settling upon him six hundred pounds a year, in bills of credit, for the whole term of the government. He told them that he did not expect to make any allowance from this to the Lieutenant-Governor, and the Lieutenant-Governor made all easy by informing the Assembly that he expected nothing either from the Governor or from them.[1]

Belcher's ambitions had much connection with the course of affairs in New Hampshire, and during his administration he often visited that Province.[2] In the existing unsatisfactory state of things there the old desire for annexation to Massachusetts unavoidably reappeared; and an urgent petition was presented to the King, praying that New Hampshire might be "joined to the Massachusetts Bay as part of the Province." Indeed, the most material issue which divided parties in New Hampshire related to the continuance of the independence of that government. The friends of Belcher desired a return to the old state of things in a complete

Relation of New Hampshire and Massachusetts.

£100 for the discovery of the authors of papers which had been distributed, defying the government to punish the rioters. (New England "Weekly Journal," of April 19, 1737.)

[1] N. H. Provincial Papers, IV. 562–572; comp. 584.

[2] In this Province, too, he followed up his habit of ingratiating himself with the Quakers. (Ibid., 597.) The little colony of Scottish Presbyterians did not find the same favor. (Ibid., 727–729.)

political union of the two Provinces.[1] As it would have brought just so much addition to his consequence, the Governor naturally was favorably inclined to this union, and a majority of the Council were his friends; but it would not do for him to avow his wish to his masters in England, as the merging of New Hampshire in chartered Massachusetts would have been the loss of a sphere for the exertion of unrestricted prerogative.[2]

The other party, which was favored by Dunbar, and which had a majority in the House, desired not only that New Hampshire should remain a separate Province, but that it should attain a still further degree of independence, by ceasing to have, as it had had for nearly forty years, the same Governor as Massachusetts. A practical difficulty in their way was the incapacity of New Hampshire to provide for its expenses, by reason of its poverty and its narrow limits.[3] And this made the establishment of

[1] "This Province is very small and very poor, and we suppose the smallest and poorest in your Majesty's dominions, ... and is utterly unable to maintain a separate Governor; . . . . . and, without the assistance and protection of the Massachusetts in case of an invasion, must in all probability be inevitably lost, with as many of the lives of your Majesty's subjects as cannot fly into the neighboring government for refuge. . . . . . If it may consist with your Majesty's royal wisdom and goodness, ... we may be joined to the Massachusetts Bay as part of that Province." (Memorial of Citizens of New Hampshire to the King in 1735, in British Colonial Papers.)

[2] "An union would be the happiest thing in the world for New Hampshire, and I wish it was possible to bring it about." (MS. Letter of Belcher to Secretary Waldron, of Oct. 4, 1731, in the Library of the Massachusetts Historical Society.) "There can't be the least hopes of obtaining it, but by a good application from New Hampshire, and I am afraid the Irish party [Dunbar's] would oppose it *manibus pedibusque*. I should think it happy for me, as well as for both Provinces." (Same to same, of Oct. 25, 1731, Ibid.)

[3] Petitions from some two hundred and fifty New Hampshire men (Register of the Privy Council, for Aug. 29, 1739) prayed that Tomlinson might not succeed in separating New Hampshire from Massachusetts; "than which," they said, "hardly any thing can be more injurious and destructive to the Province, for the Province is very small and very poor, ... and is utterly unable to maintain a separate government, and cannot do without the assistance and protection of Massachusetts" against the French and Indians. They desire to be "joined to the Massachusetts Bay as part of that Province; but,

the yet unsettled boundary a main element in the controversy. According to the extent which should be assigned to the Province, and the amount of public lands which should prove to be at its disposal, the prospect of the unionists or of the separatists would brighten.

Boundaries between the Provinces. Among the instructions brought by the Governor was one to obtain a settlement of the boundary by agreement between the two Provinces. He com-
1733. plained to the Board of Trade that Massachusetts
Jan. 13. had neglected to give proper attention to the matter.[1] The Representatives of New Hampshire, impatient and offended at the delay, resolved, without the consent of
1731. the Council, to make their suit to the King. They sent over an agent, John Rindge, who, not being
1732. disposed to remain, left his business there in the hands of one John Tomlinson, a capable and energetic merchant of London, who had formerly been in New Hampshire as a ship-master, and who now, at Rindge's instance, was made agent for the Province. Both New Hampshire parties kept up an active correspondence with the mother country, each party, and especially the respective heads of each, representing their opponents in the most unfavorable light, and the agents also being equally assiduous to justify and propagate the resentments of their
1736. principals. At length, after much discussion,[2] the
Jan. 24.[3] Privy Council directed the appointment of that commission to determine the boundaries, whose action

if that be too great a favor," then they asked to "remain under the just and acceptable administration of the present Governor," and of his successors, Governors of Massachusetts.

[1] Massachusetts had long seemed to the Board of Trade to be evading this question by procrastination. (Journals of the Board, for June 14, 21, 22, 23, July 6, 1727.)

[2] N. H. Provincial Papers, IV. 649; comp. 568, 574–577, 585, 590, 593–599, 601–606, 609–612, 653, 677, 849, 854; comp. Register of the Privy Council, for May 16, 23, and 25, 1733, Jan. 16 and 22, Feb. 14, 15, and 19, 1734, Jan. 14, March 25 and 26, June 3, Dec. 4 and 5, 1735.

[3] By its order of Jan. 24 (comp. Register, for Jan. 22, Nov. 6 and 17,

has been already described.[1] Dunbar, when he had been worsted in the local disputes, withdrew, and nursed his rage at first for nearly two years at Pemaquid, where, getting into difficulty, as usual, in the execution of his office as Surveyor of the Woods, he complained bitterly that in the support of his authority the Governor was remiss and hypocritical. He had come to entertain a hope of being appointed Governor of New Hampshire, and 1737.
he went to England to solicit that promotion. If, in respect to personal comfort, his absence was a relief to Belcher, it was the transfer of a persevering foe to a scene of greater efficiency. Belcher understood this, and wrote to the Duke that Dunbar had gone to England to May 13.
make interest against him.[2] In fact, Dunbar had scarcely reached that country when he joined with the agent Tomlinson and others in a Memorial to the July.
Duke for Belcher's removal;[3] and the representation was

and Dec. 15, 1735), the Privy Council referred the nomination of the Commissioners to the Board of Trade, who appear to have allowed Tomlinson and Paris to have the matter all their own way. (Journal of the Privy Council, for Feb. 18 and 26, March 23, 1736.) Of the parties represented on the commission, Nova Scotia, New York, and New Jersey were royal provinces, and Rhode Island had herself an unsettled boundary question with Massachusetts.

[1] Comp. Register of the Privy Council, for June 3, 1735.

[2] Dunbar recommended himself to the Board of Trade by telling them (March, 1739) that "New England might be made a very useful Colony. It is," he said, "very populous, and the people generally deem themselves independent, as is their religion. Were the Church of England encouraged, it would bring them to better principles than they now are of, being generally Republicans." (Chalmers, Revolt, II. 112.)

[3] Tomlinson and Dunbar were active fellow-workers. The Board had intrusted to the former a letter respecting the boundary, to be delivered to Belcher, if he was in New Hampshire when it arrived there, and, if not, to Dunbar. Tomlinson informed the Board (August 24) that, agreeably to this instruction, it had been delivered to Dunbar, and that Belcher had represented it as stolen, and had issued a proclamation for the discovery of the thief. He demanded it of Dunbar, who refused to give it up. When Dunbar went to England, Belcher got it from two Counsellors, who, after the proclamation, avowed their possession of it. Tomlinson expresses his hope that "their Lordships are truly sensible . . . . . of the cruel oppressions and tyranny under which his Majesty's poor distressed Province of New Hampshire hath labored, and must

July 20. warmly supported by the Board of Trade. The issue of this measure, and of others connected with it, has been already related. The last communications between New Hampshire and the Governor were not friendly. The Province was exultant, and the Governor was disappointed and embittered.[1]

In the year in which Belcher was dismissed from the governments of Massachusetts and New Hamp-
1741. shire, Joseph Talcott, of Hartford, died, having been Governor of Connecticut for seventeen successive years from the death of Governor Saltonstall.[2] During the period of Talcott's administration the chief thing to be noticed in the history of the Colony is its rapid growth, marked by the establishment of new towns. Willington, destined within the century to become noteworthy as the birthplace of one of the most eminent of American scholars, began with twenty-seven inhabitants. The settlements in quick suc-
1726. 1730. cession of Somers, New Fairfield, East Haddam,
1732. 1733. Union, Barkhamstead, Colebrook, Hartland, Win-
1734. 1737. chester, New Hartford, Torrington, Kent, Goshen,
1738. 1739. Canaan, Salisbury, and Cornwall prove the thriving condition of the community which they enlarged.

Governor Talcott in Connecticut.

Yet these territorial arrangements were not always amicably effected. In Governor Andros's time a large tract

continue to labor so long as they are under the government of a native of Massachusetts." (British Colonial Papers.)

[1] N. H. Rec., V. 24, 67, 70–80.

[2] For twenty-six years a concurrence of the two Houses had been necessary to legislative action in Connecticut. (See above, p. 228.) On the occasion of Governor Saltonstall's death, the House (whose Journal for this period is lost) refused to concur with the Council in a choice of his successor, and an Act was passed, providing that for "this special occasion, ... and to no other purpose or intent whatsoever," the two Houses should act as one body. The Convention chose Joseph Talcott to be Governor, and John Law, of Milford, to be Lieutenant-Governor, "to continue in that office till the annual election in May" (Conn. Col. Rec., VI. 432–435), at which time the election of both was renewed by the popular vote. (Ibid., 514, 515.)

about Litchfield had been improvidently granted by the General Assembly to the towns of Hartford and Windsor. When these towns proceeded to make a sale of it, the Legislature interfered, probably on the ground that the grant had by both parties been understood at the time to be merely a device for keeping the lands out of the hands of the rapacious Governor, and not as an actual transfer of the property. The towns sold the land, however, and the purchasers proceeded to survey and occupy it. It was a common interest that the settlements should be extended, and that a dispute, in which not a few persons of consequence had become interested, should be put to rest. The government entertained dispassionately the claim which had been set up, and finding it to be not without plausibility and to be enforced by independent considerations of public advantage, consented to generous terms of accommodation.[1]

1687. Jan. 26.

1726. May 26.

1727. Sept. 18.

Appeal to the King against the Connecticut laws of inheritance.

An order from the Privy Council and the Lords of Trade to proclaim King George the Second called forth warm expressions of loyalty from the Legislature, which Governor Talcott had summoned to hold a special session.[2] An Address of congratulation was sent to the King, and at the same time the Governor was charged to transmit to the agent of the Colony in England a reply to a complaint which John Winthrop, nephew of the late Governor, was understood to be urging there. Winthrop,

[1] Conn. Col. Rec., VII. 43, 44.

[2] Ibid., 120, 121. — Oct. 12, 1727, the Assembly ordered that the ceremonies which had taken place at Hartford in honor of the King's accession should be repeated at New Haven (Conn. Col. Rec., VII. 124); "that the troops in the county of New Haven, five of the eldest foot companies in the town of New Haven, and two foot companies in Milford, attend that day's service; that a treat of thirty pounds be made for their refreshment; that a quarter of a pound of powder be delivered to each sentinel; that a sufficient quantity of powder be provided for discharging three of the great guns; . . . . . that the Sheriff provide ten pounds of candles for illuminating the Court-House; . . . . . and also that he procure a barrel of good wine, at the charge of the Colony, for refreshment of the Assembly."

considering himself to be unjustly treated by the colonial courts in respect to the division of his father's estate, had gone to England to prosecute an appeal, and especially to represent that the colonial law which allowed daughters to receive real estate in the distribution of the property of an intestate person was in violation of the law of England.[1] The question was of the first importance, since, if decided adversely to the Colony, it would unsettle titles to landed property which had stood from the very beginning.[2] As yet the King's Privy Council had shown itself inclined to decide that the law of Connecticut on this subject must be disallowed, and was null. The agent was now furnished with a hundred pounds sterling, "to be improved for the use of the government in making our defence against the aforesaid complaint of Mr. Winthrop." Winthrop's wife produced to the Governor a record of

1728. Oct. 10. an Order of the King in Council, overruling that action of the Connecticut courts of which Winthrop had complained; and the Assembly ordered the Secretary to proceed to put Winthrop in possession of the land claimed by him, as soon as "the bounds and quantity of said land" should be ascertained. The situation was most inconvenient. No settlement of intestate estates could be made in the Colony with confidence that it gave a valid title. Connecticut could not be brought to accede to the determination of the Privy Council. And at length, nearly twenty years after the adverse decree of that body, the

1746. May. provincial law was sanctioned by a decision of the Council, under the advice of the crown lawyers.[3]

[1] Winthrop had conducted himself towards the Governor "insolently, contemptuously, and disorderly," declaring himself to "stand upon a par with the whole Assembly." The Assembly hereupon committed him "to the custody of the sheriff." He escaped the same night (May, 1726), and the Assembly punished him by a fine of twenty pounds. (Conn. Col. Rec., VII. 43, 44.)

[2] See above, pp. 490, 491.

[3] The case of Clark *versus* Tousey, brought before the Privy Council four years earlier, involved the question so long pending. The Assembly advanced to Tousey five hundred pounds towards the payment of his expenses,

The Assembly, which received the unwelcome intelligence of the action of the Privy Council on the law of inheritance, applied to Jonathan Belcher to go to England and associate himself in the agency for the Colony with Dummer, who was understood to be ill in health.[1] He went accordingly, and reached England at the time when the dispute of Governor Burnet with Massachusetts had increased the displeasure in the courtly circles against the Colonies. The accounts which he sent home were such as to occasion the government of Connecticut to write to him in alarm: "We are unwilling to surrender our charter, for we account it the choicest part of our inheritance, and shall not, upon any terms, be persuaded to part with the same. Therefore you will avoid all occasion of hazarding of it. Particularly we are greatly concerned respecting the conduct of the Assembly of the Massachusetts, fearing it will have an ill influence upon our affairs if that should be brought into Parliament." And the agents were instructed "to use the

1729. Oct. 9.

Alarm for the charter.

"considering that almost all the inheritances in this Colony are depending upon the settlement of intestate estates according to our ancient laws and customs, which, if they should be overruled and made void, would reduce the inhabitants to the utmost ruin and confusion." (Conn. Col. Rec., VIII. 463; comp. 506.) In October, 1730, Governor Talcott wrote to Wilks, the new agent for the Colony in London, that no intestate estate had been settled since the Privy Council's order of February, 1728.

In one of the earliest Acts passed under her provincial charter (Mass. Province Laws, I. 43), Massachusetts had made like provision to that of Connecticut "for the Settling and Distribution of the Estates of Intestates," and the law was allowed by the King's Privy Council. In 1733, an estate in Massachusetts was divided agreeably to this law by the local authorities. A brother of the deceased intestate appealed against the decision, on the ground that the distribution which had been ordered of real estate was "contrary to the laws of England," and had been so pronounced by the Privy Council in 1728, after a hearing of the same question in the case of the Connecticut law. The Privy Council dismissed the appeal (Jan. 13 and 16, 1738), the decisive consideration being that the charter of Massachusetts required that her statutes should from time to time be submitted to the Privy Council, and approved by them, as had been done in this case; while in the case of the Connecticut legislation no such consent had been given. (Proceedings of the Mass. Hist. Soc. for 1860, 64–80, 165–171.)

[1] Conn. Col. Rec., VII. 185.

utmost caution that we be not in the least measure involved with the Massachusetts when that matter comes into the Parliament." When Belcher came home as Governor of
1730. his native Colony, Francis Wilks, of London, was
Oct. 8. appointed agent for Connecticut.[1]

Yale College. The Colony continued to be generous to Yale
College. The accustomed annual gift of a hun-
Oct. 8. 1735. dred pounds to that institution was first doubled,
Oct. 8. 1741. then tripled, and then still further increased; and
Oct. 8. three hundred and ten pounds in bills of credit
1740. were voted to the church in Windham, as "satis-
May 8. faction for their temporal damages in giving up
Mr. Thomas Clap to be Rector." Time, experience, and
1729. good sense had moderated religious jealousies, and
May 8. "such dissenters as are commonly called Quakers,"
Oct. 9. and immediately afterwards Baptists, were exempted
by law from paying taxes for the support of Congregational worship, on furnishing proof that they attended a worship of their own. The Pequod Indians[2] complained of in-
1731. truders from the town of Groton on their woods
May 13. and lands, and two magistrates were appointed "to

[1] Dummer recovered his health, and in July, 1728, Belcher's appointment was withdrawn (Conn. Col. Rec., VII. 191), as was Dummer's the next year. The Assembly, "having been informed that Jeremiah Dummer . . . . . hath left the court of Great Britain, and liveth in the country, and therefore not like to be serviceable to the Colony as formerly," directed the Governor "to signify to said Dummer that this Assembly are otherwise provided with an agent, and therefore have no occasion to trouble Mr. Dummer any further in our affairs." (Ibid., 307.) — There was always a certain distrust of Dummer's sincerity, high as was the estimate justly set on his abilities. Judge Sewall records an instance of his double dealing. In his Diary for Oct. 6, 1716, the Judge enters a paper given him, he says, by Dummer, in 1711, in which Dummer expresses the wish for "Roxbury [Dudley] to be informed that he is his friend, though he must not appear for him, but rather against him."

When Belcher came to Massachusetts as Governor, Roger Wolcott and James Wadsworth were sent from Connecticut to congratulate him, and to inquire of him respecting the position of the affairs of Connecticut at court. (Ibid., 282.)

[2] Ibid., 325; comp. above, p. 479.

be their guardians and secure their redress." Ben Uncas, the Mohegan Sachem, "declared that he doth embrace the Christian religion, which is the only instance of any of the chiefs of the natives in this Colony becoming Christian, though much pains have been taken with them;" and "the Assembly, being willing to encourage so good a beginning, desired his Honor the Governor to procure for the said Sachem a coat made in the English fashion, and a hat, and also a gown for the said Sachem's wife."[1]

The Mohegan Indians.

1736. Oct. 14.

The government of Connecticut was administered frugally. The pay for Assistants was, for attendance on the General Assembly, "nine shillings and sixpence *per diem*, exclusive of the Sabbath days," and "fourpence per mile for their travel to and from the Assembly; that of Deputies was seven shillings *per diem*, exclusive of the Sabbath days, and threepence per mile for their travel."[2]

Administration and Legislation.

1729. May 8.

The paper currency was only kept by the prudent vigilance of the government from occasioning the same embarrassments and mischiefs as in Massachusetts.[3] A corporation which had been created under the name of the "New London Society, united for Trade and Commerce," presumed to issue notes similar to the colonial bills of credit. Governor Talcott convoked the Assembly in a special session, and the society's recent proceeding was declared to be illegal, and punishable like forgery

1733. Feb. 15.

[1] Conn. Col. Rec., VII. 300, 378, 519; VIII. 72.

[2] Ibid., VII. 246.

[3] May 21, 1740, the Lords of Trade called on the Assembly of Connecticut to transmit, with a printed copy of their laws then in force, "an account of the tenor and amount of the bills of credit created and issued in this government, which are now outstanding," &c. The Assembly were able to reply: "We acquaint your Lordships that about three thousand pounds of loaned bills were drawn in for interest for the year 1740; and that the whole of the said loaned bills will be discharged by the year 1742; and that the bills then outstanding, that were issued to defray the charge of government, are near or quite sunk by the taxes of the years 1738 and 1739. (Ibid., VIII. 357, 358; comp. Trumbull, II. 48.)

or counterfeiting, and its charter was repealed. It applied for a renewal of the charter, and for a loan of
May 10. money from the Colony, in order to its extrication from the embarrassments in which it was involved by this decision; but the Assembly, with exemplary wisdom, "resolved that such a society of merchants, whose undertakings are vastly beyond their own compass, and must depend on the government for their supplies of money, and must therefore depend on their influence on the government to obtain it, is not for the peace and health of the government."[1]

Vice and laziness were not leniently dealt with in Connecticut. At New Haven, Hartford, and New London were Houses of Correction, "for suppressing and punishing of rogues, vagabonds, common beggars, and other lewd, idle, dissolute, and disorderly persons, and for setting them to work." Punishment was to be applied "by putting fetters or shackles upon them, and by moderate whipping, not exceeding ten stripes at once, ... to be inflicted at their first coming in, and from time to time in case they be stubborn, disorderly, or idle, and do not perform their task, and that in good condition."[2] Lotteries were strictly forbidden, first by a proclama-
1728. Jan. 22. May 9. tion of the Governor, and then by law.[3] The legal profession was not in good repute. "Whereas many persons of late had taken upon them to be attorneys at the bar, so that quarrels and lawsuits were multiplied,
1730. May 14. and the King's good subjects disturbed," it was enacted that there should be "allowed in the Colony eleven attorneys and no more;" namely, three in Hartford County, and two in each of the others.[4] But whether it was that the law was not found to avail against the dexterity of the discountenanced profession, or for some

[1] Conn. Col. Rec., VII. 420–422, 449; comp. 454, 478.

[2] Ibid., 127–130.

[3] Ibid., 147, 161, 172, 173.

[4] Ibid., 279.

other reason, it was repealed after a short experiment.[1] The Assembly thought it prudent to have the Governor assure the Board of Trade[2] that they had not "by any premium encouraged any manufactory in this Colony."[3] But the alarm was no sooner over than they established liberal bounties for the production of silk and of hemp, and for manufacturing "canvas or duck," and "fine linen cloth."[4] In cases of epidemic disease, the law gave power to two justices to authorize constables to impress nurses, as well as to provide "other necessaries for the accommodation of the sick."[5] The necessities of the anticipated war with Spain led to an improved military system. The Governor was declared to be Captain-General, and the Lieutenant-Governor to be Lieutenant-General of the Colony's forces, and the militia, in which the highest officers as yet had been but majors, was arranged in thirteen regiments, each with the three field officers of a regular regimental organization.[6] The Assembly voted the sum of four thousand pounds for bounties for volunteers in the expedition to the West Indies, and they provided for the victualling and transportation of troops, and for the apprehension and punishment of deserters.[7]

1731. Oct. 14.

Oct. 14.

1734. May 9.

1732. May 11.

1739. Oct. 11.

1740. May 8.

July 8.

Oct. 9.

Acts for the further regulation of the militia, and "for the encouragement and better supporting the schools," were passed in the last session of Governor Talcott's service.[8] He died in the following summer,[9] and the Assembly, at its regular

1741. May 14.

Death of Governor Talcott.

1 Conn. Col. Rec., VII. 358.
2 Comp. Ibid., VIII. 22.
3 Ibid., VII. 354.
4 Ibid., 494, 495, 512, 513.
5 Ibid., 371–374.
6 Ibid., 277–279.
7 Ibid., VIII. 295, 324, 340.
8 Ibid., 379–389.

9 It fell to Talcott's lot to give his Legislature a practical lesson as to the paramount claims of public station. His wife died suddenly after a morning's session of the Houses, which had taken a recess till the afternoon. By the Constitution they could not transact business without

Oct. 8. autumnal meeting, chose Lieutenant-Governor Jonathan Law, of Milford, to serve as Governor, and Roger Wolcott, of Windsor, as Lieutenant-Governor, till the legal time for the popular election in
1742. the spring. Then, at the regular annual meeting,
May 13. it was renewed.

In the first years of King George the Second, the history of Rhode Island was uneventful. The Colony was growing, though scarcely as fast as the rest of New England.

the presence of the Chief Magistrate or of his Lieutenant, and the Lieutenant-Governor chanced to be absent and out of reach. So the stout old Governor went from his house of mourning, and finished his darkened day in the hall of council.

"May it please your Honor," said the law-makers in an address of condolence, "we, the Representatives of the Colony of Connecticut, in General Court assembled, humbly take leave, with one heart and mind, to address your Honor under the sore and awful rebuke of the Almighty, who has, by his holy and wise providence, removed from you that dearest part of yourself, the desire of your eyes, and the greatest comfort of your life, by a sudden and unexpected death; and to let your Honor know that we esteem ourselves sharers in your loss, and afflicted by your affliction, and that we do affectionately condole your Honor's lonely and widowed state, and desire with your Honor to take notice of the Divine rebuke, and to quiet ourselves with the consideration that the Almighty Lord of Hosts, all whose works are done in truth, hath done it; and would not complain of, but mourn under a sense of the heavy stroke of his holy hand; especially when we consider the subject of our present mournful meditations in the relation of a worthy consort to your Honor, or that of a mother, a mistress, a Christian friend or neighbor, in all which we should fall short of doing justice to her memory, if we should fail of pronouncing her to be virtuous, affable, tender, kind, pious, charitable, and beneficent."

And more in the same devout and tender strain; to which the revered mourner replied: —

"To Mr. Speaker and Gentlemen Representatives: —

"As every spark adds to the fire, so every fresh mention made to me of my departed companion is a fresh wound to my bleeding heart; and upon the sight of your address in condolence in the loss of her makes such impressions on me that I cannot express myself, nor speak a word, but only, with a trembling heart and hand, thankfully acknowledge your kind respects and honor done both to the living and the dead. I wish I could, in a more suitable manner, express myself to you on this solemn occasion. I hope that, in consideration of my present pressure of grief, you will cover all my infirmities with a mantle of charity; for I am, gentlemen, yours to serve, in all things that I may, to the utmost of my power." (See Mass. Hist. Col., XXI. 246–248; comp. Conn. Col. Rec., VIII. 186.

A census, made ten years since the last enumeration, ascertained the population to consist of fifteen thousand three hundred and two whites, sixteen hundred and forty-eight negroes, and nine hundred and eighty-five Indians.[1] Nineteen hundred men constituted the militia. There were five thousand tons of shipping, and four hundred sailors.[2] Such a population and such a commerce demanded facilities of interior communication, and the General Assembly licensed "Alexander Thorp, livery-stable keeper, and Isaac Casno, saddler, both of Boston, ... to set up the business of keeping stage-coaches for the transporting of goods to and from this Colony and the Massachusetts government," and gave them an exclusive patent for "improving two stage-coaches for the space of seven years, ... in regard of the great charge and expense they must be at."[3] Though most of the trade of Rhode Island passed through Boston, two vessels came every year direct from England, two from ports of Holland and Spain, and ten or twelve from the West India Islands. The value of annual exports was computed at ten thousand pounds sterling, and the ordinary yearly expenses of the government at two thousand pounds in currency. A division was made of the Colony into three counties, and to this distribution the judicial system was adjusted. Newport County was constituted of the towns of Portsmouth, Newport, Jamestown, and New Shoreham; King's County (formerly King's Province), of Westerly, and North and South Kingston; and Providence County, of Providence, Warwick, and East Greenwich.[4] The towns of Smithfield, Scituate, and Gloucester consisted of territory set off from Providence a little later.[5]

1730.

Population and industry of Rhode Island.

1731.

1736. October.

1729. June.

1731. February.

[1] Callender, Historical Discourse, 93, 94.

[2] Arnold, History of Rhode Island, II. 101, 106; Staples, Annals of Providence, 194, 198.

[3] R. I. Rec., IV. 527.

[4] Ibid., 427; Arnold, II. 97.

[5] Ibid., 102; R. I. Rec., IV. 443. Before 1674, Portsmouth, Providence, Newport, Warwick, and Westerly

On the side of Rhode Island, the jealous powers that advised the sovereign took care to straiten the borders of Massachusetts as they had done on the sides of New Hampshire and Connecticut. The patent obtained from the Council for New England by the old Colony of Plymouth gave to it lands extending westward to Narragansett Bay; but that patent could not convey jurisdiction, and the Colony never was able to supplement it by the guaranty of a royal charter. As long as Plymouth remained a separate government, the settlements which afterwards became the towns of Tiverton, Little Compton, Bristol, Warren, and Barrington, were considered as being within her limits, and were accordingly governed by her laws, and represented in her administration. When Lord Clarendon's commissioners were in New England, Rhode Island presented to them a claim to the jurisdiction of that country, founded upon the charter obtained two years before from the King, which conveyed lands "extending towards the east, or eastwardly, three English miles to the east and northeast of the most eastern and northeastern parts of the aforesaid Narragansett Bay, as the said bay lieth or extendeth itself from the ocean on the south, or southwardly, unto the mouth of the river which runneth towards the town of Providence, and from thence along the eastwardly side or bank of the said river . . . . . up to the falls called Pawtucket Falls, being the most westwardly line of Plymouth Colony, and so, from the said falls in a straight line due north until it meet with the aforesaid line of the Massachusetts Colony." The Commissioners reported to the Secretary of State that, recognizing the claim of Plymouth as being valid, they had established Narragansett Bay as the boundary between

Eastern boundary of Rhode Island.

1665.

were the only towns in Rhode Island. North Kingston and New Shoreham date from that year, East Greenwich from 1677, Jamestown from 1678, and South Kingston from 1722.

the two Colonies, "till his Majesty's pleasure should be known."[1]

No further pleasure of the King touching the question was made known, and the arrangement continued undisturbed for two generations, within which time the rights of Plymouth, whatever they were, had been transferred to Massachusetts by the charter of William and Mary. Rhode Island revived the question, and resolved to present it to the King.[2] The Board of Trade advised the Privy Council to settle it by the arbitration of commissioners to be appointed by the King from the neighboring Provinces.[3] Accordingly five commissioners were named from each of the Provinces of New York, New Jersey, and Nova Scotia.[4] After some delays five of the number met in Providence, and heard arguments on both sides, Shirley, not yet Governor, being of counsel for Massachusetts. The Commissioners' decree gave to Rhode Island the territory which has been described, rejecting her claim to about twice as much more on the north and east. Both parties were discontented, and appealed to the King; but after a full hearing of arguments an Order in Council confirmed the Commissioners' award.[5] The towns annexed received magistrates according to the system of Rhode Island.[6] Bristol and Warren were made to constitute a county with the name of Bristol. Tiverton, Little Compton, and Cumberland (Barrington) were distributed among the three old counties.[7]

1733. December. 1738. April 28. 1740. September. 1741. April. June 30. 1746. May 28. 1747. Feb. 17.

[1] See above, Vol. II. 603.

[2] R. I. Rec., IV. 431, 445, 452, 465, 486, 488, 491, 559, 560; Journal of the Board of Trade, for March 25, 26, Dec. 9, 16, 1735.

[3] Ibid., for Jan. 18, Feb. 14, April 13, 25, 28; comp. Privy Council Register, for July 20, Nov. 1, 30, 1738, Jan. 12, 1739, April 9, 1740.

[4] R. I. Rec., IV. 586 *et seq.*; Journal of the Board of Trade, for Dec. 19, 1738.

[5] R. I. Rec., V. 199–201.

[6] Ibid., 204–206.

[7] Ibid., 208.

Western boundary of Rhode Island.

The boundary on the side of Connecticut was at length determined and marked, after some final skirmishing, the result rather of old habit than of any remaining difference of opinion or purpose. Connecticut continuing to be careless about running the line "pursuant to the order and determination of his Majesty and Council,"[1] Rhode Island appointed commissioners to do that office with or without the co-operation of the sister Colony.[2] Connecticut sent men of her own, who, after some formal disputing, of not at all the same temper as that of the disputes of earlier times, agreed in marking by monuments the line which divides the friendly contiguous States at the present day.[3]

1728. May.

1739.

On the accession of the new King, the Rhode Island people sent him a loyal address of congratulation, at the same time soliciting a gift of ordnance for a work which they informed him that they had erected at Newport, — "a regular and beautiful fortification of stone, with a battery subjoined, where might be conveniently mounted sixty cannon."[4]

1727. May.

Governor Jenckes.

1732.

Governor Cranston, dying in the office which he had held for thirty successive years, was succeeded by Joseph Jenckes, of Pawtucket,[5] who held it for five years till his death. At the peril of his popularity, Jenckes maintained correct views about the danger from the flood of paper money. He refused to approve a bill "for emitting sixty thousand pounds in public bills of credit," passed when the amount of bills outstanding already exceeded twice that

1731. June.

[1] See above, p. 486.

[2] R. I. Rec., IV. 405, 411. — May 9, 1728, the Assembly of Connecticut voted immediately to run and determine the boundary line on the side of Rhode Island, "provided the Commissioners from Rhode Island shall produce an authentic copy of his late Majesty's determination of the place of said line." (Conn. Col. Rec., VII. 157.)

[3] R. I. Rec., IV. 563.

[4] Ibid., 393.

[5] Ibid., 387.

sum. He indorsed his dissent on the engrossed bill the day after the Assembly rose, which was said by the adverse party to be too late, since no valid act in legislation could take place unless while the whole Legislature was in session. A Memorial had been presented against the bill, which on their defeat the signers wished to transmit to England with a view to obtaining redress there. By way of certifying its authenticity, the Governor was induced to put it under the Colony seal, and thus it was another occasion of complaint against him that he had placed the corporate authority of the Colony in the attitude of censure of its own legislation.

He was solicited to convoke the Assembly to consider the state of things, and when he refused to do so, the Deputy-Governor took the extraordinary step of calling them together. The Assembly declared the Governor's dissent to be of no effect, chiefly on the ground which has been specified. The Governor appealed to the sovereign, desiring to be instructed, 1. whether an Act of the Assembly, not having the Governor's concurrence, was valid; 2. whether he could safely refuse the use of the Colony seal, in attestation of copies made by the Secretary to be submitted to the King; 3. whether his previous personal examination of such papers was necessary, the Secretary being a sworn officer. His application was referred in England to the law-officers of the crown, Yorke and Talbot. As to the last two points their opinion confirmed the view upon which the Governor had acted. As to the first, they said that by the colonial charter "no negative voice was given to the Governor," nor even was "any power reserved to the crown of approving or disapproving the laws to be made," and that accordingly the General Assembly, independently of the Governor's concurrence, was competent to make laws, and that the validity of laws so made depended on nothing else but their being, "as near as might be, agreeable to the laws of England,

Aug. 3.

regard being had to the nature and constitution of the place and the people."[1]

The popularity of Governor Jenckes was prostrated by this rude storm. He was displaced at the next election, being succeeded, but not till after two years, by his factious subordinate, John Wanton. During the intervening time, while the latter was continued as Deputy-Governor, the highest post was given to his brother, William Wanton, who died before the end of his second term of office.

1734.

Governors William and John Wanton.

A different radiance from that of the "New Lights" that were presently to dazzle the neighboring Colonies shone upon Rhode Island when George Berkeley came to Newport. At his Deanery of Derry, in Ireland, where his philosophical writings had given him an early fame, that fine genius and devout philanthropist had conceived the idea of establishing a college in the Bermuda Islands, for the preparation of Christian missionaries to the savages of America; and, resigning his Irish preferment, he came over to devote himself to the prosecution of that enterprise. Taking Rhode Island in his way, he awaited there the fulfilment of promises of pecuniary aid, which had been made to him by the British Ministry. But Stanhope and Walpole found other uses for the King's money, and Berkeley's generous project was starved.[2] He bought a residence in the neighborhood of Newport, and occupied it two or three years, writing there his "Alciphron, or Minute Philosopher." At and after his return home, he made valuable gifts to the colleges at Cambridge and New Haven.[3] At Newport he gave for public use a collection of books which survives

Bishop Berkeley in Rhode Island.

1729. January.

1731. September.

[1] R. I. Rec., IV. 457-461.

[2] Mackintosh, Progress of Ethical Philosophy, p. 130.

[3] See President Gilman's full account of the Bishop's bounties to Yale College, in New Haven Hist. Col., I. 147-170.

in the "Redwood Library," so called from a later benefactor.[1]

At Newport a grammar school had been maintained for nearly twenty years, and at Portsmouth school-houses had been built. At Providence another slight indication was afforded of tendency towards a salutary social change, when a school there was encouraged by the General Assembly to the extent of allowing the teacher the privilege of collecting his flock "in one of the chambers of the county house," on condition of his "keeping the glass in constant good repair," and "erecting a handsome sun-dial in the front of said house, both for ornament and use," with other conveniences "to serve the public."[2]

1716.
1723.
Education in Rhode Island.
1735. August.

In the sixth year of the administration of Governor John Wanton, a century from the foundation being then recently completed, John Callender, minister of the Baptist Church in Newport, published his "Historical Discourse on the Civil and Religious Affairs of the Colony of Rhode Island." There were then in Newport "seven worshipping assemblies, churches or societies," and in the other twelve towns twenty-six "distinct societies or worshipping assemblies of Christians, besides several places where there were occasional meetings in some part of the year, or at certain seasons." In the Colony the Baptists had twelve congregations, the Quakers ten, the Congregationalists six, and the Episcopalians five.[3] Between the Baptist churches there were diversities of opinion; the unity of the Quakers was of the

1739.
Callender's History.

[1] "Here are four sorts of Anabaptists, besides Presbyterians, Quakers, Independents, and many of no profession at all. . . . . . The town of Newport contains about six thousand souls, and is the most thriving, flourishing place in all America, for its bigness." (Letter of Sept. 5, 1728, in Stock's Memoirs of George Berkeley, 91, 92.) The fifth chapter of Professor Fraser's "Life and Letters of George Berkeley" contains accounts of Rhode Island at the time of Berkeley's residence there, and of impressions which he received.

[2] Ibid., 511; comp. Arnold, II. 41, 51, note, 59.

[3] R. I. Hist. Col., IV. 120.

vaguest kind; the Episcopal congregations at Westerly, East Greenwich, and North Kingston were small.

The breaking out of the Spanish war offered an opening for action to a seafaring people, familiar, as the Rhode Islanders were, with the islands of the West Indies. They knew how to find there opportunities for service to the King, and for enriching themselves with plunder. The Governor called for volunteers to join the expedition under Admiral Vernon, at Jamaica, and at Carthagena a small force from Rhode Island had its share of the sufferings that attended that disastrous enterprise. The preparation for it was the last public care of Governor John Wanton. He died after being placed in the chief office by seven successive annual elections. The Colonies of New England all changed their Governors at nearly the same time.

Rhode Island in the war with Spain.

1740. May.

July.

The reader of this volume has had constant occasion to observe that, from the time of the Revolution which overthrew the administration of Governor Andros and the government of King James the Second, the great early questions of New England politics had become obsolete. For a while, indeed, it seemed possible that the Protestant settlement of the English monarchy would after all be overthrown, and the despotic rule of the Stuart dynasty be re-established. But the danger, never regarded in the Colonies as considerable, was before long lost sight of. At all events, for the present there was no chance for the ascendency of a Popish policy in the British Cabinet, and the legal toleration for dissenters which came in with the Prince of Orange, and was not withdrawn under his successors, was enough, imperfect system as it was, to tranquillize the colonists as to the safety of their religious freedom. And, as they had recovered the right of legislating for themselves, under some restric-

Politics of a half-century.

tions, the complete bearing and force of which were not at first ascertained, it seemed that they might promise themselves security against the repetition of such abuses as had driven their ancestors from England, and might apply themselves with contented diligence to the ordinary pursuits of life, as communities do that are undisturbed by political injuries or apprehensions.

Under the new dynasties of the parent country, whatever of political force survived in New England was concentrated in the Colonies of Massachusetts and Connecticut. The few and feeble towns of New Hampshire constituted a royal province, unprotected by a charter, and lying at the King's mercy, except so far as Englishmen might be held entitled to the protection of English law in any and all circumstances. Plymouth no longer existed but as a part of Massachusetts. The small and ill-compacted population of Rhode Island had no policy of self-protection, except that of sycophancy to the English court, and of those disputes with its neighbors in which it might promise itself the favor of the home government, whose obvious policy it was to strengthen the feeble Colony at the expense of those which were capable of offering more opposition to encroachments on the part of the crown. Connecticut, with her charter safe, and entitled by it, like Rhode Island, to choose all her own rulers, was not liable to be corrupted by political intrigues fomented from abroad, and an eminently high tone of public integrity was maintained among her people. Authorized, within some limits practically unascertained, to conduct her own legislation, she had little to keep her relation to the mother-country in mind. Theoretically she could not make laws "repugnant to the laws of England;" but there was no effective provision for bringing her enactments under the revisal of the King's government, and, unless she allowed herself in such imprudence in respect to the English laws of trade as would alarm the cupidity of English merchants, and stimulate them to go before the Ministry with complaints, there was nothing to trouble her complete repose, or to prevent her people from passing lives of industrious tranquillity, unmolested by any public cares beyond that of providing for a fair and comfortable domestic administration. Even French and Indians did not touch the sheltered villages of Connecticut. Often she did her part not illiberally in aid of Massachusetts and even of New Hampshire, but no Indian war-path reached so far as to the dwellings of her people.

On Massachusetts, therefore, devolved substantially the protection of the interests and the principles of New England in the decades that elapsed between the Revolution of the seventeenth century and the Revolution of the eighteenth. From the same causes, Massachusetts had the same relief as her sister Colonies from the most fretting anxieties of earlier times. She was not subject, like New Hampshire, to the arbitrary discretion of the King's ministers. Like Rhode Island and Connecticut, she had a charter; though, unlike theirs, the privileges which it bestowed were hampered with onerous conditions. She had not, like them, the right to choose her own chief executive officers, but must receive them from unsympathizing men, ignorant of her affairs and wants, thousands of miles away. She had the reputation of being rich enough to be able to make the government over her a profitable job, on which account it was sought by one needy adventurer after another. Her recording officer, appointed by the King, might be expected to fulfil strictly his duty, prescribed by the charter, of reporting her enactments to the Privy Council, by which body it was not to be supposed that they would be regarded with a favorable eye. Her Governor, a placeman of the King, had a material function in constituting one branch of her Legislature. Through him, their representative and agent, the British Ministry had the nomination of officers employed in the administration and execution of the laws, and the power of arresting all obnoxious legislation.

Contemplating the dangers which lay, not hidden but patent, in such provisions, the observer of these times is less surprised at what at first view seems the captious jealousy entertained by Massachusetts of her royal Governors. Phips was a son of her own soil, — a shallow man, with friendly intentions, and incapable of occasioning alarm, even if the public attention had not been engrossed with military movements. During the little time passed by Lord Bellomont in Massachusetts, he cultivated the good-will of her people; but even then they were on their guard, and, though they made him grants of unprecedented liberality, they refused the request he was instructed to make for a fixed annual allowance. Under these two Governors the Colony felt the pulse of the parent country with a tentative legislation, and saw all its laws significant of a hankering after the old freedom remorselessly repealed. While Stoughton was at the head of affairs, the critical questions between the Province and the government at home were in abeyance. Under Dudley a definite policy of negative opposition seems to have been entered on, and his peremptory demands were met with a downright and immovable resistance. The Province would not, at the dictation of the home government, build a fort to protect an outlying waste, or establish salaries for the Governor, Lieutenant-Governor, and Judges. His persistence and that of his masters had no effect; and he desisted from it, persuaded of its inutility.

The patriots of Massachusetts must have seen with satisfaction the abilities and resolution of Dudley exchanged for the moderate capacity of Shute, and it was natural that they should esteem the time a favorable one for settling precedents for future use, and, in this attempt, for pressing an aggressive policy, as they did in the pretensions to organize the House of Representatives without the Governor's consent, to audit the public accounts, and to control the troops. In Shute's administration the normal relation created by the provincial charter between the Province and the mother country first assumed its true outline and proportions. Every threat of cancelling that instrument was an evidence of ill-will on one side, and tended to aggravate the existing jealousy on the other. But it was impossible, from the first, that the working of the new constitution should be satisfactory to both parties. As often as it favored one, it offered some annoyance to the other.

Before the first half-century of the administration of Massachusetts under the charter of William and Mary had reached its close, the most material dispute which had arisen between the Colony and the Crown was virtually settled against the pretension of prerogative. Governor Burnet and Governor Belcher brought peremptory instructions to the Province to cease holding its Governors in dependence by controlling the provision for their maintenance. The Colony would not be convinced, nor persuaded, nor intimidated. The popular branch of the Legislature, doubtfully seconded by the inconstant Council, stood firmly upon its claim. The home government hesitated, then yielded, and that which, among possible measures of protection against injustice, seemed to the patriots of Massachusetts the most material for the moment, was won by their enlightened pertinacity.

This was no triumph of good abstract theory. No maxim of political science is more indisputable than that for free governments the executive and legislative authorities must be kept distinct. Yet such is the difficulty or impossibility of preventing by special provisions all encroachment of one upon the other, that it is doubtful whether any thing can effect it when there exists mistrust between the two departments. If one apprehends an attempt at usurpation on the other's part, its natural defence is in the most extended exercise of its own powers that is any way defensible or plausible. The method is retaliated, and the contest becomes one of extreme pretensions on both sides. So it was in England in the time of King Charles the First. So it was in Massachusetts when the Legislature persisted to hold the Governor in thrall by determining his means of livelihood. So it was in the first years that succeeded the overthrow of the Slave-Power Rebellion in the United States.

Extreme as may appear some of the measures of the patriot legislators of Massachusetts in their opposition to royal Governors, it is striking to observe how they were justified by later events. To the end that executive and judicial officers may do their duty without fear or favor, undoubtedly it is true that they ought not to be dependent for their living on grants made by a legislature from time to time, wherever circumstances are such that to exempt them from this form of dependence is in reality to secure to them the disinterested guidance of their own conscience and judgment. But, most unfortunately, the constitution of government under the provincial charter of Massachusetts was such, that the people could not make their Governor and Judges independent of themselves without throwing them into the adverse interest, and making them the partial and powerful dependants of the crown. When, in the next generation after Governor Belcher's time, the Colonies were plunging into the armed contest for political independence, the champions of American rights illustrated in elaborate argument the occasions which had existed all along for keeping the Governors and Judges dependent on the people, as affording the only security against their becoming at once obsequious and powerful tools of the King, and accordingly as constituting an absolute necessity of freedom.[1] But as soon as, by the overthrow of foreign

[1] Dickinson, Pennsylvania Farmer's Letters, 89 *et seq.*

authority, it became possible to place the administrators of the chief executive and the chief judicial powers in a position of absolute independence, the importance of that arrangement as a condition of good government was cordially recognized in that Constitution of the free
1780. Commonwealth of Massachusetts which imposed the unalterable law that the salaries of her Governors and of the Judges of her Court of Final Appeal should not be liable to reduction during their term of service.

APPENDIX.

MAGISTRATES OF THE NEW ENGLAND COLONIES.

PLYMOUTH.

GOVERNOR.		DEPUTY-GOVERNOR.	
1689 - 1692.	Thomas Hinckley.	1689 - 1692.	William Bradford.

ASSISTANTS.

John Alden, 1689 - 1692.
John Freeman, 1689 - 1692.
Daniel Smith, 1689 - 1692.
Barnabas Lothrop, 1689 - 1692.
John Thacher, 1689 - 1692.
John Walley, 1689 - 1692.

MASSACHUSETTS.

GOVERNORS.		LIEUTENANT-GOVERNORS.	
1689 - 1692.	Simon Bradstreet.	1689 - 1692.	Thomas Danforth.
1692 - 1695.	William Phips.	1692 - 1701.	William Stoughton.
1697 - 1701.	Richard, Earl of Bellomont.	1702 - 1711.	Thomas Povey.
1702 - 1715.	Joseph Dudley.	1711 - 1716, 1730 - 1732.	William Tailer.
1716 - 1727.	Samuel Shute.	1716 - 1730.	William Dummer.
1728, 1729.	William Burnet.	1733 - 1741.	Spencer Phips.
1730 - 1741.	Jonathan Belcher.		

COUNSELLORS.

* William Stoughton, 1689, 1691 - 1701.
Thomas Danforth, 1689, 1693 - 1699.
John Richards, 1689, 1692.
Nathaniel Saltonstall, 1689, 1692.
Wait Winthrop, 1689 - 1717.
John Phillips, 1689 - 1692.
James Russell, 1689 - 1708.
Samuel Sewall, 1689 - 1725.
Samuel Appleton, 1689 - 1692.
Bartholomew Gedney, 1689, 1692 - 1697.
John Hathorne, 1689 - 1712.
Elisha Hutchinson, 1689 - 1717.
Robert Pike, 1689 - 1695.
Jonathan Corwin, 1689 - 1714.
Adam Winthrop, 1689, 1692.
John Foster, 1689, 1692 - 1710.
Peter Sargeant, 1689, 1692 - 1702.
Jeremiah Swain, 1689, 1690.
* John Smith, 1689 - 1692.
William Johnson, 1689 - 1691.
* Peter Tilton, 1689 - 1692.
* Elisha Cooke, 1689 - 1692.
* Isaac Addington, 1689 - 1692.
John Nelson, 1689.

* An asterisk marks the names of Counsellors chosen by the General Court in 1692, and omitted from the Board constituted by the Provincial Charter. (See above, p. 86.) Some of the new or restored Counsellors of the Charter, as Richards, Phillips, Joliffe, and Middlecot, this Court rid themselves of at the first election.

David Waterhouse, 1689.
Samuel Shrimpton, 1689.
William Brown, 1689.
* William Phips, 1690 - 1692.
* Thomas Oakes, 1690 - 1692.
Simon Bradstreet, 1692.
John Joliffe, 1692.
Richard Middlecot, 1692.
John Lynde, 1692.
Samuel Heyman, 1692.
Stephen Mason, 1692.
Thomas Hinckley, 1692.
William Bradford, 1692 - 1698.
John Walley, 1692, 1693, 1696 - 1706.
Barnabas Lothrop, 1692 - 1702.
Job Alcot, 1692.
Samuel Daniell, 1692, 1693, 1700.
Silvanus Davis, 1692, 1693.
John Pynchon, 1693 - 1702.
Isaac Addington, 1693 - 1714.
Daniel Pierce, 1693 - 1703.
William Browne, 1693 - 1713.
Nathaniel Thomas, 1693 - 1702.
John Saffin, 1693 - 1702.
Charles Frost, 1693 - 1697.
Francis Hooke, 1693, 1694.
Elisha Cooke, 1694 - 1702.
John Thatcher, 1694 - 1707.
Samuel Wheelwright, 1694 - 1699.
Joseph Lynde, 1694 - 1705, 1707 - 1716.
Samuel Shrimpton, 1695 - 1697.
Eliakim Hutchinson, 1697 - 1717.
John Appleton, 1698 - 1702.
Penn Townsend, 1698 - 1707.
Joseph Hammond, 1698 - 1703, 1705.
Nathaniel Byfield, 1699 - 1702, 1704.
John Higginson, 1700 - 1719.
Samuel Partridge, 1700 - 1714.
Benjamin Browne, 1701 - 1707.
Andrew Belcher, 1702 - 1717.
Edward Bromfield, 1703 - 1720.
Samuel Hayman, 1703 - 1705.
Samuel Legg, 1703 - 1706.
Ephraim Hunt, 1703 - 1713.
Samuel Appleton, 1703-1708, 1713, 1714.
Isaac Winslow, 1703 - 1736.
Nathaniel Payne, 1703 - 1707.
Simeon Stoddard, 1704, 1705, 1707.
John Cushing, 1706.
Ichabod Plaisted, 1706 - 1715.
John Leverett, 1706.
John Appleton, 1706 - 1723.
Peter Sergeant, 1707 - 1713.
John Cushing, Jr., 1707 - 1728.
Nathaniel Norden, 1708 - 1723.
John Otis, 1708 - 1727.
John Wheelwright, 1708 - 1732.
Daniel Epes, 1708 - 1713.
Joseph Church, 1708.
Thomas Noyes, 1711 - 1714, 1716 - 1718, 1721.
William Tailer, 1712 - 1729.
Benjamin Lynde, 1713 - 1736.
Addington Davenport, 1714 - 1729, 1734.
Thomas Hutchinson, 1714 - 1723, 1725, 1726, 1728 - 1739.
John Clark, 1714 - 1719, 1724.
Elisha Cook, 1715, 1717, 1724 - 1726, 1728.
Samuel Brown, 1715 - 1730.
John Pynchon, 1715, 1716.
Thomas Oliver, 1715.
Thomas Fitch, 1715 - 1730, 1734.
Edmund Quincy, 1715 - 1729, 1734 - 1737.
Nathaniel Byfield, 1716 - 1719, 1724 - 1728.
Adam Winthrop, 1715 - 1718, 1721 - 1726, 1728.
William Dummer, 1717 - 1720, 1722, 1738, 1739.
Samuel Partridge, 1718 - 1723.
Jonathan Belcher, 1718 - 1720, 1722, 1723, 1726, 1727.
Jonathan Dowse, 1718 - 1726, 1728 - 1730.
Paul Dudley, 1718 - 1729, 1731 - 1736.
Joseph Hammond, 1718 - 1728.
Samuel Thaxter, 1719 - 1737.
Charles Frost, 1719 - 1724.
John Burrill, 1720 - 1721.
John Turner, 1721 - 1740.
Spencer Phips, 1721 - 1723, 1725 - 1732.
Daniel Oliver, 1724 - 1732.
Symonds Epes, 1724 - 1735.
Thomas Palmer, 1724 - 1726, 1730 - 1734.
Meletiah Bourne, 1724 - 1731, 1733 - 1739.
John Stoddard, 1724, 1727, 1728.
John Clark, 1724 - 1726.
Edward Hutchinson, 1725, 1726, 1738 - 1740.
Jonathan Remington, 1727, 1730 - 1740.
Timothy Lindall, 1727, 1728.
John Chandler, 1727, 1728.
Charles Chambers, 1727, 1728.

Theophilus Burrill, 1727, 1730.
William Pepperell, Jr., 1727 - 1741.
William Dudley, 1729 - 1740.
Peter Thatcher, 1729 - 1731.
William Clarke, 1730 - 1733.
John Alford, 1730 - 1733.
Seth Williams, 1730 - 1739.
Timothy Gerrish, 1730 - 1734.
Ebenezer Stone, 1730 - 1733.
Nathaniel Coffin, 1730.
Thomas Cushing, 1731 - 1736.
Joseph Wadsworth, 1731, 1733.
John Osborne, 1731 - 1740.
Ebenezer Burrill, 1731 - 1740.
Ezekiel Lewis, 1731 - 1735.
Isaac Lothrop, 1732 - 1736.
Francis Foxcroft, 1732 - 1741.
Samuel Came, 1733 - 1741.
John Jeffries, 1733 - 1741.
Edward Goddard, 1733 - 1735.
Josiah Willard, 1734 - 1741.
Jacob Wendell, 1734 - 1741.
Samuel Welles, 1734 - 1738, 1740.
Anthony Stoddard, 1735 - 1741.
Jeremiah Moulton, 1735 - 1741.
Thomas Berry, 1735 - 1740.
Joseph Wilder, 1735 - 1740.
Ebenezer Pomeroy, 1736.
John Cushing, 1736 - 1741.
Benjamin Lynde, Jr., 1737 - 1740.
Nathaniel Hubbard, 1737 - 1740.
Richard Bill, 1737 - 1741.
Daniel Russell, 1737 - 1740.
Ezekiel Lewis, 1738 - 1740.
Samuel Danforth, 1739 - 1741.
Shubal Gorham, 1740 - 1741.
William Brown, 1740.
William Foye, 1741.
John Reed, 1741.
John Greenleaf, 1741.

CONNECTICUT.

Governors.

1689 - 1698. Robert Treat.
1698 - 1707. Fitz-John Winthrop.
1707 - 1724. Gurdon Saltonstall.
1724 - 1741. Joseph Talcott.
1741. Jonathan Law.

Lieutenant-Governors.

1689 - 1692. James Bishop.
1692 - 1697. William Jones.
1698 - 1708. Robert Treat.
1708 - 1723. Nathan Gold.
1723. Joseph Talcott.
1724 - 1741. Jonathan Law.

Assistants.

Nathan Gold, 1689 - 1694.
John Allyn, 1689 - 1696.
William Jones, 1689 - 1692.
Andrew Leet, 1689 - 1703.
John Wadsworth, 1689, 1690.
James Fitch, 1689 - 1698, 1700 - 1709.
Samuel Mason, 1689 - 1703.
Benjamin Newbury, 1689, 1690.
Samuel Talcott, 1689 - 1692.
Giles Hamlin, 1689, 1690.
Samuel Willis, 1689 - 1693, 1698, 1699.
(Fitz) John Winthrop, 1689, 1690, 1693 - 1698.
John Burr, 1690 - 1695.
William Pitkin, 1690 - 1694.
Daniel Wetherell, 1690 - 1710.
Nathaniel Stanly, 1690 - 1713.
Caleb Stanly, 1692 - 1701.
Moses Mansfield, 1692 - 1704.
John Hamlin, 1694 - 1730.
Jonathan Sellick, 1695 - 1701.
Nathan Gold, 1695 - 1708.
William Pitkin, 1697 - 1723.
Joseph Curtis, 1698 - 1722.
Richard Christophers, 1699 - 1700, 1703 - 1729.
James Fitch, 1700 - 1709.
John Chester, 1701 - 1712.
Josiah Rossiter, 1701 - 1711.
Peter Burr, 1703 - 1725.
John Alling, 1704 - 1717.
John Haynes, 1708 - 1714.
Samuel Eells, 1709 - 1740.
Matthew Allyn, 1710 - 1734.
Joseph Talcott, 1711 - 1723.
Abraham Fowler, 1712 - 1720.
John Sherman, 1713 - 1723.
Roger Wolcott, 1714 - 1718, 1720 - 1741.

Jonathan Law, 1717 - 1724.
James Wadsworth, 1718 - 1741.
John Hall, 1722 - 1730.
Hezekiah Brainerd, 1723 - 1727.
John Hooker, 1723 - 1734.
Joseph Wakeman, 1724 - 1727.
Nathaniel Stanly, 1725 - 1741.
Joseph Whiting, 1725 - 1741.
Ozias Pitkin, 1727 - 1741.
Timothy Pierce, 1728 - 1741.
John Burr, 1729 - 1740.
Samuel Lynde, 1730 - 1741.
Edmund Lewis, 1730 - 1739.
William Pitkin, 1734 - 1741.
Thomas Fitch, 1734 - 1736, 1740, 1741.
Roger Newton, 1736 - 1740.
Ebenezer Silliman, 1739 - 1741.
Jonathan Trumbull, 1740, 1741.
Hezekiah Huntington, 1740, 1741.

RHODE ISLAND.

Governors.

1689. Henry Ball.
1690 - 1694. John Easton.
1695. Caleb Carr.
1696, 1697. Walter Clarke.
1698 - 1726. Samuel Cranston.
1727 - 1731. Joseph Jenckes.
1732, 1733. William Wanton.
1734 - 1740. John Wanton.
1741. Richard Ward.

Deputy-Governors.

1689. John Coggeshall.
1690 - 1699. John Greene.
1700 - 1713. Walter Clarke.
1714. Henry Tew.
1715 - 1720. Joseph Jenckes.
1721. John Wanton.
1722 - 1726. Joseph Jenckes.
1727. Jonathan Nichols.
1728. Thomas Fry.
1729 - 1733. John Wanton.
1734 - 1737. George Hassard.
1738, 1739. Daniel Abbott.
1740. Richard Ward.
1741. William Greene.

Assistants.

John Easton, 1689.
Edward Thurston, 1689, 1690 - 1721, 1723 - 1726.
Joseph Jencks, 1689, 1696, 1708 - 1712.
George Lawton, 1689, 1690, 1714.
John Greene, 1689.
Benjamin Smith, 1689, 1696, 1698, 1700 - 1703.
Benedict Arnold, 1690.
Stephen Arnold, 1690, 1696.
John Dexter, 1690.
Caleb Carr, 1690.
John Coggeshall, 1690.
Isaac Lawton, 1690.

[The records of elections in Rhode Island are wanting from May, 1690, to May, 1696.]

Samuel Cranston, 1696.
Walter Newbury, 1696.
James Barker, 1696, 1698, 1699.
Joseph Sheffield, 1696, 1698 - 1705.
Giles Slocum, Jr., 1696, 1698 - 1700, 1703 - 1705, 1708 - 1712, 1722, 1723.
William Gibson, 1696.
Jeoffrey Champlin, 1696, 1698 - 1701, 1703 - 1715.
Nathaniel Coddington, 1698, 1703 - 1706, 1715 - 1717.
Richard Arnold, 1698, 1699.
Joseph Williams, 1698 - 1707.
John Foanes, 1698.
Walter Clarke, 1699.
Robert Carr, 1690, 1691, 1701, 1702.
Benjamin Barton, 1699 - 1702.
Joseph Hull, 1699, 1701, 1702.
Isaac Martindale, 1700 - 1702.
William Hopkins, 1700 - 1706.
John Eldridge, 1700, 1701, 1703 - 1707, 1709, 1711, 1712, 1715 - 1717.
Benjamin Hall, 1701, 1702.
Edward Greenman, 1701.
Robert Lawton, 1702.

George Hassard, 1702.
Henry Tew, 1703, 1704, 1708 - 1712.
James Greene, 1703.
Job Greene, 1704, 1712 - 1714, 1729 - 1732.
Richard Greene, 1704, 1706 - 1711.
William Wanton, 1706, 1707, 1713, 1724 - 1731.
George Brownell, 1706 - 1711.
Thomas Cornell, Jr., 1706, 1707, 1718 - 1722.
Randall Holden, 1706 - 1713, 1715 - 1719, 1720, 1722 - 1726.
Thomas Penner, 1707, 1708 - 1713, 1715 - 1717.
John Rogers, 1707 - 1712.
George Brown, 1707.
George Cornell, 1710 - 1714, 1716, 1722 - 1739.
Richard Waterman, 1713, 1719, 1727 - 1730.
Samuel Clarke, 1713, 1715, 1716.
Nathaniel Sheffield, 1713, 1714.
Jonathan Nichols, 1714, 1718 - 1726.
Joseph Whipple, 1714.
Phillip Tillinghast, 1714.
Benjamin Greene, 1714.
Jeremiah Gould, 1714, 1716, 1722 - 1725, 1736 - 1740.
John Wanton, 1715 - 1720, 1723.
James Brown, 1715 - 1722.
William Coggeshall, 1715.
John Wickes, 1715 - 1741.
Gideon Freelove, Jr., 1717.
William Anthony, 1717 - 1721, 1723 - 1738.
Rouse Helme, 1717, 1723 - 1741.
Arthur Fenner, 1718, 1721.
Stephen Hazard, 1708, 1718 - 1721.
Elisha Cole, 1718 - 1722.
Nicholas Power, 1720, 1724 - 1728, 1731 - 1733.
Andrew Harris, 1721 - 1723.
John Waterman, 1721, 1727, 1728.
Benjamin Ellery, 1722, 1740, 1741.
Francis Willett, 1726 - 1728.
William Coddington, 1727, 1728.
Samuel Vernon, 1729 - 1737.
William Smith, 1729 - 1731.
William Hall, 1729 - 1735.
John Gardner, 1733 - 1736.
John Potter, 1733 - 1735.
Philip Arnold, 1733 - 1741.
Ezekiel Warner, 1734 - 1741.
Thomas Olney, 1736.
Peter Bours, 1737 - 1741.
Joseph Fenner, 1737 - 1739.
John Chipman, 1738, 1739.
James Arnold, 1738, 1739.
Gideon Cornell, 1739 - 1741.
Richard Fenner, 1740, 1741.
John Dexter, 1740, 1741.
Christopher Phillips, 1741.

NEW HAMPSHIRE.

GOVERNORS.

1690 - 1692.	Simon Bradstreet.
1692 - 1698.	Samuel Allen.
1699 - 1701.	Earl of Bellomont.
1702 - 1714.	Joseph Dudley.
1716 - 1724.	Samuel Shute.
1728, 1729.	William Burnet.
1730 - 1740.	Jonathan Belcher.
1740, 1741.	Benning Wentworth.

LIEUTENANT-GOVERNORS.

1690 - 1692.	Thomas Danforth.
1692 - 1697.	John Usher.
1697 - 1704.	William Partridge.
1704 - 1715.	John Usher.
1715 - 1717.	George Vaughan.
1717 - 1730.	John Wentworth.
1731 - 1740.	David Dunbar.

COUNSELLORS.

John Hinks, 1692 - 1705.
Nathaniel Fryer, 1692 - 1703.
Henry Green, 1692 - 1698.
Robert Elliot, 1692 - 1716.
John Gerrish, 1692 - 1702.
William Vaughan, 1692 - 1715.
Richard Waldron, 1692 - 1698.
Thomas Graffort, 1692.
John Walford, 1692.
John Love, 1692.

Peter Coffin, 1692-1712.
John Gerrish, 1692-1709.
Nathaniel Weare, 1692-1716.
Joseph Smith, 1696-1717.
Kingsley Hall, 1698-1736.
Samuel Penhallow, 1702-1726.
John Plaisted, 1702-1716.
Henry Dow, 1702-1707.
William Partridge, 1703.
Mark Hunkin, 1710-1728.
John Wentworth, 1712-1717.
Richard Gerrish, 1716, 1717.
Theodore Atkinson, 1716-1719.
Shadrach Walton, 1716-1741.
George Jaffrey, 1716-1741.
Richard Wibird, 1716-1732.
Thomas Westbrook, 1716-1736.
Thomas Packer, 1719-1723.
Archibald Macpheadries, 1722-1728.
John Frost, 1724-1732.
Jotham Odiorne, 1724-1741.
Henry Sherburne, 1728-1741.
Richard Waldron, 1732-1741.
Joshua Pierce, 1732-1741.
Benjamin Gourling, 1732-1737.
Ephraim Dennett, 1734.
Theodore Atkinson, 1734-1741.
Ellis Huske, 1734-1741.
Joseph Sherburne, 1734-1741.
Benning Wentworth, 1734-1740.
Richard Wibird, 1740, 1741.
John Rindge, 1738.
John Downing, 1740, 1741.
Samuel Smith, 1740, 1741.

END OF THE FOURTH VOLUME.

Cambridge: Press of John Wilson & Son.

www.ingramcontent.com/pod-product-compliance
Lightning Source LLC
LaVergne TN
LVHW021059110826
845150LV00001B/122

* 9 7 8 1 4 2 5 5 6 6 3 4 0 *